Report 153

1996

Beach management manual

J D Simm (editor)
A H Brampton
N W Beech
J S Brooke

CONSTRUCTION INDUSTRY RESEARCH AND INFORMATION ASSOCIATION
6 Storey's Gate, Westminster, London SW1P 3AU
E-mail switchboard @ ciria.org.uk
Tel 0171-222 8891   Fax 0171-222 1708

CIRIA

Beach management manual
Construction Industry Research and Information Association
Report 153, 1996
© CIRIA 1996

ISBN 0-86017 438 7
ISSN 0305 408 X

Keywords		
Beach management, coastal management, shoreline, waves, sediment, beach scheme, beach recharge, beach control structures, groyne, breakwater		

Reader interest	Classification	
Beach managers, specialist and non-specialist coastal engineers and designers	AVAILABILITY	Controlled
	CONTENT	Procedural guidance and best practice
Focused on UK practice, but of use to international readers	STATUS	Committee guided
	USER	Beach managers and coastal engineers

Summary

The need for research into coastal processes, sediment transport and the performance of beaches is widely recognised in the UK. In the recent past a substantial amount of research has focused on beach behaviour, many new research projects have been planned or are underway and a number of beach recharge schemes have been successfully implemented, yet there remained a serious lack of comprehensive guidance on the management of beaches. It was clear that if economic, effective and environmentally acceptable beach management schemes were to be developed in the future then practical guidance was needed urgently.

CIRIA Research Project 483 has produced procedural guidance and set out best practice for the management of beaches characterised by non-cohesive sediments based on state-of-the-art knowledge and the results of recent research. The *Beach management manual* is structured as far as possible around the beach management process. For example, because beach schemes, which often adjust natural processes, must be designed with an appreciation of existing coastal processes, the manual begins by introducing the attributes, morphology and processes of beaches. It then goes on to consider the starting point of all successful beach management - data collection and monitoring.

With the essential elements for beach management in place, the manual sets out basic principles such as problem definition, design constraints and opportunities, likely option effectiveness, economic appraisal and environmental assessment. It also provides detailed information on the design considerations and principles associated with the various management options, including beach recharge, beach control structures and managed landward realignment, together with guidance on scheme implementation. Recognising the fact that beach schemes cannot be implemented in isolation from an overall beach management strategy, the manual concludes with a discussion about the need for and requirements of ongoing management and beach maintenance.

The *Beach management manual* represents a comprehensive source of information on beach management, without reproducing material which is readily available from other sources. It is complemented by CIRIA Report 154 *Beach recharge materials - demand and resources*.

Foreword

This manual has been produced as a result of CIRIA Research Project 483 *Beach management manual*. The manual also constitutes NRA Report 23, produced through NRA Project 446. The objective of the project was to draw together existing knowledge and experience and the results of recent research to produce detailed guidance on beach management for coastal engineers and others involved in beach management, for coastal defence purposes. The project was run as part of a wider research programme on beach management and materials. The other main element of this programme was CIRIA Research Project 482, which has produced a report on *Beach recharge materials - demand and resources* (CIRIA Report 154).

The manual was prepared under contract to CIRIA by HR Wallingford (HR), Posford Duvivier (PD) and Posford Duvivier Environment (PDE). CIRIA's Research Manager for the project was Siân John, with support from Judy Payne who managed the *Beach recharge materials* project.

The manual was edited by Jonathan Simm (HR) and compiled by the following authors.

Chapter 1	Jonathan Simm (HR), with support from Alan Brampton (HR)
Chapter 2	Alan Brampton, with contributions from George Motyka (HR), Nigel Bunn (HR) and Jeremy Lowe (HR) on morphology and processes; and Julia Everard (PDE), Chris Adnitt (PDE) and John Purviss (PDE) on environmental aspects.
Chapter 3	Peter Hawkes (HR), drawing extensively from CIRIA/CUR (1991).
Chapter 4	Alan Brampton (HR), with contributions from Tom Coates (HR) on beach data collection; Julia Everard (PDE), Chris Adnitt (PDE) and John Purviss (PDE) on environmental aspects; Grant Murray (PD) and John Cooper (PD) on geotechnical data collection; and Jeremy Lowe (HR) on databases. Advice was also provided by NRA Anglian Region and Peter Barter (Sir William Halcrow & Partners Ltd).
Chapter 5	Jonathan Simm (HR), with support from Alan Brampton (HR) and contributions from Jan Brooke (PDE) on environmental aspects; Dick Thomas (PD) on performance requirements; and Nigel Bunn (HR) on beach analysis techniques.
Chapter 6	Noel Beech (PD) and Alec Sleigh (PD), with contributions from Julia Everard (PDE), Chris Adnitt (PDE) and Jan Brooke (PDE) on environmental aspects; Dick Thomas (PD) on economic appraisal; Nigel Bunn (HR) on beach modelling; Tom Coates (HR) on control structures; Ian Meadowcroft (HR) on risk and uncertainty; and Nick Bray on recharge sources.
Chapter 7	Jonathan Simm (HR), with contributions from Nigel Bunn (HR) and Alan Brampton (HR) on beach stability and modelling; Alec Sleigh (PD) and Noel Beech (PD) on transportation, measurement, cost and construction; and Julia Everard (PDE), Chris Adnitt (PDE), John Purviss (PDE) and Albert Nottage (HR) on environmental aspects. The sections concerned with beach recharge resources and availability were provided by Nick Bray and the British Geological Survey team working on CIRIA Report 154.
Chapter 8	Jonathan Simm (HR) and Tom Coates (HR), with contributions from George Motyka (HR) on sills and beach drainage systems; Noel Beech and Alec Sleigh (PD) on cost optimisation and construction; and Julia Everard (PDE) and Chris Adnitt (PDE) on environmental aspects.
Chapter 9	Kathryn Carpenter (HR) and Chris Adnitt (PDE) on dune management; William Allsop (HR) on rock beaches; Jan Brooke (PDE) on managed landward realignment; and George Motyka (HR) on restoration of natural supply and sediment bypassing.
Chapter 10	Alec Sleigh (PD) and Noel Beech (PD), with contributions from Alan Brampton (HR) on post-project procedures; and Julia Everard (PDE) on environmental aspects.

| Chapter 11 | Jonathan Simm (HR), with contributions from George Motyka (HR) on periodic recharge, recycling and regrading; Noel Beech (PD) on structural maintenance; and Julia Everard (PDE) and Jan Brooke (PDE) on managing the beach environment. |
| Appendix A | Nick Bray. |

John Eggett (PD) provided contributions throughout on health and safety and the CDM Regulations, and Albert Nottage (HR) provided advice on environmental aspects.

Project funders

Financial support for the project was provided by:

Department of the Environment - Construction Sponsorship Directorate
English Nature
Ham Dredging Ltd
National Rivers Authority
SCOPAC
Van Oord ACZ
Welsh Office
Westminster Dredging Co Ltd.

Steering Group

Following established CIRIA practice, the research was guided by a Steering Group which comprised:

Chairman
Chris Fleming   Sir William Halcrow & Partners Ltd

Members
Andrew Bradbury   SCOPAC/New Forest District Council
Ronald Gardner (from Spring 1995)   Westminster Dredging Co Ltd
Siân John   CIRIA
Michael Owen   Consultant, representing the National Rivers Authority
Hugh Payne   The Welsh Office
Anthony Polson (until Autumn 1994)   MAFF, Flood and Coastal Defence Division
David Richardson   MAFF, Flood and Coastal Defence Division
Keith Riddell   Babtie Group Ltd
Philip Roland (until Spring 1995)   Westminster Dredging Co Ltd
Ian Townend   ABP Research & Consultancy Ltd
Neal Turner   Bournemouth Borough Council

Corresponding members
Russell Arthurton   British Geological Survey
Nick Bray   Consultant
Iain Fairgrieve   Ham Dredging Ltd
Marian Geense   CUR, The Netherlands
Jim Houston   USAE Waterways Experimental Station, CERC, US
Richard Leafe   English Nature
Robert Runcie   National Rivers Authority, Anglian Region
David Smart   Van Oord ACZ
Henk Jan Verhagen   IHE, DELFT, The Netherlands
Peter Woodhead   Department of the Environment

Contributions were also received from Terry Hedges, University of Liverpool, and Joan Pope, USAE Waterways Experimental Station, CERC.

CIRIA is grateful for the support given to the project by the funders, the members of the Steering Group and all of those organisations and individuals who have participated in the completion of a successful project. In particular, CIRIA would like to thank the USAE Waterways Experimental Station, CERC, and IHE, DELFT, for their input into the project.

Contents

List of Tables

List of Boxes

List of Figures

Glossary

In general, the terms given here are those commonly found in coastal engineering practice. Consistency with terms used in CIRIA/CUR (1991) and Thomas and Hall (1992) has been sought as far as possible. Occasionally, one term has had to be selected from a range of possible terms (e.g. beach 'recharge' rather than 'replenishment', 'nourishment' or 'feeding').

Abrasion platform	A rock or clay platform which has been worn by the processes of abrasion (i.e. frictional erosion by material transported by wind and waves)
Accretion	The accumulation of (beach) sediment, deposited by natural fluid flow processes
A Class tide gauge	One of a UK network of tide gauges maintained to the highest and most consistent standards
Amplitude	Half of the peak-to-trough range (or height)
Apron	Layer of stone, concrete or other material to protect the toe of a seawall
Armour layer	Protective layer on a breakwater or seawall composed of **armour units**
Armour unit	Large quarried stone or specially shaped concrete block used as primary protection against wave action
Asperities	The three-dimensional irregularities forming the surface of an irregular stone (or rock) subject to wear and rounding during attrition
Astronomical tide	The tidal levels and character which would result from gravitational effects, e.g. of the Earth, Sun and Moon, without any atmospheric influences
Back-rush	The seaward return of water following the **up-rush** of a wave
Backshore	The upper part of the active beach above high water and extending to the toe of the **beach head**, affected by large waves occurring during a high tide (see Box 2.1)
Barrier beach	A sand or shingle bar above high tide, parallel to the coastline and separated from it by a lagoon
Bathymetry	Refers to the spatial variability of levels on the seabed
Beach	A deposit of non-cohesive material (e.g. sand, gravel) situated on the interface between dry land and the sea (or other large expanse of water) and actively "worked" by present-day hydrodynamic processes (i.e. waves, tides and currents) and sometimes by winds
Beach crest	The point representing the normal limit of high tide wave-induced **run-up** (see Box 2.1)
Beach face	From the **beach crest** out to the limit of sediment movement (see Box 2.1)
Beach head	The cliff, dune or seawall forming the landward limit of the active beach (see Box 2.1)
Beach management plan	A formal written plan for managing a **beach** (generally for **coastal defence**) involving a selection from a wide range of potential capital, maintenance and monitoring works

Beach management scheme	A specific planned investment in a set of works for managing the **beach**. This may be a one-off project or may be phased over a number of years
Beach material	The non-cohesive material (e.g. sand, gravel) comprising a **beach**
Beach plan shape	The shape of the beach in plan; usually shown as a contour line, combination of contour lines or recognizable features such as beach crest and/or still water line
Beach profile	A cross-section taken perpendicular to a given beach contour; the profile may include the face of a dune or seawall, extend over the **backshore**, across the **foreshore**, and seaward underwater into the **nearshore** zone
Beach recharge	Supplementing the natural volume of sediment on a beach, using material from elsewhere - also known as beach replenishment/ nourishment/feeding
Beach seining	A method of fishing carried out near the **beach** using a large vertical fishing net whose ends are brought together and hauled
Bed forms	Features on a seabed (e.g. ripples and sand waves) resulting from the movement of sediment over it
Bed load	Sediment transport mode in which individual particles either roll or slide along the seabed as a shallow, mobile layer a few particle diameters deep
Bed shear stress	The way in which waves (or currents) transfer energy to the sea bed
Benefits	The economic value of a scheme, usually measured in terms of the cost of damages avoided by the scheme, or the valuation of perceived amenity or environmental improvements
Berm	(1) On a beach: a nearly horizontal plateau on the **beach face** or **backshore**, formed by the deposition of beach material by wave action or by means of a mechanical plant as part of a **beach recharge** scheme (2) On a structure: a nearly horizontal area, often built to support or key-in an **armour layer**
Boulder	A rounded rock on a beach, greater than 250mm in diameter and larger than a **cobble** - see also **gravel, shingle**
Boundary conditions	Environmental conditions, e.g. waves, currents, drifts, etc. used as boundary input to physical or numerical models
Bound long wave	Long wave directly due to the variation in set-down at the breaker line due to wave groups
Breaching	Failure of the **beach head** allowing flooding by tidal action
Breaker depth	Depth of water, relative to **still water level** at which waves break; also known as **breaking depth** or limiting depth
Breaker index	Maximum ratio of **wave height** to water depth in the surf zone
Breaker zone	The zone within which waves approaching the coastline commence breaking, typically in water depths of between 5 and 10 metres (see Box 2.1)
Breaking	Reduction in wave energy and height in the surf zone due to limited water depth

Breastwork	Vertically-faced or steeply inclined structure usually built with timber and parallel to the shoreline, at or near the **beach crest**, to resist erosion or mitigate against flooding
Bypassing	Moving beach material from the **updrift** to the **downdrift** side of an obstruction to **longshore-drift**
Chart datum	The level to which both tidal levels and water depths are reduced - on most UK charts, this level is that of the predicted **lowest astronomical tide** level (LAT)
Clay	A fine-grained, plastic, sediment with a typical grain size less than 0.004mm. Possesses electro-magnetic properties which bind the grains together to give a bulk strength or cohesion
Climate change	Refers to any long-term trend in mean sea level, **wave height**, wind speed, drift rate, etc.
Closure depth	The depth at the offshore limit of discernible bathymetric change between surveys
Coastal cell	Coastline unit within which sediment movement is self-contained
Coastal defence	General term used to encompass both coast protection against erosion and sea defence against flooding
Coastal forcing	The natural processes which drive coastal hydro- and morpho-dynamics (e.g. winds, waves, tides, etc)
Coastal processes	Collective term covering the action of natural forces on the shoreline, and nearshore seabed
Coastal squeeze	The effect when hard defences (including beaches fixed in position by control structures) interrupt the natural response of the shoreline to sea level rise, restricting landward retreat and resulting in loss of the intertidal habitat
Coastal zone	Some combination of land and sea area, delimited by taking account of one or more elements
Coast protection	Protection of the land from erosion and encroachment by the sea
Cobble	A rounded rock on a beach, with diameter ranging from about 75 to 250mm - see also **boulder, gravel, shingle**
Cohesive sediment	Sediment containing significant proportion of clays, the electromagnetic properties of which cause the sediment to bind together
Conservation	The protection of an area, or particular element within an area, whilst accepting the dynamic nature of the environment and therefore allowing change
Core	(1) A cylindrical sample extracted from a beach or seabed to investigate the types and depths of sediment layers (2) An inner, often much less permeable portion of a breakwater, or barrier beach
Coriolis	Force due to the Earth's rotation, capable of generating currents
Crest	Highest point on a beach face, breakwater or seawall
Cross-shore	Perpendicular to the shoreline
Current	Flow of water
Current-refraction	Process by which wave velocity is affected by a current

Cusp	Seaward bulge, approximately parabolic in shape, in the beach contours. May occur singly, in the lee of an offshore bulk or island, or as one of a number of similar, approximately regularly-spaced features on a long straight beach
Deep water	Water too deep for waves to be affected by the seabed; typically taken as half the **wavelength**, or greater
Deflation	Erosion of dunes by wind action
Depth-limited	Situation in which wave generation (or **wave height**) is limited by water depth
Design wave condition	Usually an extreme wave condition with a specified return period used in the design of coastal works
Detached breakwater	A breakwater without any constructed connection to the shore
Diffraction	Process affecting wave propagation, by which wave energy is radiated normal to the direction of wave propagation into the lee of an island or breakwater
Diffraction coefficient	Ratio of diffracted **wave height** to deep water **wave height**
Diurnal	Literally 'of the day', but here meaning having a period of a 'tidal day', i.e. about 24.8 hours
Downdrift	In the direction of the nett longshore transport of beach material
Drogue	Float used to track current paths at a depth below the water surface determined by the position of vanes suspended beneath the float
Drying beach	That part of the beach which is uncovered by water (e.g. at low tide); sometimes referred to as the 'sub-aerial' beach
Dunes	(1) Accumulations of windblown sand on the **backshore**, usually in the form of small hills or ridges, stabilised by vegetation or control structures
	(2) A type of bed form indicating significant sediment transport over a sandy seabed
Duration	The length of time a wind blows at a particular speed and from the same direction during the generation of storm waves
Ebb	Period when tide level is falling; often taken to mean the **ebb current** which occurs during this period
Edge waves	Waves which mainly exist shoreward of the breaker line, and propagate along the shore. They are generated by incident waves, their amplitude is a maximum at the shoreline and diminishes rapidly in a seaward direction
Epifauna	Animals living in the sediment surface or on the surface of other plants or animals
Event	An occurrence meeting specified conditions, e.g. damage, a threshold **wave height** or a threshold water level
Exponential distribution	A model probability distribution
Extreme	The value expected to be exceeded once, on average, in a given (long) period of time
Fetch	Distance over which a wind acts to produce waves - also termed **fetch length**.
Fetch-limited	Situation in which wave energy (or **wave height**) is limited by the size of the wave generation area (**fetch**)

Flood defences	See **sea defences**
Forecasting	Prediction of conditions expected to occur in the near future, up to about two days ahead
Foreshore	The intertidal area below highest tide level and above lowest tide level (see Box 2.1)
Freeboard	The height of the crest of a structure above the **still water level**
Friction	Process by which energy is lost through shear stress
Friction factor	Factor used to represent the roughness of the sea bed
Frontager	Person or persons owning, and often living in, property immediately landward of the beach
Fully-developed sea	A wave condition which cannot grow further without an increase in wind speed - also **fully-arisen sea**
GIS	Geographical Information System. A database of information which is geographically orientated, usually with an associated visual system
Gravel	Beach material, coarser than sand but finer than **pebbles** (between 2 and 4mm diameter)
Group velocity	The speed of wave energy propagation. Half the wave **phase velocity** in **deep water**, but virtually the same in **shallow water**
Groyne	Narrow, roughly shore-normal structure built to reduce longshore currents, and/ or to trap and retain beach material. Most groynes are of timber or rock, and extend from a seawall, or the **backshore**, well onto the **foreshore** and rarely even further offshore. In the USA and historically called a **groin**
Groyne bay	The beach compartment between two **groynes**
Gumbel distribution	A model probability distribution, commonly used in wind and water level analysis
Hard defences	General term applied to impermeable coastal defence structures of concrete, timber, steel, masonry etc, which reflect a high proportion of incident wave energy; cf. **soft defences**
Headland	Hard feature (natural or artificial) forming local limit of **longshore** extent of a **beach**
Hindcasting	In wave prediction, the retrospective forecasting of waves using measured wind information
Historic event analysis	Extreme analysis based on hindcasting typically ten events over a period of 100 years
Incident wave	Wave moving landward
Infauna	Animals living in the sediment
Infra-gravity waves	Waves with periods above about 30 seconds generated by wave groups breaking in the surf zone (also known as **long waves**)
Inshore	Areas where waves are transformed by interaction with the sea bed
Intertidal	The zone between the high and low water marks
Isobath	Line connecting points of equal depth, a seabed contour
Isopachyte	Line connecting points on the seabed with an equal depth of sediment

Joint probability	The probability of two (or more) things occurring together
Joint probability density	Function specifying the joint distribution of two (or more) variables
Joint return period	Average period of time between occurrences of a given joint probability event
JONSWAP spectrum	Wave spectrum typical of growing deep water waves
Limit of storm erosion	A position, typically in a maximum water depth of 8 to 10 metres, often identifiable on surveys by a break (i.e. sudden change) in slope of the bed (see Box 2.1)
Littoral	Of or pertaining to the shore
Littoral drift, Littoral transport	The movement of **beach material** in the **littoral zone** by waves and currents. Includes movement parallel (longshore drift) and perpendicular (cross-shore transport) to the shore
Littoral zone	Zone from the **beach head** seawards to the limit of wave-induced sediment movement (see Box 2.1)
Locally generated waves	Waves generated within the immediate vicinity, say within 50km, of the point of interest
Log-normal distribution	A model probability distribution
Long-crested random waves	Random waves with variable heights and periods but a single direction
Longshore	Parallel and close to the coastline
Longshore bar	Bar running approximately parallel to the shoreline
Longshore drift	Movement of (beach) sediments approximately parallel to the coastline
Long waves	Waves with periods above about 30 seconds generated by wave groups breaking in the surf zone (also known as **infra-gravity waves**)
Macro-tidal	Tidal range greater than 4m
Managed landward realignment	The deliberate setting back of the existing line of defence in order to obtain engineering and/or environmental advantages - also referred to as managed retreat
Marginal probability	The probability of a single variable in the context of a joint probability analysis
Marginal return period	The return period of a single variable in the context of a joint probability analysis
Mean sea level	The average level of the sea over a period of approximately 12 months, taking account of all tidal effects (see **tides**) but excluding surge generated by meteorological effects. Variation in mean sea level may well occur in the longer term
Mean water level	The average level of the water over the time period for which the level is determined
Mean wave period	The average wave period derived from integrating the wave energy spectrum
Meso-tidal	Tidal range between 2m and 4m
Micro-tidal	Tidal range of less than 2m
Morphologically averaged wave condition	A single wave condition producing the same nett longshore drift as a given proportion of the annual wave climate

Mud flat	An area of fine silt usually exposed at low tide but covered at high tide, occurring in sheltered estuaries or behind shingle bars or sand spits
Nearshore	The zone which extends from the **swash zone** to the position marking the start of the **offshore zone**, typically to water depths of the order of 20m (see Box 2.1)
Ness	Roughly triangular promontory of land jutting into the sea, often consisting of mobile material, i.e. a beach form
Numerical modelling	Refers to the analysis of coastal processes using computational models
Offshore	The zone beyond the **nearshore zone** where sediment motion induced by waves alone effectively ceases and where the influence of the sea bed on wave action has become small in comparison with the effect of wind (see Box 2.1)
Operational	The construction, maintenance and day-to-day activities, associated with beach management
Overtopping	Water carried over the top of a **coastal defence** due to wave **run-up** exceeding the **crest** height
Overwash	The effect of waves **overtopping** a **coastal defence**, often carrying sediment landwards which is then lost to the beach system
Peaks over threshold (POT)	Refers to the maximum value of a variable during each excursion above a threshold value
Pebbles	Beach material usually well-rounded and between about 4mm and 75mm in diameter
Persistence of storms	The duration of sea states above some severity threshold (e.g. **wave height**)
Phase velocity	The velocity at which a wave crest propagates; cf. **group velocity**
Physical modelling	Refers to the investigation of coastal processes using a scaled model
Pierson-Moskowitz spectrum	Wave spectrum typical of fully-developed deep water waves
Piezometric surface	The level within (or above) a soil stratum at which the pore-pressure is zero
Pocket beach	A beach, usually small, between two **headlands**
Preservation	Static protection of an area or element, attempting to perpetuate the existence of a given 'state'
Probability density function	Function specifying the distribution of a variable
Profile of storms	Refers to the persistence of storms coupled with the rate of change of sea state (e.g. **wave height**) within the storms
Recycling	The mechanical movement of beach sediment from **downdrift** to **updrift**
Reef	A ridge of rock or other material lying just below the surface of the sea
Reflected wave	That part of an incident wave that is returned (reflected) seaward when a wave impinges on a **beach**, **seawall** or other reflecting surface

Reflection	See **reflected wave**
Refraction coefficient	Ratio of refracted **wave height** to deep water **wave height**
Refraction (of water waves)	The process by which the direction of a wave moving in **shallow water** at an angle to the contours is changed so that the wave crests tend to become more aligned with those contours
Regular waves	Waves with a single height, period and direction
Residual (water level)	The components of water level not attributable to astronomical effects
Return period	Average period of time between occurrences of a given event
Revetment	A sloping surface of stone, concrete or other material used to protect an embankment, natural coast or shoreline against erosion
Rip current	Jet-like seaward-going current normal to the shoreline associated with wave-induced longshore currents
Risk analysis	Assessment of the total risk due to all possible environmental inputs and all possible mechanisms
Roller	Rotational eddy with a horizontal aixs driven by breaking wave action
Runnel	Channels on a beach, usually running approximately shore-parallel and separated by beach ridges
Run-up, run-down	The upper and lower levels reached by a wave on a beach or coastal structure, relative to **still-water level**
Salient	Coastal formation of beach material developed by wave refraction and diffraction and longshore drift comprising a bulge in the coastline towards an offshore island or breakwater, but not connected to it as in the case of a **tombolo** - see also **ness, cusp**
Sand	Sediment particles, mainly of quartz, with a diameter of between 0.062mm and 2mm, generally classified as 'fine', 'medium', 'coarse' or 'very coarse'
Scatter diagram	A two-dimensional histogram showing the joint probability density of two variables within a data sample
Sea defences	Works to alleviate flooding by the sea, sometimes known as **flood defences**
Sea level rise	The long-term trend in mean sea level
Seawall	Solid coastal defence structure built parallel to the coastline
Sediment	Particulate matter derived from rock, minerals or bioclastic debris
Sediment cell	In the context of a strategic approach to coastal management, a length of coastline in which interruptions to the movement of sand or shingle along the beaches or nearshore sea bed do not significantly affect beaches in the adjacent lengths of coastline
Sediment sink	Point or area at which beach material is irretrievably lost from a coastal cell, such as an estuary, or a deep channel in the seabed
Sediment source	Point or area on a coast from which beach material arises, such as an eroding cliff, or river mouth
Seiche	Standing wave oscillation in an effectively closed body of water
Semi-diurnal	Having a period of half a tidal day, i.e. 12.4 hours
Sequencing of storms	Refers to the temporal distribution of storms and therefore how they are grouped

Shallow water	Water of such depth that surface waves are noticeably affected by bottom topography. Typically this implies a water depth equivalent to less than half the **wavelength**
Shingle	A loose term for coarse beach material, a mixture of gravel, pebbles and larger material, often well-rounded and of hard rock, e.g. chert, flint, etc.
Shoaling	Decrease in water depth. The transformation of wave profile as they propagate inshore
Shoaling coefficient	Ratio of shoaled **wave height** to deep water **wave height**
Shoreline	One characteristic of the coast, often poorly defined, but essentially the interface between land and sea
Shoreline management	The development of strategic, long-term and sustainable coastal defence policy within a **sediment cell**
Shore normal	A line at right-angles to the contours in the surf zone
Short-crested random waves	Random waves with variable heights, periods and directions
Significant wave height	The average height of the highest one third of the waves in a given sea state
Silt	Sediment particles with a grain size between 0.004mm and 0.062mm, i.e. coarser than **clay** particles but finer than **sand**
Soft defences	Usually refers to **beaches** (natural or designed) but may also relate to energy-absorbing beach-control structures, including those constructed of rock, where these are used to control or redirect **coastal processes** rather than opposing or preventing them
Spit	A long, narrow accumulation of sand or shingle, lying generally in line with the coast, with one end attached to the land the other projecting into the sea or across the mouth of an estuary - see also **ness**
Standard of service	The adequacy of defence measured in terms of the return period (years) of the event which causes a critical condition (e.g. **breaching**, **overtopping**) to be reached
Still-water level (SWL)	Average water surface elevation at any instant, excluding local variation due to waves and **wave set-up**, but including the effects of **tides**, **surges** and long period **seiches**
Strand line	An accumulation of debris (e.g. seaweed, driftwood and litter) cast up onto a beach, and lying along the limit of wave uprush
Sub-tidal beach	The part of the beach (where it exists) which extends from low water out to the approximate limit of storm erosion. The latter is typically located at a maximum water depth of 8 to 10 metres and is often identifiable on surveys by a break in the slope of the bed
Surf beat	Independent long wave caused by reflection of **bound long wave**
Surf zone	The zone of wave action extending from the water line (which varies with tide, surge, set-up, etc.) out to the most seaward point of the zone (**breaker zone**) at which waves approaching the coastline commence breaking, typically in water depths of between 5 to 10 metres (see Box 2.1)

Surge	Changes in water level as a result of meteorological forcing (wind, high or low barometric pressure) causing a difference between the recorded water level and that predicted using harmonic analysis; may be positive or negative
Suspended load	A mode of sediment transport in which the particles are supported, and carried along by the fluid
Swash zone	The zone of wave action on the beach, which moves as water levels vary, extending from the limit of **run-down** to the limit of **run-up** (see Box 2.1)
Swell (waves)	Remotely wind-generated waves. Swell characteristically exhibits a more regular and longer period and has longer crests than locally generated waves
Threshold of motion	The point at which the forces imposed on a sediment particle overcome its inertia and it starts to move
Tidal current	The movement of water associated with the rise and fall of the tides
Tidal range	Vertical difference in high and low water level once decoupled from the water level **residuals**
Tidal wave	The rise and fall in water level due to the passage of the tide
Tide	The periodic rise and fall in the level of the water in oceans and seas; the result of gravitational attraction of the sun and moon

Tides

(1) *Highest astronomical tide (HAT), lowest astronomical tide (LAT):* the highest and lowest levels, respectively, which can be predicted to occur under average meteorological conditions. These levels will not be reached every year. HAT and LAT are not the extreme levels which can be reached, as storm surges may cause considerably higher and lower levels to occur.

(2) *Mean high water springs (MHWS), mean low water springs (MLWS):* the height of mean high water springs is the average throughout a year of the heights of two successive high waters during those periods of 24 hours (approximately once a fortnight) when the range of the tide is greatest. The height of mean low water springs is the average height obtained by the two successive low waters during the same periods.

(3) *Mean high water neaps (MHWN), mean low water neaps (MLWN):* the height of mean high water neaps is the average of the heights throughout the year of two successive high waters during those periods of 24 hours (approximately once a fortnight) when the range of the tide is least. The height of mean low water neaps is the average height obtained by the two successive low waters during the same periods.

(4) *Mean high water (MHW), mean low water (MLW):* for the purpose of this manual, mean high/low water, as shown on Ordnance Survey Maps, is defined as the arithmetic mean of the published values of mean high/low water springs and mean high/low water neaps. This ruling applies to England and Wales. In Scotland the tidal marks shown on Ordnance Survey maps are those of mean high (MH) or low (ML) water springs (WS).

TMA spectrum	Wave spectrum typical of growing seas in limited water depths
Tombolo	Coastal formation of beach material developed by **refraction, diffraction** and **longshore drift** to form a 'neck' connecting a coast to an offshore island or breakwater (see also **salient**)
Tsunami	Seismically-induced gravity waves, characterised by **wave periods** that are in the order of minutes rather than seconds
Updrift	The direction opposite to that of the predominant longshore movement of beach material
Up-rush	The landward return of water following the **back-rush** of a wave
Water depth	Distance between the seabed and the **still water level**
Water level	Elevation of **still water level** relative to some datum
Wave celerity	The speed of wave propagation
Wave climate	The seasonal and annual distribution of **wave height, period** and **direction**
Wave climate atlas	Series of maps showing the variability of wave conditions over a long coastline
Wave direction	Mean direction of wave energy propagation relative to true North
Wave directional spectrum	Distribution of wave energy as a function of wave **frequency** and **direction**
Wave frequency	The inverse of **wave period**
Wave frequency spectrum	Distribution of wave energy as a function of frequency
Wave generation	Growth of wave energy by wind
Wave height	The vertical distance between the trough and the following crest
Wavelength	Straightline distance between two successive wave crests
Wave peak frequency	The inverse of wave peak period
Wave peak period	Wave period at which the spectral energy density is a maximum
Wave period	The time taken for two successive wave crests to pass the same point
Wave reflection	See **reflected wave**
Wave set-up	Elevation of the water level at the coastline caused by radiation stress gradients in the surf zone
Wave steepness	The ratio of **wave height** to wavelength also known as **sea steepness**
Wave rose	Diagram showing the long-term distribution of **wave height** and direction
Wave transformation	Change in wave energy due to the action of physical processes
Weibull distribution	A model probability distribution, commonly used in wave analysis
Wind rose	Diagram showing the long-term distribution of wind speed and direction
Wind sea	Wave conditions directly attributable to recent winds, as opposed to swell
Wind set-up	Elevation of the water level over an area directly caused by wind stress on the water surface
Wind stress	The way in which wind transfers energy to the sea surface

Notation

The notation used in this manual is generally consistent with that adopted in CIRIA/CUR (1991) and thus also with IAHR/PIANC (1986). However, the user is cautioned that, for consistency, some familiar terminology may have been changed, modified or redefined.

Where symbols are used only at one point in the manual (e.g. in a Box), they may not be included in this list, but in that case a definition will be given at that point.

a, b, c	parameters of various probability distributions
C_r	reflection coefficient, H_r/H_i
c_w	air/water friction coefficient
D_e	effective particle diameter as measured by sieving
D_{e50}	median effective particle diameter as measured by sieving
D_n	nominal block diameter ($= M/\rho_r$)
D_{n50}	nominal diameter ($= M_{50}/\rho_r$)
D_z	sieve diameter, diameter of stone which exceeds the $z\%$ value of sieve curve
$E_{\eta\eta}(f)$	wave frequency spectrum
$E_{\eta\eta}(f,\theta)$	wave directional spectrum
f	wave frequency
F	fetch length
f_p	spectral peak frequency
g	acceleration due to gravity
G_s	gap between two detached breakwater structures
h	water depth
h_s	water depth at a structure
$\tilde{H} = F_n\{\tilde{h},\tilde{F},\tilde{t}\}$	dimensionless wave height prediction parameter
H	wave height
H_b	individual or regular breaking wave height
H_i	height of wave incident at beach or structure
H_o	offshore wave height, i.e. wave height in deep water
H_{os}	offshore significant wave height, unaffected by shallow-water
H_r	height of wave reflected from beach or structure
H_s	significant wave height, average of highest one-third of wave heights
H_{s_b}	significant wave height at breaking
i_w	wind-induced water surface slope
k	wave number, $2\pi/L$
K_d	diffraction coefficient
K_R	refraction coefficient

K_s	shoaling coefficient
L	wave length
L_m	wave length of mean T_m period
L_o	deep water or offshore wave length, $Gt^2/2\pi$
L_{om}	offshore wave length of mean T_m period
L_s	detached breakwater structure length
m	beach slope (= cotan α)
m_2	second spectral moment
m_0	zeroth spectral moment
N	number of waves in a storm event
N_s	relative wave height, $H_s/\Delta D_{n50}$
$P(X \leq x)$	probability less than a given value
p_a	atmospheric pressure in mbar
q	rate of supply or loss of beach material per unit length of coastline
Q	rate of longshore transport (or drift) of beach material
R_c	crest freeboard, level of crest relative to still water level
s	wave steepness or sea steepness
$S(x)$	number of individual stones moved longshore by an individual wave
t	wind duration
t_a	thickness of permeable beach material
t_B	beach thickness
T	wave period
$\tilde{T} = F_n\{\tilde{h},\tilde{F},\tilde{t}\}$	dimensionless wave period prediction parameter
T_c	average time between storms
T_m	mean wave period
T_o	relative mean wave period, $T_m(g/D_{n50})^{\frac{1}{2}}$
T_{op}	relative peak wave period, $T_p(g/D_{n50})^{\frac{1}{2}}$
T_p	spectral peak period, inverse of peak frequency
T_R	return period of a certain event
T_s	significant wave period
T_z	mean wave period derived from counting analysis
U	depth-averaged current speed
U_{rms}	root mean square bottom orbital velocity beneath random waves
U_w	average wind speed
w_s	fall velocity of isolated grains of sediment in stagnant water
X_s	distance of a detached breakwater structure from the original beach crest
z_a	static rise in water level directly due to atmospheric pressure

α	angle between the plane of the beach surface and the horizontal plane
β	angle between wave orthogonal and beach normal
β_b	angle between wave orthogonal at breaking and beach normal
β_o	wave direction in deep water
γ_{br}	breaker index or maximum H/h ratio
Δ	relative buoyant density of material considered, e.g. for rock = $(\rho_r/\rho_w)-1$
η_{max}	wave set-up at the shoreline
η_{min}	wave set-down at the breaker line
η_w	wave set-up
θ	wave direction
λ_i	internal pore-pressure penetration length
ρ	density
ρ_{air}	density of air
ρ_r	mass density of material, over-dried density
ρ_w	mass density of sea water
τ	bed shear stress
τ_c	bed shear stress due to currents
τ_{cr}	bed shear stress of threshold of sediment motion
τ_w	peak bed shear stress due to waves

Acronyms

AONB	Area of Outstanding Natural Beauty
BODC	British Oceanographic Data Centre
CAD	Computer Aided Design
CCW	Countryside Council for Wales
CD	Chart Datum
CDM	Construction (Design and Management) Regulations 1994
CE	Crown Estate, UK
CERC	Coastal Engineering Research Center, USA
CIRIA	Construction Industry Research and Information Association, UK
CUR	Centre for Civil Engineering Research and Codes, The Netherlands
DoE	Department of the Environment, England
DoT	Department of Transport, England
DTM	Digital Terrain Model
DXF	Data eXchange Format
EA	Environmental Assessment
EN	English Nature
EPSRC	Engineering and Physical Sciences Research Council, UK
ES	Environmental Statement
EU	European Union
FIDIC	Federation Internationale des Ingenieurs - Conseils
GIS	Geographical Information System
GPS	Global Positioning System
IADC	International Association of Dredging Companies
IAHR	International Association for Hydraulic Research
ICE	Institution of Civil Engineers, UK
IOC	International Oceanographic Commission
IPCC	Inter-governmental Panel on Climate Change
JNCC	Joint Nature Conservation Committee, UK
JONSWAP	Joint North Sea Wave Project
MAFF	Ministry of Agriculture, Fisheries and Food, England
MCA	Multi-Criteria Analysis
MEWAM	Methods for the Examination of Water Associated Materials
MHW	Mean High Water
MHWN	Mean High Water of Neap Tides
MHWS	Mean High Water of Spring Tides
MLW	Mean Low Water
MLWN	Mean Low Water of Neap Tides
MLWS	Mean Low Water of Spring Tides
MPCU	Marine Pollution Control Unit, appropriate local region of England or Wales
MSL	Mean Sea Level
MUFHRC	Middlesex University Flood Hazard Research Centre, England
MWL	Mean Water Level
NERC	Natural Environment Research Council, UK
NGO	Non-Governmental Organisation
NNR	National Nature Reserve
NRA	National Rivers Authority[1], England and Wales
NVC	National Vegetation Classification
ODN	Ordnance Datum Newlyn
OJEC	Official Journal of the European Communities
OS	Ordnance Survey of Great Britain and Northern Ireland
OSCR	Ocean Surface Current Radar

---

[1] As of April 1996, the functions of the National Rivers Authority (NRA), Her Majesty's Inspectorate of Pollution (HMIP) and the Waste Regulation Authorities (WRAs) were taken over, in England and Wales, by the Environment Agency, in Scotland, by the Scottish Environmental Protection Agency, and in Northern Ireland, by the Environment and Heritage Service.

POL	Proudman Oceanographic Laboratory, UK
POT	Peaks Over Threshold
RDBMS	Relational Database Management System
RFDC	Regional Flood Defence Committee, appropriate local region, England and Wales
SAC	Special Area of Conservation
SCI	Site of Community Interest
SCOPAC	Standing Conference on Problems Associated with the Coastline
SFC	Sea Fisheries Committee, appropriate local region of England
SMA	Sensitive Marine Area
SMB	Sverdrup Munk Bretschneider (wave prediction method)
SMP	Shoreline Management Plan
SPA	Special Protection Area
SSSI	Site of Special Scientific Interest
SWL	Still Water Level
TAW	Technical Advisory Committee on Water Defences (Dutch)
TBM	Temporary Bench Mark
TMA	Texel Marsden Arsloe (wave prediction method)
UK	United Kingdom
WO	Welsh Office
WWF	Worldwide Fund for Nature

1   Introduction

1.1   GENERAL PHILOSOPHY OF BEACH MANAGEMENT

This manual seeks to encapsulate the philosophy and to describe the details of good present-day beach management practice concentrating on the management of beaches for coastal defence. The philosophy described has evolved gradually as the understanding of major processes has developed. It reflects a move from a largely *ad-hoc* approach, arising out of initial inadvertent interference with beaches, to more conscious attempts to control or preserve beach attributes, whether for amenity, coastal defence or environmental reasons.

The fundamental concepts now widely accepted as forming the essential principles of the present state-of-the-art in beach management can be summarised as follows:

1.   To understand and work with natural processes. This will include:

- seeking greater understanding of the local and regional geology and geomorphology (including origins, sources and losses of beach material) and its relationship to particular beaches
- seeking greater understanding of the forces driving beach processes - winds, waves, tides, currents
- monitoring beach morphology (physical and environmental response to driving forces and sediment supply)
- understanding interrelationships, interactions and dependencies between beaches and the wider coastal environment within a framework of strategic planning.

2.   To determine coastal defence and environmental performance requirements and establish broad management strategies to meet these requirements, where necessary identifying:

- individual problems
- response options.

3.   Where required, economically justified and environmentally acceptable, to undertake improvement schemes. Such schemes may include:

- new beaches
- works such as beach recharge and beach control structures designed to change the nature or rate of existing beach processes, such works often having both initial and subsequent phases during their design life
- works designed to accommodate existing processes such as dune management or managed landward realignment.

4.   Establish, as part of any improvement scheme, detailed ongoing strategies of monitoring, management and maintenance. These strategies will require periodic review and may include:

- longshore recycling and profile regrading
- structure maintenance
- amenity-based activities such as the control of debris and blown sand.

The elaboration of these concepts forms the subject matter of this manual, which largely focuses on management of the beach as a coastal defence.

1.2 HISTORICAL CONTEXT OF BEACH MANAGEMENT IN THE BRITISH ISLES

The earliest influences by man on beaches occufred well before the Victorian era. However, it was only then that shoreline and beach management, whether deliberate or inadvertent, commenced in earnest.

Early examples of man's influence on beaches include:

• commercial sea trade and fishing activities where fishing quays and harbour breakwaters often acted as coastal groynes, trapping the longshore movement of sediment, causing beach accretion on one side of the harbour and erosion on the other (see Figure 1.1)

Figure 1.1   *Beach west of Dover Harbour, from Shakespeare Cliff, Kent (courtesy HR Wallingford)*

• waste dumping on the shore, from early examples, such as the discharge of stone ballast from sailing ships, to the later impacts of the discharge of mining waste, the latter sometimes creating whole beaches of waste material such as coal or china clay waste (see Figure 1.2)

• the extraction of gravel and sand from beaches for aggregates and other construction work

• transport routes, both road and rail, constructed along the top of beaches (see Figure 1.3), thereby limiting the free movement of beach sediment and, on eroding foreshores, necessitating protective measures or accommodation of beach roll-back by landward movement of the transport route

• glass making, using beach sand

• local groyning of beaches to protect key coastal buildings such as coastguard stations.

Figure 1.2   *Beach formed from china clay waste, Carlyon Bay, Cornwall (courtesy HR Wallingford)*

Figure 1.3   *Rail track on crest of shingle beach, Co Wicklow, Ireland (courtesy HR Wallingford)*

In the Regency - Edwardian period, a significant and more managed set of additions was made to this *ad hoc* mixture of generally inadvertent beach management/control measures which developed in the wake of the Industrial Revolution. The new measures often had a genuinely philanthropic motive and included the following approaches:

1. Large seawall and promenade structures were constructed on the crest of beaches for amenity and recreational reasons (see Figure 1.4) and in front of cliffs to prevent cliff erosion (as at Bournemouth, Dorset). These structures often caused erosion of the beaches fronting them. Beaches downdrift were also affected as their sediment supply was cut off. As a result, engineers found it necessary to introduce additional (intermediate) groynes or new promenades and groyne fields downdrift. The lengthening of the promenade at Minehead, Somerset, UK is a classic example of this.

Figure 1.4   *Amenity and recreational use of beach and promenade at Mablethorpe, Lincolnshire (courtesy Posford Duvivier)*

2. Floodbanks and outfall structures were constructed on saltmarshes to facilitate land drainage and to create high quality agricultural land (as in the Fens of Norfolk). These structures often interfered with the complex interactions between saltmarsh lands and beaches thereby causing loss of habitat and erosion.

3. Seawalls were also constructed to permit reclamations for coastal industry (power stations, refineries, etc.) requiring access to water for their processes. Again these seawalls have often had a major impact on coastal morphological processes.

4. Sewage outfalls were often constructed across beaches to reduce direct pollution of the beach, but these sometimes acted as groynes and caused accretion/erosion problems.

Beach management schemes, often consequential to the Regency - Edwardian works or uncontrolled housing developments near the shore, continued throughout the first half of the 20th century. The development of mass tourism immediately after the end of the Second World War in 1945, including the advent of holiday camps and holiday homes, led to pressures for the shoreline position, and for fronting beaches, to be fixed.

In 1945, as part of the post-war reconstruction process J A Steers was commissioned by the Government to review the coastline and its development. His report eventually led in 1949 to the Coast Protection Act with its more centralised and rationalised approach.

A key event in the national (and indeed European) approach to coastal defence occurred with the 1953 North Sea storm flood. From this time onwards public awareness became dominated by fears in respect of flooding. Local boards (now the Drainage Boards and the National Rivers Authority) were empowered to carry out works to alleviate flooding. Unfortunately, the works then implemented often hindered progress towards the more sensitive, strategic and economically efficient approach which Steers had advocated.

Whilst coastal defence became considerably more organised, in respect of beach management, the divisions of responsibility and administrative boundaries often bore little resemblance to natural process boundaries. Thus works which may have been beneficial to one authority's beaches sometimes had a detrimental effect on the beaches of an authority lying downdrift. Indeed, piecemeal solutions within one coastal authority's boundaries have often had an adverse effect on the overall integrity of their own defences.

Various local government reorganisations carried out since the 1950's have had little impact on this situation, because they have been undertaken for reasons other than beach management. However, the recent establishment of Regional Coastal Groups of operating authorities (NRA regions and maritime district councils), and the move towards producing regional Shoreline Management Plans operative across groups of authorities, is now addressing this problem. The present legislative and administrative arrangements in England and Wales are shown in Box 1.1. Somewhat different arrangements apply in Scotland and Northern Ireland.

Another relatively recent and significant development in beach management has occurred as a result of the conservation movement. In the 1970's, the National Trust started to acquire large tracts of relatively natural scenic coastline in order to preserve it and now, in conjunction with other charities such as the National Trust for Scotland, County Wildlife Trusts, Royal Society for the Protection of Birds, Wildfowl and Wetlands Trust, Woodland Trust, John Muir Trust, etc., owns or manages over 140,000ha of coastal land in Great Britain within 835 sites.

More recently, beaches containing nationally valued geology, landscape and biota have been set aside as various types of conservation area. More than 1,570,000ha of coastal land in Great Britain are designated as one or more of: Special Areas of Conservation, Special Protection Areas, Ramsar sites, National Nature Reserves, Sites of Special Scientific Interest (SSSI), Biosphere Reserves, Biogenetic Reserves, Local Nature Reserves and/or Country Parks (Keddie, 1995). Furthermore, the Ministry of Defence is responsible for over 472km of coastline, while 1525km are incorporated within Heritage Coasts some of which may coincide with the above designated sites. These sites together therefore represent a significant proportion of the 12,500km-long Great Britain coastline.

In all of these historic and more recent moves in beach management, conflicts of interest and aspiration between both public and private organisations and individuals have existed. Shoreline Management Plans (SMP) and wider coastal zone management will generally resolve major conflicts and set overall objectives. The role of beach management is to achieve the local, and beach related, coastal defence/nature conservation/public amenity/industrial objectives within the overall coastal strategy.

Box 1.1   *Coastal defence legislation and responsibilities in England and Wales*

Coastal defence is a composite term covering protection against both coastal erosion (coast protection) and flooding (flood defence). It is important to be aware of the distinction between these terms in order to understand the legislative arrangements which affect coastal defence and their implementation. Further information on coastal defence in the wider context of coastal management can be found in Section 5.1.

Flood or sea defence applies to those measures taken against flood hazard.

Coast protection applies to measures taken against land erosion and other encroachments of the sea.

The responsibilities of the Ministry of Agriculture, Fisheries and Food (MAFF) include the provision of grant aid for capital works carried out for coastal defence by operating authorities. In Wales these responsibilities are those of the Welsh Office. Detailed requirements for the publication of notices, consultations with other bodies and the conditions attached to grants are contained in the relevant grant memoranda.

Flood or sea defence
The construction, improvement and maintenance of defences against coastal flooding is undertaken by the National Rivers Authority (NRA) under the Water Resources Act 1991. The flood defence functions of the NRA (which from 1 April 1996 will become part of the Environment Agency) are controlled by 10 Regional Flood Defence Committees (RFDC). The chairperson of each RFDC is appointed by MAFF, with a majority of members being local council nominees. In addition, the NRA has powers to provide flood warning systems.

Flood defence works may also be undertaken by others, including local authorities, under the Land Drainage Act 1991. In addition, local landowners (including such bodies as Railtrack) may construct flood defence works. Joint schemes involving several authorities are possible.

Coast protection against erosion and encroachment by the sea is undertaken by maritime district councils. These authorities are empowered under the Coast Protection Act 1949 to carry out works as required for the protection of their area. Where capital schemes are concerned (excluding emergency works), councils are required to consult with: the NRA, neighbouring maritime district councils, the County Council, harbour, conservancy and navigation authorities and fisheries committees. They may also have to apply for a licence under the Food and Environment Protection Act 1985. All schemes require the approval of MAFF and specific conditions may be attached to this approval. Before MAFF can give formal approval, other relevant Government Departments, the Crown Estate, the Countryside Commission and English Nature or the Countryside Council for Wales are consulted. Proposed schemes must be advertised.

Landowners and other bodies, including Railtrack, Highway and Harbour Authorities, may also undertake coast protection works. Such bodies must normally consult the relevant coast protection authority before commencement of works (though harbour authorities have some exemptions from this).

Co-ordination
The operating authorities (NRA and maritime district councils) are responsible for identifying the need for coastal defence works and initiating schemes and studies. The NRA is required to exercise general supervision over all matters relating to flood defence. MAFF encourages Regional Coastal Groups, which now cover most of the coastline of England and Wales, to encourage operating authorities to liaise in developing coastal defence strategies in their areas.

Permissive powers
The powers governing coastal defence vested in operating authorities under the legislation are generally permissive rather than mandatory. These authorities are not therefore obliged to prevent flooding or erosion and have the option of allowing natural processes to take place without intervention.

Funding
MAFF only pays grants to eligible authorities for those capital works which can be demonstrated to be environmentally acceptable, technically sound and economically worthwhile. The rates of grant payable depend upon the needs of the area in relation to the resources available. In addition to grant aiding the initial recharge of beaches for coastal defence purposes, grant aid will be considered for any necessary subsequent replenishment, recycling and monitoring of beach material provided that the scheme is part of a long-term management plan for the relevant stretch of coastline. In most circumstances grant aid is also available for the preparation of Environmental Statements.

The residual capital costs of grant-aided schemes, the costs of all non grant-aided schemes and all revenue expenditure are financed firstly from local funds:

(a)   NRA spending is funded primarily from levies on county councils
(b)   for district council grant-aided schemes, supplementary credit approval is generally available to give the council borrowing powers to fund the residual capital costs. Slightly different arrangements apply in Wales.

For the most part local costs of coastal defences are financed ultimately by central government through the Revenue Support Grant scheme. The situation is different in other parts of the UK e.g. Scotland and Northern Ireland.

1.3 OBJECTIVES, READERSHIP AND STRUCTURE OF THE MANUAL

1.3.1 Objectives

The manual has the following objectives:

1. To draw together existing knowledge and experience and the results of recent and current research to produce detailed procedural guidance on beach recharge and beach management, as part of a coastal defence strategy.

2. To provide a comprehensive and authoritative manual of current best practice for use by beach managers and coastal engineers.

1.3.2 Readership

The manual has been designed for use by beach managers, and by consulting engineers and designers concerned with beaches characterised by non-cohesive sediments. It has been drafted to provide guidance for both the specialist and non-specialist, focusing on management of the beach as a coastal defence. In this respect, some of the general information included is intended to educate the graduate engineer inexperienced in matters of beach management. Overall the manual is intended to be informative to all readers and, within this framework, detailed information which the specialist coastal engineer will require is also provided.

A significant body of literature on the subject of beaches exists within the international coastal engineering community, including documents published or in preparation which cover experience and practice in other countries such as The Netherlands and the USA. Whilst taking full account of this experience and practice, the manual deliberately seeks to reflect UK practice in order to specifically assist UK coastal engineers and beach managers in local authorities and the NRA. However, it is also designed to be of use to a wider international audience and this is reflected by reference to international experience and techniques which are not directly applicable to the UK macro-tidal, storm wave dominated shoreline. In addition, it is hoped that the reference to UK practice and experience will provide a valuable insight to international readers, which may assist in the understanding and management of beaches elsewhere.

This manual is complementary to the recently published CIRIA/CUR (1991) *Manual on the use of rock in coast and shoreline engineering*, the CIRIA book *Seawall design* (Thomas and Hall, 1992) and the CIRIA (1990) *Guide to the use of groynes in coastal engineering*. In order to produce a comprehensive document some overlap between these publications has been necessary, for example in areas such as hydraulic loadings and the design process, and where this occurs consistency has been maintained as far as possible. As a general rule, however, the Beach Management Manual represents a comprehensive source of information on beach management, without reproducing material which is readily available from other sources.

1.3.3 Structure and use of manual

The manual has been structured, as far as possible, around the beach management process, as illustrated in Figure 1.5. The cells of this flowchart direct the reader through the manual (and thus the process) through reference to relevant chapters or sections of the manual. The approach adopted recognises that in many situations the design, construction and periodic maintenance of major management schemes may be necessary and indeed Chapters 6 to 10 of the Manual are devoted to this subject. However, because beach management (described in outline in Chapter 5) often involves interfering with or adjusting natural beach processes, beach schemes must be designed with an appreciation of existing coastal processes and their management, and these are therefore discussed in the early chapters of the manual.

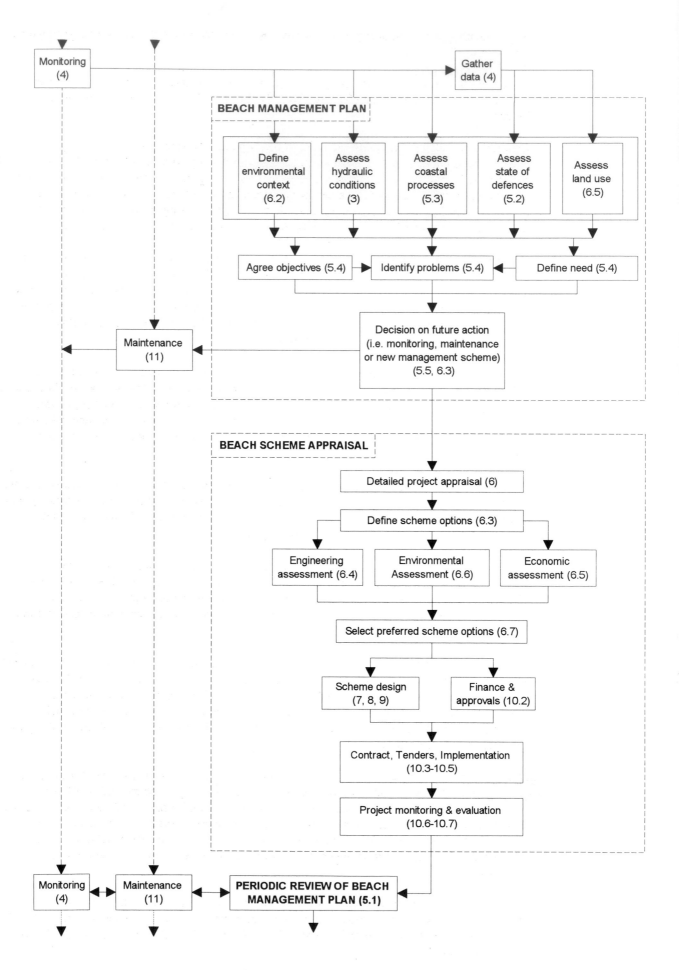

Figure 1.5   *Beach management process*

Approximate locations of specific sites in the UK mentioned in the document can be found by reference to Figure 1.6.

References to places in the *manual* generally include the country. However, if the country of the location is not stated, it can be assumed to be the UK. Within the UK, locations are given by county.

Chapter 2 provides a general introduction to beach processes, morphology and attributes, covering both physical and environmental aspects and dealing with origins of beaches and beach material, sediment transport processes and influences that modify beach development. It also includes an overview of how these elements interact in the UK context. This chapter will provide a useful introduction both to the reader coming to the subject for the first time and also to the experienced beach manager wishing to review particular aspects of beach processes.

The development and maintenance of beaches is dominated by the normal and extreme climates of the prevailing wave, tide and water level conditions. The manual addresses this subject in *Chapter 3*. The chapter provides guidance (with formulae and graphs) for estimating conditions for use in the management of beaches and the design of beach schemes. The more experienced coastal engineer may find the information on joint probabilities and climate variability, for example, of interest because it reflects latest research findings.

Chapter 4 deals with the essential starting point for all successful beach management - data collection and monitoring. The chapter covers the collection of all relevant types of data (beach profile, plan shape and sediment size) together with related environmental, seabed, hydraulic and geotechnical information. It reviews the requirements of an initial survey and subsequent monitoring. The chapter concludes with a discussion of methods of storage, analysis and appraisal of the data.

Chapter 5 describes the basic principles of beach management, setting it in the context of other management plans in the coastal zone. The chapter explains how identification of existing and future beach status and behaviour enables performance requirements to be identified and an implementation plan for beach management prepared.

Many beach management strategies will involve investment in capital schemes. *Chapter 6* details the basic elements of the appraisal and design process common to all such schemes. The chapter covers problem definition, constraints and opportunities, options for beach management and their likely effectiveness, economic appraisal, environmental assessment and scheme selection.

An important option for beach management is beach recharge. *Chapter 7* describes this subject in depth. Aspects covered include the sourcing, selection and specification of beach recharge material and the identification of the volumes required and the procedures for obtaining it. Delivery, placement and measurement techniques are also reviewed. The chapter concludes with an assessment of the environmental considerations which arise as a result of the design and construction of such schemes.

Recharge and other beach management schemes often require control structures for effective performance. *Chapter 8* provides details on the design of the plan shape and profile of such structures, indicating how types and designs may vary with tidal range and beach sediment size. Structure types covered include groynes, detached and shore connected breakwaters, modified seawalls and revetments, sills and beach drainage systems. The chapter concludes with a discussion of cost optimisation, environmental impacts and enhancements, and construction methods.

Chapter 9 looks at a broader range of beach design options and covers the subjects of dune management, rock beaches, managed retreat and adjustments to sediment supply rates. Not all of these will necessarily require a scheme of capital works, but all will require some kind of planned investment.

Figure 1.6   *County divisions of the United Kingdom*

Chapter 10 describes the practicalities of scheme implementation. The chapter covers the entire process of obtaining necessary approvals and finance, preparation of contract documents, tendering procedures and construction. It concludes by discussing post project evaluation and monitoring.

Schemes should not be implemented in isolation from the overall beach management strategy and process. *Chapter 11* closes the manual with a discussion of ongoing management and beach maintenance, whether this is associated with a capital works scheme or not. Subjects covered include periodic recycling and recharge of beach material and beach profile regrading. Maintenance of beach control structures is also discussed, as is control of blown sand and the environmental considerations associated with ongoing management.

2 Beaches: attributes, morphology and processes

2.1 INTRODUCTION

To manage beaches successfully, it is important to understand how they were formed, the processes that determine their morphology, and how they are likely to develop in the future. It is also necessary to appreciate the many attributes that a beach may have, ranging from providing a natural defence against flooding, to being important as a haven for wildlife. This chapter considers these topics.

2.1.1 Definition of a beach

In this manual, a beach is defined as a deposit of non-cohesive material (e.g. sand, gravel) situated on the interface between dry land and the sea (or other large expanses of water) and actively "worked" by present-day hydrodynamic processes (i.e. waves, tides and currents) and sometimes by winds.

Most beaches extend further landward than the highest tidal or still water level, onto a "backshore" (see Box 2.1). This area is only occasionally affected by wave action. On sandy coasts the backshore often includes an active dune system (see Section 9.1), which forms an integral part of the beach itself. Other features (e.g. cliffs, seawalls) can also affect beaches and, whilst the management of these is not discussed, their effect on beach processes is considered.

Beaches normally extend over the whole inter-tidal "foreshore", i.e. the area which is regularly covered and uncovered by the rise and fall of the tides (see Box 2.1). The seaward limit of beaches varies from site to site and from season to season at any particular location. For example, the impressive shingle barrier of Chesil Beach (see Figure 2.1) on the coast of Dorset extends only slightly beyond the lowest tidal level, at a sharp division between the mobile gravel particles and the clay seabed. Other beaches, particularly those of sand which are exposed to heavy wave action, extend much further seaward. By contrast shingle beaches may have their seaward limit well above low water, for example where they lie on a rocky foreshore (see Figure 2.2).

Other zones relevant to beaches have been identified in Box 2.1. These are believed to offer a helpful categorisation of the main zones of wave action, sediment transport and beach morphology, but the reader is cautioned against attempting to delineate the limits of these zones too precisely as they will vary significantly with many factors including location, tidal characteristics, beach sediment and level of wave action.

All natural beaches have a variety of sizes of sediment present on their surface and through their depth. Chesil Beach has a surface covering of fine gravel to coarse pebbles, but below its surface lies a core consisting of a mixture of gravel, sand and clay particles. In this manual, we have restricted attention to beaches whose surface sediment is non-cohesive, usually sand and gravel and have excluded muddy coastlines, such as saltmarshes and estuarine mud-flats. These beaches can be categorised into four principal beach types (see Figure 2.3):

- shingle
- shingle upper/sand lower
- shingle/sand mixed
- sand.

Figure 2.1   *Chesil Beach, Dorset (courtesy HR Wallingford)*

Figure 2.2   *Shingle beach on rocky foreshore, Southerndown, Mid Glamorgan (courtesy HR Wallingford)*

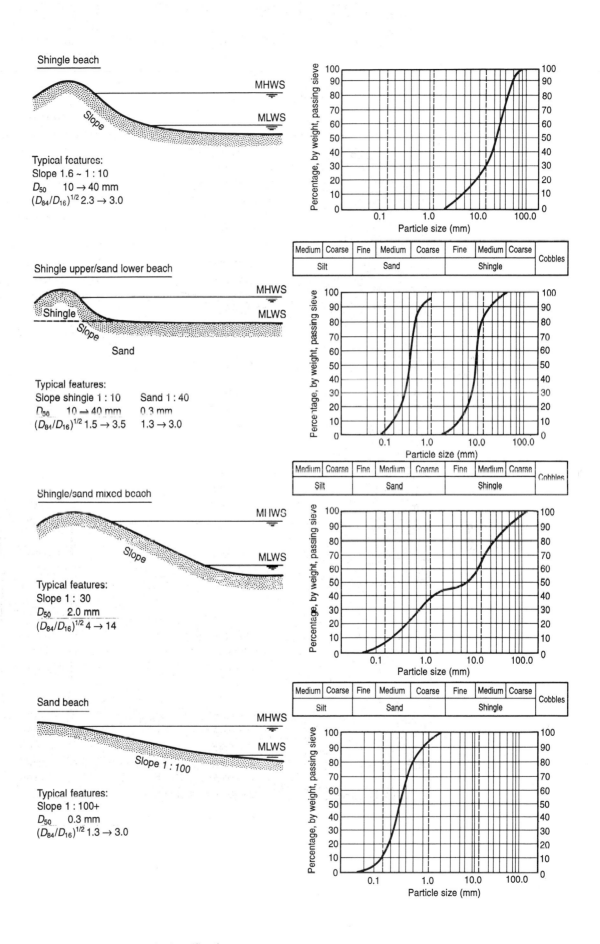

Shingle beach

Typical features:
Slope 1.6 ~ 1 : 10
D_{50} 10 → 40 mm
$(D_{84}/D_{16})^{1/2}$ 2.3 → 3.0

Shingle upper/sand lower beach

Typical features:
Slope shingle 1 : 10   Sand 1 : 40
D_{50} 10 → 40 mm   0.3 mm
$(D_{84}/D_{16})^{1/2}$ 1.5 → 3.5   1.3 → 3.0

Shingle/sand mixed beach

Typical features:
Slope 1 : 30
D_{50} 2.0 mm
$(D_{84}/D_{16})^{1/2}$ 4 → 14

Sand beach

Typical features:
Slope 1 : 100+
D_{50} 0.3 mm
$(D_{84}/D_{16})^{1/2}$ 1.3 → 3.0

Figure 2.3   *Beach classification*

Box 2.1   *Definition of beach zones*

Backshore	The upper part of the active beach above high water and extending to the toe of the *beach head,* affected by waves occurring at high water during severe storm events
Beach crest	The point representing the normal limit of high tide wave induced run-up
Beach face	From the *beach crest* out to the limit of sediment movement
Beach head	The cliff, dune or seawall forming the landward limit of the active beach
Breaker zone	The zone within which waves approaching the coastline commence breaking, typically in water depths of between 5 and 10 metres
Foreshore	The intertidal area below highest tide level and above lowest tide level
Limit of storm erosion	A position, typically in a maximum water depth of 8 to 10 metres, often identifiable on surveys by a break (i.e. sudden change) in the slope of the bed
Nearshore	The zone which extends from the *swash zone* to the position marking the start of the *offshore zone*, typically to water depths in the order of 20m
Offshore	The zone beyond the *nearshore zone* where sediment motion induced by waves alone effectively ceases and where the influence of the sea bed on wave action has become small in comparison with the effect of wind
Surf zone	The zone of wave action extending from the water line (which varies with tide, surge, set-up, etc.) out to the most seaward point of the zone (*breaker zone*) at which waves approaching the coastline commence breaking, typically in water depths of between 5 and 10 metres
Swash zone	The zone of wave action on the beach, which moves as water levels vary, extending from the limit of run-down to the limit of run-up

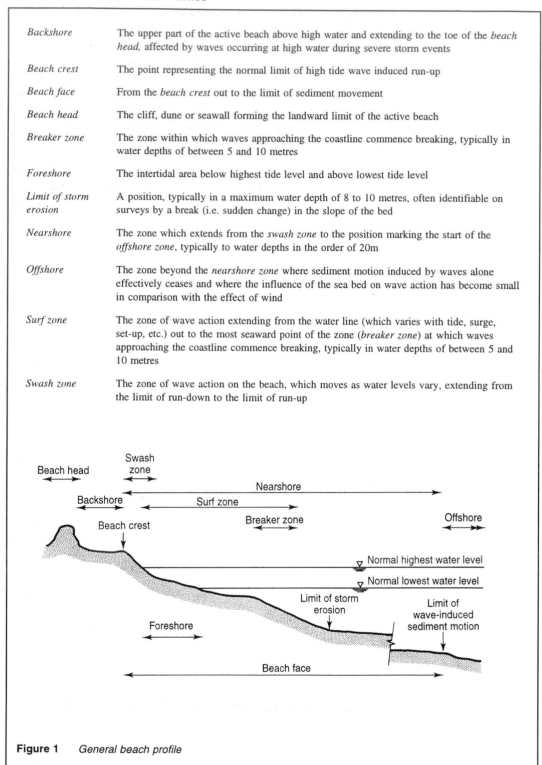

Figure 1   *General beach profile*

2.1.2   Chapter layout

Having established some basic definitions in respect of beaches, Section 2.2 considers the important features or attributes of beaches. These range from the role of beaches as defences against erosion or flooding, to their importance as areas used for recreation, or as habitats for plants and animals. Attention is then turned to the various processes affecting beaches. The morphology and development of beaches are dominated by three principal factors, namely:

- the origins and character of the beach material
- the movement of that material by waves, currents, etc.

- various "external" modifying influences such as the solid geology of the area and management of the coastline.

Whilst these three topics are inter-related, it is convenient to deal with them in separate sections of this chapter. Section 2.3 deals with the origins of beach material, and its characteristics. Section 2.4 then deals with the present-day processes which mobilise and transport that material. For simplicity it considers sediment transport on an idealised beach (i.e. a beach with an ample supply of sediment) and a simplified hydrodynamic climate (i.e. wave and tidal conditions).

Section 2.5 then discusses the large number of complicating or modifying factors, some of which usually influence the development of a particular beach. These include the effects of solid geology, of various kinds of intervention by man, and of climate change and sea level rise.

Section 2.6 discusses the concepts of sediment transport budgets, including sources and sinks of beach material, and the derived concept of units for natural divisions of a coastline into *cells* which are often appropriate units for beach management. The UK coastline is used to give examples of these concepts.

2.2   BEACH ATTRIBUTES

The following sections describe the characteristics or features of a beach which could potentially be affected in some way by management. These characteristics are presented in five groups:

- coastal defence attributes
- flora and fauna (i.e. the natural environment)
- human issues (including both human activities and features which are of interest to humans)
- environmental quality (water quality, sediment quality, debris, etc.)
- other aspects of the physical environment (e.g. geology).

The description of the characteristic is followed by a brief discussion of the various beach attributes (e.g. sediment size, beach slope, etc.) which are relevant and important to the continued well being and/or existence of that feature.

Beaches are dynamic structures; they respond to changes in the hydrodynamic conditions over short and long terms. These responses, such as overtopping and landward migration of the crest, are natural to a beach and should not be seen as negative processes. They do, however, need to be taken into account in the management of the beach. Changes in coastal processes, whether natural or man-induced, can lead to problems or opportunities at the point of the change or elsewhere on the coast.

2.2.1   Coastal defence and other physical attributes

Beaches as coastal defences

In most situations around the UK coastline, beaches form a vital part of any defence against erosion or flooding. In some locations, beaches in their natural state provide the only defence. Almost all beaches are a valuable asset to the coastline and its protection.

Beaches are a natural buffer between the sea and the land. They are efficient dissipators of wave energy and reduce the damage to the beach head and hinterland due to overtopping, flooding or direct wave action. It must be recognised, however, that a healthy natural beach, which has endured storm events for centuries may not continue to provide a satisfactory standard of defence. Massive barriers such as Chesil Beach (see Figure 2.1), or the sandy beaches along the coast of the Netherlands have been breached in the past, with subsequent serious flooding of the hinterland. Similar failures in the future could have catastrophic effects.

Some beaches are subject to overtopping in severe events and also to percolation of water through the beach structure. Gradual erosion of the solid rock platform on which beaches rest and attrition of the granular material itself can affect all beaches, as can the potential movement of material along the coast and to the landward. In the UK, most beaches now have restricted supplies of fresh material, and are therefore always liable to adjust to such movements by gradual landward migration. This tendency is reinforced by any rise in sea level relative to the land (see Section 2.5.3). If such landward movement is prevented by man-made structures (e.g. seawalls), then the consequences of erosion are likely to be serious; this has been termed "coastal squeeze".

Viewed as a naturally occurring coastal defence structure, a beach has to be assessed for the standard of protection it provides at present, and that which it is likely to provide in the future. If necessary a beach may need to be modified, for example by adding extra material, and subsequently managed to achieve the required standard. Beaches therefore need to be treated as a coastal defence in a similar manner to the existing coastal stock of seawalls, groynes, etc. Provided that management can be carried out in an appropriate and environmentally-sensitive manner, then other attributes of beaches, such as those described below, can also be preserved.

2.2.2   Flora and fauna

Beaches may provide an important nature conservation resource by way of the fauna and flora they support, either directly (e.g. the diversity of plants in a sandy beach fronting a sand dune) or indirectly (e.g. the numbers of birds which feed on species directly associated with the beach). Such beaches may be designated for their scientific importance via a number of designations. Details of the relevant designations (e.g. Ramsar sites, Sites of Special Scientific Interest (SSSI), Special Areas of Conservation (SAC), Special Protection Areas (SPA) and National Nature Reserves (NNR)) are outlined in DoE Planning Policy Guidance Note 9, Nature Conservation (DoE, 1994). The degree of protection (statutory or otherwise) and management to conserve their important features, will vary according to their designation and the land ownership, or on the scope of any management agreements.

Flora

The establishment of flora on non-cohesive beach sediments is generally limited due to the instability of the substrate for root anchorage. There are, however, some distinctive floral communities which do occur in shingle and sand beaches as well as communities which exist on the nearshore zone, such as eel grass and kelp. These latter species provide habitat for a diverse and abundant associated flora and fauna. Otherwise, those plants which do establish themselves on a shingle or sand beach generally occur above high water mark and are essentially terrestrial in character rather than marine.

To enable vegetation (e.g. strandline species, such as sand couchgrass and sea sandwort) to colonise a sandy beach there must be a source of organic matter. This is most likely to be provided by decaying seaweed and other vegetation stranded by high tides. Once vegetation is established it can tolerate a certain degree of sand deposition. The ability to withstand sand deposition depends on the species. Burial by sand actually stimulates growth in certain species (e.g. sand couchgrass and marram grass).

Beach levels are clearly important for determining the survival of vegetation, particularly because of the degree of inundation to which the plants are subjected. The types of vegetation which occur on shingle and sandy beaches have adapted to low levels of water and derive much of their water from sources other than seawater (e.g. fresh water run-off, rain, dew). They are, therefore, tolerant of only very limited inundation by seawater. Such plants are also susceptible to damage by the movement of shingle. Examples of typical beach flora are shown in Figures 2.4 and 2.5.

Figure 2.4   *Sea Kale (Crambe maritima) Pagham Beach, W. Sussex (courtesy HR Wallingford)*

Figure 2.5   *Yellow Horned Poppy (Glaucium flavum) Pagham Beach, W. Sussex (courtesy HR Wallingford)*

Invertebrates

Both the abundance and the diversity of invertebrates which inhabit sand and shingle beaches are limited due to the instability of the substrate; the abrasive nature of the sediment, a high-wave energy environment and the low levels of organic matter present.

Shingle beaches are almost devoid of life in terms of marine species, whereas sandy beaches support a variety of infauna (i.e. organisms which live in the sand). Those species which do inhabit sandy beaches are generally hard-shelled, burrowing organisms. A few marine worms have adapted to live in sand and build tubes, made of sand, around themselves in order to gain some protection.

Sediment size is of prime importance in determining the abundance and diversity of species which occur within beaches. The greater the particle size the smaller the surface area of a given volume of sediment. A smaller surface area provides less interstitial space for species to live and less space for essential oxygen and organic matter. Sediment size is also important for filter feeding species which live in sand, as different sized sediments (both large and smaller than native) introduced into a habitat, may cause clogging of respiratory surfaces.

Beach level is also an important characteristic. Invertebrates require a certain amount of tidal inundation in each tidal cycle for feeding purposes. Many species which inhabit non-cohesive sediments are filter feeders and feed only when the tide is in.

Invertebrates which utilise shingle and sand beaches include terrestrial species such as various types of flies and wasps, which make use of the substrate above the strand line. These species often provide a food source for seabirds but, when occurring in large populations, may require management where the beach has significant amenity use (see Section 2.2.3).

Birds

A number of birds use beaches as sources of food and for nesting. Birds, such as ringed plover and sanderling, are predominantly found feeding on sandy shores. As discussed above, sediment size is of prime importance in determining the presence of invertebrates and hence the availability of food for feeding birds.

Shingle and sand habitats are of importance to some birds for breeding, especially little terns and ringed plovers. The stability of the shingle and height of the beach where the birds are nesting are important in determining breeding success, as they relate to the susceptibility to flooding of the nesting areas.

Fish

Certain species of fish have adapted to life in the intertidal zone, whereas other species just rely on the intertidal zone for feeding when the tide is in. These latter species, however, generally prefer muddy sediment where prey species are more abundant. Species of fish which have adapted to life on sandy beaches include the sand goby and the lesser weever. These species feed on the sandy beach when the tide is in and remain buried in the sand when the tide is out. The major requirements of these fish in terms of beach attributes appear to be an abundant supply of food and a suitable sediment size for burrowing.

Many coastal areas are potentially of importance for the egg and larval stages of a variety of fish and/or as fish nursery areas.

Other fauna

Other animals which use the beach include marine and terrestrial mammals. Of the marine mammals, seals are the most common, coming ashore for breeding and moulting or between fishing in inshore waters. Seals often use sandy beaches for such activities, but the primary consideration is likely to be the level of isolation of the beach, rather than characteristics of the sediment. Small terrestrial mammals including rats and voles, which feed on organic material on the strandline, may also make use of the beach for scavenging purposes. This is a case of opportunistic feeding rather than selective feeding based on habitat type. Other species associated with sandy shorelines include sand lizards and a variety of specialised insects such as sand hoppers.

2.2.3 Human environment

Informal recreation

Informal recreation describes those activities which are relatively passive, involving little or no equipment. Examples include sunbathing, walking, playing, paddling and swimming. Existing beach attributes which are relevant to the continued enjoyment of these informal activities must be taken into account in the course of investigating any management initiatives. Sediment size, for example, is an important consideration at a "bucket and spade" resort where the beach is the main attraction (see Figure 2.6). Sediments should be of an acceptable recreational quality (i.e. of a size which is comfortable under bare feet and compatible to sand castle building, and/or include items of interest such as shells). Other considerations will include beach slope, desirability of a dry area of beach at high tide and access to both the beach and water. Excessively flat sand beaches can be unpopular since they entail long walks to the sea at low water.

Figure 2.6   *Fun and sandcastles (courtesy Bournemouth BC)*

Formal recreation

Formal recreation involves those activities which are active, and which require equipment for participation. Examples include powerboating (see Figure 2.7), sailing, windsurfing (see Figure 2.8), or the use of personal watercraft. Existing formal recreational uses and associated requirements of the beach, such as adequate and safe access both to the beach and the water, need to be taken account of in beach management. Beaches used for specific purposes (e.g. canoeing or surfing) should be managed to ensure that the use, if desirable, can be maintained.

Figure 2.7   *Powerboating (courtesy Bournemouth BC)*

Figure 2.8   *Windsurfing (courtesy Bournemouth BC)*

Access

The maintenance of suitable and safe access to the beach is of paramount importance if general or specific use of the beach is to be encouraged. For uses which require the transportation of equipment, slipways with safe turning circles and parking areas for vehicles and trailers are desirable.

Safety

There are a number of potential hazards associated with beaches and beach or coastal features, including the slope of the beach, the slope of the sea bed, cliff instability leading to falls, strong currents, etc.. For example, very flat beaches can be rapidly inundated on the rising tide. Conversely very steep shingle beaches can cause unsafe bathing at high water with plunging breakers and severe undertow currents. All these hazards are subject to varying levels of public perception. Such hazards can be reduced by making provision for safety measures. Safety features which are often provided include lifesaving equipment, information boards, a flag system, lifeguards and/or beach patrols and zoning for recreational uses.

Landscape

Beaches, as an integral part of the coastal zone, form an important landscape resource which should be maintained and enhanced where possible. In England and Wales, for example, certain designations cover coastal landscapes of outstanding quality. Heritage Coasts, Areas of Outstanding Natural Beauty (AONBs), National Parks and various local authority designations all serve to protect the coastal landscape, particularly in undeveloped areas.

Commercial fishing activity

Where fishing vessels are stored and/or launched from beaches, a number of beach characteristics must be considered if the activity is to be maintained. These include beach gradient, beach profile, sediment size, degree of tide coverage, beach furrows, width and gradient of vehicle access points and availability of local car parking facilities.

Fishing in the beach area is usually limited to the area below low water, where fishermen may employ trawls, dredges, nets and pots in the shallow inshore zone. The use of static gear for the capture of crabs and lobster is particularly prominent in the coastal zone around the UK. Beach seining uses the beach as an integral part of the method and can take place at any time of the tide. Although there are numerous other pressures influencing the migration of fish, some beach-related aspects may be important in this regard such as sediment size, sediment mobility, degree of fines, turbidity and wave action.

Commercial activity, tourism and adjacent land uses

In resort areas, commercial activity is often intense, both on and landward of the beach. Beach concessions and other commercial enterprises often rely on the beach because of its role in attracting tourists and visitors to the area.

Archaeology and heritage interest

Coastal areas have long provided a focus for human settlement and may therefore contain sites of important archaeological or historical significance. Features of importance which have been recognised around the UK coast include ancient submerged forests, settlements and shipwrecks. Many archaeological sites have already been lost to the encroaching sea. A managed beach may act as protection for any archaeological remains (e.g. by protecting them from erosion).

Navigation

Safe and clear navigation in inshore water is a key consideration in management of the beach, particularly if management initiatives involve reducing the water depth or causing obstruction in the nearshore zone.

Infrastructure

Telecommunications cables, oil and gas pipelines and sewage outfalls are among the facilities found around the coast, as they pass over, through, or under the land/water interface. The integrity of these assets is, in many cases, partly dependent on the maintenance of a stable and adequate beach.

2.2.4 Environmental quality

Water quality

Good water quality is a basic requirement for a resort beach and is particularly important if Blue Flag designation is to be achieved (see Box 11.4). Anything which causes an increase in the amount of material suspended, whether temporarily or in the longer term, can affect water quality. In some cases land drainage and/or sewage outfalls may affect water quality at and around the point of discharge. Tidal conditions, currents, etc. will affect the extent to which changes in water quality subsequently affect beach use, habitat value, etc.

Sediment quality

The existing quality of beach sediment is determined by particle size and by any contaminated discharges from marine or land-based sources such as storm sewage outfalls and metal laden streams. However, it is materials such as clays and silts rather than sands which typically concentrate contaminants to environmentally significant levels. The natural chemical content of sand can have an important influence on the vegetation of any associated dune systems. In particular, calcium carbonate content, largely from shell debris, affects the type of dune vegetation.

Debris

Debris (e.g. litter, jetsam and flotsam, dog faeces and sewage related debris) can often be a problem on beaches. With a tide washed beach, the sea acts as an effective cleanser for much biodegradable debris. In England and Wales, the district council is responsible for litter clearance and, under the Environmental Protection Act 1990, they are also required to undertake oil pollution cleaning operations in conjunction with the Marine Pollution Control Unit (MPCU).

2.2.5 Physical environment

Many coastal sites are of particular importance for their geological or geomorphological interest. Cliffs may be valuable because they represent particular geomorphological features or good exposures of specific rocks, and the beaches fronting them are an integral part of controlling the rate of erosion. In England, such sites may be designated by English Nature as Sites of Special Scientific Interest and/or Geological Conservation Review Sites in recognition of their value. They also represent an important educational resource.

Natural or man-induced changes in the physical processes operating on a coastline can affect these sites in a number of ways. For example beach management works can lead to:

- disruption of the natural geomorphological process of cliff erosion supplying fresh beach material
- slowing or cessation of landslip processes which are of interest in their own right, or which produce fresh exposures of rock faces/fossils

- covering of exposed rock faces and strata
- changes in the composition or amount of sediment in transport, with possible knock-on consequences for other attributes up- or down-drift.

2.3 ORIGINS AND GEOLOGICAL EVOLUTION OF UK BEACHES

2.3.1 Origins

The present day situation of all the beaches around the UK coastline is a snapshot of an ongoing evolutionary process which commenced towards the end of the last Ice Age. The last Ice Sheet covered Britain north of a line from approximately South Wales to East Anglia. North of this line many beaches are backed by boulder clay laid down under the Ice Sheet. South of this line the sediments laid down during the Ice Age are commonly fluvio-glacial sands and gravels. At this time, melt-water from the dwindling glaciers formed fast-flowing rivers which carried large amounts of sediment to the coast. As the ice-sheets continued to diminish, the volume of water in the seas and oceans increased, producing a rapid rise in sea level. The rate of rise was much greater than that occurring today and produced dramatic changes in the coastline, as, for example, the North Sea and Irish Sea basins filled with water. This advance of the seas, known as a marine transgression, left some beach material behind, stranded on the seabed in ever-deepening water. At the same time, however, some beach sediment was moved landward, building up beaches which, in places, still exist today at the maximum extent of the transgression. A good example is Chesil Beach (see Figure 2.1) which is largely the result of the last marine transgression, and is made up of relic seabed sediment to which little or no fresh supplies are presently being added. Another example is North Shore, Llandudno (see Figure 2.9), a pocket beach trapped between the rocky headlands of the Great and Little Ormes and formed of shingle moved ashore during the marine transgression.

Figure 2.9   *Pocket beach at North Shore, Llandudno, Gwynedd (courtesy HR Wallingford)*

In some areas, particularly along the south and east coasts of England, the advancing sea eroded soft sedimentary rocks at the shoreline or in shallow water (e.g. those largely comprising sands and gravels deposited in earlier geological eras). This erosion released sediment (e.g. flint pebbles, quartz sand or ironstone) which added to the stock of material for the developing beaches. Elsewhere, for example on the western and northern coasts of the UK, harder rocks withstood the erosion and formed cliffs with little or no sediment at their bases.

Sea levels started to rise rapidly at the end of the last glaciation (about 10,000 years ago), slowing about 5,000 years ago to a rate similar to that of today. As a result most UK beaches are the product of a sedimentary regime extending over many thousands of years.

2.3.2 Modern-day sources

Cliffs

The natural process of erosion of cliffs and the nearshore seabed continues to the present day. Direct wave action at the base of cliffs, leading to their collapse, is the most dramatic method of erosion, although the processes involved can be much more complicated than they may at first appear. Often the failure of a cliff is largely governed by the flow of groundwater through it, rather than purely as a result of marine action. Weathering of the cliff face by wind, rain and freeze-thaw processes can also be a factor. In the UK, as a result of the construction of promenades or coastal defences which protect the base of cliffs, the supply of fresh beach material has diminished markedly over the last 100 years or so. Many of the remaining un-protected cliffs have now become valuable conservation sites (see Section 2.2.5) and their continuing role in supplying beaches with sediment is an argument put forward in favour of not protecting them in the future. As an example, Figure 2.10 shows the coastline at Covehithe in Suffolk. The beach in the foreground is derived from the recent erosion of the glacial till cliffs a little further north. The cliffs in this photograph are themselves eroding and providing sediment for the beaches to the south.

Figure 2.10   *Beach formed from glacial till cliffs at Covehithe, Suffolk (courtesy HR Wallingford)*

Shore platforms

Erosion of the nearshore seabed continues in many areas forming *shore platforms*, which extend landward as sea level continues to rise. As this erosion continues, water depths increase, which allows larger waves to break at the toe of beaches, cliffs or man-made defences. Erosion of the shore platform is most intense in shallow water, where the wave-induced water motions at the seabed and the abrasive effects of mobile sediment are greatest. Further offshore, the erosion process is more gradual, and occurs less frequently, for example in severe storms. Individual pebbles of gravel and shingle are sometimes removed from the seabed and brought ashore by the buoyancy and wave/current induced drag forces on seaweed attached to the pebbles causing them to be pulled out of the seabed when the action of waves and currents alone would not have been sufficient to do so. This process is often known as kelp-rafting: typical kelp-rafted pebbles are shown in Figure 2.11.

Rivers

Apart from erosion of cliffs and the nearshore seabed, there are few other sources of fresh material to beaches around the UK coastline. Elsewhere in the world rivers are important sediment sources; some fast-flowing rivers in Scotland still carry significant quantities of sand and gravel to the coast, but elsewhere in the UK the river flows are too modest to do so. (Flows of silt and other cohesive material into the beach environment, from rivers and estuaries, are outside the scope of this manual.)

Other sources

Other modern-day sources of beach material exist. "Biogenic" materials, such as shell and coral fragments, are a major component of beaches in some tropical areas. In the UK the carbonate content of sand is generally low, although it can still be significant in places. For example, the beaches of South Uist in the Outer Hebrides (see Figure 2.12) are largely formed of calcium carbonate sand derived biogenically, and much of the sand blown onshore along the west coast of Devon and Cornwall is shell debris.

Figure 2.11   *Kelp rafted pebbles (courtesy HR Wallingford)*

In a surprising number of areas around the coast, beaches are formed, partly or entirely, from industrial waste products. Many of the popular tourist beaches in south-west England are made up of waste from tin mines, quarries or china clay workings (see Figure 1.2). In other places, both beaches and backshore areas are largely composed of colliery or steel-production waste. For example, Figure 2.13 shows the beach at Workington in Cumbria, which is largely composed of waste products from coal mining and steel production further south. Now that many of these industrial concerns have ceased to operate, the coastline is adjusting to the lack of fresh material by retreating landwards.

Figure 2.12 *Biogenic sand beach at South Uist, Outer Hebrides (courtesy HR Wallingford)*

Figure 2.13 *Industrial waste beach at Workington, Cumbria (courtesy HR Wallingford)*

2.3.3 Losses

Wave action

As well as considering the supply of beach material, it is necessary to consider the losses that occur, either naturally or as a result of human activity. As sediment on beaches is moved to and fro by the action of waves and tides, so it is subject to attrition. Softer particles, such as shell or coal, are abraded and broken up by contact with harder material (e.g. quartzite sand).

The finest particles are then often too small to reside on the active beach face and are winnowed out, to be transported offshore and eventually deposited in deeper, calmer water.

Wind action

On some beaches, prevailing onshore winds lift sand grains from the beach surface and carry them inshore, often to a considerable distance landward of the coast and beyond the normal dune systems (see Box 5.5 and Chapter 9.1) where they would remain as a sediment resource for the beach. Unless river flows carry these grains back to the sea, they are lost to the beach system. Several examples of this process can be given for the UK coast, the most notable being that of Kenfig, between Porthcawl and Port Talbot, in south Wales. Here a medieval village and its agricultural land, had to be abandoned because of the accumulation of wind blown sand from the beaches.

Littoral processes

Beach material may also be lost offshore into deep water as a result of natural sediment transport processes. This tends to occur at *headlands* or *nesses*, particularly affecting the finer, or less dense, fractions of the beach sediment. Such a sediment transport path may be difficult to prove, but the series of sand banks off the Norfolk coast between Great Yarmouth and Cromer are believed to have been produced by this type of process. Certainly off the coast of California, USA, a very deep chasm in the nearshore seabed is responsible for a considerable loss of beach sediment travelling along the seabed close to the coastline.

Human extraction

It is not uncommon to find that beach material is being deliberately removed by humans for a variety of purposes, as mentioned in Section 2.5.2. Whilst now becoming less common as a factor in beach losses in the UK, except in remote areas or where existing historic licences or laws permit it, this type of commercial extraction is an important issue in beach management elsewhere in the world. New licences for beach material extraction in the UK are most unlikely to be granted, unless they relate to recycling of material as opposed to its use as aggregate.

2.4 BEACH SEDIMENT TRANSPORT PROCESSES

2.4.1 Basic concepts

By the definition of a beach in Section 2.1, its sediment is mobile under the action of waves and tidal and wave-induced currents. These hydrodynamic forcing processes are complex and their evaluation for a particular site often requires specialised methods and knowledge. In keeping with the principal purpose of this chapter, a description of waves, tides and currents is not included. Instead these topics are covered in Chapter 3. In the rest of this section, attention is focused on the transport of beach material that these processes cause. Understanding how sediment is moved, and how beaches develop as a consequence, is very important to the management of beaches. This requires an introduction to some fundamental concepts.

Sediment particles are transported by stresses caused by the motion of the fluid. These stresses initiate movement of particles on the sea bed and maintain the movement of these particles once it has been initiated. This raises several questions which are fundamental to the study of beaches, for example:

- Will the particles forming the beach move under given conditions?
- How many particles will move in a given period of time?
- What is the direction of movement?
- Where and when will the particles stop moving?

These issues are now addressed.

Threshold of motion

To initiate transport, the fluid stresses have to overcome the inertia of the particles resting on the bed. For a single grain of sand on the beach surface, the threshold of motion is very low, and will be reached and exceeded under modest wave and current action. Pebbles and cobbles are obviously more difficult to move, especially if they are embedded in a layer of finer sediment which reduces flows beneath the larger particles. The geometry of the position of a particle on the bed in relation to other bed particles is therefore important. Since the geometry of each particle in a graded population will vary, there will be many individual threshold conditions. It is necessary to distinguish the threshold for individual movement (which corresponds to a few particles) and the threshold for general movement (where many particles move). In the nearshore zone, particles may be stationary under certain conditions and move under more severe conditions (i.e. the threshold of individual movement can be identified). Under breaking waves most particles tend to move continuously (i.e. conditions exceed the threshold of general movement).

For unidirectional flow the Shields curve is the most commonly used descriptor for the threshold of motion. Similar curves have now been developed for transport of sand under waves and under combined waves and currents. These have been published in a Manual of Marine Sands (Soulsby, 1994) and can be used to predict the onset of general movement in the coastal environment. A summary of the suggested prediction technique is given in Box 2.2.

Modes of transport

Once the particles are in motion there are various modes of transport. Each mode has characteristics which will determine the rate and direction of movement and the consequent morphological response. Three modes of sediment transport are generally recognized in the coastal environment:

1. Bed load - In this mode, particles roll and saltate along the bed in a layer a few particles thick above the bed. The weight of the particles is supported wholly by the bed. The collision of moving particles with those on the bed is an important mechanism for the initiation of further movement and the modification of existing motions.

2. Suspended load - In this mode, the particles are carried in suspension by the ambient water motions above the bed load layer. The weight of the particle is supported wholly by the fluid.

3. Sheet flow - If the stress due to the motion of the fluid exceeds a certain value then ripples on the seabed may be washed out and replaced by a thin moving carpet of particles of high concentration. Particle to particle interactions are very important in this mode, which is dependent upon both the hydrodynamic size of the particle and the magnitude of the fluid motions.

The hydrodynamic size of the particle is usually described by its fall velocity (see Box 2.3) which is a useful description of how a particle moves in a fluid and is used later in this manual in a number of calculation procedures. The maximum wave orbital velocity at the bed describes the magnitude of the fluid motions. These can be used to indicate the expected mode of transport for particular particles. As the wave conditions vary so will the mode of transport for any particular particle.

Box 2.2   *Threshold of sand motion*

The following procedure should be applied when determining whether or not the sand on the sea bed is likely to move due to waves and/or tidal currents.

1. Determine the threshold bed shear-stress of motion, τ_{cr}, for a given grain size.

The classical work of Shields for steady currents has been extended by Soulsby (1994) to waves, and combined waves and currents, leading to Figure 1 which represents plots of τ_{cr} versus the grain diameter d, for $g - 9.81ms^{-2}$, $s = 2.65$, temperature = 10°C, salinity = 35ppt, typical of sand in sea water, and also for sand in fresh water at 20°C.

The threshold bed shear-stress τ_{cr} corresponding to a sand of size d is simply read off from Figure 1. It must be noted that Figure 1 only applies to the threshold of motion on an initially flat horizontal bed, under the typical conditions defined above. When using other conditions, see the Manual of Marine Sands (Soulsby, 1994).

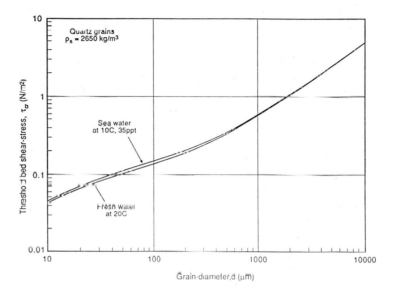

Figure 1   *Threshold bed shear-stress for motion of quartz grains of sieve-diameter d*

2. Calculate the actual bed shear-stress τ due to waves only, currents only or a combination of the two.

(a)   For currents only, calculate the drag coefficient C_D from the formula:

$$C_D = \left(\frac{0.40}{\ln (h/z_0) - 1} \right)^2$$

where h is the depth of water, z_0 is the bed roughness length (for flat uniform sand, $z_0 = D_{50}/12$)

Then calculate current-only bed shear-stress

$$\tau_c = \rho_w \, C_D \, U^2$$

where ρ_w is the density of sea water, U is the depth-averaged current speed.

(b)   For waves only, calculate $T_n = (h/g)^{\frac{1}{2}}$ (h is depth of water) and T_n/T_z (T_z is the zero crossing period)

From Figure 2 established by Soulsby (1994), determine $U_{rms} \, T_n/H_s$, using the JONSWAP curve, and then U_{rms}, which is the bottom orbital velocity beneath random waves. Note that U_{rms} can be exceeded due to the random character of the waves.

Continued

Box 2.2 *Continued*

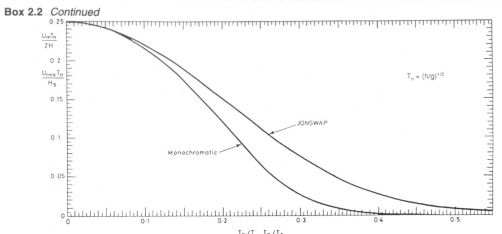

Figure 2 *Bottom velocity for monochromatic waves ($U_m T_n/2H$ versus T_n/T) and random waves ($U_{rms} T_n/H_s$ versus T_n/T_z)*

Calculate the wave friction factor f_w given by Soulsby:

$$f_w = 1.39 \left(\frac{U_{rms} \, T_z}{2\pi} \right)^{-0.52}$$

and wave-only peak bed shear-stress $\tau_w = 0.5 \, \rho \, f_w \, (U_{rms})^2$

(c) The bed shear-stress beneath combined waves and currents is enhanced by up to 70% beyond the value which would result from a simple linear addition of the wave-alone and current-alone stresses. This occurs because of a non-linear interaction between the wave and current boundary layers. The Manual of Marine Sands (Soulsby, 1994) examines the predictions from a number of models of the mean (τ_m) and maximum (τ_{max}) shear stresses throughout a wave period under combined waves and currents. Figure 3 shows these results for waves and currents travelling in the same direction ($\phi = 0°$) although it is unclear which model provides the best predictions. When investigating threshold of movement the τ_{max} should be used.

3. Compare the threshold bed shear-stress, τ_{cr}, and the actual bed shear-stress, τ.

If τ is greater than τ_{cr}, the sand grains will move.

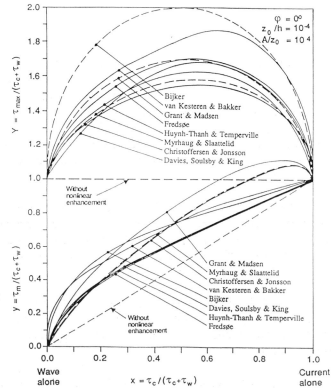

Figure 3 *Intercomparison of eight models for prediction of mean (τ_m) and maximum (τ_{max}) bed shear-stress due to waves plus a current*

Box 2.3 *Fall velocity of sand grains*

The fall velocity w_s (or settling velocity) of sand grains in water is determined by their diameter and density, and the viscosity of the water.

There are a number of formulae for calculating the settling velocity w_s of isolated sand grains in still water. Figure 1, based on a formula established by Soulsby (1994), shows curves of w_s versus grain diameter, D_e, for the special case $g = 9.81\text{ms}^{-2}$, $\rho_s = 2650\text{kgm}^{-3}$, temperature = 10°C, salinity = 35ppt, typical of sand in sea water, and for the case of sand in freshwater at 20°C.

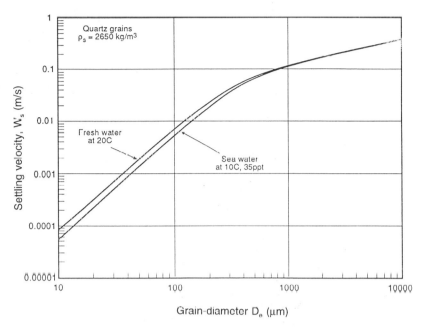

Figure 1 *Settling velocity of quartz grains of sieve-diameter D_g at low concentration in still water.*

For high concentrations or for conditions different from those defined above, see Manual of Marine Sands (Soulsby, 1994).

Transport rate and direction

The transport rate is calculated by multiplying the mass of particles which are capable of being moved (i.e. whose threshold of motion has been exceeded) and the velocity at which these particles move over the bed. In the beach environment the main agent for the initiation of movement and maintaining motion is stirring by oscillatory wave action. The mass of particles available for transport can therefore be determined from the local wave conditions. A number of relationships have been developed to predict this mass related to the shear stress applied to the bed by the wave. The applied shear stress and hence the mass of particles can be affected by the presence of bedforms (such as ripples) and vice versa.

This mass of particles will follow the oscillatory wave motion of the flows. The gross transport rate may therefore be large but the mass of particles does not move very far from where it was originally picked up. Net movements of particles, which are the agent of morphological change, are a consequence of small differences in either the onshore or offshore gross movements. A number of factors can produce this difference:

1. As waves enter shallow water their surface profile becomes more asymmetric. This corresponds to an asymmetry in the horizontal bed velocity with onshore flows of higher velocity but shorter duration than offshore flows. This tends to increase the net movement of particles onshore.

2. A local bed slope will enhance the downslope component of movement; on beaches this will tend to increase the gross offshore movement. The gross movement can also be

influenced by the presence of asymmetrical bedforms which can cause so-called *rip currents*.

3. A mean current will influence the balance of the gross movements. The net movement will be a result of the interaction of the oscillatory flows and the mean current. Such flows may be created by tides or by waves.

Factors 1 and 2 are important for determining the direction and rate of the cross-shore transport of particles; 3 is important in the determining the longshore transport rate.

Temporal and spatial scales

The coastal environment is characterized by temporal and spatial changes in currents, wave heights, the water depth and intensity of turbulence. As a consequence there are similar temporal and spatial changes in fluid motions and hence in the initiation of movement, mode, rate and direction of movement. The shortest timescales are those associated with the periodicity of the incoming waves, typically in the range of 1 to 20 seconds. These primary wave motions are often accompanied, however, by longer wave periods, in the range of 15-60 seconds and referred to as *long* or *infra-gravity* waves. On UK beaches in particular, another important periodicity is that of the tidal cycle (about 12.4 hours), which affects both the water depths and the character of the *steady* currents close to the coast. Effects at even longer timescales also occur, for example the 28-day Spring-Neap tidal cycle and seasonal effects (i.e. an annual cycle).

Of course, not all the processes affecting beaches are strictly periodic. Many of the major morphological changes on a coastline occur as a result of episodic events (i.e. unusual circumstances typically associated with severe weather). A single storm will often have more effect on the shape of a beach above the high-water mark than many months of more normal wave and tidal conditions. For this reason, it is often necessary to concentrate effort on prescribing these severe combinations of wave action and tidal level as part of a beach management exercise.

Spatial scales of sediment transport and beach morphology also vary considerably. At the shortest, wave-like ripples on a sandy beach affect the roughness of the seabed and hence the mobility and transport of the sand itself. At the other extreme, the excursion of a particle under the influence of the ebb and flood tidal currents during a single tidal cycle can be many kilometres. In between, there are many other length scales which affect the development of beaches. It is not uncommon, especially in areas of modest tidal range, to find that sandy beaches develop a set of roughly equally spaced circulation "cells" in the horizontal plane. Well-defined seaward flowing currents alternate with more diffuse and weaker landward flows, the two being connected by shore-parallel currents. Where these systems persist for any length of time, particularly where the incoming waves are consistently of near uniform height, period and direction, these circulation cells are often accompanied by spatially-regular beach forms (cusps) as illustrated in Figure 2.14. It can be appreciated that if beach material is to move along the shore through such an area, it is likely that it will do so in a rather tortuous fashion, swirling around from cell to cell, in the horizontal plane and probably oscillating in vertical position as well. On oceanic coasts subject to large swell waves, intense seaward flowing rip currents can develop (by the same process) and form a serious hazard to bathers.

To quantify the sediment transport patterns on a beach, it is clearly not easy to follow the motions of the individual particles of material as they pursue their haphazard courses over the beach. Some simplification of the transport processes is necessary, to allow the longer-term motions to be predicted without trying to understand the shorter period, smaller spatial-scale fluctuations.

Figure 2.14   *Beach cusps at Hengistbury Head, Dorset (courtesy Bournemouth BC)*

CIRIA Report 153

As a first simplification it is convenient to consider a very long, straight beach, with parallel contours and an ample supply of beach material. The complications that occur in most real situations, for example offshore islands or groyne systems, are considered in a later section of the manual (see Section 2.5).

It is then standard practice to divide the movement of sediment into two orthogonal components, namely parallel to the coast and perpendicular to it. As can be appreciated from the foregoing description of beach cusps, this too is a simplification of what actually occurs on beaches, but one which greatly assists in understanding beach development. The following two sections discuss these two components of transport. Section 2.4.2 discusses the movement of sediment parallel to the beach contours, *longshore transport* and Section 2.4.3 the movement perpendicular to the beach, *cross-shore transport*.

2.4.2   Longshore transport

General

The transport, or *drift*, of beach material along a coastline, caused principally by the action of waves and tidal currents, is the major factor in the long-term development of beaches. Galvin (1990) almost over-emphasises this point when he states:

"...all examples of shore erosion on non-subsiding sandy coasts are traceable to man-made or natural interruptions of longshore sediment transport."

However in many cases the explanation of long-term erosion or accretion is very close to that expressed by Galvin. "Long-term" development is defined as a period of at least 1 year, and more generally a period of 5 to 10 years or more. Over shorter timescales, cross-shore transport is also important. Indeed during a single tidal cycle, or a storm, the effect of the waves at the shoreline may dominate the changes in the shape of a beach. These changes can sometimes be irreversible (e.g. the breaching of a barrier beach) and thus contribute to long-term development.

Significant volumes of beach material will only be moved along the shore if there is a steady, or quasi-steady current to carry it, running parallel to the beach contours. A number of possible causes for such currents exist, but in the UK there are three main ones:

- waves which break at an angle to the beach contours
- tidal currents
- variations in breaking wave heights along the beach.

Other factors sometimes cause, or contribute to the creation of shore-parallel currents, for example wind-induced stresses and river flows.

It is important here to introduce the concepts of *gross* and *net* longshore transport. In very few situations does sediment travel only in one direction. As the winds change direction, so do the waves, with the result that on some days the beach material will be transported in one direction, only to be transported back in the opposite direction a few days, or even a few hours later. When tidal currents are important contributors to the transport process, this variability in drift direction can be even more marked. In some situations, for example when trying to maintain an open channel or trench across a beach, the transport of sediment from both directions is important. This is known as the *gross drift* and is the summation of the volumetric transport rates independent of direction.

In most circumstances however, including the development of the beach plan shape, it is the net result of the 'to' and 'fro' movements of the sediment which is more important. This is calculated by subtracting the one component of drift from the other, and is called the *net longshore transport*.

Theoretical approaches

It is only in relatively recent times that longshore sediment transport began to be quantified in terms of a volumetric transport rate, and then related to the hydraulic processes causing it. In many parts of the world, the dominant cause of longshore drift is the oblique arrival of breaking waves. On the long, straight, sandy coastline of California, USA, where tidal currents are small, and wave action is dominated by long-period swell, it is reasonable to consider only this mechanism, and much of the fundamental research into longshore transport was carried out here between 1950 and 1970. From these important investigations came a relatively simple formula, often known as the CERC equation, connecting the longshore drift rate and the characteristics of the incoming waves (see Box 2.4). This formula has subsequently been used in a number of numerical models of beach development, and hence applied at a large number of sites, often very different in character to the Californian coast. It remains a useful starting point for drift calculations even today, provided only long-term drift rates are required (i.e. on a long-term rather than day by day basis). The accuracy of the calculations, and confidence in them, is greatly increased by specific calibration for the particular stretch of coastline being considered. This topic is returned to later in this section.

Over the years the CERC formulation has been criticised on the grounds that it makes no allowance for factors such as grain-size or beach slope, which are potentially very important. It only attempts to represent one of the causes of longshore drift, namely oblique wave breaking. Also, the CERC formula provides only a "bulk" volumetric drift rate (i.e. integrated over the complete beach profile above and the below water line). In many studies, for example when designing a groyne, it is useful to have information on the distribution of the sediment transport across the beach profile as well.

As a result of this, considerable effort in recent years has gone into improving predictions of longshore drift rates and this has generated a number of variants to the CERC formula. Incorporation of the contribution to transport caused by variations in breaking wave height into the CERC formula, for example, was introduced by Brampton and Ozasa (1980), although this only remedied one criticism. Work by Kamphuis et al. (1986), van Hijum and Pilarcyzk (1982) and Kamphuis (1991) concentrated on including the effects of different grain sizes and beach slopes into bulk drift rate formulae but did not include the effect of tidal currents. A useful recent review of methods of calculating longshore transport rate using the CERC formula and its variants is presented by Bodge and Kraus (1991) who also review Bagnold's (1963) method for including the effect of tidal currents.

It is normally necessary to calculate the drift rate, Q, for a large number of different wave (and perhaps tidal current) conditions to evaluate, for example, the average annual nett longshore transport rate for a particular coastline. Originally it was not uncommon to derive a single "average" wave condition and assume it persisted throughout the year. More recently, this idea has been largely replaced by two alternatives. One is to derive climatic information on wave conditions, averaged over a number of years and present it in the form of probability tables, giving the typical number of hours that any particular set of wave/tide conditions occur. The transport rate for each combination persisting for one hour is then calculated and a weighted result obtained. This calculation generally needs to be repeated for many locations along the coastline as its orientation and position alters, e.g. with time. The second is to obtain, or derive, an hour by hour tabulation of wave (and tidal) conditions and simply calculate the drift at each hour. This latter approach has advantages when examining variations in drift rate from year to year, or when modelling beach evolution in areas where significant changes in beach orientation occur rapidly (e.g. in groyne bays).

Box 2.4   *Potential longshore transport rate*

Waves breaking at an angle to a beach cause longshore transport of beach sediment. The waves have a potential for moving sediment which can be calculated using for example the CERC formula below. If the beach face is covered with mobile beach material over the complete active profile then the potential rate will be realised, otherwise the actual longshore drift rate will be smaller.

The CERC Formula relates the immersed weight potential longshore sediment transport rate I and a longshore wave energy flux factor P_L by

$$I = KP_L \tag{1}$$

where K is an empirical coefficient of proportionality, and

$$P_L = (EC_g \sin\theta \cos\theta)_b \tag{2}$$

The subscript b refers to breaking. The energy density E and group celerity C_g at breaking are given or approximated by linear-wave theory as

$$E = \frac{1}{8}\rho_w g H_b^2 \tag{3}$$

$$C_g = \left(\frac{gH_b}{\gamma_{br}}\right)^{\frac{1}{2}} \tag{4}$$

where ρ_w = fluid density, g = gravitational acceleration, H_b and θ_b = wave height and angle at breaking, and $\gamma_{br} = H_b/h_b$, where h_b = water depth at breaking. Eq. 1 is then

$$I = \frac{K}{16\sqrt{\gamma_{br}}} \rho_w g^{3/2} H_b^{5/2} \sin(2\theta_b) \tag{5}$$

To obtain the volumetric longshore transport rate, Q, the following equation is used

$$Q = \frac{I}{(s-1)\rho_w g a'} \tag{6}$$

where s = specific density of sediment relative to the density of the fluid medium and a' = the ratio of the solid volume to the total volume of the sediment. In practice, s and a' are taken as about 2.65 and 0.6, respectively.

The proportionality constant, K, was originally recommended (in the Shore Protection Manual 1977, 1984) as taking a value of 0.77 for typical sandy beaches. This value is, however, designed to be used when the wave height, H_b, is given as a root mean square wave height (H_{rms}). If significant wave height, H_s, is used then the equivalent value of K should be 0.32.

Although this value of K is a reasonable estimate for average sandy beaches, there is a dependence of the K coefficient on sediment grain size (see Kamphuis' formula, Section 7.2.2). For shingle beaches the appropriate value of K is much smaller (by a factor of between 10 and 20).

Calibration of longshore transport calculations

Existing sediment transport formulae or models, applied without specific adjustment for a site, can at best give order-of-magnitude estimates of the volumetric rates of transport. This is a result of the complex nature of the processes being modelled and the simplifications and assumptions which have to be made. By calibration against actual site measurements and an understanding of the limitations of the methods, the accuracy of estimates can be greatly improved.

Direct measurement of transport rates in the field has been attempted many times, over the years, using a variety of methods. On shingle beaches, where the sediment is moved as a bed load, sediment "traps" have been deployed to record drift rates under measured wave and tidal conditions, with some success (Chadwick, 1988). As with many other techniques, however, such experiments can only be carried out under modest wave activity and for a limited time period. The devices themselves affect the local sediment transport regime, and beach profile changes due to cross-shore transport can complicate the measurements.

Tracer techniques, which have proved useful in measurements of flows and sediment transport in pipes and rivers, have also been applied in beach situations. Difficulties arise, however, because of the dispersion that occurs in the highly energetic surf-zone. Much of the tracer material is randomly distributed both across the surface of the beach and through a considerable depth of the sediment deposits, often making it difficult to identify a net transport direction, let alone to quantify the rate of movement. The situation is simpler on a shingle beach, and improved tracer techniques, such as the Southampton University Electronic Pebble System, have been developed recently which show promise.

Estimating the transport of sediment travelling as a suspended load under breaking waves is understandably even more difficult and only very limited success has been achieved. Experiments of this type are largely designed to help understand the processes involved rather than to quantify the transport along a particular beach during particular wave and current conditions.

As a consequence of these difficulties, estimates of transport volume are usually made using measurements of the effects of longshore drift, e.g. the build-up of material against large structures such as breakwaters and harbour arms, recorded rates of growth of natural features such as spits and inlet shoals, or less directly by the measurement of infill rates or dredging volumes in harbour approach channels.

These approaches suffer from the disadvantage that changes in beaches are related to the variations in longshore drift rather than to the drift rate itself. If a very long groyne or breakwater which can be assumed to trap all the sediment moving alongshore is not present, and this is often the case, then some uncertainty in the net sediment transport rate is inevitable. This is more of a problem on sandy coasts, where much of the drift is carried as suspended load, and especially where tidal currents contribute to the transport, because significant transport takes place well outside the wave breaker zone.

It must also be appreciated that the calculation of the volume of material that has accumulated on, or eroded from a beach is also problematical. Two particular points are crucial. Firstly, it is important to realise that the net longshore transport at any site can vary considerably from year to year; this is reflected in the variations in the position of the high water line on a beach. It is worthwhile obtaining information on coastline positions on a number of dates, so that long-term trends (which will only become apparent after several decades) can be separated out from shorter-term fluctuations.

Secondly, whilst it is relatively easy to measure changes in beach elevation, difficulties arise in converting this to a volume change as both the landward and seaward limits of change need to be defined. The seaward limit poses the greatest problem and it is necessary to use the concept of "closure depth" to achieve this conversion. It can be defined using analysis of beach profiles (provided they continue far enough underwater), as the ratio of the change in cross-sectional area divided by the advance or retreat of the high water line (or another convenient contour). Often, however, insufficient data is available for this type of analysis, and the closure depth has to be estimated by experience, using information on beach profiles at various locations along a coast. Whichever method is used, it is normal to carry out sensitivity tests to examine the effects of errors in the closure depth on the longshore drift calculations.

Other factors can also complicate calibration of longshore transport rate computations. In real situations, there are often man-made structures, for example groynes, whose effect on the drift cannot be easily accounted for. In the UK, many beaches are a mixture of sand and shingle, and in places the two types of material may have a nett longshore transport in opposite directions, because they occupy different parts of the beach profile. Finally, as discussed in Section 2.5, sometimes there is insufficient beach material to satisfy the potential longshore transport that waves and tidal currents would otherwise create. In this circumstance, the changes in beach plan shape will be much smaller than expected on the basis of the calculations. Artificially adding material to such a coastline will result in much greater drift rates than occur naturally.

Despite these difficulties, rates have been calculated for a number of sites around the UK, as listed in Table 2.1 below. In the UK, nett longshore drift rates are rarely greater than 250,000 cubic metres/year for sand beaches, or more than 50,000 cubic metres/year for shingle beaches. If calculated drifts are larger, the site conditions should be carefully re-examined.

Table 2.1 Typical net annual transport rates around the UK (CIRIA, 1990)

Location	Beach material	Net longshore transport rate m³/year
Lancing, Sussex	Shingle upper/ sand lower	52,000 W→E
Hornsea, Humberside	Shingle upper/ sand lower	200,000 N→S
Pevensey Bay, Sussex	Shingle	40,000 W→E
Cromer, Norfolk	Shingle upper/ sand lower	100,000 W→E
Walcott, Norfolk	Sand	340,000 N→S
Teignmouth, Devon	Shingle upper/ sand lower	25,000 E→W
Bournemouth, Dorset	Shingle upper/ sand lower	25-50,000 W→E

Effects on beach plan shape

The practical significance of longshore drift lies in the resulting changes in the plan shape of a coastline and its beaches. As a general rule, beaches will tend to adjust to a position where the nett longshore drift is minimised, so that the beach faces into the prevailing waves. In small bays, beaches often achieve this configuration readily, but on more open coastlines a beach may never adjust to the orientation which makes the nett drift rate negligible.

The link between longshore transport of sediment and beach plan shape can be explained by a simple mass continuity approach, illustrated in Box 5.6. If there is a small variation in the sediment transport rates passing through nearby sections of a coast, the beach locally accretes or erodes to compensate for the variation. If a long harbour breakwater or groyne is built across a beach, preventing sediment transport past or over it, then the nett transport rate at that point becomes zero. This produces a dramatic variation in the drift rate compared to the open beach on either side, and hence a corresponding change in the beach plan shape (see Figure 2.15).

Calculating the longshore transport rate on a beach, and predicting its evolution has been an area of great interest and effort for over 40 years, well before the time when wave conditions could be reliably forecast. A number of methods are now available, with varying degrees of sophistication and limitations.

The simplest models can only deal with a "nearly straight" beach, assume that everything depends on just one variable (i.e. distance along the shoreline) and predict the changing position of a single representative beach contour. These simple methods are the so-called One-line beach plan shape models. As the years have passed, various additions to these models have been developed to allow for the effects of structures such as groynes, breakwaters, seawalls, etc, whilst retaining the original basic concept (e.g. Hanson and Kraus (1989), Brampton and Ozasa (1980)).

One-line models, however, cannot deal with cross-shore transport and beach profile changes, and this led to development of so-called 2-line and Multi-line models (see Bakker *et al*, 1970, Perlin and Dean, 1983). In these, the position of more than one beach contour is predicted, hence providing information on the beach profile. The concepts of the beach being nearly straight and everything depending on just one space dimension were usually retained, but extra equations were incorporated to predict the changes in the beach profile as the incident wave conditions changed. This leads, for example, to a better way of estimating the efficiency of a groyne in retaining beach material. Even so, the calculations of the changes in beach plan-

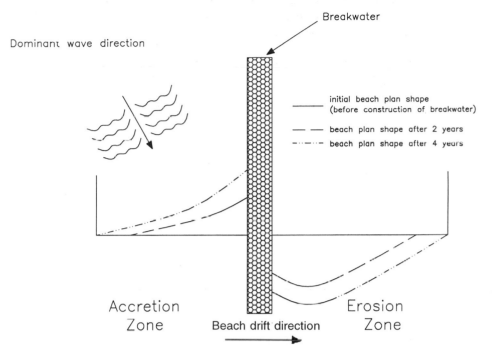

Figure 2.15 *Effect of a breakwater on the beach plan shape*

shape and profile shape are not truly linked. The three-dimensional beach morphology changes are predicted by two separate modules, each operating in two-dimensional space (plan and beach cross-section respectively).

Such simple approaches do not adequately deal with many real situations, for example where beaches have a strongly curved plan-shape, and research continues into better methods for more complex shorelines. This has resulted in "2DH Coastal Area" models, which calculate waves, currents and sediment transport at grid points covering a plan area covering the coastline and nearshore seabed, i.e. in two dimensions in the horizontal (2DH). These types of model are usually built up using more or less standard modules describing the constituent physical processes, as follows:

- a wave field model
- a wave-driven force computation on the basis of radiation stresses or wave energy dissipation
- a depth-integrated current model which describes the depth-averaged velocity field without vertical resolution
- a sediment transport formula or a depth-integrated suspended load model which describes the depth-averaged sediment concentration without vertical resolution
- a sediment balance module which computes the bed level changes from the divergence of the transport field.

Combining these components, however well-understood on their own, yields a new dynamic system whose behaviour is still poorly understood. Coastal area models contain a multitude of non-linear elements (e.g. advection, bottom friction, transport model), which each may lead to non-linear instability in their numerical computation. Consequently, the model may suddenly start producing nonsensical results or become unstable after a seemingly stable and sound computation over a long period of time.

In addition to such numerical problems, it is still necessary to simplify some of the processes to keep computational effort and expense within reasonable bounds. The 2DH Coastal Area models also require much more sophisticated input data (e.g. wave and tidal conditions, information on sediments) than the simpler models described above.

Despite the difficulties, these new models are producing encouraging results, and are likely to improve still further in the near future. Some of the models, for example, deal with the interaction between changes in the plan shape and in the profile shape of beaches in a much better way than in the older Multi-line models. For further details, the reader is recommended to consult the special issue of Coastal Engineering, 21, December 1993, entitled *Coastal Morphodynamics: Processes and Modelling*.

2.4.3   Cross-shore transport

As waves move onshore they are modified by a number of processes such as shoaling and refraction. There is a consequent spatial variation in the fluid motions at the bed. This is reflected in changes in the mode, magnitude and direction of sediment transport. These spatial changes are apparent in the morphological response of the beach profile. Four major hydrodynamic regions within the nearshore zone can be identified (see Box 2.1 and Figure 2.16):

1.   Offshore to breaker zone - in this zone waves begin to shoal (see Section 3.4.1) as they are influenced or "begin to feel" the bed. Flows at the bed become large enough to initiate the movement of particles. Initially the mode of transport is predominantly bed load. As the wave continues to shoal the flows increase in intensity and the suspended load increases. Ripples are formed which are parallel to the wave crests and sediment is suspended above them.

2.   Breaker zone - as the wave approaches the breaker zone the near bed velocities become very high and the ripples are washed out. The predominant mode of transport is sheet flow over a flat bed. Onshore of the breaker zone the stirring of the bed is much greater.

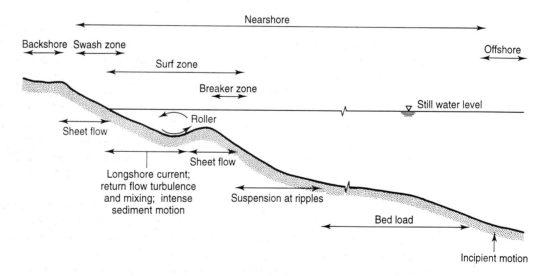

Figure 2.16   *Hydrodynamic regions of the beach*

3.   Surf zone - this zone is characterized by turbulence generated by the breaking waves, downward jets of the breaking waves impinging on the bed and large-scale horizontal roller movement. Large amounts of material are suspended in the water column, the concentration being much greater than further offshore. There are strong indications that the amount of suspended load is correlated with long-period oscillations, which are of the order of 100 seconds), rather than with individual short-period waves. Wave-induced currents are present along with the oscillatory wave motion. In addition there is often a return flow offshore. The presence of large amounts of suspended material and strong currents results in high transport rates. Ripples are usually absent from the surf zone indicating the presence of sheet flow.

4. Swash zone - this interface between the dry and wet areas of the beach is important for the understanding of event driven accretion and erosion. Both long-period oscillations and short-period waves may be important in this zone. Sediment moves in high concentrations as sheet flow under swash and backwash.

The variation in the processes across the beach results in characteristic beach profiles. The form of the beach profile will then have a feedback role in modifying the subsequent shoaling waves. On beaches with a significant tidal range (most UK beaches) the temporal variation in mean water level will result in a spatial shift of the whole hydrodynamic pattern. The different zones will migrate across the beach profile during the course of a tide. This will modify the beach profile, tending to smooth out features, such as bars which occur frequently in other parts of the world. Variations will also occur through time as the incident wave conditions change, for example creating "summer" and "winter" profiles.

Effect on beach profiles

While longshore transport is the primary mechanism for changes in beach plan shape, cross-shore transport is the means by which the beach profile changes. The response time of beaches to variation in cross-shore transport can be as small as one tidal cycle (during storms) or as large as six months (seasonal variations). Predictions of beach response are very important for coastal designers and managers and it is therefore not surprising that much research has been carried out into this subject. Two types of profiles have been distinguished. The winter profile is commonly associated with offshore transport, with sediment being transported seawards to form a bar at or below the low water line. This bar subsequently migrates landwards under calmer weather, to form a summer profile, distinguished by the presence of a berm at the wave swash limit. Such profile variations can be classified according to the sediment size and to the deep water wave characteristics (wave height and wave length).

Of greater relevance to beach management is the prediction of the actual response of various initial (pre-storm) beach profiles under a given set of wave and tidal level conditions. At Medmery, West Sussex for example, a severe storm cut a massive shingle ridge back from a width of 20m to 3m within one high water stand, prolonged by a surge. During the same period a wide shingle beach at Hayling Island, Hampshire was overtopped as a result of elevated water levels (see Figure 2.17), allowing larger waves to reach the coastline without breaking (causing rapid profile re-adjustment). Response predictions will not only give the likely beach cut back during such a storm, but also enable the likelihood of overtopping to be predicted. When considering both natural beaches and beach recharge (see Chapters 5, 6, and 7) this will enable an appropriate crest height and beach width to be determined.

Predicting the response of shingle beaches to storms is an important tool in the coastal engineering armoury and numerical models can now reproduce beach profile changes quite accurately, provided that the time element is not significant (i.e. beach profile adjustment is assumed to occur within the duration of the storm). On the basis of extensive flume experiments a similar semi-empirical tool is now available for determining the response of a beach and dune system to storm wave attack. Corresponding empirical tools also exist for evaluating sand beach/dune profile evolution during storms, mainly developed in the USA and the Netherlands. More recently, process-based morphological response profile models have been developed for sand beaches (Roelvink and Brøker, 1993). More information on all these models can be found in Section 5.3.

On a longer time scale beach losses can occur as a result of offshore sediment transport by wind induced currents, or in an onshore direction by wind transport onto dune systems. Such losses are not easily quantifiable due to a poor understanding of the physical processes involved and the rapid changes in these "forcing parameters" with time. Quite often recourse is made to a sediment budget analysis, a description of which can be found in Section 2.6.

Figure 2.17   *Surge at Hayling Island, Hampshire (courtesy HR Wallingford)*

2.4.4   Dunes

Dunes are created by the accumulation of wind-blown sand transported landward from the backshore and the higher portion of the inter-tidal foreshore. To successfully trap and retain this sand, dunes rely on vegetation, especially certain species of grasses, which both reduce the wind velocity close to the dune face allowing deposition, and retain moisture which increases the threshold of motion of the sand grains.

Dunes located on the backshore of a sandy beach are important in the development of the profile of that beach. They provide a capacity to store more sand than can be accommodated on the foreshore of the beach itself. They act as a reservoir of material which is available during storms and, if necessary, enables the beach profile to adjust to a flatter profile, and absorb the incoming wave energy. A well-stocked dune system also acts as a direct and cost-effective defence to flooding during extreme storm events. In addition, damage to dunes during storms is usually repaired naturally; which does not occur with man-made defences. As a consequence of these advantages, large parts of the coastline in The Netherlands are protected from flooding by a maintained dune system. In the UK, dunes are less prevalent. According to Ranwell and Boar (1986) about 9% of the coastline of England and Wales has dunes, and for about 25% of this frontage the dunes are the sole or partial provider of sea defence.

In favourable conditions, such as experienced on the Costa Doñana in Spain, dunes may reach 90m in height. In the cooler, wetter conditions around the British Isles, dune heights are less spectacular. A typical fully developed dune may reach perhaps 15m, with a maximum height of about 30m. The rate of accretion of dunes depends on the strength and persistence of the onshore winds, the rate of drying of sand particles on the beach surface and backshore, the growing conditions for dune-building vegetation, and on available sand supplies. Quantative evidence for the natural rate of dune build-up is rarely available, but Ranwell and Boar (1986) quote a vertical accretion rate of about 20cm/year at Newborough Warren, implying that a dune may take 75 years to reach its full height at this location. Work on establishing models of dune growth is continuing, principally in the USA and The Netherlands. It is clear, however, that the accretion process can involve hundreds or even thousand of cubic metres per linear metre of coast during a single year, hence comparing in scale to major artificial beach recharge exercises.

It follows from the above discussion that reducing the capacity of dunes to accrete during favourable conditions is likely to increase the risk of damage and flooding to properties and land behind the dunes in severe weather. Where dunes act as the sole, or part, of the flood defence along a coast, effort should be put into the preservation or enhancement of the dunes.

In addition to their role in modifying beach processes, dunes are often important wild-life habitats. Further discussion of dunes and their management can be found in Section 9.1.

2.5 MODIFYING INFLUENCES ON BEACH DEVELOPMENT

2.5.1 Effects of the solid geology of the coastline

The discussion in Section 2.4 of sediment transport processes and the resulting development of beach morphology, was based on two simplifying criteria, namely that there was a plentiful supply of mobile sediment, and that the beach was long and straight. In practice there are few sites in the world, let alone the UK, where the beaches satisfy these criteria.

In many places, there is simply insufficient sediment available for a beach to achieve either the plan or profile shape that might be expected on the basis of the *potential* sediment transport at those sites. More often, however, the solid geology of the coastal area and the nearshore seabed, affects the development of beaches. This may be the result of direct effects, for example, by blocking sediment transport pathways, or indirectly, perhaps by modifying the wave or tidal current patterns in the nearshore zone. These effects are considered in this section.

The most obvious effects are on the plan shape of beaches. Sometimes more difficult to appreciate are the effects on beach profile. In the following paragraphs, a few of the commonest beach forms are described (see Figure 2.18) and the description of these is followed by a discussion of the effects of solid geology on beach profile. The study of natural beaches and their formation, is however a large subject in its own right and the reader is referred to King (1972) for further information on this topic.

Pocket beaches (see Figures 2.9 and 2.18)

As marine action erodes the coastal land mass, it is not unusual for a jagged coastal plan shape to develop, as softer rock is removed from between less easily eroded outcrops. As a result, bays develop between these harder features, often trapping sediment and thus leading to the formation of a beach. The plan shape of the beach depends on the geology of the rocks and sediments both above and below water, and can vary from virtually straight (e.g. Whitesand Bay, Dyfed, Wales) to almost circular (e.g. Lulworth Cove, Dorset, England). In small pocket beaches, the beach plan may not change dramatically even if the offshore wave direction changes; this is because the shoreline wave conditions are dominated by wave diffraction around the headlands at either end of the bay. From this has evolved the idea of "headland control", a technique for controlling beach form by building artificial headlands to produce strongly curved pocket beaches. In larger bays, material often moves to and fro along the beach, altering its plan shape in response to varying angles of wave attack.

Tombolos (see Figure 2.18)

An island or reef situated just offshore has a dramatic effect on the wave conditions along a beach. As a consequence, material is swept into the sheltered area behind it forming either a *salient* in the beach plan shape, or sometimes allowing a neck of sediment to deposit, connecting the island to the beach. This feature is known as a tombolo, after a particularly impressive example on the Tuscany coast of Italy (Tombolo di Orbetello). In general, tombolos are found most commonly in areas of very low tidal range, where the complicating effects of tidal currents and changes in the water level are small.

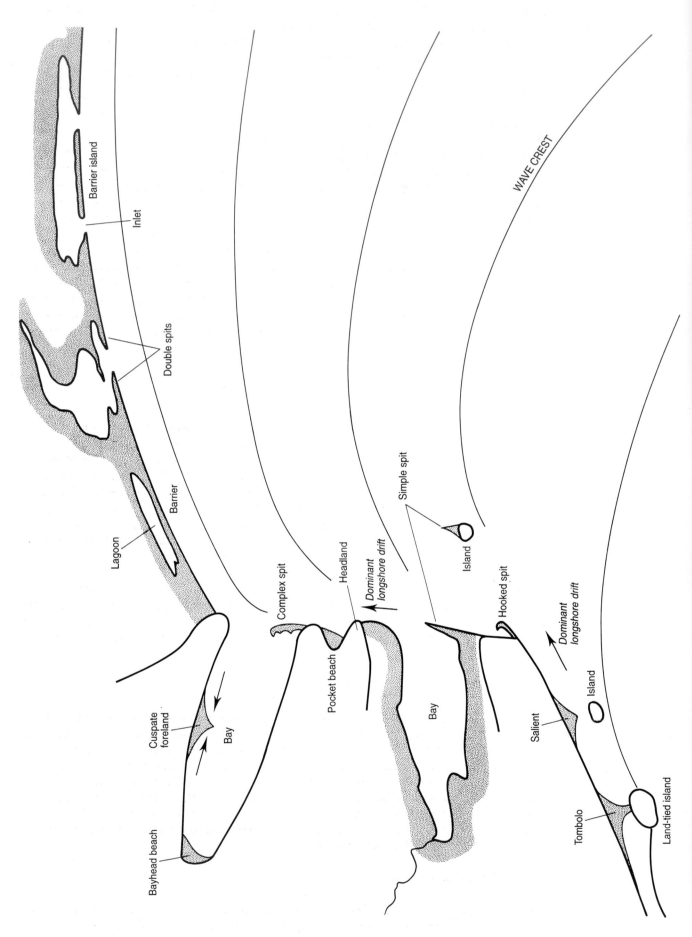

Figure 2.18   *Coastal features*

In the UK the term is also extended to cover similar features linking two islands together, for example the sand bar between Gugh and St Agnes, Isles of Scilly. The shape of a tombolo is even more dominated by wave diffraction around the offshore island than in small pocket beaches and, as a result, the beach plan shape is very stable. The construction of artificial offshore islands or reefs, known as detached breakwaters, has therefore been a standard approach to beach control in many countries, particularly in Japan and around the Mediterranean Sea.

Cuspate forelands (see Figure 2.18)

A small island well offshore will not normally form a complete tombolo, but will often cause a salient to form in the more sheltered area. Such a feature may also be caused by a sand or shingle bank as well as by a rock outcrop. Intriguingly cuspate forelands, also known as cusps or nesses, can form without such offshore features; a good example of which is Dungeness, Kent, on the south coast of England. There is, as yet, no full explanation of these features where they occur on an otherwise relatively straight coastline. It seems that they are more common when the prevailing wave climate has two opposing directional components, each at a considerable angle to the beach normal. Where cusps or nesses are not associated with a fixed feature, such as an offshore reef, they have a tendency to migrate along the coast due to perturbations in the rate of longshore drift. Large features, especially those of shingle such as Dungeness and Orford Ness in Suffolk, have moved along the coast in the past, but slowly. Small features, such as Caister Ness and Benacre Ness on the East Anglian coast, however, have been much more volatile and as they have migrated, difficulties have arisen in managing the adjacent coast.

Spits (see Figure 2.18)

Where valleys open onto a coast, any associated rivers or estuaries affect the movement of sediment along the shoreline and hence the shape of the beaches on one or both sides at the opening. The result is often a finger of beach material, extending from the main beach into or across the mouth of the river or estuary, which is known as a spit. These features can take a variety of forms, depending on both the hydraulic processes and the local geology. They are often of considerable geomorphological interest, since they provide historical evidence of past shoreline positions. They also often separate out distinct types of coastline and hence ecological habitats. As a consequence many such spits are designated Sites of Special Scientific Interest.

As spits extend across the mouth of a river or tidal inlet, they gradually shift the deep water entrance channel in the downdrift direction. In some situations the spit then is breached by the channel breaking through it, often re-establishing itself on a previous location. The severed end of the spit then rapidly attaches itself to the coast on the other side of the inlet, producing a *double spit* (see Figure 2.18).

Barrier beaches (see Figures 2.1 and 2.18)

In many places around the coast of the UK, longshore drift has carried beach sediment across the seaward end of valleys, first forming a spit, and later a complete divide or barrier between the low-lying valley floor and the sea. Chesil Beach (see Figure 2.1) is a fine example of such a beach form. Typically such beaches were initially backed to the landward by a lagoon, though many have subsequently been artificially drained in recent times. For these beaches in particular, the processes of groundwater flows and percolation are extremely important in maintaining their form. Despite an often impermeable core (due to settling out of fines), barrier beaches in a natural state are generally able to gradually shift landward, in response to rising sea level for example, whilst retaining their integrity.

Effect of reefs on beach profile

On many tropical coasts a nearshore coral reef will trap sand on its landward side and destroy most of the incoming wave action by causing it to break. As a result, the beach slope between the reef and the shoreline is generally rather steep, and certainly much less variable than it would have been without the reef. In the UK, a few similar examples of offshore reefs do occur, for example the Beerpan Rocks in Dorset east of Bournemouth, but often their effectiveness at modifying beach profiles is greatly reduced by the large tidal ranges.

Effect of substrate on beach profile

It is not unusual to find that a gently sloping shore platform occupies much of the nearshore zone, and sometimes the lower part of the inter-tidal foreshore as well. These shore-platforms may be formed within a range of rock types, ranging from extremely durable igneous and metamorphic lithologies (see Figure 2.19) in the north and west of the UK, through to more easily eroded limestones, chalk and clays in the south and east (see Figure 2.20). These platforms adopt a much shallower slope than mobile sand or gravel under wave action, so that the underwater profile of the beach usually terminates at a more or less distinct line on the platform. The level of this division between the beach material and the platform will vary depending on wave conditions, tidal level and the amount of mobile material available. Any granular material found on the platform beyond this point will typically be extremely mobile, lying as it does on a hard substrate and being subject to wave turbulence. Where such material does exist, it is usually in the form of a patchy, thin veneer filling in any depressions in the rock platform. On softer rocks, the presence of the mobile sediment provides an agent for abrasion of the platform with the oscillatory currents under waves agitating the material and moving it to and fro across the sea-floor.

Figure 2.19   *Hard shore platform at Nash Point, S. Glamorgan (courtesy British Geological Survey)*

As noted in Section 2.3, this gradual attrition of a shore-platform can supply the beach with fresh material. Along much of the coast between Selsey Bill in West Sussex and Brighton in East Sussex, for example, the erosion of the chalk platform provides considerable numbers of flint pebbles, which can be identified by their covering of chalk which rapidly disappears in the abrasive environment of the active beach. However, for each pebble derived by this process, a much larger volume of the platform has been removed. This lowering of the platform increases water depths (and hence wave heights) at the toe of the beach and lowers the "cut-off" level between the mobile material and the platform itself. Under these dual influences, a beach will either need a greater volume of mobile material to retain its character, or will need to move landward onto a higher part of the platform. It seems likely that the process of erosion of the shore-platform is at the root of many of the coastal and beach erosion problems around the

Figure 2.20 *Clay platform underlying beach at Huttoft, Lincolnshire (courtesy Posford Duvivier)*

south and east coasts of England, affecting both clay substrates (e.g. Medmery Beach, Hampshire) and chalk platforms (e.g. Seaford, Sussex).

Effect of natural sediment traps

A deep hole or canyon close to a shoreline will form a potential sediment trap and thus denude downdrift beaches. Such features have less dramatic effects around the beaches of the UK than the deep canyons off the Californian coast, but still may be present and have an influence, especially in the areas of harder rock in the north and west. An example of these deep features is provided by numerous paleo-river valleys which cut deep channels into the sedimentary rocks during the period of low sea levels associated with the last glaciation. These valleys have now been drowned by the rise in sea level. Some have been filled during the subsequent marine transgression (e.g. the Tees estuary) whilst the infilling of others continues to this day (e.g. the Humber estuary). Interestingly, many have apparently not been infilled at all (e.g. the deeps off St Catherine's Point, Isle of Wight), although the present-day hydraulic environment would seem to encourage such a process. It can be deduced under these circumstances that there must be little available sediment within the vicinity.

Indirect influences due to modification of waves and currents

Apart from direct influences on beach processes, seabed features can have a marked effect on waves and tidal currents and thus indirectly affect beaches. The extremely rugged seabed off the western coast of the Outer Hebrides reduces an extremely energetic offshore wave climate to a rather mild nearshore one. Isolated features, either lying above or below the general level of the surrounding seabed will also have the potential to alter wave conditions at the shoreline, although this effect is only likely to be noticeable if the feature is large (in the order of 100m diameter) and lies in the nearshore zone (typically less than 20m water depth in the UK).

2.5.2   Effect of human intervention on beach development

Virtually all the geological effects of solid geology on beach development mentioned in the previous section have parallels in the effects caused by human intervention. For example, as noted in Section 2.5.1, man has often deliberately tried to replicate the effects of headlands and offshore islands to control beaches. In addition, the dredging of the nearshore seabed, particularly for navigation channels, has produced effects similar to those caused by natural deep depressions in the seabed. Where these intervention measures have been taken, however, it has often proved necessary to carry out further maintenance either to the structures themselves, or to compensate for the effects they have had (e.g. periodic dredging of navigation channels). A number of the most important (i.e. largest scale) of these human impacts are summarised below.

Coastal defences

One of the major impacts on the behaviour of beaches is the long-term cumulative effect of constructing seawalls and groynes, which have been in place for 100 years and more in many parts of the country.

The construction of seawalls can have a variety of effects on the coastline and adjacent beaches. Walls built in front of the base of cliffs not only protect land at the top of the cliff and reduce sudden cliff-falls, but they also prevent the eroding cliff from contributing fresh material to the beach, with the resulting sediment starvation along the downdrift coast.

In the short term, at least, wave reflections from seawalls (see Figure 2.21) can affect the level of the beach in front of it, and hence cause greater wave attack on the wall itself. The question of whether this leads to a continuing long-term lowering of beach levels is a more complex question, not yet fully answered. In many situations, for example, the beach level seems to have almost stabilised in front of seawalls, and although the wave reflections are very strong, the beach has apparently adjusted to the new environment.

Using a seawall to fix one stretch of coastline and reducing its ability to be eroded at the same rate as adjacent frontages, can lead to the formation of artificial promontories. For example, at Sheringham, Norfolk, the late 19th century walls have resulted in the natural alongshore movement of material being severely disrupted, so that the actual drift along the town frontage is now considerably less than the potential rate. As a consequence, the unprotected coastline to the east has retreated more rapidly than that west of the town. With the formation of a "dog-leg" in the coastal plan-shape, shingle can now be transported to the east, but not to the west, resulting in the effect of a one-way drift "valve".

Construction of groyne systems can and does have a similar impact, tying up beach material resources, especially shingle, in one area whilst starving the downdrift beaches of their supply of sediment. The long-term effect of groyning long stretches of coast can also severely reduce the rate of longshore drift. This leads to the situation that if the supply of material is artificially increased (e.g. by recharge) then the rate of drift is also dramatically increased from the normal measured value. Other coastal structures such as harbours and jetties can have similar effects.

A further impact of groyne construction is the creation of both seaward-flowing rip currents and circulation cells both of which have a length scale similar to that of the groyne spacing. Such currents can lead to offshore losses of fine-grained beach sediment, as well as diminishing the efficiency of the groynes themselves.

Commercial removal of beach material

Although now fortunately in decline in most of the UK, beaches were often used as convenient sources of material for a wide range of commercial activities. Quartz sand is used in glass-making and iron foundries. Both of these industries have extracted material from UK beaches in the past, often leaving considerable coastal protection problems in their wake (e.g. at Portobello, Edinburgh). Other types of sand contain important minerals (e.g. baryte) and beaches are used as a convenient source for this ore. Carbonate sand is extracted from beaches, together with seaweed, and used as a fertiliser in some parts of the UK, for example, on the western seaboard of the Outer Hebrides.

Figure 2.21   *Wave reflections at seawall at Bray, Co Wicklow, Ireland (courtesy HR Wallingford)*

Sand and gravel are still also extracted from beaches for aggregate used in construction (e.g. in Devon and Cornwall) and also for other purposes, such as in "pebble mills" for grinding spices. Larger pebbles and cobbles were also frequently used for facing walls or houses.

In some cases this extraction of beach material causes no great difficulties and is therefore likely to benefit the local community, which otherwise would be faced with the extra cost of importing bulky material to do the same task. Elsewhere, however, the extraction may well threaten the stability of the coast, or affect its character. For example in parts of the West Indies, the demands of the tourist industry encourage the construction of accommodation and roads. The traditional sources of building materials, however, are the same beaches which helped to attract the tourists in the first place.

Material may also be added to the beach by tipping. Quarry waste, steel slag and colliery waste have all been tipped directly onto beaches. For example, at Easington, Durham, the beaches have been completely altered by the addition of many millions of tonnes of colliery spoil. Though the Easington spoil is now being removed by wave action, it may be many decades before a natural beach appearance is reached.

Waste has also been tipped into rivers which have then carried the material downstream to the beach. The size grading and mineralogy of these tipped deposits will often be quite different from the natural beach material and so the beach response will be different.

Dredging

Dredging around the coast of the UK is strictly controlled. This is because the dredging of the seabed, either to create safe navigation channels, or to obtain commercially valuable materials such as sand and gravel, may have a two-fold impact on nearby beaches. First, a change in the seabed contours can affect hydraulic processes both locally and further afield. Both tidal flows and waves can be affected. The extent of these changes will depend on the relative increase in water depth caused by the dredging. Problems may be caused by the dredging of deep channels in shallow water close to the coast, usually for navigational access to a port or harbour. In this case the change in the seabed levels is usually permanent, since depths have to be maintained indefinitely. In extreme cases, waves may reflect from the channel flanks, altering the wave climate along the coast.

The second impact can result from the abstraction of sediment itself, either for commercial sale, or to improve navigation. In either case, there is a danger of removing material which otherwise contributes to the natural development of the beaches in the area. As before, this effect is greatest when dredging takes place in shallow water, particularly for navigation, where sediment is regularly mobilised by waves or tidal currents.

Disposal of material offshore also occurs. This may be to dispose of material dredged from harbours, or other unwanted material, which is generally deposited in specified areas so that it does not have any significant effect on the nearby beaches. Material has also been deposited to provide an offshore source of beach recharge material or to act as wave breaks. Research is currently under way to assess such beneficial disposal.

Beach material bypassing or re-cycling

Increasingly beach development is being managed and controlled by large-scale intervention in natural transport processes. Large scale re-cycling operations, such as that carried out at Seaford, Sussex, are capable of matching and opposing natural transport processes (see Figure 2.22). In the USA and Australia, in particular, systems involving the use of fixed pumps are used to move sediment from one side of a harbour or tidal inlet to the other, to help stabilise the position of the local beaches (see Section 9.5).

2.5.3   Effects of climatic changes and sea level rise

Until recently, there has been a tendency, when considering the development of a coastline and its beaches, to assume that the present-day natural processes affecting that development are constant (i.e. that wave and tidal conditions will not vary very much from year to year or from decade to decade). One consequence of the current debate on potential climate change, due to pollution and the "Greenhouse Effect", has been to focus attention on the validity of just such assumptions. It is often implied that the greatest threat to the future development of the coastline is the predicted increase in mean sea levels. In the long-term future (i.e. 50 years or more) this indeed may be the case. However, it has also become clear that other predicted effects, such as changes in wave conditions, may be even more important in the short-term.

The stormy winter of 1989/90, which resulted in considerable damage to the coastline around England and Wales, brought changes in wave conditions into the collective consciousness of coastal managers. There now is no doubt that the North Atlantic and the North Sea have become stormier in the last few years. Whilst this trend alone can have dramatic consequences on beaches and their development, it is less widely appreciated that there has also been a subtle change in wave directions as well. This can bring about very substantial changes in the rates of longshore drift and there is ample evidence already that beaches on the south and east coasts of the UK have suffered considerably as a result.

A typical response of a natural beach is to "roll back" (i.e. move landwards gradually) as the sea level increases. This is a positive characteristic of the beach as it allows it to respond naturally to the new climatic conditions. Problems occur when this roll back is constrained, either by a structure, a phenomenon known as "coastal squeeze" or by the limited volume of

Figure 2.22   *Nourished beach at Seaford, E. Sussex (courtesy HR Wallingford)*

beach sediment. The management choices when this occurs are: to do nothing and allow the beach to react naturally, to import new material to maintain the present beach position or to remove the obstacle, allowing roll-back to continue. The possible implications of climatic variations on each of these management options therefore need to be carefully considered when setting a strategy.

2.6   SEDIMENT BUDGETS AND COASTAL CELLS

2.6.1   Sediment sources and sinks

In order to help understand beach erosion and accretion and the processes causing them, it is useful to introduce the concept of a sediment budget. This is essentially a balance of sediments within a specified length of coast, based on the application of the principle of continuity of mass. Evaluating the sediment budget involves identifying and quantifying the gains of sediment (from the so-called *sediment sources*), the losses (*sediment sinks*) and the transport processes linking them. An important element in determining the budget is the attempt to balance the gains and losses, and deciding on the accuracy and completeness of any such quantification. For example, if the budget does not balance, this may be because an important sediment source or sink has been overlooked, or has been inaccurately evaluated. Alternatively, the transport processes (by waves, tidal currents, etc.) may have been incorrectly calculated. Without a reasonably balanced budget, there is a danger that important processes have been overlooked, leading to subsequent difficulties or mistakes in managing the beach.

The objective of the sediment budget calculation is to explain long-term changes in beach material volumes from point to point along the coastline being considered. If the beach is eroding, then the quantities of material arriving at that beach must be less than those departing. Accretion occurs where the supply of sediment outweighs the losses. By identifying the various elements contributing to the budget, both appropriate and inappropriate management techniques often become apparent. The first step in a sediment budget is to identify the relevant elements, namely sources, sinks, sediment types, and transport mechanisms.

Typical sources of sediment are:

* erosion of shore platforms, cliffs, and other backshore areas
* river borne sediment
* addition of biogenic material (i.e. calcium carbonate), such as shell fragments
* net long-term transport from the offshore seabed or from an adjacent stretch of coastline
* wind blown material from inland sources
* additions of material by human agencies (e.g. beach recharge, the nearshore disposal of dredged spoil, and industrial waste tipping).

Typical sediment sinks are:

* deposition in estuaries, tidal inlets, harbours and associated dredged areas (e.g. approach channels) and around beach structures (e.g. in the lee of detached breakwaters)
* overwashing of beach material, i.e. sediment carried over the beach crest in severe storms
* transport of wind-blown sand to the landward
* net long-term transport into deep water or to an adjacent stretch of coastline
* abrasion and chemical decomposition of beach material, particularly industrial waste products
* removal of material by human agencies (e.g. aggregate extraction, navigation dredging, removal of beach sediments during beach cleansing operations, removal of sand and shingle washed onto promenades during storms and removal of wind-blown sand).

Having identified the main types of sources and sinks, it is the necessary to consider the various sediment transport mechanisms. The major types of transport are:

* longshore transport by wave action
* cross-shore transport by wave action
* transport caused by tidal currents
* transport by other steady or quasi-steady currents (e.g. wind-induced circulation)
* wind transport of sand
* transport by human agencies e.g. recycling operations or bypassing of harbours and tidal inlets.

The various elements of a sediment budget are shown in diagrammatic form in Figure 2.23, taken from the Shore Protection Manual (CERC, 1984). Generally it is not possible to define in advance the relative importance of the elements of a sediment budget for a particular shoreline. Contributions which are unimportant in some parts of the world may be crucial in other areas. Some general guidance for conditions in the USA are presented in the Shore Protection Manual (Table 4-16), based on the likely magnitude of the various elements compared with the gross and nett longshore drift rates.

An important cautionary note concerning the use of sediment budgets is that quite often net long-term losses or gains from deep water (i.e. offshore) can only be estimated by assuming they make up any discrepancies in the remainder of the sediment budget. If such quantities are large, then it is probably wise to question the accuracy of the other calculations, unless convincing evidence for long-term net transport to or from deep water can be found.

It should be borne in mind that existing sediment transport formulae may only have an accuracy of ±50%. Other elements such as the transport caused by tidal currents, or wind action, will have even greater uncertainty attached to their calculation. Interpretation of sediment budgets, therefore, has to be carried out with considerable care. It is often necessary to carry out sensitivity tests for some of the elements and sometimes it has to be concluded that the existing data are not sufficient to carry out a full budget analysis. This latter conclusion in turn may indicate the need for further data collection (see Chapter 4).

A sediment budget can be drawn up for any required length of coast, for example, the frontage of one local authority. However, given the various difficulties that can and do occur, as indicated above, the task is made much easier by a careful choice of the start and end points along the coast. Often the largest contribution to beach erosion and accretion is that caused by

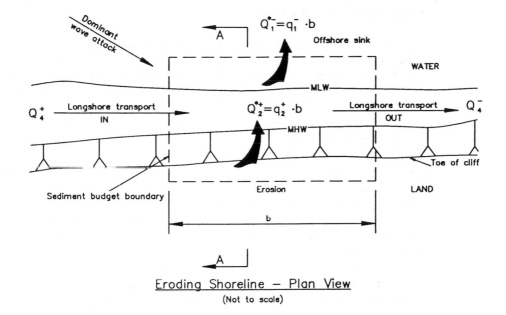

Eroding Shoreline – Plan View

(Not to scale)

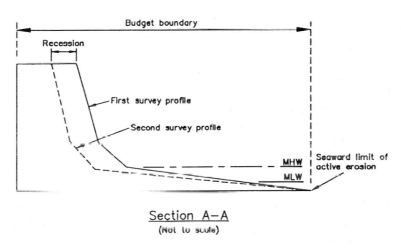

Section A–A

(Not to scale)

Figure 2.23   *Sediment budget (CERC, 1984)*

variations in longshore transport of beach material. It is therefore sensible to define the boundaries of an area for which the sediment budget is to be calculated, at points where the longshore transport rate is known, or where the net drift rate is zero. This leads on to the concept of a coastal or sediment *cell*, as a basis not only for examining beach processes, but as a way of dividing up the coastline for management purposes

2.6.2   Regional divisions and sediment cells

Until recently the management of beaches has been carried out within small stretches of coastline, with coast protection works being almost always carried out to address a particular localised problem. This approach has led to a proliferation of downdrift erosion problems, particularly at the junction between protected and unprotected stretches of coast (see Figure 2.24 - Chewton Bunny, Christchurch Bay). With the setting up of Regional Coastal Groups (see Box 1.1) and with the commitment of MAFF, NRA regions and maritime local authorities in preparing Shoreline Management Plans, this situation is now changing radically in England and Wales. There is now a requirement for works to be carried out within the context of coastal cells, so as to minimise adverse effects on adjacent stretches of coastline. There is also an increasing trend for larger schemes to be carried out, so as to deal with the problems of a particular coastal frontage in a less piecemeal manner. In terms of beach management the

Figure 2.24   *Junction of protected and unprotected coastlines at administration boundary of Chewton Bunny, Christchurch Bay, Dorset (courtesy English Nature)*

concept of "coastal cells", that is a division of the coastline into units within which sediment movement is self-contained, is a very important one.

The definition of a coastal cell, within the context of beach management, is a frontage within which longshore transport and cross-shore transport of beach material takes place independently of that in adjacent frontages. This definition is applied strictly to non-cohesive beach material whose movement is generally restricted to the backshore, foreshore and nearshore zones (see Box 2.1).

The definition of a cell as described here has been established from the viewpoint of the movement of sand and shingle along beaches and the nearshore zone, taking into account the likely consequences of interfering with that movement. Had the main concern been the management of muddy shorelines, estuarial sediments, etc., then the divisions prescribed here would be inappropriate. Indeed it should be stressed that if estuarine processes are being evaluated then the concept of a coastal cell almost certainly breaks down. There is hence no universally applicable division of the coastline into cells. Different boundaries will be needed for different interest groups. The division of the UK coastline shown in Figures 2.25 and 2.26, is thus strictly applicable to beaches comprised of non-cohesive sediments.

For sand and shingle beaches the boundaries between major (regional) cells are usually major headlands. Such headlands should be littoral drift divide points and ideally be bare of beach material (so that any onshore movement is forced either to one side or the other of a headland and is not deflected in its path by any coast protection works in adjacent frontages). An ideal cell boundary is Portland Bill in Dorset. Interfering with the movement of beach material on one side of the Bill will not cause problems on the other (indeed beach material types on either side of Portland Bill are distinctly different).

Sediment sinks are points at which sediment transport paths meet so that beach material tends to accumulate (see Section 2.6.1). This happens naturally in well sheltered areas, such as deeply indented bays or major estuary mouths. Provided that sediment transport is strongly one dimensional and towards the sink, then interference with beach process on one side of a sink will not normally affect beach movements on the other. A good example of this type of coastal cell "boundary" is the mouth of The Wash.

CIRIA Report 153

Figure 2.25 *Boundary of major cells - England and Wales (Motyka and Brampton, 1993)*

The size of coastal cells may be very large. For example between Flamborough Head and The Wash the alongshore transport of sediment is only partly interrupted by the River Humber (fluorescent tracer studies have shown that material can be transported southward from Spurn Head in Humberside to the Lincolnshire coast). Such cells may therefore encompass many

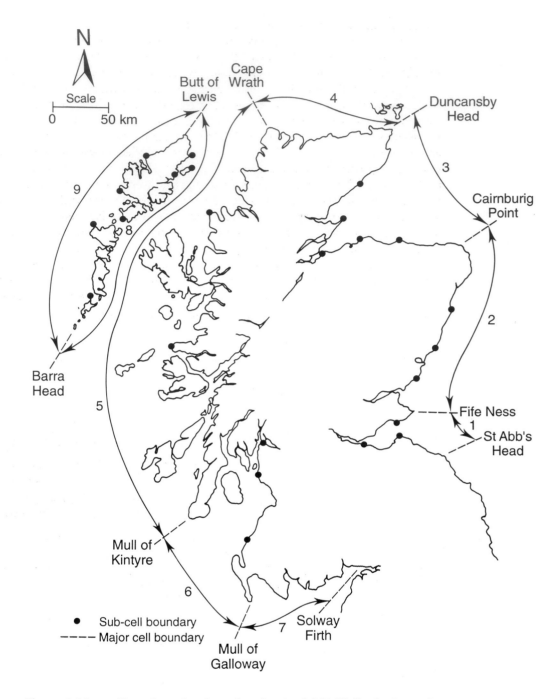

Figure 2.26   *Boundary of major cells - Scotland (HR Wallingford, 1995)*

coast protection authorities and other interested bodies. On the other hand, individual cells may be very small due to the strongly indented, embayed nature of the coastline (e.g. Sennen Cove, Cornwall). For the purposes of efficient beach management it is useful to distinguish major cell boundaries from smaller individual cells.

Regional and local coastal cells

The coastline of England, Scotland and Wales has been be divided into 20 regional coastal cells (see Figures 2.25 and 2.26), although further sub-division is feasible, particularly in Scotland because of the strongly indented coastline and lack of interaction between the widely separated beaches of the west coast. Sub-divisions can be made most easily at headlands, although several major estuaries are effective sinks for beach sediments and qualify as zero nett transport boundaries.

Within regional cells there exists a variety of smaller but still essentially independent sub-cells forming a sensible basis for the management of beaches. Two illustrations are given of these smaller cells (see Figures 2.27 and 2.28). Figure 2.27 shows the frontage from Selsey Bill, West Sussex, to Beachy Head, East Sussex, which is the western end of Regional Cell No 4. The littoral drift divide at Selsey Bill makes this a natural choice for a cell boundary. From the Bill eastward there would be a continuous transport of beach material from west to east if it were not for the presence of groyne systems and harbour arms and jetties. The harbours of Shoreham-by-Sea and the marina at Brighton are major obstacles to drift, although they do not eliminate it entirely. None of these extend sufficiently far seaward to significantly affect sediment transport over the seabed and hence do not qualify for status as cell boundaries. The predominance of swell wave activity from the south-west allows some "leakage" of material from west to east, but there is insufficient action to transport material in the opposite direction. The heavy arrows in Figure 2.27 indicate that some of these harbours are one-way valves for littoral transport (the smaller thin arrows indicate the nett sediment transport direction). Beachy Head at the eastern end of the frontage is a major headland, but is not a barrier to the drift of shingle. However, consideration of the wave climate and sediment transport processes indicates that material is transported eastward around the headland but rarely in the opposite direction. The amount of by-passing is small and the headland can therefore be considered as a sub-cell boundary. It has the status of being a one-way valve for littoral transport.

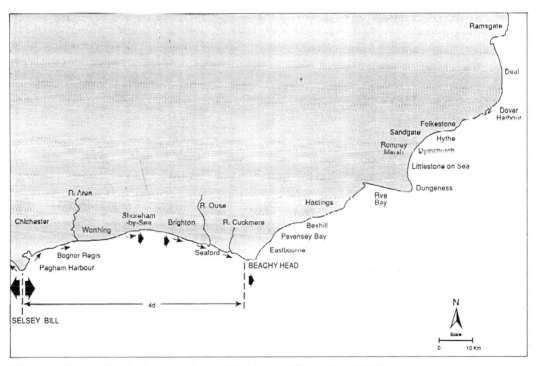

Figure 2.27   *South Downs sub-cell (Motyka and Brampton, 1993)*

Figure 2.28 is a further example of a sub-cell, situated at the northern end of Regional Cell No 5. The sub-cell boundary at Sheringham is considered to be a drift divide for the transport of shingle on the upper beach. Here there is no dramatic change in the orientation of the coastline. However, the concavity in plan shape and the distribution of waves about an orthogonal to the general coastal alignment, results in a nett westerly drift to the west and a nett easterly drift to the east of Sheringham. In this particular area, the position of the drift divide tends to shift from time to time due to relatively small changes in wave conditions. From Sheringham to Hunstanton the drift is to the west, as shown by the orientation of shingle spits, sand spits and other features which indicate a nett westerly drift. From Hunstanton to Snettisham the coastal fringe comes increasingly under the influence of the shelter provided by the mud flats in The Wash. The shingle spit from Hunstanton southward terminates at Snettisham Scalp, which is considered to be a sediment sink and a natural boundary to this coastal cell.

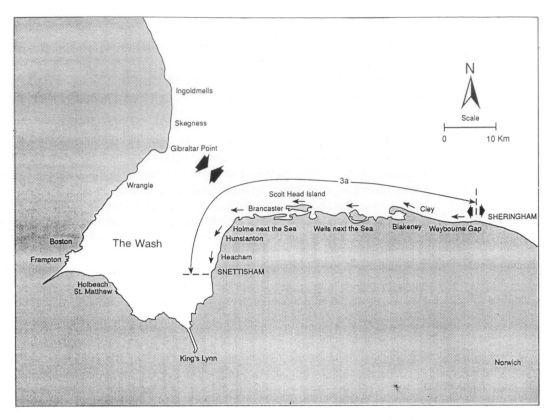

Figure 2.28   *North Norfolk sub-cell (Motyka and Brampton, 1993)*

Geological character of the UK coastline

The natural divisions of the UK coastline described are the result of geomorphological processes over millions of years. The varied nature of the UK coastline and its beaches is a reflection of the underlying geology. The rocks range from very old and extremely hard Pre-Cambrian lithologies, in the Outer Hebrides, through to much more recent (Quaternary) softer sedimentary deposits forming the coasts of south-east England.

The UK land mass is undergoing a gentle lifting due to regional tectonic processes (acting over millions of years) and glacial isostatic rebound (acting over the last few thousand years). North of a line from the island of Anglesey, Gwynedd to the Tees in Cleveland these effects results in an uplift of up to a few millimetres per year, while south of this line the land surface is subsiding at about the same rate. Coupled with a world-wide increase in the volume of sea-water (eustatic sea-level rise) and tectonic movements this is producing a rise in sea-level relative to the coastline of about 3mm/year in south-east England. The rates of sea-level rise have been well documented by both tide gauges and by analysis of coastal landforms. In this more densely populated south-eastern corner of England, therefore, the rocks forming the coast are not only more readily eroded by marine action but are experiencing the greatest rate of sea-level rise. In addition, the major rivers in this area are rather slow-flowing, and bring little or no fresh sand or shingle to the coast.

Conversely, in the north-west of Scotland, where the rocks are still re-bounding after the weight of ice was removed following the last Ice Age (isostatic uplift), the often rocky coastlines are rising relative to sea-level. In this case, where the rocks are older and more durable, the problems due to sea-level rise are generally absent. Rivers such as the Spey and Findhorn in Grampian are also still providing coarse-grained sediment to the coast in parts of Scotland.

Hydraulic character of the UK coastline

As well as its very varied geological character, leading to a great diversity of beach types, the UK coastline also experiences a complex hydraulic regime. The relatively wide and shallow continental shelf of north-west Europe leads to the creation of large tides, reaching a maximum amplitude in the upper Bristol Channel around Avonmouth, Avon, where a mean Spring tide has a range of about 12 m. Accompanying these large tides are often substantial tidal currents which can modify the transport of beach material on open coastlines and are important in transporting sediment in estuaries and tidal inlets. Such currents may be important even where the tidal range is modest, or small, as at Swanage where the mean Neap tide range is only about 0.5m.

The tidal regime is further complicated by atmospheric effects, including pressure and wind, which in the relatively shallow seas around the UK coast can produce large differences (residuals) between the predicted and observed tidal level. For example, around the south-east coast of England, where both the English Channel and the North Sea coast form funnels concentrating the tidal energy, tidal surges often exceed 1m in height and this can produce testing conditions for a beach if surge and high water coincide. Details of how to obtain extreme water levels around the UK coast are described in Section 3.1.8.

The wave climate also changes character around the UK coastline. In the far south-west, for example, the coastline is exposed to the north-east Atlantic, which has one of the most hostile wave climates in the world. Even in areas where the *fetch* over which the wind can generate waves is limited, for example in the Irish Sea, gales often produce significant wave heights in excess of 5m in most years. Existing available data around the UK coast is described in Section 3.3.4.

2.7   IMPLICATIONS FOR BEACH MANAGEMENT

The preceding sections of Chapter 2 provide a brief introduction to beaches, concentrating on the UK coastline. The remainder of this report deals with the many, and often complex, issues which have to be dealt with when managing beaches. It is therefore appropriate to summarise briefly the key components of the preceding chapter and their implications for beach management. First, it is important to recognise that all beaches have a range of characteristics and attributes, and that their role as a component in the defence of the land from the depredations of the sea is only one of these. A good beach management scheme will preserve or enhance as many of a beaches attributes as possible.

It is also vitally important, before embarking on any active management, to understand the origins and evolution of a beach. The plan shape and sediment of a natural beach always depend upon the solid geology, and geological evolution of the solid rocks of the coastline. The long, straight, parallel-contoured beaches preferred by numerical modellers are very rare! In reality, almost all coastlines are complicated by rocky outcrops and irregular seabed contours. These produce spatially-varying wave and tidal conditions, and curved beach plan shapes. The type and quantity of beach sediment also depend greatly on the geological (and human) history of an area rather than just present-day processes. Historical legacies have to be considered, and combined with detailed modelling of the water and sediment dynamics, if the past and likely future development of a beach is to be understood.

Modelling waves, tides, the sediment transport they produce, and the resulting changes in beach morphology is an extremely challenging task. Whilst great strides have been made in recent years, using both numerical and scale physical models, much remains to be refined and verified. Whilst the response of a beach in the short-term (i.e. a few hours or days) can be calculated, the models available for predicting its long-term evolution (i.e. a few years or decades) are rather crude. Our knowledge of the wave climate around the UK coastline is imperfect, and the effect of changes in that climate are only just being appreciated. In view of all of this, historic records of beach changes, and continued monitoring, are vital in predicting beach evolution.

Finally, effective and sustainable management of a beach has to be based, in most cases, on a wider understanding of the coastline within which it is set. This will often involve the development of a sediment budget.

A beach cannot be managed as a coastal defence without an adequate volume of sediment. It is therefore crucial to identify the natural source of that sediment, to assess the losses from the beach and the supply to it. Usually new sediment is only generated by the erosion of cliffs or the nearshore sea bed, and is transported to a beach by longshore currents generated by waves and tides. Losses of material from a beach are normally also as a result of longshore transport, although there may be losses offshore and by gradual abrasion. Such losses along the coast, however, will generally form a supply of material to another beach. From a national or regional viewpoint, therefore, the historic remedy of preserving one beach by beggaring its neighbour is rarely sensible.

If sea levels continue to rise, beaches will require more material than at present to remain in the same position. Alternatively, it will be necessary to allow them to retreat landwards, although in many places this option would be unacceptable and impracticable. The essence of beach management, therefore, is to ensure an adequate amount (and type) of beach material at all points along a coastline where a beach is required, at reasonable cost, and without causing unwarranted environmental damage.

3 Hydraulic conditions

Hydraulic boundary conditions which are relevant to the management of beaches comprise:

- wave climate (i.e. the distribution of wave height, period and direction)
- currents (i.e. the distribution of current speed and direction)
- water levels (i.e. the distribution of still water level).

Information on wind velocity, groundwater flow and fluvial flow may also be relevant in some circumstances.

Extreme values may be important for design purposes, but the complete range of values (overall distributions) is more important for many beach processes which continue during any conditions above those at the threshold of motion of beach sediments. As this threshold is generally quite low, the majority of the complete distribution is significant. Seasonal and/or long-term changes in any of the prevailing hydraulic conditions (both overall and extreme), and information on the persistence of high values and natural inter-annual variability, may also be important.

The principal relationships between the relevant hydraulic conditions are shown in Figure 3.1. The figure should also give some guidance as to which hydraulic parameters need to be determined in any particular case.

Combinations of two or more parameters often determine their impact on beach development. In these cases not only do the separate parameter distributions have to be determined, but a correlation analysis may be necessary to establish the joint probability of the two or more parameters acting together. Potentially the simultaneous occurrence of all six variables listed above could be important in estimating the instantaneous longshore drift rate.

This chapter describes concepts, indicates which parameters are important in different circumstances, suggests data sources and provides outline methods for deriving numerical results. More theoretical detail on wave generation and transformation processes are given, for example, in CIRIA/CUR (1991) and CERC (1984). Throughout Chapter 3, sub-sections contain details on the most cost-effective methods for derivation and procurement of hydraulic data.

3.1 WATER LEVELS

Water levels are perceived to be less critical in the management of beaches than in the design of coastal structures. However, water levels are important in a number of ways:

- overtopping of a beach crest by waves depends on the still water level and thus affects the standard of protection offered by the beach
- the force on a sea wall partially protected from waves by a mobile beach depends on the still water level
- the new beach profile produced by storm wave action depends on the still water level
- the beach sediment may be different at different levels, in turn meaning that the rate of wave- and current-induced drift is dependent upon the still water level
- the wave height may be limited by breaking before arrival at the beach
- groundwater levels in the beach and beach head will be affected by changes in still water level
- the practicality of construction and maintenance will be affected by the overall water level regime
- the level of wave impact on sea walls and thus the response of the fringing beach is directly influenced by water level.

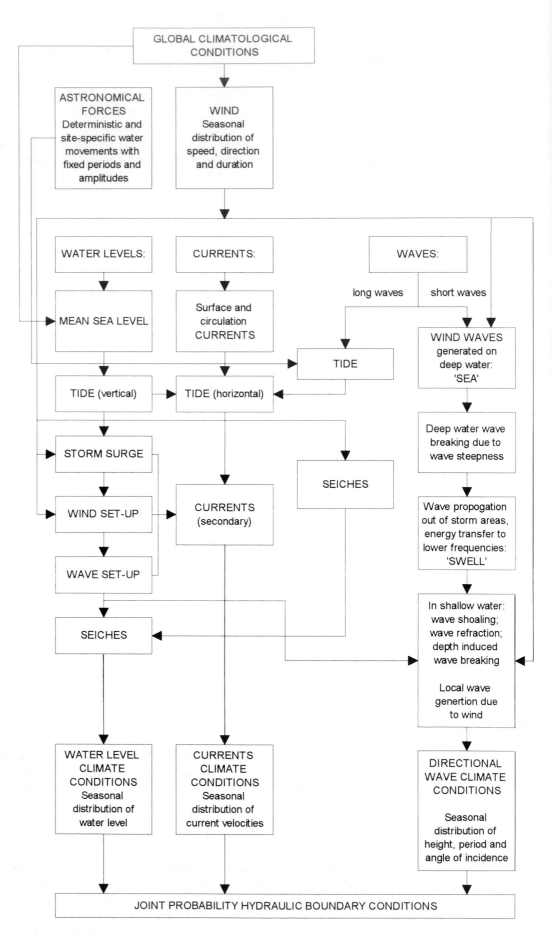

Figure 3.1 *Hydraulic boundary conditions*

There are various components of water level which need to be considered. As well as astronomical tides and very rare seismic (tsunami) effects, there are several meteorological components ("residuals") of water level. These residuals comprise storm surges, wind set-up, wave set-up and seiches. The major effect determining water level at any one instant, around the UK at least, is the astronomical tide which can be predicted accurately well in advance.

Meteorological and seismic effects are not predictable more than, at best, a few days in advance, and even then the predictions are very uncertain.

Some of the components of water level are partially correlated (i.e. a higher or lower value of one component will lead to a higher or lower value of another component). Correlations often arise between components of meteorological origin such as storm surge, wind set-up, wave set-up and even seiches. There can also be some correlation between these components and astronomical tidal level in shallow areas. For example, surges may propagate differently in different water depths and in different currents.

Usually the two most important components of water level at any one moment are astronomical tide and storm surge. The former is cyclical with a period dependent on the relative significance of astronomic forces at a particular location (see Section 3.1.2); for most of the UK the period is 12.42 hours on average. The latter component occurs intermittently, typically as individual events with durations of the order of a day or so, peaking about mid-way through those periods. The variation with time of water level due to astronomical tide and storm surge is illustrated in Figure 3.2.

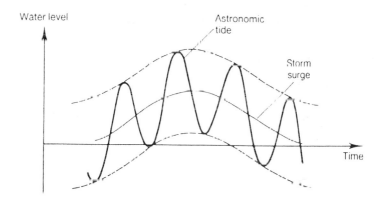

Figure 3.2   *Variation in water level due to storm surge and astronomical tide*

3.1.1   Mean water level

For coastal waters in open communication with the sea, the mean water level (MWL) can often effectively be taken as a site-specific constant, being related to the mean sea level (MSL) of the oceans. In some areas, for example the eastern Mediterranean, the mean sea level varies slightly with the time of year, in a predictable way.

Most countries have a national datum level, which is often approximately equal to the MSL, for example Ordnance Datum in the UK. Chart Datum conversely, as used by the British Admiralty, represents the Lowest Astronomical Tide, which varies significantly from one place to another.

3.1.2   Tides

The basic driving forces of tidal movements are astronomical and therefore entirely predictable, which enables accurate prediction of tidal levels and currents. Since tides are a long wave phenomenon, resonance and shoaling effects caused by geography and bathymetry can lead to considerable amplification of tidal levels in shallow seas and estuaries. Tidal range, approximately equal to twice the tidal amplitude, is generally below 1m in open oceans, increases slightly towards the continents and may increase considerably in shelf seas. Large amplifications are found, for example, in bays along the coasts of England, France and Wales (spring tidal range up to 12m) and in the Bay of Fundy, Canada (spring tidal range up to 13m), while a 4-5m spring tidal range is common for the southern North Sea. The predictive character of tides can be useful when timing of critical operations and manoeuvring during construction is needed.

Tides are predominantly generated by the fundamental gravitational attractions of the Moon and Sun which are proportional to their masses and to the inverse square of their distances from the Earth. Although the Moon is much smaller than the Sun, it has a bigger influence on tides because it is much closer to the Earth. In particular, the timing of the tide is associated with the relative position of the Moon rather than with the time of day, and advances at about 48 minutes a day. Another consequence of the Moon's orbit relative to the Earth is that the tide generating forces of the Sun and Moon are continually moving in and out of phase. Near full moon and new moon, the Sun and Moon pull together to give larger, Spring tides. Smaller, Neap tides are produced at around first and third quarter moons when the Sun and Moon oppose each other. The Spring-Neap cycle is about two weeks.

The orbits of the Sun and Moon are not circular so tides also vary on a seasonal basis with the largest tides of the year occurring at the Spring and Autumn Equinoxes. Minor variations also occur over an 18.6 year cycle due to the variable angular disposition of the Sun and Moon. Even the major planets have a small effect, but these are not important for beach management.

The dominant tidal components have periods of approximately half a day (semi-diurnal tides) and a day (diurnal tides). Dominant semi-diurnal tidal components include principal lunar (M_2, period 12.42 hours) and principal solar (S_2, period 12.00 hours). Dominant diurnal components include principal lunar diurnal (O_1, period 25.82 hours) and luni-solar diurnal (K_1, period 23.93 hours). Specific coastline geometry (e.g. of channels, bays, estuaries) and bottom friction can generate frequencies equal to the sum or difference of basic frequencies. The contributions of these secondary frequencies may be significant. McDowell and O'Connor (1977) give a good description of the mechanics and practicalities of tidal motions, especially near to the coast.

Other aspects of tides and the obtaining of tidal data are discussed in Sections 3.1.8 to 3.1.10.

3.1.3 Storm surges

Local minima of atmospheric pressures (depressions) cause a corresponding rise of MWL (similarly, high pressures cause reduced water levels). Mean air pressures at sea level are 1013 millibars (mbar) approximately. In the storm zones of higher latitudes ($\geq 40°$) variations from 970 to 1040mbar are common, while in tropical storms pressures may drop to 900mbar.

The height of the corresponding static rise of MWL (z_a, in metres) is:

$$z_a = 0.01 \ (1013 - p_a) \tag{3.1}$$

where p_a is the atmospheric pressure at sea level, in mbar.

Due to dynamic effects, however, the rise in water level can be amplified significantly. When the depression moves quickly, the elevation of the water level moves correspondingly as a storm surge. A storm surge behaves as a long wave with a wave length approximately equal to the width of the centre of the depression, typically 150-800km. The height of these long waves may increase considerably due to shoaling. For example, along the coasts of the southern North Sea, storm surges with a height of 3m have been recorded. In practice the term "storm surge level" is sometimes used loosely to include the astronomical tidal component and other meteorological effects.

3.1.4 Wind set-up

Shear stress exerted by wind on the water surface causes a slope in the water surface (see Figure 3.3) as a result of which wind set-up and set-down occur at downwind and upwind boundaries, respectively.

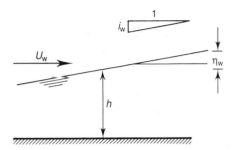

Figure 3.3   *Wind set-up*

If the water depth and wind field are constant as shown in Figure 3.3, the wind-induced gradient (i_w) of the still-water surface can be estimated from:

$$i_w = c_w(\rho_{air} / \rho)U_w^2 /(gh)\tag{3.2}$$

where U_w = wind speed
h = water depth
ρ, ρ_{air} = mass density of sea water and air (1030,1.21kg/m^3)
c_w = air/water friction coefficient (0.8×10^{-3}-3.0×10^{-4}) - values increase with wind speed (Abraham *et al*, 1979).

The resulting maximum wind set-up (η_w) at the downwind coast or shoreline is:

$$\eta_w - i_w F/2\tag{3.3}$$

where F = fetch length.

In practice, and without calibration data, equations (3.2) and (3.3) can only provide a guide as to the likely wind set-up, due to uncertainties about the value of c_w and the choice of representative values of h and F. If possible, site-specific measurements of surge, from which wind set-up can be estimated, should be made on a few windy days, from which to infer a site-specific calibration of the equations for use in subsequent predictions.

3.1.5 Wave set-up

Wave set-up is caused by energy dissipation due to shoaling of the incoming waves (see Figure 3.4). For small amplitude sinusoidal waves the wave set-up can be roughly approximated by linear wave theory.

Referring to the wave conditions at the breaker line, the theory enables the derivation of the following approximate relationship, which can be used as a first estimate of wave set-up:

$$\eta_{max} = 0.3\gamma_{br}H_b\tag{3.4}$$

where γ_{br} = breaker index or maximum H/h ratio (Section 3.4.1)
H_b = wave height at the breaker line (regular waves).

H_b can be found by applying a wave model to the local bathymetry, using deep water waves as a boundary condition.

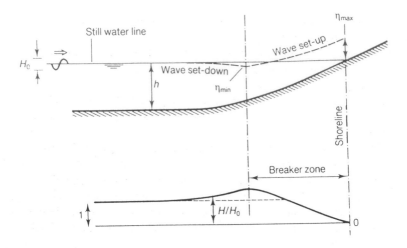

Figure 3.4 *Wave set-up*

3.1.6   Seiches

A seiche in a body of water is a standing wave oscillation of the water surface with the natural frequency of oscillation for that water body. It is normally observed in completely enclosed water bodies such as lakes and seas. Thus when a long wave traverses the water body it is reflected from the end and the interference with the original wave results in a standing wave pattern. However, if a body of water such as a bay or estuary is open at one end, then reflection may again occur at the open end and standing waves can be observed. One famous location for seiches is in the Adriatic Sea where the water level at Venice can display oscillations for considerable periods.

It is very difficult to estimate the amplitude of a seiche because it depends in general on how close the forcing frequency is to the natural oscillation frequency. If they are close then large amplitudes may occur (e.g. the tidal amplitude in the Severn estuary). If an oblong lake is suddenly subject to a steady wind along its long axis, then the maximum rise in water level is considerably higher than that which would be obtained by a simple balance between water slope and wind force. The maximum would be twice as large as the increase in level caused by wind set-up (see Section 3.1.4) alone.

3.1.7   Tsunami

Tsunami are seismically induced gravity waves, characterised by wave lengths that are in the order of minutes rather than seconds. They often originate from earthquakes below the ocean, where water depths can be more than 1000m, and may travel long distances without reaching any noticeable wave height. However, when approaching coastlines their height may increase considerably. Due to the large wave length, increases that result from shoaling and refraction coming inshore from significant water depths can be calculated using shallow-water wave theory. Wave reflection from the relatively deep slopes of continental shelves may also be an important consideration.

A method for estimating the height and frequency of tsunami is given in CIRIA/CUR (1991). However, it is unlikely that this component of water level would be important in the management of UK beaches, except perhaps where the beaches protect very sensitive installations such as nuclear power stations.

3.1.8   Design extreme water levels

Still water level is defined as the average sea surface elevation over an area at any instant. It excludes localised variations due to waves and wave set-up, but includes tidal elevations and surges (and long period seiches, if any). It would be possible to calculate extreme surges and astronomical tides separately, to derive the correlation between the two, and then to combine them. However, in practice, it is only the overall still water level which is measured and which is of interest. It is therefore most convenient to consider it as a single parameter, recorded at the peak of the tide. This also avoids the complication of separating out the surge and of determining the correlation between surge and predicted tide.

There are many long-term sets of water level data around the UK which have been analysed (Graff, 1981; Coles and Tawn, 1990; POL, 1995) to predict extreme water levels at about 50 specific locations. In practice it will rarely be necessary for a designer to attempt extremes predictions from raw data. Although a method for this is given in CIRIA/CUR (1991), it is generally better to work from the reliable published extreme water levels (e.g. POL, 1995) and to convert them to the site of interest. Any uncertainty involved in calculating extreme water levels in this way is usually small compared to uncertainties associated with prediction of extreme wave conditions and to an assessment of their correlation with extreme water levels. An approximate method for deriving extreme water levels based on published extreme values for another nearby location is given in Box 3.1. This method works well in bays and estuaries, but should be applied with caution around convex coastlines such as the Suffolk/Norfolk coast.

Box 3.1   *Simple approach to correlating extreme water levels*

An approach to deriving a first estimate of a probability distribution of extreme water levels for a site for which there is only basic astronomical tidal information is to correlate this site with one nearby for which both tidal data and extreme water level predictions are available. Correlation is then achieved by assuming (Graff, 1981) that the following ratio is the same for the two sites:

$$\frac{\text{Extreme level - mean high water spring (MHWS) level}}{\text{Spring tide range (MHWS - MLWS)}}$$

Where available and appropriate, a slightly more accurate estimate can be achieved by replacing spring tidal range in the above ratio by the sum of the principal semi-diurnal tidal components, $M_2 + S_2$ (see Section 3.1.2 for definitions).

3.1.9   Sources of water level data

Low cost software is available from hydrographic water level data suppliers for those engineers wishing to predict astronomical tides for themselves. At present, this can only be done for sites at which the tidal harmonic constituents have been established from measurements. A planned enhancement will permit direct predictions at intermediate locations by interpolation of the harmonic constants. However, it is not usually necessary for the user to carry out tidal predictions, because tables are composed on a routine basis and issued yearly by port or coastal authorities and by national admiralties (the US and British Admiralties, in particular, have extensive data files). These provide high water (HW) and low water (LW) levels and times for major ports, usually one year ahead, but they can also be used to derive site-specific tidal constants needed for further prediction at intermediate sites. Charts and tide tables also include typical tide curves to enable predictions to be made for intermediate water levels between high and low water.

In the majority of UK studies, only the astronomical tide (as given in Tide Tables) and/or the overall still water level (as measured by tide gauges) will be considered. In most situations, wind set-up is a small component of the water level, wave set-up is very localised, and tsunami are so rare that they are not significant in beach assessment. Where storm surges and seiches are significant, they will automatically be included in tidal measurements, and for most practical purposes they need not be separated out. In most situations it will not be necessary to commission tide gauge recording or any "new research" into water levels, but merely to carry out an informed review of existing data. Some sources of tidal and water level data are listed below:

• open literature on extreme water levels (for extreme total water levels, see Section 3.1.8)
• Admiralty Tide Tables and Charts (for astronomical tidal ranges)

- Proudman Oceanographic Laboratory (for measured or predicted water level data, for the A Class tide gauge network (see Figure 3.26), bespoke analyses and the Permanent Service for Mean Sea Level)
- others: consultants, universities, port authorities, local authorities, specialist literature.

Where water level recording is necessary, one should bear in mind the following points. The gauge location should be permanent, accessible, and not subject to interference by vandals or wave action. For measurement of surges and/or sea level trends, the instrument would need to operate for an indefinite period. For reliable derivation of local tidal constituents, it is necessary to have continuous tidal observations for at least a year. However, reasonable estimates can be made from as little as 14 days of data if there are constituents from a site nearby based on a longer record. Analysis of tidal data is not trivial: extraction of surges requires a knowledge of the astronomical tide and analysis of tidal constituents requires specialist software.

3.1.10   Timing of high water levels

A useful property of the tides to remember when planning to inspect a beach or to do work is that mean high water of Spring tides (MHWS) at a given location always occurs at about the same time of the day. The MHWS timing at another place will be different, and the typical Neap tide (MHWN) timing will be about 6 hours different from the MHWS timing. For example MHWS at the River Tees Entrance, Cleveland, occurs at about 0500h and 1700h (GMT) each Spring-Neap cycle and MHWS at Walton-on-the-Naze, Essex, occurs about 8 hours later at 0100h and 1300h (GMT). Please note that these times are typical for the two locations: for actual tide times the user should refer to Tide Tables. Perhaps more important for carrying out work on beaches is the timing of the most extreme low waters, and whether or not they occur during daylight. Figure 3.5 is a map of Britain indicating which coasts have MLWS at approximately midnight and mid-day, and which have MLWS at about 6 a.m. and 6 p.m.

3.1.11   Water level forecasts

The Storm Tide Warning Service is run by the UK Met Office as a flood forecasting service funded by MAFF. A tidal model is run alongside the weather forecasting model, to predict storm surges. When the predicted total water level (i.e. astronomical tide plus surge) exceeds a given threshold for any particular division of the coast, then a warning is issued. Authorities may then put into practice their flooding contingency plans.

3.2   TIDAL CURRENTS

Although waves are usually the dominant cause of beach movement, currents, associated with the propagation of the tide and other origins, should also be considered. Currents determine the directions of drift outside the surf zone, and a nett longshore current may cause a significant nett annual littoral drift. Tidal currents are more important in terms of their ability to transport sand than shingle. This is due to shingle tending to be found higher up the beach where currents tend to be reduced, and to shingle having a higher threshold of movement than sand. The roles of waves, tides and currents are inextricably linked in determining the unique character of every beach. The variation of water levels and the associated water movements also serve to distribute and disperse effluent, flotsam and jetsam.

3.2.1   Current generation, modulation and influence

Current generation processes

Coastal and estuarine waters are free to move in response to any applied force. The most important of these are the following, naturally occurring ones:

- the gravitational forces of the Sun and Moon which generate the tides
- wind stresses which produce local wind generated currents and wind surges

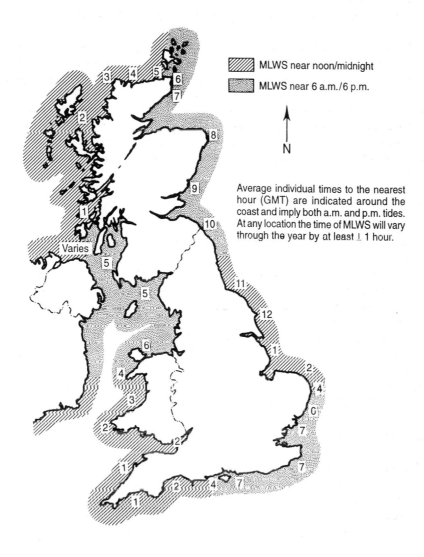

Figure 3.5 *Approximate timing of MLWS around Britain*

- waves which generate nett mass transport as a result of vertical profile and wave breaking and wave set-up effects
- atmospheric pressure gradients which produce pressure surges
- the gravitational force of the Earth (this does not in fact generate currents directly but it is nevertheless a very important force which converts differences in water level and differences in pressure and density into water movements)
- although not strictly a force, river discharge is a localised cause of currents in and around estuaries.

Modulation of flow

There are other forces which can modify existing currents but do not themselves generate them:

- Coriolis effect due to the Earth's rotation causes an existing current to deflect to the right in the northern hemisphere and to the left in the southern hemisphere. Coriolis is responsible for generating the characteristic rotating tidal systems in the North Sea, Irish Sea and English Channel, whilst in the absence of Coriolis (i.e. near the Equator) a simple, linear tidal propagation is produced

- bed shear stress (friction) dissipates energy and slows the flow
- centripetal accelerations create secondary circulations in water flowing round a bend.

Flow and transport processes

The two main flow and transport processes are bed shear stress and turbulent mixing. The underlying agent of both these is the fluid viscosity. The friction (bed shear stress) experienced by a viscous fluid depends on the roughness of the bed. Bed shear stress drags bed sediment in the direction of flow. Turbulence, generated as a result of instability of the viscous shear flow, lifts sediment from the bed which is carried away by the flow in suspension. Erosion of the bed is likely in areas of high bed shear stress and intense turbulence. Sediment carried away by the flow may be deposited in areas where bed shear stress and turbulence are low. Wave orbital motion and wave breaking increase the bed shear stress and turbulence, thereby greatly enhancing erosion of the bed and sediment transport.

Turbulence, by mixing other suspended and dissolved substances through the water column, is also an important element of dispersion. Natural decay processes such as coliform mortality or atmospheric cooling also contribute in the dispersion process.

3.2.2 Derivation and measurement of currents

Description of currents

Currents can be described over a given time scale by a time-mean magnitude, direction, and spatial and turbulent variability. In addition, current velocities vary in a vertical sense over the water depth and, except for density- and wind-induced currents, the vertical distribution of velocities is usually described by a logarithmic function.

Data on current velocities can be obtained by direct measurement, or by use of numerical and physical models, although in the case of models, boundary condition current measurements may be required. Information on currents can be obtained from the following sources.

Use of charts and tables

In many countries, coast or port authorities or the Admiralty provide tables and charts of current velocities, based on observations in the vicinity of main shipping routes, river mouths and estuaries. These are useful so long as it is recognised that surface velocities may, for wind- and density-induced currents, differ significantly from the velocities closer to the bottom.

Sources of data include the British and US Admiralties, who hold data on currents in many strategic marine areas all over the world. In particular, Admiralty Chart "Diamonds" and Tidal Stream Atlases, are widely used. Marine and offshore activities have also often necessitated current (and other) measurements, but such data may be in the private domain and difficult to obtain.

Use of analytical methods

When current data are available from one or more nearby locations, the currents for the site concerned might be estimated from correlation. However, only for tidal or wind-induced currents can a reliable relation be assumed between neighbouring locations. Correlation factors for one or more other locations can be derived from a limited number of simultaneous measurements, but the sites to be correlated must show good similarity with regard to geography (e.g. alignment of coastline, exposure to wind and waves, location relative to river mouths, bays, breakwaters) and bathymetry. For the derivation of currents (unlike the prediction of extreme water levels), interpolation and extrapolation should be the last resort because current patterns do not vary linearly from place to place, due to the irregular nature of the coastline.

Some situations permit derivation of useful analytical expressions for currents. Examples include:

- the tidal current in the entrance of a harbour basin or estuary, where if the geometry allows for schematisation by a simple rectangular shape, the storage equation (based on continuity only) can be used to relate the current velocity to the (known) water levels and width and length of the basin
- longshore and density currents which may allow for an analytical approach, but rarely without any empirical support.

Use of tidal flow models

Increasingly, numerical tidal flow models are used to predict current flows. The models use three-dimensional seabed bathymetry, and most (but not all) work with depth-averaged flow velocities. The models require boundary conditions usually taken from a coarser grid model, but perhaps from charts or atlases. Usually, results from the models are collected over complete tidal cycles, perhaps representing a neap tide, a spring tide and a surge tide. The models provide information on the variability of water surface elevation and current velocity both over the modelled area and over the tidal cycle. Tidal flow modelling requires specialist software and experience and is best left to consultants with appropriate expertise.

On an opportunistic basis, tidal data may be available from previous model studies which cover a fair proportion of the UK coast.

Current recording

Normally a 14-day programme, to cover the spring/neap cycle, is sufficient to record current velocities at discrete fixed locations. The choice of location is important and multiple placements at different depths may be required.

Flow tracking methods or OSCR deployments are required to establish current patterns over a wider area. Drogues can be deployed to follow currents at different depths over short time periods (e.g. one tide cycle). OSCR is a radar-based system which can be used to measure surface water movements over longer time periods.

3.3   DEEP WATER WAVE CONDITIONS

This section considers offshore waves, seaward of the nearshore zone within which shallow water wave transformation processes become important. Here, typically in >20m of water, the waves are not limited by water depths and are therefore generally described as deep water waves.

Often these wave conditions will be altered during their propagation through the nearshore zone before arrival at the beach where they are to be applied. Generally, therefore, it will be necessary to modify these wave conditions using methods described in Section 3.4.1 before using them in beach calculations.

At most sites it is both convenient and realistic to consider wave generation in deep water quite separately from wave transformation in shallow water. The former can be considered to occur seaward of some particular position or depth contour, typically 15-20m for open coast sites, and the latter to occur landward of that boundary. However, there are a few locations, where the shallow coastal waters extend a long distance offshore, at which this assumption is not valid and where a hybrid approach to wave generation and wave transformation may be necessary.

Long wave phenomena such as tides and storm surges are, for engineering purposes, treated as quasi-static water level components rather than as waves (see Section 3.1).

An extreme wave condition may be needed for determining the standard of protection afforded by an existing or recharged beach. It can be specified in terms of a wave height, a wave period, and where necessary a wave direction, with a given return period. The concept of a design extreme wave condition is relevant in the context of management of beaches, as the condition may cause a short-term response in the beach, involving a change in profile, overtopping or damage to a structure lying landward of the beach. However, unlike a fixed structure, the beach may well recover naturally from the action of an extreme wave condition unless longshore response or other factors have permanently reduced the available volume of beach material.

The long-term behaviour of beaches is often more dependent on the overall wave climate than on the design extreme wave condition. On sand beaches, for example, both longshore and cross-shore transport may occur during a high proportion of the total time, in even quite modest sea states. The longshore drift at any particular time will be dependent upon wave height, period and direction, and at different times may move sediment either left-to-right or right-to-left along the beach. In order to predict the overall longshore movement of beach material throughout the year, it is therefore necessary to have good information on the overall wave climate. Because of the sensitivity to wave direction (see Figure 3.25) it may be necessary to use quite sophisticated methods for determining the deep water wave climate and to perform the calculations on a site-specific basis. This requires the use of a directional wave recorder or a wave hindcasting model.

3.3.1   Definitions and parameters

Types of wave condition

Particular wave conditions may be specified in different ways, depending on the methods used to derive them and on their intended use, as follows:

1. *Regular waves* repeat indefinitely, each wave being identical to the others. They are defined by a peak to trough wave height (H), a peak to peak wave period (T) (or alternatively wave length (L)) and a direction of propagation (θ).

2. *Long-crested random waves* are uni-directional but include a range of wave heights and periods. The random wave height is usually defined by a significant wave height (H_s), which is approximately equal to the average height of the highest one third of the waves, and an average wave period (T_m). A fuller description of the sea state is given by the frequency spectrum ($E_{\eta\eta}(f)$), which gives the distribution of wave energy as a function of frequency.

3. *Short-crested random waves* additionally include a range of directions, defined in terms of the standard deviation of wave energy propagation direction or some other standard spreading function. A fuller description of the sea state is given by the directional spectrum ($E_{\eta\eta}(f, \theta)$), which gives the distribution of wave energy as a function of frequency and direction.

Short-crested waves provide the best representation of true ocean waves, but there may be insufficient information from which to specify them in detail, or they may be over-detailed for the subsequent analysis steps.

The use of particular wave conditions is appropriate for design (extreme) wave conditions where only a small number of return periods and wave direction sectors are to be considered. However, for the estimation of long-term longshore drift rates, it is necessary to have more information on the overall wave climate. As a minimum, it is necessary to have information on the distribution of wave height and direction for, say, the highest 20% of wave conditions. A seasonal breakdown of conditions may be necessary for operational and planning purposes. Ideally the information on wave climate would comprise the overall and seasonal distributions of H_s, T_m and θ. However, in practice the information is easier to handle if expressed as a distribution of H_s and θ only, together with a standard relationship (e.g. a fixed "wave steepness") between H_s and T_m.

Forecast wave conditions may be required for operational purposes, for planning site activities on a day-to-day basis. Forecast weather and wave data is routinely available from the UK Meteorological Office for times up to 36 hours ahead, with updates every 12 hours.

Spectral description of waves

In general, an observed wave field can be decomposed into a number of individual wave components, each with its own frequency ($f = 1/T$) and direction (θ). The distribution of wave energy as a function of the wave frequency is commonly presented by means of the one-dimensional wave-energy density spectrum, denoted as $E_{\eta\eta}(f)$.

A variety of semi-empirical wave spectra have been presented, each having their specific range of applicability. Two of the most widely used are the spectrum described by Pierson and Moskowitz (1964) and JONSWAP (Hasselmann *et al*, 1973), both of which are shown in Figure 3.6. In the figure, the peak frequency (f_p) is a characteristic parameter which is defined as the frequency of peak energy in a wave spectrum. The peak period T_p is the inverse of f_p. F is the fetch length, also discussed in Section 3.3.4.

The Pierson-Moskowitz (P-M) spectrum represents a fully-developed sea in deep water. The JONSWAP (J) spectrum represents fetch-limited sea states, i.e. growing seas.

CIRIA/CUR (1991) describes the TMA modification to the JONSWAP spectrum for use in a wave generation area of limited water depth. It also describes how several different wave height and period parameters may be derived from the spectrum, of which the most relevant are:

$$H_s = 4m_0^{1/2} \tag{3.5}$$

$$T_m = (m_0/m_2)^{1/2} \tag{3.6}$$

where m_0 and m_2 are moments of the spectrum $E_{\eta\eta}$.

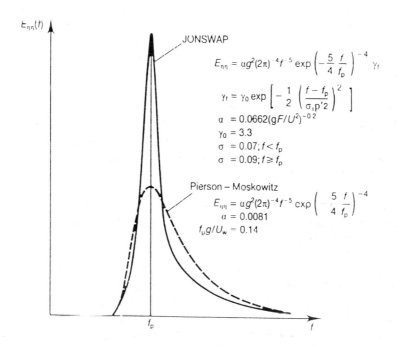

Figure 3.6 *Pierson-Moskowitz and JONSWAP spectra*

Wind-sea and swell

Wind-sea refers to wave energy generated within a limited area (up to about 1000km radius) by winds occurring relatively recently (within the preceding day or so). These wave conditions can be predicted from information on winds occurring within the previous couple of days within a few hundred kilometres of the position of interest.

Swell refers to waves which have moved well away from the area in which they were generated. Generally these wave conditions cannot be predicted from information on local wind conditions. In practice, the distinction between wind-sea and swell is not always clear or relevant, and different organisations use slightly different definitions of swell (Hawkes *et al*, 1995). A distinction may be made between "young swell" originating within the same basic wind system as would have produced any locally generated waves and "old swell" arriving from distant unrelated storm areas.

Around the UK, wind-sea usually has larger wave heights than swell, but swell has higher wave periods than wind-sea. Swell tends to arrive from directions where the fetches are very long (1000km or more), whereas severe wind-sea may come from a greater range of directions. Some parts of the UK coast from which there is no long fetch, for example north Wales, are protected from swell. Other parts, particularly those such as the north Cornwall coast exposed to Atlantic wave conditions, receive far more swell.

Almost by definition, there can be little or no correlation between wind-sea and "old swell" although one might expect a degree of correlation between wind-sea and "young swell". They may occur together, but it is more likely that extreme swell and extreme storms will be uncorrelated except for the fact that both are likely to occur in winter. The correlation between wind-sea and swell and its relevance and application in coastal engineering are the subjects of on-going research.

Superficially it may seem that storm seas are more important than swell in coastal defence work. However, the longer wave periods associated with swell can sometimes cause greater overtopping and/or movement of beach material than the higher wave heights associated with wind-sea.

Wind-sea and swell will provide *alternative* design extreme wave conditions, both of which may be important in some circumstances. In cases where wave climate has been synthesised from local wind data, it may be necessary to add a background swell component. For long-term beach response, dependent on the total wave climate, the effects of wind-sea and swell should be combined.

Alternative sources of wave energy

Some very long period oscillations in the sea surface elevation, such as seiches, storm surges and tides, might be considered as waves for some purposes, but here they are categorised as components of the water level and are considered in Section 3.1. However, "long waves", derived from the varying wave set-up as wave groups arrive at the coast, are best categorised as a wave phenomenon. These waves (see Section 3.4.1) have small heights, but long periods, of the order 30 seconds to several minutes. On a beach, these long waves modify the processes caused by the wind-sea and swell, for example producing long period variations in set-up and in longshore currents. The relative phasing of the long waves and the groups of wind waves can also affect the movement of sediment, particularly at right-angles to the beach contours.

3.3.2 Wave statistics

This section addresses the long-term (e.g. seasonal or annual) distribution of significant wave height, mean wave period and mean wave direction, as this may be important in determining beach behaviour. In practice (e.g. in physical modelling or numerical prediction of beach profiles) it may be possible only to test in detail a small number of specific wave conditions.

This section also suggests ways in which a small number of representative wave conditions may be selected.

The distribution of heights and periods for individual waves within a stationary sea state is of little importance in beach management, but information on this subject is available in CIRIA/CUR (1991) or CERC (1984). Conversely, the order in which different sea states occur within a period of time, i.e. the persistence, profile and sequencing of storms, is more important for beaches, where damage may accumulate over a period of time, than for fixed coastal structures.

Methods for compilation of long-term wave climates

The significant wave height is usually assumed to be constant during each hourly or three-hourly measurement or prediction period. For most purposes the long-term distribution of wave climate can be determined from simple histogram analysis of all the available measurements or predictions. In doing so it may be necessary to weight the observations if one season of the year is under- or over-represented in the sample.

There are several possible enhancements to this approach.

1. If the data covers only a short period of time, for example one year, there may be doubt about whether or not the period was representative of longer term conditions. With reference to some longer term source of data, for example wind measurements, the period of the wave observations can be compared with longer term conditions and subsequently modified as necessary.

2. A theoretical, probability density function can be fitted to the data to smooth out the observations. Following this, extreme values can be estimated from the fitted distribution.

3. The available data may be of high quality, but still be inadequate in terms of period of observations, position of observations, lack of data on wave direction or lack of information on wave spectrum. A site-specific wave hindcasting model could be calibrated against the available data and then re-run for a longer period and/or a second location so as to overcome the inadequacy of the data.

4. The available wave data may come from more than one population, perhaps characterised by distinctly different wave steepnesses and/or different wave directions. It may help the subsequent analysis, if these populations can be separated out.

Distribution of significant wave height

There is no theoretical argument in favour of the use of any particular probability density function in all situations. However, in the majority of cases the Weibull Distribution (see Box 3.2 and Figure 3.7) provides at least as good a fit to H_s data as any other candidate distribution.

Distribution of significant wave height and period

The distribution of both significant wave height and wave period are important in determining beach response to wave loading. A typical sea steepness ($2\pi H_s/gT_m^2$) for the highest few percent of wave conditions may be helpful later in assigning a wave period to an extreme wave height.

Several authors have given theoretical functions for the joint distribution of wave height and period. Perhaps the best known formulation is that used in the enhancement procedure for ship observed wave data (Hogben *et al*, 1986). However, in practice the joint distribution is usually obtained directly from sequential measured or hindcast wave data.

Box 3.2   *Three-parameter Weibull Distribution*

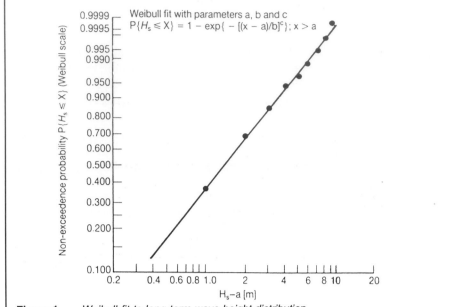

Figure 1   *Weibull fit to long-term wave height distribution*

The three-parameter Weibull Distribution is defined by the following relationship:

$$P(H_s) = 1 - \exp\left[-\{(H_s - a)/b\}^c\right] \tag{1}$$

where H_s =   significant wave height
    P =   probability less than H_s
    a, b, c are parameters to be found

Rearranging and taking logs twice, this becomes:

$$\log\{-\log(1 - P(H_s))\} = c\{\log(H_s - a) - \log b\} \tag{2}$$

Writing

$y = \log\{-\log(1 - P(H_s))\}$
$x = \log(H_s - a)$

x and y can be plotted on linear scales.

Alternatively, and more conveniently, appropriate graph paper is available (or can be prepared) with a logarithmic scaling following Equation (2). The parameters of the distribution are calculated after plotting the various exceedance levels on this Weibull scaled graph paper (see Equation (2)) and drawing the best fit straight line through the points. As a check, this procedure can be reproduced by a computer program and the results compared.

Wave heights and periods determined from a series of 3-hourly recordings can be presented in a scatter diagram which gives the fraction of waves found within each of a number of pre-defined classes of H_s and T_m (see Figure 3.8). The scatter diagram is created by counting over a long period of time, covering a range of storm conditions, so as to determine the total number of individual sea states falling within classes ΔH_s and ΔT_m.

Distribution of significant wave height and direction

Wave direction (θ) in the approaches to the coast is important in determining propagation behaviour, and wave direction in the surf zone is important for sediment transport. Littoral transport formulae include a term dependent upon the wave direction relative to the coastline.

In deep water well offshore, waves will generally come from a very wide range of directions. Information on wave direction can be obtained from direction sensing wave recorders, wave hindcasting models and wave observations by shipping.

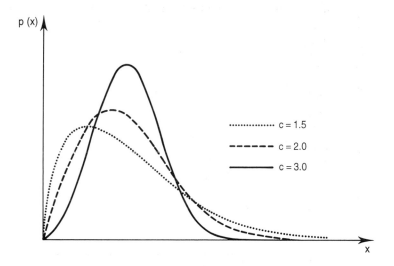

Figure 3.7 *The two-parameter (a–o) Weibull Distribution*

It is convenient to present the distribution of H_s against θ either as a scatter diagram (see Table 3.1) or as a wave rose (see Figure 3.9). The scatter diagram is potentially more useful if subsequent calculations are to be undertaken, whilst the wave rose gives a more immediate visual impression of the distribution.

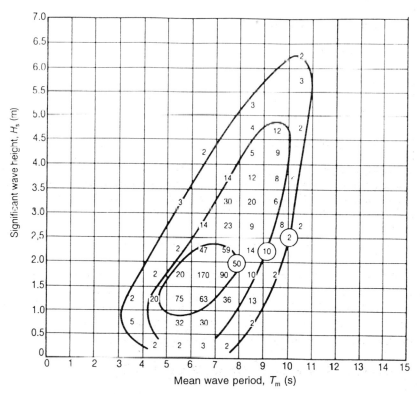

Note: Figure in circles on heavy contour lines indicate percentage of observations falling outside a particular contour line.

Figure 3.8 *Scatter diagram (parts per thousand) indicating joint distribution of H_s and T_m*

Table 3.1 Example of wave height/direction scatter diagram
Data in parts per hundred thousand
Significant wave heights in metres

H1 to H2		P(H>H1)	Wave angles in degrees North											
			-15 15	15 45	45 75	75 105	105 135	135 165	165 195	195 225	225 255	255 285	285 315	315 345
0.00	0.25	0.9397	719	1312	3280	2799	1645	1255	1122	1263	1205	3708	2640	632
0.25	0.50	0.7239	181	338	5621	4317	2291	1581	1322	1258	1960	8039	767	260
0.50	0.75	0.4445	5	15	3561	3440	1489	923	886	952	2173	6340	39	15
0.75	1.00	0.2462	0	4	1009	629	208	174	144	137	1222	5001	2	0
1.00	1.25	0.1609	0	0	305	252	36	11	6	43	734	4678	0	0
1.25	1.50	0.1002	0	0	33	28	9	2	0	2	200	3191	0	0
1.50	1.75	0.0656	0	0	0	4	1	1	0	0	73	2253	0	0
1.75	2.00	0.0422	0	0	0	1	0	0	0	0	35	1344	0	0
2.00	2.25	0.0284	0	0	0	0	0	0	0	0	15	1351	0	0
2.25	2.50	0.0148	0	0	0	0	0	0	0	0	2	447	0	0
2.50	2.75	0.0103	0	0	0	0	0	0	0	0	1	534	0	0
2.75	3.00	0.0049	0	0	0	0	0	0	0	0	1	168	0	0
3.00	3.25	0.0032	0	0	0	0	0	0	0	0	0	208	0	0
3.25	3.50	0.0012	0	0	0	0	0	0	0	0	0	46	0	0
3.50	3.75	0.0007	0	0	0	0	0	0	0	0	0	48	0	0
3.75	4.00	0.0002	0	0	0	0	0	0	0	0	0	5	0	0
4.00	4.25	0.0002	0	0	0	0	0	0	0	0	0	2	0	0
4.25	4.50	0.0001	0	0	0	0	0	0	0	0	0	7	0	0
4.50	4.75	0.0001	0	0	0	0	0	0	0	0	0	0	0	0
4.75	5.00	0.0001	0	0	0	0	0	0	0	0	0	7	0	0
Parts per thousand for each direction			10	18	147	122	60	42	37	39	81	398	37	10

Storm persistence and sequencing

Some beach responses are sudden and occur only in extreme sea conditions. However, most beach processes, such as longshore or cross-shore drift, are more gradual and continue even during quite commonly occurring sea conditions. The impact on the beach builds up over a period of time, and may reverse in direction from time to time. For example, beaches tend to steepen during winter and to flatten during summer. If there were a concentration of one particular wave condition, then that may have a different impact upon beaches than a more evenly distributed long-term wave climate. Hence the interest in storm persistence, profile, sequencing and distribution throughout the year.

The distribution of storms varies from one place to another. Their occurrence may be linked to the hurricane season, the monsoon season, or to the very regular passage of atmospheric depressions. In most cases the best way to assess the impact of storm distribution is to work with long-term hindcast wave data. The distribution and persistence of storms, as well as of wave height, period and direction, will then be explicitly represented without having to be specifically analysed or described. In predicting the temporal development of a beach under the action of such wave data, the natural variability of the sea will automatically be represented.

Storms can be identified conveniently from time series data using a Peaks Over Threshold (POT) approach (see Section 3.3.2). They can be described in terms of their time for development and decay, their persistence time above the threshold, their peak wave height, and their associated period of calm after the preceding storm. Analysis might consist of examining the probability of higher than average peak wave heights or durations occurring in successive storms, or the joint distribution of peak wave heights and calm durations between storms. Storm profiling and sequencing is a topic worthy of further research, but the results will vary from one location to another and it may therefore be difficult to provide generally applicable guidelines. Hedges *et al* (1991) introduced some definitions (reproduced in Figure 3.10) relating to storm persistence, profile and variability, and applied them to wave data hindcast in Liverpool Bay.

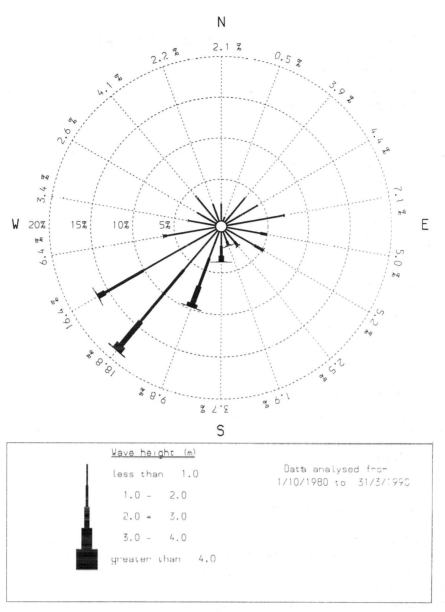

Figure 3.9 *Typical wave rose*

In the absence of long-term hindcast wave data, a reasonable assumption would be that the most severe storms all occur during the winter, at random intervals, and that they each develop and decay over a period of a day or so. The peak wave height during a storm is usually and realistically assumed to persist for a period of about 3 hours. A typical storm profile would then involve a gradual increase in wave height (from some mean winter value) over a period of 16 hours (t_r in Figure 3.10), a constant peak wave height for 3 hours, and then a 16-hour decline (t_d in Figure 3.10) in wave height.

The wave period (T_m) associated with a given storm peak wave height (H_s) is usually determined with reference to a standard wave steepness ($2\pi H_s/gt_m^2$). Where possible, this steepness is derived from the top few per cent of predicted (or measured) wave conditions, but otherwise a typical value of 0.06-0.065 can be used.

Design extreme wave conditions

In practice, prediction of extreme wave conditions (extremal analysis) is based on the processing of significant wave height data only. Any treatment of wave period is usually based on the assumption that wave height and wave period are strongly correlated, perhaps being related by some constant wave steepness. Any treatment of wave direction is usually based on a "conditional analysis", the condition being that the wave records analysed have directions

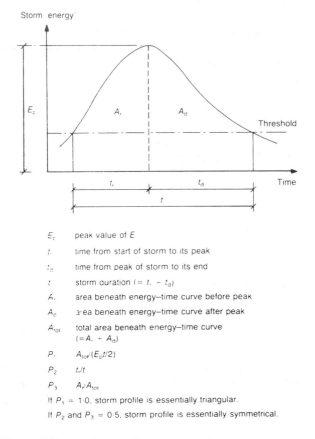

E_r	peak value of E
t_r	time from start of storm to its peak
t_d	time from peak of storm to its end
t	storm duration $(= t_r - t_d)$
A_r	area beneath energy–time curve before peak
A_d	area beneath energy–time curve after peak
A_{tot}	total area beneath energy–time curve $(= A_r + A_d)$
P_1	$A_{tot}/(E_p t/2)$
P_2	t_r/t
P_3	A_r/A_{tot}

If $P_1 = 1.0$, storm profile is essentially triangular.

If P_2 and $P_3 = 0.5$, storm profile is essentially symmetrical.

Figure 3.10   *Storm shape parameters*

within a particular angular sector. In other words, wave data within different direction sectors are considered as being members of different populations which can be analysed separately.

The standard procedure in the analysis of extreme statistics of significant wave height, H_s, is as follows.

1. Select the data for analysis.
2. Fit a distribution to the data.
3. Compute return values from the fitted distribution.
4. Compute confidence intervals.

For extraction of storm wave height data, the Peaks Over Threshold method is recommended. In this method only the storm peak wave heights above some chosen threshold (e.g. $H_s = 3$m) are used in the extremal analysis. It is recommended that the wave height threshold is chosen such that the average number of data values per year (typically 5-10) above the threshold is equal to or less than the average number of storms per year (typically 10-20). For areas where there is a strong seasonal variation of storms, an appropriate threshold can be obtained by the requirement that one storm per year from the calmer season is to be included in the data set.

The method of moments can be used for the estimation of the parameters of the distribution. The method works by equating statistical moments (mean, standard deviation, skewness etc.) of the model distribution to the moments of the observed distribution. The number of statistical moments used is equal to the number of parameters of the model distribution. Several model distributions are described in Appendix 5 of Tucker (1991), together with the relationships between the moments and the parameters of the distributions.

CIRIA Report 153

As mentioned in Section 3.3.2, the Weibull Distribution usually provides a good fit to the data, whether storm peak wave heights have been extracted or the entire distribution of H_s (for each population) is used. However, some alternative candidate distributions are given in Box 3.3.

Box 3.3   *Theoretical extreme value probability distributions*

The following theoretical extreme value probability distributions are commonly used for fitting the long-term distributions of wave height, water levels etc.

Gumbel
$$P(X \leq x) = \exp\left[-\exp(-ax + b)\right]$$

Weibull
$$P(X \leq x) = 1 - \exp\left[-\left(\frac{x - a}{b}\right)^c\right]$$

Log-normal
$$p(x) = 1/(Ax \sqrt{\pi}) \exp\left[-\left(\frac{\ln x - b}{a}\right)^2\right]$$

Exponential
$$P(X \leq x) = 1 - \exp[-(x - a)/b]$$

where $P(X \leq x)$ is the probability distribution function, i.e. the probability that X will not exceed x, $p(x)$ is the probability density function of x and $p(x) = Dp/dx$.

The return value $x(T_R)$ is the threshold value equalled or exceeded on average once during a time interval T_R (the return period). Knowing T_R, $P(x(T_R))$ can be found from Equation (3.7), which in turn allows $x(T_R)$ to be determined from a fitted distribution such as described in Box 3.2.

$$P(x(T_R)) = 1 - T_c/T_R \qquad (3.7)$$

where T_c is the average time between storms.

An alternative way of looking at an event with a given return period is to consider that (for $T_R \geq 5$ years) the probability of its occurrence in any one year is approximately equal to $1/T_R$. For example, a 10000 year return period event is equivalent to one with a probability of occurrence of 10^{-4} in any one year. BS6349 Part 7 (1991) gives a diagram for conversion between return period and probability of occurrence in any given number of years. Table 5.3 contains similar information in tabulated form.

Assuming that the input wave height data are accurate, the uncertainty in the computed return value $x(T_R)$ is believed to depend mainly on:

- inherent statistical variability i.e. sampling variability
- uncertainty due to possible improper choice of extreme value distribution
- uncertainty in the computation of significant wave height due to a record of limited length.

At least one complete year of wave height data is required, but for reliable extremes predictions 5 or 10 years are necessary.

Relationship between different measures of wave period

Many different definitions of wave height and period are described in IAHR (1986). However, whereas wave height is usually defined in terms of a significant wave height (H_s), three or four different measures of wave period remain in common use.

T_m is the *mean* wave period derived from integration of the energy spectrum. This is the mean wave period measure used by most spectral wave models and most modern wave recorders. T_z is the equivalent parameter obtained by counting analysis based on a series of individual zero-upcrossing waves. Its value is almost identical to T_m.

T_p is the spectral *peak* wave period. Its value is usually reported (in addition to T_m) by spectral wave models and modern wave recorders. It is also the wave period approximated in ships observations of wave conditions. The ratio between T_m and T_p varies between about 0.65 and 0.9, from one location to another, from one wave direction to another and from one storm to another. Only for the ideal case of fully-developed waves in the open ocean does it automatically take the theoretical value of 0.78. However, in practice, and in the absence of site-specific data, it would be reasonable to assume $T_m = 0.8 T_p$.

The significant wave period (T_s) is still in occasional use, particularly with predictions derived from older wave forecasting curves. It is defined in a similar way to H_s, as the average period of the highest one-third of the waves. Its value usually falls somewhere between T_m and T_p.

3.3.3 Wave generation by wind

Physical processes

Phillips (1957) showed that the turbulence associated with the flow of wind near the still water surface would create travelling pressure pulses. These pulses generate waves travelling at a speed appropriate to the dimensions of the pressure pulse on an otherwise flat water surface. Wave growth by this process is most rapid when the waves are short and when their speed is identical with the component of the wind velocity in the direction of travel.

Miles (1957) showed that the waves on the sea surface must be matched by "waves" on the bottom surface of the atmosphere. The speed of air and water must be equal at the water surface. Within a shear zone of this type, energy is extracted from the mean flow of the wind and is transferred to the waves. The magnitude of this transfer at any frequency is proportional to the energy already present at that frequency. Growth is normally most rapid at high frequencies and is significantly affected by any pre-existing waves.

Sea development during storms

Like individual waves under the influence of wind, the wave spectrum also evolves with time, gaining energy from the wind and being attenuated by friction, breaking, etc. As well as changes in the overall energy of a spectrum, energy is continuously being redistributed to the lower frequencies. A developing sea tends to have a narrow spectrum (see JONSWAP spectrum in Figure 3.6), whereas a fully-developed sea has a broader spread of energy across different frequencies (see Pierson-Moskowitz spectrum in Figure 3.6)

When a wind continues to blow at the same strength upon a fully-developed sea, there is no further change in the spectrum. However, if the wind speed increases, growth begins again, whilst if the wind speed falls, the energy begins to decay to lower (swell) frequencies.

Wind statistics

Where wave data are not available or for some reason are not adequate for the intended purpose, hindcasting from wind records may be the only way to achieve an estimate of the wave climate. Around most of the UK coast, sequential wind records in digital format are available from about 1970 onwards. It should be noted that on land, records may easily show a 10-20% reduction in wind speeds (due to increased surface roughness) compared to values measured over water.

Wind velocities over water may also be obtained from ships observations or from the archives of weather models. In both these cases, individual records may be unreliable, but the large volume of data makes them a good source of site-specific ocean wind climate data.

Wind climate data can be conveniently expressed as a scatter diagram of wind speed against direction (see Table 3.2) or as a wind rose (see Figure 3.11). Typically wind velocities will be divided into Beaufort speed ranges and 30 degree direction sectors.

The parameters needed for simple conversion of a stationary wind condition into an equivalent wave condition are the wind speed, the wind direction and the wind duration. In practice the wind speed and direction will vary over a typical duration of ten to twenty hours, and average values need to be computed. Any direct information on wind duration (or persistence) which may be available from the original records is lost when the data is summarised in scatter diagram or rose format.

Table 3.2 Example of wind speed/direction scatter diagram

Mean wind speed		Percentage number of hours with winds from												
knots	m.p.h.	350°-010°	020°-040°	050°-070°	080°-100°	110°-130°	140°-160°	170°-190°	200°-220°	230°-250°	260°-280°	290°-310°	320°-340°	All directions Total
						DECEMBER								
Calm														2.5
1-3	1-3													9.7
4-6	4-7	0.4	0.7	1.2	2.6	3.2	1.4	1.6	1.3	0.5	0.4	0.7	0.9	14.9
7-10	8-12	0.2	0.9	1.2	1.6	2.5	2.6	3.1	2.5	2.1	1.1	1.8	0.9	20.5
11-16	13-18	0.1	0.8	1.6	1.5	2.5	2.1	4.3	4.0	5.4	3.7	2.4	0.6	29.0
17-21	19-24	0.1	0.2	0.3	0.6	1.3	0.5	1.1	1.9	2.6	2.5	0.9	0.2	12.2
22-27	25-31	0+	0+	0.2	0.4	0.7	0.2	0.2	1.1	2.0	1.9	0.5	0.2	7.4
28-33	32-38				0.1	0.1			0.1	0.3	0.6	0.1	0+	1.3
34-40	39-46								0+	0+	0.1	0.1	0+	0.2
41-47	47-54										0+			0+
48-55	55-63													
56-63	64-72													
>63	>72													
TOTAL		0.8	2.6	4.5	6.8	10.3	6.8	10.3	10.9	12.9	10.3	6.5	2.8	97.7
										Percentage number of hours missed				2.2
						YEAR								
Calm														6.1
1-3	1-3													17.2
4-6	4-7	0.6	1.2	1.7	2.0	2.3	1.6	1.5	1.4	1.9	2.0	1.7	1.3	19.2
7-10	8-12	0.4	1.3	2.1	1.8	1.9	1.9	2.5	2.5	3.6	2.9	2.8	1.4	25.1
11-16	13-18	0.2	0.7	1.7	1.3	1.2	1.4	2.6	2.6	3.7	2.9	2.5	0.8	21.6
17-21	19-24	0+	0.1	0.4	0.4	0.4	0.3	0.7	0.8	1.1	1.1	0.6	0.1	6.0
22-27	25-31	0+	0+	0.1	0.2	0.1	0.1	0.1	0.3	0.6	0.5	0.2	0.1	2.3
28-33	32-38				0+	0+	0+	0+	0+	0.1	0.1	0+	0+	0.2
34-40	39-46						0+	0+	0+	0+	0+	0+	0+	0+
41-47	47-54									0+	0+			0+
48-55	55-63													
56-63	64-72													
>63	>72													
Total		1.2	3.3	6.0	5.7	5.9	5.3	7.4	7.6	11.0	9.5	7.8	3.7	97.7
										Percentage number of hours missed				2.2

There are three main ways in which wind data can be prepared for use in wave predictions:

1. A standard probability function, for example the Weibull Distribution, can be fitted to the hourly wind speeds (either within one direction sector or overall). The fitted distribution can then be extrapolated to hourly extreme values using methods described in Section 3.3.2. The hourly values can then be converted to equivalent speeds for different durations, as necessary, using the speed conversion factors listed in Table 3.3. This method is appropriate only for "design wave conditions".

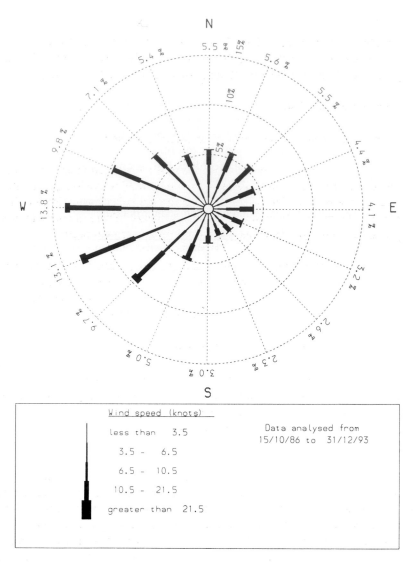

Figure 3.11 *Typical wind rose*

Table 3.3 Wind speed (U_w) conversion factors related to duration of wind speeds

Time base (hours)	Factor (-)
¼	1.05
½	1.03
1	1.00
3	0.96
6	0.93
12	0.87
24	0.80

2. Wind information in scatter diagram or wind rose format can be broken down into percentages of data within certain classes of speed and direction. To be conservative, a very long duration can be assigned to each category of data, so that in effect the later wave predictions will be "fetch-limited". This approach is reasonable for estimating the directional wave climate, but the neglect of wind duration may tend to over-predict wave heights.

3. Sequential (i.e. hour by hour) wind speeds and directions can be used as input to wave hindcasting models (e.g. Hawkes, 1987; Hedges *et al*, 1991). If suitable wind data and the necessary software are available, this approach is the most accurate method of converting wind data into equivalent wave data. Most hindcasting models take account of the actual

variability of the wind records hour by hour, as well as time-averaged values. (More sophisticated hindcasting models can use *wind field* data as input, but this approach is only practical within specialist institutions such as the UK Meteorological Office.)

Wave prediction methods

There are several general types of wave prediction method.

1. Design curves based on an effective fetch, a wind speed (some methods prefer the more theoretically correct *wind stress*) and a wind duration, yielding a significant wave height and a wave period. The wave height is limited either by the fetch (when the duration is long) or by the duration (when the fetch is long). There is also a limiting sea state (for any given wind speed) beyond which no further growth occurs.

2. The simplest directional spectral computer models assume a constant wind velocity over the wave generation area, whose shape and size may be specified or may be idealised. The models calculate a frequency and direction spectrum which may be integrated to yield wave height, period and direction parameters at the position of interest.

3. More complex spectral wave models may:

   - allow the wind velocity to vary across the generation area
   - take a boundary wave condition to represent swell entering the generation area
   - simulate growth and decay of storms
   - incorporate some wave transformation processes
   - provide predictions over a wide area.

Any of these approaches may be used in the time dependent form necessary for accurate wave climate prediction. That is they may be re-run repeatedly for one time step after another as the wind conditions change. The methods may be used in either "forecast" or "hindcast" mode depending on the source of the wind data. The hindcasting may be done over a period of just a few days (the duration of a single storm) up to many years (for wave climate prediction). The manual design curve approach is inconvenient for use over periods of more than a day or so, whilst the necessary wind data for longer periods of hindcasting may not be readily available. Long-term wave climate hindcasting is probably best left to one of a few specialist UK institutions, for example the Meteorological Office which holds an archive of such hindcasts from its operational forecast models.

Empirical wave growth formulae are based upon the relation between the "characteristic" wave and the "standard wind field". This wind field is given through the average wind speed (U_w), the fetch (F, the distance to the coast, measured in the upwind direction) and the duration (t) of the wind field. An optional additional characteristic parameter is the water depth (h), which is usually assumed constant.

A fully-developed sea has, for a given U_w, reached its maximum wave height and period. In a fetch-limited or growing sea at least one of the parameters, F, t or h poses a limiting condition to the actual sea. Using g/U_w^2 and g/U_w as scale factors for H, F and h and for t and T, respectively, the empirical wave growth formulae are usually written in a dimensionless form as $\tilde{H} = F_n\{\tilde{h},\tilde{F},\tilde{t}\}$ and $\tilde{T} = F_n\{\tilde{h},\tilde{F},\tilde{t}\}$. These relations are given in CERC (1973), which also addresses determination of an effective fetch (fetch reduction due to fetch width). For design purposes, diagrams have been prepared to estimate H_s and T_s of the expected wave field, at a given fetch (F) and wind speed (U_w). The diagrams (WMO, 1988) are given in Figure 3.12 (deep water) and Figure 3.13 (shallow water). The reader should note that CERC (1984) contains wave prediction curves based on an intermediate calculation of wind stress, whose reliability for all situations has been questioned, particularly for extreme events.

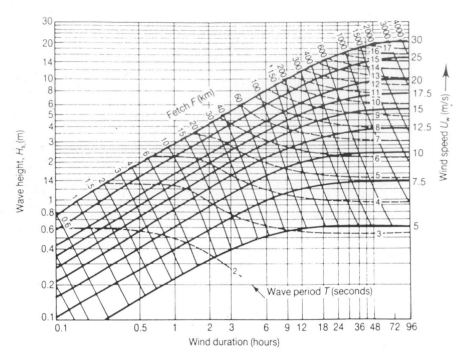

Figure 3.12   *Deep water wave forecasting diagram for a standard wind field*

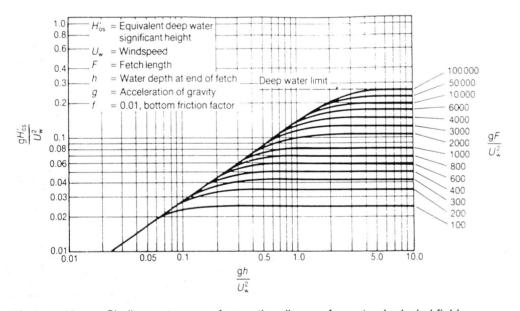

Figure 3.13   *Shallow water wave forecasting diagram for a standard wind field*

Spectral methods also offer means to estimate sea growth. Suitable prediction curves for wave height and period, based on the JONSWAP spectrum are given in Figures 3.14 and 3.15. It should be noted that waves thus obtained must be modified, if appropriate, to take account of possible shallow water effects (see Section 3.4.1).

Wind wave growth may continue landward of the deep water zone, in areas where shallow water wave transformation is also taking place, although at most sites this is not significant. This may be of concern where the shallow coastal waters extend for a long distance offshore.

The problem can be partially overcome by careful selection of a deep water wave prediction point perhaps within the shallow water area.

At a limited number of sites (e.g. within the Solent) waves generated along restricted fetches, where the shape of the body of water influences the wave direction, may be important. Here

CIRIA Report 153

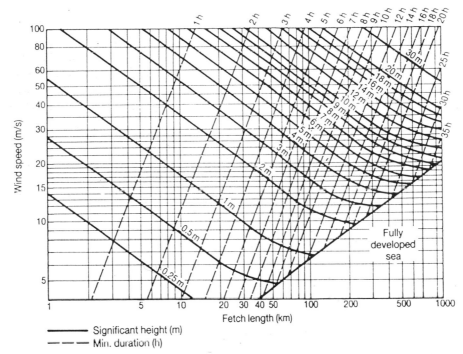

Figure 3.14 *Prediction of significant wave height from wind speed for JONSWAP spectrum*

methods of predicting locally generated waves originally developed for use in inland waters and reservoirs may be of assistance. Methods are presented in a new edition of the ICE Floods, Waves and Reservoir Safety Guide (Department of the Environment (DoE), in press) for calculating a significant wave height, H_s using a simplified Donelan/JONSWAP equation. H_s is calculated as $U_{wf}F^{0.5}/1760$ where U_{wf} is the factored over-water wind speed in m/s and F is the fetch length in m. Further details on the application of the method, including the derivation of the factored design wind speed, U_{wf}, from basic wind speed data, can be found in DoE (in press).

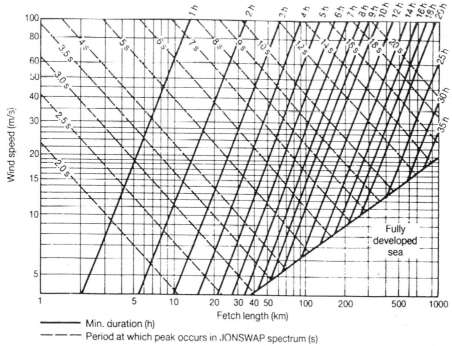

Figure 3.15 *Prediction of peak wave period from wind speed for JONSWAP spectrum*

Swell waves

Around some parts of the UK large swell waves may provide an *alternative* design condition to severe storm waves. They may also introduce a separate background component of wave action causing a different impact on the beach to the wind waves. They are therefore potentially important.

The distinction between wind-sea and swell is often blurred, except perhaps where a wave spectrum has two distinct peaks. It can be difficult to extract swell data from measured wave data in an objective and useful way. It is impossible to predict swell from local wind records, since by definition the two are uncorrelated.

Swell wave activity is routinely logged during ships observations of weather and wave conditions, providing some readily and cheaply available information on swell. However, visual observation of swell is difficult and the observations cannot be considered very reliable.

The most reliable source of swell data in deep water are the global wave models run by some meteorological agencies. These fully spectral models have access to spatially and temporally varying wind field data and their global grids allow wave energy to build up, propagate and decay in a realistic manner. The archives of such models contain data from which information on swell can be extracted. Indeed, the UK Meteorological Office routinely separate and archive the wave predictions into wind-sea and swell. This information is commercially available.

This archived data has recently been used to derive representative extreme swell conditions for the English and Welsh coasts. The resulting report (Hawkes *et al*, 1995) includes tables of deep water swell wave height conditions, for a range of wave periods and return periods for off-the-shelf use in wave transformation models almost anywhere around England and Wales. The report shows the same information in atlas format, which gives an immediate visual impression of the importance of swell at different locations. For example, Figure 3.16 shows the variability of the 1-year return period swell significant wave height around England and Wales.

3.3.4   Sources of wave data

Five main sources of information on wave statistics are available for the UK Continental Shelf. These are derived from wave measurements, visual observations, hindcast data synthesized from numerical wave models, satellite remote sensing and wave climate atlases. In most areas, wave conditions are less well defined than water levels, and it is often necessary to undertake site-specific wave predictions.

Wave measurements

Measured wave data from instruments in the sea are the most direct and accurate means of determining waves but, due to the cost of deploying and monitoring wave recorders, they are only available at a few locations and then only for a few years duration. In general, wave measurements are mainly used to validate numerical wave models which can then be used to hindcast long-term directional wave climate data. The British Oceanographic Data Centre (BODC) at the Proudman Oceanographic Laboratory, Bidston, Merseyside, maintains a global inventory of measured wave data (MIAS, 1982) on behalf of the International Oceanographic Commission. A review and catalogue of instrumental wave recording sites around England and Wales has been given by Brampton and Hawkes (1990). The fact that waves have been recorded and catalogued gives no guarantee that the data will be available for re-use in other projects. There is no data banking system, and data may be irretrievable due to commercial confidentiality or poor archiving.

Where wave recording is to be commissioned, it should be carried out by one of a small number of specialist contractors over at least a six-month winter period. The instrument location should be representative, in terms of wave climate, of the area of interest, and preferably away from fishing and navigation zones. For measurement of extremes and/or wave

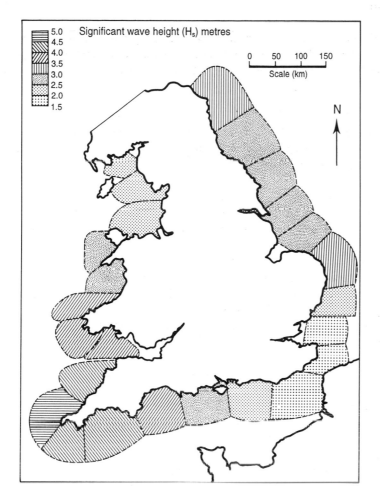

Figure 3.16 *Variability of the 1-year return period swell significant wave height around England and Wales*

climate trends, a long deployment would be necessary. The type of wave gauge (staff, pressure sensor, wave rider, etc.) is dependent on the water depth, the expected size of the waves and the availability of moorings and shore facilities. Analysis of wave data is a fairly specialised task best left to the wave recording contractor.

Visual wave observations

The largest data base of waves consists of visual observations from ships and offshore platforms. Various compilations of these statistics have been produced in the form of atlases. Although individual observations are not as precise as measurements, long-term climate statistics derived from the large data sets of visual observations are believed to provide a useful representation of the climate of a sea area. Swell and wind-sea components are logged separately, each in terms of height, period and direction.

Wave data on the UK Continental Shelf (and elsewhere in the world) are available from staff at the Meteorological Office at Bracknell who can retrieve and summarise visual observations in any specific area and period, to provide a reasonable guide to the local wave climate. This is a rapid and inexpensive source of data, but it cannot provide the site-specific detail which may be necessary for coastal work.

Synthetic wave data

An increasing and useful source of information is now available from numerical wave models operated routinely by national meteorological agencies. This source of wave data, whose accuracy is limited by the physical processes in the wave model and specification of the wind field, offers the best possibility of providing detailed wave information on a regular spatial grid.

The current (1995) UK Meteorological Office European wave model operating over the North Sea has remained essentially unchanged since July 1986. It is a second-generation depth-dependent model operating on a grid 0.25 degree latitude x 0.4 degree longitude. The hindcasting wind and wave fields have been archived from all versions of the model in use since 1977. This data is commercially available.

Around most of the UK there are about 20 years of wind data available for use in simplified wave hindcasting models, based on local wind data. A disadvantage of such models is that they neglect wave energy arriving from outside the immediate area of interest (i.e. swell). However an advantage is that they can be calibrated and validated against local wave measurements. The 20 years of sequential data can be used to examine wave climate, extreme waves, littoral drift rates, structural responses and any natural variability or trend in the above. Several consultants offer this type of bespoke wave modelling service.

A catalogue of synthetic wave data, covering existing wave predictions around England and Wales, is available (Ramsay and Harford, 1995).

The UK Meteorological Office European wave model also provides deep water forecast data up to 36 hours ahead, which may be useful in planning site activities. MAFF and NRA funded a study to assess the use of this type of data, in conjunction with local wave transformation modelling, for operational use at the coast.

Remote sensed data

Remote sensed wave data from earth satellites can also give useful information over the oceans. Estimates of 50-year return values of significant wave height around the British Isles have been made by Carter (1993) using the radar altimeter in GEOSAT.

Most wave data so far analysed and presented have been from the GEOSAT mission from 1985 to 1989. In the future, the satellite ERS-1 (launched in 1991) and other missions are likely to add to our knowledge of the spatial variation of wave heights over the ocean. At present, this source of information is of limited use in coastal studies, but it will become of increasing importance in wave climate studies.

Wave climate atlases

In a major collation of global wave data, Hogben and Lumb (1967) compared visual observations with data from Ocean Weather Ships equipped with wave recorders. In an extension of this work, known as *Global Wave Statistics*, Hogben *et al* (1986) developed parametric relationships between wind speeds, wave heights and periods, in order to maximise the information provided by the larger numbers of wind speeds available from most oceans. However, by its very nature the method produces results which are representative of rather large areas, and so this work probably represents the limit to which parametric methods can be taken for the definition of wave climate from visual observations.

Two publications by the Department of Energy (1984 and 1990) respectively provide contours of extreme individual wave height and extreme significant wave height around the UK. A third Department of Energy publication (1991) is a wave climate atlas for the UK. It contains information on the distribution of wave height and period for each season and overall in the form of contours.

These atlases do not contain enough detailed site-specific information for coastal design purposes. However, they do provide good data on the general variability of wave conditions in deep water around the UK. They may be adequate for feasibility calculations. The information on variability could be used to convert detailed wave climate information, which may be available for some nearby location, to equivalent data at the site of interest.

3.3.5 Deep water wave breaking and diffraction

Besides wave generation by wind, very few processes need to be taken into account when waves are in deep water. Only three principal factors may need to be considered:

1. Deep water breaking occurs when a certain limiting wave steepness is exceeded. Steepnesses using significant wave height and peak wave period rarely exceed one-twentieth. This factor is, of course, implicit in the empirical wave growth formulae.

2. Wave reflection and diffraction by islands, rocks, etc. (see Section 3.4.1).

3. Energy transfer between frequencies (see Section 3.3.3).

3.4 SHALLOW WATER WAVE CONDITIONS

Much of the previous Section 3.3 on deep water wave conditions applies equally well to shallow water conditions. The following are perhaps the most significant differences between deep water and shallow water wave conditions:

1. In deep water, the most important processes in the development of the wave field are usually energy growth from the wind, deep water wave propagation, and eventual decay of wave energy. Conversely, in shallow water, the main processes in the transformation of waves are shoaling, depth-refraction, current refraction, friction, breaking, diffraction and reflection.

2. In deep water, there are several sources of wave data (see Section 3.3.4). Except where data is available on an opportunistic basis from previous studies, none of these sources is likely to provide direct information on shallow water wave climate at any particular site.

3. The nearshore wave climate will usually come from transformation of the deep water climate or from bespoke nearshore wave hindcasting or measurements.

4. In the open ocean waves may come from any direction. As the waves approach the shore, refraction turns their direction of propagation towards the shore normal. The range of wave directions in shallow water will therefore be much smaller and some offshore wave directions may be unimportant in terms of their contribution to the nearshore wave climate. Wave heights tend to be reduced during propagation towards the coast, and some waves may be depth-limited by breaking. However, wave periods are often almost unchanged from deep water to the coast.

5. In deep water, extreme conditions are derived from wave climate data. In shallow water, extremes may come from transforming offshore extremes or from extrapolation of nearshore climate (if available).

6. With the emphasis on beaches, it is important to be able to predict the inshore wave directions accurately. At many sites around the UK, the necessary accuracy can only be achieved using 3D bathymetry and fully spectral wave models.

3.4.1 Wave transformation processes

The processes described for deep water do not cease to occur in shallow water, but they become much less important than the additional wave transformation processes occurring in shallow water. In the very shallow water of the surf zone, all the transformation processes become non-linear. However, for practical purposes, linear models are adequate for several of the processes, namely:

- refraction
- shoaling
- diffraction
- reflection
- interaction with currents.

The following, conversely, are usually classed as non-linear surf zone processes:

- wave breaking
- seabed friction
- development of long waves.

With the exception of seabed friction and long waves, the topics in this section are described at length in CIRIA/CUR (1991) and CERC (1984), which include simple calculation methods. Only the most commonly used methods and the most relevant details will be repeated here.

Calculations are usually carried out using site-specific computer models of wave transformation, preferably working with a fully spectral representation of the deep water (boundary) wave conditions. Different numerical models simulate different combinations of shallow water processes, and the choice of model may vary from one site to another. Advice on the subject of model selection is given in Hawkes and Jelliman (1993) and in HR Wallingford (1994).

Refraction

Refraction is the change in the direction of wave propagation. This generally arises due to the changes in wave propagation velocity when waves propagate in varying water depth. In this situation, the direction of wave incidence (β) relative to the beach inclines towards the direction normal to the local depth contours. This usually implies that the wave crests tend to become more parallel to the coastline when approaching shallower water (see Figure 3.17). The corresponding change in wave height (relative to the deep water wave height, H_o), caused by redistribution of energy along the wave crests, is usually expressed in the refraction coefficient, K_R.

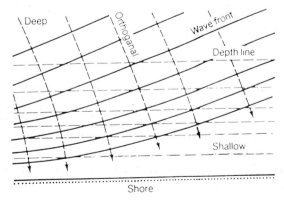

Figure 3.17   *Depth refraction on a foreshore*

Applying linear wave theory to a regular wave with wave number k ($= 2\pi/L$) and direction β_0 in deep water, the local wave direction β at a water depth h is found from:

$$\beta = \arcsin \{\sin(\beta_0) \tanh(kh)\} \tag{3.8}$$

and the corresponding refraction coefficient, K_R, in the case of straight parallel bed contours, from:

$$K_R = \sqrt{\{\cos(\beta_0)/\cos(\beta)\}} \tag{3.9}$$

For irregular seas, a representative effective K_{Reff} value can be obtained from curves given in CIRIA/CUR (1991) reproduced from Goda (1985).

Refraction can also occur without water depth changes due to changes in wave propagation velocity arising from the presence of a varying current field (see Section 3.4.1).

In practice, manual refraction calculations are rarely undertaken, but rather they are either carried out using numerical wave models or they are built in to the coastal response calculations.

Shoaling

Shoaling is a change in wave height due to waves propagating into different water depths and this is a separate effect to changes in wave height which may be a consequence of changes in wave direction arising from refraction. The effect is normally expressed in terms of the shoaling coefficient, K_s, which is defined as the local wave height relative to the deep water wave height H_0. Using linear wave theory, K_s, can, for a given wave period, be written as a function of water depth:

$$K_s = \frac{1}{\{[1 - (2kh/\sinh(2kh)] \tanh(kh)\}^{0.5}} \tag{3.10}$$

In practice, manual shoaling calculations are rarely undertaken, but rather they are either carried out using numerical wave models or they are built in to the coastal response calculations. Refraction and shoaling are often considered together in numerical models as both involve linear responses to changes in water depth.

CIRIA/CUR (1991) includes curves for calculation of shoaling coefficients on plane and composite slopes of different steepness.

Diffraction

Propagating waves, impinging on obstacles such as piles, breakwaters, headlands and islands, interact with these structures. The resulting wave field around the structures generally shows a marked change relative to the undisturbed wave field. The resulting change of wave height, relative to the original undisturbed wave, is expressed by the diffraction coefficient (K_d). There is also a change in wave direction in the lee of the structure (see Figure 3.18). A diffraction analysis is often performed by using numerical models, as alternatives are only available for very simple geometries.

Design curves for calculation of K_d are given in CIRIA/CUR (1991), reproduced from Goda (1985). These diagrams give the ratio between diffracted and undiffracted random waves, for a single breakwater and a breakwater gap, as a function of position, wave length, wave direction and directional spread.

Figure 3.18   *Wave diffraction around terminal groyne (courtesy HR Wallingford)*

Reflection

For structural design, wave reflection generally occurs when waves are propagating onto breakwaters, seawalls and beaches. Where reflection occurs, orbital (bed) velocities can be calculated based on the combined effect of incoming and reflected waves. Reflected waves can be added to the incoming waves using the principle of superposition, so long as linear wave theory is being used.

Reflection coefficients, usually specified in terms of the ratio between reflected and incident wave heights, depend on the slope and surface of the reflecting structure.

One situation where reflection is important is in the case of a submerged beach fronting a vertical sea wall. Damage to the beach can be significantly increased by strong reflections from the wall. However, reflections are not usually considered explicitly since most design methods are given in terms of the *incident* wave conditions. The predicted structural responses will already incorporate an allowance for a typical degree of reflection. Incident wave conditions may, however, sometimes include a component of waves reflected from submerged channels and other seabed and coastal features remote from the beach being considered.

Wave-current interaction

When waves propagate through an area with spatially varying currents, they can be affected in height, length and direction. Generally an increasing following current will "stretch" the waves, reducing their height and increasing their length, and vice versa for an increasing opposing current. If there is a change in the component of current speed normal to the direction of wave propagation, then refraction will occur, causing a change in wave direction. The magnitude of these effects depends on the wave direction, wave length and the spatial changes in current velocity. The shape of the wave spectrum, both as a function of frequency and of direction, may be changed by interaction with currents. Further details are given in Hedges (1987).

Apart from the simple case of waves and currents moving along a single axis (e.g. Department of Energy, 1977), wave-current effects are too difficult to assess manually. However, as the effects are linear, they may be incorporated into refraction models, many of which have the option to include current-refraction effects.

Although current fields vary spatially and temporally at most sites, their effects on waves tend to balance out over a tidal cycle. In practice it is only necessary to model such effects where currents are unusually strong, for example in channels or near to estuary mouths.

Wave breaking

The general topic of non-linear surf zone processes is reviewed by Dodd, Bowers and Brampton (1995). The processes involved are non-linear in that they depend on wave height and in that there may be some movement of wave energy between frequencies. Descriptions of wave breaking, wave attenuation due to friction and the development of long waves are given in the remainder of this section.

Wave breaking (see Figure 3.19) occurs mainly due to two criteria, related to depth or steepness, each limiting the maximum wave height. While depth-induced breaking is usually the determining factor in shallow water, the limit of steepness should still be considered.

Figure 3.19   *Wave breaking on a beach (courtesy HR Wallimgford)*

The breaking criterion due to water depth is normally given by a useful non-dimensional parameter called the breaker index (γ_{br}), defined as the maximum wave height-to-depth ratio (H/h):

$$H \text{ limited by depth:}\quad H/h \leq [H/h]_{max} = \gamma_{br} \tag{3.11}$$

γ_{br} has a theoretical value of 0.78 for regular waves. However, it should be noted that γ_{br} is not constant, but ranges roughly between 0.5 and 1.5 depending on beach slope, beach roughness and wave period, while for irregular waves (represented by H_s) typical values are found to be $\gamma_{br} = 0.5\text{-}0.6$. Higher values tend to occur with higher beach slopes and with longer wave periods.

Most surf zone wave and beach numerical models incorporate at least a simple check on wave breaking, for example where waves are depth-limited by wave breaking before arrival at the toe of a beach. The check may merely involve reduction of the significant wave height after breaking to 55% of the water depth. Some models use a slightly more sophisticated method in which attenuation due to breaking is applied more gradually and realistically. The manual equivalent is either to use the 55% criterion on fairly flat beaches or to use design curves in

CIRIA/CUR (1991). These diagrams give γ_{br} for random waves as a function of wave period and bed slope.

Seabed friction

Wave energy is lost in shallow water in the shearing boundary layer close to the bed, where the cyclic wave-induced currents attempt to move the sediment on the bed. The rate of energy loss depends mainly on wave height, wave length, water depth and bed roughness. Calculations of friction effects are uncertain, being very sensitive to assumptions about the state of the seabed and to the method used.

In the quite unusual situation of a uniformly shallow wave generation area, wave prediction formulae and design curves, similar to those used for deep water wave prediction, are available for use in limited water depths. The *Shore Protection Manual* (CERC, 1984) contains modifications due to Bretschneider and Reid (1953) of the SMB wave forecasting formulae and design curves (reproduced as Figure 3.13) for use in shallow water. The more recent TMA spectrum is a modification of the JONSWAP spectrum for use in limited water depths.

In the more usual situation of deep water waves suddenly entering shallow water and encountering frictional attenuation at some distance from the coast, a depth-limited wave prediction formula may be used to provide a guide to the wave height at a point near the shore. However, this approach tends to under-estimate wave heights if the depth used is that at the prediction point.

Figures 3.12 and 3.13 provide deep and shallow water wave height forecasting curves based on the widely used SMB wave prediction method and Bretschneider modification for friction (CERC, 1973) assuming a typical "friction factor" of 0.01. Both diagrams require a wind speed and a fetch or duration as input, and both give about the same significant wave height for a high water depth (h in Figure 3.13). Calculation of frictional attenuation is very uncertain, but a reasonable estimate can be made by applying Figure 3.13 more than once. For example, predictions could be extracted for i) deep water (h=100m, say), ii) a typical water depth over the wave generation area, and iii) the limited water depth at the prediction point. A sensibly weighted average of the three predictions could then be taken as an estimate of the most likely significant wave height remaining after frictional reductions. The brief descriptions of wave breaking and seabed friction effects provide methods for calculation of wave height. However, the reduction in wave energy may not be uniform across the spectrum. The depth-limiting or saturation spectrum may also be important in determining the spectral form in the surf zone, if that is required. Tucker (1994) gives theoretical methods, supported by field wave data, for the spectral form just within the surf zone.

Long waves

Even in a stationary sea state, individual wave heights vary, and it is common for groups of large waves to occur, especially where some swell wave activity is present. Beneath these wave groups, the mean sea level is lowered (set-down). Between the groups, where the wave activity is less intense, the mean sea level is rather higher (set-up). These alternating areas of set-up and set-down produce a long period wave motion, of period typically 30 seconds to several minutes. These oscillations give rise to "bound long waves" (i.e. "bound" to the wave groups in the wind-sea); these long waves typically have a modest height, of perhaps 10-30cm around the UK coast. The long waves propagate with the wave groups, and become more important as they reach the shoreline. Whilst the "primary waves", i.e. the wind-sea and swell, are largely destroyed by breaking and frictional effects, the long waves are not, and are therefore "liberated" when the primary waves break. Much of the long wave energy is reflected, leading to a partial standing wave pattern, known as "surf beat". Collectively, these bound and free long waves are also referred to as "infra-gravity waves". If the waves approach a beach obliquely, the long waves can cause modifications to the longshore currents, and also form "edge waves", which travel along the beach, and are often trapped within the nearshore zone. Many research workers feel these edge waves are responsible for the formation of beach cusps which often occur on swell-dominated beaches of low tidal range (see Figure 2.9).

Long waves also produce variations in both the set-up and the run-up in the surf zone caused by the primary waves. The long period oscillations in these effects can cause both greater damage to, and overtopping of coastal structures. In addition, the relative phasing of the long waves and the primary wave groups can have a significant effect on the suspension and transport of beach sediments. This effect has attracted considerable interest in recent years. In a recent paper (Hardisty, 1994), for example, it was advocated that in storm wave conditions, such long wave motions dominate the movements of sediment perpendicular to the shoreline, moving it either onshore or offshore depending on the relative phasing between the water movements and the suspension of sediment they produce. Some researchers also consider that surf beat is one of the most important parameters in the dynamics (or stability) of breaker bars on a beach profile. Whilst the potential importance of long waves is therefore clear, the same author points out that adequate mathematical models for either the hydrodynamics or sediment processes under such waves still have to be developed.

3.4.2   Wave statistics in shallow water

Much of what was written in Section 3.3.2 for wave statistics in deep water remains valid and will not be repeated here. Only the differences from deep water will be emphasised.

It is important that shallow water wave data for use in beach modelling should include accurate information on wave direction, and that it should provide wave climate data, as well as extremes. As stated for deep water, the distribution of individual waves within a stationary sea state is not important for use in beach calculations.

Since it may be impractical to run a large number of tests in any beach modelling, the concept of a morphologically averaged wave condition is introduced. This is a single wave condition, which when run for a specified period of time gives the same volume of littoral drift as the net drift expected over a longer period (one season or one year, for example), during which time a range of wave heights and directions would occur.

Long-term distribution of wave height

There is less theoretical argument in favour of the Weibull Distribution (see Section 3.3.2) than in deep water. This is because the highest sea states will be more influenced by shallow water effects than the smaller ones, and in an extreme case where waves are limited by breaking, there may be a clearly defined upper limit to wave height.

In practice, the Weibull Distribution continues to work adequately in fairly shallow water not subject to wave breaking, and it is recommended that any attempt to use model probability distributions be limited to this situation. If it is necessary to use model distributions closer to the shore, then the Weibull distribution can still be used. However, after fitting and extrapolation, those waves which would have broken should have their heights reduced to some limiting value.

Long-term distribution of wave height and period

The description given in Section 3.3.2 applies equally well in shallow water, except that the upper tail of the wave height distribution may be limited by breaking. For practical purposes the same type of joint distribution can be used in shallow water (well seaward of the surf zone), as would be used in deep water.

Long-term distribution of wave height and direction

The description given in Section 3.3.2 applies equally well in shallow water, except that the upper tail of the wave height distribution may be limited by breaking, and the wave directions may be limited to a small range close to the shore normal.

Spectral description of waves

The description given in Section 3.3.1 applies equally well in shallow water, except that the shape of the frequency spectrum may be slightly changed and the directional band width may be much reduced by shallow water effects. For practical purposes the same type of frequency spectrum can be used in shallow water (well seaward of the surf zone), as would be used in deep water. However, it will usually be necessary to modify the directional spectrum (if any) to allow for the sheltering effects of the land and for refraction effects.

Design extreme wave conditions

In most situations where there is information on the shallow water wave climate, the methods described in Section 3.3.2 for derivation of deep water extremes can still be applied. However, the nearer the wave prediction point is to the surf zone, the less the Weibull Distribution is likely to provide a good fit to the data. If the fit is poor, another model distribution (see Box 3.2) could be tried, but it is unlikely that this would provide a significantly better fit. For this reason, it is wise to restrict extremal wave analysis to positions well outside the surf zone.

In water depths where waves are close to breaking, the extreme wave height may be depth-limited. In this situation it is better to determine the *water depth* as accurately as possible and then to calculate the extreme wave-height based on a breaking criterion (see Section 3.4.1). Where the wave height is severely depth-limited, the design inshore wave height may occur much more often than the design offshore wave height. For example, all offshore waves, with return periods in excess of, say, 1 year may result in the same inshore wave height. However, the same would not necessarily be true of the wave period which is less strongly limited by the water depth.

A more common approach to prediction of extreme wave conditions in shallow water is to transform the deep water extreme conditions from offshore to inshore, using a suitable numerical model. The advantages of this approach are that it is usually easier to calculate extremes in deep water and that there is no need to determine the shallow water wave climate. A potential disadvantage is that the "event" which causes a deep water extreme with a given return period will not necessarily cause an inshore extreme with the same return period. An example of this is where an inshore site is protected by a headland from the full force of the largest deep water waves.

Morphologically averaged wave conditions

For design calculations only a very small number of wave conditions (often only one) have to be analysed. In beach modelling, the sediment may be in motion a high proportion of the time in a wide range of wave conditions. Even if the wave climate could be discretised into a small number of bands of wave height and direction, there would still be quite a large number of conditions to be analysed. It may be impractical to run a large number of tests in some forms of beach modelling, for example when using a physical model. It may therefore be convenient in some situations to be able to represent the wave climate by a much smaller number of wave conditions (perhaps only one).

The concept of a morphologically averaged wave condition is introduced. This is a single wave condition which, when run for a specified period of time, gives the same volume of littoral drift as the net drift expected over a longer period (one season or one year, for example) during which time a range of wave heights and directions would occur.

The annual net littoral drift rate can be estimated by applying a simple formula (see Sections 2.4.2 and 7.2.2) in turn to each element of a wave climate, taking account of the frequency of occurrence of that element. The overall result would be expressed in terms of an average net volume of drift in one direction or another. A morphologically averaged wave condition, when applied for a specified period of time, causes the same volume of drift. Three main parameters are needed to specify this wave condition, namely wave height, wave direction and duration of application. As there are three parameters, there are an infinite number of possible morphologically averaged wave conditions. In practice, the duration and one of the other two parameters are chosen, perhaps based on the operational constraints of a physical model, and the third is then determined. Most institutions working in wave and beach modelling have simple software packages to carry out these calculations, but they can be applied manually.

The morphologically averaged wave condition might then be used in tests intended to be representative of average beach behaviour over a whole year. This approach should be used with some caution. The total drift (left and right) may be very much larger than the amount of material moving in the morphologically averaged wave condition and one of the two components (left or right) would not be directly represented at all. In addition the condition is most appropriate to open beaches or to beaches controlled by simple sloping groynes. Substantial structures such as detached breakwaters may only allow longshore transport to occur under storm conditions, so a single wave condition which represents the full range of conditions may not simulate the transport regime correctly.

3.4.3 Summary of wave data sources and uses

Figure 3.20 summarises the sources of deep water wave data, their transformation to the coast and their use in beach calculations. The data gathering, wave and beach modelling, and interpretation of results, is usually done on a site-specific basis and requires some experience. Readers without the necessary experience should seek specialist advice or perhaps sub-contract the work to a consultant offering this service.

3.5 JOINT PROBABILITY OF WAVES AND WATER LEVELS

Derivation of "climates", i.e. the long term distributions of winds, waves, currents etc, is considered in earlier sections. The joint occurrence of, say, wave heights and periods or wave heights and directions, is automatically included in the resulting predictions. A method for determining the joint occurrence of current and wave climates is given in Section 3.5.8. Apart from this, Section 3.5 concentrates on more extreme (or design) events outside the range of occurrences covered by the climate data and the earlier sections of this chapter.

3.5.1 Introduction

Overtopping and damage to coastal structures are usually associated with times of both large waves *and* high water levels. It is therefore important to consider both parameters in the design and assessment of coastal defences. The relative importance of large waves and water levels in a particular situation depends on the particular coastal response being considered. For example, groyne stability is largely dictated by wave height, whilst overtopping is more sensitive to water level and wave period, and beach response is a function of both water level and wave condition.

The volume of data available around the UK, means that extreme water levels can be calculated quite reliably. The intermittent nature of wave recording and the variability of wave conditions in coastal waters, mean that prediction of extreme wave conditions is slightly more difficult and uncertain. However, one equally important aspect, which is sometimes not explicitly addressed in design, is the correlation between high waves and high water levels: in other words how likely is it that the two will occur simultaneously.

There are two main reasons why the occurrences of large waves and of high water levels may be correlated. The first and more general reason is meteorological: certain weather conditions, for example westerly storms in the English Channel, will tend to produce both high waves and high surges. However, since the astronomical component of water level is usually much larger than the surge component, any such correlation may be modest. The second and more localised reason is due to the behaviour of waves in the nearshore zone: shallow water wave transformations, particularly in very shallow water, are dependent upon water depth. If the wave prediction point is very close inshore or protected by sand banks, then wave conditions may be depth-limited, in which case there would be a strong correlation between large waves and high water levels.

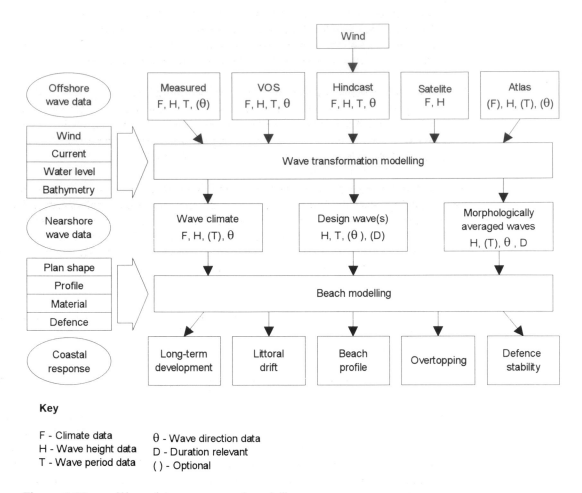

Figure 3.20   *Wave data sources and modelling*

Correlation varies from site to site and from one storm direction to another. As with wave predictions it is usually necessary to assess joint probability on a site-specific basis.

The concept of a return period when dealing with joint probabilities is less straightforward than when dealing with a single variable. A joint probability extreme can be defined in terms of the probability that a specific wave height will be exceeded at the same time as a specific water level will be exceeded. For any particular return period, there will be a range of combinations of wave heights and water levels, each of which is expected to be equalled or exceeded once, on average, in each return period. For example, one could consider a very severe wave condition with a modest water level, or a very severe water level with a modest wave condition - both will occur and both may have the same combined return period. This definition is helpful in interpreting and assessing correlation, and in expressing results in terms of two primary variables. Only one combination will be a "worst case" in terms of run-up, overtopping or damage, but it may be necessary to test several combinations in order to find that worst case. Other definitions of return period may be more useful and appropriate where it is possible to work directly in terms of the probability of the coastal response variable. These are based either on integration of the joint probability densities (for example for risk analysis) or on direct extrapolation of the response variable itself.

Joint probability extremes can be calculated and presented either offshore or inshore. Offshore results are applicable over a larger area, but may need to be transformed inshore before further use. Inshore results are more site-specific, but may be applicable only in one small area. Wave predictions and joint probabilities are often calculated as a function of direction. This is important, since general exposure to waves, correlation between large waves and high water levels, and transformation inshore, may all be dependent upon storm direction.

A joint probability assessment requires, at least, a good knowledge of the distribution and extremes of waves (alone) and water levels (alone). A competent person, armed with this knowledge, could make an intuitive assessment of the correlation between high waves and high water levels and a good estimate of the joint probability extremes.

A full and objective joint probability assessment requires more good quality data and techniques, and at present requires the specialist knowledge and software available from only a small number of consultants. At least several years of simultaneous water level and (usually hindcast) wave data are required in order to make a detailed assessment of correlation and of its possible dependence upon storm direction and severity.

Hawkes and Hague (1994) describe several theoretical and practical approaches to joint probability analysis. They also include a comparison of the results derived from different methods and limited validation against field data on the occurrence of damage at sea defences. POL (1995) extending the work of Coles and Tawn (1990) have refined the prediction of the joint probability of tides and surges, and hence that of extreme water levels around the UK, considering not only the correlation between tides and surges at individual A Class tide gauges, but also the spatial correlation between nearby gauges.

Further MAFF-funded research is now under way to develop a robust method for extrapolation of joint probability *densities*, and to validate and provide an inter-comparison of new and existing methods against both synthetic and field data.

3.5.2   The independent and dependent cases

The joint probability of two variables (X and Y) is given by the likelihood ($0 \leq P(X \geq x$ and $Y \geq y) \leq 1$) of variable X being not less than a given value x, at the same time as variable Y being not less than a given value y. X and Y may refer to still water level (SWL) and significant wave height at each successive high water. Two trivial cases of joint probability are complete dependence and complete independence. Two variables, SWL and H_s, are completely dependent if a given water level always occurs at the same time as a given wave height, H_s, when the return periods of each of the two variables would be equal, i.e.:

$$P(\text{SWL} \geq x \text{ and } H_s \geq y) = P(\text{SWL} \geq x) = P(H_s \geq y) \tag{3.12}$$

On the other hand if they are completely independent then there is no correlation between them and the joint probability is simply the product of the two marginal probabilities, i.e.:

$$P(\text{SWL} \geq x \text{ and } H_s \geq y) = P(\text{SWL} > x) \cdot P(H_s \geq y) \tag{3.13}$$

In the case of waves and water levels, the assumption of complete dependence would lead to a very conservative design since the 100-year event would have to comprise a 100 year wave condition coupled with a 100-year water level. Conversely, the assumption of independence would lead to under-design in some cases, since any increase in the probability of high wave heights at times of very high water levels would have been ignored. The correlation between waves and water levels will usually lie between the two extremes of complete dependence and complete independence. The two will be partially dependent, to an extent best determined from analysis of actual data.

Often, only conditions at high water are of interest, and at most locations peak surge levels persist for less than half a day. Therefore, conditions at each successive high water (706 per year) can conveniently be taken as independent and assumed to persist over the duration of high water, accompanied by wave conditions which (subject to depth limitations) will persist over the tidal cycle. Therefore, for arithmetic purposes in combining probabilities, a 1-year return period event, for example, has a probability of occurrence of 1/706. As the independent and dependent cases are simple to calculate, it may be worth deriving them early in any project. Treating these as the most optimistic and most pessimistic scenaria respectively, may help in judging the value of any more detailed joint probability analysis. The same reasoning can be applied to events with slightly longer durations (e.g. 6 or 12 hours) provided that an allowance is made for the varying water level during a tidal cycle.

3.5.3 Intuitive methods of analysis

The simplest method for assessing correlation is an intuitive one based on general experience and the shape and size of the sea area around the prediction point. The assessment may conclude that there is a modest correlation and, for example, that high waves and high water levels with a 100-year joint return period are 10 to 100 times *more* likely to occur together than the assumption of *independence* (see Section 3.5.2) would suggest. It may conclude that there is a strong correlation and, for example, that high waves and high water levels with a 100-year joint return period are only 10 to 100 times *less* likely to occur than the assumption of *dependence* (see Section 3.5.2) would suggest. (The probability ratio between the independent and dependent cases is 706 × 100.)

As an example, combinations of wave heights and water levels (each specified in terms of its marginal return period) with a joint probability return period of 100 years are given in Table 3.4. It is intended that *all* combinations of waves and water levels with a given degree of correlation will be tested for *each* design consideration in turn, in order to find the worst case for each one. The table compares the combinations that would be appropriate for different assumed degrees of correlation between wave heights and water levels. A "correlation factor" is introduced here: it is the ratio of the actual joint probability to the value that would be associated with independent variables.

The suggested minimum correlation factor is 2, since any less would be rather risky without more detailed calculations. This would be appropriate where waves and water levels were expected to be independent. Correlation factor 20 represents a modest level of dependency, appropriate if some correlation is expected even if there is no particular evidence for it. Correlation factor 100 represents well-correlated conditions such as one might expect where strong winds moving along a narrowing sea area would produce both high surges and high waves. Example areas of such correlation might be the eastern English Channel and Severn Estuary during westerly storms, and the southern North Sea during northerly storms. The strong correlation factor 500 represents a dependence level that would be unusual around the UK. It might be appropriate in an area where a strong correlation between surges and wave heights would be expected, and where the astronomical tide is low.

This simplified approach is not intended as an adequate substitute for a rigorous joint probability study. However, it does provide a guide to the relative importance of wave height and water level in determining the joint return period. It is offered for use in studies where the alternative would be to take no specific account of joint probability.

3.5.4 Analytical methods of analysis

The best method, if constraints on time, budget and data permit, is to examine several years of simultaneous wave and water level data in order to assess correlation and to derive joint probability extremes. This allows the correlation analysis to be performed in a similar objective scientific manner to that which would be applied to the wave and water level predictions. The correlation is determined by scatter diagram analysis of pairs of values of wave height and water level at each high water over a period of several years.

Lines joining areas of the scatter diagram with an equal density of observations can then be thought of as probability contours. Any skewness in the contours would be indicative of correlation (dependence) between the two variables.

As examples, Figures 3.21 and 3.22 are scatter diagrams of surge against significant wave height, for high waters during periods of over ten years. Figure 3.21, for a point just off Hythe in Kent, demonstrates *negative* correlation between high waves and high surges. In this situation the largest wave heights would tend to coincide with negative surges. Conversely, Figure 3.22, for a location at the outer edge of Christchurch Bay in Hampshire (although water

Table 3.4 Combinations of conditions with a 100-year joint probability return period for different assumed correlation factors

Water level return period (years)	Wave condition return period (years) for a correlation factor given below			
	2	20	100	500
0.02	14	100	---	---
0.05	6	57	---	---
0.1	2.8	28	100	---
0.2	1.4	14	71	---
0.5	0.6	6	28	100
1	0.28	2.8	14	71
2	0.14	1.4	7	35
5	0.06	0.6	2.8	14
10	0.03	0.28	1.4	7
20	---	0.14	0.7	4
50	---	0.06	0.28	1.4

Note: It is assumed that there are 70 600 high tides in 100 years. The extremes are expressed in terms of their marginal return periods. The four alternative example levels of dependency are "none", "modestly correlated", "well correlated" and "strongly correlated" (see Section 3.5.3).

levels are calculated for a position close to the entrance to Christchurch Harbour), demonstrates *positive* correlation between high waves and high surges. In this situation the largest wave heights would tend to coincide with positive surges.

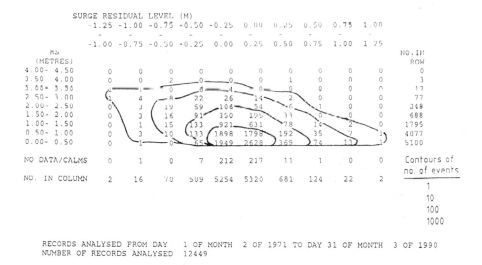

Figure 3.21 *Example probability contours demonstrating negative correlation between surge and significant wave height (off Hythe, Kent)*

The return period approach to wave heights and water levels

The return period of any particular combination of wave height and water level can be estimated, from first principles, directly from scatter diagram data. The number of occurrences of data exceeding a given wave height threshold at the same time as exceeding a given water level threshold can simply be counted and compared with the total length of the data set. For example, a combination of wave height (y) and water level (x) exceeded (i.e. SWL $\geq x$ and $H_s \geq y$) one hundred times in ten years would have a return period of 0.1 year, and another one exceeded ten times in ten years would have a return period of 1 year. There will be several combinations of wave heights and water levels corresponding to any given return period. With a long-term data set of, say, ten years, it is possible to draw contours for the most commonly occurring events, with return periods of up to about one year.

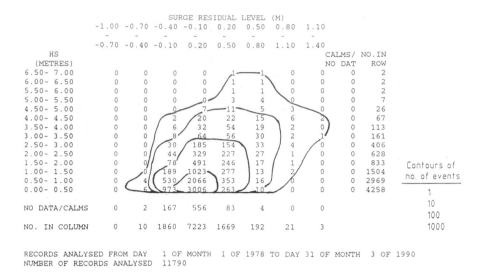

RECORDS ANALYSED FROM DAY   1 OF MONTH 1 OF 1978 TO DAY 31 OF MONTH 3 OF 1990
NUMBER OF RECORDS ANALYSED 11790

Figure 3.22   *Example probability contours demonstrating positive correlation between surge and significant wave height (Christchurch Bay, Dorset)*

Probability contours of rarer events could then be sketched in, retaining the shape of the known contours. The spacing between the extrapolated contours should be approximately equal for each factor of ten (or any other convenient factor) increase in rarity of event represented. So, for example, the one, ten and hundred year return period contours should be drawn so as to have roughly the same shape and spacing. The positions of the contours as they meet the x- and y-axes are fixed by the values of the marginal extremes, i.e. the extreme water levels (for all waves) and the extreme wave heights (for all water levels).

As an example, Figure 3.23 is a scatter diagram of water level against significant wave height, for high waters during a period of about 10 years, off Shoreham in Sussex. Probability contours for return periods of 0.1 and 1 year are drawn in directly from the data. Marginal extremes are determined so as to fix the positions of the higher return period contours on the x- and y-axes. Contours for higher return periods are then drawn in using the manual extrapolation procedure described above. Having determined the positions of the contours, several combinations of wave heights and water levels with a given joint return period can be extracted for subsequent use in design, assessment or further modelling. It should be noted, however, that not all combinations of wave height and water level which may be calculated for a given joint return period will result in the same degree of response or failure (hence the move towards the methods described in Sections 3.5.5 and 3.5.6).

Alternatively, extremes can be determined more objectively by extrapolating wave heights for increasingly rare water levels, and water levels for rare wave heights. This involves setting a series of thresholds (x_i, $i = 1$, n) for (say) water level, and performing extremes analysis only on the wave height data *above* the threshold, for each threshold in turn. The resulting extremes distribution (for threshold x_i) $P(H_s \geq y)$ also forms part of the joint extremes distribution as $P(H_s \geq y$ and $SWL \geq x_i)$. By combining these extrapolations, contours can be constructed joining combinations of wave height and water level with equal joint return periods.

The extrapolated joint density approach

This approach models and extends the joint probability contours without particular reference to the return period of events. This is more appropriate for risk analysis, where the emphasis is on calculation of the probability of a particular response, as opposed to design where particular input parameter values may be needed. Risk analysis is often applied to assessment of existing situations.

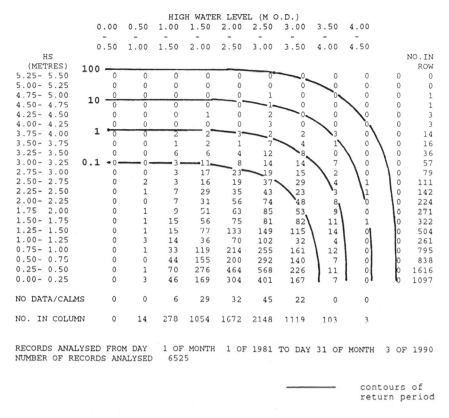

Figure 3.23 *Example of manually drawn extreme joint probability contours of water level and significant wave height (off Shoreham, W. Sussex)*

Figures 3.21 and 3.22 are examples of joint probability density contours drawn manually within the body of the data. These contours could be extrapolated manually by eye. Alternatively, model probability distributions (for example the Weibull or Normal distributions) can be fitted to each of the individual variables, with another equation to define the degree of correlation between them. If this is possible, then the positions of the extrapolated contours can be determined objectively from the extreme values of the fitted distributions and correlation equation.

MAFF-funded research is under way to develop methods of transforming real wave and water level data into simpler bi-variate Normal distributions whose joint statistics are already well known. Methods will be developed to change the actual marginal distributions for the input variables into Normal distributions. Once the joint probability statistics have been computed for the Normal distribution, the results will be transformed back to equivalent results for the original distributions. In principle, this method is not limited to two variables, i.e. wave height and water level, and wave period could be added as a third independent variable.

The coastal responses of interest (e.g. structural failure, overtopping etc) are then determined by integration over the joint probability contours. This approach is more mathematically rigorous than the return period approach, and it is more amenable to extension to more than two primary variables. It is unfortunately more difficult to use by non-specialists but has the benefits of comparability with the easier combined probability methods described below.

3.5.5 Combined probability methods

It is quite common to calculate joint probability extremes in fairly deep water offshore and then to assume that they are applicable over quite a wide area. Before use at the coast, it may be necessary to transform these conditions inshore and then to assess the ability of the sea defences to withstand each combination of waves and water levels at the inshore point.

If only a small number (up to about three) of inshore locations and only a small number of design variables (e.g. overtopping) are of interest, then the joint probability results can be expressed in a more directly useful form.

For a given return period, all the combinations of offshore wave conditions and water levels could be converted into, for example, rates of overtopping at a particular location (if overtopping is the critical consideration). This would indicate which combination of offshore conditions is critical, in terms of overtopping, and this combination could then be highlighted for use by the coastal engineer. This method of results presentation has its advantages. However, it should be used with caution, since conditions highlighted as above would have very specific application. At nearby sites, or for alternative variables (run-up or force), it is likely that some other combination of offshore waves and water levels would be critical in design.

Alternatively, the design variable(s) of interest at the inshore site(s) of interest could be continuously hindcast for whatever period of wave and water level data is available. For example, if there were 20 years of simultaneous wave and water level data available, it could be used to hindcast (i.e. to produce a value for every hour) rates of overtopping directly at an inshore site of interest. This is the only practical method of incorporating wave period as an independent variable in the analysis, in addition to wave height and water level. The rates of overtopping could then be examined and used to infer a probability distribution and extreme values for use in design.

This direct hindcasting approach is a useful way of carrying out and presenting the results from a joint probability assessment: instead of a rather unwieldy table containing several combinations of offshore conditions, it produces a single overtopping extreme as required by the designer. However, this approach should be adopted with some caution. The behaviour of the defence may change dramatically under extreme values of one or more of the input variables, for example from gentle erosion to overtopping or retreat. In this situation of a discontinuous coastal response function, the direct hindcasting approach may give a misleading design prediction. Also, results presented in this way may not be applicable at similar sites nearby, and would not provide equivalent values of *any* other variable (wave height, water level, run-up or whatever). If results were required later for some other variable, or some other point, or perhaps even to test a modified wall design, it would probably be necessary to repeat the entire hindcasting exercise, since no general results would be available.

3.5.6   Design with joint waves and water levels

Joint probability analysis results can be expressed as a range of combinations of wave conditions and water levels, each with the same return period. Each one is expected to be exceeded once, on average, in each return period. In designing or assessing a structure, one would need to ensure that it could withstand every combination of wave height and water level for the return period being used. In other words, for each coastal response variable of interest, each combination of extreme water level and wave condition should be tested, to determine the worst case for each response variable.

Alternatively, the results of a joint probability analysis may be presented in the form of a climate scatter diagram (e.g. Figures 3.8 and 3.21-23) with or without extrapolated joint probability density contours. This form of presentation is more appropriate for building up a probability distribution of a coastal response variable, found by integrating the response function over the joint ranges of each of the primary input variables. Examples are beach plan shape development (primarily as a function of wave height and direction) which may continue during even quite commonly occurring conditions, and risk analysis (primarily as a function of nearshore wave height and water level) where the overall probability of a given response is to be calculated.

If the wave heights and water levels are derived for a location other than the point at which they are to be applied, some adjustment of values may be necessary. The most obvious case is the need to modify wave conditions calculated offshore to allow for shallow water transformations prior to their arrival at coastal defences. If wave periods are required these can be assigned to particular significant wave heights based on a typical wave steepness ($2\pi H_s/gT_m^2$) for storm waves. If wave direction is important, perhaps in wave transformation or in coastal response, then separate calculations may need to be done for each direction sector of interest.

The degree of correlation between large waves and high water levels varies between different locations and different wave direction sectors, and even between offshore and nearshore. (Some illustrations of this are given in Hawkes and Hague, 1994.) It may therefore be inappropriate to assume that the most severe sea states offshore will give rise to similarly severe conditions at the coast. On open coasts, where the largest waves offshore also give rise to the largest waves inshore, then the correlation with high water levels will be similar for both situations. However, where waves are strongly depth-limited before arriving at the sea defences, then wave period (and perhaps therefore a different type of sea condition) may be much more important nearshore than offshore. Also, for locations protected by headlands from the largest offshore waves, the nearshore situation may be different to offshore. For example at Cardiff, South Glamorgan, swell waves from the west (which give rise to the largest wave heights in the Outer Bristol Channel) are correlated with high water levels, but the locally generated waves (which give rise to the largest wave heights at Cardiff) are uncorrelated with high water levels.

Joint probability analysis will normally be based, even if indirectly, on measurements taken during recent years, assuming that they are representative of longer term conditions. If the wave conditions or water levels are known to be subject to any long-term variations (such as a rise in mean sea level) or if the period of measurements is known to be unrepresentative, then allowance should be made for this (see Section 3.6.1).

3.5.7   Design with joint waves and currents

Here again it may well be worth carrying out a joint probability analysis, as waves usually demonstrate a clear physical interaction with currents, one example being current refraction (see Section 3.4.1). In addition, waves and currents often have a common driving force in wind and the waves themselves may induce further currents. In such cases the current velocities will not be independent of wave height and other wave-related parameters such as orbital velocities.

3.5.8   Wave climate from joint waves and tides

The cross-shore response of a beach is strongly influenced by both waves and water levels. The longshore drift is strongly influenced by wave direction and continues during even quite commonly occurring sea conditions. The propagation of waves in the nearshore zone may be affected by the tidal level and by the current field, both of which vary during the tidal cycle.

To obtain an accurate nearshore wave climate, it would be possible to hindcast the nearshore wave conditions hour by hour, taking account of the water level and current field as it varies hour by hour. A more practical approach, however, is to transform the offshore climate to inshore, en bloc, for a small number of tidal states. This approach would be appropriate for analysis of continuously occurring processes, such as beach development, as opposed to those occurring only in extreme conditions. A littoral drift rate is calculated for each separate wave climate, matched with the corresponding current data. The overall wave climate and littoral drift rate are then computed by taking a representative average of the separate nearshore wave climates and drift rates. The tidal states chosen might be high water, low water, mid-flood and mid-ebb for Neap and Spring conditions.

3.6   CLIMATE VARIABILITY

Where the design of beaches is concerned, it will not be appropriate to design the initial profile for long-term sea level rise, as most schemes will involve periodic recharge or recycling of materials which can be used to make future adjustments as required. This is one of the major attractions of beach management for coastal defence. The emphasis should be on making assessments of the additional material which may be required in the future when considering the overall cost of long-term beach management strategies. However, given the gradual nature of the rise, there will be instances where there will be an element of natural adjustment, though there may also be long-term destabilisation if, for example, such adjustments lead to a steeper beach profile. In any case, changes in storm duration, intensity, frequency or dominant direction may well be much more significant for beach management than a relative sea level rise.

3.6.1   Sea level rise and climate change

Increasing water level

Mean sea level rise over the last century is a well documented phenomenon (IPCC, 1990). Long-term measurements show a typical rate of rise of 1-2mm/yr. Gradual slight changes in land level produce apparent regional variations in the rate of rise, from a higher than average rate in the south-east of England to a lower than average rate in northern Scotland.

Many institutions are involved in research on sea level rise and its implications. For several years there have been many varied predictions of an imminent increase in the rate of mean sea level rise. A certain proportion of the predicted rise is already thought to be committed regardless of any corrective action which may be taken, but there is some sensitivity to future actions in pollution control etc. The present consensus is that in future the rate of rise will increase to about 5mm/yr, with some regional variations, although as yet there is no evidence of this accelerated rise having started.

The method of allowance for future sea level rise may vary from one application to another. Therefore, it is usually most convenient to calculate and quote water levels at present day values, and then to make a separate adjustment for any expected future changes.

MAFF advises coastal engineers to take account of expected sea level rise when designing or assessing sea defences. However, predictions of future changes in sea level are uncertain and are frequently updated, and any such changes will be gradual. As a result of this, sea level rise is often considered on a contingency basis rather than as a firm commitment. For example, rather than designing sea defences now for a half-a-metre rise in sea level over the next century which may never occur, designers may instead prepare contingency responses for review when evidence of accelerated sea level rise is more definite. MAFF (1993) (see Box 3.4) gives recommendations of rates of sea level rise to be assumed for different parts of England and Wales.

In the absence of any evidence to the contrary, any increase in mean sea level is likely to cause an equal increase in all other water levels, including extreme water levels. To make allowance for sea level rise in beach management, instead of using present day sea levels, one might take the sea level expected to exist either mid-way through the design life of the beach or at the end of its design life. Beach management should also take account of possible long-term adjustment of beach levels and nearshore bathymetry as relative mean sea levels gradually change.

Box 3.4   *Rates of future relative sea level rise for England and Wales (MAFF, 1993)*

NRA Region	Allowance
Anglian, Thames, Southern	6mm/year
North-West, Northumbria	4mm/year
Remainder	5mm/year

As well as a change in mean sea level, there is a possibility of changes in tidal ranges. Long-term tidal measurements show slight past trends in this respect, which may continue into the future. However, as evidence for changing tidal ranges is limited, it is not yet necessary to take account of this risk in design.

Tidal oscillations consist of many superimposed harmonics, the largest of which is the M2 component with a period of just over 12 hours. However, the longest harmonic has a period of 18.6 years, which for a location with a high tidal range such as the Severn Estuary, can provide a significant decadal variation in the highest water levels. This astronomical variation should not be confused with long-term sea level rise.

Future climate change will influence weather patterns, which in turn may influence the size and frequency of storm surges, in turn influencing the total water level and risk of flooding. However, as evidence for changing storm surges is limited, and as any change could equally well be for better or for worse, it is not yet necessary to take account of this risk in design.

Changes in winds and waves

Mean wave heights in the North Atlantic have increased by 1-2% per year since 1960 with no corresponding increase in mean wind speeds. Figure 3.24 shows mean wave heights and extrapolated 50-year return period wave heights based on complete years of data from long-term wave measurements at Seven Stones off Cornwall, UK. Mean wave heights in the North Sea also increased between 1960 and 1980. Derived extreme wave heights have also increased, but not as rapidly as mean wave heights.

Small changes in locally generated waves from year-to-year, predicted by a wave hindcasting model (Jelliman *et al*, 1991), were closely matched by corresponding changes in the wind data from which the waves were derived. This implies that the *general* pattern of winds and storminess has not changed much over the last twenty years, but that small changes in wind speeds and directions may have occurred.

Some additional tests involving changes in wave direction showed some very gradual changes in mean wave direction over periods of 10-30 years. The potential effect on littoral drift of the change in mean wave direction was shown to be very significant (see Figure 3.25), although the drift rate changes cannot be quantified reliably.

Further site-specific analysis (Brampton, 1993) showed that some of the temporal changes predicted by the wave and drift models are probably genuine. Hindcasting of waves and annual drift rates were carried out for five locations on the south coast of England and the results were compared with actual beach behaviour. At Shoreham in West Sussex, Pevensey in East Sussex and Hythe in Kent, net drift rates during the winter of 1989-90 were higher than at any time during 1981-90, both in the numerical model and in reality. Conversely, at Hurst Castle in Hampshire and at West Bay, Dorset, drift rates during the winter of 1989-90 were not out of the ordinary, either in the model or in reality. The numerical methods correctly predicted a *reversal* in the direction of net sediment transport at West Bay between 1974-82 and 1982-90, as confirmed by site observations and beach measurements.

Models of future climate tentatively suggest that changes in wind conditions will be small. Around the UK the proportion of westerly winds is predicted to reduce, the proportion of easterly winds to increase, and mean wind speeds to increase slightly. There are some slight inferences that the proportion of westerly winds and the number of storms in the North Atlantic may reduce following global warming. A significant increase in the proportion of waves (and winds) coming directly towards the North Sea coasts of the UK is predicted (Jelliman *et al*, 1991) for the future, although not necessarily any increase in extreme wave heights. A significant decrease in the proportion of waves (and winds) coming directly towards the Atlantic coasts of the UK is predicted for the future, although again not necessarily any decrease in extreme wave height.

There is no need for immediate action to raise or strengthen coastal defences. However, coastal engineers should be prepared to re-assess their coastal defences at regular intervals, and to be responsive to any evidence of accelerated climate change. Regional databases, such as that commissioned by NRA (Anglian Region) permit a rapid assessment and management response to any new information on climate change. Several more localised re-assessments, for example in southern England and in North Wales, have taken place recently, prompted by the severe storms in October 1987 and in winter 1989/90.

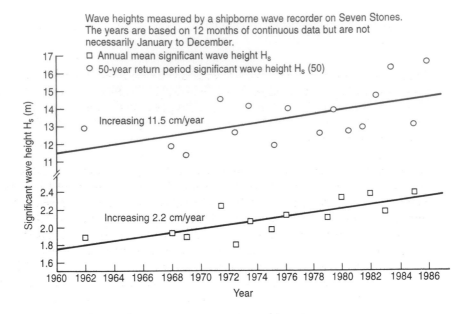

Figure 3.24   *Variation in annually averaged H_s (Seven Stones 1962-86)*

3.6.2   Historic extreme events

Most analysis of hydraulic environmental conditions is based on long-term continuous data sets of wind, water level, current or wave data. In this context, long-term could be anything between 1 year for wave data and 100 years for tide gauge data. Usually the information is worked up into a distribution from which design and/or climate data is extracted. This approach deals with representative conditions rather than actual events.

Historic event analysis is an alternative approach in which individual recorded events are considered. There are two main purposes. One is to include severe storms which would otherwise not be considered due to their occurring outside the period of availability of the long-term data. The second is to numerically reproduce an event (or period of time) for which there is good information on the beach response, to assist in understanding of the processes involved and/or calibration of a combined wave and beach model.

Types of event

Characteristics of events of interest might include one or more of the following:

* occurrences of high waves, or swell
* occurrences of high water levels, or surges
* overtopping and flooding
* damage to sea defences
* falling beach levels
* damage to property, or death.

Once the criteria are established for events of interest, the search may be carried out either locally or regionally, and over either a shorter or longer sampling period. Normally the criteria will be set so that the search produces a maximum of ten such events.

Sources of data

There are several sources of data which can be used either to help identify historic events or to provide further information on events already identified.

Weather records go back over 100 years. Much of the data before about 1970 is available only in paper format, and there may have been many changes in measuring techniques and locations. Nevertheless this information is reliable and can be recovered fairly easily from meteorological archives. This type of information can be scanned for unusually low pressures or high wind velocities.

Tidal level records go back over 100 years at a few stations around the UK, and in most cases a breakdown into separate astronomical and surge components has already been performed. There are presently about 40 A Class tide gauges in place around the UK (see Figure 3.26) and perhaps a further 60 locally owned gauges. This type of data can be scanned for unusually high total water levels or surges.

Measured wave data is patchy both in time and in spatial coverage. Site-specific wave model data tends to cover a longer period of time and a greater density of locations. Lists of measured and hindcast wave data around England and Wales are given in two separate HR Wallingford reports (Brampton and Hawkes, 1990; Ramsay and Harford, 1995). Existing measured or hindcast wave data may be available for re-use on an opportunistic basis from about 1960 onwards. A more consistent source is the archives of operational wave forecasting models but such data may only be available from about 1986 onwards. This type of data can be scanned for unusually large wave heights or periods. Other sources include the memories and personal records of local residents, local and national papers, local and national authority archives and flood marks, any of which might typically provide information going back about fifty years. Much of this information will be subjective, highlighting impacts such as injuries, flooding and damage to coastal structures, rather than being based on scientific measurements. Dhérent and Petit-Renaud (1994) provide a methodology, with example results, for the use of archival resources collected over a period of 350 years, for climate history research.

Uses of data

In a general sense, historic event analysis can effectively extend the length of a data set used for more intensive analysis, or at least put that data set into a longer term context. For example, there may be 20 years of measured water level data and hindcast wave data in digital format for derivation of wave and water level statistics. Historic event analysis, perhaps based on recorded flooding of a sea wall over a period of 100 years, might be used to identify the worst ten storms over the 100-year period. If the main 20-year data set did not contain exactly two of these worst 10 events, then it might accordingly be judged a more or less severe period than average.

Coastal modelling might include the derivation of extreme waves and water levels, and prediction of the coastal response in terms of damage or overtopping. If the historic event analysis was based on well documented local damage reports, then predictions of waves, water levels and coastal responses at the same times and dates could be used to calibrate and validate the modelling procedures.

Design conditions are usually based on a specified return period (or frequency of occurrence per year). Historic event analysis could be used to provide reassurance that the return period approach led to a design based on conditions comparable with any known events with similar frequency of occurrence.

3.7   HYDRAULIC MODELLING

Many institutions run numerical models of one type or another for tides, waves and beaches. A much smaller number have physical modelling facilities. For both physical and numerical modelling, the bathymetry may be two-dimensional (flume and profile models) or three-dimensional (basin and gridded models). Similarly the wave conditions may be regular, long-crested random or short-crested random.

The expense involved in physical modelling cannot be justified for the preliminary stages of design, but is usually a cost-effective way of refining a preferred scheme or comparing two or three equally favoured schemes. Where physical modelling is undertaken to refine a coastal scheme, it will usually have been preceded by numerical modelling as a means of selecting preferred schemes.

3.7.1 Numerical modelling of water levels and currents

Numerical models are essentially tools to solve a set of mathematical equations for the variable(s) of interest (e.g. the depth mean current velocity), the equations in turn being a schematic description of the real underlying processes. One-dimensional flow models usually perform well for average currents in well defined current systems with pronounced flow concentrations (e.g. channels and rivers) but in most situations two- and three-dimensional flow models will be required, and here the choices of schematisation and computation schemes are important for realistic results.

Perhaps the most important factor to bear in mind with numerical models is to ensure that the applied boundary conditions (water levels, including tidal and wind/wave-induced velocities, and treatment of bottom boundaries) are correct. When models are used to solve questions related to sediment transport, spatial variations in water levels and currents may be important.

3.7.2 Physical modelling of water levels and currents

Physical modelling is an important option for complicated (usually three-dimensional) current patterns for which the boundary conditions can be reproduced in the laboratory. Physical modelling can be particularly useful in a number of situations:

- where interference of currents and waves is concerned
- where verification of (or comparison with) a numerical model is required
- if a physical model can be built and operated at a competitive cost in relation to other options.

3.7.3 Numerical modelling of waves

Most reliable numerical wave models for prediction of nearshore wave conditions are based on linear wave theory and incorporate, as a minimum, representation of refraction, shoaling and profiled bathymetry. Some models:

- include one or more of the additional processes of breaking, frictional attenuation, diffraction, currents, reflections, wave growth and development of the spectrum, as necessary
- use a full 3D bathymetry and a full directional spectrum, which are usually necessary in beach modelling, except perhaps where the nearshore contours are approximately shore parallel
- work with a full wave climate, which is usually necessary in beach modelling, rather than just a small number of wave conditions which may be adequate for assessment of extreme conditions.

Another approach to wave modelling is based on energy tracking through a bathymetric grid. Again, different models include different physical processes, and discretise the seabed and wave spectrum differently. This approach allows a more sophisticated analysis of the non-linear effects of breaking, frictional attenuation and spectrum development.

The choice of wave model will depend on the quality of the input data, the intended end use of the results, the physical processes expected to be important, and the time and budget available for the analysis. Some physical aspects of the nearshore environment are difficult for most wave numerical models, for example complex bathymetry, deep water channels, wave breaking and rapidly varying currents. It is important to be aware of any significant processes which are being neglected or over-simplified, before embarking on numerical modelling, which may later give a false impression of the accuracy of the calculations.

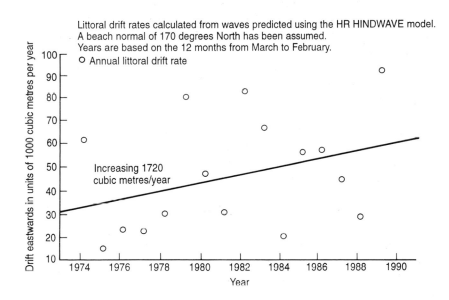

a Variation in drift rate

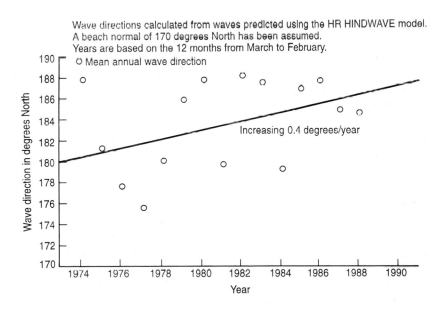

b Variation in drift direction

Figure 3.25 *Potential variation in annually averaged littoral drift (Littlehampton, W. Sussex 1974-90)*

Figure 3.26 *Existing A class tide gauge network around the UK (courtesy MAFF)*

Beach managers will rarely have direct access to a wide range of numerical models, and where necessary will sub-contract the work to one of a small number of specialist consultants. Advice on the selection of an appropriate numerical wave model is given in Hawkes and Jelliman (1993) for named models and HR Wallingford (1994) for generically described models.

3.7.4   Physical modelling of waves

Physical wave models can be used as a predictive scale model for the prototype scheme or to calibrate or validate a numerical model. This validation may be particularly important where the waves are severely reduced by friction and breaking effects before arrival at the beach, a situation not well handled by numerical models. Physical models may be used to simulate wave transformation, but more importantly they are used to determine the (fairly short-term) coastal response, i.e. beach profile, overtopping, one year of net annual drift etc.

As wave direction is so important in determining drift rates, it is usually necessary to work in a basin and to test a number of wave spectra from different directions. Ideally, a full directional spectrum would be used, but very few institutions have the necessary facilities. Three dimensional wave and beach modelling is very much more expensive than equivalent numerical modelling, and so should only be used when justified by the value of the scheme being assessed.

Physical modelling is not recommended for the direct modelling of long-term beach development, although it may be useful when carried out in conjunction with numerical modelling.

4 Data collection and monitoring

4.1 GENERAL APPROACH

Managing a beach effectively requires data. Measurements or observations of the beach itself are obviously needed, data are required on the attributes of the beach described in Section 2.2, and sometimes it is also necessary to include measurements of other factors, for example waves, tides and weather conditions which dominate beach development.

Data are required for three main reasons:

* to identify spatial and temporal trends, determine their significance, and help to understand their causes
* to provide information to assist in the assessment and design of management strategies
* to appraise the performance and impacts of the adopted beach management methods.

A clear distinction must be made between an initial survey of the whole beach system at a particular moment in time, and monitoring of the beach system as it varies with time. The initial survey should be as detailed as possible, as it will be compared with measurements of the system made in the future. A desk study of existing data should be undertaken prior to specifying the initial survey to ensure that the new data covers all sensitive areas and that work is not repeated unnecessarily.

Monitoring is an ongoing exercise in data collection. Comparisons of monitoring data with that from the initial baseline survey enable the performance of new management strategies to be judged. Ideally the measurements made during the monitoring programme should be a sub-set of those made for the initial survey. This allows the build up of a consistent time series, which eases comparison. The monitoring programme also needs to be flexible to allow for different rates of change; the frequency and resolution of the measurements should reflect the duration and physical dimensions of the processes being measured. Many of the attributes of a beach also alter seasonally and so information at various times throughout the year will be required. Identifying long-term trends in beach attributes (and beach-influencing factors, such as wave and tidal conditions) will require data over several years.

It is important that data collection is cost-effective, i.e. that the value obtained justifies the effort involved. Measurement methods need to be chosen bearing in mind required accuracy and cost. Experience has shown that enthusiasm (and funding) for monitoring soon diminishes unless the information obtained from monitoring is made available promptly and in a readily comprehensible form. Before adding information obtained from monitoring to the database, however, it is essential that the data is quality checked. Results obtained must be analysed and presented in a suitable way, ideally determined at the same time as the monitoring programme itself is specified. Information on trends, determined by the analysis of baseline time series data, can help to ensure that erroneous monitoring data is identified and, where feasible, corrected. Well presented results can be of interest not only to the beach manager, but to a wider audience, particularly the local population and their elected representatives. There is also value to be gained from such data collection by the scientific community and planning authorities.

In order to design a suitable data collection system for any particular beach, the following key questions must be answered.

Why is it important to collect data?

The reasons to collect data can be summarised as follows:

1. Understanding the past - short-term fluctuations and long-term trends in the behaviour of the beach and in the hydraulic regime need to be identified to understand the development

of a beach. Without this information it is often difficult to identify precisely the causes of change and is certainly much more difficult to predict future changes.

2. Identification of present problems - monitoring changes of the beaches allows the early identification of changes in the beach response. This may confirm the year-to-year stability or health of the beach and may provide reassuring confirmation of beach recovery or regrowth. Perhaps more importantly, data can be used to detect when beach levels have fallen to a critical level which could lead to unwanted overtopping, damage to the backshore or undermining of sea walls. Monitoring may also be significant for the maintenance of other important beach attributes (e.g. to limit damage to important ecological habitats).

3. Programming management operations - monitoring can assist in the timing of existing management schemes. Beach recharge schemes, for example, may be programmed with enhanced confidence if the beach is closely monitored.

3. Predicting future solutions - data are required to calibrate and validate physical and numerical models which may be used for predicting the future development of a beach, hence assisting in the design of appropriate solutions to any particular problem. Information may also help justify the expense of future beach management, for example, by quantifying numbers of tourists and the recreational use of beaches.

4. Monitoring solutions - whatever their nature, soft beach management schemes will need to be monitored much more carefully and frequently than hard defences. The information will assist, for example, in post-project evaluations and in understanding the environmental impacts of schemes. It may also suggest better methods of tackling problems in the future.

Which data should be collected and what are the priorities?

In general, the precise details of the data that need to be collected as part of a beach management exercise will depend upon the specific site and its character. A preliminary assessment of the site is often necessary to design a suitable data-collection programme. This should identify the information already available, the further variables to be measured and the level of accuracy and resolution required. Accuracy and resolution will govern the choice of instruments and methodology that are appropriate. Possibilities for data collection will almost always exceed the budget available. As a consequence it is often necessary to set priorities and to concentrate effort on the most vital information.

It is important to consider what information is already being collected, or generated, which proposed monitoring might duplicate. For example, certain parts of the UK coastline are well served by tide gauges (see Section 4.2), therefore it may be unnecessary to initiate a local tide level measurement system. Similarly, local conservation groups may already be collecting ecological data which could form part of the environmental assessment of a scheme (before or after installation).

The following topics are presented in their likely order of priority for data collection:

1. Beach levels, sediments and attributes.

2. Geotechnical site investigation.

3. Land, underlying strata and nearshore seabed.

4. Tidal currents and wave conditions close to the beach.

5. Tidal levels, offshore waves, winds, etc.

When and where should the data be collected?

Data have to be collected in a systematic and planned manner if maximum benefit is to be derived. The choice of sampling interval in time and space is dependent upon the process being studied. For example, to identify any seasonal variation in beach levels against a seawall, it will be necessary to survey them at least four times a year, at regular intervals. In the longer term, once seasonal variations have been established, a twice yearly monitoring regime is likely to suffice. If, however, post-storm beach levels are of interest, a more flexible fast-response approach to survey will be required. Similarly, thought needs to be given to the locations at which data are gathered. As an example, it may be preferable to survey beach levels along the base of a seawall, i.e. a longitudinal section, rather than having closely spaced cross-sections, especially if the beach is groyned. The locations of any previous surveys should also be considered; more reliable comparisons can be made when the data collection location is consistent. The frequency and location of environmental, seabed and geotechnical surveys also need to be considered carefully (see Sections 4.3, 4.4, 4.5).

It may be necessary to adjust the data collection programme over time if conditions change at the site, or more importantly if the survey programme adopted is not providing the information required. Analysing the data is a vital part of any data collection exercise, rather than a post-script to it.

How should the data be stored and analysed?

No universal consensus exists on the best way of storing beach monitoring data. Almost all data have a geographical location, so a Geographical Information System (GIS) is a powerful tool to store, collate and analyse information. This approach has been adopted by some UK coastal authorities. Monitored data will also usually vary with time e.g. hour by hour synthetic wave or tidal level data. An important part of the analysis of the information gathered, therefore, involves time-series analysis, for example to separate the short-term fluctuations from any long-term trends. For such time-series data storage and analysis, personal computer (PC) storage systems such as spreadsheets, Computer Aided Design (CAD) and simple bespoke databases can perhaps be used more simply than GIS if the geographical referencing is less important. Simplicity of storage, retrieval and analysis are key to effective data management. The coastal manager rarely needs more than a simple method of inputting data, viewing the data in graphical or numeric form and the ability to compare with alarm or threshold conditions. This can usually be achieved with spreadsheet, CAD or simple database type programs which are widely available and easy to use. However, if a coastal authority has elected to use a GIS system, perhaps for wider reasons e.g. drainage data, coastal data can also be stored, viewed and compared on it so long as staff are correctly trained in its use.

It is important that analysis is carried out as new data are entered into the database, and up-to-date summaries of the results are made available to interested parties. Apart from maintaining an interest in the data collection, prompt analysis has other advantages. Although the data should have been checked before being input, erroneous data (for example, beach levels) can be identified after loading by prompt analysis which will reveal surprising or unrealistic changes. If the analysis is delayed, the opportunity may soon be lost because of the rapid variation in beach levels with time.

Of course, if levels have dropped rapidly for example, it should equally be possible to compare them with pre-defined alarm levels, and hence take prompt action to start to remedy the developing situation.

A vital part of any analysis of data is the presentation of results in a convenient form that can be appreciated by non-technical individuals and groups, as well as providing a summary for the beach managers themselves. The requirement for such output from the data collection programme needs to be defined in advance and developed in the light of experience.

Prompt interim analysis of the data does not, of course, preclude the in-depth analysis required when a solution to a problem is being considered. Thought must, therefore, be given to subsequent uses of the information as well; for example, it may be necessary to pass on some of the information to specialists for more sophisticated analyses and, therefore, standard output formats will be helpful.

How should a data collection programme be started?

The practicalities of starting up and sustaining a data collection programme will be almost as site-specific as the beaches themselves. The perceived importance of beaches, and their management, to the local community or the region, and the resources available for that management, are both critical factors. It is rarely possible to start a long-term monitoring exercise without prior justification, usually expressed in benefit-cost terms.

Several stages are normally needed prior to starting a beach monitoring programme. First, the need for the information has to be established, usually to non-technical fund holders. Then it is important to review what information already exists and where the gaps are. This leads on to consideration of the needs for further information, and whether it can be obtained in a short-term programme of monitoring (this is often the case for the hydraulic forcing processes of waves and tides), or whether longer-term monitoring is required.

Having set the objectives of a data collection programme, a decision will need to be made on the required accuracy and frequency of the information for the baseline and monitoring surveys. The methods for storing, analysing and disseminating the information also need to be specified at this stage. In this context, the role of Coastal Groups may be particularly relevant, since it is often possible to decide on a set of measurements of wider value than for one beach or stretch of coastline; for example, simultaneous tidal level and current measurements to calibrate a regional tidal flow numerical model.

It is then necessary to estimate the costs of the programme and ideally to place financial values on the likely benefits that will accrue. The benefits, of course, come from improving the efficiency, or cost, of beach management and thus avoiding losses or making economic gains as a result. It is important at this stage to investigate the possibility of finding partners to assist in the sometimes expensive business of monitoring.

4.2 BEACH DATA COLLECTION

4.2.1 Programme planning

Beaches are constantly changing in response to the various processes and factors which control them. Successful management of a beach requires that the processes should be identified and changes should be monitored. The data should be analysed and appraised following a carefully planned ongoing data collection programme. The aim of the programme should be to understand the beach responses and to identify potential problems, thereby allowing management to be proactive rather than reactive. Monitoring should be undertaken on any coastline where there is a potential risk of flooding or erosion that threatens significant property or infrastructure and it is essential for the post-construction assessment of any new beach works or management scheme.

The programme should include:

- recording observations
- taking fixed aspect photographs
- measurement of beach profiles and plan shapes
- analysis of beach sediment samples
- determination of the sediment budget
- environmental data collection
- aerial photography
- bathymetric survey.

This work must be undertaken in conjunction with the monitoring of waves and water levels, as well as the collection of geotechnical, bathymetric and tidal current data.

Prior to establishing a field programme, a desk study should be undertaken. Information relating to the geological and historical development of the beach is vital to understanding the present situation and therefore to the planning of the programme. Sources of information include:

- geological memoirs and maps
- published research papers
- local universities and colleges
- Ordnance Survey sheets
- Admiralty Charts, including collector charts
- previous beach surveys
- engineering drawings and records
- historic photographs, both aerial and ground
- press reports and local knowledge
- satellite imagery.

Particular attention should be paid to the nearshore and backshore geology, and to the impact of coastal structures and dredging.

Planning of an effective programme of fieldwork must take account of a number of factors. Beaches respond rapidly to changes in environmental conditions, therefore field work must be undertaken sufficiently often to reveal short term variations as well as long-term trends. At the outset surveys should be undertaken monthly and immediately after any significant storm events. This level of monitoring should be maintained until an understanding of the processes and factors controlling the beach has been developed and the potential for seasonal and storm related variations, the areas of particular concern, and the sediment sources and sinks have been identified. Once these requirements have been met then the survey frequency and extent can be reduced, but systematic post-storm observations should be continued to ensure that any unexpected developments can be appraised quickly. An example of an ongoing monitoring programme for the beaches and coasts of NRA Anglian Region is given in Box 4.1.

The following sections expand on the general methods and management of beach data collection. Detailed descriptions of equipment and techniques are not included, but a number of useful references are appended. As a general point, all observations, measurements and photographs must include a reference time, date and location. Where possible they should also reference the recent wave conditions and the state of the tide. These references will ensure that data appraisal can be completed effectively.

4.2.2   Site inspections

The simplest form of monitoring a beach is by regular inspections of the coastline. As with any other form of monitoring, however, the value of this technique is greatly enhanced if the inspections are well-specified, and the information obtained is recorded and analysed in relation to previous inspections. The use of photographs and pre-prepared checklists or record-sheets is a good way of increasing the value of such inspections. Inspections will vary according to the site and the particular concerns of the beach manager, but they should include the collection of information on:

1. Beach changes, for example:
    - beach levels against sea-walls, groynes, etc.
    - evidence of erosion of dune faces, or steep scarps at the beach crest
    - exposure of the solid shore-platform in the inter-tidal zone.

2. Beach texture, for example:
    - deposition or loss of sand covering a shingle upper beach
    - deposition of mud on the lower beach face.

Box 4.1 *Shoreline Monitoring Programme, NRA Anglian Region*

The NRA Anglian Region Shoreline Monitoring Programme includes various strategic elements to gain a long-term overall picture of the behaviour of the coastline:

- beach surveys
- bathymetric surveys
- aerial survey
- shoreline inspections
- water levels
- modelled wind and wave data
- measured tide/waves in estuaries.

Some details of these surveys are as follows:

Beach level surveys are carried out at 1km intervals along the whole of the open coast, on 350 survey lines, twice a year during January and again July/August. This is a continuing programme which commenced in July 1991.

Bathymetric surveys are undertaken July/August once every 4 years, North Norfolk was surveyed bathymetrically in 1991, Suffolk/Norfolk in 1992, Essex in 1993 leaving Lincolnshire to be surveyed in 1994 before repeating North Norfolk in 1995 and so on. This programme is also extending into estuary locations with the Blackwater being surveyed in 93/94.

Aerial surveys are undertaken annually for the whole coast and additional areas to this required for other projects have been added to the main survey thereby improving efficiency.

Shoreline inspections commenced in early 1992 and are undertaken by District Staff. They consist of two elements; beach inspections which record beach sediments, dip measurements and an overall summary of the beach changes and structure inspections which record details on the structure and a general overview of the structure condition. Photographs taken during the inspections are noted on the inspection sheets. A specialist, proprietary software package is used to store and retrieve this as well as beach level data, and wind, wave and water level data.

Single wave/tide recording contracts have been carried out in estuaries, commencing with the Blackwater in 1993/94. These recordings provide previously lacking empirical data.

Scheme specific monitoring is being undertaken on a more concentrated basis than the 1km-surveys already undertaken for 18 Capital Projects, surveying lines at a more frequent interval. This work is at the request of Project Engineers and is co-ordinated through the Shoreline Management Group to ensure consistency of data and to improve value for money by amalgamating contracts and using the expertise built up by the Group for Contract Document specification.

Biological survey work is also being specified and managed by the Shoreline Management Group, covering invertebrates, vegetation birds and sediments. Contracts are currently operating in the Colne and under way for Hunstanton/Heacham, Bathside Bay and the Yare.

3. Damage to structures, for example:
    - missing groyne planking
    - spalling or abrasion of concrete walls
    - displacement of rock armour
    - exposure of structure foundations.

The timing and frequency of such inspections will vary, depending on the vulnerability of the coastline and the need for active management. It is important to repeat inspections as frequently as possible to observe the natural fluctuations in beach morphology and the ability of the beach to recover from storm events. Inspection of beach structures should be undertaken immediately after a severe storm event, when the lowered beach levels allow inspection of areas normally buried. Recent damage can be assessed and appropriate actions can be taken.

4.2.3 Beach profiles

Beach profiles comprise surveyed section lines perpendicular to either the shoreline or to a pre-determined baseline. They are used to quantatively establish beach response to storm events, beach recovery rates, long-term volume changes, areas of potential flood or erosion risk and the potential envelope of cross-shore elevations. If beach profiles are combined with nearshore bathymetric surveys, then morphological changes across the full zone of wave influence can be assessed. Rapid appraisal of profile data is vital for determining whether management works are required and for establishing some of the design constraints for the works.

When establishing profile lines or station points it is vital to ensure that they can be easily re-established for successive surveys. The profiles must have a defined bearing and must be tied to independent control points. Control points should be established inland of areas which might be subject to erosion during the course of the monitoring programme. It is desirable, but not always possible, to set out a common baseline for adjacent profile lines. Figure 4.1 illustrates possible baseline situations.

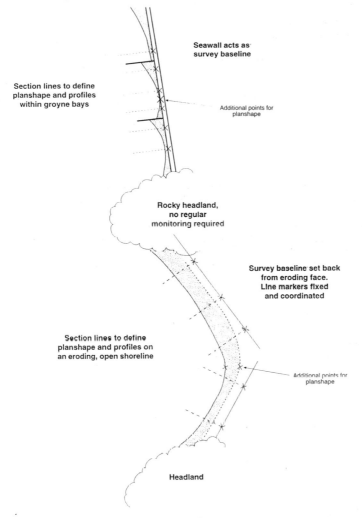

Figure 4.1   *Survey baseline*

Beach profiles can be surveyed (see Figure 4.2) using traditional levelling, a total station or Global Positioning System (GPS). Line and level surveys may provide distorted results due to the methods of measuring the chainage on steep-faced beaches. Total stations provide undistorted XYZ data in an easily processed format. GPS technology is in use for a number of regular monitoring programmes and will become more widespread.

The location of the profile lines should be carefully considered. The density of the lines should be sufficient to provide adequate coverage of the beach. On long open beaches the lines may be spaced at intervals of a kilometre or more with allowance made for nearshore features, such as bars, banks and troughs, which may result in localised variations. On groyned beaches it may be necessary to survey lines on either side of the groynes and at the centre of the bays, though not all groyne bays need to receive the same density of coverage (due to the repeatability of the bay plan shape in a groyne field). Profile lines for general monitoring should not be taken immediately adjacent to structures, as localized scour can mask the more general beach form; a separation of about 5-10m is normally sufficient. Profiles taken adjacent to structures may be of value if information is needed on scour.

Figure 4.2   *Beach profile levelling in St. Clements Bay, Jersey, Channel Islands (courtesy HR Wallingford)*

Supplementary shore parallel profiles are of great value, particularly at the toe and crest of the beach if Digital Terrain Models (DTMs) are to be used in data analysis. It should be noted that DTM analysis will require a much greater density of survey points to prevent the apparent accuracy of the displayed data from masking the limited coverage of the actual data.

The extent of the lines is important. Surveys should identify boundaries between the mobile beach toe and bed rock and the crest and sea wall/cliff, if appropriate. The landward end should reach beyond the expected point of storm wave influence. On natural coast lines this may require the surveying of sand dunes, the backs of shingle ridges or the top of eroding cliffs. The seaward end should extend to at least the level of MLWS, or further if conditions allow the staff person to enter the surf zone safely. Bathymetric surveys should overlap the beach profile and extend it out to a depth below which wave induced transport is negligible, typically between 5 and 10m below Chart Datum (CD). Bathymetric surveys generally require the use of specialist equipment and are therefore completed less frequently than beach profiles. However, they are valuable in defining long term and storm induced transport patterns.

Photographs of the beach should be taken from fixed positions in conjunction with surveys. Photographs are particularly useful for identifying small-scale features, such as cusps or other changes in beach material type (see Figure 4.3), which might influence the data interpretation. They can also be used to record beach development adjacent to structures or in areas not covered by the fixed profile lines. Development of such features may be analysed by adding profiles to the monitoring programme if the baseline survey is sufficiently detailed.

During survey analysis, and particularly volume calculation, it must be remembered that vertical accuracy is usually ±20mm for topographic surveys and ±150mm for bathymetric surveys. Plan position is usually ±0.2m and ±1m respectively. Care is also required in selecting an appropriate profile envelope when analysing changes in volume (Clayton, 1977).

CIRIA Report 153

Figure 4.3   *Changes in beach type and profile gradient, Sheringham, Norfolk (courtesy HR Wallingford)*

4.2.4   Beach plan shape

The beach plan shape (see Chapter 2) is normally characterised by one or more longshore lines defined by tidal levels (i.e. MHWS, MSL, MLWS) or by the beach crest. Beach plan shapes can be used to monitor storm response and long-term volume changes and to determine areas of potential risk.

Monitoring techniques depend on the length of coastline to be considered and the types of beach. Aerial photographs can be very useful in obtaining a general understanding of long lengths of coastline and photogrammetric analysis of stereo pairs can provide data for volume calculations or mapping, though they cannot be used to identify changes below water level. Photogrammetry can be accurate provided that good ground control is established, and the photography is at a suitable scale. Photography taken at a scale no larger than 1:2500 is needed to provide ±100mm vertical accuracy; typically vertical accuracy is between ±100 and ±150mm. However, costs are high and elevation resolution is poor, particularly on wide sand foreshores. Surveys conducted every five years and before and after major works, would be sufficient to provide a qualitative record of beach development. Costs could be shared with adjacent authorities. The photographs alone provide an excellent record of the coast which can often be of value many years after the flight. Photogrammetry, which is often much more expensive than the flight itself, can always be carried out at a later date provided ground control can be established. Satellite imagery is a another source of plan shape data. Yet another approach is that currently being employed by the NRA which has been surveying the coastline of England and Wales every 3 months since 1993 using similar equipment to that used in satellite imagery but deployed in a light aircraft (the CASI system). Ground control measurements are taken using the NRA's own survey craft and, whilst the surveys are primarily for coastal water quality modelling, data on shoreline position, suspended sediment pathways and (to a limited extent) nearshore bathymetry can also be gleaned from the measurements.

Plan shape definition can also be derived from beach profile data, though profiles at fixed locations may miss important longshore features. Ideally high density topographic survey data should be used to form digital terrain models, however, this method is very time consuming and expensive if it is to be repeated regularly or if a large area is to be covered. A sensible compromise is to use beach profile data supplemented by surveys of particular points of interest, such as the positions of severe beach crest cut-back or accretion. If a total station or GPS, is used to measure profiles, then additional points can easily be added. If traditional levelling is used, then points can be measured as offsets from a baseline as illustrated in Figure 4.1.

Features such as spits, tombolos and barriers are best surveyed by spot levelling and analysed with DTMs. DTMs should be used with caution if the data is of low density coverage.

4.2.5   Beach response near structures

Beaches in the immediate vicinity of groynes, breakwaters and sea walls are subject to very rapid change as a result of wave and current interactions with the structures. Scour can cause unexpectedly high rates of littoral drift and during extreme events can cause catastrophic damage by undermining foundations. This is the cause of a very high percentage of sea wall failures in the UK (Thomas and Hall, 1992). Damage of beach control structures by wave action, such as the removal of armour units from the crest, can modify beach response. Deposition of fines in the lee of structures can similarly be a problem, particularly on amenity beaches. Monitoring such localised responses allows beach managers to be proactive in their maintenance programme, thereby reducing the potential for costly damage. It also provides useful design information for future schemes on similar sites.

If beach response is varied, then a formal programme of measurements may not be effective. Recorded observations and fixed aspect photographs are more likely to provide the information required. Dip measurements can be taken relative to stable points, such as groyne crests or sea wall steps. Observations should include such things as exposure of foundations or underlying strata, evidence of terminal scour, areas of deposition, spacial and temporal variations in sediment type and evidence of structural damage.

This work should be carried out in conjunction with beach profiling, but must be more responsive to storm events. Measurements and observations of waves and currents in the immediate area of the structures should also be undertaken to assist in understanding and therefore predicting the beach responses. As with all other beach monitoring, the records should include basic data such as date, time, tidal state and recent wave and wind conditions.

4.2.6   Beach material sampling

Beach material sampling is undertaken to determine seasonal or long-term changes in beach composition, sources of materials, appropriate recharge materials where required and to provide design information for coastal models. A beach sampling programme must be planned to cover potential variations cross-shore, longshore, vertically and seasonally. Vertical and seasonal variations are particularly important on mixed or shingle beaches. Unlike profile and plan shape surveys there is little to be gained from frequent surveys after the beach composition has been satisfactorily defined. Observations and photographs taken in conjunction with other field work will normally provide sufficient information to detect any long term changes in composition. The exception to this is post-recharge monitoring, for which regular sampling may help to identify whether the recharge material was appropriate, or whether a finer or coarser material should be used for future maintenance 'top ups'. It is also useful to monitor the rate of abrasion where crushed rock nourishment has occurred.

Sampling methods are straightforward. Samples should be collected from the surface and from depths of up to 1m below the surface. The size of sample depends on the particle size and the need to obtain statistical validity; 1kg is ample for sand, while much greater quantities are required to achieve a statistically valid sample containing cobbles up to 100mm. Samples larger than about 10kg are obviously impractical if large numbers of locations are involved in the survey, but care must be taken to try to achieve a representative sub-population. Photographs of a 1m square scale lying on the beach are useful as supporting evidence for analysis.

Obtaining sub-surface samples may require mechanical assistance, but care should be taken not to disturb the sample area by first driving over it.

Sample analysis can be undertaken by a commercial soils laboratory. The laboratory should provide a description of the material using standard terminology, a grading curve, the median particle size (D_{50}) and the spread (D_{85}/D_{15}). More detailed analysis can be carried out by specialist laboratories to determine the mineralogy, which can be useful in determining the provenance of the beach material, though the results may be inconclusive as the sources may be diverse and will often include heterogeneous glacial deposits.

Beach sampling should be undertaken in conjunction with nearshore sampling and a study of the underlying nearshore and back shore geology. Further details of field and laboratory methods can be found in British Standards (1975, 1981 and 1984) and in specialist publications (Dyer, 1979, for example).

4.2.7 Establishing a sediment budget

A sediment budget is the sediment transport volume balance for a segment of the coast. Sediment quantities can be categorized according to the sources, sinks, sediment types and processes involved (see Section 2.6). Definition of a sediment budget will assist in:

* identifying the relevant forcing conditions, processes and factors affecting the beach
* estimating transport volumes and rates for design purposes
* monitoring the success of any management schemes.

In general, coastal managers are interested in wave or tidally induced longshore and cross-shore transport. However, in some situations wind transport and dredging can be important processes. Consideration must be given to all potential sediment types from fines to cobbles.

The methods for estimating the sediment budgets combine predictive techniques (Section 4.5) with desk studies and field measurements. All of the methods are subject to large uncertainties and require the involvement of specialist assistance.

Desk studies involve analysis of available records such as Ordnance Survey maps, existing beach surveys and aerial photographs to build up a time series of beach positions allowing long-term development of the beach planshape to be analysed. The construction of substantial cross-shore structures, such as training walls or breakwaters, can cause the build up of beach material which may be measurable by analysing successive maps or photographs. Alternatively, cliff erosion rates can be converted into transport volumes. Unfortunately these situations may not be applicable or may be misleading.

Field measurements of plan and profile shape can be more reliable, particularly at sites where a monitoring programme has been in place for a number of years. Comparisons of successive beach plan shapes measured near cross-shore structures can be used to estimate drift.

Another, potentially more reliable approach, is to deploy tracers to identify sediment transport paths. In the past radioactive, fluorescent, coloured or metallic tracers have been used. More recent techniques include the use of magnetic sand particles (Van der Post and Oldfield, 1994) and electronic pebbles (Voulgaris et al, 1994). Tracer studies are only of significant value if they are extensive in terms of the amount of tracer deployed, the coverage of the beach (both horizontally and vertically) and the time over which the survey is run. Tracer surveys must be combined with the measurement of waves, water levels and beach profiles to provide a complete picture of the shoreline situation over the survey period for comparison with the long-term conditions.

4.3   ENVIRONMENTAL DATA COLLECTION

4.3.1   General considerations

The following sections set out the various types of environmental data which might be needed in order to assess, evaluate or monitor the environmental characteristics of the existing beach for the purpose of a beach management initiative. In all cases, in common with other types of information, existing environmental data held by the various agencies with interests in and around the particular area of the investigation should firstly be identified, collated and reviewed. Statutory and non-statutory bodies, non-governmental organisations (NGOs), universities and other educational establishments, local interest groups and members of the public all hold information which will potentially be of high value to any environmental investigation.

In addition to data held by the local authority or NRA in Britain, organisations including port authorities, the Sea Fisheries Committees and others may hold similar relevant information, sometimes going back over a number of years. NGOs are often a valuable source of information and statistics, as are other local interest groups (e.g. local wildlife trusts or archaeological societies, sailing clubs and wildfowling groups). Local universities and colleges may have collected, collated and possibly processed potentially useful data. In the latter cases, care may be needed to ensure the accuracy of the data, particularly if the circumstances under which it was collected indicate that there was no quality control (e.g. data collected for a student project). Finally, members of the public may be able to provide information which, when verified, can help to develop an understanding of the environmental parameter(s) being investigated. This information may be collected via public meetings, questionnaire surveys, meetings with local residents, etc..

Box 4.2 lists examples of British agencies who may hold data in respect of various environmental characteristics. Consultation with such agencies is discussed in detail in Section 6.6.2.

If insufficient information exists within the study area to facilitate a baseline assessment of (e.g. the status of) a certain environmental characteristic(s), original survey work may be required. This survey work should be carried out in advance of any management or construction activity and should, ideally, take place over a number of years prior to any potentially major change being instigated. This period of survey enables an assessment to be made of any natural fluctuations in population, community structure, abundance, distribution, etc. The amount of survey work required is, however, site specific and will depend to some extent on the nature and scale of the proposed works or activity. In all cases, the collection of baseline data needs to provide sufficient information to enable the comprehensive prediction of impacts and the assessment of their significance, as well as a baseline against which to measure any change.

Once impacts have been predicted, it may (in certain situations) be necessary to continue the survey work as a monitoring exercise during the management or construction activity, to ensure that any damage to the environment is indeed minimised or that environmental benefits are, in fact, being realised.

On completion of any management or construction activity, or between stages of a programme of activities, it is important to carry out subsequent monitoring of some or all of the parameters previously surveyed. Such monitoring for the purposes of comparison with the previous (or predicted) situation, is important for assessing the recovery of a site following the activity or construction process and/or for assessing any beneficial impacts which may have occurred as a result. Ongoing surveys associated with monitoring will also provide valuable information to assist in the future prediction of impacts relating to proposed schemes in the same (or similar) locations.

Box 4.2   *Example sources of British data on environmental characteristics of the existing beach*

Environmental parameter	Primary information sources
Flora/invertebrates/birds/fish/ fauna	English Nature, Scottish Natural Heritage, Countryside Council for Wales, Royal Society for the Protection of Birds, Royal Society for Nature Conservation, Wildfowl and Wetlands Trust, Woodland Trust, British Association for Shooting and Conservation, National Trust, Marine Conservation Society, Joint Nature Conservation Committee, Local Wildlife Trust, British Trust for Ornithology.
Recreation (informal and formal)	District and Regional Council, County Council, Sports Council, Ramblers Association, Royal Yachting Association, British Water Ski Federation, Personal Water Craft Association, National Federation of Sea Anglers, British Association for Shooting and Conservation.
Safety	Health and Safety Executive, District and Regional Council (Environmental Health Officer, Safety Officer).
Landscape	Countryside Commission, Countryside Council for Wales, District Council, Scottish Natural Heritage.
Commercial fishing activity	Ministry of Agriculture Fisheries and Food, Scottish Office Agriculture and Fisheries Department, Sea Fisheries Committees, National Rivers Authority, Sea Fish Industry Authority, Local Fisherman's Associations.
Commercial activity, tourism and adjacent land uses	District and Regional Council, Tourist Board, County Council, Chamber of Commerce, Sports Council.
Archaeology and heritage	English Heritage, Royal Commission for Historic Monuments of England, Cadw (Wales), Department of National Heritage, County Archaeologist, District Council.
Navigation	Port Authority, Harbour Commissioners, National Rivers Authority, British Waterways, Trinity House.
Infrastructure	British Telecom, British Gas, Electricity Plcs, National Grid, Water Company, District Council, County Council, Regional Council, British Pipelines Agency, Ministry of Defence.
Water quality	National Rivers Authority, District Council, River Purification Board.
Sediment quality	Port Authorities, Ministry of Agriculture, Fisheries and Food, Local Universities, District and Regional Council (Environmental Health Officer).
Coastal and hydrological processes	National Rivers Authority, Internal Drainage Boards, English Nature, Countryside Council for Wales, Scottish Natural Heritage, District Councils, Ministry of Agriculture, Fisheries and Food, Welsh Office.
Geological interests	English Nature, Countryside Council for Wales, Scottish Natural Heritage, British Geological Survey

4.3.2   Natural environment

Flora

In order to evaluate beach management initiatives, data will often be required on the type, abundance and distribution of vegetation at a particular site. These data are generally collected using the standardised National Vegetation Classification (NVC) and are assessed in terms of the abundance and dominance of type of vegetation in a given area.

Existing data for the flora on sandy beaches are generally limited to sand dune surveys. Such data is usually available from the relevant nature conservation agencies (see Box 4.2 for agencies).

If no data exists for a site, a thorough botanical survey may be required following NVC guidelines. The seasonal variation of plants is such that surveys should be carried out during the growing season, which is generally May to September. Outside these times it may still be possible to carry out a survey of certain habitats, but identification will be more difficult and certain plants may not be present. Typical vegetation survey guidelines are shown in Box 4.3.

Box 4.3 *Typical vegetation sampling and analysis techniques and equipment*

a) The size of quadrat to be used should be 1m x 1m square.

b) Transects should be established at regular intervals at right angles to the shoreline.

c) For each transect line an agreed number of quadrats should be established on a random basis.

d) For each quadrat, all vascular plant species should be identified and abundance recorded.

e) A photograph of each quadrat should be taken at the time of survey.

f) A photograph of each transect should also be taken from the nearest elevated point.

g) The species list for the community recorded in each quadrat should be compared to standard reference lists provided in the NVC, and the community classified wherever possible.

h) The distribution of plant communities should be mapped (using the NVC) utilising quadrat data and, if appropriate, aerial photographs. Changes in the extent of plant communities in different parts of the beach since previous vegetation mapping should be assessed and evaluated.

Invertebrates

In some cases, data may be required on the abundance, diversity and distribution of invertebrates within a site. Existing data are generally limited for invertebrates, but data may be available where coastal defence or other schemes have been proposed or carried out. Where no data exist, it may be necessary to carry out baseline surveys to establish the invertebrate communities present at a site. This should involve a visual assessment of epifauna and sampling to assess the distribution of infauna. A visual assessment is usually carried out over the whole site (depending on size). Sampling is carried out along transects from highwater mark to low water mark. A typical sampling procedure is given in Box 4.4.

In certain circumstances, where a more detailed study is required, it may be necessary to carry out meiofaunal analysis.

Data should be collected throughout the year, ideally for a number of years to enable seasonal changes to be assessed. Abundance of organisms is generally at its highest in the summer and autumn, and at its lowest in winter and spring. This is, however, dependent on the species.

Box 4.4 *Typical littoral sampling procedure and equipment*

a) Identify and record sample sites along permanent transects.

b) Take replicate samples of the sediment at the exact location of each sample site.

c) Sampling should be carried out.

d) Larger macrofaunal species could be sampled by digging an area, of about 1m^2, at each sampling location, to a depth of approximately 30cm. The sediment should be separated to reveal any large individuals.

e) Samples should be placed in plastic bags and a numbered ID tag added. Site location, time, date and sampler's name should be recorded.

f) Samples should be analysed in a laboratory to identify the species present.

g) Samples should be sieved prior to analysis.

h) Identify species to assess diversity and abundance.

Birds

Data on bird populations may be available from the national or local bird organisations or trusts. If data does not exist, surveys should be carried out during the winter months (October to March) with the shoreline, depending on length, being divided into sections. The surveys should ideally be undertaken twice a month to coincide with spring and neap tides. Counts should be undertaken two hours before and two hours after low tide. Where data does not exist on breeding birds at a potential shingle or sand breeding site, the area should be surveyed during the main breeding season (April to July). Approximately two visits to the site each month should be undertaken with species, obvious pairs, singing birds and birds with young, being recorded.

Fish

Any existing data on commercial fish species and abundance are likely to come, via fisheries interests, from the national authority, sea fisheries committees, local angling clubs or local inshore fishermen. As fish are such mobile species, it is very difficult to conduct survey work in a limited time. Given the nature of the species likely to be present in the nearshore zone, survey work may involve fishing techniques such as dredging or trawling, but such techniques can have a destructive effect on the communities living in the beach sediment. It is, therefore, recommended that data is collected from local anglers as far as practicable, or that alternative non-destructive techniques such as seine netting or diving are employed.

Other fauna

Other fauna, such as seals and otters, will rarely be encountered on sites where beach management is proposed. These are elusive species, selecting beaches which are seldom, if ever, used by the public. It is therefore unlikely that a survey will be required to assess the distribution of such species.

4.3.3 Human environment

Informal recreation

Data on the type and intensity of informal recreation are often not available. Some indication of the numbers of visitors to a resort can be established from published hotel and guest house accommodation records or visitor attractions (e.g. visitor centres, castles and museums). These types of data are usually held by the relevant local authority. Other proxy indicators of intensity of use include seaside "pay and display" car parks and data from beach concessions (e.g. deck chair or equipment hire). These data, again available from the local authority, will also help to indicate seasonal use of the area, highlighting the length of the season, popular weekends and holiday periods.

For more accurate data on the intensity and type of use of the beach, information can be collected through the use of counts and/or surveys. Data should ideally be collected over a period incorporating weekends and weekdays during the summer (high) and also low and "shoulder" seasons. Information collected should include, *inter alia*; number of adults, number of children, types of activity and level of participation, time, date and prevailing weather conditions.

Formal recreation

Data on the type and intensity of formal recreational activities are sometimes more widely available than that for informal pursuits. Potential sources of existing data include the relevant local authority and local clubs, the latter providing information on membership and number of active participants.

For more accurate or current data, on-site summer (and winter if appropriate) surveys and counts could be carried out. Questionnaire surveys could also be utilised to establish the pattern, seasonal variations in and intensity of use by both local sports clubs and non-affiliated users. Anecdotal evidence from beach officers (e.g. wardens, patrols, etc.) may also be used as a basis for further studies.

Access

Data on the number, use and quality of accesses should be available from maps or from the relevant local authority and/or landowners. If suitable data are not available, on-site surveys and inspections will be required.

Safety

Information on hazards at a particular site (see Section 2.2.3) and on the safety equipment either required or currently in use should be available from the Safety Officer within the local authority. On beaches which have attained European Union Blue Flags or Seaside Awards (a Tidy Britain Group Initiative), a record should also be available of accidents and incidents occurring on the beach, facilities, and during activities, etc.

Landscape

Information on some characteristics of the landscape will be available from national agencies or local authorities. Alternatively, it can be interpreted from local plans which may contain protective or enhancement policies.

Commercial fishing activity

Information concerning the type and intensity of use of both the beach and inshore zone by fishermen can generally be obtained through discussions with local fishermen and/or through regular site visits. If insufficient data are available from such sources, original data may need to be collected on fishing activity. The time frame in which such fish surveys or fisheries monitoring is carried out may be crucial to the success or accuracy of the work, and it should also be noted that there are difficulties in extrapolating existing activity to future years, or between different seasons.

Commercial activity, tourism and adjacent land uses

Information on commercial activities, concessions and adjacent land uses, etc. should be available from the local authority or direct from those responsible for the commercial activity.

Archaeology and heritage

Information on archaeology and heritage interests should, in the first instance, be collected from the relevant local authority. In the absence of such data, survey work should be carried out to establish not only the extent of any existing archaeological remains, but also to consider the archaeological potential of the beach zone. The nature of any subsequent survey work will, in each case, depend on the results of previous studies, therefore the final requirements can be very different from site to site. Surveys in the subtidal zone may need to be undertaken by divers, but these would usually only be required when other evidence suggests a high potential for submerged features. Archaeological survey work should be commissioned and monitored in consultation with the relevant authority.

Navigation

Local port or navigation authorities and harbour masters are among the groups who may hold information on nearshore navigation or navigational fixtures in the beach zone.

Infrastructure

Appropriate local, regional or national organisations can provide details of the nature and location of their infrastructure facilities, for example the companies responsible for utilities.

4.3.4 Environmental quality

Water quality

Water quality data and discharge information for England and Wales are usually available from the public registers and reports on discharge consents of the NRA. Water quality information for recreational beaches, particularly European Union (EU) bathing water beaches, is available from local authorities. If no existing or recent data are available but such information is needed, data collection will be required. On EU bathing water beaches, appropriate techniques/methodologies should be used. Typical survey requirements for other situations are set out in Box 4.5.

Box 4.5 *Typical water and sediment quality sampling and analysis procedures for background monitoring and assessment*

a) Identify and record permanent sampling locations.

b) Measure and record in-situ parameters (e.g. pH, Eh, dissolved oxygen, temperature) with calibrated portable analytical equipment.

c) Collect sufficient water/sediment in pre-prepared decontaminated containers, with sample preservative if necessary.

d) Record site location, time, date, sample reference and sampler's name.

e) Prepare and analyse samples. The procedures to measure and record the range of chemical and microbiological parameters, as required, should follow standard methodology (e.g. Standing Committee of Analysts: Methods for the Examination of Water Associated Materials (MEWAM)).

f) Quality control should be practised during fieldwork, laboratory analysis and data handling and interpretation.

For a background survey on water quality, data should be collected throughout the year as they can vary considerably over space and time. It is important to detect any trends in water quality that may be dependent, in part, on the effects of seasonality. Alternatively, if an emergency survey has to be carried out, the duration of the survey would necessarily be shorter, with a higher density of sampling sites and a greater sampling frequency.

Sediment quality

Existing sediment quality is generally not measured because non-cohesive beach sediment pollution is rare. Some information may be available from specialist research reports, although its use may be limited. Particle size information is useful in determining whether or not there are fine materials in the sediment. Such analyses may have been carried out during coastal geomorphology studies. The carbonate content of sands and sand dunes may be available from specific reports on dune systems.

If no information is available on beach sediment, sample analyses could be carried out to gain information on particle size distribution, mineralogy and carbonate content and any other physico-chemical parameters pertinent to the beach or criteria in question. The basic strategy for sediment sampling and analysis is similar to that for water quality assessments. Typical sediment sampling and analysis procedures are set out in Box 4.5. Beach sediments are less susceptible to seasonal influences, however, and thus one or two sample surveys should be sufficient to gain a basic understanding of a sediment's characteristics.

Debris

Information on the type and quantity of debris on the beach should be available from the local authority (who are responsible for litter clearance) or possibly regional water companies, who may undertake debris surveys.

4.3.5 Physical environment

Coastal processes

The data required to ensure a satisfactory understanding of the processes operating at the coast, and hence identify the interdependency between the existing physical process regime and the various coastal environmental assets, are discussed in Section 2.2.

Geology and geomorphology

In order to assess whether or not there are any important geological or geomorphological resources at a particular site, consultation should be undertaken with the county agencies for nature conservation, local natural history groups, etc. The British Geological Survey may also hold relevant information. If original survey work is required, this should take the form of a site inspection to establish the location, nature, extent and significance of geological and geomorphological interests at and around the site.

4.4 NEARSHORE SEABED CHARACTER

Few beaches terminate at or above the low water mark; most continue into the nearshore zone. Even if the beach itself does not extend beyond the foreshore, there are usually a number of features of the nearshore zone which affect it. The beach manager, therefore, usually requires information concerning the seabed in the nearshore zone, especially if it is changing over time. There are three main topics of interest, namely the bathymetry (i.e. underwater topography) of the nearshore zone, the sediments and their disposition over that zone and finally any evidence for the transport of those sediments, for example, bedforms. The following sections consider these topics in turn.

4.4.1 Bathymetry

The bathymetry of the nearshore zone is of interest to the beach manager for a number of reasons. First, many beaches extend to a considerable distance below the lowest tidal level. For the purposes of calculating beach material volumes, it is necessary to carry out hydrographic surveys of the submerged part of the beach profile. Figure 4.4 shows cross-sections taken for the nourished beach at Seaford, Sussex. The division between the shingle beach face and the chalk shore platform is clearly identifiable, between about 4m and 5m below Ordnance Datum Newlyn (ODN) around Britain.

Other features of the nearshore seabed may also be important, such as the gradual lowering of the level of the shore platform suspected as being a cause for long-term beach erosion in many places on the east and south coasts of the UK (see Chapter 2). Comparison of historical and modern-day seabed levels in the nearshore zone may demonstrate this trend. In areas of hard rock, these changes are likely to be exceedingly slow and surveys even decades apart will reveal no changes. In softer lithologies, the changes will be more rapid, but even so the inevitable inaccuracies of normal hydrographic surveying may make it difficult to resolve such changes, at least for many years.

Many beaches are also affected by the presence and movements of banks of seabed sediment, or of channels produced by tidal currents, the latter particularly in the vicinity of the mouths of estuaries or tidal inlets. These movements are often much more rapid than the gradual erosion of shore platforms and in some circumstances occur so often that it is financially impractical to carry out surveys frequently enough to fully record (or understand) them. Changes in banks

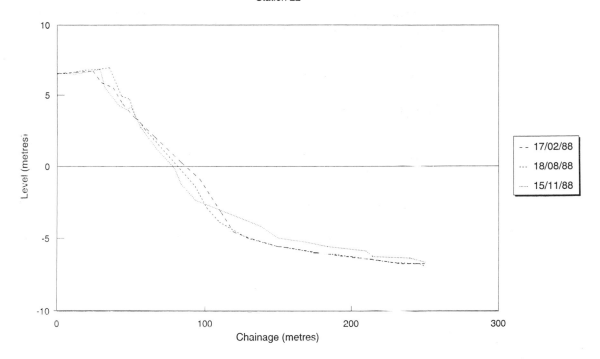

Figure 4.4   *Variations in beach cross-sections measured at Seaford, E. Sussex*

and channels cause changes in both the waves and tidal currents in their vicinity and further landward, which in turn affect beaches and their development.

Two common situations are worth specific mention. The first, illustrated in Figure 4.5, shows the effects of a meandering deep water channel moving into an estuary or tidal inlet. As the channel changes alignment, moving closer to the shore on one side of the inlet mouth, currents along that beach will be increased; wave action is also likely to be increased on that part of the coast, as the beach is pinched between the channel and the shoreline. Finally, the presence of the channel directly affects the underwater portion of the beach profile, with the steeper slopes assisting the wave-induced undertow carry beach material offshore.

A second common effect is the result of a change in the height of sand banks, either some distance offshore (e.g. off Great Yarmouth), or just seaward of an estuary mouth (often referred to as the entrance bar). These banks alter naturally, for example seasonally, or as a result of a major fluvial flood. They also react to reclamations, or natural siltation within an estuary. These features provide a natural breakwater for the coast, reducing the incoming wave energy, particularly at times of low tidal level but they are often important throughout the tide. A reduction in the height of such bars or banks will therefore produce increased wave activity at the shoreline and possibly beach erosion. In many other countries wave heights at the shoreline are affected by rock or coral reefs and these changes in wave height also have to be measured if beach development is to be understood.

If a sandbank changes position, by moving alongshore, then this can provoke a corresponding reaction in the coastline, with the beach material tending to follow the bank; a ness or cusp in the lee of the bank will hence migrate along the coast to maintain its position relative to the bank.

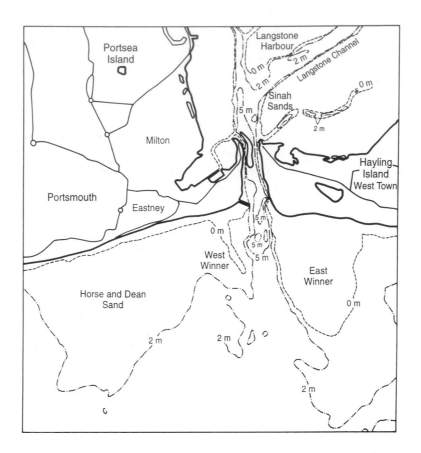

Figure 4.5   *Meandering channel, Langstone Harbour, the Solent, Hampshire*

Survey methods

By surveying the nearshore zone the past evolution of a beach becomes easier to understand. The survey information itself is directly useful, for example in establishing numerical models of waves and currents in the nearshore zone. Repeated surveys, in appropriate circumstances, will help quantify and explain beach changes.

In the first instance, it is sensible to obtain historical information on the nearshore seabed contours. In the UK, the best starting point is the Hydrographic Office of the Admiralty at Taunton in Somerset. This organisation holds large numbers of charts, both modern and historical, for the UK coastline and much of the rest of the world as well. Published Admiralty Charts are designed specifically for navigation and as such tend to emphasise high points on the seabed (i.e. minimum water depths in any area). It is, therefore, preferable to obtain the more detailed *collector charts*, produced from the original survey data, which contain much more detail on seabed levels. Admiralty Charts provide depths below a Chart Datum, usually taken as the predicted lowest astronomical tidal level. This can be related to a land-based datum (i.e. ODN in the UK) and it is often convenient to do so, for ease of comparison with topographic surveys of a beach. Particular care is needed in areas of rapidly changing tidal range (e.g. the Bristol Channel) since the Chart Datum is not necessarily horizontal, i.e. a fixed distance below ODN. Historical charts may also be reduced to different datum levels as the predictions of lowest astronomical tide level change. Occasionally, other sources of bathymetric charts are available, for example from port or harbour authorities or previous coastal studies. Time spent identifying these previous surveys is often well spent, since accurate bathymetric surveying in the nearshore zone is difficult and expensive.

Not surprisingly, charts produced for navigation tend not to contain detailed information in very shallow water. It is often necessary to commission specific surveys to cover the nearshore zone (i.e. beyond the low water mark) out to the deeper water area where charts provide the required information. Such surveys are rarely easy, because of waves and currents, changing tidal levels, and the difficulties of precise position fixing. These problems are made worse by the need to use craft which can operate in areas of shallow water. Generally, this means the use of shallow-draft boats, which are more easily disturbed by wave action. Other options, such as the use of hovercraft have been advocated, but are only used rarely.

Surveys should be carried out in such a manner that it is possible to compare the hydrographic survey of the foreshore (i.e. above low water mark) with a topographic survey of the same area. The surveys should be tied into the same grid and datums as land surveys. More advanced position fixing systems such as GPS or trisponders and digital echo-sounders linked to computer surveying packages allow nearshore hydrographic surveys to be carried out quickly and accurately. Surveys need to be carefully planned with as much knowledge of local conditions (tides, currents, etc.) as possible. Even under ideal conditions a vertical accuracy of ±150mm and horizontal accuracy of ±1m are considered satisfactory. Tidal control is a particular problem and the surveyors must ensure that the tide gauge or tide pole is located at an appropriate location allowing for local variations in tide levels. Surveys are often hampered by material, such as weed, suspended in the water and causing rogue echo sounder reflections.

The required frequency, spatial coverage and accuracy of the surveys also needs to be considered, since both have direct implications on the costs involved. In highly dynamic situations (e.g. near an estuary mouth) or where it is important to account for the total volume of material on a beach (e.g. following an artificial nourishment) then surveys may need to be carried out at 6-month intervals, or even more frequently. Additional surveys should also be carried out immediately following significant storm events. On rocky coastlines, where the seabed offshore is unlikely to change rapidly, then a single survey may suffice for many decades (as is the case for many navigational charts).

The required spatial coverage and accuracy of the surveys will depend considerably on the purpose for which the data are needed. For a nourished beach such as Seaford for example, the hydrographic survey was set up as a seaward extension to the topographic beach surveys (i.e. with information collected on standard cross-section lines along the coast).

For other purposes, for example setting up numerical models of waves or tidal currents in the nearshore zone, it may be appropriate to concentrate survey efforts on particular areas, for example across channels or sandbanks. By concentrating resources, the frequency of surveys can be increased without reducing accuracy. As with beach surveys, the accumulated volume of survey data will enable modest variations to be averaged out, hence revealing any underlying trends.

The accuracy of position fixing and of depth measurements, will vary depending on the particular site, the weather conditions, instrumentation used and the skill of the surveyors. Specialist advice needs to be taken, in general, to ensure that the appropriate survey is specified for any particular site.

4.4.2   Seabed sediments

Examining the nature and disposition of sediments on and beneath the nearshore seabed will often assist understanding of the origins and development of a beach. Investigations of sediment deposits in the nearshore zone will sometimes show quite a close similarity to the local beach material. The question then arises as to whether the sediment interchanges between the seabed and the beach, or whether there is a predominant net transfer of sediment from one to the other. If material is being lost from a beach to an offshore deposition area, the most common situation, then the possibility of intervention, namely recycling material back to the beach, becomes worth considering. If the beach is being fed by an offshore source of material, then clearly this situation needs to be preserved and perhaps enhanced. Indications of the direction of sediment transport are discussed in Section 4.4.3 below.

In some situations, particularly on the Atlantic seaboard of the UK, there will be very little sediment in the nearshore zone, except in the underwater part of the beach. As a consequence, sediment is more likely to be lost offshore than gained from the seabed and this often serves to emphasise the geological relict nature of the beach (see Section 2.3). On coasts in areas where the rocks are sedimentary in origin, the presence and distribution of sediment on the seabed (or the lack of it) can provide useful clues concerning the sediment budget for the beaches. For example, many nearshore banks of sediment would appear, on a casual inspection, to be part of the general sediment system for that coastline (i.e. formed of similar sediments to those in the beach) and probably interchanging material with it. For this reason, it might be assumed that both the beaches and offshore bed features were formed by the same hydraulic processes.

Some of the sediments forming beaches and the seabed offshore may have formed due to accretion over the past few thousand years or during post-glacial, glacial or pre-glacial times. The conditions under which these sediments were laid down may have been very different from modern conditions though their lithology may be similar to modern sediments. An example of this are late glacial gravels within river valleys which presently only carry fines or mud. Care must therefore be exercised when evaluating sediments from beaches or from offshore to ensure that the sampled unit is part of the modern sedimentary regime and not part of an older or relic unit. Anomalous grain size, colour, lithic content and consolidation may be indicators of an older relic unit.

It is therefore important to distinguish between relic and present day material. Both exist and their relative importance at a particular site needs to be assessed.

Survey methods

A great deal of information on the nature, origins and present day movements of seabed sediments can be obtained by suitable survey methods (see McQuillin and Ardus, 1977). There are two classes of method for obtaining information on seabed sediments; those which give data on surface sediments and those which give data on the sub-surface sediments. Each class can be further sub-divided into direct sampling and remote-sensing techniques.

Surface sampling techniques include:

- surface grab sampling, using grabs collecting samples up to 30kg in weight followed by visual inspection of samples or particle size analysis; echo sounding interpretative software can extend the usefulness of grab sampling
- side-scan sonar, which can be used to identify bedforms (see Section 4.4.3) and the sediments forming the seabed.

Analysis of the particle size distribution and sorting of sediment derived by grab sampling can be used (Gao *et al*, 1994) to give information on sediment transport pathways. Although this technique is still being developed it can be useful when combined with other information, such as bedforms.

For assessments of the origin of superficial sediments, geotechnical subsurface investigations can prove very useful and a description of some frequently used techniques is given in Section 4.6.

4.4.3 Sediment transport and bedforms

The presence of sediment on the seabed does not necessarily imply that it is mobile. Sand, gravel and coarser material on the seabed may be lithified into an immobile mass by a matrix of finer sediments and biological organisms. As a consequence the threshold of motion is high and may not be reached even during severe storms and tidal flows. Often large areas of the seabed are colonised by marine flora and fauna and the presence of such wildlife gives a good indication of the lack of mobility of the seabed sediments.

Sediment shows evidence of its mobility by being moulded into bedforms on the seabed. The smallest of these are ripples, as commonly observed on the foreshore of a sandy beach. These are usually shorted-lived features, reflecting conditions which may have only lasted for a few hours in the recent past. As the mobility of sediment increases (e.g. under stronger currents or larger waves) the size and persistence of the bedforms also increases (see Figure 4.6).

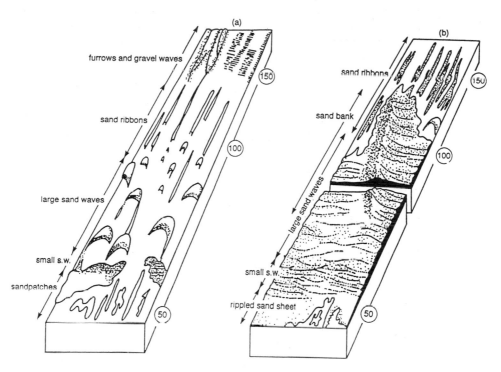

Figure 4.6   *Size and persistence of bedforms (from Stride, 1982)*
(a) low sand supply (b) abundant sand supply

The smaller of the more persistent bedforms may reflect only recent sediment transport conditions, such as those present during part of the tidal cycle or during the most recent storm. The larger forms indicate a longer term sediment transport pattern and, usually, the net direction of that transport. Care has to be taken since these bedforms may, like the sediment, be relic features and hence not indicate present-day sediment transport patterns.

Other features may also indicate sediment transport patterns over the seabed. The pattern of sediment infill into dredged areas (e.g. navigation channels) can provide useful information. Distributions of sediments showing decreasing or increasing grain size trends may indicate a direction of transport. Detailed analysis of the composition of the sediment, using naturally occurring minerals which act as tracer particles, can also indicate transport paths. Finally, a number of experimental techniques exist to study at least the short-term movements of seabed materials, such as fluorescent or radio-active tracers, seabed drifters, etc.

The sediments of the seabed surface and the bedforms into which they are moulded reflect the hydrodynamic conditions at the seabed. The information they provide is generally a net direction and a qualitative indicator of volumetric rates of sediment transport. They do also give a starting point for numerical models of sediment transport over the seabed, which can provide further information on the mechanisms involved.

4.5 WIND, WAVE AND TIDAL CLIMATE DATA COLLECTION

The importance of the hydraulic processes of wave and tides in the development of beaches has been described in Chapter 2. In a beach monitoring programme, therefore, it is clearly essential to have a good knowledge of these factors. Whether it is necessary to carry out long-term measurements of waves and tides is, however, open to doubt. The initial step is always to establish what information is already available (i.e. previous measurements) and what information is likely to be available in future (i.e. without carrying out measurements oneself).

Sources of wave, water level and current data are described in Chapter 3, with methods of measurement, analysis and interpretation for different situations. However, the special case of measurements near structures is covered in more detail below.

4.5.1 Wave and current measurements near structures

The interactions between waves, currents and coastal structures are complex and not well defined in theory. Local beach response is therefore difficult to predict, even with the use of numerical or mobile bed physical models. Good quality records of waves and currents near structures, in conjunction with beach response monitoring, will improve the reliability of the prediction models. However, these records can be difficult to obtain as the environment can be very hostile, particularly when breaking waves are present and the areas of interest may be very restricted in both time and location.

Wave processes in the vicinity of structures include diffraction, refraction, reflection, transmission, impact and overtopping. Measurements of any of these processes in the field requires specialist equipment and knowledge, much of which is still in the development stage and is not available for general use. Some information on recent research can be found in Box 4.6.

Box 4.6   *Wave monitoring near coastal structures*

Wave monitoring near coastal structures has undergone recent development in the UK. Methods have been developed for the measurement of reflected wave energy seaward of structures and refracted/diffracted energy in the lee of structures. Techniques include spectral and directional analysis using data from arrays of up to 6 transducers mounted on the seabed. This data will be used in the development of predictive models to improve the design of shallow water structures (Chadwick *et al*, 1994 and Bird *et al*, 1994).

Work on breaking wave impact pressures on coastal structures has also been undertaken (Kirkgoz, 1995, Crawford *et al*, 1994, Allsop *et al*, 1995). Investigations have included the effects of accretion levels and the scale effects introduced when measuring wave impacts in physical models.

Overtopping of seawalls has been investigated at length in physical models, but has rarely been measured in situ. Field measurements of overtopping by individual waves have been obtained recently for a site in North Wales (Herbert, 1995) with some success, but as yet the results and analysis have not been published.

Important information on wave processes can also be gathered from direct observation. This applies particularly to overtopping and wave transformation around and through structures. The use of video recording can be very useful as a means of developing a database for later analysis. Observations are much more useful if they are combined with continuous monitoring of wind velocity, water levels and incident waves at some point further offshore.

Measuring and observing currents around structures can be undertaken more easily than wave measurements. Currents are generated by waves or tides and can therefore vary significantly with time and location. They can be measured over time at discrete points or as flow paths. A measurement programme that combines both methods is most appropriate in the presence of structures.

Flow paths can be monitored by deploying surface floats or sub-surface drogues. These can be anything from oranges to sophisticated devices tracked by radar or other electronic signalling systems. As the purpose of monitoring is to provide flow velocity data for predicting beach response, then sub-surface drogues are more useful as they follow near-bed, rather than surface, flow. The field programme must be extensive enough to allow tidal currents to be monitored over complete ebb- and flood-cycles on both spring and neap tides, and must allow observation of currents over a substantial area, say 150m updrift and downdrift, and up to 50m offshore. Where possible, the programme should also attempt to monitor wave induced currents, which are generally only of interest close to the structure, say within 20m, but can be very varied depending on incident wave conditions.

Point measurements can be made by deploying directional current meters (see Figure 4.7) for one or two spring-neap tidal cycles. Flow path monitoring can be used to indicate suitable point locations, though these will be restricted by the requirements of the available equipment. The meters will need to be bottom mounted for stability and to monitor nearbed currents. As the breaker zone is a very hostile environment due to wave forces and suspended sediment then only very robust electromagnetic or acoustic doppler type equipment can be used. Specialist knowledge is required to achieve successful data collection. Current monitoring must be combined with measurements of incident waves, water levels, wind velocities and beach/nearshore topography.

Figure 4.7   *Directional current meter (courtesy HR Wallingford)*

4.6   GEOTECHNICAL DATA COLLECTION

The principal objective in undertaking geotechnical data collection for a beach management project is to derive a comprehensive understanding of the geological and geomorphological make up of the coast, beach and foreshore. Such information will be used to:

• facilitate analysis of coastal processes (e.g. to assess erodibility of soils or the nature of processes that have led to their distribution)
• aid an assessment of coastal erosion and deposition
• provide input parameters for the design of works.

Section 4.6.1 outlines the basic procedures required for site investigations and Section 4.6.2 reviews various methods for recording data and carrying out measurements with particular reference to marine operations.

4.6.1   Site investigation

Good site investigation practice follows the standard procedures described in BS 5930: 1981 Site Investigations (being updated 1995) and the series of publications Site Investigations in Construction by the Site Investigation Steering Group (1993) of the Institution of Civil Engineers. Other helpful advice can be found in Weltman and Head (1983). These guidelines can be summarised to four easily definable steps which are now described in turn.

Desk study

The purpose of the desk study is to assemble all the available existing and published data on a particular site. The general information required for a desk study is described in Appendix A of BS 5930: 1981 Site Investigations and potential sources of information are indicated in Appendix B of BS 5930 and in Dumbleton and West (1976). Of particular interest in the preliminary phases of an investigation for a beach management project are:

- present day and historical Ordnance Survey maps held in libraries such as the British Museum and the Bodleian, Oxford
- geological maps and memoirs held by the British Geological Survey
- recent and historical aerial photographs
- Local Authority information (library and museum records)
- existing ground investigations.

The results of the study should provide the preparatory information required by the specialist who executes the site reconnaissance.

Site reconnaissance

A rigorous visual examination of the site should be undertaken at the earliest opportunity and be carried out by a suitably qualified and experienced geotechnical engineer or engineering geologist (Appendix I of Site Investigation in Construction; Part 2, Planning, procurement and quality management, provides outline definitions of geotechnical personnel). Appendix C of BS 5930 provides notes and guidelines on the preparation and execution of a site reconnaissance.

A site reconnaissance is best performed on foot and it is essential to carry a site or district plan which can be marked up with observations as the reconnaissance progresses. The need to plan the visit to coincide with suitable tides is obvious but often overlooked.

Particular attention should be paid to omissions or alterations to the features described on maps or plans, be they topographical, geological or man made. Photographs taken during a site reconnaissance often identify details missed by the naked eye and are always more cost effective than a return visit.

Detailed observations should be made of the nature and characteristics of the exposed strata on the beach, foreshore or coastal cliff and a preliminary judgement made on the susceptibility of the foreshore strata to erosion. Any evidence of surface water, springs or ground water flow should be recorded.

Detailed examination and special studies

Based on the results of the site reconnaissance and the data available from the desk study, an evaluation will be made of the need for a more detailed examination or special study of the ground conditions, geology or geomorphology. The most appropriate methodology will be determined by the scope of the project, problems to be addressed and available budget.

Further detailed examination might include topographic surveys, geological mapping, aerial photography and, more rarely, geophysical surveys (Griffith and King, 1985). Geological maps of the majority of the UK coastline produced by the British Geological Survey are available at scales of 1:50,000 or 1:63,360 (1 inch to 1 mile) and tend to have sufficient detail for preliminary interpretation of local geology. Aerial photographs may have been recovered as part of the desk study. Most of the UK coastline has already been photographed from the air to prepare and revise Ordnance Survey maps and monitor coastal erosion.

The desk study and site reconnaissance may have revealed that a more detailed ground investigation is required with fieldwork incorporating the drilling, logging and sampling of boreholes and trial pits as illustrated in Figure 4.8. Section 4.6.2 describes the application of various methods and at this stage reference should be made to the recommended procedures in the document Site Investigation in Construction, Part 2; Planning, procurement and quality management. All work should be executed in accordance with BS 5930: 1981, Code of Practice for Site Investigations.

On completion of the detailed ground investigation laboratory testing of recovered samples should be carried out. BS 1377 Parts 1 and 2, 1990 describe the standard procedures for preparation of samples and classification testing.

Figure 4.8   *Beach sampling (courtesy Posford Duvivier)*

Interpretation

The final step of the investigation is to assimilate, review, correlate and interpret all the recovered data. The results of this step will be input to the evaluation of the most appropriate beach management strategy. The key factors that may affect design decisions will be:

- the nature, extent and depth of beach deposits
- characteristics of beach substrata, their origin and weathering profile
- coastal cliff stability and rate of erosion (see ICE (1991), and Hoek and Bray (1977))
- tidal lag in the variation in groundwater levels, saline intrusion and groundwater conditions.

4.6.2 Methods

There are many factors to consider before selecting the most suitable procedure for geotechnical site investigation. An informed decision must be made based on the information required for a particular project and a knowledge of the limitations of the most practicable method of acquiring the information. This section describes the more common methodologies.

Shallow trial pits

It is possible to examine in detail the condition of the ground both vertically and laterally in the exposed sides of the trial pit. Disturbed samples can be recovered for classification and particle size analysis in a laboratory.

Clearly trial pits are only practicable as part of a land-based investigation. Trial pits are a quick, efficient and relatively cheap method of executing a near-surface sub-strata investigation. As many as 10 trial pits can be excavated, logged, sampled and backfilled in a working day.

Vibrocoring

Vibrocoring is a technique for recovering samples of the seabed to depths of up to 10m below bed level although it is commonly used for more limited penetrations. However it may be difficult to deploy a rig in very shallow water as the vessel may sit on, or push against, the rig. It comprises a tubular piston (which may or may not have a cutting shoe liner and catcher) which is vibrated into the sediments from a frame lowered to the seabed by a cable. It is a rapid and cost effective technique for recovering shallow samples of sea bed materials, particularly sandy deposits. It is of limited use in gravels, except when cores with very wide barrels are employed.

Light cable percussion (shell and auger)

This technique is probably the most common method of drilling a borehole for the purpose of investigating ground conditions in the UK. For a beach or coastal investigation on land, the rigs can be dismantled and towed by a light vehicle and therefore access often dictates the practicability of the method.

For an investigation over water, or in the inter tidal zone, the cable percussion rig can be mounted on to a floating pontoon or jack-up barge. The rate of progress over water tends to be much slower than on land and the costs for boring, sampling and in-situ testing (Clayton, 1993) reflect the increased difficulty of handling tools and stringing casing between the deck and sea bed. If performed from a floating pontoon progress may be governed by the tide or weather.

Light cable percussive boring techniques are suitable for most soils and soft rocks. Tools used in cable percussion boreholes bring up samples which are generally only suitable for identifying and classifying the recovered lithology. Procedures for sampling and in situ testing are described in BS 5930. Where good recovery in hard ground or rock is required, cable percussion boreholes are often advanced using rotary coring techniques (Weltman and Head, 1983).

Cone penetration tests

There are two types of cone penetration test using either a static or dynamic drive mechanism. The static penetration test utilises a standard cone which is pushed into the ground at a constant rate while the resistance of the cone tip is measured. It is also possible to measure the combined resistance of the cone and push rods or the cone and an outer sleeve. Advanced electronic penetrometers fitted with transducers can record cone resistance, friction and excess pore pressure at the cone tip in a continuous profile. Although no sample is recovered, a very accurate profile of the soil and its characteristic properties can be interpreted from the results (Meigh, 1987).

For investigations over water the static penetrometer rig can be mounted on a jack-up barge in a similar manner to the cable percussion equipment. Alternatively, purpose-built static penetrometer units have been developed for lowering to the sea bed from floating plant to investigate ground to depths of at least 5m depending on the conditions.

The dynamic penetration test simply involves the continuous driving of a rod and standard cone into the ground and measuring the distance driven against the energy applied (ICE, 1988). The technique is often used on land based operations to provide in fill data between boreholes or trial pits and is an extremely cheap and efficient method of investigating large areas. Dynamic penetration testing is rarely undertaken for marine work because the additional cost of static penetration tests are marginal in relation to the mobilisation costs.

Standardisation has been achieved in BS 1377: Part 9, 1990 which describes the two main types of test established in Europe.

Rotary core drilling

Rotary core drilling is the traditional method of investigating hard ground or rock. In beach management projects this may be required to confirm the characteristics of the bedrock and in particular its weathering profile. Drill rigs are most commonly truck-mounted and are not particularly manoeuvrable where access is difficult. In the beach or coastal environment, restrictions similar to those for cable percussion rigs apply. Where one is coring partially cemented, weak, weathered materials, considerable expertise is required to recover cores of satisfactory quality.

For marine investigations, rotary coring can be performed from a floating pontoon or jack-up barge. However, the quality of the drilling and the recovery of samples can be greatly affected by waves and a rising or falling tide, so jack-up barges are more commonly used.

Geophysical surveying

Geophysics is a specialised subject distinct from geology and geotechnics. Where a geophysical survey is required the advice of an organisation that specialises in this work should be sought. Geophysical surveys are rarely sufficiently independent of a borehole investigation, but are cheap and will provide general information on ground conditions over a large area relatively quickly. Most methods will identify anomalies where materials have markedly different properties and so will assist in targeting more detailed investigations.

On land, the most commonly used geophysical methods are seismic refraction or resistivity techniques and over water continuous profiling using seismic reflection is often more appropriate (International Geological Society Engineering Group, 1988).

Seismic refraction can be difficult to interpret when the velocity of shock wave transmission in near surface layers is greater than in underlying materials. This commonly occurs in beaches of dense gravel overlying clays. Resistivity surveys rely on matching results with idealised conditions which may be complicated by saline intrusion of the ground water in a coastal region.

For geophysical investigations over water or in the inter tidal zone, seismic reflection techniques are adopted which rely on an extension of the echo sounding principle to identify sub-seabed stratification resulting from variations in the acoustic reflection characteristics of different materials. Without borehole information, it is often hard to distinguish between materials with similar characteristics and, in shallow water, reflectors near the surface may be difficult to identify with confidence. However, the relatively low cost, high speed and wide coverage often justify the use of a geophysical survey at an early stage of an investigation or to interpolate between widely spaced boreholes.

Instrumentation

Instrumentation can be used to monitor the properties of the beach and associated structures with time. It can provide specific information on gradual movement or deterioration of a particular element. The following are commonly adopted applications of monitoring.:

- coastal slope stability
- coastal structure stability (e.g. retaining wall, wave walls)
- groundwater and salinity changes.

Table 4.1 summarises the methods and the type of information they provide.

The following key factors must be considered when designing an instrumentation programme:

- instruments must be protected from damage by vandalism and exposure to the elements
- the responsibility for monitoring and maintenance of the instruments must be made clear
- allowance must be made in the budget for both instrument installation and maintenance.

Table 4.1 Geotechnical instrumentation for monitoring properties of beaches and associated structures

Method	Brief description	Information provided
Inclinometers: manual electrolevels	Vertical profile in a borehole with manual or electronic recorded displacement. Effective in areas of slope stability.	Displacement/time on vertical profiles.
Extensometers	Embedded rods which measure change in length.	Displacement/time for lateral or inclined movement.
Settlement posts	Vertical posts placed on horizontal plates at the base or within areas of fill embankments. In some cases may be isolated from surrounding fill. Provide a reference level for settlement monitoring.	Settlement/time or settlement/depth profile for embankments or fill.
Piezometers	Of various types but hydraulic or pneumatic types can provide continuous monitoring of some pressures and groundwater levels.	Groundwater and soil pore pressure/time records. Maybe in response to tide or construction changes.
Load cells	Measurement of loads in specific elements of a structure.	Performance of structures e.g. retaining walls.
Continuous water conducting meters	Instruments for monitoring conductivity and hence salinity over time. May be installed permanently or lowered down wells periodically.	Monitoring of saline intrusion and changes with time.
Ancillary equipment: datalogger	Digital instruments for logging continuous or cyclic data from transducers; data are stored and down loaded for analysis at intervals.	Logging.

4.7   DATA STORAGE AND ANALYSIS

To manage a beach successfully, an accurate picture of the actual response of the coastal processes is required. As outlined in Section 4.1.1, data are required in four key areas:

- understanding the past - data are required to identify short-term fluctuations and long-term trends
- identification of present problems - data are required to monitor alarm levels

- predicting the future solution - data are required to calibrate and validate physical and numerical models for future solutions
- monitoring the future solution - data are required to monitor the solution, particularly with 'soft' engineering schemes.

The collection of data in a dynamic system, such as a beach, is necessarily a continuous task as the system state and response are continuously changing. It involves measuring a large number of variables over a larger geographic area than of immediate concern to the present-day manager. The result is that, in a well-planned monitoring programme, a large amount of data will be collected from a variety of sources. It is, therefore, essential to plan carefully the storage of these data in a form which makes further analysis most efficient. Collecting data for their own sake is not always the best plan; a well designed programme should have a clear objective and methodology. Figure 4.9 shows a simple example methodology for storing and analysing beach profile data.

4.7.1   Software

The methodology shown in Figure 4.9 can be implemented using spreadsheet, CAD and simple bespoke databases. Choice may depend upon the available computing expertise. Many people are familiar with spreadsheet programs and it is possible to develop worksheets to perform required tasks. Visualisation of the data is extremely easy, however numeric and report analysis is more difficult. The disadvantage is that spreadsheets are not optimised to manipulate large amounts of data. As the database increases in size the speed of the spreadsheet may be reduced. In addition, spreadsheets lack some of the functionality associated with database programs.

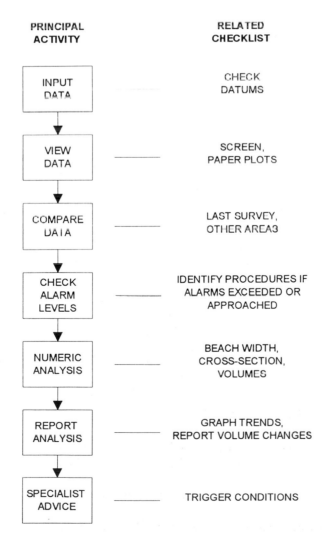

Figure 4.9   *Flow chart for storing and analysing beach profile data*

CAD programs can be used to store information with geographical locations plus details of attributes. The presentation of geographical data is very easy. Other types of display, such as time series and comparison between variables is more difficult. The database functionality of CAD programs may be limited.

Both spreadsheet and CAD programs are simple and flexible; however, they are more limited in functionality that a bespoke database with routines written specifically to analyse and present beach data. This may also include simple predictive models to allow the identification of alarm levels and forecasting of future beach response, such as future beach volumes and levels. The databases are also tailored to the particular requirements of data having both temporal and spatial elements and allow, for example, temporal data such as waves and water levels to be analysed and compared seasonally with site-specific threshold exceedance values.

4.7.2   Geographical Information Systems (GIS)

A GIS is a software package for the acquisition, storage, retrieval, manipulation and analysis of spatially referenced data. The most sophisticated GISs are expensive and require considerable processing power and storage capacity, whilst basic systems are also available for use on desk-top PCs at a modest cost (from a few thousand pounds upwards in 1995 UK prices). Despite this wide cost range, all systems are based on two essential components:

1. A database capable of storing and retrieving information about the mapped data, which is referenced by geographical position and other search criteria. Some systems include an internal database but most now include interfaces to external relational database management systems (RDBMS).

2. A visualization system capable of displaying spatially-referenced data (e.g. maps) and interrogating the mapped data for coordinate information. Other graphics, such as graphs, photographs and video images may also be displayed.

It is important to distinguish how a GIS represents data, either as raster or vector, and also to distinguish whether the data are structured or unstructured. The method of representation is fundamental to the type of information that can be recorded and the analysis that is possible. Box 4.7 describes the differences between the types of data representation. These distinctions are very important and fundamental to system choice. The purpose to which the GIS will be put dictates what data representations are required.

The functionality of the GIS must be considered when selecting a GIS system. Again, there must be a clear understanding of the proposed use before a system is purchased and of how, and by whom, the system will be maintained, updated and accessed.

Data input

There are a large number of different data storage and transfer formats, both for raster and vector data. It is essential that the input and output formats supported by the selected GIS are compatible with those used by external suppliers of data (e.g. OS map format). Similarly, the ability to input and output Data eXchange Format (DXF) files allows a direct interaction with CAD packages. The GIS must also provide efficient methods for inputting data derived from site surveys and modelling studies. This information could be in the form of figures, photography, maps, tables, text as well as computer files.

Data management and processing

Before data input to a GIS can be analysed for a particular purpose it is usually necessary to perform some type of pre-processing. This may include coordinate transformation, rescaling, joining, clipping and edge-matching of polygons, conversion to raster data or to vector data. Many of these processes are fundamental to GIS and are usually offered as standard functions within a package, although this is not always the case.

Box 4.7   *GIS data representation*

Vector and raster data

Vector data consist of points or a series of connected points defining lines, networks and polygons specified in a continuous coordinate space. This method of representing data is very economical in terms of computer storage and precisely locates the data, allowing accurate calculation of lengths and areas. Vector information may be stored in layers which can be overlaid to examine the relationship between features. Output from Computer Aided Design (CAD) packages is normally vector data. A very large proportion of the Ordnance Survey large-scale maps have been digitised and are available in vector format.

Raster data consists of a regular grid of cells of picture elements (pixels) that may be coloured to represent features or characteristics. Lines can be represented in this way but accuracy is limited by the pixel resolution. This representation is very effective for spatial analysis but can involve a high overhead in computer storage unless compressed in some way. Raw raster data basically only provides a backdrop and requires further processing to allow analysis, although a number of raster-based GIS packages now permit full analysis, which is useful when processing images such as those obtained from satellites. Note that a computer screen always *displays* pictures as raster pixels whether the *representation* of the data within the system is vector or raster.

Structured and unstructured graphical data

Structured data have associated topology (i.e. the computer "knows" what the points, lines or areas are and "understands" how they relate to one another). With structured data, the screen graphics can interact with the analysis functions and database queries. *Unstructured* graphical data can be used by the system to generate a picture but no analysis or query operations. Scanned maps or photographs used as backdrops are usually unstructured.

A typical application utilising these distinct representations is a raster backdrop of a base map or base photograph with vectors representing features superimposed on top. The raster backdrop may be unstructured, although not always, while the vector overlay will be fully structured with topology, allowing spatial analysis and retrieval of attribute (associated) data from the database.

Data analysis

Examples of standard GIS spatial analysis functions based on vector data are:

- area and perimeter calculations
- overlaying and merging of polygons
- summing of spatially coincident values
- generation of thiessen polygons (assigning area characteristics using point data)
- buffering of features (defining zones of influence around a point, line or area)
- point-in-polygon (the geographical occurrence of one feature within another).

Database operations

The ability to carry out spatial queries is what differentiates a GIS from conventional databases. These processes include simple data retrieval using spatial delimiters (windows or proximity measures) and Boolean operators (AND, OR, NOT, etc.) to locate, display and tabulate cases where particular conditions are satisfied. The following questions are typical of the types of query a GIS may be used to perform:

- are there any wave measurements within 10km of this location?
- what are the seabed surface deposits at this location?
- where is survey station 24B?
- what type of sea wall is at this location?
- what type of sediments are found near revetments?

Three dimensional surface modelling

Surface modelling can provide three-dimensional representation of recorded data or model output. This may be used for further analysis such as contouring, slope analysis and volume estimation (e.g. volume above some threshold such as MHWS) or for visualization purposes.

Applications

It is vital to recognize that whatever GIS product is selected, any particular application (such as beach management) requires that the basic GIS functions, described above, must be used to build the specialist processes needed to meet the requirements of that application. This may involve building links between the GIS and external software and numerical models. It may also be necessary to develop completely new functions tailored to a particular application. The ease with which this application development can be achieved is as important as the availability of the generic functions themselves. Many GIS products allow the user to build menus and icons for complex bespoke operations, providing a seamless join with the main system.

Purchasing GIS functions that may prove to be of little use is a real possibility, particularly in the early stages of development. Potential purchasers need to ask the question: does the application envisaged really require all the spatial analysis functionality of a full GIS, or would access to a relational database through a graphical user interface suffice? To avoid obtaining unnecessary software, a modular system offers the basic functions as a starting point and more specialist functions can be obtained as required by subsequent development. This modular feature is offered by several of the most widely used GIS products.

Following development of the application software it will be tempting to expect immediate benefits from the system. A GIS is useless, however, without the data which it was designed to handle. It has been estimated that typically up to 75% of the final cost of implementing GIS is due to data entry. Experience from existing GIS sites suggests that it is realistic to expect a lead time of at least 12 months before significant interrogation of the system will be possible.

Once the GIS is operational, data entry and maintenance will become a major commitment, without which the system will quickly fall into disuse. This is likely to require significant resources, in both time and money.

4.8   APPRAISAL OF MONITORING RESULTS

The principal objective of the monitoring described above is to provide information of value in the efficient management of a beach. More precisely, this involves:

* reviewing the information obtained
* deciding what further monitoring is necessary
* deciding whether any (different) management of the beach is necessary.

This section of the report concentrates on the former two topics, leaving the interpretation of the data for decisions on beach management to Chapter 5.

4.8.1   Review of information obtained

A first step in appraising a monitoring exercise is to decide whether the required information has actually been collected and whether it has then been analysed and the results made available to the correct audience. In this context, it is important to have a clear statement of the requirements of a monitoring exercise beforehand, by means of a pre-determined set of quality criteria. In many cases, specialist advice on the initial specification of surveys should be sought before starting monitoring.

These quality criteria will vary depending on the type of information collected. As an example, before starting to measure a beach profile, it will be necessary to decide on the accuracy of the levels (vertically) and on the initial location and orientation of the profile line (again defining the accuracy required). Experience has shown that much of the value of such surveys can be lost simply because, for example, the location of the origin of the profile has not been defined using a National Grid (or equivalent) co-ordinate system. It is also important to periodically review any temporary bench marks used for beach surveying. Calculated beach volumes, for example, will change dramatically if the level of a Temporary Bench Mark (TBM) is not constant (for example due to ground settlement). Much beach profile data in the UK has also been devalued by loss of TBMs, for example as defences are re-built or coastal roads re-surfaced (see Clayton, 1977). At the same time, it may well be wasteful to specify unnecessary accuracy in the beach levels; given the size of individual pebbles, or sand ripples, a vertical accuracy better than 10mm is impractical. In practice an accuracy of 50mm is usually entirely adequate, and will not affect the subsequent understanding of beach behaviour. If beach profiles are to be surveyed at 3-monthly intervals, it is probably equally unimportant if the surveys are delayed by a few days to allow easier surveying (e.g. at low water during daylight hours), although if post-storm profiles are required then the surveys must be completed as soon after the peak of the storm as possible (e.g. the following low tide).

It is equally important that any information collected should be analysed promptly and the results of that analysis stored safely, as well as the information itself. The former requirement allows possible re-surveying to be carried out if results are surprising (e.g. in comparison to earlier surveys). The latter is often neglected, but is important in the context of beach management since it may be many years before the full value of a data-set can be appreciated. Long-term trends in beach levels, for example, many be effectively masked by the effects of a few years of untypical weather. As already noted, therefore (see Section 4.2.3) great care is required in selecting appropriate baseline and monitoring beach profile "envelopes".

It is therefore best to set up, at the same time as setting up the monitoring programme and as part of the beach management strategy, a clearly defined approach to analysis of results. The approach currently adopted by NRA Anglian Region as best practice and implemented on the Mablethorpe to Skegness frontage, of the coast of Lincolnshire, is illustrated in Box 4.8 as an example worthy of consideration. The idea of establishing critical beach levels, or cross-sectional areas, is a widely used concept which helps to draw attention to potentially serious drops in beach levels. Such thresholds can be set using information on the levels of sea wall foundations, or using numerical modelling of likely beach profile response and overtopping in severe storms.

Finally, as with many other aspects of beach management, it is likely that the cost-effectiveness of a monitoring exercise will come under scrutiny from time to time. Much of the value in monitoring lies in its ability to demonstrate the behaviour of a beach to a wide audience, perhaps to provide re-assurance that a particular management strategy is succeeding, or to show that other action needs to be taken. Apart from ensuring that the information obtained is disseminated to those interested in a beach, it will also be wise to periodically consider the implications of changing the frequency, or required accuracy of a particular monitoring programme, or even abandoning it. This topic is considered in more detail next.

4.8.2 Deciding on further monitoring

If a beach is being actively managed, for example by periodic nourishment or re-cycling, some beach monitoring is likely to be carried out indefinitely. In a few other situations, however, a monitoring campaign may only need to last for a limited period, for example with pocket beaches; although this does not eliminate the possibility of repeating such a campaign at some stage in the future. In practice the decision about the nature and frequency of further monitoring will depend both on what is monitored and the specific character of the site (see also Chapter 11). Box 4.9, which describes the monitoring at Seaford in East Sussex, shows how different approaches were adopted for the monitoring of beach profiles and wave conditions.

Box 4.8 *Analysis of beach profile monitoring on Mablethorpe to Skegness frontage, Lincolnshire*

Area and volume calculations

On receipt of survey data, survey lines (seawall to offshore) are placed in a spreadsheet database. Beach areas and volumes are then calculated automatically. At present beach volumes are calculated for three 'slices' - above High Water, High Water to Low Water, below Low Water. Individual sub-areas and volumes in each of these slices (A_1, A_2, A_3, and V_1, V_2, V_3) are integrated across the beach profiles (see Figure 1 below).

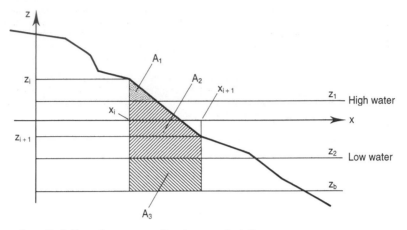

Figure 1 *Definitions for cross-sectional area calculations*

The automated calculations in the system show variations between surveys (i.e. in time) of any or all of these and also variations in space (i.e. along the beach).

Comparison with critical areas/volumes

Critical areas/volumes are also set up for each profile. Each time the analysis is run (i.e. after every survey) the system will identify any profiles where the beach has a smaller area/volume than the critical (see Figure 2 below). At some locations it may be that other factors may be as important as beach volume. For example, beach levels at a seawall may be the critical parameter. In this case, a comparison of such levels is included in the automatic routines, with the system flagging up any profiles showing significant variations or failing to meet a critical level.

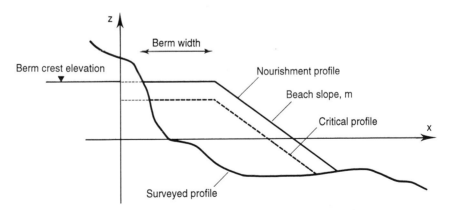

Figure 2 *Definitions of various beach profiles*

Results obtained from the database analysis are also shown on an area map to help identify longshore and geographical trends. Analysis reports produced after each survey include an interpretive section which will use the analysis to 'track' longshore movement of beach material between profiles.

A decision on whether to continue monitoring will normally depend on whether the further data could affect the management of a beach. Hence on a beach which is stable or accreting, there will often be no need to continue monitoring (although it may be prudent to review the situation every few years). Even if extra data are required, it is good practice to review present monitoring practice every few years to decide whether alternative methods are available, or whether the specification can be changed, to provide the information needed at lower cost. This review should also extend to the analysis and presentation of results from a monitoring exercise.

Box 4.9   *Monitoring programme for shingle beach recharge scheme at Seaford, E. Sussex*

The Seaford scheme has been mentioned previously (see Section 4.4.1) and a cross-section of the beach is presented in Figure 4.4. The capital works for placing the initial beach recharge were completed in 1987. Different approaches have been adopted to the monitoring of beach levels and waves.

Beach levels

Beach levels have been monitored since before the recharge was carried out, although the number of beach cross-sections surveyed have been modified in the light of experience and analysis. It is likely that such surveys will continue for many years, to check on the success of the recharge and guard against any problems arising and remaining undetected.

Waves

Before the recharge was carried out a wave measurement campaign was undertaken, lasting for just over one year. This, together with numerical modelling, was sufficient to understand the wave climate for this coast and it has not been necessary to continue such monitoring.

5 Putting beach management principles into practice

5.1 MANAGEMENT OF THE COAST

5.1.1 Beach management in context

In some instances, beach management is undertaken as a unique initiative for which a need has been identified by a managing agency. In other cases, beach management may need to be undertaken alongside or as part of the implementation of a more strategic initiative. There are a large number of such initiatives, all of which can potentially influence or interact with beach management (see Figure 5.1). These include local plans, coastal zone management plans, shoreline management plans, catchment management plans and management plans for specific sites such as National Nature Reserves (NNR). Of these, beach management is most likely to take place in the context of a shoreline management plan or a specific site management plan. Many such management initiatives have been developed in response to a recognition of the value of proactive planning (as opposed to reactive responses).

The following sections describe the various interests and management responsibilities for the coast, and the associated coastal management plans and initiatives in more detail. The scope and extent of most of these plans is summarised in Table 5.1 and Figure 5.2.

5.1.2 Background

Numerous agencies currently undertake management activities at the coast. These diverse agencies include those with responsibility for:

- coastal defence
- pollution control
- conservation
- control of development on land
- regulation of development of the sea bed
- regulation of activity on and in the sea.

Not surprisingly, there is an equally diverse range of legislation and regulation affecting the above interests. The publication prepared for the Department of the Environment reviewing coastal planning and management (Rendel Geotechnics, 1993) provides detailed information on this subject.

The overall co-ordination of these various management interests in an attempt to ensure that they can co-exist in a sustainable fashion, is known as coastal zone management. The need for better coastal zone management was recognised by the UK Government's Report on *Coastal Zone Protection and Planning*, from the House of Commons Environment Select Committee in 1993.

Arguably many of the historic problems associated with coastal defence have arisen from a lack of strategic management of the coast. Coastal defence schemes have often been developed in response to an urgent need (sometimes in itself a function of inappropriate development) over a limited length of coast and have not been able to benefit from a full awareness of long-term trends and of the scheme's interaction with the wider coastal regime. In terms of coastal defence, therefore, a good system of coastal management will *inter alia* be based on a sound programme of monitoring carried out in a coordinated fashion by the relevant local coast protection authority and flood defence authority (see Chapter 3) and on an understanding of coastal processes over an area which is not confined by administrative boundaries. The detailed reasons for such an approach have already been identified in Chapters 2 and 3 (see in particular Section 2.6).

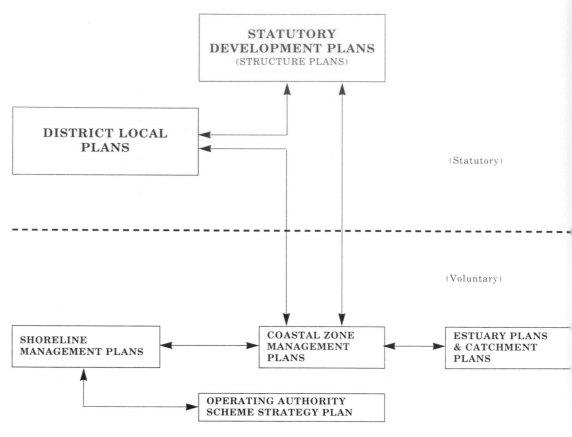

Figure 5.1   *Relationship between management plans (MAFF, 1995)*

Table 5.1 Management plans affecting the coast (adapted from MAFF, 1995)

	Beach Management Plan	**Shoreline Management Plan**	**Coastal Zone Management Plan**	**Catchment Management Plan**
Primary Purpose	Strategic planning for control of beaches and the beach environment.	Strategic planning for coastal defence.	Framework to help resolve competing pressures in the coastal zone.	Strategic planning of NRA functions.
Main Issues Covered	Coastal defence Recreation Environment.	Coastal defence.	Development Recreation Landscape Environment Navigation Coastal Defence etc.	Flood defence Water resources Navigation Conservation Fisheries Pollution.
Extent and Boundaries	Management Unit	Sediment cell/ subcell.	Varies: may focus on specific areas such as estuaries or longer stretches of open coast.	Main river catchments.
Lead Authority	Maritime District Council or NRA (in collaboration with other members of the relevant coastal group).	Maritime District Council or NRA (in collaboration with other members of the relevant coastal group.)	District or County Council, Borough Council or other interested organisation.	NRA.

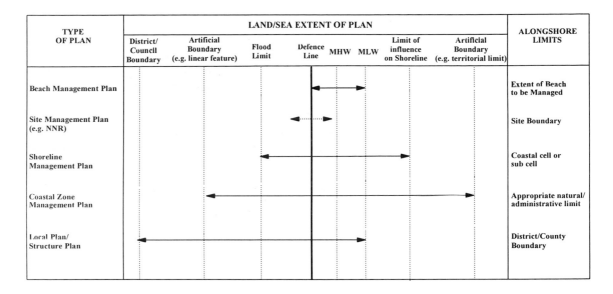

Figure 5.2   *Land/sea extent of management plans*

5.1.3   Local plans

Local plans and other development plans (e.g. structure plans), which provide a statutory framework for decision-making on development for the local authority, may make reference to the desirability or otherwise of protecting or promoting the use of the coastal area. Local plans may also contain policies which relate specifically to certain sites or types of development along the coast. They do not generally deal with problems that extend beyond their own administrative boundary. Similarly, because of the limit to which the local authorities' jurisdiction extends, local plans do not generally cover the area seaward of mean low water mark.

5.1.4   Coastal zone management plans

Non-statutory coastal zone management plans, which may be contained within or overlap with administrative boundaries, are increasingly being prepared by (or for) groups of interested organisations, most or all of whom have management responsibilities at the coast. In many cases coastal zone management plans are being developed because the issues facing development and resource use at the coast (including use of the water area) are perceived as being different to the more general terrestrial planning issues covered in development plans.

Coastal zone management plans can vary enormously in their level of prescriptiveness, from a broad strategic planning framework to a detailed action plan targeted at those responsible for the day-to-day management of the resource. Coastal zone management plans, like local plans, can cover a broad range of interests (economic, social, environmental, commercial, etc.) and, indeed, coastal zone management planning policies relating to the area above Mean Low Water (MLW) may be adopted into the relevant statutory plan(s). However, they also extend seawards beyond mean low water mark to cover fisheries activities, water sports, etc. Although the limit is usually closer inshore, in some cases the spatial coverage of the coastal zone management plan could extend seaward as far as the territorial limit.

Along the coast, the coastal zone management plan coverage may be dictated by administrative boundaries. Inland, administrative boundaries may also be the limiting factor. Alternatively a particular contour or a linear feature (road, railway, etc.) may be selected as an artificial yet convenient boundary, or attempts might be made to define the zone where there is significant interaction with, or impacts on, the coastline.

5.1.5   Shoreline management plans

Shoreline management plans, which are also non-statutory and which may also be contained within or overlap administrative boundaries, are being developed to provide a strategic, long-term approach to the provision and/or management of coastal defences. The aim of a shoreline management plan is to produce a strategy for coast protection and/or flood defence that will satisfy technical requirements by providing strategic defence options in the medium to long term, in an environmentally acceptable and economically efficient manner. The spatial coverage of a shoreline management plan generally extends from a defined erosion or flood risk limit on the landward side, out to the maximum seaward limit of influence on the shoreline. The limits up and down the coast will usually be defined on the basis of the coastal processes operating. Wider effects, up and downdrift, and offshore, should also be considered as these can influence beach development even though they are outside the area of beach or seabed being influenced.

In England and Wales, shoreline management plans should be developed in accordance with the MAFF (1995) guidelines, the procedure from which is summarised in Box 5.1. These plans are being developed on a sediment cell basis (see Section 2.6).

Box 5.1   *Procedure for the production of a shoreline management plan (MAFF, 1995)*

Key issues to be considered

- coastal processes
- coastal defences
- land use and the human and built environment
- natural environment

Stage 1 - Data Collection and Objective Setting

- identify all those with an interest in the area
- collate and analyse data on all key issues
- set management objectives for the Plan area

Stage 2 - Appraisal of Coastal Defence Strategic Options

- define management units
- appraise strategic coastal defence options
- consult on the preferred strategic coastal defence option(s)
- compile the Plan

5.1.6   Beach management plans

Beach management is, again, more limited in its spatial land/sea extent, although the alongshore extent of the area covered by the plan will relate to the beach to be managed and may overlap administrative boundaries. As discussed elsewhere, beaches are an integral part of coastal defence. In order to serve that purpose they must be maintained with sufficient proportions so that they can meet coastal defence, as well as other requirements, now and in the future. Beach management is the process of managing the beach, whether by monitoring, simple intervention (e.g. sand fences, litter clearance, etc.), recycling, renourishment, or the construction and maintenance of beach control structures such as groynes. A beach management plan should therefore set down the detailed strategy for management of the beach in order to achieve an agreed policy, normally that defined in the relevant shoreline management plan. Specific guidance on the preparation of Beach Management Plans for England and Wales, prepared in discussion with MAFF and the Welsh Office, is given in Box 5.2.

The specific content of the plan should avoid *ad hoc* solutions to localised problems unless absolutely necessary in the short term. Instead, it should be based on a vision, or best estimate, of how the beach will perform in a number of years from the inception of the plan. Planning requirements related to shoreline retreat suggest that this vision should extend some 75 years

Box 5.2 *Preparation of beach management plans in England and Wales*

1. Beach Management Scheme Appraisal

The project appraisal of any beach management scheme should consider the technical, economic and environmental appraisal of different options, including beach management options, generally tested against a 'do nothing' approach, and carried out in the same way as for a capital works scheme.

After identifying the relevant beach management unit, the promoting authority should establish clear overall objectives for the beach management scheme and identify any specific constraints to its implementation. The appraisal will take account of historical development of the beach and benefit from the results and analysis of previous monitoring.

Development of the appraisal will involve, amongst other things, consideration of the nature of the beach, its major functions, material composition, the natural forces acting on it and its response to both routine and extreme events, including the influence of any structures. An important element of the appraisal will be a sensitivity analysis which will need to examine the response to storms and, in particular, sequences of storm events, to develop the design and procedures required to achieve appropriate standards of protection. It should result in the definition of allowable operating limits and action levels required to deliver the scheme objectives.

The appraisal should also establish the nature and frequency of monitoring required to inform the management process. The full appraisal should be carried out at intervals to take account of improved knowledge and changed circumstances (MAFF require one at least every five years for renewal of scheme approval).

2. Operational Beach Management Plan

An operational beach management plan will set out, for local managers and operational staff, the work to be undertaken. This will be in similar detail to a capital scheme specification, though the actual work involved will probably be more flexible. It will, for example, set out the objectives of beach management, define the allowable operating limits to maintain functionality, specify the method and frequency of monitoring and define any action levels for further work. It should also set out the procedures to be followed where works are required, including the identification of sources of material, where appropriate, and not the environmental considerations which are to be taken into account.

into the future. In reality, accurate predictions over such a long period are extremely difficult and in practice, as Box 5.2 indicates, regular revision of the plan will be required taking account of collected monitoring data (see Chapter 4).

The development of a beach management plan should follow the sequence indicated in Figure 5.3.

5.1.7 Site specific environmental management plans

In addition to the various plans discussed above, site specific environmental management initiatives may cover part or all of the area of a beach management plan. Of particular relevance in the UK are the management initiatives for stretches of Heritage Coast, or for Sites of Special Scientific Interest, Special Protection Areas and Special Areas of Conservation which include an area of foreshore. Many coastal National Nature Reserves are the subject of management planning initiatives (e.g. Newborough Warren National Nature Reserve in Gwynedd). Other site specific plans could include those for tourism and recreation use/development.

5.1.8 Management terms

Any or all of the above plans could potentially identify deliberate management of beach processes as (part of) the preferred management option, albeit for very different reasons (e.g. coastal defence, tourism, ecology).

As part of the process leading up to the identification of a preferred management regime, most plans will have defined goals and objectives for the coast. Any goals and objectives (and policies/actions/etc.) which have already been defined and possibly agreed by the responsible authorities will clearly provide an important starting point for beach managers. Where no such strategic initiatives exist, however, the setting of such objectives represents an important first

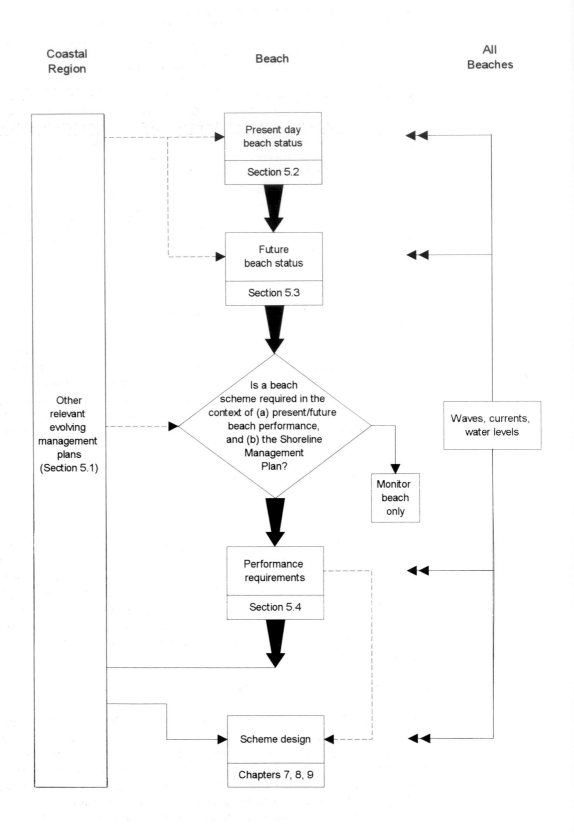

Figure 5.3 *Flow chart for beach management*

step in the beach management process. The definition of coastal management terms is provided in Table 5.2.

Table 5.2 Coastal management terminology

Term	Definition	Example
Goal	Broad, long-term aim, or vision, of the Management Plan. Goals encompass the holistic management of the coastal resource.	To achieve an integrated and sustainable system of management and development within the coastal zone.
Objective	Specific, shorter term target for attaining goals. Objectives may focus on specific environmental parameters or on achieving a particular goal.	To achieve an adequate standard of coastal defence which is technically, economically and environmentally acceptable.
Policy	Statement setting out agreed guidance on a particular issue or range of issues. Policies provide the framework within which future decisions will be taken.	To promote "natural" systems of coastal defence (e.g. beaches, sand dunes, etc.).
Action	Detail on what needs to be done by whom, and when, in order to achieve a particular objective (or an element of that objective).	To nourish the beach at location x; to monitor the physical and biological characteristics of the intertidal area.

5.2 PRESENT-DAY BEACH STATUS

An evaluation of the present-day status of a beach (and its likely future development - see Section 5.3) is fundamental in deciding whether to actively manage a beach, or to refrain from intervention. Many of the attributes of a beach alter seasonally. Consequently a full evaluation will require information at various times throughout the year. Identifying long-term trends in beach attributes (and beach-influencing factors, such as wave and tidal conditions) will require data over several years and reference should be made to the detailed recommendations in Chapter 4 when establishing a data collection strategy.

5.2.1 Value as a coastal defence

Sole or part defence

Concern about the past, or likely future, performance of a beach as a coastal defence is the most common reason for needing to manage a beach. This may be because the beach is the sole defence against the flooding or erosion of a coastal area. In most vulnerable parts of the UK, however, beaches lie in front of "built" defences. Here they partly absorb some of the energy of the incoming waves and hence reduce the damage and/or overtopping of those structures. Whether the beach is the sole defence or only part of it, it will be important to assess its effectiveness in this role and whether that is likely to reduce in the short to medium-term future.

Health of beach and beach profile

It is important to differentiate between the general "health" of a beach and its function in coastal defence. A beach may be at a very low level and the volume of material within it may be reducing, but this does not necessarily mean that any management of the beach to improve the standard of defences is warranted. This may be because there is no need for defences (e.g. in front of a hard-rock cliff), or because the beach does not contribute usefully to the performance of the defence structures behind it. Although unusual, in some areas, beaches may even detract from the standard of defence by causing abrasion to the structures.

Very often, however, if a beach is at a low level and/or declining, then the coastal defences in that area will be adversely affected. The most common concerns regarding the beach as a defence relate to the reduction of performance in one of the following situations:

1. In front of built defences, where the beach is required to:

   - provide cover to the face, and particularly the toe, of the structures
   - reduce the depth of water immediately in front of structures, hence limiting the maximum wave height that can impact on them
   - adjust under the incoming waves, both absorbing some of their energy and altering the slope of the seabed in front of the structures, so altering the likelihood of overtopping.

2. Where the beach is the sole defence and must be of sufficient dimensions to:

   - provide sufficient volume of beach to allow full beach profile adjustment under extreme wave attack
   - limit the volume of water flowing over or through the beach in the landward direction
   - prevent wave action eroding the land or cliff base behind the beach
   - protect the underlying geology from erosion (e.g. veneer beach).

To examine the functionality of a beach as a coastal defence, its cross-section must be considered. The height and width of its crest, the gradient of its seaward face, and the water depth at the toe of the beach are all important parameters in assessing its likely performance under severe storm conditions.

Changes in beach profile

Unlike conventional structures, beach profile parameters will change over time. Changes in the plan shape of a beach caused by an unusual wave direction may reduce the volume of material under a cross-section at a critical point (e.g. down-drift of a groyne). Seasonal fluctuations in slopes and upper beach levels often have created a low, gently sloping beach prior to the onset of a severe storm. The beach will change shape during the storm itself, so the duration of an extreme event also becomes important. Predicting the future shape and performance of a beach as a coastal defence is therefore more complicated than for a built defence structure.

Adequacy of beach as a defence

The adequacy or inadequacy of a beach as a defence can often be established by examination of its performance in the past. A beach which has failed to prevent overtopping in a particularly severe storm event may still be providing an adequate standard of defence for the area behind it. It is important to bear in mind the probability of such a severe event recurring before concluding that the defences must be improved. However, a beach which is found to have been overtopped in modest conditions, or which frequently falls to a level which exposes the foundations of a seawall, is clearly unlikely to be regarded as adequately functioning as a coastal defence on its own even though it is contributing to the total performance of the defences.

Conversely, it must be remembered that even a massive beach which has endured storms for centuries may be on the verge of becoming inadequate as a defence if sea-levels continue to rise. If the monitoring of a beach or an examination of historical records reveals a long-term reduction in the beach dimensions, then this inadequacy is even more likely to occur.

The present day value of a beach as a coastal defence relates mainly to its performance under certain future design events. As the beach will also be changing as a result of long-term processes which will affect its performance under such future design events, predictive techniques are essential tools to establish the beach's future status (see Sections 5.3, 6.2 and Chapter 7, where predictive techniques are described in detail). The interaction between the present and the future can be seen by examining the steps required to assess how a beach will meet the performance requirements listed above under (see "Health of Beach" above) specified design conditions. These steps are as follows:

1. Using the envelope of beach cross-shore profile data collected as part of the monitoring programme (see Chapter 4), identify one or more likely typical beach cross-shore profiles prior to the design event, allowing for seasonal fluctuations.

2. Derive any long-term trends in beach cross-shore profiles and longshore planshape (using, if possible, both analysis of historic beach data and predictive modelling if beach data is inadequate).

3. Combine (1) and (2) to identify likely future winter cross-shore profile. In the absence of better information it may be necessary to simply take the latest survey results (i.e. assume that the beach will be in the same state as at present when an extreme event occurs). Wherever possible, however, the statistically derived information on seasonal changes and secular trends should be used to predict a likely beach shape some years in the future.

4. Assess the behavioural response (often in combination with a built defence structure) of the present and predicted future beach profiles during a number of different extreme events (e.g. combinations of wave conditions and tidal levels). In this context responses include run-up, overtopping and any short-term erosion of the beach (and of any dunes behind) and consequent forces on, or hydraulic responses to, seawalls at the rear of the beach. Predictions of the performance of the assumed beach (and any defence structure) during an extreme event may then be carried out either with the aid of a scale physical model, or with a numerical empirical or theoretically-derived simulation method.

5. Assess the likelihood of beach recovery after a number of different extreme events.

Identification of critical beach conditions

The analysis procedure described above can be used to identify a series of response levels related to the degree of beach response. These can be identified (see Figure 5.4) as warning limits, action limits and failure limits.

The example given in Box 4.8 in Section 4.8.1 gives an indication of the type of approach with surveys where reducing beach volumes (possibly split into categories as in Box 4.6) would indicate:

- where volumes fall below a warning limit, there is a need to increase the frequency of monitoring and to plan future works
- where volumes fall below an action limit, there is a need to implement immediate recharge or other remedial work.

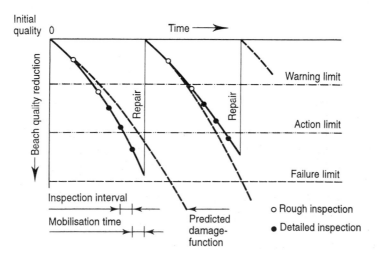

Figure 5.4   *Condition-based response to falling beach volumes*

5.2.2   Environmental audit

In order to establish the present day status of the beach in environmental terms, the environmental data discussed in Sections 4.2.1 to 4.2.7 should be collated and consultation undertaken as appropriate in order to prepare maps to indicate the location, extent and significance of features of environmental interest within the study area. Existing environmental problems and both desirable and undesirable trends should be identified.

5.2.3   Beach status report

The results of the assessment of present day beach status described in the detailed manner outlined above can be usefully summarised for management purposes in a beach status report. In this report, the results of the assessment of the importance of the beach as a coastal defence and its environmental importance should be preceded by descriptions of:

- the original beach formation (sources of material, etc.)
- the relationship of the beach to adjacent parts of the coast
- the historical development of the beach morphology and attributes (using maps and old photographs as appropriate)
- ongoing management practices or changes in, for example, dredging for navigation or navigation channel training works.

It should conclude by clearly identifying existing or historic problems and future trends, both desirable and undesirable.

5.3   PREDICTING FUTURE BEACH BEHAVIOUR

Before contemplating a management strategy for a section of coastline it is important to consider the likely future response of the beaches in both the long-term and under extreme conditions. The tools available to assess the future behaviour of the existing beach include:

- analysis of historic data in the context of coastal forcing, where beach processes are continuing in a consistent manner
- defining the coastal forcing and beach and coastal characteristics to predict the beach processes and consequent beach response.

Techniques for evaluating coastal forcing parameters (winds, waves, tidal currents and water levels) are described in Chapter 3 and for assessing and measuring beach characteristics (as defined in Chapter 2) are given in Chapter 4.

Whichever method is chosen, it should be noted that the development of a beach in general shows short-term (order of days) fluctuations superimposed on longer-term trends (order of years). Changes in the width of a beach at a specific location can be caused by the adjustment of the local beach profile in response to changing wave and tidal conditions. It can also be caused by alterations to the plan shape of the beach. In general, short-term changes are most likely to occur as a result of changes in the beach profile. Longer-term changes result from a redistribution of beach material along the coast due to variations in longshore drift causing beach plan shape changes. There is a link between the two processes and it should be remembered that any measurement of beach positions and levels will represent the combined effect of the two processes.

The methods of analysis of historic survey data should take account of the short-term fluctuation. It is often useful, for example, to plot, against time, the beach cross-sectional area at a particular section or the distance of a particular beach level contour in front of the seawall. If regular surveys have been carried out it may then be possible to identify trends of erosion or accretion. Individual profile locations should, however, not be considered in isolation. A loss in beach material from one profile section may coincide with a gain in material further along the coast. On a groyned beach it is also useful to calculate (from surveyed profiles) the volume of beach material within a groyne bay and plot the changes in this volume with time. This has the advantage that where the beach is rapidly reorientating itself to the current wave direction, the effect of redistribution of beach material within the groyne bay is filtered out from the long-term trend of beach volume change.

The two types of question likely to be asked by managers with responsibilities for the coast are of the form:

1. What will happen to the beach and any defences behind if they experience a severe storm?

2. How will the beach respond in the long-term?

The following two sections address these questions and explain the ways in which the predictions for the future response of the beach can be made.

5.3.1   Assessing response to severe events

In assessing the response of the beach to severe events there are a number of features which may become apparent:

* storm waves have a tendency to draw material down a beach whereas less steep swell waves tend to build the beach back up
* for sand beaches the material drawn offshore may form a bar
* permeable shingle beaches respond, in profile, more quickly (i.e. within a few hours) than sand beaches and if there is enough width of beach, they will form a storm crest
* for shingle beaches the crest height will depend on water level, wave height and period (often, many ridges may be seen down a beach face corresponding to crests formed by different storms)
* profile changes of a beach can cause a significant recession of the high water line and often expose a seawall behind the beach to more severe wave action.

Monitoring of beach profiles after a storm provides useful information on the current standard of protection and will help to calibrate future models. Since beaches are a natural form of coastal defence, it is often instructive to look at the crest heights (especially of shingle beaches) that have formed on nearby healthy beaches exposed to similar wave and water level forcing. This will provide a first estimate of extreme run up levels. Figure 5.5 gives an indication of the run-up level on a sand beach, with the talus forming a distinct scarp at the cliff toe.

The prediction of beach profiles after storms is usually carried out using models which can be divided into three main categories.

* parametric numerical equilibrium beach profile models
* process-based numerical morphological response beach profile models
* wave flume and wave basin physical models.

The rest of this section describes the different types of model and their mode of application.

Parametric numerical equilibrium beach profile models

Parametric beach profile models are semi-empirical models, based on observations of beach response either in the field, or in the laboratory. From these observations, one or more equations are derived which characterise the equilibrium beach profile shape (see Box 5.3 for a model of sand beaches, Box 5.4 for a shingle beach model and Section 6.4 for further information and equations). The equations involve variables such as the water level, the wave height and period, the size of beach material, etc. As with all empirically based models they are straightforward to use and provide useful results within their range of applicability. They are, however, limited to predicting results for situations that are within the range tested or observed in the experiments from which they were derived. In this regard, since the Powell model was developed from flume tests, it is only valid for normal incident waves; for oblique wave attack the model could still be used if the incident waves were adjusted to "equivalent normal waves" having similar wave run-up characteristics to the oblique waves. Formula for the run-up are given in CIRIA/CUR (1991).

Figure 5.5   *Sand beach run-up features at cliff toe, Easton Bavents, Suffolk (courtesy HR Wallingford)*

Process-based numerical morphological response beach profile models

The second type of numerical model for beach profile prediction concentrates on modelling the physical processes themselves. It calculates the water movements first, then the sediment transport they produce and finally the morphological changes. By their very nature, these models are much more complicated and require much greater computational effort. They are able, however, to predict the time-history of a changing beach profile, and this is important when wave or tidal conditions are altering rapidly, so that the beach does not have time to fully adjust to the ever-changing situations. A good recent review of the state-of-the-art of these models may be found in Roelvink and Brøker (1993)

Wave flume and wave basin physical models

Despite the great advances made in such modelling and the economic advantages of working with computational models, there are still many situations where physical scale models have an important, even a vital role to play (see Section 6.4.1 and Box 6.3). For example there are complex interactions between a beach and existing or proposed structures, computational models may not have been sufficiently calibrated or may not in fact reproduce all the important physical processes. In these situations a physical model may be more appropriate but must be carefully designed to account for the scaling of waves and beach sediment.

Box 5.3   *Empirical equations to predict sand beach profile response*

<u>Dean profiles</u>

The empirical Bruun (1954) hypothesis was supported on theoretical grounds by Dean (1977, 1987) to give a post-storm sand beach profile of the form

$$h = Ax^{2/3}$$

where h is the depth below storm surge level
             x is the distance offshore
and A is a constant 'shape factor' (depending on the length units used)

Dean (1987) has given a relation for A in terms of the fall velocity w

$$A = 0.067w^{0.44},$$

where w is in cm/s, x and y in metres.

The fall velocity can be calculated as described in Box 2.3. Dean (1991) has also expressed A directly in terms of grain size (see Box 7.6 for details).

Improvements to the approach are presented by Dean (1991), Larson (1991) and Work and Dean (1991).

<u>Vellinga's (1982) dune erosion prediction equations</u>

The erosion profile is described by

$$\left(\frac{7.6}{H_{0s}}\right)y = 0.47\left[\left(\frac{7.6}{H_{0s}}\right)^{1.28}\left(\frac{w}{0.0268}\right)^{0.56}x + 18\right]^{0.5} - 2.00$$

in which H_{0s} is the significant "deep water" wave height (m)
             w is the fall velocity of the sediment in stagnant water (m/s)
             x is the distance from the dune foot, in seaward direction (m)
             y is the depth below storm surge level (m)

The erosion extends from $x = 0$ and $y = 0$ (dune foot at storm surge level) down to a depth of $y = 0.75H_{0s}$, where

$$x = 250\,(H_{0s}/7.6)^{1.28}\,(0.0268/w)^{0.56}$$

Seaward of this position a uniform bottom slope of 1:12.5 is assumed down to the point of intersection with the initial beach profile, whereas the landward slope of the dune front (for x < 0) is taken as 1:1.

By using the idea of a closed sediment balance, this profile - that is related to the storm surge level - can be fixed in space. This is achieved by shifting the horizontal position of the computed storm profile relative to the initial pre-storm profile until there is a balance of volume between the eroded dune and the quantity of sand drawn down, as shown in Figure 1 below.

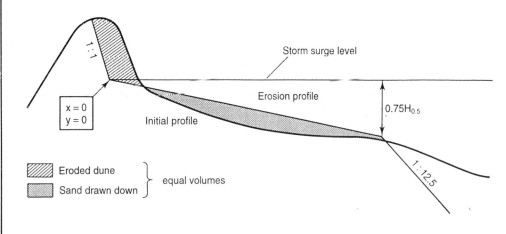

Figure 1   *Sand beach/dune system storm erosion/accretion balance*

Combination of techniques

It is also possible to combine physical and numerical models, together with field measurements, to greatly improve predictions. The laboratory experiments can be used to help calibrate numerical techniques, which in turn can be used to provide accurate predictions of the beach profile development.

This is a rapidly developing field and latest research and experienced advice should be consulted before using any particular combination of physical modelling, numerical modelling or field data collection technique.

5.3.2 Assessing gradual, long-term changes

In the long term, the principal cause of significant progressive changes in beaches is that of variations in the rate of longshore transport. However, significant long-term changes can also arise from cross-shore processes. An example of the latter is the gradual erosion of the base platform and steepening of the beaches on the Holderness coast, such as those shown in Figure 5.6.

Figure 5.6   *Beach on the Holderness Coast, Humberside (courtesy HR Wallingford)*

The use of regression analysis of long-term beach observations (see Chapter 3), particularly of the positions of high and low water marks, can yield valuable information here. It is preferable if a volumetric analysis is carried out to assess the sediment budget. From the available profiles one calculates the volume of beach sediment in a coastal section. This volume is plotted as a function of time and a regression analysis shows whether there is a long-term loss or gain of sediment. It is important to choose the boundaries carefully over which to calculate the volume. The landward boundary should be far enough landward not to be influenced by severe storms or in many cases it can be chosen as the position of an existing seawall. The seaward boundary should be chosen at a depth below which little sediment movement occurs (the closure depth). A practical boundary is a water depth of approximately twice the deep water significant wave height during for example the 1 in 1 year storm (checking whether the most seaward position occurs during high or low water conditions). The positions of moving bars should be considered when deciding on the boundary of the control volume. The movement of these bars should not disturb the analysis.

It is often useful to calculate the volume not just as one figure per profile but in horizontal and vertical slices. A greater understanding of the volume changes with time will thus be obtained and inaccuracies in the calculations due to movement of bars can be spotted and eliminated.

If only the variation in position of a specific contour is available, then this can be used for regression analysis, but the results can be misleading due to the effect of shorter-term changes in the profile. The distribution of the beach volume over the profile will be dependent on the wave and water level conditions in the days preceding the measurements. Fluctuations in the position of a single contour can be larger than the erosional trend that is being investigated. It is therefore recommended that analysis of variations in a specific contour should only be carried out if there is not enough information for a volumetric analysis.

Once any historical survey data has been analysed it may be important to model the longshore drift regime. This is particularly important if changes are to be made to structures in the coastal zone that may affect the waves or block a proportion of the drift.

The first stage in understanding the present beach processes is to estimate the annual potential open beach drift rate at a series of locations along the coast from the wave climates at these points. It is important to calculate the drift produced by a complete annual average wave climate, not just a single condition, since long-term changes in the beach planshape are dependent on the proportion of waves from different directions. It is also useful to have a measure of both the gross and the net drift rates to guide an appropriate choice of coastal protection measure that may be required. To calculate the longshore drift rate an energy-based formula (see Section 2.4.2 and Box 2.4) should be applied to each wave condition making up the wave climate. Such a formula relates the drift rate to a high power of the wave height together with a function of the direction of the waves relative to the beach normal.

Spatial variations in drift are caused by changes in the wave exposure along the beach or changes in the beach orientation. Man-made structures can also interfere with the drift, sometimes producing their own drift microclimate (Figure 5.7).

It is not actual drift rates but differences in drift rate that lead to areas of accretion or erosion, so by looking at the differences in drift rate along the coast and considering all other potential sources and sinks of material, a sediment balance can be drawn up and used to estimate locations and rates of erosion. It is usually important to put the study area into context by considering the sediment balance over the whole littoral cell, identifying the sources of supply of beach material and areas of erosion and accretion. Box 5.5 lists possible sources of supply and loss of beach material which need to be considered in a sediment budget calculation.

In the case of a beach with restricted sediment supply or a coast with shingle on the upper beach and sand on the lower, the cross-shore distribution of longshore drift must also be calculated to determine the proportion of the drift that occurs on the part of the beach where there is mobile material. The cross-shore distribution of drift produced by a particular wave condition can be estimated from an empirical distribution measured in the laboratory or the field. Figure 5.8 shows one such distribution for shingle beaches from Coates and Lowe (1993). The offshore distance from the run-up limit is non-dimensionalised by dividing by the distance offshore of the breaker point. The graph then shows the proportion of the total longshore drift occurring at each point down the beach face. To calculate the long-term cross-shore distribution of longshore drift a number of the individual distributions must be summed corresponding to the different wave heights and directions occurring at different tidal levels. In each case both the magnitude of the overall drift and the position of the breaker point will be different.

Box 5.4   *Parametric model for shingle beach profiles*

A parametric model for shingle beach profiles has recently been developed by Powell (1990) based on an extensive series of 131 model tests at HR Wallingford, UK, designed to simulate the behaviour of shingle beaches. The schematised beach profile is shown in Figure 1 and may be applied for the range $20 < H_s/\Delta D_{n50} < 250$. The model has not yet been fully validated against field data, but appears to give realistic results.

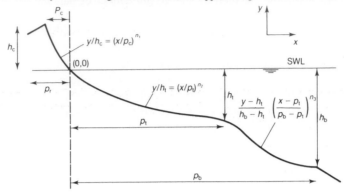

Figure 1 *Schematic shingle beach profile*

The parametric model is described by the following equations which should be read in conjunction with the definitions in Figure 1. The model is presented here to enable the designer to make first estimates. Profiles are, to some extent, duration limited and Powell (1990) suggests a method for accounting for this, but also concludes that complete reprofiling will occur within only 500 waves.

Basic beach profile prediction

1. Run-up limit, p_r

    $$p_r/H_s = 6.38 + 3.25\ln(H_s/L_{om})$$

2. Crest position, p_c

    $$p_c D_{50}/H_s L_{om} = -0.23(H_s T_m g^{1/2}/D_{50}^{3/2})^{-0.588}$$

3. Crest elevation, h_c

    $$h_c/H_s = 2.86 - 62.69(H_s/L_{om}) + 443.29(H_s/L_{om})^2$$

4. Transition position, p_t

    For $H_s/L_{om} < 0.03$:

    $$p_t \cdot D_{50}/H_s L_{om} = 1.73(H_s T_m g^{1/2}/D_{50}^{3/2})^{-0.81}$$

    For $H_s/L_{om} \geq 0.03$:

    $$p_t/D_{50} = 55.26 + 41.24(H_s^2/L_{om}D_{50}) + 4.90(H_s^2/L_{om}D_{50})^2$$

5. Transition elevation, h_t

    For $H_s/L_{om} < 0.03$:

    $$h_t/H_s = -1.12 + 0.65(H_s^2/L_{om}D_{50})^2 - 0.11(H_s^2/L_{om}D_{50})^2$$

    For $H_s/L_{om} \geq 0.03$:

    $$h_t/D_{50} = -10.41 - 0.025(H_s^2/D_{50}^{3/2}L_{om}^{1/2}) - 7.5 \times 10^{-5}(H_s^2/D_{50}^{3/2}L_{om}^{1/2})^2$$

6. Wave base position, p_b

    $$p_t/D_{50} = 28.77(H_s/D_{50})^{0.92}$$

7. Wave base elevation, h_b

    $$h_b/L_{om} = -0.87(H_s/L_{om})^{0.64}$$

8. Curve 1, crest to still-water level

    $$\frac{y}{h_c} = \left(\frac{x}{p_c}\right)^{n_1}$$

    where

    $$n_1 = 0.84 + 23.93H_s/L_m \quad \text{for } H_s/L_m < 0.03$$

    and

    $$n_1 = 1.56 \quad \text{for } H_s/L_m \geq 0.03$$

9. Curve 2, still-water level to transition

    $$\frac{y}{h_t} = \left(\frac{x}{p_t}\right)^{n_2}$$

    where

    $$n_2 = 0.84 - 16.49H_s/L_{om} + 290.16(H_s/L_{om})^2$$

Continued

Box 5.4 *Continued*

10. Curve 3, transition to wave base

$$\frac{y-h_t}{h_b-h_t} = \left(\frac{x-p_t}{p_b-p_t}\right)^{n_3}$$

where

$$n_3 = 0.45 \quad \text{for } H_s/L_{om} < 0.03$$

and

$$n_3 = 18.6(H_s L_{om}) - 0.1 \quad \text{for } H_s/L_{om} \geq 0.03$$

Position of predicted beach profile

The cross-shore position of the predicted beach profile may be established shifting the profile until a simple balance of cross-sectional areas about the initial beach profile is established. This, of course, assumes that the net longshore transport across the section is zero.

Correction for effective beach thickness, t_B

To be applied when $30D_{50} \leq t_B \leq 100D_{50}$. For values of $t_B < 30D_{50}$ the beach is destabilised. Correction R_{cpc} applies only to beach crest position, p_v.

$$R_{c_{pc}} = \frac{p_c(t_B/D_{50})}{p_c(t_B/D_{50} \geq 100)} = 6646 H_s/L_m(t_B/D_{50})^{-1.68} + 0.88$$

Correction for depth-limited foreshore

Correction factors necessary for positional parameters when $H_t/h_w > 3$, and for elevation parameters when $H_s/h_w > 0.55$.

Correction factor

$$R_{c_d} = Par_{meas}/Par_{pred}$$

where the predicted parameter value uses the wave conditions at the toe of the beach based on Goda (1985) and h_w = depth of water at toe of beach.

Depth-limited wave height: $H_{s_k} = 0.12 L_{om}[1.0 - \exp(-4.712 h_w(1.0 + 15 m^{1.33})L_{om})]$

Depth-limited wave length: $L_{m_k} = T_m(gh_w)^{1/2}$

1. Upper profile limit correction $R_{c_d} = 1.08(H_t/h_w) + 0.72 \quad \text{for } 0.3 < H_s/h_w < 2.5$

2. Crest position $R_{c_d} = 3.03(H_s/h_w) + 0.12 \quad \text{for } 0.3 < H_s/h_w < 2.5$

3. Crest elevation correction $R_{c_d} = (H_s/h_w) + 0.41 \quad \text{for } 0.55 < H_s/h_w < 2.5$

4. Transition position correction $R_{c_d} = 0.007(L_{om}/h_w)^{1/2} \quad \text{for } 40 < L_m/h_w < 130$

5. Transition elevation correction $R_{c_d} = 1.0 \quad \text{for } 0.55 < H_s/h_w < 2.5$

6. Wave base position correction $R_{c_d} = 1.08(H_s/h_w) + 1.31 \quad \text{for } 0.3 < H_s/h_w < 0.8$
    $R_{c_d} = 0.20(H_s/h_w) + 0.28 \quad \text{for } 0.8 < H_s/h_w < 2.5$

Figure 5.7   *Drift micro-climate behind fishing quay at Broadstairs, Kent (courtesy HR Wallingford)*

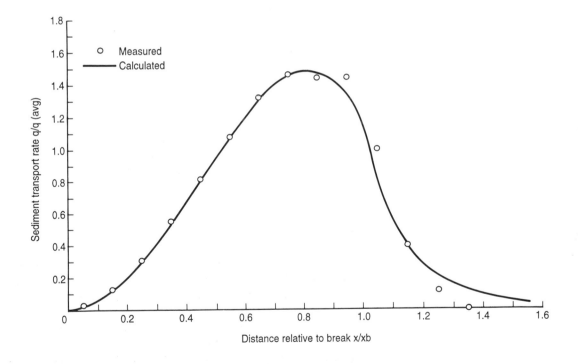

Figure 5.8   *Cross-shore distribution of longshore drift on a shingle beach*

Box 5.5   *The budget of littoral sediments (Komar, 1976)*

CREDIT	DEBIT	BALANCE
Longshore transport into area	Longshore transport out of area	Beach deposition or erosion
River transport	Wind transport out	
Sea cliff erosion	Offshore transport	
Onshore transport	Deposition in submarine canyons	
Biogenous deposition	Solution and abrasion	
Hydrogenous deposition	Mining	
Wind transport onto beach		
Beach nourishment		

Figure 1 shows a schematic example of a sediment budget with supply from an imbalance in the littoral drift (S_1-S_2), erosion of the cliffs, S_{cf}, and the sediment load of the river, S_r. Losses of sand occur into a submarine canyon, S_{cy}, and by sand being blown inshore onto the dunes. This example illustrates how engineering works such as stabilising the cliffs or damming the river (and thereby reducing its sediment load) can cause beach erosion.

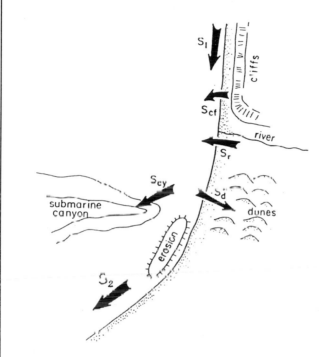

Figure 1   *Illustration of sediment budget components (Komer, 1976)*

The cross-shore distribution of longshore drift on sand beaches is quite dependent on the beach profile (adjusting in response to any change in beach profile) and will be very different depending on whether there are bars in the surf zone or not. A number of numerical models (often described as 'energetics based' models) are available to predict this distribution. These models generally first calculate the transformation of waves through the surf zone, they predict longshore currents and finally use these to calculate sediment transport. A good review of the cross-shore distribution of longshore drift is given in Bodge (1989).

Once longshore drift rates have been calculated, the long-term development of the beach can be modelled using a one-line beach planshape numerical model. This type of model is quite simple in principle so can be applied to long stretches of coastline for long periods of time. The basic principle of the model is that it first calculates the drift rate at each point along the beach taking into account the local beach orientation and the incident wave conditions. The effect of structures in modifying the waves and/or the drift rate can be included. The model applies a continuity of sediment calculation whereby the difference in drift rate into and out of a cell is equated to a volume change of the beach within the cell. From this volume change an advance or recession of each segment of coastline is calculated (see Box 5.6) and the calculation continues with the new coastline shape. To predict the long-term evolution of a coastline this method must be employed instead of just calculating instantaneous drift rates because as the beach builds out or erodes the orientation changes causing a change in the drift rate. Beach planshape models have also been developed from one-line models into multi-line models. Instead of requesting the plan shape of the coastline with a single contour, these models use a number of contours. The principles of the model are the same except that the beach profile at each point is assumed to change with the wave conditions, usually represented by simple empirical relationships, such as those in Box 5.3. The main advantage of these models is that it is possible to include the effect of changes in beach profile near structures, for example the steepening of the beach as it builds out on the updrift side of a groyne and the consequent changes in the efficiency of the groyne.

Although it is difficult to model the long-term response of a beach using a 3D wave basin model, it is often useful to employ an interactive modelling technique combining both physical and numerical models. The physical model can be used to model the detailed development of a short section of coast under a number of individual wave conditions. Information from this model can be used to calibrate a numerical model of the whole of the frontage that will be run for a complete time series of say 20 years. This interactive approach is described in more detail in Section 6.4.1.

Both numerical and physical modelling results will need to be adjusted to allow for factors not directly related to beach sediment transport, such as the reduction of sediment feed arising from the protection applied to eroding cliffs or the damming of rivers.

5.3.3 Sensitivity to climate change

When considering the future development of a beach it is important to examine the sensitivity of the predictions to possible future climate change and variability using appropriate deterministic models (including those set up for analysis of the present day situation). These factors are discussed below.

Relative sea level rise

Extreme design conditions must allow for relative sea level rise based on all relevant land and sea movements. Estimates of rates of relative sea level rise have been discussed in Section 3.6. When considering the long-term equilibrium of an unconstrained beach, the Bruun (1962) rule provides a simple method of assessing the retreat of the beach as a response to sea level rise (see Box 5.7). The main disadvantage of this simple equilibrium profile approach is that littoral drift is not taken into account. It is also important to appreciate that the coastal sea bed formations, as well as the land, are subject to long-term ecological change.

Change in wave climate directionality

If climate change causes a shift in wave directions, then longshore drift rates and the equilibrium coastline shape can be altered. In some circumstances a shift of only a few degrees can make a significant difference to the stability of a coastline. It is worth testing the sensitivity of predictions to changes in the proportion of waves arising from the various possible directions. This will allow for natural variability from year to year in the wave climate. Although at the time of preparation of this manual it is not yet certain, there is some evidence of climate change causing a shift in wave directions on the South Coast of the UK and a consequent change in drift. It will be many years before it can be proven whether this is part of a climatic change trend or within normal variability. Nonetheless, medium-term changes in drift have had noticeable impact on some South Coast beaches. For example at West Bay on Chesil Beach in Dorset, there has been a reversal of drift over the last 10 years causing changes of the order of 25 metres in the beach width in places. This highlights the importance of sensitivity testing to the wave direction.

Box 5.6   *One-line beach plan shape models*

If the longshore transport rate (Q) varies along a coast, then over time (t) the cross-sectional area (A) of the beach at any position (x) along the coast will change. This can be expressed in the following equation for the preservation of beach material:

$$\frac{\partial Q}{\partial x} = \frac{\partial A}{\partial t}$$

The changes in cross-sectional area will bring about a corresponding advance or retreat of the beach contours perpendicular to the coastline.

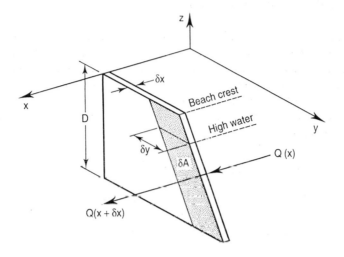

Figure 1   *Schematic of a one-line beach plan shape model*

The change in area (∂A) is equal to the change in position of the beach contours (∂y) multiplied by a representative depth (D). This results in the more common form of the above equation:

$$\frac{\partial Q}{\partial x} = D\frac{\partial y}{\partial t}$$

In practice, the beach profile will *not* advance or retreat by the same amount at all depths (as shown above). It is usual to consider the movement of one particular contour, say the high water mark, and this gives rise to the terminology of a "one-line" beach plan shape model. The depth D in the above equation is known as the "closure" depth. It can be difficult to evaluate, and may vary along the coastline. Ideally it should be evaluated by analysis of past beach changes, but often has to be approximated using beach cross-section surveys, bathymetric charts and previous experience.

5.3.4   Impact on environmental resource

In order to establish the environmental consequences of future beach behaviour, the data discussed in Section 4.3 should be collated and the results of the coastal process studies described in the rest of Section 5.3 should be considered. This evaluation can be achieved through one or more of the following: computer or physical modelling (see Section 6.4), review of past trends and predicted future trends, and/or discussions with interested parties. Of particular interest will be the future development of the coast as a result of the natural coastal processes operating, and the effects of any existing structures, etc. on that regime.

5.4 PERFORMANCE REQUIREMENTS

If having evaluated likely future beach performance, it appears to be necessary to implement some kind of beach management scheme, then the objectives of the scheme must be defined. Factors to be considered are:

- the life required of a scheme
- risk of failure
- the standard of defence consistent with achieving an appropriate benefit/cost ratio
- constraints and opportunities in respect of the environment
- the provision of maintenance.

Box 5.7 *Bruun rule relation between beach retreat and sea level rise*

The simplest mathematical method for predicting shoreline erosion caused by sea-level rise, first proposed by Bruun and know as the Bruun rule (1962, 1983), is based upon the principle of the beach equilibrium profile (see Box 5.3). The equilibrium principle is that, for a given wave climate and grain size, the beach will attain a predictable profile equilibrium. With a rise in sea-level, material will be eroded from shallow water and transported seawards to be deposited offshore on the seaward end of the profile, thus maintaining the equilibrium profile, as shown in the figure below. This 2-dimensional equilibrium profile holds for beaches on a gently sloping shoreline and, as described in Box 5.3, has the formula:

$$h = Ax^{2/3} \tag{1}$$

where

h	=	water depth
x	=	horizontal distance from shore
A	=	constant dependent upon grain size and on the length units used for x and h

Given an equilibrium profile of length l and a sea-level rise of Δs, the theoretical deposition required to re-adjust the profile is $l\Delta s$ (see Figure 1). The profile is assumed to be in materials balance (i.e. the amount of sediment moving in and out of the system is in equilibrium). The only way in which the material for deposition can be obtained is by a shoreward movement. To balance the deposition $l\Delta s$, a shoreward erosion of $ha\Delta y$ is required (where ha is the depth of exchange of material and Δy the shoreline recession). The shoreline retreat is therefore approximated as:

$$\Delta y = l\Delta s/ha \tag{2}$$

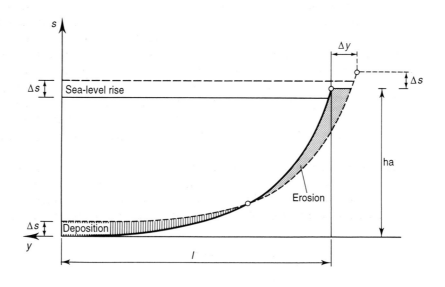

Figure 1 *Beach profile sections showing readjustment to sea level rise*

5.4.1 Life of a scheme

In different aspects of the management process the term "life" is used in a number of ways. For clarity the following can be defined:

- *Working life* - the length of time that the scheme actually lasts and is capable of functioning as required.

- *Component life* - the length of time that a particular system component lasts before requiring replacement.

- *Design life* - the minimum length of time a beach management scheme is designed to last.

In many cases of beach management substantial maintenance may be required to ensure that the actual working life is long enough to meet the required design life.

The choice of design life requires careful consideration and regard for the marine environment in which it will function. The use of a long design life may result in a very costly scheme. A shorter design life may be predetermined by expected changes in the use of the land protected or may show financial advantage even after provision is made for future replacement. It is usual for the design life chosen to be the economic optimum solution by which the functional requirements can be met (see Section 5.5). The choice is often strongly influenced by the availability of inexpensive local materials which are of limited durability. It may be found that the shorter design life leads to a cost-effective scheme with provision for future replacement.

Design life is different from the return period for design conditions. The latter relates to the risk of design conditions being exceeded (see Section 5.4.2). A sea defence with a life of 30 years may for instance be required to resist overtopping by a 1 in 100-year water level.

5.4.2 Probability of failure

Phenomena such as winds, waves, tides and surges are fundamental factors in the behaviour of beaches. Extreme values of these are therefore essential design criteria in the development of beach management and details of their calculation are given in Chapter 3. However, there are frequently no absolute maximum values of these phenomena (although there are exceptions such as when wave height is depth limited). In circumstances when there is no realistic maximum, the solution is to choose extreme values which are very rare. It follows, therefore, that there is a finite chance that the design conditions will be exceeded during the life of the beach management scheme. For convenience this probability of exceedance is normally characterised by the "return period" (T_R). An event with a return period of T_R years is likely to be exceeded, on average, once in T_R years. The most appropriate return period should be chosen in consideration of the consequences of exceedance (e.g. overtopping and consequent flooding).

As referred to in the previous section, the return period selected for the various design criteria should not be confused with design life. For example, if the return period of any extreme event is set the same as the design life, then there is a 63% chance that the extreme event will be exceeded before the end of the design life, according to the equations:

$$P = 1 - \left(1 - \frac{1}{nT_R}\right)^{(L \times n)} \tag{5.1}$$

or

$$T_R = \frac{1}{n} \times \frac{1}{1 - (1 - P)^{1/(L \times n)}} \tag{5.2}$$

where P = probability of the extreme event being exceeded during the design life, L = design life and n = number of events per year (e.g. considering extreme high waters, $n = 706$ = number of tides/year). Table 5.3 shows calculated probabilities for a typical range of these various factors and an example of this methodology is given in Box 5.8.

Table 5.3 Probability of exceedance of a design event

Return period (years)	Design Life (years)														
	2	3	5	10	20	30	40	50	75	100	200	300	400	500	1000
2	0.63	0.78	0.92	0.99	1.00	1.00	1.00	1.00	1.00	1.00	1.00	1.00	1.00	1.00	1.00
3	0.49	0.63	0.81	0.96	1.00	1.00	1.00	1.00	1.00	1.00	1.00	1.00	1.00	1.00	1.00
5	0.33	0.45	0.63	0.86	0.98	1.00	1.00	1.00	1.00	1.00	1.00	1.00	1.00	1.00	1.00
10	0.18	0.26	0.39	0.63	0.86	0.95	0.98	0.89	1.00	1.00	1.00	1.00	1.00	1.00	1.00
20	0.10	0.14	0.22	0.39	0.63	0.78	0.86	0.92	0.98	0.99	1.00	1.00	1.00	1.00	1.00
30	0.06	0.10	0.15	0.28	0.49	0.63	0.74	0.81	0.92	0.96	1.00	1.00	1.00	1.00	1.00
40	0.05	0.07	0.12	0.22	0.39	0.53	0.63	0.71	0.85	0.92	0.99	1.00	1.00	1.00	1.00
50	0.04	0.06	0.10	0.18	0.33	0.45	0.55	0.63	0.78	0.86	0.98	1.00	1.00	1.00	1.00
75	0.03	0.04	0.06	0.12	0.23	0.33	0.41	0.49	0.63	0.74	0.93	0.98	1.00	1.00	1.00
100	0.02	0.03	0.05	0.10	0.18	0.26	0.33	0.39	0.53	0.63	0.86	0.95	0.98	0.99	1.00
200	0.01	0.01	0.02	0.05	0.10	0.14	0.18	0.22	0.31	0.39	0.63	0.78	0.86	0.92	0.99
300	0.01	0.01	0.02	0.03	0.06	0.10	0.12	0.15	0.22	0.28	0.49	0.63	0.74	0.81	0.96
400	0.00	0.01	0.01	0.02	0.05	0.07	0.10	0.12	0.17	0.22	0.39	0.53	0.63	0.71	0.92
500	0.00	0.01	0.01	0.02	0.04	0.06	0.08	0.10	0.14	0.18	0.33	0.45	0.55	0.63	0.86
1000	0.00	0.00	0.00	0.01	0.02	0.03	0.04	0.05	0.07	0.10	0.18	0.26	0.33	0.39	0.63

The probability of failure of structures which form part of a management scheme is often easier to define than the probability of beach failure because the estimation of the exact beach profile at the time of an incident (i.e. a particular storm event) depends on predictive techniques (see Sections 5.2 and 5.3). In practice, failure of a beach may also occur as a result of a series of moderate events or prolonged weather from a particular direction.

This probability theory is used in the evaluation of potential damages and hence of the benefits derived from undertaking a particular scheme. This is discussed further in Section 6.5.

5.4.3   Risk assessment

The previous section outlined a method for predicting the probability of a scheme failing during its design life. Risk assessment is the process of analysing the probabilities and consequences of failure in order to arrive at a more complete description of the performance of a scheme. Risk assessment can thus help to identify hazards and failure mechanisms that might otherwise go unnoticed.

"Risk" is defined as:

$$R = P. c$$

where P is the probability of failure due to a specified hazard and c is a measure of the consequences. Risk assessment is closely related to benefit-cost analysis (see Section 5.5).

Box 5.8   *Probability of exceedance and return period: examples*

A beach scheme with a design life of 50 years is to protect developed land from flooding.

It may be considered that, because of the nature of the development which is to be protected, overtopping due to an excessively high water level would be very serious. An acceptable probability of exceedance may therefore be selected as 10% in the life of the sea wall.

In this case, to establish the appropriate return period,

$$T_R = \frac{1}{n} \times \frac{1}{1-(1-P)^{1/Ln}}$$
$$= \frac{1}{706} \times \frac{1}{1-(1-0.1)^{1/(50 \times 706)}}$$
$$= 475 \text{ years}$$

As a second example, if one considers a sea defence system with a design life of 50 years, and a design wave condition with a return period of 100 years. Then the corresponding probability of exceedance

$$= 1 - \left(1 - \frac{1}{100 \times 2920}\right)^{50 \times 2920} = 0.39$$

Note: it is assumed in analysis that a wave condition lasts 3 hours (see Section 5.4), i.e.

$$n = \frac{365 \times 24}{3} = 2920$$

The general stages in a risk assessment are:

1.   Identify hazards i.e. potential causes or triggers of failure.

2.   Formulate failure mechanisms.

3.   Calculate failure probabilities.

4.   Quantify the consequences.

5.   Calculate risk.

In carrying out this assessment process, the use of event trees or fault trees (see Figure 6.2) are often helpful to track links between contributory events or causes.

Having completed a risk analysis, the total risk inherent in a scheme is the integration of risk over all hazards and all failure mechanisms, although normally only a small number of each will be significant enough to justify detailed analysis.

Risk is normally expressed in annual terms. The units of risk depend on the consequence being considered. Different consequences may have different units and may be impossible to compare objectively. Examples of possible consequences include:

- stress and anxiety
- damages or loss of property
- loss of human life
- human injuries
- regression of beach
- loss of infrastructure
- loss of beach control structure
- environmental loss
- impact on other coastal sites.

There is a wide range of methods for risk assessment. Qualitative methods enable relative risk to be assessed by categorising probabilities and consequences, often using verbal descriptions. In this way relative risk of different schemes can be compared. Quantitative risk assessment is based on calculating failure probabilities and quantifying consequences. The more sophisticated methods involve time-series predictions over the lifetime of the scheme.

This enables a very complete model to be devised, including management rules on which future decisions can be made and long-term changes in climate taken into account. These risk models are often run probabilistically - each prediction is an example of what may happen, with an associated probability. Repeating many scenarios, this type of model can explore possible combinations of input parameters to give probability distributions of the required result variables.

Acceptable risk

The calculated risks of project options can be compared with each another or with a semi-objective standard, generally known as "acceptable risk".

There are several ways in which criteria (such as defined standards of service - see Section 5.4.4) for acceptable risk can be expressed. Some examples are discussed below:

1. Probability that service criteria will not be met. It is likely that the acceptable probability level will depend on the consequences of failure, from minor inconvenience or slight damage to loss of life or extensive damage to property.

2. Economic risk. The expected loss due to failure of a scheme may be expressed in economic terms and assessed as part of a benefit - cost appraisal.

3. Risk of death or injury. Criteria of acceptable risk may be established by examining risks from the other activities or hazards. Criteria may be expressed in terms of risk to an individual, or the number of fatalities or injuries incurred by the population as a whole.

5.4.4   Standard of service

The aim of beach management is to provide a service or services in respect of one or more requirements which include coastal defence, conservation, amenity and a number of other functions. It is important for the responsible authorities to assess whether the standard of service provided in each of these areas is satisfactory at present, in terms of the *benefits* produced (see Section 6.5.1). There is a need for the authorities to provide an overall assessment of the standard of service at a regional level. This does not remove the requirement for detailed economic, environmental and engineering appraisal for individual schemes once the regional needs are identified.

In the UK the NRA have played a leading role in pursuing regional and national initiatives which allow planning level assessments of the standard of protection, currently provided by flood and coastal defences, in terms of the protection of property. Work has also extended to cover environmental assets. NRA have adopted the term 'standard of service' for the standard of protection related to flood defence.

The NRA process requires the classification of the assets to be protected, to a common basis, so that a consistent approach can be developed. NRA have chosen to use "house equivalents" (HEs). In terms of potential flooding damage, which is taken as a measure of the value of the asset at risk, an HE is defined as "the average cost of flooding damage suffered by an average house which is at risk of flooding". HEs have not eliminated the need for benefit assessments valued in monetary terms but have been utilised by the NRA for certain management applications. Following on from this classification, the NRA have developed a system of land use banding based on the total number of HEs protected per kilometre of defence.

On this basis broad indicative standards of service can be identified and assessed for each length of defence. However, these target standards are only indicative and other criteria, such as the MAFF/Welsh Office economic *decision rule* for England and Wales, will be used to set the eventual standard on a particular frontage. Box 6.4 (see Section 6.5.3), reproduced from the MAFF (1993a) Project Appraisal Guidance Notes, sets out this decision rule and gives indicative standards of protection for different categories of land use. The "design" standard of protection of a beach can be quantified in terms of its capacity to resist meteorological events of a given return period. Usually such an assessment will require the use of mathematical or physical models (see Section 5.3).

5.4.5 Adjacent coast and foreshore

The importance of taking a broad view in assessing coastal works, particularly in terms of their impact on coastal processes, has been discussed earlier in this section and in Section 2.6. Perhaps the most important single aspect in this regard is the potential impact on adjacent coasts.

The major morphological mechanism of sediment transport acting on beaches is longshore transport. Providing more material (through nourishment) to be transported or reducing the amount of transport with beach control structures will have a significant impact on longshore transport and on the adjacent shoreline. For example, there have been a number of cases where groynes have been built to trap sand or shingle in order to enhance the beach and where, as a result, the supply of material to the adjacent beach has been starved and has led to erosion. On the other hand, wholesale beach recharge can also produce problems if rates of longshore supply are increased, with the potential for adverse impacts (e.g. the covering of valuable environmental assets, disturbance to fauna or blocking of river outlets). In defining the functional requirements of a beach management scheme the minimisation of downdrift impacts should therefore be given a high priority.

5.4.6 Environmental requirements

When performance requirements are being determined for a particular site, environmental needs should also be considered. In addition to features of environmental interest in the intertidal area, the needs of which are considered in Section 2.2, other environmental assets might be effectively protected by the beach in its role as a coastal defence. Environmental assets at risk from flooding or erosion could include sites of nature conservation interest, archaeological or heritage features, formal or informal recreational facilities, etc. In some cases, sites designated under the Birds Directive, 1979, or Habitats Directive, 1992, may require a high standard of protection because of their unique characteristics or their vulnerability to damage or destruction. However, the decision will vary on a case by case basis depending on the view of the country conservation agency. For example a freshwater site designated as a Special Protection Area which is currently protected from saline inundation by a healthy beach may require a high standard of protection. In environmental terms, a lower standard of protection may be appropriate to areas of ground that are subject to frequent overtopping and where any plant species present are salt tolerant.

Some archaeological features may be able to tolerate limited inundation providing they are not exposed to wave attack. Others may require a higher standard of protection if there is risk of damage by salinity or prolonged inundation. In other cases, an environmental resource may depend on the maintenance of the status quo situation (e.g. a brackish habitat dependent on overtopping or seepage). The key characteristics which will determine the standard of defence required by environmental assets protected by the defences are, therefore, their vulnerability to damage, their dependence on the existing regime, their ability to recover (within a reasonable time period) from any damage caused by flooding or erosion, their uniqueness (or replaceability) if they are likely to be lost permanently and the quality of the environment which would replace them.

Finally a further example of an environmental requirement may be the prevention of pollution. The beach, in its role as a coastal defence, may therefore be required to prevent environmentally unacceptable material (e.g. a waste tip located behind the beach) being eroded and subsequently introduced into the mobile sediment zone.

5.5 PREPARATION AND IMPLEMENTATION OF BEACH MANAGEMENT PLANS

The scope of a beach management plan can be very wide ranging. It may simply cover the monitoring and maintenance of a beach (see Chapters 4 and 11). Alternatively it may require the implementation of a beach management scheme involving capital works and subsequent maintenance together with extensive engineering and environmental monitoring.

The steps in the preparation and implementation of a beach management scheme are:

- definition of the problem followed by an engineering, environmental and economic appraisal of possible solutions (see Chapter 6)
- the design of the preferred solution (see Chapters 6, 7, 8 and 9)
- the implementation of the solution (see Chapter 10)
- the implementation of ongoing management and maintenance of the solution (see Chapter 11).

These steps are discussed in detail in the chapters identified above.

A typical beach management plan is shown in Figure 5.9. This plan is for the Hunstanton to Heacham flood defences, and illustrates the monitoring and maintenance cycles that should be undertaken following the initial management scheme that entailed a major recharge of the beach.

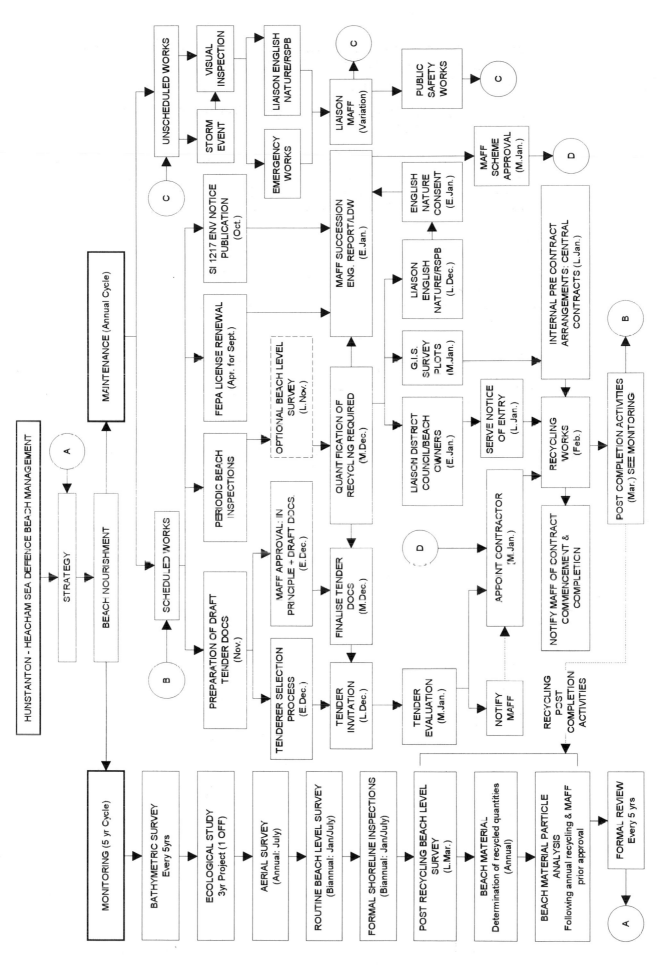

Figure 5.9   *Hunstanton to Heacham sea defence beach management flowchart (courtesy NRA Anglian Region)*

6 Elements of appraisal and design

6.1 GENERAL APPROACH

Sometimes monitoring and management of an existing beach resource indicates that it will be necessary to develop a formal beach management scheme. In this situation and where a completely new beach is required, it will be necessary to select an appropriate scheme. This chapter is concerned with the appraisal and development of a project up to the selection of the preferred scheme. It focuses on project options involving some form of beach management but it is recognised that during the appraisal stage of a project, options which exclude beach management would also be examined. Methods for detailed design of the preferred scheme are dealt with in Chapters 7, 8, 9 and 10.

A flow chart illustrating the interaction between the various tasks, leading to preparation of the preferred design is given in Figure 6.1.

6.1.1 Definition of the problem

Beach management may be sought for a number of reasons. In the majority of cases it is viewed as a means of providing coast protection or flood defence while possibly offering other environmental improvements. As such, the beach, as an integral part of a design, is more than just a means of solving a problem, it also provides opportunities. Nevertheless, the reason for adopting beach management is usually driven by the need to provide protection. More occasionally other factors may take precedence, for example in the design of harbour or reclamation works, where such works might have an impact on existing beaches. Alternatively there may be a desire to enhance an existing beach to improve tourism potential.

Whatever the initiative for the beach management scheme, there will always be issues or problems to be resolved. Moreover, the designer must decide whether a beach scheme is the right solution for the problem. This decision requires a clear and precise definition of the scheme objectives.

Determining the problem is not always straightforward. Sometimes the problem may be quite different from that initially perceived or involve a much more serious underlying problem. For example, a common coastal defence problem is that of waves and shingle overtopping seawalls during storms. This is a nuisance to the frontagers (those owning, and often living in, property immediately landward of the beach) and can cause some damage to the immediate infrastructure. One solution might appear to be to raise the seawall crest level to reduce overtopping. However, the root cause of the problem might actually be low beach levels. This in turn could eventually lead to undermining and failure of the seawall. If the seawall protects low lying land, then the losses in the event of a breach could be many times greater than those arising solely from overtopping. This example shows how the manifestation of a problem can disguise a potential catastrophe, and illustrates the need for correct definition of the problem.

Fault trees can be drawn to aid the identification of problems. Each fault tree is designed to cover the range of relevant parameters and processes according to the specific problem. Figure 6.2 gives an example of a fault tree for flow over a seawall. The figure shows the progression from alternative causes to the resultant effect, i.e. flow over the wall; in this example one possible cause of the problem is lowering of the beach. It is, of course, possible that the effect arises from more than one cause. However, the approach outlined enables alternative "failure" modes to be identified and for each mode an event tree can be prepared to enable the probability of failure in that mode to be assessed (see Section 5.4 above).

Thus, the initial part of a project appraisal is concerned with defining the problem. This will entail consideration not only to the physical manifestations of the problem, but also give an understanding of it in a broad context, both geographically and in chronological terms (e.g. will the problem worsen with time?). In essence, defining the problem entails an evaluation of what

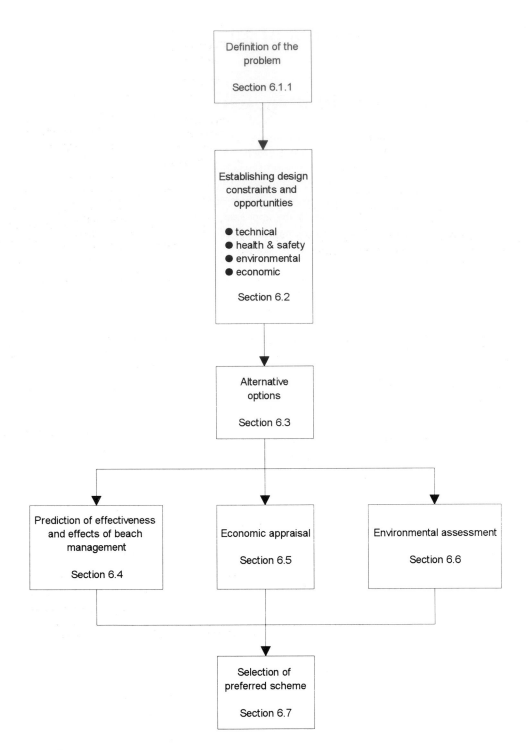

Figure 6.1 *Scheme appraisal stages*

will happen if no action is taken (i.e. if no works are carried out). This evaluation includes engineering, environmental and economic considerations, which are dealt with elsewhere in this chapter.

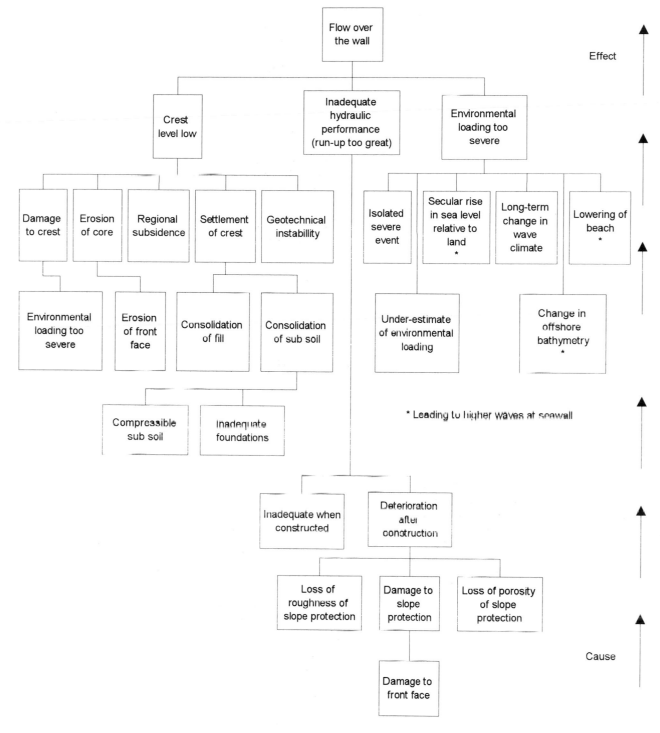

Figure 6.2 *Fault tree: events leading to flow over seawall*

6.1.2 Advancing the scheme

From a definition of the problem, an understanding of the hydraulic, environmental and human constraints and an understanding of the management objectives, it will be possible to shortlist those options which are technically viable. Fundamentally, there are two types of solution which can result:

- remove the cause of the problem
- respond to the symptoms of the problem.

Frequently the problem results from a cause which cannot be controlled; in such cases, schemes for mitigating the symptoms must be considered. The generation of alternative solutions for such schemes and the initial screening of these against technical criteria are discussed in Section 6.3.

Those schemes which are technically viable should be examined in terms of engineering, health and safety, environmental and economic criteria as discussed elsewhere in this chapter. The "do nothing" case (see Section 6.3.2) provides the basis for comparing the alternative schemes. This is the process of project appraisal described in MAFF (1993a) which culminates in the selection of a preferred design (see Section 6.7).

Project appraisal in coast protection and sea defence must entertain all the viable options, even though some may be rejected early in the process. Pro-active beach management may not form part of every option that is considered in coast protection and sea defence, but is generally a component of most options and the other options will generally require some form of beach management plan even if it is an agreed "do nothing". The remainder of this chapter is concerned with the elements of appraisal and preliminary design of the various options in the context of beach management, other (non beach design) options are also alluded to but not discussed in detail as these are dealt with by other specific texts (e.g. CIRIA/CUR, 1991, and Thomas and Hall, 1992).

6.2 ESTABLISHING DESIGN CONSTRAINTS AND OPPORTUNITIES

A large number of criteria influence the implementation of a beach management project. In this context "implementation" is taken to include the appraisal, planning, design, capital works (construction), operation and maintenance of any given scheme. As a scheme progresses, some of these factors are obviated (e.g. certain constraints during construction may not apply once the works are in place). During the appraisal and initial development of a project, however, it is important to consider all the criteria which are relevant at every stage. These criteria may present constraints or provide opportunities in the design.

This section discusses the various constraints and opportunities that should be examined at the start of a project. It should be noted that these criteria rarely act independently of each other and it is thus necessary to examine the interaction of one with another. This entails thorough overall management and coordination of the various elements of the appraisal and initial development of any given scheme.

6.2.1 Physical constraints and opportunities

The appraisal and design of a beach management project requires, as input, data on the physical setting and processes active at the site of interest. This section outlines the parameters relating to hydraulic and ground conditions that are needed and the reasons for seeking such information. The derivation of design data is covered in Chapter 3 and 4.

Water levels

Information on water levels is required for a wide range of applications including:

- analysis of coastal processes
- analysis of cross-shore movements of sediment
- evaluation of standards of performance (e.g. allowable maximum overtopping)
- ground water influence
- flood risk assessment
- practical considerations (i.e. construction and maintenance).

Water level data (see Section 3.1) will include information to describe the normal astronomical tides and information on extreme water levels. The latter includes both astronomical tide and meteorological surges. In conjunction with wave data, extreme water levels are used to assess the overtopping and breaching of coastal structure and shingle ridges. Once a defence has breached, the subsequent risk and frequency of inundation (through the breach) depends on the return periods of water levels higher than the invert of the breach.

Sea level rise (see Section 3.6.1) must be included in the prediction of normal and extreme water levels in the future. Past sea level trends can also be allowed for in the derivation of extreme water levels based on historic data. Generally this has the effect of slightly increasing the estimate of extreme levels in the future.

Wave conditions

Wave parameters are sought as essential input in the derivation of coastal processes, including both longshore and cross-shore transport, and for determining standards of defence for existing and proposed coastal structures. Two categories of data are required, which describe the wave climate and extreme values.

Wave climate (see Sections 3.3 and 3.4) data comprises the directional distribution of wave heights and wave periods at a site. This climate usually refers to the extreme as well as the average annual conditions and is based on several years' observations (usually of wind data from which waves are hindcast). The data is used to derive longshore transport of sediment - a knowledge of the annual drift enables long-term beach changes to be calculated.

Annually averaged wave climate data are also used to evaluate the typical cross-shore profiles of the beach. It is usually necessary, however, to predict the cross-shore profile subject to extreme values corresponding to the condition, or standard of service, at which the design is targeted. As the cross-shore response of a beach is strongly influenced by both waves and water levels, the joint probability of occurrence of the two processes must be considered (see Section 3.5). Waves in the nearshore zone become significantly influenced by tide level; hence the wave climate and extreme waves are a function of the tide level. This factor can significantly increase the computational effort in deriving accurate estimates of the alongshore sediment transport which, of course, occur over a range of tide levels.

Tidal currents

Tidal currents (see Section 3.2) are more important in terms of their ability to transport sand than shingle. This is due, in part, to the fact that shingle is generally found in the upper part of the beach where currents are usually reduced by shallow water effects and by flow separation off coastal features. Moreover, shingle has a higher threshold of movement than sand. In some instances however, currents can be the predominant sediment moving force. This may happen where a tidal channel meanders close to the shore. In such cases current meter data will be sought. Generally, however, the influence of currents relative to waves should be assessed on the basis of existing data in order to gauge the value and scope of a dedicated measurement campaign.

Ground conditions - general

Required data on ground conditions include that on both mobile deposits and the substrata. Data will describe the depth, distribution and character of the beach, foreshore and possibly the nearshore seabed, the landmass and adjacent cliffs.

Existing beach sediments

Data on the existing mobile sediments are needed to assess its mobility (i.e. particle size distribution) and density, and to aid identification of its origin (i.e. by matching with possible sources). The level, depth and distribution of the sediment is important as this constitutes the existing volume of material available, for which the present standard of defence can be derived.

Underlying strata

The stratum immediately beneath the mobile sediments can be responsible for the long-term lowering of the beach. At several locations around the UK coast this is known to happen due to the progressive erosion of the clay stratum beneath a "thin" mobile beach. Thus, the abrasion characteristics of the underlying materials are important. The strength of these materials is also important for deciding on construction methods (e.g. the depth and character of underlying rock determines the feasibility of piling).

Cliffs

The geological make-up of cliffs is of interest principally in two respects:

- erodibility
- as a source of sediment.

An understanding of the erosion characteristics of cliffs would be gained not only on the basis of geological data but also from historic records such as aerial photographs and maps. Cliff erosion, although often described in terms of a long-term rate of retreat, is frequently characterised by intermittent landslipping events. Thus understanding of the erosion process is important. It should also be noted that their erosion by the action of the sea is conditioned by other factors such as the widths of beach, longshore transport and coast protection works. These factors may therefore have changed with time, and data relating to these must be included in the information gathered to assess cliff erodibility.

Sediment release

As cliffs erode, sediments are released to the shore. The proportion of sediment that is retained on the shore as useful beach building material depends on the sedimentary make up of the cliff fall. Where the bulk of the material consists of clay, which can break down into fines and be lost offshore, the yield of material for beach sediment may actually be quite small.

6.2.2   Environmental constraints and opportunities

Section 2.2 sets out the type of environmental assets associated with beaches and indicated those attributes which are of particular importance to maintaining and/or protecting such assets. Environmental requirements may constrain some beach management activities or options, or lead to a requirement for mitigation or compensation measures if the impact is deemed potentially significant. Conversely, beach management may provide opportunities to further protect or even enhance environmental assets. Table 6.1 illustrates some examples of environmental constraints and opportunities associated with beach management initiatives.

Each management initiative will possess a different set of characteristics and, therefore, exert a different set of effects on the environment. Some, such as noise generated during construction, may be readily quantified, whilst others, such as the effect on shore bird populations of reductions in available feeding/roosting areas cannot be predicted with such accuracy. Indeed, prediction of the impact of coastal schemes in general is often complicated by the highly dynamic nature of the existing environment subject as it is to the vagaries of winds, waves and tides.

The basic techniques of the environmental impact assessment procedure are described in Section 6.6. Further details of the likely environmental impacts and opportunities associated with the various beach management techniques described in this manual are presented in the relevant parts of Chapters 7, 8, 9 and 11. It should be emphasised here, however, that these sections do not attempt to provide a definitive listing of all possible impacts and mitigation measures, but instead present a broad overview of the issues.

Table 6.1 Environmental constraints and opportunities

Beach Attribute	Environmental Characteristic	Example of Constraint	Example of Opportunity
Sediment size	Flora and fauna	Avoid displacement or degradation of existing species	Protect/enhance back-beach vegetation (e.g. sand dunes)
		Seasonal working required by nesting needs of bird population	Covering of clay exposures may increase species abundance
		Maintain slope, drying zone, etc.	Create nesting site for birds
	Informal recreation	Maintenance of "similar" material to ensure continuation of existing use	Provision of improved sediment size for desired use
		Wind-blown sand	
Sediment colour	Landscape	Protection of site of accepted landscape value	Re-instatement of landscape value for scarred or blighted coastline
	Flora and fauna	Maintenance of existing bird habitat	
	Recreation	Maintenance of aesthetic value of beach/coastal landscape	
Access	Various human activities, including fishing	Maintain access points during works, with particular seasonal requirements	Improve access to beach
	Long sea outfall	Structure needs to be maintained in position to enable discharge of surface water or other water	Combine structure with a beach control structure
Beach slope (offshore)	Navigation	Need to maintain safe inshore navigation	Removal of hazards
Beach slope (onshore)	Informal recreation	Maintenance of gentle and safe slopes	Provision of hazard warning boards
	Formal recreation	Maintenance of safe access and quick vessel launching	
	Commercial fishing activity	Maintain gradient for vessel launching and landing	Provision of usable beach slope
Tidal inundation	Informal recreation	Acceptable width of drying beach	Provide expanded drying beach enabling increased use
Chemical composition	Flora and fauna	Resistance of back-beach vegetation	
		Need for calcium carbonate	
	Various human uses	Acceptable levels of "contaminants" in any placement material	

6.2.3 Financial and economic constraints

The terms finance and economics should not be confused. Finance relates to cashflow. For example, financial constraints on a project are limitations to the amount of money that can be spent and financial benefits are monetary benefits that may accrue from a scheme, such as increased cashflow earnings. Economics relates to value, expressed in monetary terms. For example, economic costs of a project represent the value of property and services used in the implementation of a project. This may or may not involve money changing hands (the use of land by siting a coastal defence upon it will have an economic cost, even though it may not actually involve finance because it may already be owned by the agency building the defence).

Financial constraints

Clearly financial constraints, or budgetary limitations, are very important in the selection of a scheme. There are obviously considerable attractions in choosing the cheapest option for coastal defence. However, this may well have to be tailored to suit limitations in budget, such as in the case when one capital scheme requires a higher rate of spending than an alternative, which, while more expensive overall, allows expenditure to be phased to suit available funds. Financial constraints, if any, must be defined early in the appraisal stage to allow a sound evaluation of alternatives.

Economic constraints

It is normal for public expenditure to be scrutinised to ensure that it presents good value for money. Economic appraisal is therefore required which seeks to evaluate the economic costs and economic benefits resulting from each option and, on this basis, to assess:

- whether the work is economically justified (i.e. whether economic benefits exceed economic costs)
- which option is the best in economic terms.

Economic appraisal is dealt with in MAFF (1993a) and discussed in Section 6.5. The need to provide good value for money in economic terms is fundamental to the appraisal of beach management strategies. In the U.K. it is a prerequisite for obtaining central government grant aid for all coastal defence schemes.

6.2.4 Availability of beach recharge material from potential sources

If beach recharge is likely to be required, a recharge material source needs to be identified and adequately classified. It is necessary for the following six key aspects of the source to be determined:

- the location of the source
- the characteristics of the source material (i.e. grading, colour, shape, susceptibility to attrition, etc.)
- whether there is a sufficient volume of the material available for the scheme
- whether the volume required may be extracted to suit the programming of the beach recharge works
- the unit cost of obtaining the material
- the environmental effects of material extraction.

The last of these should already have been taken into account if the source is already licensed and is to be worked within its current licensing conditions.

These key aspects are inextricably linked to other aspects of the beach recharge scheme, such as design, scheme cost, environmental and amenity benefits and disbenefits, and programming, as illustrated in Figure 6.3. For example, if the design of the rock groynes in the scheme are altered by lengthening from existing groynes on the frontage, this may have the effect of increasing the volume required (due to the flatter beach slope), but may allow a reduction of the particulate size of the beach material to permit use of a particular source. This is particularly important with shingle beaches where the indigenous sediments can rarely be emulated exactly. However the longshore transport and general coastal process implication of such a beach material size change must also be fully evaluated.

Similarly, the location of the source and its characteristics may affect the environmental value of the scheme. A land-based source might have a lower amenity value, due to its colour, size and shape, than a sea-dredged source. Alternatively, a sea-dredged source will have to be checked for contamination, particularly if being placed close to shellfish grounds.

Clearly, the programming of the beach recharge works is of great importance and incompatibilities may arise if an urgent project requires material from a source which has yet to be licensed, or whose licensed extraction rate cannot be uplifted to provide the material at a fast enough rate.

There are many other linkages of the types described above and illustrated in Figure 6.3. For this reason it is essential that consideration of alternative sources is initiated at a very early stage of the coast protection or flood defence development and not left to be carried out at some later date when many of the scheme details have been fixed. Failure to give due consideration to material source and availability in the initial stages can result in costly redesign and delay in project implementation.

6.2.5 Construction

There are a number of factors affecting the construction of a scheme which must be considered early in the appraisal and planning in order to permit reliable estimation of costs and to ensure that:

(i) It is technically viable to build the scheme safely (see Section 6.2.7).

(ii) The impacts of construction have been identified and can be mitigated if necessary.

At this stage of the scheme development, it is always worthwhile discussing these aspects with contractors experienced in the type of work to be undertaken.

The working areas required during construction must be identified and established. Essentially two types of area are involved:

- the active construction area i.e. the beach; this may also include nearshore areas where plant is operating and backshore areas where works related to coastal defences are underway as part of an overall scheme including a beach management scheme
- areas allocated for such things as site offices, plant and materials storage.

The latter usually entails the allocation of area(s) adjacent, or near, to the beach in order to facilitate plant and material access. Among other practical factors that must be considered are the proximity to services such as fresh water and electricity.

Access to site for construction plant and materials is an important consideration. Bulk materials, such as sand, shingle or armour rock are usually delivered by sea. Floating plant will generally be used to unload and place these materials; this might include pipelines and floating hoses in the case of sand and shingle. A number of factors must be considered when assessing the feasibility for such marine operations including the seabed and foreshore bathymetry, the tidal range and the wave climate. Changes to the foreshore levels during construction must be allowed for. These might be in response to changing weather, or as a direct consequence of the works (e.g. beach recharge).

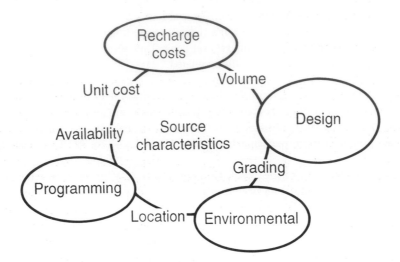

Figure 6.3 *Relationship between material source and other design constraints and opportunities*

Marine operations are susceptible to weather conditions and also depend on the location and exposure of the site in question. A study of the likely wave climate will indicate "weather windows" when marine plant can be safely deployed and operated. Tidal currents can also influence the undertaking of marine operations and are usually a significant factor in the planning of works involving diving.

Intertidal working, whether land-based or from floating plant, is affected by the tidal characteristics of each site. At a given location, high and low water of Spring and Neap tides tend to occur at the same time of day and therefore have a predictable relationship with daylight hours (see Figure 3.5). These characteristics can be advantageous or disadvantageous depending upon the operation; low tides in daylight hours assist land-based operations, while high tides in daylight hours assist marine operations, such as disposal close to shore.

Usually, some plant must be delivered by road. This might include, for example, vehicles for redistributing sand or shingle along the beach, or forming it to a specified profile. Some materials may also be delivered by road to form seawalls, groynes or other elements of the scheme. As with other types of civil construction work, it will be necessary to confirm that the roads and route can sustain the construction traffic, both physically and in terms of impact on other road users and the local community. Physical constraints such as traffic controls, bridges, weight limitation and tunnels may dictate the route for construction traffic. Sometimes it is necessary to upgrade a section of road, or an existing track, for construction purposes. During planning and possibly during appraisal, the road and highway authorities would be consulted.

The working constraints on the delivery, deployment and operation of plant imposed by the factors mentioned above will place limits on the size and type of plant used (e.g. the draft of vessels and the maximum tonnage of lorries). The choice of plant and the proposed method of working will also be influenced by their impact on the environment. Factors which would be considered here will include the following, but may include more factors depending upon the specific circumstances:

- noise from plant
- safety/risk to public
- public access to working areas
- fishing interests, water quality, avoidance of land or marine pollution
- increased turbidity during dredging and placing of materials
- seasonal or daily work periods
- impact on local businesses, tourism and recreation.

Adverse impacts, in most of these areas can be mitigated by careful choice of plant and working practice and by keeping the local community informed and aware that it is for their eventual benefit (see also Sections 6.6.2, 7.8, 7.9.2 and 10.2.4).

6.2.6 Maintenance

Maintenance of a beach scheme can entail the periodic redistribution of beach sediments; this might involve, for example, transporting shingle from one end of a bay to the other, or reforming the crest of a shingle beach when earlier storms have formed high ridges. Maintenance may also entail attendance to the hard structures. On a less frequent basis maintenance can also include further recharge of the beach. In the latter case the criteria governing future beach recharge are likely to be similar to those affecting the capital works - indeed, future recharge can actually be thought of as a part of the capital works programme.

Where maintenance measures are of a minor nature, for example beach profile redistribution, then some rather different criteria may apply. Site access will again have to be considered, as circumstances may have changed from the time of undertaking the capital works, e.g. due to construction of new hard structures. Whereas temporary works could be readily incorporated during capital works, constraints on plant availability or economics may preclude their use for maintenance. Maintenance methods must, therefore, be examined during the planning and design of a project so that practical provisions can be incorporated in the scheme and/or the frequency of maintenance measures determined.

As with capital works, the impacts of maintenance works on the environment must be assessed (see Section 6.2.2 above).

6.2.7 Safety

Under the Construction (Design and Management) Regulations 1994 (the CDM Regulations) the design of any beach scheme must give adequate regard to the need to avoid foreseeable safety risks during construction and to combat, at source, risks to the health and safety of any person carrying out construction or maintenance work.

6.3 ALTERNATIVE OPTIONS

This section outlines alternative methods for coast protection and flood defence, including beach management. Having defined the problem, a review of all alternative methods is important at this stage (see Figure 6.1) in order to formulate a series of candidate project or management options. Each of the alternatives considered can be coarsely screened at this stage using engineering, environmental and economic criteria. Initial screening of options can often usefully be carried out using a technique such as multi-criteria analysis (see Box 6.1) and will enable attention to be focused on those proposals which are sufficiently viable to warrant further evaluation. This section highlights the technical features of various options to aid this initial screening process.

6.3.1 Changes to beaches

Beach management in the context of this manual is an option for mitigating flooding and erosion of the coastal area by controlling changes in the movement of material in the backshore, foreshore and nearshore zones. The nature of these changes has been outlined in Chapter 2 and their assessment and prediction covered in Sections 5.2 and 5.3. For the purposes of the definition of any specific beach management option, these changes can be broadly classified as being either of a short or long term nature as follows:

Box 6.1 *Multi-criteria analysis (MCA)*

The method consists of making a matrix, with the various alternatives listed horizontally (I to V in the tables below) and the selection criteria listed vertically. A ranking of alternatives is made with respect to each criterion. The rankings are expressed by a mark using a predefined scale (e.g. 0, 1, ..., 10), as shown in the simple example table below.

Example of an MCA (weight factors are given in the table below)

Criteria	I	II	III	IV	V	Weight
A Beach volume	2	5	1	1	8	1
B Environmental impact	7	7	6	2	2	4
C Construction time	9	0	5	4	1	2
D Maintenance	8	8	3	1	1	3
E Risk level	6	3	10	7	5	3
F Initial cost	6	5	3	6	6	3
Resulting ranking	108	81	83	59	54	

Introduction of weighting factors improves the method, and these factors can be adjusted by agreement (e.g. within the project management team or with a group of interested parties as part of a policy analysis process). A more objective approach to determining weighing factors which can also be carried out by the project management or policy analysis team is to assign priority to one or all possible pairs of criteria. For example, the more important criterion in a pair can be assigned the value 1 and the less important a value 0, then, as shown in the table below, weight factors can be found by adding up the weightings for each criterion. An alternative approach follows the same procedure but uses scores of 2, 1, and 0 where in this case 1 represents equally important criteria.

Criteria	A	B	C	D	E	F	Weight
A	-	0	0	1	0	0	1
B	1	-	1	1	0	1	4
C	1	0	-	0	0	1	2
D	0	0	1	-	1	1	3
E	1	1	1	0	-	0	3
F	1	0	1	0	1	-	3

Short-term changes

Short-term changes to the beach profile will occur during a storm or during prolonged periods of wave action from one direction. This can lead to a movement of material cross-shore and alongshore.

Long-term changes

Long-term changes generally take place over several years (or tens of years) and can be due to a number of reasons including:

- climatic changes (e.g. directional changes in wind patterns or increased storminess)
- sea level rise
- changes in the rate of sediment supply
- changes to offshore bathymetry
- impact of coastal structures.

These long-term changes can be caused by either external influences or influences within the frontage under consideration.

6.3.2 Beach management options

Before viable engineering options for the management of the beach can be formulated, it is first necessary to gain an understanding of the coastal processes affecting the beach and its behaviour under extreme climatic conditions (see foregoing chapters especially Sections 5.3 and 5.4; see also Section 6.4 following). With this knowledge it will then be possible to predict the effectiveness of possible options and also to establish likely maintenance requirements. The possible environmental effects of each option will also need to be considered (see Section 6.6). In assessing the options, the impact that a scheme may have on adjoining lengths of the coastline is also an important aspect (see Sections 2.6 and 5.4.5).

In the broadest terms there are two fundamental options:

1. Do Nothing - this option means no defence works are undertaken and therefore no expenditure is incurred. It should be examined for the following reasons:

    *   as a baseline for gauging the benefit of the "do something" options
    *   as a viable option in cases where intervention is not warranted or may aggravate the situation.

2. Do Something - this option may include:

    *   do minimum - this involves carrying out minimal maintenance work; it may, but does not necessarily, maintain the existing standard of defence
    *   maintain standard - this involves carrying out work to maintain the existing standard of defence
    *   improve standard - this involves carrying out work to improve the existing standard of defence.

Work in these cases may involve measures which remove the cause or mitigate the effect of the problem without actually removing it. The latter may involve works either within or remote from the beach frontage under consideration.

6.3.3   Do Something options

The range of measures available to manage a beach are illustrated in Figure 6.4. Each measure is discussed briefly below.

1. Remove the cause of the problem (often termed "indirect measures" since they may not involve engineering works on the frontage in question).

Measures to remove the cause of the problem could include the following:

*   controlling the quarrying of beach sand/shingle, or the dredging of material in the nearshore zone
*   removal of relic structures interrupting the supply of material to the frontage (see Section 9.4.1)
*   retreat from updrift cliff protection, thus reinstating sediment supply.

2. Mitigate the effect ("direct measures" involving some form of engineering works on the frontage in question and often described as a "beach management scheme").

The range of possible measures available to mitigate the effect of a problem are described below. Although each measure is described separately, in practice, solutions are often developed which combine aspects of a number of these measures.

Beach maintenance (see Chapter 11)

Beach maintenance involves works that maintain the present attributes of the beach. Works that may be undertaken include:

*   structural repairs to beach control structures
*   maintenance of public accesses
*   removal of wind-blown sand, seaweed

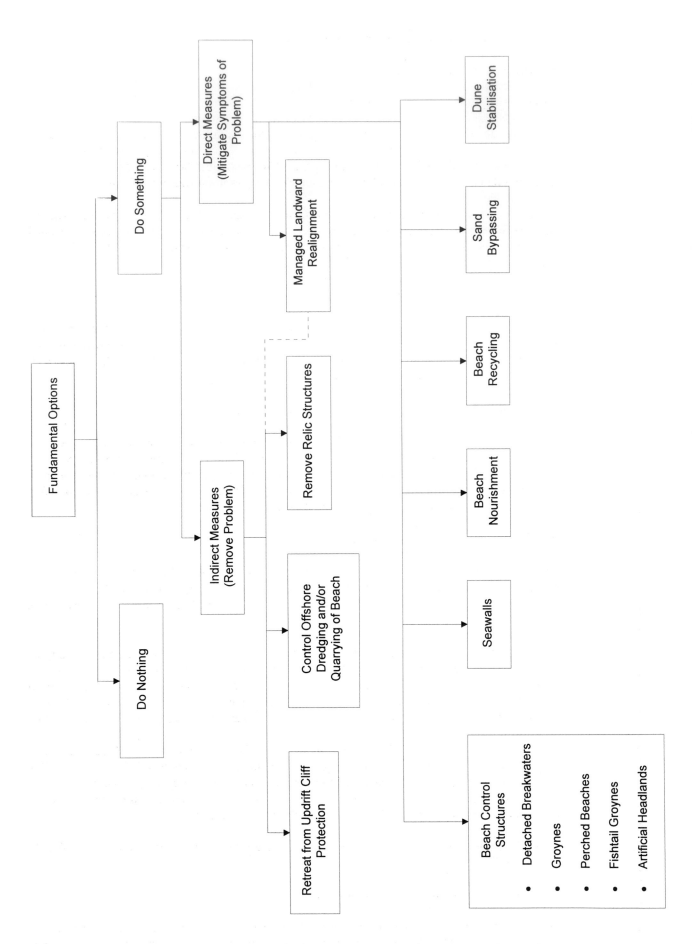

Figure 6.4   *Range of beach management options*

- maintenance of safety equipment and public notices
- litter clearance
- beach profile redistribution.

Dune management (see Section 9.1)

Over long lengths of the UK coastline the prime protection against the sea is provided by sand dunes (see Section 2.4.4). Dunes are formed from wind-blown sand and provide a valuable natural reservoir of beach material which will provide protection during storms. Their deterioration can pose substantial problems for the long-term management of a beach.

There are a number of techniques which preserve or enhance the dunes, including the planting of grass, construction of fences and restriction of public access. These techniques are designed to improve the ability of the dunes to trap and retain windblown sand. Further detailed information on this subject is given in Chapter 9.

Beach recycling (see Figure 6.5a and Section 11.2)

Beach recycling involves the collection of material from a downdrift location and transporting it to the updrift end of a beach frontage on a regular basis. Recycling may be undertaken using land or seaborne transport depending upon access, tidal range, beach levels and the quantity of material requiring recycling.

Sand/shingle bypassing (see Figure 6.5a and Section 9.5)

The construction of breakwaters and other shoreline structures can interrupt the longshore transport of material and cause erosion of the downdrift shoreline. To restore the supply of material, measures can be taken to transfer or bypass the sand from the updrift to the downdrift side of the structure. Methods used to undertake bypassing include the installation of specially designed fixed plant, floating plant (dredgers) or land-based equipment.

Beach recharge (see Figure 6.5a and Chapter 7)

Beach recharge is the replacement of sediment lost from a beach or the addition of new sediment to increase the volume of the beach. The recharge should be designed to accommodate beach changes, both short-term and long-term (see Section 6.3.2), and provide the requisite level of protection.

Material used for recharge will generally be in the sand to shingle size range. Its availability in the required quantities and grading and within a reasonable travelling distance from site are important considerations (see Section 6.2.4). Material is usually obtained from offshore sources and brought to site using seaborne transport, although there is the possibility of using inland resources and land transport (e.g. crushed rock from a quarry for recharge of a shingle beach).

As a beach recharge will continue to be subject to the shoreline processes which caused the original problem, then it is likely that ongoing maintenance of the beach will be required. This may involve periodic top up recharges using imported material or recycling of the existing material from downdrift or offshore deposits. Alternatively, beach control structures can be constructed to reduce transport by altering the shoreline processes.

A special form of beach recharge is the formation of a rock beach. This is discussed in detail in Section 9.2.

Groynes (see Figure 6.5b and Section 8.2)

Groynes are shore normal structures designed to reduce longshore transport and retain beach material. The shoreline between groynes reorientates towards the dominant wave direction and as a consequence longshore transport rates are reduced. This continues until the groyne bay

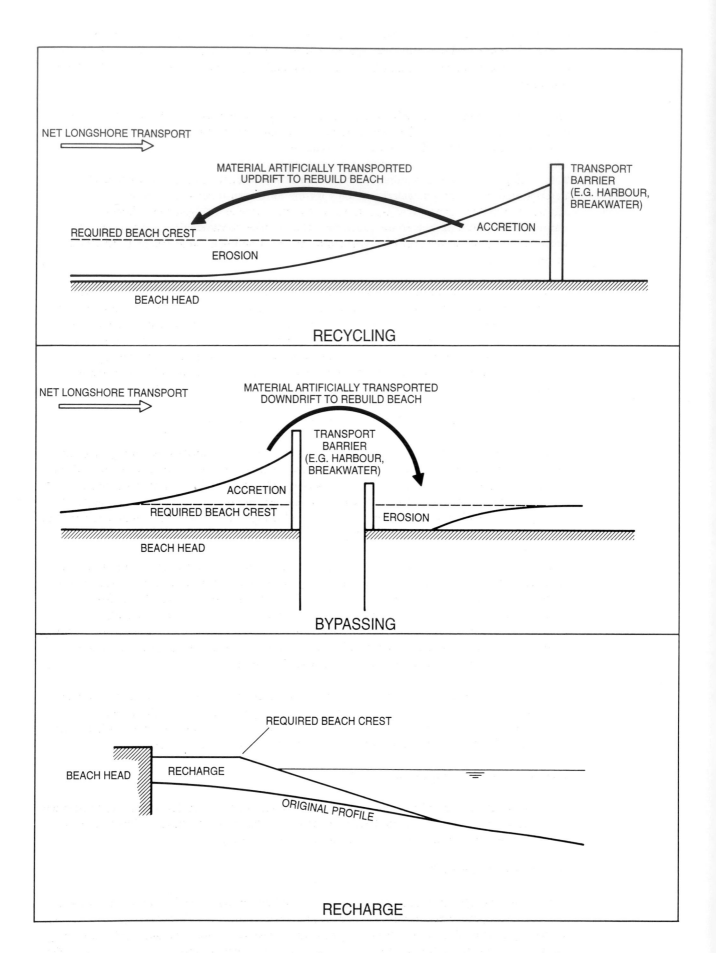

Figure 6.5a *Schematic diagrams of engineering options*

becomes full and transport is then restored by movement over and/or around the end of the groynes. Long groynes can also be used to deflect currents away from the shore. Groynes do not reduce loss of material in an offshore direction and may even increase losses under storm conditions.

The effect of groynes on shingle beaches is reasonably well understood. However, on sand beaches the effect of wave generated currents and turbulence within the groyne bays becomes more significant and the effect is less well understood.

In the UK groynes have generally been constructed from timber, sheet piles or concrete although in recent years increasing use has been made of rock. Alternative forms of construction include open stone asphalt and cribwork. Groynes are generally aligned approximately perpendicular to the shoreline. They can be constructed singly as terminal structures for a beach recharge or, more commonly, as a multi-structure "field" to protect a length of coastline.

An adaption of the conventional groyne is the shore connected breakwater (see Figure 6.5b) which utilizes wave diffraction effects behind the shore parallel section to retain beach material. If these structures are sufficiently large, then they may be designed to establish stable bays along the shoreline by confining the alongshore sediment movements. Such schemes might accept some erosion at the centre of each bay in order to realise the overall stable bay configuration. Both groynes and detached breakwaters generally require a beach recharge to reduce downdrift impacts.

Detached breakwaters (see Figure 6.5b and Sections 8.3 and 8.4)

Detached breakwaters are shore parallel structures designed to dissipate wave energy and reduce the level of wave activity at the shore. They cause sediment deposition in their lee by reducing longshore drift and offshore transport. They are placed either singly to protect a specific coastal location, or as a series of segmented breakwaters to provide protection to a longer frontage. The breakwaters are normally constructed using a rubble mound with an outer armour layer and a crest level which may or may not extend above high water.

Detached breakwaters can induce very strong changes to the coastal process regime and so a thorough appreciation of their likely impact is a prerequisite to their use. This is especially so in the macro-tidal conditions found around the UK coast where experience of detached breakwaters is limited. They do, however, offer a practicable method for stabilising the shoreline, particularly when used together with nourishment which helps to counter the tendency for the beach to erode opposite the gaps between structures. In the majority of cases, a beach recharge is required as part of a detached breakwater scheme.

The orientation of detached breakwaters towards the most severe wave direction can provide additional protection under these extreme conditions. Depending upon the directional distribution of the wave climate, breakwaters can be orientated so as to minimise their impact on the normal longshore transport whilst still providing protection from storms.

Sills (see Figure 6.5b and Section 8.6.1)

Detached structures may also be used to form a continuous shore parallel submerged breakwater or sill designed to reduce offshore losses by supporting the toe of the beach. This technique produces a perched beach, generally formed by a beach recharge.

Seawalls (see Section 8.5)

Historically, seawalls have been the most widely used option for coastal defence. They have been built along the coastlines to either protect the land from erosion and flooding or to provide an amenity function. Typically they comprise either massive vertical retaining walls or sloping revetments or a combination of these structural forms (see Section 8.5). In the U.K., many date back to Victorian times when they were originally built for amenity purposes. These were later

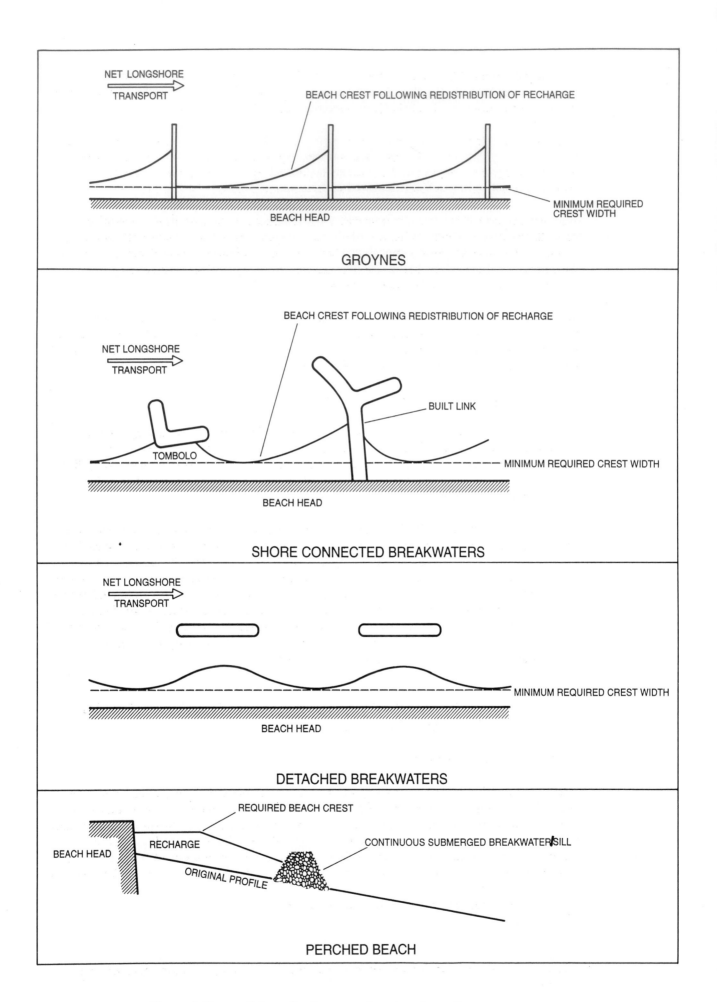

Figure 6.5b *Schematic diagrams of engineering options*

strengthened to provide a defence function as the beach receded. Some of these seawall strengthenings coincided with further extensive programmes for seawall construction during the 1930s and following the 1953 floods of the east coast.

Although seawalls provide a secure defence, they cut off the possible inshore supply of material to the beach and can encourage the localised scouring of the beach in front of the wall where the wall is regularly exposed to the sea (see Section 8.5.2). As they can have a substantial impact on the coastal processes, their use as an option requires careful consideration.

With extensive seawall construction having been completed in the past, new or modified seawalls are generally built to improve the hydraulic performance of existing walls whilst retaining their historic amenity function. They may, however, also be considered in situations where beaches are naturally stable and have an adequate supply of material entering the frontage but where a secondary line of defence is required.

When utilising a seawall considerable care must be taken to ensure that its construction does not have long-term and detrimental consequences for the management of the beach. In such a situation it may be found necessary to combine the use of a seawall with some other system of beach management (e.g. groynes, beach recharge).

Managed landward realignment (see Section 9.3)

Managed landward realignment (managed retreat) is an alternative coastal management option which can yield favourable benefit-cost ratios, whilst conserving natural processes by minimising the impact of coastal squeeze. It involves retreating inland from the existing line of flood defence or coast protection, while monitoring and maintaining an awareness of the consequences of the landward realignment.

As, by definition, managed landward realignment entails the loss of some land area which was previously defended, then it will normally only be considered where the existing defence is no longer viable. The landward realignment option may entail removing infrastructure, roads or seawalls from a shingle bank, cliff top or dune system. The landward realignment option will probably require the provision and maintenance of defences at the retreated position although it may be feasible to allow the beach to retreat to a stable alignment in which it will form a natural defence. However, the landward realignment defences can potentially be less substantial than the former primary defence as the wider beach profiles gained through retreating will absorb a greater proportion of the incident wave energy.

6.4 PREDICTION OF EFFECTIVENESS AND EFFECTS OF BEACH MANAGEMENT SCHEMES

6.4.1 Beach modelling

Numerical and physical models are important tools for assessing the future response of a beach. Often there is limited historical data available for trend analysis and anyway it is prudent to consider a number of different future scenarios such as climate change. When trying to predict the effects of proposed new beach management methods, whether they involve physical structures or new management actions, it is even more important to use models since there is no corresponding historical record of the prototype situation. The types of model available include:

- qualitative models based on observational experience
- numerical models
- physical models.

This section compares the different types of model and their usage for addressing different concerns.

Qualitative Models

The main 'model' in this category is direct observational experience of the site (see Sections 5.3.1 and 5.3.2) to identify historical trends but also to investigate geological, geomorphological and biological indicators that provide information on the dominant processes. For example, the orientation of spits and sand banks can show the drift direction as can identifying the source of beach material by comparing its composition with that of nearby eroding cliffs. When new coastal management methods are considered, such as beach recycling or construction of control structures, past experience at similar sites can give useful information for a conceptual design. These methods require experience and a broad appreciation of coastal processes, but are important as the starting point for more detailed and site specific investigation using physical and/or numerical models.

Numerical models

There are a number of types of numerical model (see Sections 5.3.1 and 5.3.2) each representing a selection of the physical processes that are operating in the coastal system (a detailed description of which are given in Section 2.4). A successful numerical modelling study will often combine two or more models, each representing part of the physical processes. It is important to take notice of the assumptions that each model makes when interpreting the results. By employing a suitable combination of models the effects of most relevant processes can be covered.

Numerical beach models have the advantage that they are not usually limited by the area they can model or the timescales over which they can operate. They can model the response of the beach to a real sequence of wave and tidal conditions, not just the individual combinations tested in a physical model. There may be uncertainties due to lack of calibration data and due to incomplete representation of physical processes, but sensitivity analysis can provide further confidence in the resulting conclusions.

An overview of numerical beach models and the way they can be used together is given in Box 6.2. Fuller details of models to assess short- and long-term beach response are given in Sections 5.3.1 and 5.3.2. Numerical methods for assessing beach recharge volumes are described in Section 7.3. Finally, details of water level, current and wave modelling are given in Sections 3.7.1 and 3.7.3.

Physical Models

Physical models are not just a scaled-down replica of reality; they are designed to correctly represent the important physical processes. A 3D mobile bed wave basin model will correctly represent the effect of waves and sometimes also tidal currents in moving the beach sediment. Well-defined scaling relationships define the differing scales of length, time, sediment size and sediment transport rate. The response of shingle beaches can be modelled accurately using these relationships. However, sand beach models are more difficult to interpret, since the scaling laws are less certain and they tend to form ripples which do not scale correctly. The details of scaling techniques are beyond the scope of this manual.

Physical models are constrained by the size of model facility available, the range of sediment sizes that can be represented, the length of time for which they can realistically be run and the number of different wave directions that can be tested. They are, however, very good at representing complex interactions between waves, currents, bathymetry and structures, as well as the links between cross-shore and longshore sediment transport processes. Finally they provide visible results that can be understood by the lay-man as well as by engineers. Box 6.3 summarises the types of coastal physical model and their uses. Details of physical models of water levels, currents and wave disturbance are given in Sections 3.7.2 and 3.7.4.

Box 6.2 *Numerical models of beach response*

Models of beach response fall into three broad categories. These are now described, together with indications as to when it might be appropriate to use each type of model.

Beach profile models

Profile models are used to assess the short-term response of cross-shore beach profiles to wave events (typically storm or swell events) of durations in the order of hours to a few days. Two main types of model exist:

- *empirical curve fitting models* based on field or physical (see Box 6.3) modelling data. Such models include those of Dean (1977, 1987 and 1991) and Vellinga (1982) for sand beaches and dunes (see Box 5.3) and that of Powell (1990) for shingle beaches (see Box 5.4).

- *process-based morphological response models*, so far only developed for sand beaches. These include a full description of the wave and sediment transport processes in the cross-shore direction. These are discussed in Section 5.3.1 and a good summary of the state of the art is given in Roelvink and Brøker (1993).

Input hydraulic conditions for these models will comprise sequences of individual wave conditions (and water levels), such as might be measured by a wave recorder or generated from a wave forecasting model. See Chapter 3 and, in particular, Figure 3.20 for further details.

Beach plan shape models

Plan shape models are used to predict the long-term plan shape response of beaches over periods in the order of months to years. They are of three main types:

- *empirical curve fitting models*, such as the crenulate bay models of Silvester (see Box 8.6) and the Berenguer and Enriques (1988) Spanish pocket beach model (see Box 8.5)

- *1-line models* (Brampton and Osaza, 1980; Hanson and Kraus, 1989) which predict the changing position of a single representative beach contour. The basis of such models is described in Box 5.6 and the longshore transport formulae which they require are discussed in Section 2.4.2 and Box 2.4.

- *multi-line models* (Bakker et al, 1970; Perlin and Dean 1983) which predict the position of more than one beach contour and are discussed further in Section 2.4.2.

Input wave data for such models might comprise an annual wave height/period/direction climate expressed by a sequence of waves and water levels or, in the simplest cases, by a single representative wave condition and water level.

Fully integrated combined models

These are aimed at predicting coastal area response in the short to medium term i.e. days to years. They are of two main types (see also Section 2.4.2):

- *combined profile and plan shape models*, often combine a process-based morphological cross-shore response model (as described above) with some form of 1-line or multi-line model and, therefore, involve restrictions on the amount of longshore variability which they can accommodate (e.g. the coastline cannot have abrupt changes in direction)

- *gridded-area process-based morphological space response models* which provide a full integrated description of the cross-shore and and longshore response.

As input they require a spatial description of wave conditions, tidal currents, water levels, sediment characteristics, etc.

Interactive approach

Table 6.2 compares the strengths and limitations of physical and numerical models. In many cases a combined modelling approach can balance the weaknesses and strengths of physical and numerical models. The models can be run interactively with cross-calibration of the results.

As an example, numerical drift modelling can be used to predict long-term drift rates on an existing beach. The results can be used to decide on test conditions in a physical model of a

Box 6.3   *Coastal physical models*

This box describes the different types of coastal physical model, their range of application and considerations necessary for the design of a physical model study.

<u>Types of Physical Model</u>

2D Wave Flumes
Rigid bed wave flume models are often used for assessing:

- the stability of structures such as seawalls or cross-sections of breakwaters made from rock or concrete armour units
- overtopping of seawalls
- wave transformation and reflection.

Waves are generated by a paddle at one end of the flume and calibrated using measurements from a wave probe at a fixed position. Normally a computer generated sequence of random waves with a given spectrum (e.g. JONSWAP or Pierson Moskowitz) is used in preference to monochromatic waves. The approach bathymetry is rigidly moulded in concrete to accurately represent the shoaling and breaking of waves before they reach the structure. Specially scaled model armour units or rocks must be used to model the stability correctly.

Mobile bed flume models are used to represent:

- beach profile response to storms
- the interaction of beaches with structures such as seawalls or submerged sills
- the effect of using different gradings of nourishment material on the beach profile.

Again the mobile beach material must be chosen to obey the correct scale laws. In the case of shingle beaches a lightweight sediment such as graded anthracite is often used.

3D Wave Basin Models
Rigid bed wave basin models enable prediction of:

- wave transformation and disturbance behind structures such as breakwaters
- wave-generated current and circulation patterns
- stability of breakwater heads.

Long-crested random waves from a selection of fixed directions can be generated using mobile wave paddles, although tests should be organised to minimise the number of paddle moves required. If directional spreading of the waves is important, short-crested multi-element paddles are used. The bathymetry of the area of interest is usually moulded in concrete and wave and current probes placed at appropriate points in the model.

Mobile bed wave basin models are used for representing:

- beach interaction with structures
- beach plan shape as well as profile changes.

In these models the mobile scaled sediment is usually formed to the correct initial profile over the top of the upper part of the rigid, moulded bathymetry.

Considerations necessary for the design of a physical model study are:

- the objective of the model tests should be clearly defined at the outset
- the dominant processes to be modelled should be identified so that the correct type of model can be chosen and the correct scaling laws applied
- the area to be modelled must be chosen and balanced against the model scale that will allow it to fit into available wave basin facilities.

short section of a proposed series of coastal defence structures. The physical model will represent the detailed beach response near the structures under a selection of wave conditions. Measurements from the physical model can then be used in a numerical model of the whole frontage containing a number of similar structures, modelling the long-term development of the whole coastline.

Table 6.2 Comparison between numerical and physical models

Aspect modelled	Ability of technique to model aspects	
	Numerical Modelling	**Physical Modelling**
Complexity:		
Complex bathymetry	Need to use sophisticated models	Strong
Complex structures	Limited by theory or calibration	Strong
Logistics:		
Quickly	Good	
Cheaply	Good	
Scales:		
Long time scale	Good	Limited by resources
Large length scale	Good	Limited by resources
Sediment transport:		
Transport rates and patterns	Limited by theory, needs calibration	Transport patterns well represented but rate uncertain due to scale effects
Beach morphology	Requires state-of-the-art models for complex situations	Shingle beach morphology well represented though timescale uncertain
Beach interaction with structures	Limited by theory	Good if at large enough scale
Boundary conditions:		
Ease of application	Very flexible and can drive from a coarse grid model	Can be difficult to apply
Varying wave forcing	Very flexible to continuously vary wave forcing	Difficult to vary direction throughout a test

6.4.2 Response in extreme conditions

When considering specific beach management schemes, whether involving new structures, beach recharge or other management actions, it is important to consider the beach response to severe events. The techniques for this evaluation have been described in Section 5.3.1 and Section 6.4.1, but the following basic procedure should be followed to calculate a minimum profile cross-section such that the beach can withstand severe events:

1. Decide on the standard of protection, remembering to use joint probability test conditions of combined wave height and water levels, not just the individual extremes (see Section 3.5 for details).

2. Model beach profile response using one of the following:

   - parametric numerical model (e.g. those described in Boxes 5.2 and 5.3)
   - process-based numerical model
   - flume model.

   Note that the beach interaction with structures (toe scour, etc.) must be considered (see Section 8.5.2).

3. Calculate overtopping, extensive formulae for which are given in CIRIA/CUR (1991) and Thomas and Hall (1992), based on the modified beach profile as determined by beach profile response modelling. If the beach levels at a seawall are decreased in a storm, the overtopping of the seawall will be increased.

6.4.3 Gradual changes in beaches

The long-term performance of a beach management scheme often has more to do with progressive changes in the beach instead of the response to individual severe events. These progressive, long-term changes are usually caused by changes in longshore transport. Beach plan shape models can be used to investigate the long-term development of the beach. Techniques for evaluating these changes have been discussed in Sections 5.3.2 and 6.4.1 but the following factors should be considered (see Section 2.4.2):

1.   When designing a system of beach control structures or beach recharge, imposition of fluctuations in the drift rate along the coast should be avoided as much as possible.

2.   Start by investigating an open beach, then, if necessary, add the minimum of structures to help even out the drift rates.

3.   Consider recycling, or periodic beach recharge, as an alternative to control structures.

4.   Consider gross, as well as net, longshore drift, since this can affect the likely fluctuations in beach planshape. Structures can sometimes worsen the situation by acting like a one-way valve, allowing drift past as the beach builds up but preventing it returning.

5.   When modelling the long-term development of a beach, a wave climate will give the proportion of time each condition occurs but it is also important to investigate the sensitivity of predictions to various wave sequences.

6.4.4   Reaction of adjacent beaches

It is important to consider the impact of the scheme on the rest of the littoral cell and not just confine investigation to the area of immediate concern. Obviously a beach management solution that merely transfers the problem further along a coast may not be a good solution. The following possible effects should be considered and possibly modelled:

- reduction of supply (or possibly increases in the case of beach recharge) to adjacent areas
- downdrift erosion
- the need for a smooth transition at the end of a scheme (see Figure 6.6), or to finish the scheme at a natural boundary.

6.4.5   Prediction of maintenance requirements

If a beach recharge scheme is implemented, it may require emergency or regular planned maintenance (see Chapter 11). It is important that this is considered when the scheme is being designed and allowance made for the likely future costs. It is possible to predict the likely maintenance requirements from the results of the beach plan shape modelling work. The following points should be considered when carrying out the modelling:

1.   Areas of accretion within a scheme may be used as a source of recharge for areas which are eroding (e.g. recycling of material from one end of a beach to the other).

2.   It may be possible to minimise initial post-placement losses by anticipating the future beach development.

3.   There is a balance between the quantity of each recharge and the interval between successive recharges. Often the rate of loss of beach material decreases with time and with beach volume. Modelling of the beach will help to optimise costs of planned maintenance.

4.   Regular monitoring is important to check whether the scheme is behaving as predicted, and to anticipate the need for future maintenance, possibly via further modelling calibrated against the monitoring data.

5. Emergency maintenance may be required following storms. This may involve altering the beach profile (perhaps scraping the beach up) as well as physical maintenance of groynes, repositioning rock and replacing timber.

6.5 ECONOMIC APPRAISAL

The application of economic appraisal to publicly funded projects is described in HM Treasury (1991) and its application to flood and coastal defence is defined in MAFF (1993a). More detailed guidance on the valuation of costs and benefits is given in Parker *et al* (1987), MUFHRC (1990) and Penning-Rowsell *et al* (1992). As a result of the guidance given in these references, this section is limited to a broad discussion of the principal elements of economic appraisal.

In principle, the appraisal should follow the sequence given below (MAFF, 1993a):

1. Undertake a reconnaissance-level appraisal of likely costs and benefits; their scale will usually indicate whether it is worth proceeding.

2. Identify the options which in practice must cover a range of standards of service.

3. Identify, quantify and wherever possible, value the costs, benefits and uncertainties of each option. Quantatively discuss non-quantifiable cases and benefits.

4. Discount costs and benefits which can be valued in monetary terms.

5. Weigh up the uncertainties.

6. Weigh up any unquantified effects.

7. Assess the balance between options.

8. Identify the preferred option.

The purpose of the appraisal is to investigate the economic worthwhileness of a scheme and to identify the economic optimum through the assessment and comparison of costs and benefits. In this search for the economic optimum, the comparison should not be confined to different types of solution (e.g. beach recharge versus groynes versus detached breakwaters), but should also explore the consequence of, *inter alia*, different defence standards and different phasing or timing of the work. The analysis, at least for the purposes of supporting an application for grant aid in the UK, should view the economics from a national viewpoint. Local or regional benefits should not be included. For example, the avoidance of the loss of an amenity in one town when an amenity elsewhere could generate similar replacement benefits, typically expressed in terms of annual revenue, as described in Section 6.5.1, at no extra cost. Equally all national costs and benefits should be included whether relating to publicly or privately owned assets, the latter sometimes being of national importance.

6.5.1 Benefits

The value to the nation of investing in beach management schemes lies, for the most part, in the avoidance of damage that would otherwise be incurred. Categories of benefits are likely to include avoidance of:

- damage to property (building, furnishing, stock, etc.) and loss of land
- disruption to traffic
- loss of utilities
- increased pressures on emergency services
- loss of recreational benefits
- loss or deterioration of environmental resources.

All of these can be valued, via the use of the available guidance referred to above, although the estimation of recreational or environmental benefits will require a specific evaluation using environmental economics. A contingent valuation survey (Penning-Rowsell *et al*, 1992) may be useful to help place money values on environmental benefits but such a study should be undertaken carefully to ensure that it is sufficiently reliable to form a reliable part of the analysis.

The benefits of a scheme should be valued and their timing assessed, for the whole duration of the design life of the scheme. They should then be discounted to give their value at the base date (normally chosen to be at or just before the start of the design life) and totalled to give the present value (PV) of benefits.

It should be noted that the above list of benefits is not exhaustive and may not include some indirect or intangible benefits which are site specific. Additionally, it may also be necessary to evaluate possible disadvantages e.g. the loss of beach following the construction of a rock revetment.

6.5.2 Costs

Costs should include all costs that will be incurred as a result of the scheme, such as:

- those associated with initial and subsequent construction (including administration, engineering, investigation, design, compensation, etc.)
- compensation costs
- all maintenance, monitoring and operational costs
- possible costs of major repairs
- consequential costs e.g. costs associated with stengthening downdrift defences.

Costs already incurred, or to which the nation is already committed, should be regarded as 'sunk costs' and omitted from the economic analysis. Costs should make no allowance for inflation, but should use the same base date as those used for the benefits. As with benefits, all costs appropriate to the scheme should be discounted to the same base date and added up to give the total present value of costs.

6.5.3 Scheme comparison

Benefits and costs should be determined for the beach management options identified in Section 6.3.2 and Figure 6.4. These can be summarised as follows:

- "do nothing" - which assumes that no further expenditure takes place and evaluates the consequent damages
- "do something" - do minimum - the benefits and costs of the minimum feasible level of investment are determined - normally this would simply involve maintenance to attempt to preserve the status quo
- "do something" - maintain or improve standard - various direct and indirect options.

Cost-benefit analysis then allows the comparison of all possible different schemes and the comparison of any one with the "do nothing" situation, on the basis of those benefits that are calculable. Schemes may be phased in order to spread the capital cost over a period of years. The spreading of the capital cost should be set against increased overall costs which may arise from issues such as multiple mobilisation and administration costs. Higher initial construction costs may lead to lower maintenance costs and to a longer design life.

MAFF (1993a) gives guidance on scheme comparison for coastal defences in England and Wales, as required by Central Government. The ratio of benefits to costs may be considered for economic comparison of alternatives and a "Decision Rule" is also given in MAFF (1993a) to assist with determining the economic optimum (see Box 6.4). In other circumstances, the net present value of scheme costs is sometimes used as the basis for comparison, often where the benefits of scheme options are similar or deemed to be similar. International lending agencies often use the internal rate of return (the discount rate at which present benefit equals present cost) which is derived from the investment.

Box 6.4   *Project appraisal decision rule (MAFF, 1993a)*

The decision rule follows a series of steps taking maximisation of the benefit-cost ratio as their starting point. It is expected that, under most circumstances, the option with the greatest average benefit-cost ratio will represent the final choice. In some circumstances this option may fall short of the indicative standard of protection. If it does, the rule then goes on to examine whether an option which would more closely approach the indicative standard of protection (see Table below) would be justified. The justification depends on the additional benefits purchased by the additional cost of increasing the scale of the project, i.e. the incremental benefit-cost ratio. Provided this additional investment is robustly worthwhile in its own right, i.e. the incremental benefit-cost ratio comfortably exceed unity, an increase in scale for standards of protection reasons is justified.

I   Examine the average benefit-cost ratios of all options. If none is at least unity, reconsider scope of options or abandon proposal.

II   Identify the option with the greatest average benefit-cost ratio that is at least unity. If this option meets or exceeds the indicative standard, it is the final choice. If not, proceed to III.

III   In order to determine whether an increase in scale would be economically efficient, examine the next option with a higher standard of protection than identified in II. Provided its average benefit-cost ratio remains at least unity, consider switching to this option if its incremental benefit-cost ratio comfortably exceeds unity under plausible values for main variables. If this option meets these conditions and meets or exceeds the indicative standard, it is the final choice.

IV   However, if the choice under II or III falls short of the indicative standard, choose the option that most closely approaches the indicative standard, provided the average benefit-cost ratio of that option is at least unity and its incremental benefit-cost ratio comfortably exceeds unity, and both ratios are robust to likely variations in key variables.

Current land use	Indicative standard of protection (return period in years)
High-density urban containing significant amount of both residential and non residential property	200
Medium-density urban. Lower density than above, may also include some agricultural land	150
Low-density or rural communities with limited number of properties at risk. Highly productive agricultural land	50
Generally arable farming with isolated properties. Moderately productive agricultural land	20
Predominantly extensive grass with very few properties at risk. Agricultural land of low productivity	5

6.5.4   Uncertainty and sensitivity

Results of an economic appraisal are sensitive to the inputs supplied. The values of inputs may not be known precisely for various reasons. Three sources of uncertainty are:

1.   Parametric uncertainty, or statistical uncertainties in the value of variables. For example, for a coastal defence scheme, relevant variables may include beach material properties affecting predictions of erosion rates and property values affecting the assessment of benefits. Parametric uncertainty can generally be reduced by more detailed data collection.

2.   Uncertainty arising from the random nature of the loadings on the system, such as waves. Many loads affecting beaches depend on meteorological factors and cannot be precisely predicted in advance.

3. Systemic uncertainty, or the possibility that the model or procedure used to make predictions is itself incomplete or erroneous.

Uncertainty should be reduced, where possible, to an extent such that the effort of achieving greater precision is unlikely to make a difference to the scheme selection.

Sensitivity testing can be carried out to test the impact of error in input data on the result. This approach is recommended to ensure that the result of the appraisal process is robust in the face of uncertainties. The question of how much variation to apply to inputs remains open. Penning-Rowsell *et al* (1992) imply that the preferred option should be "robust" to "relatively extreme" values of variables to which the appraisal is most sensitive. This clearly leaves room for subjectivity. MAFF (1993a) gives some additional guidance, stating that the preferred option should remain the preferred option under sensitivity testing and should satisfy the basic economic criterion for "a realistic range of values of key variables".

The issue of uncertainty is likely to be of particular importance to beach schemes, because of the complexity and incomplete understanding of the processes involved. Probabilistic predictions of beach response and hence whole-life scheme costs and benefits take account of the degree of uncertainty in input values, together with the sensitivity of the output to variations in inputs. Data values, load variables and model parameters are specified as probability distributions, and these can be used to produce a probability distribution for the outcome. Input probability distributions may be based on data or expert opinion or judgement. This can be used to establish an expected value and confidence levels of different degrees of error. MAFF (1993a) draws attention to the probabilistic approach and recommends it in certain circumstances.

A full implementation of probabilistic appraisal would involve many of the techniques of risk assessment (see Section 5.4.3), such as identification and formulation of hazards and probabilistic time-series prediction using Monte Carlo sampling methods to establish probability distributions of costs and benefits for the life of the scheme. There may also be the need for additional sensitivity analysis.

6.6   ENVIRONMENTAL ASSESSMENT

Any new beach management initiative whether in the form of ongoing maintenance or a new scheme (e.g. beach recharge) may affect the existing environmental characteristics of the beach. Impacts may be beneficial or damaging and may occur during construction or maintenance operations. In Sections 6.6.1 and 6.6.2, the Environmental Assessment process is briefly described and the role of consultation is outlined. Section 6.6.3 deals with the preparation and contents of an Environmental Statement.

The specific environmental constraints and opportunities in the design, construction and operation of schemes are covered within the relevant chapters of the manual which deal with specific aspects of beach management schemes. Particular attention is given to this point in Chapter 7, on beach recharge, which has been covered in less detail previously.

6.6.1   Appraisal process

Environmental Assessment (EA) is an appraisal technique used to identify and evaluate the potential impacts of a proposed development on the natural, human, chemical and physical environment. An EA will normally be required where the development is likely to have significant effects on the environment by virtue of factors such as its nature, size or location.

EA comprises a number of discrete steps and should always be initiated at the feasibility stage. Its purpose is to identify environmentally unacceptable options and to highlight the option(s) which cause least environmental damage or degradation. EA should not be used as a damage limitation exercise. Environmental and engineering considerations should be integrated throughout the assessment and design process to ensure that the design minimises adverse

environmental impacts and provides opportunities for enhancement as far as possible.
Figure 6.6 demonstrates the EA process while Figure 6.7 illustrates the context in which EA is used for coastal defence works.

Firstly in the EA process, a preliminary data collection and consultation exercise should be used to identify environmental features or characteristics of interest along the coast (scoping exercise). This process may involve the collation and review of existing information and/or a first round of consultation with parties with an interest in the study area. Some baseline field survey, usually limited, may also be required. The scoping exercise should consider the possible consequences of the scheme on the natural, human, chemical and physical environment.

Once possible environmental impacts have been established, their significance should be evaluated through a more detailed process comprising one or more of the following: consultation, site investigations, modelling, comparison to standards and literature reviews. Any potential impacts upon characteristics of the existing environment should be evaluated in the following terms:

- beneficial or adverse
- short- or long-term
- reversible or irreversible
- local or regional
- direct or indirect
- cumulative aspects.

Impacts should be identified and evaluated for both the construction and operational phases of any beach management scheme. Impacts experienced during the construction phase are generally expected to be short-term, whilst some of the impacts during the operational phase are likely to be long-term.

Where potentially significant adverse impacts are identified, possible mitigation measures should be examined and discussed with the relevant parties. In addition, enhancement opportunities should also be investigated (see Section 6.2.2). All residual impacts (i.e. those impacts outstanding after mitigation measures are implemented) must be determined and documented in the environmental report (or Environmental (Impact) Statement) in order to establish the scheme's overall acceptability. Monitoring work, liaison requirements with local bodies, and contractual requirements (i.e. mitigation, monitoring or enhancement measures to be included in the contract specification) should similarly be recommended.

Box 6.5 describes the EU regulations (which cover England and Wales) governing the undertaking of Environmental Assessments and the production of Environmental Statements.

The CIRIA manual on Environmental Assessment (1994) provides further details on the appraisal process, as do the MAFF guidelines *Coastal Defence and the Environment* (MAFF, 1993d).

6.6.2   Consultation

An essential part of the environmental assessment process comprises an extensive consultation exercise involving, among others, local authorities, nature conservation bodies, commercial agencies and representatives of other groups within the study area (e.g. recreational or sports clubs). Such consultation can help to identify and collect information (e.g. unpublished data) which might otherwise be unavailable. It also demonstrates to interested parties that they are being involved in the decision-making process. Potential consultees, both statutory and voluntary, would generally be the same as those who might be able to supply information (see Box 4.2 for example).

Consultation also plays a vital role in the identification and evaluation of potential impacts in the study area. In addition to informing interested parties of the various options for beach management/coastal defence, the consultation exercise can play an important educational role

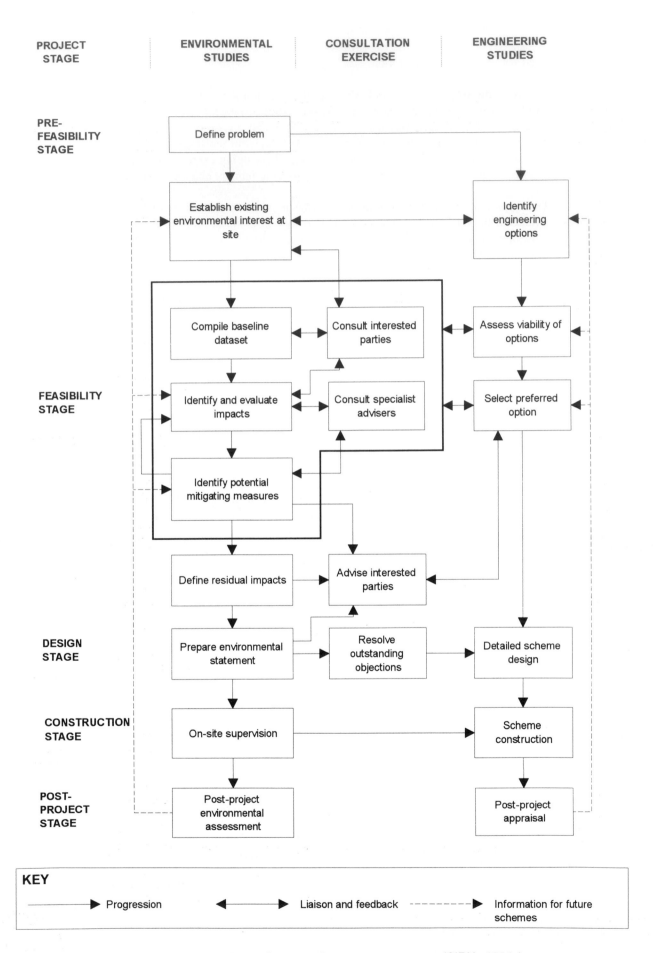

PROJECT STAGE	ENVIRONMENTAL STUDIES	CONSULTATION EXERCISE	ENGINEERING STUDIES

PRE-FEASIBILITY STAGE

Define problem

Establish existing environmental interest at site

Identify engineering options

FEASIBILITY STAGE

Compile baseline dataset

Consult interested parties

Assess viability of options

Identify and evaluate impacts

Consult specialist advisers

Select preferred option

Identify potential mitigating measures

Define residual impacts

Advise interested parties

DESIGN STAGE

Prepare environmental statement

Resolve outstanding objections

Detailed scheme design

CONSTRUCTION STAGE

On-site supervision

Scheme construction

POST-PROJECT STAGE

Post-project environmental assessment

Post-project appraisal

KEY

→ Progression   ◄——► Liaison and feedback   ------► Information for future schemes

Figure 6.6   *The environmental assessment process (CIRIA, 1994c)*

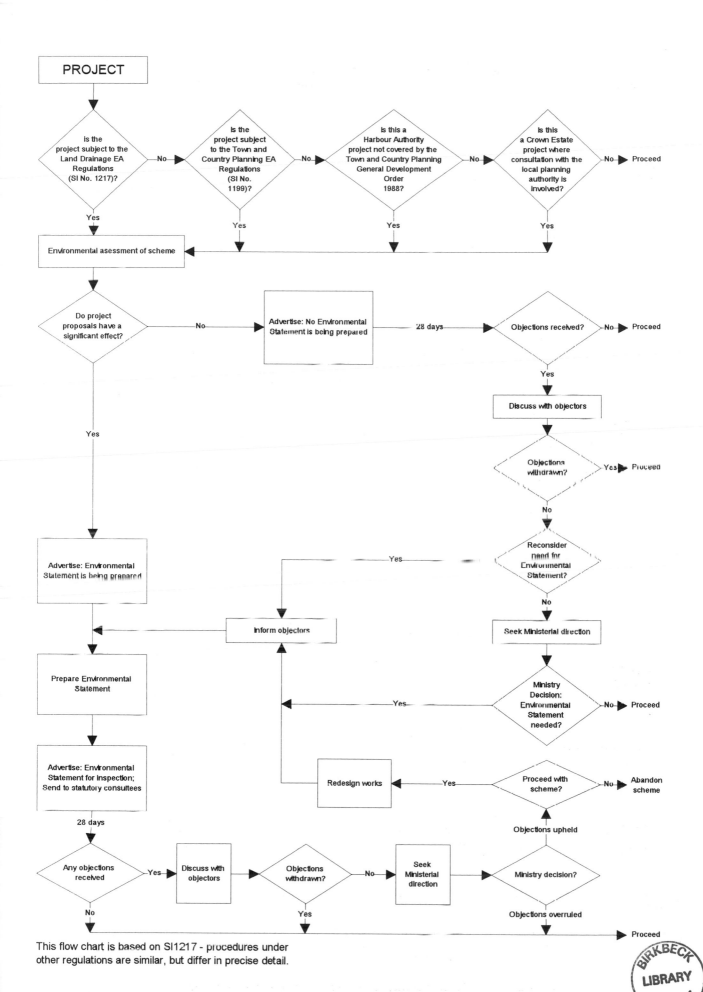

This flow chart is based on SI1217 - procedures under other regulations are similar, but differ in precise detail.

Figure 6.7   *The context of EA procedures for coastal defence works (MAFF, 1993d)*

CIRIA Report 153

(e.g. explaining how a healthy beach absorbs wave energy). A consultation document, presentations and/or meetings can be used to explain the coastal processes and how the various types of defence tackle the problem most effectively. Such an approach develops understanding and enables consultees to make more informed, reasoned comments. In recognising and wherever possible accommodating the interests and objectives of affected bodies it would be the intention that a scheme that is acceptable to all parties could be promoted. Involving interested agencies in a way which stresses that their representations will be taken on board should similarly aid the smooth implementation of a scheme affecting a resource (i.e. beach) for which public acceptability and support is important because of the wide range of interests.

6.6.3   Environmental Statement: preparation and contents

Where an Environmental Statement (ES) is required, this document should be prepared in accordance with the relevant statutory instrument under which the environmental assessment is required. The EC Directive (85/337/EEC) and associated British regulations also require that the ES contains specific contents (see Box 6.5). These requirements are detailed in the CIRIA manual on Environmental Assessment, but in brief the ES should include the following components:

* a description of the proposed development
* data identifying and assessing the effects of the development on the environment
* a description of the significant environmental effects
* a description of the measures taken to avoid, reduce or remedy any adverse effects
* a non-technical summary.

For coastal defence schemes an EA may be required under one of two statutory instruments (SI) implementing the EC Directive on the assessment of environmental effects 85/733/EEC. For flood defence works the SI 1217 Land Drainage Improvement Works (Assessment of Environmental Effects) Amendments Regulations 1988 apply. Where new works are proposed which would involve planning permission, SI 1199 Town and County Planning (Assessment of Environmental Effects) Regulations 1988 apply. SI 677 (1994) which is an amendment to SI 1199, adds coast protection works to the assessment regulations.

Guidance on the EA process and on the preparation of the ES is available in published guides (DoE, 1989; MAFF, 1993c and 1993d; CIRIA, 1994).

6.7   SELECTION OF PREFERRED SCHEME

Following the initial coarse screening of options carried out using multi-criteria analysis or a similar approach (as described in Section 6.3) and a detailed review of the potential effectiveness, costs, benefits and environmental impact of those options which survive the coarse screening, a preferred scheme can be selected. For most coastal defence schemes in the UK this will follow the MAFF economic/performance decision rule (see Section 6.5.3). Where non-UK government funders are involved, other kinds of economic/performance decision rules may be used. In all cases, there may be reasons why economically attractive options may be rejected on environmental or political grounds. It is important that all options are considered fairly, and to an approximately equal level of investigation, to avoid rejecting any one option before its full potential has been explored.

Having selected a preferred scheme, the evaluation of that design can then proceed to a more detailed level. The remaining chapters of this manual give more detailed information on the design of specific elements of schemes and their implementation, which may also prove useful when evaluating, comparing and selecting options.

Box 6.5   *EU requirements for an Environmental Statement*

ANNEX III

INFORMATION REFERRED TO IN ARTICLE 5 (1)

1. Description of the project, including in particular:

   - a description of the physical characteristics of the whole project and the land-use requirements during the construction and operational phases,

   - a description of the main characteristics of the production processes, for instance, nature and the quantity of the materials used,

   - an estimate, by type and quantity, of expected residues and emissions (water, air and soil pollution, noise, vibration, light, heat, radiation, etc.) resulting from the operation of the proposed project.

2. Where appropriate, an outline of the main alternatives studied by the developer and an indication of the main reasons for his choice, taking into account the environmental effects.

3. A description of the aspects of the environment likely to be significantly affected by the proposed project, including, in particular, population, fauna, flora, soil, water, air, climatic factors, material assets, including the architectural and archaeological heritage, landscape and the inter-relationship between the above factors.

4. A description[1] of the likely significant effects of the proposed project on the environment resulting from:

   - the existence of the project

   - the use of natural resources

   - the emission of pollutants, the creation of nuisances and the elimination of waste;

   and the description by the developer of the forecasting methods used to assess the effects on the environment

5. A description of the measures envisaged to prevent, reduce and, where possible, offset any significant adverse effects on the environment.

6. A non-technical summary of the information provided under the above headings

7. An indication of any difficulties (technical deficiencies or lack of know-how) encountered by the developer in compiling the required information.

---

[1]   This description should cover the direct effects and any indirect, secondary, cumulative, short, medium and long-term, permanent and temporary, positive and negative effects of the project.

7   Beach recharge

It is recognised that a healthy beach is probably the most effective form of sea defence since, provided that it is not constrained by space or material supply limitations, it has the ability to adapt its shape naturally to changing wave and tidal conditions and dissipates wave energy. Many natural beaches have suffered erosion due to a man-made restriction to supply: coastal dunes have been built on and knocked down, eroding cliffs stabilised, and the material supply from updrift beaches reduced by coastal defence works. Beach recharge is a method of restoring beaches and thus their coastal defence as well as their amenity function, see Figure 7.1.

Figure 7.1   *Creation of an artificial shingle beach by recharge, Penmaenmawr, Gwynedd (courtesy HR Wallingford)*

There are three main situations where beach recharge may be deployed:

1. In areas of the coast which are experiencing losses of beach material and there is a shortage of incoming drift. In such circumstances it will be necessary to replenish the beach and it may also be appropriate to try to reduce the drift out of the area to increase the life of the scheme. This can be achieved by the use of beach control structures (see Chapter 8) or by periodically recycling the material from the downdrift end of the beach back to the updrift end.

2. On any beach which is acting as a self-contained coastal cell (i.e. a complete system with little sediment input or output) but redistribution of the beach material is occurring. Some areas of the beach may be accreting while others are eroding. In such circumstances beach recharge can be used in the badly affected areas, possibly in conjunction with control structures designed to regulate the fluctuations in drift.

3. For the purpose of enhancing or retaining the recreational value of the area by creating a wider beach or, following land reclamation such as the construction of a promenade, a similar beach further seaward.

Some of the advantages and disadvantages of beach recharge are summarised in Box 7.1. It can be employed both in a one-off scheme or as part of a staged or progressive strategy, the extent of recharge tending to be greater in a one-off scheme. The predicted recharge interval can be tuned to optimise the balance between capital and maintenance costs.

Box 7.1   *Advantages and disadvantages of beach recharge*

Advantages
Can be aesthetically pleasing
Is usually environmentally friendly
May enhance the recreational value
Less likely to cause erosion problems downdrift

Disadvantages
High monitoring and maintenance commitment
May change sediment transport characteristics
Possible problems with availability of suitable material - competition with aggregate industry
Need to obtain a licence for new offshore borrow areas
More difficult to obtain public acceptance as a coastal defence

The sections of this chapter outline design considerations and principles for a beach recharge scheme as well as practical implementation and environmental considerations. Subjects covered include:

- availability and sourcing of recharge material (Section 7.1)
- selection of material size, grading and mineralogy (Section 7.2)
- determination of a recharge volume (Section 7.3); this must be determined to provide a given standard of protection against severe events (see Section 5.3)
- specification and testing (Section 7.4)
- procedures for obtaining recharge material (Section 7.5)
- transportation of the material to the site and placement (Section 7.6)
- measurement and costs (Section 7.7)
- construction aspects (Section 7.8)
- environmental considerations (Section 7.9).

7.1   SOURCING RECHARGE MATERIAL

7.1.1   Alternative sources

There are essentially five main categories of sources for recharge material. These are:

- existing licensed offshore extraction areas
- offshore extraction areas, presently unlicensed, for which a specific licence is to be obtained for the scheme (or a series of schemes)
- navigational dredging projects, including port and harbour developments
- land-based natural sand and gravel deposits (including re-cycled material) and quarried rock
- secondary aggregates, being by-products from industrial processes, wastes and demolition materials.

Many of the beach recharge schemes implemented to date have used the first category. However, due to the demand on existing licensed reserves and competition with the construction industry, there is an increasing tendency for sources to be considered from the other categories. Some of the advantages and disadvantages of using the above categories are outlined in Box 7.2. Dredging equipment available for winning material from a marine source is described later in Box 7.14.

Box 7.2 *Examples of advantages and disadvantages of alternative material sources*

---

1. Existing licensed offshore extraction areas

Advantages:
May be possible to obtain material within short timescale
No exploration costs involved
Outline specification of material usually available for design
Usually possible to identify material suitable for beach use

Disadvantages: No guarantee that sufficient material will be available when required
Lack of suitable material may lead to lengthening of project and cost increase
Cost may be high during periods when construction activity is high
No control over material availability

2. Unlicensed offshore extraction areas

Advantages:
Known overall volume of reserves
Consistency of source for the future
Control over whole operation
Planned maintenance made easier
Material normally suitable for beach use

Disadvantages: Length of time required to obtain licence
High initial costs of exploration and licensing of specific extraction areas
Possible chance of failure to obtain licence
Specification not determined until end of exploratory stage
Unknown working conditions may be placed on the licence

3. Navigational dredging projects

Advantages:
Material often same as beach material if sites are close
Re-use of dredged material highly desirable on environmental and economic grounds
May have large cost advantages
Total volume available known

Disadvantages: More difficult to arrange suitable contractual terms
Material has to be accepted as dredged
Concurrent dredging and recharge operations difficult to arrange
Rejection of unsuitable material may lead to unfinished recharge

4. Natural land-based sources

Advantages:
Gives wider selection of materials for smaller schemes
Availability at short notice

Disadvantages: Particles are often sharper than sea dredged material, giving steeper slopes in initial stages
Colour and shape may be aesthetically undesirable
Delivery by road vehicles often environmentally unacceptable

5. Secondary (by-product) aggregates

Advantages:
Often available in large quantities and at low or nil cost

Disadvantages: Colour and shape may be aesthetically undesirable
Delivery to site, even by sea, may increase costs to an unacceptable level

Note: Other possible environmental advantages and disadvantages are discussed in Section 7.9.

7.1.2   Influence of scheme size

Past experience has demonstrated that the size of a scheme, in particular the volume of beach material required, will influence the choice of source. Schemes may be broadly split into three size ranges:

- volumes of up to 100,000m^3
- volumes between 100,000 and 300,000m^3
- volumes in excess of 300,000m^3.

Those schemes in the smallest size range have the greatest opportunity for choice of source. Schemes requiring less than 50,000m³ of material can often obtain this material either from a land-based source, from navigation dredgings (e.g. from a maintenance campaign or capital dredging works) or from a licensed marine source. As the volume increases, road transport becomes more of a problem, maintenance dredging becomes less likely to supply an adequate quantity and a licensed marine source becomes the more likely choice.

In the intermediate range, between 100,000 and 300,000m³ of material, a licensed marine source is likely to be chosen for UK schemes. Volumes within this range may well be available from one or more licensed extraction areas at a suitable distance from the site and without the need for increasing the extraction rate beyond the maximum annual tonnage permitted. Occasionally a channel dredging project will supply the desired volume, but the opportunities for this are limited.

For volumes in excess of 300,000m³ there is an increasing likelihood that insufficient material will be available from the annual tonnages permitted from licensed areas, which tend to be around 500,000 tonnes per year around the UK. The maximum permitted in an individual year may be increased (an "uplift") as long as the total extraction does not exceed certain limits (see Section 7.5), but the alternative of finding a new source is likely to be the better option. The only practical alternative to finding a new source is for the project to be lengthened, with construction occurring over a number of seasons.

7.1.3   Influence of scheme location

The location of a scheme is also likely to affect the source selection process. Schemes within reasonable sailing distances of the existing licensed marine areas will tend to be supplied from these areas. Licenced areas around England and Wales are located predominantly on the South and East coasts, with a few sites situated in the Bristol Channel and in the North West. A major portion of the Welsh coast, the South West and North East of England are currently devoid of licensed marine sources. Existing marine sand and gravel resources off the South, East and West coasts of England and Wales are shown in Figures 7.2, 7.3 and 7.4, which also indicate the location of licensed areas. It is important to note that these figures indicate the total physical resource, they do not give an indication of the workable resource.

Further information on the distribution of marine materials around the coast of England and Wales may be obtained from CIRIA Report 154 *Beach recharge material - demand and resources* (CIRIA, 1996).

The demand for these marine resources has also been estimated in CIRIA (1996). A summary of the results of this assessment is shown in Box 7.3 and is compared with the "potentially workable resource". An estimation of the latter resource was obtained from calculations of volumes of material in the grid squares shown in Figures 7.2 to 7.4, which excludes all material within 0.5m of the seabed and material in grid squares dominated by fines (material less than 0.125mm in diameter).

Information regarding the sources of land-based materials which might prove to be suitable for beach recharge are also given in the above-mentioned CIRIA publication. From this work it is possible to obtain a picture of the distribution of various sources of natural quarried materials as well as major sources of secondary aggregates. Generally, the superficial (drift) deposits lie to the east of the country, whilst the quarried rock sources tend to lie in the west.

CIRIA (1996) provides collated information on the total marine resources to aid beach recharge scheme planning. It does not obviate the need for detailed prospecting should a possible marine source be identified, but it will help beach managers decide whether recharge is an option in a particular location by identifying the general distribution of regional sources.

Box 7.3   *Anticipated future demand for beach recharge material for the coasts of England and Wales compared with potentially workable resources*

The anticipated total demand for beach recharge material for England and Wales from 1995 to 2015 has been estimated by CIRIA (1996). The approach used was necessarily simple and relied on a number of broad assumptions. Material estimates for potential capital and maintenance recharge under present day conditions were made for 19 sites around the UK coastline for which beach recharge may be a practical solution to coastal defence. In addition, future climate change and sea level rise were considered, initially for several specific sites and then on a regional basis.

The 19 sites were selected using the following criteria, in approximate order of importance:

* availability of wave climate and beach profile data
* geographical distribution
* representation of sand and shingle beaches
* potential for implementation of a recharge scheme
* representation of different risk categories
* and representation of different sized schemes.

Estimates of the capital recharge requirement for the sand beach sites utilized a 2-dimensional sand morphodynamic model, whilst the parametric model described in Box 5.3 was used for the shingle beaches. Estimates for maintenance recharge requirements were based on estimates of potential longshore drift (see Box 2.4) with modifications for the effect of structures based on experience from existing UK sites. Wherever possible, comparisons were made between the simple estimates made for the project and estimates made using more rigorous methods for sites that are currently under design or have been recently completed.

Extrapolation to the whole coastline involved identifying all of the frontages for which beach recharge schemes might be completed within 20 years and representing each of these by one of the 19 selected sites, modified by taking the following factors into consideration:

* likely phasing of construction
* use of beach control structures
* impact of downdrift losses as feed to adjacent beaches
* variation in exposure to wave action
* variation in tidal range and risk of storm surge damage
* uncertainty in methods.

The anticipated total demand estimates for both sand and shingle for each of the twelve coastal areas considered (shown in Figure 1), are presented in Table 1, where they are compared with the potentially workable resource estimated as described in Section 7.1.3 and, in considerable detail, in CIRIA (1996).

Table 1   Comparison of regional recharge demand for England and Wales from 1995 to 2015 with resource estimates

Region	Estimated demand (m³ × 10⁶)					
	Anticipated total UK demand to 2015 Mm³			Potentially workable resources Mm³		
	Shingle	**Sand & Gravel**	**Sand**	**Shingle**	**Sand & Gravel**	**Sand**
Tyne-Tees	6	1.1	16.0	0.07	0.13	30.3
Yorks-Humber	3	0.6	11.9	not investigated		
Wash	2.1	0	15.4	75.5	69.7	434.0
East Anglia	8.6	0.6	9.5	224.0	150.2	5552.9
Thames Estuary	97.5	13.3	53.2	90.9	367.4	3373.9
English Channel E	64.4	6.7	25.6	225.4	92.1	761.6
English Channel W	2.9	0	1.6	0.02	0.9	42.8
Bristol Channel S	0.7	0	18.9	150.1	57.6	3466.6
South Wales	0	0	44.8	6.1	22.1	256.0
North Wales	1.5	0	9.9	9.2	48.0	324.4
Lancs & Cheshire	0	0	10.3	0	0	128.3
Cumbria	0.7	0	6.4	not investigated		

Continued

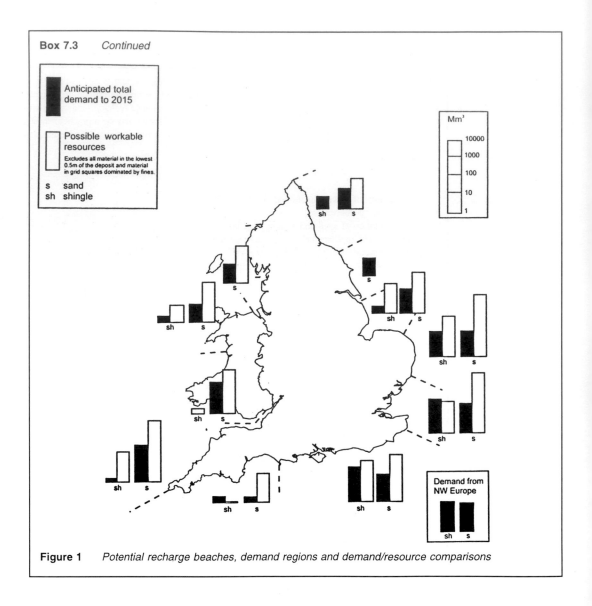

Figure 1   *Potential recharge beaches, demand regions and demand/resource comparisons*

7.1.4   Material availability

When a potential source of material has been identified, it is important to obtain a realistic assessment of its availability to the recharge project. Material from licensed marine sources is used mainly as a supply of aggregate for the construction industry, in particular for making concrete. Large beach recharge projects require volumes of aggregate which are often of the same order as annual permitted maximum which may be abstracted from a licensed offshore block.

In times of recession, when construction activity is relatively low, much of the permitted licensed marine aggregate tonnage is available for recharge schemes. However, as the construction industry becomes more active, so the competition for aggregate becomes more acute. In such circumstances, less material may be forthcoming for beach recharge schemes, the material may be made available at a higher cost or the availability may depend on the aggregate producing licensee being granted an uplift on the annual permitted tonnage. In times of high construction activity a further constraint may be that the option of screening out fine material is not available. This is because only normal trailer hopper suction dredgers may be available to "raise" the material, the specialised aggregate dredging vessels which can carry out screening being dedicated to other tasks.

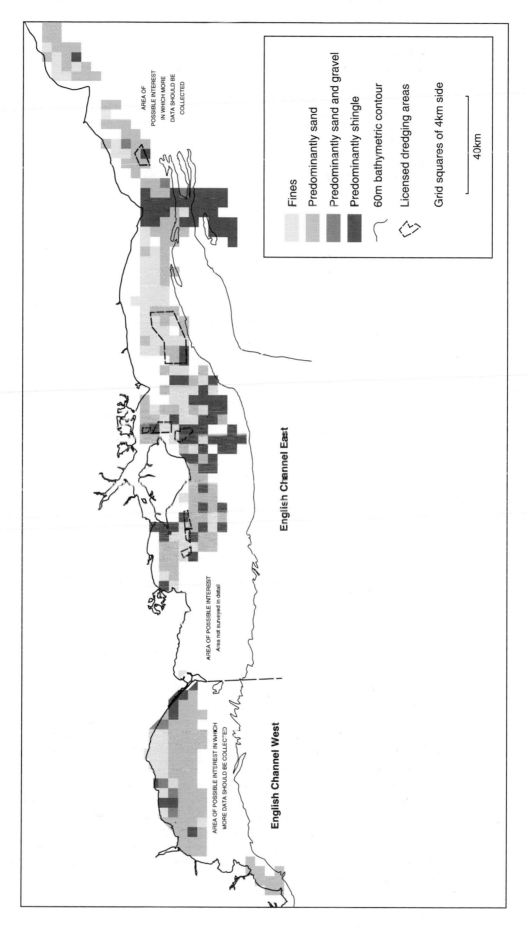

Figure 7.2 *Distribution of sand and gravel resources off the south coast of England (CIRIA, 1996)*

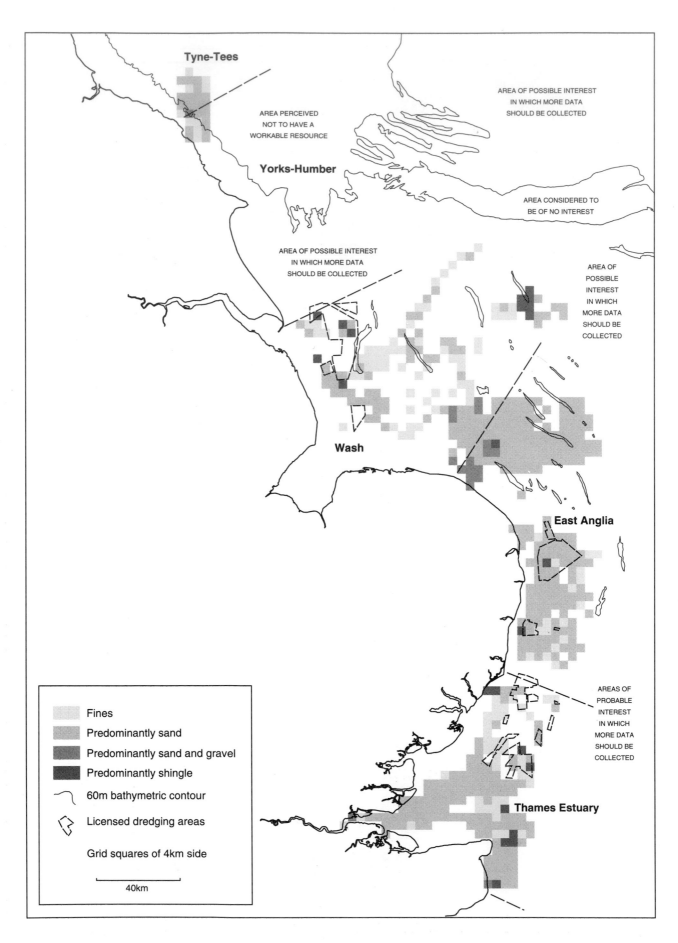

Figure 7.3 *Distribution of sand and gravel resources off the east coast of England (CIRIA, 1996)*

Figure 7.4   *Distribution of sand and gravel resources off the west coast of England and Wales (CIRIA, 1996)*

7.2 SELECTION OF MATERIAL SIZE, GRADING AND MINERALOGY

It has long been recognised that the selection of material size is one of the most important decisions for a beach recharge scheme. It is now widely recognised that material grading can be as influential in its effect on beach stability and response. When designing a beach recharge scheme from available material sources, the four main issues in terms of performance as a coastal defence are:

- beach stability
- sediment dynamics
- durability
- recreational aspects.

The last aspect is discussed in Section 7.9, along with other environmental considerations that should be taken into account.

7.2.1 Classification system

Before discussing the main issues, it is worth briefly mentioning the various classification systems for describing material size. In the UK the British Standards Institution (BS) classification is widely used and has been adopted for figures throughout the manual. The classification is defined in Table 7.1 where the standard BS Sieve sizes are also defined. An illustration of its use is given in Figure 7.6.

Table 7.1 BS Material size classification

Material		Material size (mm)
Clay		< 0.002
Silt	Fine	0.002 - 0.006
	Medium	0.006 - 0.02
	Coarse	0.02 - 0.06
Sand	Fine	0.6 - 0.02
	Medium	0.2 - 0.6
	Coarse	0.6 - 2.0
Gravel	Fine	2.0 - 6.0
	Medium	6.0 - 20.0
	Coarse	20.0 - 60.0
Cobble		> 60.0

Other systems include the Unified Soils Classification and the Wentworth Classification; these are defined in Figure 7.5.

7.2.2 Beach stability

Since sorting of the natural beach material will have occurred over many years, the natural material size and grading at a particular site will provide a good guide to what material will be stable. It is usual to employ material of a similar or coarser size and grading to ensure stability. Due to restrictions in the availability of material, this may not be practicable, technically or economically. Alternatively there may be a desire to replace an existing shingle beach with sand or vice versa. Whatever the material size and its relation to that of any existing beach, design methods are required to determine the stability of the resulting beach. These methods are presented in Section 7.3. This section addresses the processes and factors that need to be considered before the design methods in Section 7.3 are employed.

Firstly, cross-shore sediment transport and resulting changes in the beach profile must be considered. It is well known that there is a direct linkage between sediment size and average

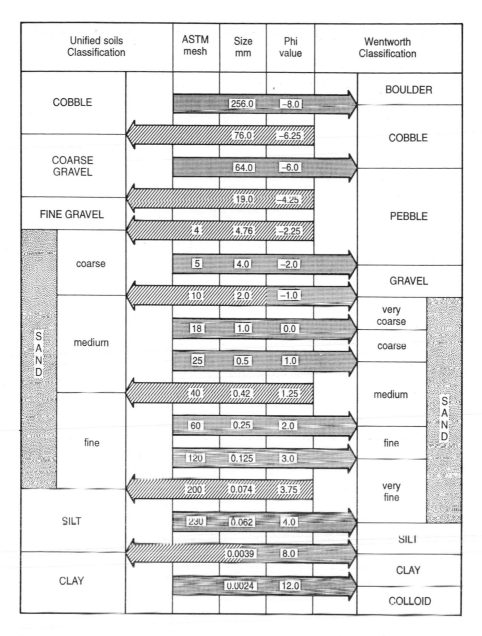

Figure 7.5   *Material grain size scales and classification systems (CERC, 1984)*

beach slope, with finer sediment lying at a flatter slope. Table 7.2 gives typical beach slopes for different mean grain sizes. In general a beach of a given grain size will adopt a flatter slope in an area exposed to a severe wave climate or steep waves than it would with more moderate waves.

Table 7.2 Typical beach slopes for various mean sediment sizes

Sediment type	Median sediment size D_{50} (mm)	Mean beach slope		
Sand	0.2	1:50	-	1:100
	0.3	1:25	-	1:50
	0.5	1:20	-	1:40
Shingle	5.0	1:8	-	1:15
	10.0	1:7	-	1:12
	25.0	1:4	-	1:8

Sand beaches lie at a relatively shallow slope, since the majority of sediment carried up by the wave run-up returns in the backwash, so there is no hydro-dynamic mechanism for steepening.

Shingle beaches are more permeable so much of the run-up percolates down into the beach reducing the backwash, allowing material to be deposited higher up the beach and thereby steepening the slope. However a widely graded shingle (or mixed sand and shingle) beach will be less permeable and therefore rest at a flatter angle even though the median grain size (D_{50}) may be the same. This effect of grading on beach slope is quantified in Powell's equilibrium slope method (see Box 7.10 in Section 7.3).

Recharged beach profiles must be matched to the size and grading of the recharge material otherwise there will be a rapid initial adjustment towards the natural equilibrium slope which, if the beach has been placed at too steep an angle, will result in rapid erosion of the upper beach. Over a period of time as the beach is re-worked by wave action, it is likely that the recharge grading will evolve to become more typical of that of a natural beach. Therefore whilst it is necessary to ensure that the design profile for a beach recharge is commensurate with the material size and grading being used, it is also important that the designer is aware of the potential for changes in beach profile behaviour as the beach grading evolves towards a more natural state.

In addition to changes in the profile of a recharged beach, there may be losses due to longshore transport. In fact this is likely to have been one of the mechanisms responsible for loss of the beach in the first place. The CERC formula for longshore transport rate in the Shore Protection Manual (CERC, 1984) does not contain any explicit dependence on sediment grain size although there is a site-specific calibration parameter K_1. Kamphuis (1991) gave the following empirical expression for drift on sand beaches indicating that longshore transport rate, Q, will increase as sediment size decreases. Although this expression is reported to be applicable to both sand and shingle beaches, most of the data from which it was derived was representative of sand beaches.

$$Q = 6.4 \times 10^4 \, H_{sb}^2 \, T_p^{1.5} \, m_b^{0.75} \, D_{50}^{-0.25} \, \sin^{0.6}(2\beta_b) \qquad (7.1)$$

where
H_{sb} = significant wave height at breaking
T_p = peak wave period
m_b = beach slope (= $\tan\theta$)
D_{50} = mean grain size
β_b = angle between wave orthogonal at breaking and beach normal.

The dependence on sediment size is, however, weakened since finer sediment will rest at a flatter slope and the slope term in Kamphuis' expression acts in the opposite way to the sediment size term. It is therefore recommended that Kamphuis' relationship is only applied to sand beaches. For shingle or cobble beaches, experience suggests that longshore transport rates are about 15-20 times less than for sand as calculated using the CERC formula. Consequently if a shingle beach is being replaced by a recharged sand beach (which may be attractive from an amenity point of view), serious consideration needs to be given to losses due to longshore transport.

Even if the beach recharge material is identical to that on the natural beach, longshore transport rates may increase since the recharged beach might extend into deeper water whereas there may have been a restricted supply of beach material available to be transported on the original beach. In many situations around the UK coast, there is a lower sand beach with an upper shingle beach. The proportion of wave energy being dissipated on the shingle beach will increase if the shingle is recharged, pushing its toe into deeper water. Section 5.3 shows how the cross-shore distribution of potential longshore drift can be calculated and used to determine the drift rate on the shingle part of the beach. Existing beach control structures such as groynes may become less efficient with a wider or higher recharged beach. They may therefore need to be extended or replaced.

Beach Coarsening

Beach coarsening occurs when beach recharge is undertaken using material larger than the native material. It can be carried out with the deliberate aim of armouring a beach to make it more stable under conditions where natural erosion processes cannot be modified and would otherwise result in the rapid loss of native beach material. It may also be the result of the availability of material that is larger than the optimum required by the designer.

The improvement in the hydraulic characteristics of a beach as a result of coarsening can be achieved on both sand and shingle beaches. Box 7.4 describes a sand beach recharged with a mix of sand and shingle, while Box 7.5 describes a situation in which shingle was introduced to a predominantly sand beach.

Box 7.4   *Sand coarsening - Sand Bay, Avon*

A very effective beach management scheme was carried out in 1983/84 at Sand Bay, near Weston Super Mare, where a coarse sand intermixed with a proportion of shingle was used to create a relatively steep upper beach berm on an otherwise very flat, long sandy/muddy foreshore.

Sand Bay is contained between two headlands so that loss of material through alongshore transport was negligible. The main problem was that with the large tidal range and the severe wave exposure there was a danger that recharge material would be dragged down and intermixed with the fine sand, silts and muds which comprise the flat lower foreshore.

In this case recharge material was obtained from two marine sources, one containing a high proportion of gravel while the other contained sand. The nourishment material was dredged and discharged by pipeline onto the upper part of the beach from when it was redistributed by bulldozer to form a 20m berm with a seaward slope of 1:10.

The mixture was considerably coarser than the native material but there were still sufficient fines for some material to be blown landwards. The backshore was therefore stabilised by means of fencing and introduction of marram grass. The beach is now considerably steeper than the original and presents a valuable amenity, being exposed even at high tide.

Box 7.5   *Shingle coarsening - Highcliffe, Dorset*

At Highcliffe, Dorset, beach coarsening was carried out on a predominantly sandy foreshore backed by unstable cliffs of banded clay, sand and flint. Protection to the base of these cliffs had formerly consisted of a sloping timber revetment. With persistent beach lowering, this revetment became increasingly overtopped and damaged by waves. In 1984 a decision was made to import gravel from local quarries so as to form an artificial storm beach and rock groynes were constructed to retain this material in place. The reason for putting the gravel in place was to attract finer particles to the beach. The scheme has proved its success in subsequent years and after topping up operations and a major extension of the groyne system in 1991/92 the shingle beach is providing a high degree of protection, with the cliffs being protected from direct wave action. Ongoing monitoring of the beach has shown that the shingle has remained more stable along the eastern length, where narrowly graded material (15-40mm) was placed, relative to the western end, where more widely graded sand and gravel was placed. Minor top-ups have been required in the west.

Beach coarsening is normally restricted to beaches which have been badly eroded and are failing to give an adequate level of backshore protection. It is unlikely that such a method would be appropriate on amenity beaches, subject to only minor beach erosion.

Beaches which are close to tidal inlets, where the tidal current or wave regime has dramatically altered as a result of changed inlet bathymetry, and the onshore migration of tidal channels etc, are areas where this form of management could be used. Beaches where persistent coastal erosion has resulted in general foreshore lowering (i.e. by the erosion of the substratum) are clearly also candidate areas. The coast of eastern England, along which there are many stretches of coast affected by steepening of the intertidal zone, could generally be improved by beach recharge, and beach coarsening may play an important role in improving the long term stability of the beaches, coarser beaches generally being stable at steeper slopes (see Table 7.2).

Beach coarsening has occurred fortuitously at a number of South Cornwall beaches as a result of the discharge of china clay waste through rivers onto adjacent beaches, one example being Carlyon Bay near the clay exporting port of Par. At this site the clay waste has resulted in a wide beach of material which has properties somewhere between a coarse sand and a fine gravel. The material is fairly angular and therefore very free draining and it forms a very stable beach under normal wave conditions. Under severe conditions, the material becomes banked up in a similar manner to a shingle upper beach and forms an efficient protection against wave overtopping.

Beach coarsening can be successfully used under a wide variety of conditions. It can certainly be used in areas where the longshore transport of sediment is small but onshore/offshore movement is high and needs to be restricted. It can also be applied to open beaches where there is a need to reduce the longshore transport rate, without recourse to extensive control structures (see Chapter 8). Under conditions of high drift, gravel or small rock is a suitable material for providing a protective carpet at the base of sand dunes, as commonly occurs on the beaches of West Wales for example. The obvious constraints to this type of management is the impact it may have on public amenity, and the risk to local flora and fauna from the coarse and relatively mobile material.

With this type of management, there is a need for extensive pre- and post-project monitoring, not only from a coastal processes viewpoint but also to assess possible ecological impact. At present, little is known about the likely environmental impact or of the likely performance of this type of management, so site specific impact studies are necessary.

7.2.3 Sediment dynamics

Once placed on a beach, recharge material will be re-worked by the waves and tidal currents and sorted to some extent. Especially on sand beaches, part of the finer fraction may be lost through toe wash-out or winnowed from the beach face. Initial losses of fines are likely to be greater when recharge material is pumped ashore from a dredger since the pumped slurry contains a high proportion of water which may carry the fines offshore. The wash-out of fines from the recharge site can have long-term effects on the adjoining benthic or inter-tidal ecosystems (see Section 7.9). On shingle beaches, where there is a fair proportion of fines in the recharge material, there will be a migration of the finer fraction into the core of the beach during the sorting process. Although this will result in less volume loss of fines, it will lead to a less permeable surface layer of the beach, resulting in a flatter equilibrium slope and restricting the ability of the profile to build a crest to withstand storms.

Recharge material with a wider grading than the natural beach generally behaves less well. This is partly due to the higher proportion of material at the finer end of the grading. However, experience from a recent shingle beach recharge, for example at Hayling Island (Clare, 1988), has shown a tendency for a loss of the coarsest fraction in an offshore direction. This was confirmed in an aluminium tracer experiment by Nicholls (1985). It is believed that the oversized particles, which protrude from the surface, are plucked out of the matrix and transported offshore. By contrast, in a naturally graded beach the surface is armoured by the interlock between particles of varying sizes.

7.2.4 Durability

Beaches are active structures with their material continually being moved by the waves and tides. Rounding and weight loss in the beach environment is dependent on the shape and mineralogy of the beach material. Around the UK most marine sources of sand and gravel have a high quartzite content and are relatively hard. The gravel and sand banks are often relict coastal or fluvial features so the material will already have been rounded. Weight loss from rounded particles is much reduced from the rate of weight loss occurring in irregular particles such as crushed quarry rock. Here the weight loss can be envisaged as taking place in two overlapping stages:

1. Removal of asperities on irregular particles principally by impacts.

2. Gradual wearing away and rounding of the particles once the asperities have been removed.

The first process will occur relatively quickly leading to an initial rapid reduction in particle weight. At a later stage the second process will begin, progress and eventually dominate the degradation process. Sources of beach recharge can be compared for weight loss by abrasion mill tests in accordance with methods described in CIRIA/CUR, (1991). An example of weight loss of crushed quarried carboniferous limestone is given in Table 7.3.

Table 7.3 Carboniferous limestone beach recharge weight loss (Penrhyn Beach, North Wales)

In-service life	weight loss	shape
1 year	2%	sub-angular
3 years	10%	sub-rounded
5 years	14%	sub-rounded
10 years	24%	rounded
15 years	30%	well-rounded

This material from a local North Wales quarry was placed on Penrhyn Beach. The wear after 3 years was assessed and used to calibrate the timescale of abrasion mill tests and to extrapolate likely weight loss into the future (Poole, 1993). With limestone the lost weight is removed from the beach as a fine dust. Other rock types will degrade to form sand-sized sediment that may remain on the beach and not be completely lost. In such a situation, the beach may not lose as much weight but the grading will be altered and the volume decreased due to a greater packing density.

The shell content of a beach recharge material is important from the durability point of view since shells will degrade faster and, because of their shape and lower density, are more likely to be winnowed out from the beach. Other contaminants, such as coal or chalk, will again degrade quickly. Clay will be eroded and particles lost through suspension.

7.3 DETERMINATION OF RECHARGE VOLUME

The quantity of material required for a beach recharge scheme will need to be determined taking into account both coastal defence and amenity considerations.

The new beach profile is usually designed to ensure that it provides an adequate standard of protection during a severe storm, for example using numerical modelling methods (see Section 5.3). In most situations, allowance also has to be made for the likely losses of beach material over time due to longshore drift and also cross-shore losses. A balance has to be struck between the amount of material placed initially, and the future maintenance commitments, i.e. periodic "top-up" operations. It may also be necessary to consider the dimensions of the beach produced (e.g. plan area, slope), and the type of beach material, in terms of the recreational value of the coastline.

Methods of varying degrees of complexity have been developed to determine recharge volumes and these are described below.

1. Simple methods, which are appropriate where the correct material is available to restore a beach to historically recorded levels, or to match existing healthy beaches nearby.

2. Methods based on calculations of the response of a typical beach profile to design wave/ tidal level conditions, taking into account sediment sizes or gradings which are different to the native beach material, and which would therefore result in a different beach profile shape (e.g. slope, crest level).

3. Detailed computational or physical modelling considering both the plan shape and profile of the new beach, the need for control structures (e.g. groynes), and the maintenance strategy.

These approaches are now discussed in the following sections.

7.3.1   Simple recharge calculation methods

Learn from nature

The simplest method, i.e. comparing the present day beach with a healthy beach in the same area (or indeed with the state of the same beach in previous years when it was itself healthy), should always be attempted as a first step. It is also worthwhile making enquiries about previous beach recharge schemes in the same general area, or of beaches of similar material type as part of this simple approach.

The crest height and width, the slope and the lower limit of the existing beach profile should be compared with those on a healthy beach, of similar exposure, in the same area. This will allow the required increase in cross-sectional area at a number of locations to be determined. At this stage, a simple allowance for future sea level rise and different tidal levels should be incorporated into the desired crest height. This will lead to a good first estimate of the quantity and type of material required to produce a beach in keeping with the natural coastline. Information can also be gathered on the size and grading of the indigenous beach material (remembering to sample at a number of locations over and below the beach surface).

If a sufficient quantity of similar material can be obtained at reasonable cost, and losses from the new beach in future years due to longshore drift are likely to be small, or easily made good, then this may be all that is required to determine the recharge volume. However, this situation is uncommon. A lack of an 'ideal' beach for comparison, a lack of good quality, long-term monitoring, or difficulty in locating material of similar grading are likely to require the use of predictive models (See Section 7.3.2).

The Dutch Design Method (Verhagen, 1992)

In The Netherlands, most beach recharge is carried out to combat progressive coastal erosion. The Dutch also have a long period of good monitoring data from which to calculate past losses. Hence the method employed for designing most beach recharge schemes in The Netherlands is:

1. Regularly (at least once a year) measure beach profiles for a period of at least 10 years.

2. Calculate loss of sand in m^3/year per coastal section.

3. Add 40% to account for losses as the profile adjusts to allow for the increased exposure of the recharge profile.

4. Multiply this quantity by a convenient lifetime (e.g. 5 or 10 years).

5. Place the material between the low-water-minus 1m line and the dune foot on sandy beaches. Shingle beach recharge should in most cases be concentrated on the upper part of the beach.

The method is simple, implicitly allowing for both cross-shore and longshore losses but it does require good quality profile measurements over a long period. It also assumes that the recharge material is a good match to the 'native' beach material.

7.3.2   Profile design methods: sand beach recharges

A number of alternative methods are given here. However, experience in the USA, an excellent objective summary of which may be found in Davison *et al* (1992), suggests that no one of these methods should be used in isolation. Instead, as many as possible should be used to indicate the potential range of recharge volumes that may be required. Caution should be adopted when using these methods not to infer that coarser materials will necessarily last longer than native material.

1.   Dean's equilibrium profile method (Dean, 1991)

This is the most widely used method of its type in the USA. It concentrates on determining the volume of recharge sand of a given grain size that will need to be placed on a beach to increase the dry beach width by a given amount The method is described in Box 7.6.

2.   Pilarczyk, van Overeem and Bakker (1986) equilibrium slope method

The equilibrium slope method of predicting recharge volume of sand beaches considers the reshaping of the active profile in response to prevailing hydraulic conditions and the depth to which the profile will develop. The method is described in Box 7.7.

3.   "overfill factor" or "overfill ratio" methods

These methods, developed for sand beaches, assume that the native material at any particular site represents the most stable sediment grading for the site specific environmental conditions. They go on to assume that the beach volume is sorted by the wave and tidal processes to eventually adopt a grain size distribution similar to the native material. They also extend the generally accepted principle that coarser grain sizes are often more stable to the extent that coarser materials of a similar (log-normal) distribution will last longer than the native material when used as a recharge; this extension still waits to be proven with any reliability.

Given these principles, these methods quantify the extent of overfill required to mitigate these losses. Box 7.8 gives one such methodology by Krumbein and James (1965). James (1975) modified the approach to account for the stability of the coarser fraction and produced the first graph in Box 7.9 to calculate an adjusted overfill factor, R_A. To determine the periodic recharge requirements James defined a recharge factor, R_J, as the ratio of the rate at which the recharge material will erode relative to the rate at which the native beach material is eroding. The set of curves on the second graph in Box 7.9 show the relative values of R_J for various combinations of recharge and native materials. The greater the value of R_J the greater the frequency of recharge.

James's methods have been widely used in the USA and perhaps almost as widely criticised, particularly in respect of their predictions of recharge life via the R_J factor (Davison, 1992). For this reason, the reliability of James's methods must therefore be questioned and they should only be used in combination with other corroborative techniques. Their use should not be extended to shingle beaches as the results, which were applied to one project in the UK, have proved to be misleading; an alternative approach for shingle beaches, which is believed to be more reliable, is given in Section 7.3.3 and Box 7.10.

7.3.3   Profile design method: shingle beach recharges

An equilibrium slope method was derived by Powell (1993) specifically for shingle beaches recharged with sediment of a dissimilar grading. The method was based on results of laboratory model tests carried out at HR Wallingford. Although comparison between predicted and field data was carried out and yielded encouraging results for shingle sized sediments, a more extensive comparison including temporal variations in natural beach profiles will be necessary to improve confidence in the model results. This method, described in Box 7.10, can take account of the difference in wave climate from site to site.

Box 7.6   *Dean's equilibrium profile method*

Dean proposed that beach profiles develop a characteristic parabolic equilibrium profile given by:

$$h = Ax^{2/3} \tag{1}$$

where h is the depth below still water for any given horizontal distance, x, from the shoreline, both measured in metres. A can be expressed (Dean, 1991) as:

$$A = 0.21\, D^{0.48} \text{ where } D \text{ is the grain size in mm} \tag{2}$$

Other formulae for A are given in Box 5.3.

Figure 1 below shows three different types of profile depending on the relative values of A for the native and recharge (fill) material. The intersecting profile intersects the native profile before the closure depth, d. The non-intersecting profile, although steeper than the native profile, does not intersect before the closure depth. For the submerged profile, the fill material is finer than the native material and insufficient volume has been added to increase the dry beach width. In the following figures subscript N denotes a parameter relating to native material and subscript R denotes one relating to recharge material. R_c indicates the berm crest height and Y the increase in dry beach width.

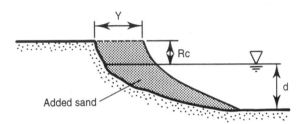

a) Intersecting profile; recharge grain size, D_R > native grain size, D_N ($A_R > A_N$)

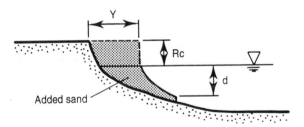

b) Non-intersecting profile; recharge grain size, D_R < native grain size, D_N ($A_R < A_N$)

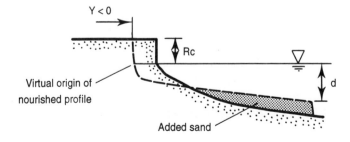

c) Submerged profile; recharge grain size, D_R < native grain size, D_N ($A_R < A_N$)

Figure 1   *Generic types of recharged profiles*

Continued

Box 7.6   *Continued*

Procedure
Determine the closure depth d as:

$$d = 1.75\,H_s \tag{3}$$

where H_s corresponds to the nearshore significant wave height with a frequency of occurrence of 12 hours per year.

Select a berm crest height, R_c, and required increase in dry beach width, Y.

Determine A_R and A_N from equation (2) for the fill and native material respectively.

Determine whether the profiles are intersecting or non-intersecting using (4):

$$Y\left(\frac{A_N}{d}\right)^{3/2} + \left(\frac{A_N}{A_R}\right)^{3/2} \quad \begin{array}{l} < 1 = \text{Intersecting,} \\ > 1 = \text{Non-intersecting} \end{array} \tag{4}$$

If they are intersecting, use the following equation (5) to calculate the volume V required per metre run of beach to advance the shoreline by distance Y:

$$V = R_c Y + \frac{A_N Y^{5/3}}{\left[1 - \left(\frac{A_N}{A_R}\right)^{3/2}\right]^{2/3}} \tag{5}$$

If the profiles are non-intersecting use equation (6):

$$V = R_c Y + \frac{3}{5}d^{5/2}\left[\left[\frac{Y}{d^{3/2}} + \left(\frac{1}{A_R}\right)^{1/2}\right]^{5/3} A_N - \left(\frac{1}{A_R}\right)^{3/2}\right] \tag{6}$$

CAUTION: THIS METHOD SHOULD NOT BE USED IN ISOLATION (SEE SECTION 7.3.2).

Box 7.7   *Beach recharge design (Pilarczyk, van Overeem and Bakker, 1986)*

This method bases the recharged profile on the present native profile, but if the grain size of the recharge material is different from the native material the profile steepness is altered according to the following relationship.

$$\ell_R = \left(\frac{w_N}{w_R}\right)^{0.56} \ell_N$$

where w =   fall velocity (calculated as described in Box 2.3)
                ℓ =   distance offshore of a given depth contour
subscript   N   =   denotes native material
subscript   R   =   denotes recharge material.

Note: For common beach sand of diameter D between 0.15mm and 0.85mm, Hallermeier (1981) gives the following approximation for fall velocity w (in cm/s):

$$w = 14D^{1.1} \text{ (where } D \text{ is in mm).}$$

If the recharge material is coarser than the native material, i.e. $w_R > w_N$, then the profile of the recharged beach is steeper than the original profile shown in Figure 1 below. The converse effect applies to recharge materials finer than native sediments.

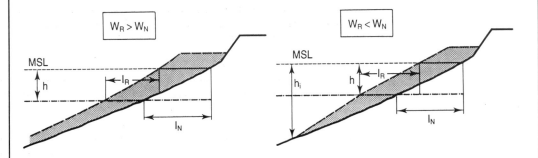

Figure 1   *Effect of grain size on profile steepness (Vellinga, 1982)*

The above profile is used down to a cutoff depth, h_c, of the active beach defined by Birkemeier's (1985) re-evaluation of Hallermeier's (1978) work as:

$$h_c = 1.75 \, H_s$$

where H_s corresponds to nearshore wave conditions and is the local significant wave height with a frequency occurrence of 0.137% (i.e. 12 hours per year).

Beyond this depth the recharge beach thickness is assumed to decrease linearly within a transition zone until it intersects the original profile at an intersection depth h_i, given by $h_i \approx 3H_s$ (Figure 2).

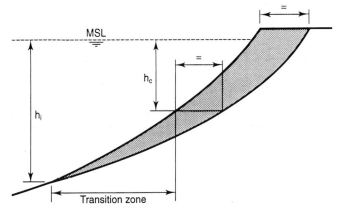

Figure 2   *Profile of beach fill: recharge sand equal to native sand*

CAUTION: THIS METHOD SHOULD NOT BE USED IN ISOLATION (SEE SECTION 7.3.2).

CIRIA Report 153

Box 7.8 *Critical overfill ratio for sand beaches (Krumbein and James, 1965)*

Krumbein and James (1965) established a method for estimating the additional quantity of recharge material required if the recharge and native sediments were dissimilar. The methodology involved multiplying the required volume of beach material, assuming a natural grading, by a critical overfill ratio, $R_{\phi crit}$ to determine the quantity of recharge material over and above that required by the absolute dimensions of the proposed recharge works. The derivation of $R_{\phi crit}$ is given below:

$$R_{\phi crit} = \frac{\sigma_{\phi R}}{\sigma_{\phi N}} \exp\left[- \frac{(M_{\phi N} - M_{\phi R})^2}{2(\sigma_{\phi N}^2 - \sigma_{\phi R}^2)} \right]$$

where

ϕ	$=$	$-\log_2 D$ (D = sediment diameter in mm)
M_ϕ	$=$	$(\phi_{84} + \phi_{16})/2$, larger values of M denote finer material
σ_ϕ	$=$	$(\phi_{84} - \phi_{16})/2$
ϕ_{84}	$=$	84th percentile in phi units
ϕ_{16}	$=$	16th percentile in phi units
subscript R	$=$	denotes recharge material
subscript N	$=$	denotes native material

The $R_{\phi crit}$ calculation cannot be applied to all the possible combinations of recharge and native sediment gradings. The Shore Protection Manual (1984) provides a table setting out four basic relationships between recharge and native materials, and concludes on the applicability of the $R_{\phi crit}$ method. This is presented in Table 1 below.

Table 1   Applicability of the $R_{\phi crit}$ calculations

Category Case	Relationship of Phi Means	Relationship of Phi Standard Deviations	Response to Sorting Action
I	$M_{\phi R} > M_{\phi N}$ Recharge material is finer than native material	$\sigma_{\phi R} > \sigma_{\phi N}$ Recharge material is more poorly sorted than native material	Best estimate of required overfill ratio is given by $R_{\phi crit}$
II	$M_{\phi R} < M_{\phi N}$ Recharge material is coarser than native material		Required overfill ratio is probably less than that computed for $R_{\phi crit}$
III	$M_{\phi R} < M_{\phi N}$ Recharge material is coarser than native material	$\sigma_{\phi R} < \sigma_{\phi N}$ Recharge material is better sorted than native material	The distribution cannot be matched but the fill material should be stable; may induce scour of native material fronting toe of fill.
IV	$M_{\phi R} > M_{\phi N}$ Recharge material is finer than native material		The distributions cannot be matched. Fill loss cannot be predicted but will probably be large.

CAUTION: THIS METHOD SHOULD NOT BE USED IN ISOLATION (SEE SECTION 7.3.2).

Box 7.9   *Adjusted overfill factor, R_A and renourished factor R_J for sand beaches (James, 1975)*

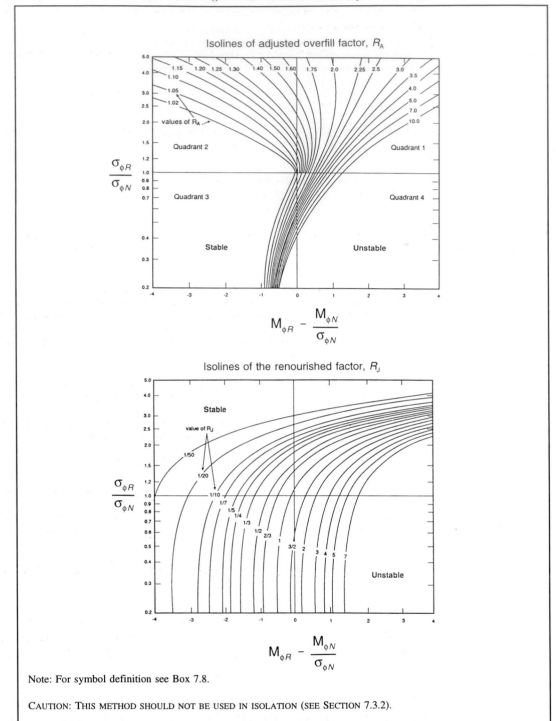

Note: For symbol definition see Box 7.8.

CAUTION: THIS METHOD SHOULD NOT BE USED IN ISOLATION (SEE SECTION 7.3.2).

Box 7.10   *Powell's equilibrium slope method for dissimilar shingle beach recharge*

The recommended procedure is:

1. Identify possible sources of recharge material and undertake surveys in sufficient detail to establish the extent of variations in material size and grading within the resource area.

2. Determine the wave climate at the recharge site and calculate a range of design wave conditions corresponding to a selection of appropriate return periods.

3. Establish an 'equilibrium' slope envelope using the range of design wave conditions and likely recharge sediment characteristics from the following equation:

$$\sin \theta = 0.206 \left(\frac{H_s}{L_m}\right)^{-0.124} \left(\frac{D_{84}}{D_{16}}\right)^{-0.223} \left(\frac{H_s}{D_{50}}\right)^{-0.174}$$

where θ is the angle between the beach slope and the horizontal, H_s is the significant wave height at the toe of the beach, H_s/L_m is the sea steepness at the mean period, T_m, and the sediment gradings (D_{16}, D_{50} and D_{84}) refer to the recharged material.

4. Select an appropriate slope from within the derived envelope. The selection procedure may make use of probabilistic techniques to assess the most cost-effective or lowest risk option, or may simply result in a mean or extreme lower slope being employed. If the latter option is adopted, it should be recognised that if the design 'equilibrium' slope is too shallow it will result in a very costly scheme and one which may, under mild conditions, also suffer a pronounced onshore movement of material, resulting in a beach that is much wider at the shoreline than originally intended.

5. Calculate a design crest level which will usually be set at or above the 2% wave run-up exceedance level. This level could be obtained by the application of suitable formulae such as those set out in Box 5.3.

6. Select an appropriate beach width either to provide the standard of defence required taking account of maintenance commitments or to meet amenity or recreational requirements.

It should be noted that the three terms of the equation in 3 predict that:

- steeper (storm) waves cause a beach to flatten whereas shallow (swell) waves build a steeper beach
- wide gradings give a flatter slope
- higher waves generally give flatter beaches whereas the larger the mean grain size, the steeper the beach.

7.3.4   Detailed computational or physical modelling of a recharge scheme

The methods described in Sections 7.3.1, 7.3.2 and 7.3.3 are more suitable for studies and the design of small schemes. For larger schemes, where an improved understanding of the coastal process is likely to refine the recharge volume, then computational or physical model tests may be undertaken.

In the UK, beach recharge volumes have almost always been refined in recent years by the use of site-specific modelling techniques. Simpler methods, as described in Sections 7.3.2 and 7.3.3, are generally applied in initial feasibility studies.

Most major recharge schemes in the UK have achieved or exceeded their expected performance, and as a result, this method of beach management is well-regarded. In the USA, however, many schemes have been criticised. Often, because of an inadequate post-project monitoring programme, it has been difficult to decide whether a nourished beach has behaved as expected.

Where schemes in the UK have failed to perform adequately, the cause has been the movement of sediment along the coastline, leading to loss of beach volume in the area where the recharge was carried out. Although many schemes have been monitored, it is often difficult to obtain that information. There is no evidence, however, that significant problems have arisen because the desired beach profile shape has not been achieved.

Better analysis and publication of the monitoring results for beach recharge schemes should be an important objective for coast protection authorities in the UK. In particular, comparisons should be made between the expected and actual performance of recharge schemes, with any major discrepancies being noted, and if possible explained.

7.4 SPECIFICATION AND TESTING OF MATERIAL

Specifications for beach recharge schemes are discussed in Section 10.3.5. This section deals specifically with the specifications of the beach recharge material.

7.4.1 Selection of grading

The grading selected needs to take account of the design considerations set out in Section 7.2 above. However, it must also reflect the range of materials that are actually available for the project.

If it is possible for a client to obtain a dredging licence, then the grading specification which is imposed on the contractor must reflect the material actually available at the source and, unless prescreening by the dredger is envisaged with its attendant disadvantages, then the material must be accepted "as-supplied". Suitable site investigation and trial dredging will identify variations in grading across the licensed area and it may be necessary to specify a particular part of a licensed dredging area for a particular project.

More commonly, use will be made of nearby licensed marine sources for commercial abstraction of aggregate, general information about the location of which may be obtained in the UK from the Crown Estate. Information on the material gradings available from these sources will need to be obtained from the licence holder. A common and practical approach to specification, is to obtain size gradings from the various economically accessible sources and reflect those in the grading envelopes that are included in any specification. It is essential however to avoid insisting on adhering to a particular grading curve and to provide sensible limits of variation which should be as broad as possible within the constraints of the scheme design, permitting inclusion of all likely suitable materials. The bi-modal nature of many of the coarser beach and recharge materials should be recognised (see Figure 7.6) and effort concentrated on the larger fraction, with the smaller size material only being specified as a maximum percentage by weight of the total. If available sources simply do not match the design requirements, then the design approach will have to be modified. It is thus essential to obtain these grading curves as soon as possible when attempting to establish the feasibility of a beach recharge project. An example of a typical approach adopted for a 200,000m^3 shingle recharge scheme on the south coast of England is shown in Box 7.11.

An alternative approach to providing fixed grading envelopes at tender stage is to provide a broad indication of D_{50} size required and then, depending on what is offered by the tenderer, to fix the material size more precisely when drawing up the contract.

In the UK, many dredgers have the ability to sort material as it is loaded and so coarser or finer gradings than native seabed sediments can be obtained, but at a cost. Such screening of material is only permitted on some abstraction licences around the UK and has the significant long-term disadvantage that the unwanted fraction dumped back onto the seabed tends to render the remaining material less suitable for use in future beach recharge schemes.

Another source of recharge material for smaller projects, although a decreasing reserve, are land-based gravel pits. In the UK, details of pits and quarries located near to a particular site may be found in the latest annual Directory of Quarries and Pits published by the Quarry Management journal. Small shingle recharge projects can also make use of oversize rejects, available from commercial processing for aggregates of material from marine or land-based gravel sources. If use of such material is envisaged, then the specification must again reflect availability.

Box 7.11 *Grading specification approach adopted for shingle recharge scheme at Elmer, W. Sussex*

This box presents the pre-specification procedures for the calculation of required Beach Recharge Gradings for a shingle recharge scheme at Elmer, East Sussex.

Initially, some 70 samples of existing beach were taken at Elmer. These were taken from various locations along the frontage, across the beach from the top of the shingle bank down to the single/sand toe and at various depths at each location. Figure 1 below shows typical grading curve results from four depths at one location near the top of the beach. This indicates the variation throughout the depth of a relatively stable natural shingle bank. It is considered ideal to attempt to match this grading by supplying new material that will reflect this existing make-up.

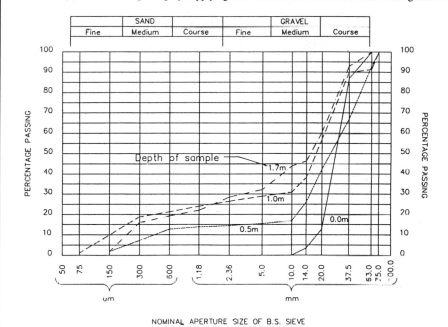

Figure 1 *Typical grading of existing beach material*

Details of gradings of recent dredgings from the local source, the Owers Bank, were also obtained because it was assumed that it was the source any contractor would prefer to use if available. Indications from the dredging companies were that adequate spare capacity was available from this source under existing licences.

Figure 2 below represents an example of a grading curve for these dredged materials. The curve shows beach material as dredged and the possible grading that could be achieved by screening during the dredging process.

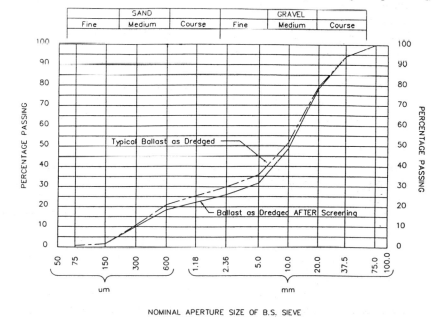

Figure 2 *Typical gradings of materials from Owers Bank source in the English Channel*

Continued

From discussions with the dredging companies, it was apparent that coarser gradings could be achieved by careful selection of the dredging areas; it can be generally assumed that there will be a loss of fines during a marine delivery process, irrespective of the delivery method (split barges or pumping).

The required envelope was determined, having made due allowance for all this data, and the success or otherwise of previous recharge schemes and the various gradings used on them. In particular, it was important to ensure that the material requested was available and that the grading supplied would not be alien to the environment into which it was being placed.

Figure 3 below shows the required grading envelope for the Elmer scheme and also the grading of a typical sample of material that was actually supplied by the contractor.

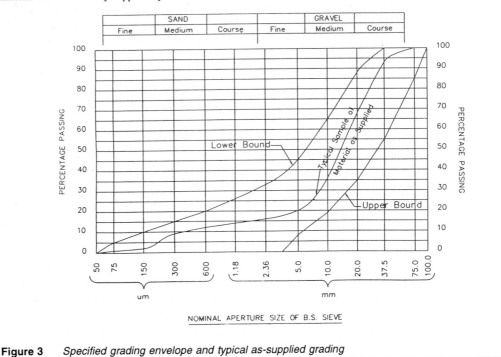

Figure 3   *Specified grading envelope and typical as-supplied grading*

In some cases, such as in North Wales, land-based crushed quarried rock may be the only available source of coarse material for beach recharge. In this case the grading specification will need to reflect the aggregate sizes which are being commercially produced in the area or at least the production equipment available in local quarries. The selected grading will also need to reflect the initial rapid rate of wear such materials experience and appropriate testing for wear carried out. Where the beach is used for amenity purposes, an initially rapid rate of rounding may be advantageous (see Section 7.2.3).

7.4.2   Limits on oversize and undersize material

Having selected an appropriate grading or range of gradings for a particular project, there should be control on the material actually supplied to meet the design requirements. However, whilst this may be possible for land-sourced materials, it must be acknowledged that it is difficult to control the grading of marine-sourced materials. Controls on grading are in general limited to selective sourcing and on-board grading-washing.

Once grading envelopes have been set, the proportion of undersize or oversize material that may be permitted can be defined in various ways. The traditional approach has been to assume that a particular section of beach is represented by a sample (or group of samples combined) and to take the proportion of the sample falling outside the grading curve as a measure of the undersize proportion of that part of the beach. The equivalent volume of material in that part of the beach represented by that proportion is then generally excluded for payment. Section 7.4.3 gives further details on sampling and testing, and Section 7.8 information on measurement.

Limits on undersize material are important in the case of shingle, where the undersize limit set will effectively define the maximum amount of sand in the grading. This limit must be achievable in the light of available sources and methods of production. With sand recharge, it is important to avoid the inclusion of excessive proportions of cohesive material.

Limits on oversize material will clearly be necessary in the case of sand recharge, particularly for amenity beaches. They will also be needed in the case of crushed rock sources provided for amenity beaches. They may also be relevant in avoiding material which may be preferentially lost from the surface of the beach in a gap-graded material.

However, having set reasonable specification limits based on the available material, if under or over-sized material is supplied, then the design requirements or design life of the scheme may be prejudiced. In deciding whether to reject such material it should be recognised that it is both costly and difficult to remove once it has been placed on the beach.

In order to avoid, as far as possible, this contentious area, the undersize and oversize limits should be as wide as possible and determined from envelopes of all relevant available grading curves (see Section 7.4.1) with sensible tolerances applied. Guidance should be sought from suppliers where possible on the likely variation on an individual grading.

7.4.3   Sampling and testing for grading

Whilst it must always be recognised that the contractor has less than total control over the material being supplied, it is still essential to take and analyse samples for payment purposes and also to provide data to assess the performance of the beach. Such samples should be taken at regular intervals throughout the course of the project. The only way to determine whether the "on-the-beach" grading specification, described in Sections 7.4.1 and 7.4.2 above, is being achieved is to sample the placed material at regular intervals across and through the depth of the beach as work progresses. Samples may be taken as material is being placed into the beach or subsequently by means of trial pits dug through the beach. If the latter approach is adopted testing should be as soon as possible after a section of beach is completed. Rates of sampling for shingle are commonly in the range of 1 to 3 samples per 1000 cubic metres delivered and placed on the beach. Consideration should also be given to sampling and testing aboard the dredger.

Historically beach designers have allowed a *de minimis* figure of between 5 and 10% of samples not to comply with the grading requirements. Payment deductions may be made in the case of non-compliance in proportion to the amount of material failing, less the proportion allowed to fail. However, such deductions are frequently the source of much dispute, particularly for marine-sourced materials, and should be avoided wherever possible by appropriate specification and sourcing of material.

7.4.4   Other sampling and testing

In addition to checks for grading, analysis for potential contaminants in recharge material such as heavy metals, organics, oils and the presence of high levels of fine material may be required. Other tests on the intrinsic properties of the material could include such measurements as density, water absorption, rate of wear. These should generally only be carried out once at or before source approval stage. Thereafter tests only need to be repeated if there is some indication that the nature of the material has changed to such an extent that one of these parameters has changed.

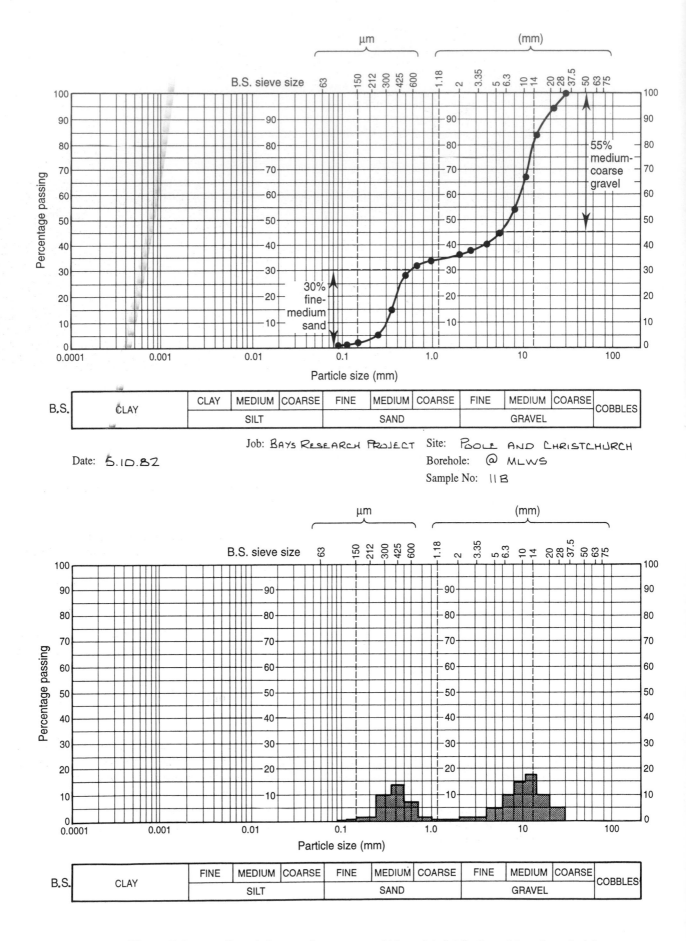

Figure 7.6 *Cumulative grading curve and bi-modal distribution of beach material*

Figure 7.7   *Placing sand recharge on Mablethorpe to Skegness frontage, Lincolnshire (courtesy Posford Duvivier)*

7.4.5   Mechanical grading and washing

Materials produced from land-based rock quarries are generally crushed and graded. Washing and grading processes are also frequently employed in land-based gravel pits.

By contrast, it is likely to be an extremely expensive and difficult process to contemplate washing or grading of marine-dredged aggregates at the beach site. It is to be much preferred to select an appropriate source or adjust the design to suit available sources. Alternatively mixed material sources offshore can be screened by aggregate dredgers, where the licence conditions allow this, to remove oversize material or a proportion of undersize.

Designers contemplating washing in order to reduce the sand content of recharge material for a shingle beach should be aware that there is no known practical benefit from so-doing. There is probably more advantage to place additional material on the beach to compensate for the proportion which is sand, rather than to attempt to remove it. In practice, rapid sorting takes place under wave action through the top one metre or so of a gravel beach and this effectively removes most of the sand.

Mechanical grading is only likely to offer marginal benefits. Experience has shown that there is no advantage to be gained from creating thin layers of beach material increasing in average size towards the beach surface. Such layers are highly susceptible to being stripped off due to differences in permeability between layers and the consequential uneven hydraulic pore pressure gradients which are generated. Expenditure on mechanical grading is unlikely to be cost effective and the noise and inconvenience required to achieve the layered effect may cause considerable nuisance.

7.5   OBTAINING RECHARGE MATERIAL - UK PROCEDURES

A diagrammatic outline of the development of a beach recharge scheme in the UK is shown in Figure 7.8. In this diagram the considerations described in Section 7.1 above will have been taken into account in cells A and B, to enable a preferred source to have been identified. The remainder of this Section relates to cell C.

Cell C covers the planning and licensing procedures required to enable the material identified from the preferred source to be brought to the site. The requirements will vary depending on the type of preferred source and the quantity of material required. Hence, the procedures will also depend on these. A brief review of the requirements for each source type is given below, followed by detailed procedural advice in later sections.

It should be noted that the length of time taken to satisfy the various statutory requirements and licensing arrangements will vary considerably and may range from a few months in the simplest case to two years or considerably more if new licences are sought (see Section 7.5.2).

7.5.1   Material from existing licensed marine sources

If the material is to be brought from an existing licensed marine source and can be obtained within the constraints of the current licensed maximum annual extraction tonnages, then no further licensing of the source is necessary. Virtually all sand and gravel dredged from licensed areas within territorial limits and the Continental Shelf of the UK is owned by the Crown Estate and extraction licences are granted by them. Currently all licences are held by aggregate extraction companies, but a number of applications from clients involved in beach recharge schemes are being processed.

In view of the licences currently granted, clients wishing to use materials from licensed sources merely have to put their works out to tender to suitable contractors and the industry will provide the material to the site. However, discussion with contractors and the Crown Estate is recommended in the preliminary stages to determine material suitability and the royalty chargeable.

If the licensed source, or sources, selected for the scheme are not able to provide sufficient material within their permitted annual extraction tonnages, it will be necessary for the licensee(s) to obtain an uplift on the permitted annual tonnage. Depending on licence conditions, uplifts of up to two times the maximum annual extraction may be granted by the Crown Estate. Permission will normally be granted if the licensee has "rolled over" some of the previous years' quota, but no material may be taken in advance of the maximum allowable. Figure 7.9 illustrates this principle.

Figure 7.9 also shows that, if the licensee wishes to extract more than twice the annual maximum, his application has to be referred by the Crown Estate to the DoE for a new Government View, as if the application was for a new licence. The Government View Procedure is described in more detail in the next section. As the documentation and studies relating to most existing licensed areas are already available, a Government View for an uplift in these areas may possibly be carried out in a relatively short period, without a new environmental assessment being carried out.

7.5.2   Material from a new licensed marine source

When it is intended that a new marine source should be identified and licensed, the following procedure is adhered to in the UK:

- a suitable source to explore is identified and then an application is made to the Crown Estate for an exploration licence
- if a licence is granted, potential licensee carries out exploratory work to determine optimum area for production, often in a two-stage exploration process

- if suitable material is found in sufficient and workable quantity, potential licensee holds pre-application discussions with the Crown Estate, who consult with others. Applicant decides whether to prepare Environmental Statement (ES)
- application submitted to the Crown Estate, if applicant decides to proceed
- the Crown Estate carries out informal consultations and advertises proposals
- the Crown Estate provides DoE/WO with detailed proposals and checks whether an ES is required
- the Crown Estate pass application to DoE/WO for formal Government View, together with list of agencies and others who have commented
- DoE/WO consult other Government Departments, interested parties and applicant, and give Government View
- if Government View is positive, the Crown Estate will grant a licence.

The process set out above, from advertisement of proposals onwards, will take a minimum of 30 weeks, but with most schemes now requiring an ES, the procedure is likely to take considerably longer. A period of two years is generally reckoned to be more realistic and if the environmental or hydrodynamic regimes of the potential extraction area are complex, a period of between 3 to 5 years might be required. The most important aspects of this procedure are set out in Appendix A.

7.5.3   Material arising from navigation dredging

Recent large recharge schemes involving the use of material arising from navigation dredging have been initiated by the navigation authorities and not the promoters of the recharge schemes. Major navigation dredging and port improvement schemes are often implemented much more rapidly than coastal defence works. Hence the initial incentive to use navigation dredgings from large schemes for beach recharge is likely to be a result of the navigation authorities' obligations to find a beneficial use for the dredged material. Only perhaps when small recharge volumes are required is it likely that the coastal authority will prompt the navigation authority to carry out some dredging.

Although the use of navigation dredging for beach recharge schemes may be difficult to organise, this solution to finding recharge material has considerable environmental benefits and should be actively encouraged. The two major benefits are that:

- the navigation dredgings will not be disposed offshore, thereby reducing disruption to local fisheries and the environmental effects of the disposed material, and
- no offshore material extraction is required, with similar benefits.

Beach recharge schemes using navigation dredgings have been successfully completed at Bournemouth in Dorset and Harwich in Essex (see Boxes 7.12 and 7.13) (Appleton, 1991; Turner, 1994; Allen, 1994; Ash, 1994). For both schemes, the following key aspects led to successful arrangements being set up between the navigation and coastal authorities:

- early discussion between the coastal authority, navigation authority, the MAFF Regional Office, English Nature and others as appropriate
- willingness of coastal authority to accept material "as dredged", unless at great variance from desired specification
- great attention paid to setting up workable contractual arrangements for both coastal and navigation authority, in particular keeping the dredging and recharging contracts separate from one another
- willingness of coastal authority to innovate specific financial arrangements to overcome budgeting difficulties arising from short time frame.
- good liaison throughout all stages with local interests, particularly fishermen.

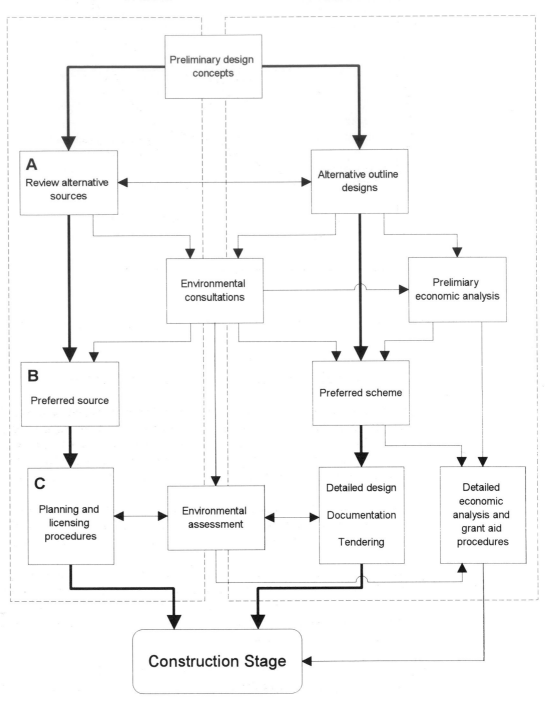

Figure 7.8 *Overall beach recharge implementation flow chart showing scheme and material source development*

The time required to arrange a beach recharge scheme satisfactorily using navigation dredgings will depend to a large extent on the programming of the navigation dredging. The navigation authority will need to obtain the necessary consents, which, in addition to those normally required for a beach recharge scheme (see Section 10.2.1), might include the local Harbour or Port Act, the Coast Protection Act 1949 (with respect to DoT consent under Section 34) and the Harbour Works Acts (Environmental Effects - No 2) Regulations 1989. A major capital dredging project may have a lead-in time of some 12 to 18 months, but the requirement to remove small volumes of suitable material under maintenance works may arise quite rapidly.

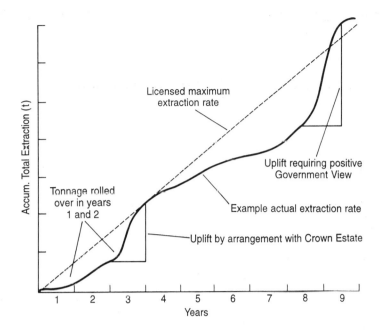

Figure 7.9 *Example aggregate extraction under Crown Estate and Government View procedures*

7.5.4 Material from natural, land-based deposits

The most common land-based sources are operating quarries and sand-pits. These sources are usually exploiting marine deposits, glacial wash-out or bedrock fragmented by blasting and crushing. The latter produces a more angular material than the naturally worn marine and glacial products. The ore of angular material must take account of rate of wear and balance amenity considerations (i.e. rapid rounding) with durability considerations.

Although obtaining the material may be relatively straightforward, there are two aspects which require careful consideration. The transport of the material and the extraction of the material when the source has not been approved under the Town and Country Planning Act 1990.

In many cases the coastal authority will also be responsible for the planning aspects of the proposed scheme. It will, thus, be necessary for the authority to consult with its planning committee to ensure that the supplier of the material to the site will be able to obtain consent for the necessary transport arrangements. Transport of large volumes of suitable beach material may cause environmental problems, such as:

*   suspension of undesirable quantities of dust in dry periods
*   spillage of aggregate, particularly large stones, onto the public highway, causing danger to other vehicles
*   excessive noise in specific areas or at certain times of the day
*   damage to public roads, causing obstruction to other road users and leading to the need for reinstatement of the roads
*   unacceptable delays to other traffic due to the number, size and speed of the trucks carrying the aggregate to the site.

Box 7.12 *Bournemouth Borough Council use of dredgings from Poole Harbour, Dorset*

In 1970 and 1974/75, Bournemouth BC conducted two beach recharge campaigns using respectively 89,000m³ and 1,404,000m³ of medium-sized sand dredged from two different, licensed borrow sites.

By careful appraisal of the results of the monitoring work carried out over the years from 1974 to 1988, it became obvious that provision was needed for a third beach recharge scheme in the early 1990's.

The required material was offered to Bournemouth BC in the spring of 1988 by Poole Harbour Commissioners who were planning a substantial deepening of the Swash Channel, the main navigational approach to Poole Harbour, for the new generation of cross-channel vehicle and passenger ferries.

The estimated quantity of required beach material was approximately 1 million cubic metres and that was the same as the quantity of material to be liberated from the bed of the Swash Channel, allowing for roughly 15% losses.

The work, carried out over two winter periods during 1988/89 (see Figure 1) and 1989/90, enabled beaches with critical beach levels to be recharged in advance of a planned provision, within a local authority budget and rolling programme of works.

Figure 1 *Recharge operations in progress on Bournemouth beach, Dorset, March 1989 (courtesy Bournemouth BC)*

7.5.5 Material in the form of secondary aggregates

The only known use of secondary aggregates (e.g. china clay sand, colliery spoil, power station ash and metalliferous slags) as beach recharge material is a small volume of oversize material from sea-dredged sources. This was purchased at the processing yard of an aggregate company. No records of any other secondary material having been obtained for beach recharge have been identified. However, it is possible that, in the future, shortage of suitable natural materials may alter the economics and secondary aggregates could prove to be more attractive.

The main consideration for secondary aggregates, if such a source is found to be cost-effective, is the transport of the material (see Section 7.6). However, other concerns may also arise. For instance, waste sand from the English China Clay works in the South-West, which has been considered on a number of occasions, contains a percentage of fine material which would be released during placing or subsequent re-working and which may affect the environment.

Box 7.13 *NRA Anglian Region use of dredgings from Harwich Harbour, Essex*

Work has been carried out by the NRA (Anglian Region) to protect eroding saltmarsh on the northern side of Horsey Island, Essex. A volume of 100,000m³ of sand and gravel dredged from the navigation channel at Harwich Harbour was pumped onto the muddy foreshore (see Figure 1). Apart from protecting the saltmarsh from wave action, the mound of dredged material also provided a nesting site for a colony of Little Terns (*Sterna albifons*) one of Britain's rarest sea birds. No adverse environmental effects on the saltmarsh were identified.

Figure 1 *Dredged material placed in front of eroding saltmarsh (courtesy HR Wallingford)*

7.6   TRANSPORTATION TO SITE AND PLACING

There are two basic techniques for the transportation and placing of material for beach recharge, these may be described as "hydraulic" and "dry" methods. Hydraulic methods are generally used for material obtained from marine-based sources and dry methods for material obtained from land based sources, but there can be exceptions to this. Both techniques usually employ bulldozers to place fill to the final beach profile.

7.6.1   Hydraulic methods

Although transportation to site and placing of material may be regarded as separate operations the are, nevertheless, closely linked and interrelated activities. The basic options for the combined operation of transportation and placing are discussed below and a short description of the types of dredging plant likely to be used is included in Box 7.14.

Dredged material is pumped through a pipeline from the borrow area to the site

Where the borrow area is close to the site, material may be dredged and pumped directly onto the beach. This technique usually employs either a cutter suction or suction dredger to lift and pump the material to the beach. If pumping distances are considerable (i.e. several kilometres) additional booster pump stations may be required.

Using this technique, it is likely that in addition to the material sought fine material dredged from the borrow area will be placed on the beach. This will result in increased material losses from the beach and the creation of a plume of fine material away from it. Pumping material into bunds may reduce these losses by lengthening the flow path between the point of discharge and the water's edge. After filling, bunds should be levelled fairly quickly to the desired beach profile so as to minimise subsequent losses.

Box 7.14 *Dredging equipment*

Dredging can be undertaken using a variety of equipment including:

- Trailing Suction Hopper Dredger - a vessel that has the ability to load its own hold (or hopper) by means of a draghead and suction pipe trailed over the side of the vessel. Loading takes place with the ship underway and discharge is by bottom dumping or pump discharge.

- Cutter Suction and Suction Dredgers - these dredgers are generally pontoon mounted and comprise either a cutter or suction head and dredging pumps. They are generally dumb (not self propelled) and dredging only takes place when they are moored using a combination of spuds and winches. They can discharge into barges or, over limited distances, pump material directly to site. Large examples of these dredgers may be of ship-type rather than pontoon construction.

- Mechanical dredgers - these include the following:

  - Bucket Dredger (a pontoon comprising a bucket chain on a movable support ladder; the buckets cut material from the seabed which is then lifted by the ladder for discharge, via a chute, into a barge),

  - Grab Dredger (a grab crane and bucket mounted on a pontoon),

  - Dipper Dredger (a face shovel mounted on a pontoon), and

  - Backhoe Dredger (a backhoe excavator mounted on a pontoon).

Trailing suction hopper dredgers and to a much lesser extent, cutter suction and suction dredgers are used for winning material for beach recharge projects. Mechanical dredgers are not used for beach recharge but may undertake sediment bypassing and navigational dredging.

Trailing suction hopper dredgers can typically dredge in water depths ranging from 10 to 30m and have hopper capacities from around 300 to 12,000 cubic metres although vessels with capacities over 6,500 cubic metres are rare. When dredging sands and gravels loading times are typically between 30 and 60 minutes.

The main advantages and disadvantages of these two types of dredger are listed in Table 1 below.

Table 1 Advantages and disadvantages of trailing suction and cutter suction dredgers

Type of Dredger	Advantages	Disadvantages
Trailing Suction Hopper Dredger	• Can work in adverse weather • Can deliver material directly to site • Moderate mobilisation costs	• Sensitive to seabed debris • Supply of material is not continuous
Cutter Suction and Suction Dredger	• Can operate in shallow water • Relatively high output with continuous operation	• Sensitive to sea conditions • Relatively high mobilisation costs

Dredging operations around the UK will be subject to the terms and conditions of the production licence issued by the Crown Estates' Commissioners. The licence will require the use of the Crown's Electronic Monitoring System for monitoring dredging activities.

Dredged material is transported by hopper between the borrow area and a remote discharge point where it is pumped ashore through a pipeline

This is probably the most frequently used technique for beach recharge (see Figures 7.7 and 7.10). A trailing suction hopper dredger (see for example Figure 7.11), with pump ashore equipment, is loaded at the borrow area and sails to the head of the pipeline for discharge. The connection between the dredger and the pipeline may be made in a number of ways including the use of a riser pontoon and a self-floating flexible pipeline (see Figure 7.12). The choice of connection will depend upon the exposure of the site and availability of plant and equipment. If a long pipeline is employed, it may be necessary to install either a floating booster station or, if space permits, a booster station on the deck of the dredger. Where a long stretch of coastline is to be nourished, two or more pipelines may be installed to avoid excessive pumping distances and to ensure that operations continue during pipeline moves.

Dredged material is transported by hopper between the borrow area and a rehandling site where it is dumped; the material is then re-dredged and pumped ashore through a pipeline

This technique may be used in situations where high continuous output is required or where no self-unloading trailing suction hopper dredgers are available.

Figure 7.10   *Beach recharge being placed alongside Shakespeare Cliff reclamation, Dover, Kent (courtesy Eurotunnel)*

Material is loaded at the borrow area then transported and dumped onto a rehandling site using a trailing suction hopper dredger or barges. Generally the rehandling site will be chosen close to the beach, in a sheltered location to avoid excessive losses. It may simply comprise an area of the seabed or sometimes a pre-dredged pit. The material is then lifted from the rehandling site and pumped ashore through a pipeline using either a cutter suction or a suction dredger.

The double handling of the fill material will result in the wash out of almost all fine particles (silt fraction) before placing on the beach. The environmental consequences of these losses and also losses from the rehandling site during a storm should be carefully considered as they may preclude the use of this method.

Figure 7.11   *8,225 m³ hopper capacity trailing suction dredger HAM 310 (courtesy Ham Dredging)*

Dredged material is transported by hopper between the borrow area and site and directly discharged onto the beach from the bow of the vessel

A method which involves discharging or spraying material from the bow of a trailing suction hopper dredger can be used for beach recharge. This technique, generally known as "rainbowing", requires the use of a shallow draught dredger so that the discharge occurs as close to the foreshore as possible.

Dredged material is transported by split-bottom hopper between the borrow area and the site and dumped on the lower beach at high water

If there is a large tidal range at the site, it may be practicable to dump material on the lower beach at high water directly from the dredger or after transfer to a bottom dump or flat top barge. To complete the placing operation, land-based plant may be used at low water. This method may be limited to smaller projects and emergency works because of restrictions on the draught (and therefore capacity) of hopper barges and dredgers that can be used.

Inside figure labels:
- Ballast infill (beach)
- High water
- Low water
- Sea bed
- Variable length new foreshore

Figure 7.12 *Artist's impression of shingle beach construction at Seaford, E. Sussex in 1987 (courtesy Zanen Dredging)*

7.6.2 Dry methods

Material removed from a quarry or other land-based source can be delivered to site by road, rail or possibly a conveyor system. Road vehicles are likely to provide the cheapest form of transport.

For transportation by road, a traffic management scheme should be established in conjunction with the local highway authority and police, this should cover the following:

- permitted number of deliveries per hour
- steps to avoid convoys
- use of radios to control vehicle movements
- definition of preferred routes
- restriction on parking adjacent to the site
- permitted working hours
- covering of loads with sheeting.

7.7 MEASUREMENT AND COST

7.7.1 Measurement

The overall objective of a method of measurement is to provide a fair and equitable method of payment for work carried out satisfactorily.

Unless the work is to be undertaken on either a lump sum or daywork basis, a method of measurement is required so that the payments due to the contractor can be determined. The method of measurement will, in general, involve either volumetric or weight measurements. For land sourced materials, measurement may take place after loading or after placing on the beach. For marine source material, there are four stages within the dredging and placing cycle at which records for measurement can be taken. These are discussed below:

1. On the sea bed - Volume changes during dredging due to potential losses of fine material during these operations make measurement on the seabed using pre and post dredgings survey inappropriate. This method is, therefore, generally not adopted for beach recharge projects.

2. During dredger loading - With suction dredgers an evaluation of the dredged quantity can be obtained from measurement of velocity and concentration of solids in the intake pipe. It is generally recognised that measurement using flow and concentration meters (errors of the order of ± 10%) is not sufficiently accurate to form the basis of payment. This method is therefore not recommended.

3. In the hopper - Measurement after the dredger has been loaded can involve an assessment of either the volume or weight contained in the hopper. The hopper volume is determined by measuring the level of material in the hopper and calculating the volume using special loading tables supplied by the manufacturer. The hopper weight is determined by measuring the light and loaded draught of the vessel and establishing the corresponding vessel displacements. Both methods give acceptable results with sands and gravels and are therefore appropriate for beach recharge projects.

4. On the beach - Measurement on the beach involves pre- and post-placing surveys from which the volume of material placed can be calculated. The method is straightforward and suitable for use on beach recharge projects.

Methods 3 and 4 are, therefore, considered appropriate methods of measurement for a beach recharge project. The choice between these two methods depends on the nature of the project and the preferred allocation of risk, between the employer and the contractor, regarding losses from the beach during construction.

Losses from the beach during placing (sometimes called "run-off") are directly affected by the contractor's working method. Measurement by method 4 excludes these losses and therefore encourages efficient working methods. Method 3, on the other hand, includes these losses within the measurement.

Losses, at the beach, resulting from wave action are difficult to quantify and in any case may only be short-term with material subsequently returning to the beach. A method of measurement that recognises this may provide a fairer allocation of risk and result in better value for money. For example, it may be appropriate to measure sections of the beach (such as groyne bays) as the work progresses.

Further details on beach recharge losses are given in Box 7.15.

Box 7.15 *Beach recharge losses*

The mechanical removal of material from a borrow area and its transport and distribution over a beach, will usually entail significant losses in volume. Greatest losses will occur when using sea-dredged aggregate and smallest losses will be associated with land-based recharge operations. The project designer needs to assess the likely magnitude of such losses at an early stage of design recognising that in practice actual losses will be highly site-specific. For example, dredging sand and gravel for recharge material may result in the leaching of fines and some smothering of seabed flora and fauna. An Environmental Assessment may therefore need to be carried out to determine the potential impact of dispersal of fines. Similarly, material may be lost during handling operations and its 'fate' may need to be examined by simulating the dispersal of fines by waves and tidal currents. All such studies need to be made at the feasibility stage of design.

Recharge material, immediately after placement on the beach, is also prone to rapid dispersion. It may therefore be necessary to carry out predictions of the weather window for placement operations and to assess the likely dispersion of material both offshore and in a longshore direction.

Losses of recharge material thus need to be assessed during the following phases of a beach management programme:

(1)   Losses during construction

•   during winning operations

•   during the transfer of material from the borrow area to the beach. Losses will be significantly increased if the operations involve double handling (for example when dumping material into a pit or onto a spoil mound) prior to pumping it ashore by pipeline

•   during the currency of the contract or to the point of agreed completion of a beach length (typically a groyne bay). Losses can be high as a result of beach drawdown by storm wave action, since material settling out beyond the low water mark is in most contracts, deemed to be a loss.

There is little in the way of firm guidance on the likely volume losses during construction. Contractors have reported that losses of the order of 20-25% of hopper volume can be expected from the time the material has been loaded on to the ship to the time it is delivered and placed in its final position on the beach. However, since the density of material in the hopper is likely to be of the order of 10-12% less than the original in situ material due to bulking, about half of these losses can be attributed directly to volume change or compaction during placing on the beach. At Hayling Island, Hampshire, eventual beach recharge densities were measured at around 2.1T/m³ for the placed recharge material. Equivalent densities and required tonnages elsewhere in the process can be deduced from the suggested loss and bulking percentages. Generally, losses during dredging operations need not be considered directly by the Client as they are usually borne by the Contractor.

(2)   Losses during initial beach adjustment

Beach losses may continue during the first few years after completion of the recharge scheme, as the material becomes sorted by wave and tidal action to a condition of dynamic equilibrium. If the beach material is similar in character to the native material, the losses may not be great. At Portobello, for example, the total beach volume was measured at 600,000m³ after completion of the first recharge operation in September 1972. By March 1988 beach monitoring had shown that the total beach volume had fallen to 570,000m³, an average loss of less than 2,000m³ per year.

For mixtures of dissimilar sediments (i.e. mixtures of sand and shingle with two distinct gradings) losses may be high and adjustment may take place several years after placement. This is especially so for recharge materials which have been compacted, and in some cases partly cemented during beach reprofiling operations. Beach readjustment may be prolonged under these conditions and may still be taking place 5 or more years after recharge, by which time up to 30-40% of the recharge volume may have been lost.

(3)   Longer term losses

As a result of gradual dispersion (by littoral drift, gradual offshore loss, etc.), recharge material will undergo long-term losses in volume. These losses can be assessed using numerical modelling of beach plan shape or beach profile change and have been addressed elsewhere in this manual. Details of the modelling techniques relevant to the assessment of beach transport, both longshore and cross-shore, can also be found in Chapter 5 of the manual.

7.7.2　Construction costs

The cost of beach recharge varies widely and is determined by many factors, these include:

- size of project - there are obvious economies of scale with a large project
- bathymetry of borrow area and site - this will determine the maximum size of dredger than can be deployed on the project, pumping distances, etc.
- travel distance between borrow area and the site - this can affect the types of dredger that can be used on the project and the method of transport; if unloading operations are restricted by the tide then travel distance will also determine the number of trips that a dredger can complete within each tidal cycle
- recharge material - this will determine the pumping power and also affect maintenance costs with coarser material causing greater wear and tear to the dredger, pipelines, etc.
- estimated losses (see Box 7.15)
- availability of dredgers - the dredgers available to complete a project will affect the cost
- degree of exposure of site to weather conditions - this will determine the type of dredger that can be used on a project, the downtime and the season within which the work can be carried out
- third party requirements - any restrictions placed on dredging operations will have a direct influence on the overall cost of a project. These might include local authority requirements for public access to the beach.

It is obvious that the above factors are interrelated and that the estimation of beach recharge costs is a complex process. For this reason the contractor should be given as much freedom as possible over the choice of plant and working methods so that competitive prices are obtained during the tender procedure. There are, however, likely to be engineering and environmental factors which will require the application of certain restrictions.

The units costs for a number of shingle beach recharge schemes are shown in Table 7.4. It should be noted that scheme costs are strongly influenced by the factors discussed above and therefore the table provides only a broad indication of the likely range of costs.

The costs discussed so far in this section are construction costs and not overall project costs. The latter are discussed in general terms in Section 8.7.1.

7.7.3　Compensation

In building and construction generally, as with other activities which are carried out in the public arena, compensation may be payable where the works adversely affect or disrupt the interests of others.

In England and Wales both the Water Resources Act 1991 and the Coast Protection Act 1949 include specific provisions for the award of compensation to those affected by works carried out under this legislation. Claims within these provisions would normally be made by the individuals or companies concerned against the promoting authority and realistic estimates of legitimate claims, taking account of the intended approach and methods of working, should be included in scheme appraisals where they represent real economic loss. Some payments, such as those for loss of production, whilst completely legitimate and payable from project funds may not represent a cost to the project in strict economic terms if, for example, the lost business is likely to be transferred elsewhere.

In the case of beach management schemes, the areas of concern to affected parties may be very extensive and include fishing interests and other users of the seabed and nearshore area, all of whom will need to be taken into account. Compensation issues away from the immediate interest of the works (for example, at the marine sediment source site and along the travel corridor between the source and the beach) are complex and will require particular consideration.

Table 7.4 Unit costs for a range of shingle beach recharge projects since 1980

Date	Location	Fill volume (10^3m³) as placed on beach	Actual unit cost (£/m³)*
1979/80	Elmer	39	9
1980/81		41	
1993		150	3
1980	Church Norton Spit		
1983	Bexhill	152	
1985	Hayling Island	470	5
1985	Highcliffe	44	
1992		17	
1987	Glync Gap (Bexhill)	50	9
1987	Seaford	1500	4
1988	Shoreham	25	4
1990		71	5
1989	Whitstable	110	
1989	Bognor Regis	25	14
1990	Hastings	250	6
		101	12
1990/91	Heacham/Hunstanton	400	17
1991	Aldeburgh	40	
1992	Felixstowe	70	
1992	Shakespeare Cliff	65	9
1992	Sandgate/Folkestone	133	9

* Note: Costs given are actual historic figures to the nearest pound and have not been adjusted to allow for inflation.

7.8 CONSTRUCTION ASPECTS

During the feasibility and design stages of a beach recharge project careful consideration should be given to the control and planning of site work. The following points should be considered:

1. Existing drainage outfalls - these structures may require extension to avoid the head from being buried by the recharge scheme. Such work may be completed under an advance works contract. Similar comments would apply to any seawater intake structures.

2. Undersea cables, sewage outfalls, etc. - enquiries should be made to establish the location of all pipelines, cables etc. and any special arrangements for working in the vicinity of such installations determined. As an example, a dredger would not be allowed to discharge into a pipeline located within the effluent plume from a sewage outfall because of the risk of pumping contaminated water onto the beach.

3. Pipeline fabrication areas - if long steel pipelines are to be used to discharge material onto the beach, then consideration should be given to the provision of a suitable fabrication site.

4. Onshore working areas - the permitted number and extent of onshore working areas needs to be considered at this stage. This will depend largely on the use of the beach by tourists and other third parties.

5. Restrictions on noise and nuisance - restrictions on noise and the use of floodlighting should be considered carefully, as beach recharge is generally undertaken continuously (i.e. 24 hours per day).

6. Public safety - measures necessary to prevent the public entering areas where beach recharge is taking place should be considered. This may include the use of safety fencing, warning notices and personnel to patrol the boundary of the working area. The contractor will require land access to the beach and it may be necessary to cordon off a corridor along the beach for this purpose.

7. Disposal of unsuitable material - arrangements for the disposal of material found to be unsuitable for beach recharge should be considered at this stage.

8. Winter working - beach recharge works can be badly disrupted during periods of adverse weather. The working season normally runs between mid-spring and late autumn. For an exposed site, a decision to plan the works over the winter months should be carefully considered as it will undoubtedly have a significant cost effect and safety risks may be unacceptably high. The benefits to the overall project (e.g. to tourism) must also be sufficiently increased to justify the extra costs (MAFF, 1993a).

9. Cessation of work over winter - where work is suspended over a winter period it may be considered necessary to establish a suitable location and detail for the temporary termination point of the works. However, where feasible, it is preferable to allow the contractor to decide when and where work is suspended for the winter.

10. Third Parties - full liaison should take place with all interested parties to establish their requirements in relation to the project. Third parties will include local and county councils, beach user groups, all fishing interests, coastguard, Royal National Lifeboat Institution, Trinity House, local navigation authorities, sailing clubs, etc.. The above list is unlikely to be exhaustive and there will undoubtedly be a number of project specific interest groups to consult. This is dealt with further in Section 6.6.2 and Box 4.2.

11. Public Liaison - if beach recharge is taking place in an urban area or on a popular tourist beach it may be appropriate to hold regular public meetings during the period of construction.

7.9   ENVIRONMENTAL CONSIDERATIONS

By attempting to emulate natural processes of sediment replenishment, beach recharge can, if employed appropriately, be one of the most environmentally friendly forms of beach management. Nevertheless, a variety of potentially adverse, as well as beneficial, impacts on environmental characteristics may be associated with recharge schemes.

Section 2.2 sets out some of the primary beach attributes on which environmental interests or uses depend. In selecting material for recharge, it is therefore essential that factors such as sediment size, shape, smoothness and colour are carefully selected to avoid adverse impacts on recreational use or ecological interest. Similarly, in designing the beach, particular attention must be paid to both the onshore (access) and offshore (recreational water use) slope of the beach and to the width of the drying beach. Opportunities for environmental enhancement should also be explored. Finally, chemical testing should be carried out in order to ensure that the materials to be used for recharge are not contaminated, for example as a result of previous waste disposal activities.

In order to identify and evaluate potential impacts of beach recharge, baseline and monitoring surveys, as described in Section 4.3, will be required. The following sections discuss some typical potential impacts on features of the natural, human, chemical and physical environments. Examples of typical impacts during the recharge and subsequent operational phases of beach recharge schemes are summarised in Tables 7.5 and 7.6. These sections also indicate some of the measures which might be taken to mitigate adverse environmental impacts (see Box 7.16).

Finally, at the end of the section, brief consideration is given to the need to properly assess potential impacts of beach recharge on the source or donor sites as a consequence of the extraction of material.

Table 7.5   Typical potential environmental impacts of beach recharge schemes during the construction phase

Potential Impact	Nature of Impact + Positive — Negative
Natural Environment	
Disruption/damage to habitats due to smothering	—
Destruction of habitat	—
Human Environment	
Disruption of informal and formal recreational usage	—
Restrictions on access	—
Public hazard as a result of construction activities	—
Visual impairment of landscape	—
Disruption to commercial activities and land use	—
Local employment generation	+
Disturbance to archaeological sites	—
Interference with inshore navigational requirements	—
Disturbance to infrastructure facilities	—
Environmental Quality	
Introduction of contaminants from pumping water and/or recharge material	—
Turbidity due to fines in run-off water	—
Physical Environment	
Disruption/destruction of geomorphological or geological features as a result of construction activities	—
Scouring brought about by the large volumes of water used in hydraulic pumping	—

Note: Impacts on the source or donor site are discussed in Section 7.9.5

Table 7.6 Typical potential environmental impacts of beach recharge schemes during the operational phase

Potential Impact	Nature of Impact + Positive - Negative ± Positive or Negative
Natural Environment	
Increased sediment supply to site and/or downdrift habitats	±
Creation of new habitats	+
Human Environment	
Boost to local economy	+
Leisure/amenity resource enhancement	+
Reduced risk of flooding/coastal erosion	+
Preservation of archaeological sites through covering	+
Environmental Quality	
Turbidity due to run-off during recharge	-
Physical Environment	
Changes in sediment transport regime	±
Covering of geological exposures	±

7.9.1 Principal impacts of beach recharge on the natural environment

Flora

Potential impacts on flora include those caused by smothering vegetation with recharge material. A potential impact also exists where eelgrass beds or algal communities exist in the nearshore zone adjacent to, or downdrift of, a beach recharge scheme. If the sediment for recharge contains a significant amount of fines, these fine particles may cause an increase in turbidity and sedimentation in the nearshore zone. Such impacts could be mitigated against by ensuring that the imported sand has a small proportion of fines, and by careful control of plant movements (e.g. access by vehicles through dunes).

Invertebrates

The significance of any smothering of existing invertebrates in the sand or shingle depends on a number of factors including the importance of the existing community in terms of species present and their distribution, abundance, rarity, levels of tolerance to environmental disturbance and likely recolonisation rates.

Mitigation measures could involve only recharging a relatively small section of beach at one time to enable recolonisation to occur and/or controlling the rate of deposition (e.g. reducing the depth of sediment put onto a beach at any one time).

Birds

Bird populations are likely to be affected by the construction phase rather than the operational phase of a beach recharge scheme. Potential impacts include disturbance and damage to habitat and a reduction in numbers of invertebrates which provide a source of food for birds.

Mitigation for beach management works in terms of the above impacts could entail minimising disturbance to sensitive habitats (e.g. sand dune or shingle); reinstating any damaged areas; and timing the works to avoid sensitive times of year (e.g. nesting) in ornithologically important areas.

Box 7.16 *Environmental mitigation measures, Mablethorpe to Skegness, Lincolnshire, beach recharge*

Mitigation measures recommended for the proposed beach recharge scheme along the Lincolnshire coast included:

- marked, signed access points to prevent damage to dunes (see Figure 1) caused by vehicles or plant
- timing of recharge works in resort areas to avoid peak holiday season
- notice boards and leaflet distribution to advise local people and holiday-makers of need for and duration of works
- issue of Notices to Mariners to ensure water users are warned of works
- careful routing of construction traffic to avoid safety hazards in town centres and on narrow lanes
- litter control on wider area of drying beach.

Figure 1   Dunes on Mablethorpe to Skegness frontage, Lincolnshire (courtesy Posford Duvivier)

Fish

Activities which will have an impact on the fish communities are essentially those affecting the invertebrates (see above) which attract the fish to the intertidal area. Sediment size distribution is also of importance for the species of fish which burrow into the sediment. Significant impacts might be anticipated if the sediment size distribution differs significantly from that which presently makes up the beach, detrimentally affecting an important population.

Other fauna

Impacts on marine and terrestrial mammals are limited as most of the species are mobile and will not be affected by beach recharge schemes. However, it is important that any sensitive habitats near or adjacent to the site are left undisturbed or, if it is necessary to use such areas, minimum damage is caused and the site is reinstated.

7.9.2 Principal impacts of beach recharge on the human environment

Informal recreation

Adverse winter weather conditions often mean that coastal defence work has to be undertaken over the spring and summer period (April-September in the UK), when calmer sea conditions allow work to be carried out in the intertidal zone and on the line of defence. Where beach recharge is undertaken on popular resort beaches, the potential for conflict during the construction phase is high. Beach recharge operations are likely to have an impact on beach users by restricting the area of beach available for use and/or access along the beach (see Figure 7.13).

Figure 7.13   *Beach disturbance during recharge at Seaford, E. Sussex (courtesy Babtie Dobbie)*

There are various measures which can be employed to reduce the impact of such works, including the provision of alternative points of access; providing safe and easy access over the pipelines used for pumping beach material ashore via stepped platforms; and restricting operations to small stretches of coast wherever this is viable. Where possible, however, recharge operations should be timed to avoid the most heavily used lengths of coast during the peak holiday season.

It is generally accepted that construction work will cause some disturbance, however, an informed public is usually a more tolerant public. Problems and delays are more acceptable if the relevant affected parties are kept informed. An information board should be displayed prominently at all sites. In addition, leaflets might be distributed to local households or updates provided on local radio. The information thus presented should include: a timetable of works; an explanation of how the works will be phased; a schedule of working hours; the area of work at a particular time; and a contact name, address and telephone number. It is also worth noting that construction works have a curiosity value in their own right.

Formal recreation

Beach recharge operations can often have a short-term adverse impact on formal types of recreation, particularly as regards access to the beach and the sea. As far as possible, where existing access is restricted by construction work, alternative access should be provided for trailered boats and other equipment. Lines and pipelines coming ashore from dredgers should be clearly buoyed and lit and information boards should be posted informing recreational water users of the location, nature and duration of works and any potential navigational hazards.

Access

Impacts and mitigation measures regarding access to the beach and sea are generally described above. As far as possible, alternative access should be made available where construction works restrict existing access, whether for people, boats, commercial users, etc. All accesses must be reinstated following completion of any scheme.

Figure 7.14 *Excavation in shingle beach, Hayling Island, Hampshire (courtesy HR Wallingford)*

Safety

As already indicated in Section 7.8, safety impacts must be an important consideration, particularly during any large plant movements on the beach (e.g. the movement of bulldozers for mechanical reworking of the beach material, see also Figure 7.13). Construction works have a high curiosity value, particularly among children. During beach recharge operations the public should be kept away from the immediate area around the point of discharge because of the strong force of water and sediment output. Although it is not always practical to keep the public off the beach, measures must be employed to reduce the potential for incidents. Mitigation measures should include fencing to divide access areas from construction sites and clear signs indicating risk of injury. Good site management, safe routing of site traffic, restriction of access to some areas of beach via fencing or scaffolding, and/or the provision of personnel to patrol the beach may be appropriate.

Care should also be taken during beach recharge operations to avoid unmarked hazards such as large holes (see Figure 7.14) or areas of stockpiled material on the beach and intertidal area,

Figure 7.15   *Cliffing of recharge material, Seaford, E. Sussex (courtesy Babtie Dobbie)*

and other debris associated with removal of old structures (e.g. groynes). Strict controls on waste disposal and careful site management on the beach are essential. In addition, beach cliffing can occur on a nourished beach, leading to a potential hazard which should be removed by mechanical plant (see Figure 7.15).

Landscape

Site offices, construction plant, dredgers anchored offshore and pipelines will all have an impact on the landscape to varying degrees. Recharge works will, however, generally be short-term and can, in fact, add an atmosphere of interest and activity to the area. A compact and tidy site should mitigate against any significant land-based adverse impacts.

Commercial fishing activity

Impacts on the fishing industry as a result of a beach recharge operation are likely to occur from one of three situations: direct disruption to fishing activity effectively resulting in a loss of fishing ground; disruption to launching and landing operations on the beach itself; and indirect impacts on the industry through damage or disruption to the wider marine environment.

Mitigation measures include the establishment of "access corridors" and "waiting areas" to physically separate the recharge operation and local fishing activities; the use of Notice(s) to Fishermen, national fishing press and local press to disseminate information about works; and the use of water-based "liaison skippers" to ensure an immediate response to potential incidents.

Severance of the beach access point (e.g. slipway) and/or the launching site, perhaps by the feeder pipe, may make it impossible for fishermen to launch their vessels from the usual location. Careful positioning of the feeder pipe, the provision of suitable access over the pipe, or the arrangement of an alternative access can mitigate against such impacts.

CIRIA Report 153

During the construction phase of a beach recharge scheme, the works may influence the local fishing activity through damage or temporary disruption to the marine environment. Such impacts may reduce the local presence of certain fish. However, impacts such as an increase in turbidity and smothering of food sources are likely to be short-term during and immediately after construction operations only.

Commercial activity, tourism and adjacent land uses

Many holiday resorts rely on return visits by tourists and holidaymakers. Large-scale disturbance could therefore potentially have an impact upon the tourism trade, and subsequently the local economy and employment if the works make visitors consider going elsewhere next year. Mitigation measures such as those outlined in the above sections should be implemented during the construction phase in order to minimise disruption as far as possible, particularly in areas relying on beach trade (e.g. seaside concessions). On completion, beach recharge will provide a sound and secure sea defence to the hinterland, encouraging continued investment in the area. An enhanced beach may also attract more tourists to the area with subsequent longer term beneficial impacts on commercial activity and trade.

Residential areas and businesses may experience some disruption during the construction period of a beach recharge scheme. In an attempt to make many of the environmental impacts (e.g. disturbance, noise, dust and general inconvenience) more acceptable, it is important that the public are kept informed. Hoteliers and businesses should be given clear information, preferably in writing, well in advance of the ensuing works.

Archaeology and heritage interests

Coastal archaeological sites can be damaged by heavy plant and machinery. Sites should be avoided or protected with a layer of imported material or matting. An on-site archaeologist may also be required to supervise work in sensitive areas.

Navigation

During construction works as part of a beach recharge project, inshore navigation activities may be adversely affected. Perhaps the most commonly encountered problem involves disruption and an increased hazard to recreational craft and fishing vessels. The significance of the potential impact will be dependent on the site characteristics including both recreation and fishing activity in the area and also the particular recharge operation. Mitigation measures (e.g. Notices to Mariners, Notices to Fishermen, posters and other forms of information dissemination) can be adopted to ensure that all vessels or craft are aware of the works and the potential hazards. If necessary, with the consent of affected parties, temporary exclusion zones may be established around the works.

Infrastructure

Impacts of beach recharge operations on infrastructure facilities are unlikely to be significant assuming that the technical mitigation measures available to a developer are implemented. A newly recharged beach may result in an outfall pipe being unable to discharge at the location or depth for which it was designed. Although the problem must be addressed in site specific terms, it is likely that the pipe could be extended and still serve the same purpose. The same solution may be possible for a water intake pipe. Buried facilities may be afforded an increased lifespan by being given an increased level of protection from beach erosion.

7.9.3 Principal Impacts of beach recharge on environmental quality

Water quality

A reduction in the water quality of the nearshore water may be generated by the movement of the sand slurry into the sea water during and immediately after recharge. As indicated earlier, any such impact is likely to be localised and short-term. Consultation with the National Rivers

Authority would be necessary to ensure the impact does not contravene the transparency requirements under the Bathing Water Directive.

During recharge, water would generally be abstracted to allow sand to be pumped ashore. The area from which this water is abstracted must be carefully selected (e.g. away from sewage outfalls) to ensure no adverse environmental impacts are caused in the recharge zone as a result of polluted water being pumped ashore.

Sediment quality

Prior to material placement, the sediment must be tested for a range of contaminants including metals, organics and oils. In cases where there are significant levels of contamination in the proposed material (as assessed by comparison to accepted standards), an alternative material source must be identified.

Debris

No litter debris, waste material, etc. should remain on the beach during or after the construction phase. All accidental waste spillages during construction (e.g. oil) should be cleaned up prior to the re-opening of the beach to the public.

Once a recharged beach becomes operational, it may be that more formal and informal recreational use of the area will occur and lead to a progressive increase in the amount of litter/debris left on the beach. A significant increase in beach litter may require either the provision of more facilities, or additional management activities such as beach cleaning.

7.9.4 Principal impacts of beach recharge on the physical environment

Coastal processes

The adoption of a beach recharge scheme (or use of beach control structures - see Chapter 8) could alter the coastal process regime in a particular area. Increased (or reduced) material movement downdrift of a site may potentially affect the type of natural or human environmental assets described elsewhere in Section 2.2.2 and 2.2.3. On-site monitoring of sediment movement is therefore essential. This may result in a requirement for controlling structures. Comprehensive modelling of sediment movements may also facilitate mitigation against adverse impacts.

A possible impact of pumping is associated with the possibility of scouring. Thus, wash-out of fine materials from the site can alter the geomorphology (e.g. produce a coarser grain size distribution and steeper beach profile) and ecology (e.g. disrupt the biota which is often very sensitive to grain size composition) of the area.

Geology

Important geological exposures may be given increased protection by a beach recharge operation. In a situation where peat exposures, for example, are regularly subject to wave attack as a result of the removal of the sand covering, the placing of a permanent sand layer on the beach will protect the site from further erosion. A potentially adverse impact may however, result if compaction occurs due to the weight of overlying sediment or if important geological exposures used for education purposes become inaccessible due to covering.

Grain size

Whatever the source of recharge material employed, it is unlikely to be of precisely the same grain size distribution as that at the site to be recharged. A significant mismatch in this regard may give rise to various impacts. Thus, for example the introduction of coarser material on to the beach may reduce the amount of wind-blown sand reaching sand dune communities thereby starving these systems of an essential sediment supply. Conversely, if the material employed for recharge is too fine, continued wash-out will occur from the recharge site; a process which can have significant, long-term impacts on the intertidal and sub-tidal biota both at the site of recharge and at downdrift sites.

To minimise effects such as those described above, great care should be given to the selection of recharge material with appropriate grain size characteristics for the site concerned.

Land-based extraction

Potential environmental impacts associated with the extraction of land-based minerals are discussed in CIRIA (1994c) "Environmental Assessment". A number of potential impacts will need to be considered if land based sources are to be utilised including increased traffic volume and movements, visual intrusion, loss of valuable land, damage to archaeological features and hydrological considerations (see Section 7.5.4).

7.9.5   Potential impacts of the extraction of material for beach recharge

Beach recharge schemes can create significant disturbance at the source or donor site from which the recharge material is obtained.

Marine extraction

Under current procedures in England and Wales, potential environmental impacts on the marine environment as a result of sand or gravel extraction from marine sources are considered as part of the Government View procedure (see Section 7.5.2 and Appendix A). The DoE/Welsh Office can require that an Environmental Assessment is prepared if significant environmental impacts are anticipated. Early consideration of potential impacts is essential as data may need to be collected before impacts can be properly evaluated. Some potential environmental impacts are detailed in Table 7.7.

Table 7 7   Potential adverse impacts on the marine environment associated with material extraction

Natural Environment

Disturbance, removal or alteration to the substrate on which a variety of species depend

Disturbance to fish/shellfish resource (e.g. migration routes, feeding or spawning areas)

Human Environment

Conflict with other users (e.g. commercial fishing, military activities, commercial shipping, recreational vessels etc.).

Disturbance to features of archaeological or heritage interest (e.g. wrecks)

Environmental Quality

Disturbance or resuspension of fine materials or contaminants

Physical Environment

Alterations in wave climate, local hydrography, water circulation

Alterations in the pattern of coastal erosion or deposition

8   Beach control structures

8.1   INITIAL CONSIDERATIONS

The coastal processes which give rise to the need for beach management schemes will continue after such schemes have been implemented. If a scheme is implemented with no control structures installed to modify the processes, then any beach loss is likely to continue, and may even accelerate if the volume of mobile sediment has been increased by recharge. Depending on the shoreline situation, this ongoing erosion can be addressed in two ways: the first is to undertake maintenance recharges at regular intervals, while the second is to integrate beach management with construction of beach control structures, which will modify the erosion processes, resulting in a more modest beach recharge programme. This chapter describes control structures and discusses their applications and impacts. Other useful publications which will supplement this text are referred to. Three texts of particular importance are the *Manual on the use of rock in coastal and shoreline engineering* (CIRIA/CUR, 1991), the *Guide to the use of groynes in coastal engineering* (CIRIA, 1990) and *Seawall Design* (Thomas and Hall, 1992). These publications provide guidance on detailed design which is beyond the intended scope of this manual. In addition, readers should refer to the American publications, the *Shore Protection Manual* (CERC, 1984; new edition in preparation) and *Engineering design guidance for detached breakwaters as shoreline stabilization structures* (CERC, 1993), though the applicability to the UK coastal environment should be considered.

For the purposes of this manual, beach control structures are defined as man-made works designed to reduce net long-term loss of beach material due to longshore or offshore transport. Control structures include groynes, detached breakwaters, shore connected breakwaters, seawalls, sills and beach drainage systems. These works may have secondary advantages such as improving navigation channels, providing safe mooring sites for small craft or for creating amenity facilities. Apart from seawalls, the control structures are not intended to provide direct shore protection. If the controlled beach is not expected to provide full protection to the beach head (i.e. the line defining maximum allowable cut back under design storm conditions), then secondary defences such as set-back revetment may be necessary.

Design of control structures should be integrated with beach design and management to maximize the advantages that they can offer and mitigate potential detrimental impacts. Reduction of longshore transport along a length of the shoreline must cause a reduction of input to the sediment budget of adjacent lengths with consequent erosion (see Figure 8.1 where a terminal groyne had been in place for many years prior to the construction of the present groyne and other control structures). Therefore it is fundamental that the acceptable level of impact on adjacent shorelines is determined. Design of structures within the context of an overall shoreline management strategy is normally appropriate, though often more difficult to achieve. It is only appropriate to disregard other parts of the shoreline in situations where the shoreline to be protected forms an independent littoral process unit (e.g. pocket beaches on a hard cliff coastline as described in Section 2.6), or where a considered decision has been made to allow retreat in an area of low value.

Other detrimental impacts should also be considered. Many forms of structures are visually intrusive. Structures can affect the shoreline ecology by changing localised wave and current regimes and by altering the human use of the area; examples include damage to inshore shell fisheries, loss of rare shingle beach plant communities, loss of unique algal communities, and development of cohesive sediment communities on formerly rocky or sandy shorelines. Beach control structures may also alter the use of the shoreline for commercial and leisure use; submerged structures may create navigation hazards, protected areas will allow deposition of mud and silt, large expanses of sand can be subject to wind transport, structures could represent a public hazard, and localised currents and wave focusing may be hazardous to swimmers.

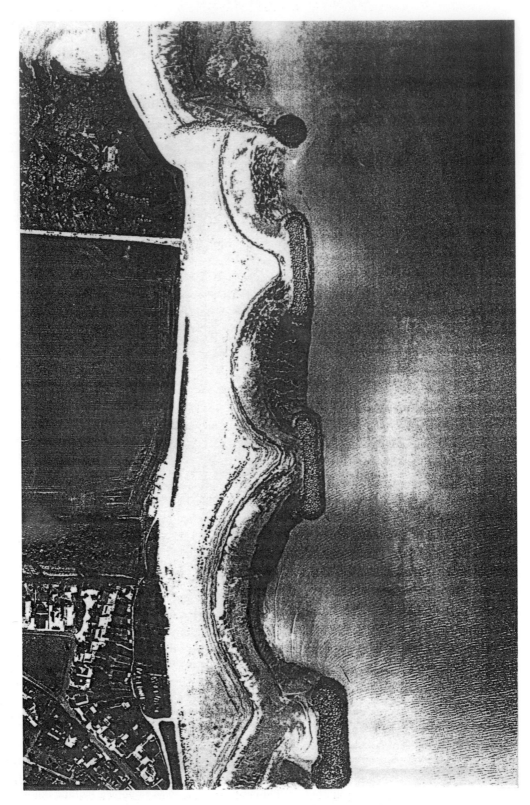

Figure 8.1   *Detached breakwaters and terminal groyne on a shingle beach at Elmer,
W. Sussex (courtesy Arun DC)*

Finally, the problems of attempting to control different types of beach material should be
understood. Shingle transport is dominated by wave action and is primarily limited to a
relatively narrow zone of the beach and to a limited elevation above the sea bed, and therefore
various control structures can be used successfully. Sand transport, in contrast, can be

CIRIA Report 153

dominated by either waves or tidal currents, can take place at any point from the backshore dunes (wind transport) to depths of over 10m and at any level in the water column due to suspension. Wide flat sand beaches in meso (2-4m) or macro (>4m) tidal situations can only be controlled effectively by using massive structures that would influence the whole foreshore to at least low water, although more modest structures can be used to influence sand movement across the high tide zone.

Prior to commencing the design process for beach control works, the scheme appraisal (see Chapter 6) must determine the aims and requirements for the works. Consideration should be given to a number of points, including:

- Does the backshore need equal levels of protection along the full frontage or are there sensitive points needing increased protection?

- What are the risks of not managing the beach, and what are the potential benefits?

- Is the main problem potential flooding or erosion?

- Is it important to maintain the longshore drift rate to downdrift frontages or is storm protection more critical?

- Is there a secondary line of defence?

- Is a change to the shape of the coastline acceptable, with areas of reclamation and areas of loss, or must the present shoreline be maintained?

- What level of risk is acceptable to the local community?

- What benefits exist to justify any investment?

- Can beach control structures also be used for navigational purposes?

- What changes to the natural and human environment are acceptable?

- Can the aims be achieved through regular beach management operations without control structures?

- What methods of construction and materials are available and practical?

- How will post-construction maintenance and/or modification be undertaken?

Once these points have been considered, then the designer can begin the process of selecting the optimum approach to developing a beach control scheme using one, or several, of the types of structure listed in Table 8.1, taking account of the situation in which the structures are required and their advantages/disadvantages. The reader should also refer to Section 8.8, Tables 8.6 and 8.7 and Box 8.12 for guidance on the environmental impacts and approaches to mitigation which should be taken into account in the structure selection process.

The following sections consider each type of control structure, giving general guidance on their use and, where possible, specific design procedures. When using the design guidance in this manual, the coastal engineer should recognise that every scheme will have site specific characteristics and will probably require numerical and/or physical modelling for full evaluation and optimisation. The chapter concludes with sections on cost optimisation, environmental considerations and a brief discussion of construction methods.

Table 8.1 Guidelines for application of control works

Structure type[1]	Situation	Advantages[2]	Disadvantages[2]
Groynes	- Shingle - any tidal range - Sand - micro-tidal only - High gross drift, but low net - Low vertical sided structures suitable for low wave energy - Large mound type structures suitable for high wave energy	- Allows for variable levels of protection along frontage	- Can induce local currents which increase erosion, particularly on sand beaches - Vertical structures potentially unstable with large cross-structure beach profile differences - Requires recharge to avoid downdrift problems
Detached breakwaters	- Shingle - any tidal range - Sand - micro-tidal only - Dominant drift direction - Constant wave climate, not storm dominated - Creation of amenity pocket beaches or salients	- Allows for variable levels of protection along frontage	- Large visual impact particularly with macro-tides - May cause leeward deposition of fine sediment and flotsam - Strong inshore tidal currents may be intensified - May cause hazardous rip currents - Difficult to construct due to cross-shore location - Difficult to balance impact under storms and long-term conditions - Difficult to balance impact on both shingle and sand transport
Shore connected breakwaters	- Shingle - any tidal range - Sand - limited effect with macro-tides - Dominant drift direction - Any wave climate - Strong shoreline tidal currents ("fishtails" only) - Creation of amenity pocket beaches	- Allows for variable levels of protection along frontage - Can be used to create amenity features - Longshore and cross-shore control	- May cause leeward deposition of fines and flotsam - Little design guidance at present
Seawall/ Revetments	- Sand or shingle - Any tidal range, any wave climate - Low gross drift rate - Provides secondary line of defence where beach can not be designed to absorb all wave energy during extreme events	- Well developed design methods - Provides equal protection along frontage - Can be designed to support a sea front development	- No drift control - May become unstable if erosion continues
Sills	- Shingle or sand - Low wave energy - Low and variable drift - Submerged with micro-tides, regularly exposed with macro-tides	- Creates perched beach - Reduces shoreline wave climate	- Storms may remove beach irreversibly - Level of protection reduces during storm surge events
Beach drainage systems	- Sand beaches, normally up to the high water line - Any tidal range - Any wave climate or drift rate	- Responds to beach developments	- Limited experience of use - Long-term maintenance may be expensive - Risk of failure during short duration, extreme storms

Notes:

(1) The guidelines given above assume that the structures are either built in conjunction with a beach recharge or that downdrift frontages are not dependent on continued longshore transport

(2) In addition to the above considerations a range of other environmental issues, described in Section 8.8, need to be taken into account

8.2 GROYNES

8.2.1 Definition and general guidelines

Groynes are long, narrow structures built approximately normal to the shoreline. They extend across part, or all, of the intertidal zone, and may have small lateral extensions to the seaward end or head (Figure 8.2). Groynes are normally built in groups, known as groyne systems or fields, which are designed to allow continued longshore transport. They can also be single structures designed as total barriers to transport (i.e. terminal groynes), though structures of this type tend to be classified as shore connected breakwaters. Groynes can be built with permeable sloped faces of rock, asphalt or concrete armour units, or with impermeable vertical faces of masonry, concrete, sheet piles or timber. Their purpose is to interrupt longshore transport, causing a build-up of beach material on their updrift side, until transport can resume over or around the structure. If downdrift erosion is a potential problem, then a recharge scheme should always accompany groyne construction.

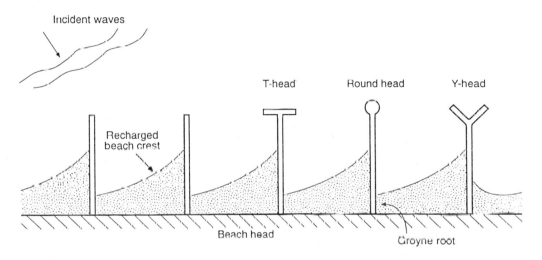

Figure 8.2   *Definition of groyne terminology*

Groynes are very common on UK beaches (CIRIA, 1990), but are subject to some controversy as to their effectiveness (Fleming, 1990). As a general guideline, groyne systems are appropriate to frontages where the existing shoreline must be maintained and where there is a low net, but high gross drift.

Schemes on shingle beaches have been more successful than those on sand beaches, and vertical sided groynes have been shown to be efficient only on shorelines which are exposed to moderate or low-energy wave climates (say, $H_s < 2m$). Examples can be quoted of existing groyne systems which successfully contradict these guidelines, but often these are on sites which would have relatively stable beaches with no control structures at all and the groynes only serve to reduce short-term variations in beach response. Large terminal groynes are probably only practical on shingle beaches, and should only be installed where longshore drift can be cut off with no detrimental effect to the downdrift shoreline, (e.g. adjacent to dredged navigation channels).

Groynes on sand beaches are not intended to trap all longshore drift, but to control a sufficient part of the beach profile to protect against severe erosion of the upper beach. This is achieved by reducing the currents that run along the beach.

8.2.2   Effect on beach development

Groynes provide a direct physical barrier to longshore transport and are intended to effectively alter the orientation of the beach to be more closely aligned to the dominant wave conditions, hence reducing longshore drift. Beach material transported towards a groyne will be deposited against the updrift side. This updrift deposition will continue until the wave and tidal processes are sufficient to re-establish transport over or around the groyne. The beach will then develop a sawtooth plan shape, which will vary with wave conditions.

The effectiveness of a groyne as a barrier will depend on the type of beach material, the wave climate, the tidal regime, the dimensions and the hydraulic characteristics of the groyne, and, in the longer term, the stability of the substrata and the durability of the groyne materials. As the wave climate is subject to large variations due to changing wind conditions, then the design of groynes will always be a compromise between providing for beach stability under long-term and extreme sea states. A well designed groyne system will give rise to a minimum of beach volume change from a fully eroded condition following severe storms to a fully developed condition under swell conditions.

At present there are no simple and reliable methods for the design of groynes. Field experience, numerical models and physical models must be combined with environmental studies to produce outline designs which are likely to be successful. Numerical models are available to predict the effect of wave activity on beach planshape in the presence of groynes, including the effect of varying tidal ranges. However, they are limited by significant simplifications relating to transport processes over and around groynes (e.g. suspension of sediment allowing transport over elevated groynes, cross-shore wave induced currents, tidal currents, redistribution of the transport distribution curve between the beach crest and the toe of the active beach). Similarly cross-shore numerical models and physical modelling techniques have their limitations (Brampton and Goldberg, 1991; Powell, 1990; Coates 1994). The complex interactions between waves, currents and structures are not sufficiently well understood to allow complete confidence to be placed on the model algorithms and scaling relationships which have been developed. However, in practice, appropriate calibrations can limit the impact of these uncertainties on the design processes.

An example of beach development due to groyne construction is given in Figures 8.3a and 8.3b. Comparison of the beach in 1987 and 1994 shows that the groynes have been very successful in gathering and retaining beach material.

8.2.3   Design considerations

Material type

Groynes can be constructed from a number of materials, the choice of which depends on the requirements and limitations applicable. Table 8.2 summarises the advantages, disadvantages and potential applications of different construction materials. Account should also be taken in selecting groyne materials of their likely environmental impact and whether this can be mitigated. Guidance on the use of materials can be found in BS 6349: 1984, Code of Practice for Maritime Structures, Part 1 General Criteria (British Standards, 1984). Specific information on the use of timber is covered by BS 5268: 1977, The Structural use of Timber, while the use of rock is covered in the previously referenced CIRIA/CUR (1991) *Rock Manual*. Reference should also be made to recent research results from HR Wallingford regarding stability of cross-shore structures under breaking waves (Jones and Allsop, 1994, see Box 8.1) which suggests that standard rock size design methods for structures on shallow slopes (e.g. Hudson formulae, Van de Meer's methods) will under predict rock requirements for steep beaches by a substantial margin.

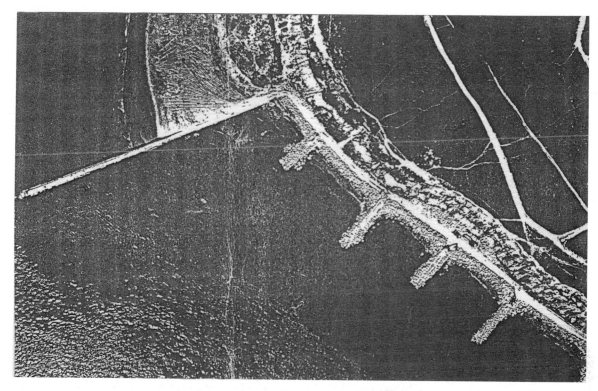

Figure 8.3a   *View in 1987 of groynes constructed at Hengistbury Head, Dorset (courtesy Bournemouth BC)*

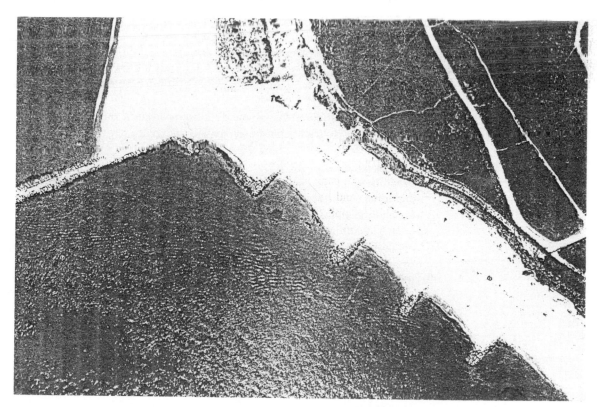

Figure 8.3b   *View of Hengistbury Head, Dorset, in 1994 showing natural beach accumulation (courtesy Bournemouth BC)*

Groyne design - shingle beaches

Recent research using physical models at scales of 1:17 and 1:50 (Coates and Lowe, 1993 and Coates, 1994) on shingle beach response to various groyne types and configurations has led to a number of guidelines to supplement those presented in earlier publications.

1. Influence of construction material type - vertical groynes were found to perform equally to equivalent rock mound groynes under swell and moderate storm conditions (up to $H_s = 2m$). However, under more severe storm conditions, the interactions of waves and wave generated currents with the impermeable, vertical groyne faces caused local upper beach erosion. This erosion could cause the groynes to be outflanked where there is no secondary defence.

   No evidence was found to suggest that rock groynes can be spaced more widely than equivalent vertical groynes. However, rock groynes can be built to a higher profile which would allow wider spacing relative to low timber groynes.

2. Crest level of groynes - assuming equal length from beach head to seaward toe, the most effective groynes under all conditions were found to be high rock structures, sometimes referred to as rock *bastions*. Effectiveness in this case is related to the change in beach volume between a full eroded state under severe storm conditions and fully accreted state under moderate swell waves. Minimising changes in volume will ensure that recharge material placed within a groyne bay is conserved while any new material is able to continue down drift.

   The crest of groynes (see Figure 8.4) should be set about 1m above the design storm beach profile across the breaker zone so that they act as a significant barrier to transport under storm conditions. Significant longshore transport of shingle can occur over groyne crests. Reliable field data is not yet available to quantify this transport, but model research suggests that transport can occur over groynes which stand up to 1m above the beach, and that groynes with a crest of only 0.25m above the beach do not form significant barriers to drift when the offshore wave height (H_s) is around 2m.

   The design beach profile which is used for crest level calculations needs to be set to reflect the influence of varying water levels and alongshore plan shape movements as the beach responds to different wave directions. A terminal groyne will clearly require a crest level based on the most seaward beach profile position required on its updrift side.

   The berm elevation of the groyne does not need to be any higher than the berm elevation of the beach, as no significant transport will take place above this level.

3. Groyne length - groyne length is not a simple concept. The landward end is taken as the beach head, or the beach position beyond which erosion is not acceptable under the design conditions. The seaward end is less easily defined. Many low-level groynes extend well beyond the length over which they influence transport and therefore their physical length is greater than their effective length. Available research (Coates, 1994) suggests that groynes on shingle beaches are only effective to the point at which their crest intersects with a depth of approximately 0.75 H_b (breaking wave height) below the water level. This relationship is, unfortunately, only useful in non-tidal situations. For tidal situations, the effective length varies with water level. In view of the difficulty in defining an effective length, the concept of a simple ratio of spacing to total length is of little value. A more easily defined and consistent parameter is the berm length: the distance from the beach head to the point where the groyne profile drops below the beach crest level during the design storm (see Figure 8.4). This definition is also an over-simplification, as it does not account for the slope of the groyne from the berm to its seaward toe, although this slope is normally designed to be the approximate mean of the envelope of beach profile slopes for the location (see Figure 8.4).

Table 8.2 Groyne construction materials

Type/ Material	Advantages	Disadvantages	Suggested applications
Vertical timber	- Possible post-construction adjustment	- Cost and availability of hardwoods - Environmental restrictions on hardwood sources - Susceptible to physical abrasion and biological attack - Vertical construction does not absorb wave or current energy - Current induced beach scour pits along face and around head - Unstable if large cross-groyne differentials in beach elevation develop or if large crest heights are required - Difficult to construct below MLW - Require maintenance	- Low to moderate energy shingle beaches with low net drift
Rock mound	- Hydraulic efficiency due to energy absorption - Re-usable material - Simple construction methods - Underwater construction possible - Post-construction adjustment easy - Stable, durable - No size limit	- Availability and transport of suitable rock - Structures may be hazardous to swimmers and other beach users - Accumulation of debris within structure - Bed layer required if substrate is mobile	- Low to high energy sand or shingle beaches with low net drift in areas where suitable rock is available - Good for terminal structures
Concrete units	- Hydraulic efficiency due to energy absorption - Stable, durable - Availability of materials	- Rigorous construction methods required - May be hazardous to swimmers and scramblers - Accumulation of debris within structure - Bed layer required if substrate is mobile	- Low to high energy sand or shingle beaches with low net drift, in place of rock - Good for terminal structures
Vertical concrete/ masonry	- Availability of materials	- No post-construction adjustment - Expensive and complex construction particularly below MLW - Near vertical construction does not absorb wave or current energy - Maintenance required	- Low to moderate energy beaches with low net drift - Good for terminal structures
Steel sheet piles	- Rapid construction - Can be placed below low water	- Vertical construction does not absorb energy - No post-construction adjustment - Suffer from abrasion; resulting jagged edges are a safety hazard - Suffer from corrosion	- Can be used to form foundation and sides of concrete structures, particularly below MLW
Gabions	- Low cost, rapid construction - Hydraulically efficient	- Not durable - Particularly susceptible to vandalism - Only suitable for small structures	- Low energy sand or shingle beaches with low net drift
Rock-filled crib work	- Low cost due to smaller rock - Hydraulically efficient	- Movement of rocks can damage crib-work	- Low to moderate energy sand or shingle beaches, with low net drift .
Grouted stone or open stone asphalt	- Low cost	- Prone to settlement problems - Susceptible to abrasion	- Low to moderate energy sand or shingle beaches, with low net drift, on stable substrate
Rock apron around timber	- Increase energy absorption of existing vertical structures	- Interfaces subject to abrasion due to different interactions with waves	- Refurbishment of old vertical groynes on low to high energy shingle or sand beaches with low net drift

Box 8.1 *Rock-armoured beach control structures*

The cross-section of rock-armoured beach control structures is generally based on methods developed for permeable rubble breakwaters (described in CIRIA/CUR *Rock Manual*, 1991). Calculations of armour size are based on the use of the Hudson or the Van der Meer formulae given as equations 5.43-5.46 therein. The Van der Meer method is however only valid for normal wave attack, so the size of armour on the outer ends of groynes or breakwaters must be calculated using the Hudson equation with values of the K_D coefficient derived for roundheads in the *Shore Protection Manual* (CERC, 1984).

Some rubble groynes and revetments on steep shingle beaches (slopes around 1:6 - 1:10) have experienced higher levels of damage than predicted by these methods (Allsop *et al*, 1995). Recent laboratory tests (Jones and Allsop, 1994) were conducted in a wave basin with random waves to describe the armour response on four rock armoured structures on a steep shingle beach of 1:7:

1 a bastion or roundhead groyne with a constant crest level armour slopes at 1:2
2 an L-shaped groyne, formed from the bastion groyne, by building sideways form the seaward end
3 a groyne with an inclined crest (higher at landward end, lower at seaward end) and armour slopes at 1:2
4 a simple 1:2 rubble sea wall slope.

Armour displacements were measured by profiling over the structure. For most test conditions the damage significantly exceeded that predicted by Van der Meer's equations for normal attack on simple trunk sections. The increase in damage (see Figure 1) was so severe that the armour might need to be two times heavier than on a conventional structure. Modifications to the Van der Meer formulae have been suggested for structures on steep shingle beaches. The modified formula for plunging waves shown in Figure 1 may be written:

$$H_s/\Delta D_{n50} = 4.8 P^{0.18} (S_d/\sqrt{N})^{0.2} \xi_m^{-0.5} \tag{1a}$$

and the modified formula for surging waves as:

$$H_s/\Delta D_{n50} = 0.77 P^{0.18} (S_d/\sqrt{N})^{0.2} \sqrt{\cot\alpha_s} \; \xi_m^P \tag{1b}$$

where

P = Van der Meer's permeability factor, typically varying between 0.1 and 0.6
N = number of waves in a storm event
α_s = slope angle of face of structure
S_d = dimensionless damage parameter
ξ_m = Surf similarity parameter = $\tan\alpha_s/\sqrt{(2\pi H_s/g \; T_m^2)}$

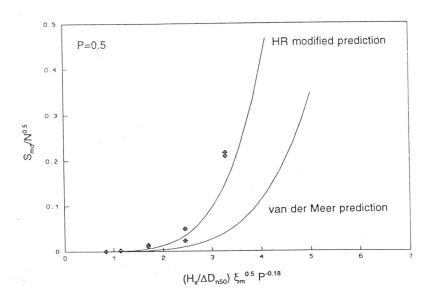

Figure 1 *Damage to structures on steep beach slopes under normal wave attack*

The relative increase of damage indicated by these equations should be anticipated for all rock armoured structures built on beaches of slope between 1:6 to 1:10. Some further allowance must also be made for the reduced stability of armour on the curved parts of the structures. The most exposed zones may require further increases in armour size, with relative increases similar to those predicted for breakwater roundheads.

4. Groyne spacing - groyne spacing must be designed to ensure that the beach head is not exposed to wave action at any point within a groyne bay under the design conditions. This design criterion may vary according to the local situation and the presence of an effective secondary defence. As the beach orientation will tend towards the wave direction at breaking, then the designer must first establish from the range of possible directions the breaking direction of waves which will cause the most severe beach crest cut back. From this information the worst case beach orientation can be derived, after which the designer must optimise the balance between groyne berm length and spacing. This optimisation must consider the marginal cost of increasing groyne length, the cost of recharge material and the desirability of having fewer large structures or more small ones (Figure 8.4).

5. Groyne head extensions - groyne head extensions formed of rock (see Figure 8.5) can be beneficial in terms of improving groyne efficiency. If groynes are built entirely on shingle then current induced scour around the groyne head tends to be of little importance. Consequently small 'T' or 'Y' extensions will have little effect other than to encourage a very limited amount of accretion due to redistribution of wave energy by diffraction. The material used for the extension would be better used to raise and extend the main groyne. However, if the groyne extends across a shingle upper beach down to a sand lower beach then scour can lead to structure instability, and head extensions can be used to dissipate local currents.

    Large head extensions at an elevation above MHWS can be advantageous as they modify the incident waves extending the longshore influence of the groyne. This allows the groyne spacing to be increased and the total number of structures to be decreased. Typically, such extensions have a length of about half the design storm wavelength. Structures of this type can also influence nearshore tidal currents. They are more closely related to connected breakwaters than to traditional groynes (see Section 8.4).

Groyne design - sand beaches

Groynes are generally only effective as beach control structures on sand beaches in micro-tidal, low wave energy environments where the spacial distribution of wave and tidal current transport across the foreshore is limited. Sand beach groynes are not normally intended to trap all the longshore drift but should be long enough to control a sufficient part of the beach profile to protect the upper beach from severe erosion. The material accreting along the upper beach often contains a high proportion of coarse sand, shells and shingle (gravel), and may have a steeper profile than the main beach. The following guidelines may be used for the outline design of groyne fields.

1. Influence of construction material type - on low wave energy beaches vertical groynes will perform equally to equivalent rock groynes. If groynes are to be used on sand beaches exposed to larger waves, then rock is generally considered to be more effective due to the inherent reduction in reflectivity and greater stability of large structures. Localised wave generated currents around vertical groynes can cause severe scour which can be controlled by placing a rock apron in critical areas.

2. Crest level - as sand is transported in suspension throughout the water column, then the higher the groyne crest (up to the beach berm level) across the surf zone, the more impact it will have on longshore transport. As a minimum the designer should determine/predict the envelope of potential sand beach profiles and then set a groyne crest level which follows the berm level, and, seaward of the berm, follows about 1m above the slope of the upper limit of the envelope. The design should allow for the predicted reorientation of the beach caused by the groynes.

3. Length - as with crest level, a groyne which extends across the full surf zone at a high level will have a greater impact than a short, low structure. However, as large groynes may be neither practical nor desirable, then the following design approach is suggested.

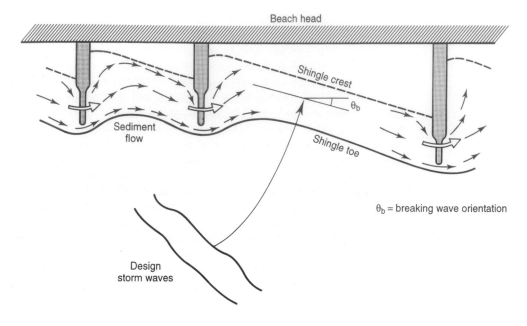

Typical currents in groyne system

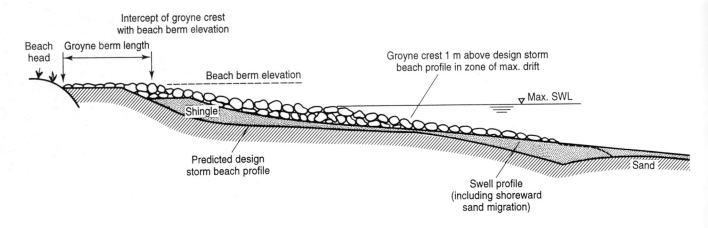

Typical rock groyne profile

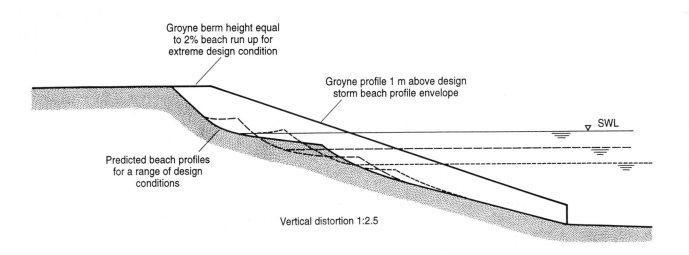

Typical timber groyne profile

Figure 8.4   *Groyne design sketches for shingle beaches*

Choose a wave height and period representing a moderate summer (swell) wave climate when the beach is building up. Calculate the position of breaker zone at mean high water tide level and select a length of groyne which extends seaward of this zone. If there is a solid wall or revetment at the beach head, groynes should extend to meet it. Any gap will result in severe scour in extreme storms. On beaches without seawalls etc., groynes should be extended well landward of the anticipated beach crest position (under storm conditions).

4. Spacing - the spacing of groynes on sand beaches can generally be greater than on shingle beaches since sand beaches do not re-orientate themselves as rapidly. Numerical modelling will normally be required to determine an appropriate range of beach orientations from which to establish the length and spacing of any groyne bay.

Construction and maintenance

In addition to the hydraulic considerations, groyne design must consider construction and maintenance requirements. A number of questions must be addressed, most of which are applicable to any form of beach structure. These are set out, as a checklist, in Table 8.3.

Figure 8.5   *Rock groyne extension, Pagham Beach, W. Sussex (courtesy HR Wallingford)*

Table 8.3 Beach control structures construction and maintenance checklist

- Suitability of sub-strata to support structure
- Tidal windows for maintenance (especially lower beach)
- Access to seafront for plant and materials (by land or sea)
- Access along beach during construction
- Access along beach for maintenance and emergency works following construction
- Flexibility for modifying structures in response to post-construction monitoring (Section 10.6)
- Availability and suitability of materials
- Availability of suitable plant and workforce
- Ability to dismantle and rebuild structure in response to emergency/damage

8.2.4 Recharge of groyne field

Groyne construction and beach recharge operations need to be phased appropriately to ensure a minimum of disruption to the environment and to the local community. To reduce losses of recharge material, it is normal to commence operations from the downdrift end of the scheme. Both groynes of each groyne bay must be completed before commencing the recharge. The precise timing of each operation will depend on the anticipated construction rate for the groynes relative to the rate of supply of beach material. As groyne construction is a land-based operation, and large recharges are generally sea-based, then there should be scope for simultaneous operations.

The required volume of recharge material within each bay can be estimated, in conjunction with groyne design, using numerical models of beach plan shape and beach profiles (see Sections 5.3 and 6.4) based on the design wave conditions. For shingle beaches the numerical models can be combined with a wave basin physical model to optimise the groyne layout and the beach volume. Designers should be aware of the limitations of the models and should make use of experienced coastal engineers to advise in this complex area of beach management.

8.3 DETACHED BREAKWATERS

8.3.1 Definition and general guidelines

Detached breakwaters are shore parallel structures that provide coastal protection by reflecting, dissipating, diffracting and refracting incident waves, and therefore reducing wave energy and littoral transport in their lee. Material deposited in the zone of reduced wave energy forms a bulge in the shoreline, known as a *salient*; if downdrift impacts are not important, then the salient may be allowed to develop until it is attached to the structure at high water forming a *tombolo* (Figure 8.6). The structures may be single, designed to protect a short length of coastline, or multiple unit systems designed to protect an extended frontage. They are generally built of rock or concrete armour units. If a recharge scheme is not undertaken in association with breakwater construction, then erosion of surrounding beaches will normally occur.

Detached breakwaters on an open beach are intended to reduce, rather than halt, the local potential rate of longshore drift. To achieve this, waves must be able to act on the full length of the leeward beach over that part of the tidal cycle during which the bulk of the transport occurs. If this is not achieved, a tombolo will form; the beach drift will be halted in the lee and may eventually resume along the seaward face. In this case the structure becomes shore connected and its effect on the shoreline is modified (see Section 8.4). This latter situation may be desirable if the intention is to create a pocket beach or to reclaim part of the foreshore.

Detached breakwaters as beach control structures have only been introduced in to the UK since about 1980, but have been used extensively for a number of years in Japan, the USA, Singapore and around the Mediterranean. In general, their use outside the UK has been most common on sand beaches in micro to meso-tidal situations with fetch-limited wave conditions, and in estuaries to promote saltmarsh development. In some situations structures have been designed primarily to create amenity beaches in situations where downdrift responses are not important. A recent publication by the US Army Corps of Engineers (CERC, 1993) presents much of the available research and field experience. In the UK, detached breakwaters have been used as single structures at Leasowe Bay in the Wirral, Cheshire (Barber and Davies, 1985) and Colwyn Bay in Clwyd, and as multiple structures at Elmer in West Sussex and Sea Palling, Norfolk. With the exception of the Sea Palling site, these structures have all been in macro-tidal situations, with both sand and shingle beaches; the only associated recharge has been at Elmer. Recent research has been undertaken on the impact of single structures on shingle beaches using physical models (Coates, 1994) and extensive monitoring is under way at the Elmer site to provide validation data for numerical models of wave response to pairs of structures and to record long-term beach developments. Some of the phenomena observed at the Elmer site are briefly discussed in Box 8.2, and illustrated in Figures 8.7a and 8.7b.

Box 8.2   *Observations from the detached breakwater scheme at Elmer, W. Sussex*

Evidence from field monitoring of beach response at Elmer has shown some of the potential problems associated with detached breakwaters on shingle upper/sand lower beaches. The structures were designed to provide flood protection under severe storm conditions. Consequently they act as barriers to longshore transport under more normal conditions. The structures were also designed on the basis of shingle transport processes being independent of sand transport, and of sand deposition being of limited importance. The result of these design assumptions has been very effective protection of the immediate shoreline, with sand and shingle accretion above the anticipated rate. The sand that has been deposited in the lee of structures has increased the dissipation of wave energy and further decreased the longshore transport of shingle. The result is likely to be a long-term loss of shingle volume downdrift of the site.

In general, breakwaters are suited to coastlines that require higher levels of protection at sensitive points and do not have sensitive downdrift beaches, as long-term predictions of transport response is uncertain. They are particularly well suited to frontages where the development of additional beach area can be justified for recreational/amenity purposes. They can be effective on micro and meso-tidal sand beaches, but can be used with any tidal range on shingle beaches. Under macro-tidal conditions, particularly in areas affected by significant storm surges, the structures will be very high and consequently can have a serious visual impact. Submerged reef structures can be used in meso-tidal conditions, though their effectiveness at reducing wave energy may be limited, particularly in the event of a storm surge.

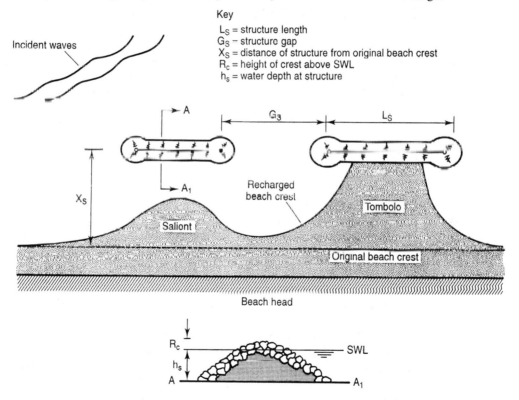

Key

L_S = structure length
G_S = structure gap
X_S = distance of structure from original beach crest
R_c = height of crest above SWL
h_s = water depth at structure

Figure 8.6 *Detached breakwater terminology*

Design of detached breakwaters on an open beach must endeavour to achieve a satisfactory compromise between the (sometimes conflicting) criteria regarding requirements of storm protection and long-term beach stability, between the responses of shingle and sand on mixed beaches and the problems of integrating the beach response over the full tidal cycle.

There is evidence that potentially hazardous rip currents may develop around breakwaters under certain tidal conditions (Coates, 1994) and that structures which are too large, too close together or too close to the shoreline, can cause deposition of fine sediment, natural flotsam and pollutants. Exacerbation of unsightly and odorous seaweed deposition along the south coast of England is an example of the latter.

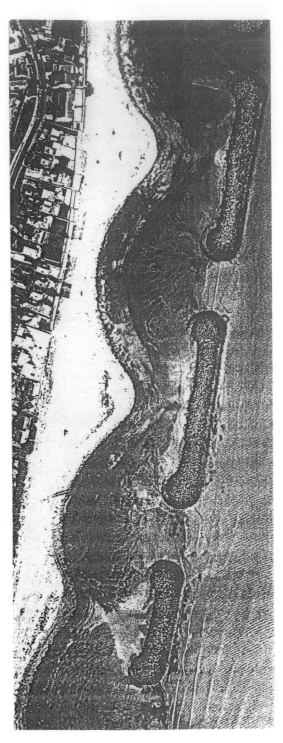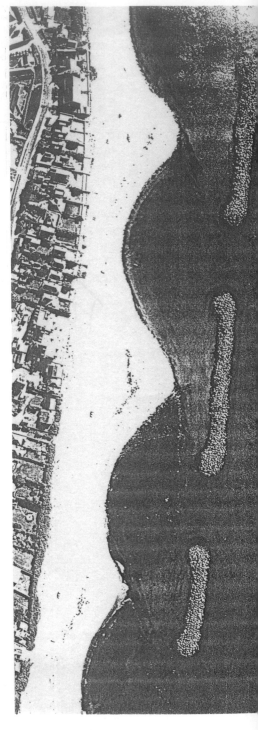

Figure 8.7   *Detached breakwaters at Elmer, W. Sussex, at low (a) and high (b) water level;
note the accretion of fine material across the lower beach (courtesy Arun DC)*

8.3.2   Design approach

Detached breakwaters give rise to an area of reduced wave energy in their lee. In situations of oblique wave attack, they will cause beach material to be deposited as the wave induced longshore transport forces decrease. If the beach has not been recharged, then this deposition will be at the expense of the adjacent beaches on an open frontage. If the beach has been recharged, then the beach manager will wish to retain the recharge material while not altering the existing drift. It should be noted that the structures cannot modify drift along the beach to seaward, so the designer must consider what width of the foreshore is to be affected.

The influence of a detached breakwater on beach development depends on the structure length, freeboard, distance offshore and orientation relative to the dominant wave directions; in the case of multiple structures the influence is also dependent on gap length. Recent research (Coates, 1994) has shown that, in theory, single detached breakwaters can be designed to retain shingle recharge material while allowing the natural drift to continue on a beach with a strongly dominant drift direction. At present this design approach is embryonic, but further work could provide a general method. Box 8.3 presents the approach and limitations. It should be noted that the breakwater can only be designed to achieve the correct efficiency where the drift is reasonably constant in direction and rate. If the drift is dominated by extreme events, particularly where these may be generated from a variety of directions, then it will not be possible to optimise design and an alternative form of control should be considered.

This design approach is only applicable to shingle beaches. Guidelines for sand beaches can be found in the previously referenced CIRIA/CUR and CERC publications (CERC, 1993, CIRIA/CUR, 1991). Box 8.4 presents some of the concepts of detached breakwater design proposed in CERC (1993) and Box 8.5, also included in CIRIA/CUR (1991), presents the Spanish micro-tidal pocket beach approach. Designers must be aware of the differences between the micro-tidal sand beach situations considered by CERC and the meso or macro-tidal sand and/or shingle beach UK situations in which tidal currents can play a significant role in the transport of sand and where the mobile beach may be nearly a kilometre wide. Winthrop Beach, Massachusetts has the largest tidal range of all the breakwater scheme locations quoted by CERC, at 2.7m. The scheme comprises 5 rock breakwaters with lengths of 91m and gaps of 30m, set about 300m offshore. A small salient beach was formed above the high tide level behind one breakwater. Tombolos developed at low tide level behind 4 of the structures. If the amenity value of the beach is not considered, then the scheme would not be justified on a benefit/cost basis; the rock required to retain the small salient could have provided greater shoreline protection with a much lower risk of failure if it had been used to form a revetment along the existing seawall. In many UK situations the tidal range is greater than 2.7m and so structures would have to be longer, higher and further seaward than those at Winthrop Beach. Although such schemes could be possible, it is unlikely that they could be justified unless a substantial amenity value could be placed on the beach.

Design procedures for multiple breakwaters on shingle beaches have only reached an embryonic stage. Available guidelines are based on limited field experience, engineering judgement and physical model tests at HR Wallingford (Coates, 1994). Designers must consider the potential variations in beach plan shape and the drift rate along the full length of the protected shoreline. Physical model tests suggest that the drift rate in the lee of multiple emergent breakwaters is similar to the rate for single structures of the same dimensions, assuming the gap lengths are equal to, or greater than, the structures lengths. Information on short gap lengths is not available, but wave - structure interactions will cause the rate to reduce as the gap reduces to some threshold value. The beach crest plan shape will develop towards the wave front pattern in the lee of the breakwater gaps; numerical models are available to predict these patterns, but not the associated drift rates. Future research developments will extend the physical model results and the numerical model capabilities to produce a practical design approach. At present designers must rely on advice from experienced coastal engineers and the interactive use of numerical and physical models.

Box 8.3 *Example of an initial design for detached breakwaters on shingle beaches*

This example design approach is based on recent research at HR Wallingford (Coates, 1994) in which a range of breakwater configurations were tested in a scaled physical model under a limited number of sea conditions. All tests were undertaken with a wave height of 2m (H_s) and a wave direction of 23° relative to the initial shoreline at a depth of 5m. The model simulated a typical UK situation of a shingle upper/sand lower beach at a scale of 1:50.

The method allowed the potential drift rate of shingle in the lee of the structure to be reduced to match the actual drift rate along the beach under the design conditions. Therefore, the downdrift loss of material will equal the updrift input, and any recharge material will be retained. The efficiency figure presented below assumes storm wave periods ($H_s/L_m=0.06$).

Method

1. Derive potential shingle drift rate (Q_p) for frontage, based on wave climate and assuming unlimited supply of shingle (see Section 2.4.2).

2. Estimate existing or required shingle drift rate (Q_o) (see Section 6.2) and determine the required efficiency of structure as $\eta = (1 - Q_o/Q_p) \times 100$.

3. Use efficiency plot to determine the range of dimensions which will allow the actual drift rate to continue.

4. From this range, select the optimum combination of freeboard (R_c), length (L_s) and offshore distance (X_s) to achieve the secondary aims of the structure e.g. safe small craft mooring, extreme storm protection for sensitive frontage location.

Note that this approach assumes that the site is subject to a relatively constant drift rate and direction, and it does not consider the potential for deposition of fines in the lee of the structures.

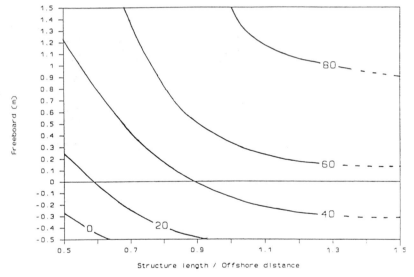

Figure 1 *Efficiency contours relative to structural variables*

This was an example approach to the design process which may be useful in other similar situations. Note that potential bathymetric changes of the sand lower beach (present in many instances) were not included, neither were field data available to validate the model results. The approach is for single breakwaters, or for coasts where the breakwaters are sufficiently far apart to be considered to act as single breakwaters.

8.3.3   Design considerations

The design approach discussed above assumes that the breakwaters will be constructed as permeable rock mounds parallel to the existing shoreline. Although these assumptions apply to most existing breakwaters, there are a number of variables which should be considered.

Materials

Rock is a very satisfactory material for breakwater construction, assuming that it is durable and economically available in the required size. Concrete armour units, either single layer or random placed, can replace rock. Both materials must be carefully designed and specified to ensure stability under the design storm conditions.

Box 8.4 *Design concepts for detached breakwaters on sand beaches (CERC, 1993)*

The geometry of detached breakwaters and the resulting beach response can be described by a number of fundamental parameters. These are shown in Figure 8.6. In particular the breakwater length, L_s, the gap width, G_s, the offshore distance of the breakwater, X_s, and the depth of water at the breakwater, h_s, are important in determining the morphological response, characterized by the salient amplitude. A number of dimensionless groups of these parameters can be used to describe the beach response. The ratio L_s/S_s (breakwater length to gap width) characterizes the ability of the structures to block incident wave energy; X_s/h_s (offshore distance to depth of water at the breakwater) represents the influence of the structure location in effecting shoaling and diffraction of the incident wave energy. Essentially as the ratio of L_s/S_s decreases and X_s/h_s increases, more wave energy can penetrate behind the breakwaters. The effect of wave energy on the beach response has been characterized into five different categories:

(a) PERMANENT TOMBOLOS (PT) - very little wave energy reaches the shore and the protected beach is stable. There is very little transport along the shore landward of the breakwater. Littoral transport may be displaced into deeper water, seaward of the breakwater.

(b) PERIODIC TOMBOLO FORMATION (PTF) - one or more breakwater segments are periodically backed by tombolos. This is primarily due to variability in the wave energy reaching the lee of the individual segments. During periods of high wave energy, tombolos may be severed from the structure resulting in salients. During low wave energy periods, the sediment accretes and the tombolo reforms. The longshore effect of this type of planform may be periodic trapping of littoral material followed by the release of a 'slug' of sediment. Even in a relatively stable scheme, only some segments may be backed by tombolos, due to alongshore variability in the amount of energy behind the breakwater system.

(c) WELL-DEVELOPED SALIENTS (WDS) - this occurs when higher wave energy reaches the lee of the structure and is characterized by a balanced sediment budget. Longshore moving material enters and leaves the scheme at approximately the same rate. In addition, rip current development within the gaps is unusual.

(d) SUBDUED SALIENTS (SS) - in this case the shoreline sinuosity is not as obvious and the salients are smaller. The beach may periodically store and release sediment. Although the quantity of material retained in the scheme may remain generally balanced through time, there will be periods of increased loss or gain and the uniformity of the beach plan can not be guaranteed.

(e) NO SINUOSITY (NS) - if high wave energy reaches the beach, including the area directly in the lee of the breakwaters, the beach plan shape may not reflect the presence of the structures. Replenished beach material may actually serve as a source of material for downdrift beaches.

The relation between these different planshape categories and the breakwater geometry is shown in Figure 1. Tentative limits for each of the main plan shapes in indicated, however these are based on limited prototype data.

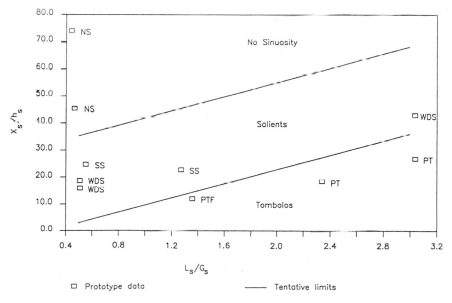

Figure 1 *Effect of breakwater layout on morphological response of sand beaches*

If the breakwaters are to serve a dual function (i.e. protection of moorings or amenity platform, as well as shore protection) then a composite structure comprising a solid crest platform with a hydraulically effective seaward face would be needed. Attention must be paid to the detailing of the interface of materials as differential loadings may cause damage.

Box 8.5 Design of pocket beaches based on Spanish micro-tidal experience

Berenguer and Enriques (1988) published a useful set of design equations for pocket beaches where the tidal range is less than 1m based on an analysis of 24 Spanish beaches such as Rihuete Beach, Murcia, shown in Figure 1. With reference to the definition sketch (a), the following relations were obtained:

$$A_0 = 2A_1$$
$$A_1 = 25 + 0.85S$$
$$X.B_0 = 2.5A_1^2$$
$$S_p = X.B_0 - (\pi A_1^2/2)$$
$$\text{or } S_p = 0.376X.B_0$$

where S_p is the maximum stable surface area of the beach.

In addition, a graphical relationship was developed between the cross-sectional surface area of the gap ($S.d_g$) and the dimensions of the resulting beach ($A_1^2.D_m^{1/2}$), as shown in (b), where S, d_g and A have dimensions in metres and D_m, the mean sand grain diameter, is in millimetres.

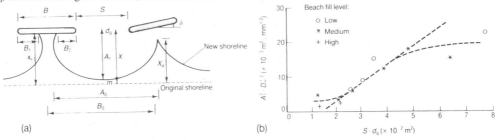

(a)   (b)

Figure 1 *Rihuete Beach, Murcia, Spain, after creation of pocket beaches (courtesy Director Gen. Ports & Coasts, Spain)*

Frontages affected by low wave energy conditions can be protected by other novel materials such as lattices of car tyres or barge hulks, but consideration should be given to their appearance, environmental impact and durability.

Dimensions

The design method presented in Box 8.3 provides an example method for determining a suitable range of combinations of breakwater length, freeboard and offshore distance to achieve a dynamically stable shingle beach. Consideration should also be given to other design factors which are influenced by the structure dimensions. These include their cost, their influence on the amenity use of the shoreline, and the construction methods.

The cost of the structures is primarily governed by the volume of material required. This volume can be optimised for each situation. Shifting the position of the structure seaward will increase the depth of the toe, and therefore the total height, and will also necessitate an increase in length and/or freeboard to maintain the efficiency. Similarly a decrease in freeboard will require an increase in length or a shift landward. Where an extended length of shoreline must be protected, then the size of individual structures must be balanced against the total number of structures.

The dimensions and location of the breakwaters may also be influenced by the construction methods. If rock is to be delivered by barge, then there may be advantages in working as far down the beach as possible, and vice versa for land-based delivery. Access and transport difficulties along the beach may also influence the number and location of structures.

As with all beach control structures, attention should be paid to the detailing of the toe and ends. These are points at which turbulence due to waves or currents may cause scour of the beach and structural instability. The *Manual on the use of rock in coastal and shoreline engineering* (CIRIA/CUR, 1991) provides useful guidance.

Orientation

Structure orientation is dependent on the wave climate. If there is a strongly dominant wave condition, responsible for both long-term transport and extreme storm conditions, then breakwaters can be oriented parallel to the wave fronts. In many coastal situations, however, waves may approach from a range of directions and a shore parallel orientation provides a compromise solution.

Environmental considerations

Generally speaking, detached breakwaters are visually intrusive but they can be used to enhance the amenity value of the beach and sea front. Apart from the rather subjective attractions of breaking up long featureless beaches into small embayments, there are other, more tangible, benefits. Beach users are not obstructed by cross-shore structures, and protected water is available for swimming or launching and mooring small boats. The salients provide a stable area of beach that can be used for seasonal parking or the setting up of beach huts and kiosks to service beach users. The breakwaters provide possibilities for creating small islands although the public safety due to lack of access during high tide levels and currents between the structures should be considered (see Section 8.8)

8.3.4 Recharge

Detached breakwaters will give rise to salients separated by embayments. To prevent unwanted erosion within embayments and to ensure a rapid development of a dynamically stable beach, the recharge material should be placed to the anticipated planshape and profile immediately after construction of each breakwater.

Post-construction monitoring will reveal any unanticipated changes in the coastline. The breakwater should be modified if necessary with the use of reusable construction materials such as rock or randomly placed armour allowing minor modifications to be made. If the losses or gains are modest and seasonal, then a recycling operation or a minor maintenance recharge programme may be sufficient to ensure that the beach achieves the design objectives.

8.4   SHORE CONNECTED BREAKWATERS

8.4.1   Definition and general guidelines

Shore connected breakwaters include a variety of hybrid structures which do not fit easily into the categories of groynes or detached breakwaters. They combine cross-shore and longshore elements, and are connected to the shoreline either by a structural link or by the development of the beach into a permanent tombolo (see Figures 8.8 and 8.9). This manual only considers structures designed for shoreline management, but similar principles apply to harbour breakwaters which influence beach development. As these structures all tend to be substantial, they are generally constructed from rock or concrete armour units. In most situations these structures will not provide sufficient beach protection unless a recharge scheme is included.

Breakwaters are normally designed to reduce longshore transport by promoting the development of dynamically stable beaches between pairs of structures, or in conjunction with natural features, and to reduce wave attack in their lee. The length and profile shape of the cross-shore arm can be used to determine the drift rate. Structures which extend across a subsstantial part of the inter-tidal zone can be applied to areas where the erosion of downdrift beaches is not a significant factor and where discrete points along the shoreline require greater protection than the intervening lengths. Less extensive structures can be designed to allow drift to continue. In general, the principle of creating dynamically stable beaches is most appropriate to coastlines with a dominant wave direction, as storm waves from secondary directions can cause severe short-term erosion in the centre of the bays and in the lee of the structures. They can function on both sand and shingle beaches, though the need to extend across the majority of the mobile beach profile may make their use uneconomic in wide meso- or macro-tidal sand beaches. Like detached breakwaters, shore connected structures create areas of reduced wave and tidal energy in which fine sediments and pollutants can accumulate creating a potential public hazard and causing a local alteration to the ecology. However, such problems can be overcome by predicting the final beach shape and recharging with sufficient sand and shingle to achieve this and hence eliminate accumulation of fine-grained material.

8.4.2   Effect on beach development

Shore connected breakwaters are intended to form dynamically stable bays by reducing and reorientating incident wave energy before it reaches the critical parts of the beach and, if they extend sufficiently seaward, by deflecting tidal currents offshore. Incident wave energy is either reflected or dissipated directly by the seaward face of the structure, or is transmitted, diffracted or refracted towards the shoreline. Unlike detached breakwaters, the structures are intended to prevent any transport on the landward side, thus resulting in the formation of stable bays with upper beach plan shapes defined by the incident wave fronts. Changes in wave direction will cause the planshape to vary, so the designer must allow for the required protection level under the dominant storm wave direction, but must also recognise the potential for redistribution under storms from other directions; this is particularly so for structures with no built link, as severe erosion may cause the tombolo to break down.

Transport seaward of the structures will continue, but can be virtually eliminated, if required, by extending the cross-shore element of the structures to the low tide line.

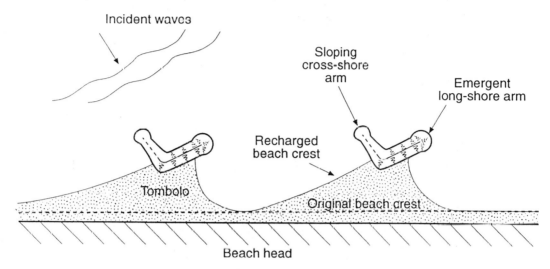

(a)   Connected by tombolo

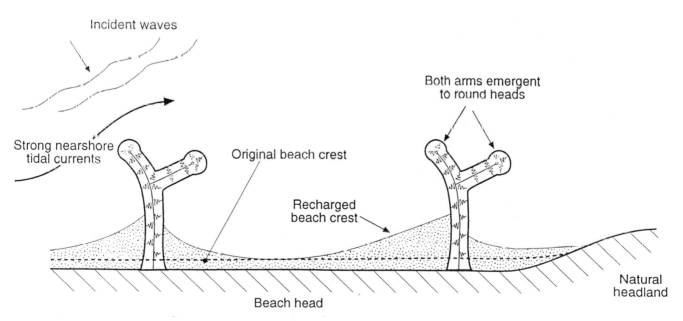

(b)   Connected by built link

Figure 8.8   *Shore connected breakwaters*

8.4.3 Design considerations

Materials

As with most substantial coastal structures, rock or randomly placed concrete units are suitable construction materials. Specification of size, and slope, must ensure stability under storm conditions. Guidelines on outline design are presented in CIRIA/CUR (1991). Reference should be made to recent research results regarding stability under breaking waves on steep beaches (Jones and Allsop, 1994, see Box 8.1).

Shore connected breakwaters offer scope for combined amenity and beach control functions. Composite structures with public access platforms can be considered, particularly if the increased beach area created by the embayment is to form a leisure facility. Forces on and damage to all elements of composite structures must be carefully considered at the detailed design stage.

Figure 8.9   *Shore connected breakwaters with built links to the backshore, Llandudno, Gwynedd (courtesy Welsh Office)*

Dimensions

The design of breakwaters with a built link to the beach head is based on the experience of several sites around the UK. At these sites strong inshore tidal currents influence longshore transport across the lower sand beach. As a consequence, the whole structure extends further offshore, and has a substantially higher cross-shore arm, than would be necessary to control a beach where tidal currents were not a factor.

If tidal currents are not significant, then the structure can be shifted inshore, the (built) shore link can be reduced or removed, and the cross-shore arm elevation can be lowered. In this situation, the shore link is replaced by the beach recharge material forming a tombolo in the protected lee of the longshore arm, while the cross-shore arm serves to control wave induced transport in a similar manner to a groyne. The following guidelines maybe used to estimate dimensions for structures without a built shore link but physical modelling is strongly recommended to achieve design optimisation:

1. Cross-shore arm - design of the cross-shore arm follows the principles of rock groynes, but with the landward part of the groyne berm omitted (see Section 8.2). When the beach is fully developed transport of excess material will occur over and around this arm.

2. Longshore arm - the crest of the longshore arm is horizontal and must be sufficiently high to minimise wave energy transmission by overtopping; if beach transport occurs in the lee of the structure, then there is a risk of a net loss of beach recharge material. The crest elevation can be taken as the beach crest elevation under the design storm condition. Crest lengths must be of the order of half the design wave length.

3. Layout and spacing - the length of the longshore arm, the cross-shore width of the tombolo and the spacing between structures must be balanced to achieve the required level of protection in the bays while optimizing costs. These dimensions will be influenced by such things as the wave climate, the existing sediment budget, and the nearshore tidal currents. As no detailed guidance is available, then designers should make use of a wave basin physical model to optimise layouts.

Orientation

The wave climate dictates the optimum orientation of both arms of the structure. The cross-shore arm should be normal to the expected beach orientation updrift of the structure. If the wave climate has a single dominant storm or morphological direction, then the longshore arm can be orientated parallel to the wave fronts, while structures subject to attack from a range of directions should be built parallel to the original shoreline.

The principles controlling the spacing of shore connected structures under typical (i.e. macro-tidal) UK conditions have not been developed, although preliminary model studies have been completed (DeVidi and Coates, 1995). For micro-tidal, sand beach dominated wave action, reference can be made to work by Hsu and Silvester on *headland control* as set out in Box 8.6. An example of a recent application of this approach on the coast of the United Arab Emirates is shown in Box 8.7.

8.4.4 Recharge

Recharge material should be placed to the anticipated dynamically stable beach planshape and profile immediately after installation of the structures. This is essential in the case of structures without a built shore link, as the recharge tombolo forms the shore connection in this case. This anticipation of the future beach shape reduces both the short-term accumulation of mud/weeds etc. and the risk of sand being drawn into the lee of the structure, eroding adjacent parts of the shoreline.

There is also scope for placing varying sizes of beach sediment along the frontage, with sand in the lee of structures, grading up to coarse shingle in more exposed areas. In this situation the designer must carefully anticipate the potential changes in beach profiles and planshape under different wave conditions. A beach scheme of this type has been carried out on a shingle beach in the UK, but was not entirely successful in predicting the eventual disposition of beach material.

As with all control schemes, ongoing post-construction monitoring will allow performance to be assessed and modifications to be made to optimise the beach planshape.

8.5 MODIFIED SEAWALLS AND REVETMENTS

8.5.1 Definition and general guidelines

In this section, seawalls and revetments are taken to include all continuous, shore parallel structures that are intended to provide a final line of flood or erosion protection and are designed to absorb some wave energy. They range from vertical walls modified with a rock or armour unit face, through simple, sloped structures to permeable timber fences. They do not provide direct control of longshore transport, but can have a significant influence on beach levels due to their impact on cross-shore beach processes. For simplicity, the term seawall will be used to describe all of these structures.

Seawalls define the seafront of many coastal towns and also protect long lengths of low lying land and soft cliffs. Many were intentionally built within the active intertidal zone in order to allow promenades to be developed. Others were built along the backshore as a final line of defence, but subsequent foreshore erosion has brought some of them into contact with wave action. In general, beach management schemes should be designed to ensure that waves do not reach the wall, except under extreme conditions when the walls may be required to act as a final defence. If there is an existing wall, then it may need to be made structurally sound and/or more able to absorb, rather than reflect, wave energy. If there is no wall, then consideration should be given to the potential advantages of installing one, including risk reduction, reduction in the volume of beach recharge and provision of public access. A set-back wall (see also Section 9.3) designed to retain flooding under extreme conditions may well be preferable to a wall within the normal active beach zone. As seawalls do not control longshore processes directly, then it is likely that other structures will be included in a beach recharge scheme. Readers are referred to the CIRIA publications *Seawall Design* (Thomas and Hall, 1992) and *Old waterfront walls* (Bray and Tatham, 1992) for detailed guidance on design and maintenance.

8.5.2 Effect on beach development

When designing a beach recharge scheme in the presence of an existing seawall or designing a new seawall behind a beach, the effect of wave/seawall and seawall/beach process interactions on beach development should be estimated. Many concerns have been expressed in regard to the impact of seawalls on beach development, some of which are valid and others of which are not. Dean (1986) provided a classic assessment of these which is reproduced as Table 8.4.

Wave/seawall interactions

Wave/seawall interactions can give rise to increased local turbulence, resulting in high levels of sediment suspension and the potential for localised scour.

If the seawall has a reflective, rather than an absorbent profile, and if beach levels are low enough to allow regular wave contact with the wall, then a long-term scour problem is likely and the stability of the wall foundation may be reduced. However, if the seawall has an energy absorbing profile, or if the beach is sufficiently well formed to allow only occasional wave/wall interaction, then any erosion is likely to be short-term (see Kraus and Pikley, 1988). Wave attack on seawalls can also result in overtopping and potential flood damage, and the design should ensure that this risk is minimised even in the event of a significant loss of beach material.

Box 8.6   *Principles of headland control (Hsu et al, 1989)*

Headland control

Headland control is a system of coastal management in which structures are used to generate alternating headlands and crenulate bays which are in equilibrium with the incident waves. Hsu *et al* (1989) have suggested the idea that crenulate-shaped bays can be kept in equilibrium by use of a system of headlands. Persistent waves which dominate littoral processes for the stretch of coast are diffracted around the upcoast headland and refracted in such a way as to arrive normal to the shoreline of the bay along its entire periphery. Littoral drift is therefore reduced to a minimum and the shoreline remains stable with respect to longshore drift. The concept is based on the observation of natural crenulate bays which appear to be in equilibrium with the incident wave climate. Relationships for the equilibrium form have been developed from model tests and measurements of natural bays. The equilibrium form is judged to have been achieved when no further sediment is received into the bay, waves break simultaneously around the bay periphery and the beachline is static (Figure 1).

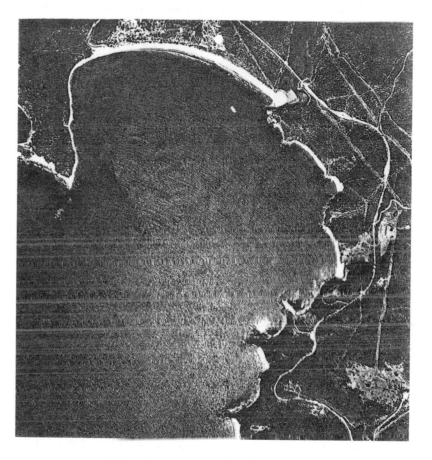

Figure 1   *Waves entering Twofold Bay, Victoria, Australia, showing simultaneous breaking along beach periphery (courtesy Silvester)*

Figure 2 is a definition sketch of a static equilibrium bay showing the variable involved. The incident wave crests impinging at angle β to a straight beach, designated as length R_o, will erode it until the curved outline is reached. The final shape will have a downcoast tangent parallel to the wave crest line at the point on the headland where diffraction occurs. The shape of the curved beach when stable is dictated by the fact that it takes an equal time for any diffracted and refracted wave to reach the periphery. Hsu *et al* (1989) provide design curves for the calculation of the final equilibrium slope in terms of R/R_o versus the radius angle θ for a specified wave approach angle β (R is the radius from the diffraction point to the beach for a specified angle of θ).

Continued

Box 8.6   *Continued*

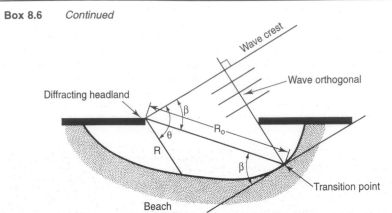

Figure 2   *Definition sketch of a static equilibrium bay showing variables involved*

Waves are diffracted around the upcoast headland and the control line is defined between this headland and the transition point (Figure 2). At the transition point, the tangent to the beach is parallel to the offshore wave crests. The control line has length R_o and is angled (β) to the wave crest line. The method of Hsu *et al* (1989) uses these two parameters to determine the equilibrium bay shape defined as pairs of values (R,β). Figure 3 gives the relationships between R/R_o and θ for each value of β. For ease of use, these ratios (R/R_o) are tabulated in Table 1 where linear interpolation between the 5° increments of β can be used.

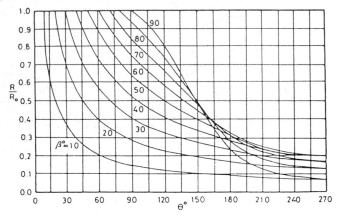

Figure 3   *R/R_o versus θ for varying β*

Table 1   Arc ratios R/R_o for a range of β and θ

β/θ	30	45	60	75	90	120	150	180	210	240	270
10	0.37	0.26	0.20	0.17	0.15	0.12	0.10	0.10	0.08	0.08	0.08
15	0.53	0.38	0.30	0.25	0.21	0.17	0.15	0.14	0.12	0.11	0.11
20	0.70	0.50	0.40	0.33	0.28	0.23	0.20	0.17	0.15	0.13	0.13
25	0.85	0.61	0.48	0.41	0.34	0.27	0.24	0.21	0.18	0.16	0.16
30	1.00	0.72	0.57	0.48	0.40	0.32	0.28	0.23	0.20	0.18	0.17
35	-	0.82	0.65	0.55	0.47	0.37	0.31	0.26	0.22	0.19	0.19
40	-	0.91	0.73	0.62	0.42	0.41	0.34	0.28	0.23	0.20	0.20
45	-	1.00	0.80	0.68	0.58	0.46	0.38	0.29	0.24	0.21	0.20
50	-	-	0.87	0.74	0.64	0.80	0.40	0.31	0.24	0.21	0.21
55	-	-	0.94	0.80	0.69	0.54	0.43	0.32	0.24	0.21	0.20
60	-	-	1.00	0.87	0.74	0.58	0.45	0.32	0.24	0.21	0.20
65	-	-	-	0.91	0.79	0.62	0.46	0.31	0.23	0.20	0.19
70	-	-	-	0.96	0.84	0.66	0.48	0.30	0.22	0.18	0.17
75	-	-	-	1.00	0.88	0.70	0.48	0.296	0.20	0.16	0.15
80	-	-	-	-	0.92	0.74	0.49	0.27	0.18	0.14	0.13
85	-	-	-	-	0.97	0.78	0.49	0.25	0.15	0.12	0.10
90	-	-	-	-	1.00	0.81	0.49	0.23	0.12	0.09	0.07

Further information and other references on the subject of headland control can be found in Silvester and Hsu (1993).

Box 8.7   *Use of equilibrium bays, Al Mamzar Beach Park, Dubai, United Arab Emirates*

The Al Mamzar beach park lies on the border between Dubai and Sharjah in the United Arab Emirates. A large area of seabed was reclaimed seaward of the natural shore and a recreational beach frontage was required. Due to the scarcity of suitable beach sand it was necessary to form the basic reclamation geometry including the "equilibrium bays" in dredged coral and to place a 1-2m thick veneer of sand over the formation in the beach areas. The bay shapes were designed in accordance with the theory of Silvester and Hsu using nearshore wave conditions derived using conventional wave refraction methods. Typically the 1-in-1 year wave is of the order of 3.5m with a period of 7 seconds (T_z) and the maximum tidal range is 2.0m (LAT to HAT). Downdrift impacts were not a design constraint. The beaches have, at the time of writing, been performing satisfactorily for 5 years and post-construction monitoring has shown that little beach movement has occurred following initial profile adjustment.

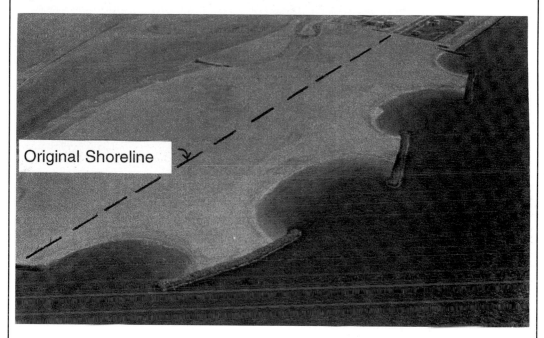

Original Shoreline

Figure 1   *Bays soon after construction (courtesy Sir William Halcrow & Partners)*

Effect of vertical seawalls on shingle beaches

Research has been undertaken by Powell and Lowe (1994) on the effect of wave/seawall interactions on the beach profile, for coarse sediments. For vertical seawalls, four different types of scour/reflection behaviour have been identified, with the occurrence of a particular type depending on the local wave conditions and water depth. A qualitative model is shown in Figure 8.10 in which the four different response types are presented:

1. Type I - initial beach level is high relative to the wave height, reflected energy is low, high onshore movement, low offshore movement, reflection coefficient, C_r, low and constant through time.

    The beach responds in much the same way as a natural beach. The seawall plays little part in the beach processes as it is not under direct wave attack.

2. Type II - combination of beach levels and wave heights is such that there is marginal scour, reflected energy is low, predominant onshore transport, some offshore transport, C_r decreases through time.

    Initially there is scour at the toe, however, over time, the beach can build up due to the predominant onshore movement of material. As the beach level increases so the amount of reflected energy, and hence the proportion of onshore to offshore transport, decreases. Given sufficient time the beach levels can build up to the Type I condition.

3. Type III - initial beach level is low, relative to the wave height, reflected energy is high, low onshore movement, high offshore movement, C_r increases through time.

Table 8.4 Assessment of some commonly expressed concerns relating to coastal armouring (Dean, 1986)

Common concern	Assessment	Explanation of assessment
Coastal armouring placed in an area of existing erosional stress causes *increased* erosional stress on the beaches adjacent to the armouring	TRUE	By preventing the upland from eroding, the beaches adjacent to the armouring share a greater portion of the same total erosional stress
Coastal armouring placed in an area of existing erosional stress will cause the beaches fronting the armouring to diminish	TRUE	Coastal armouring is designed to protect the upland, but does not prevent erosion of the beach profile waterward of the armouring. Thus an eroding beach will continue to erode. If the armouring had not been placed, the width of the beach would have remained approximately the same, but, with increasing time, would have been located progressively landward
Coastal armouring causes an acceleration of beach erosion seaward of the armouring	PROBABLY FALSE	No known data or physical arguments support this
An isolated coastal armouring can accelerate downdrift erosion	TRUE	If an isolated structure is armoured on an eroding beach, the structure will eventually protrude into the active beach zone and will act to some degree as a groin, interrupting longshore sediment transport and thereby causing downdrift erosion
Coastal armouring results in a greatly delayed post-storm recovery	PROBABLY FALSE	No known data or physical arguments support this
Coastal armouring causes the beach profile to steepen considerably	PROBABLY FALSE	No known data or physical arguments support this
Coastal armouring placed well back from a stable beach is detrimental to the beach and serves no useful purpose	FALSE	In order to have any substantial effects on the beaches, the armouring must be acted upon by the waves and beaches. Moreover, armouring set well back from the normally active shore zone can provide "insurance" for upland structures against severe storms

The toe depth increases with time and there is a general lowering of beach levels. As the beach level decreases, so the amount of reflected energy, and hence the proportion of onshore-to-offshore transport, increases. Given sufficient time, the beach levels can reduce to the Type IV condition.

4. Type IV - initial beach level is very low, relative to the wave height, reflected energy is high, predominantly offshore movement, C_r large and constant through time.

    Scour is small compared to water depth. The movement of material is low in both the onshore and offshore directions due to the large depth of water, relative to the wave height. Eventually a dynamically stable situation is attained from which, regardless of the incident wave conditions, the beach cannot recover its former levels.

Generally response Types I and II are associated with beach accretion while Types III and IV correspond to scour. Constructive beach building (Type I and II) occurs at a similar rate to Type III scour with about half of the profile development occurring during the first 100 waves. Type IV scour, being associated with greater depths of water at the wall, occurs at a slower initial rate though for all response types a quasi-equilibrium position is reached quite quickly i.e. within about 3000 waves.

Beaches can move through a negative feedback loop, with decreasing reflection coefficient, from a Type II to Type I situation. Starting from a Type III situation, a beach will move through a positive feedback loop, with increasing reflection coefficient, to a stable Type IV situation.

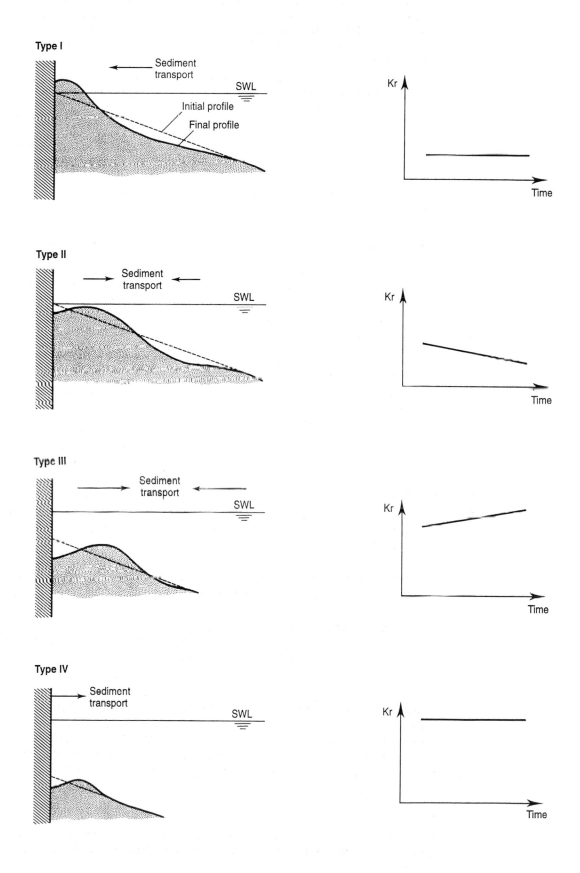

Figure 8.10 *Classification for scour response types*

CIRIA Report 153

Box 8.8 below presents some guidelines for estimating toe scour in coarse sediments $(5mm < D_{50} < 30mm)$ at vertical seawalls. However, these guidelines are limited in their application and designers should take advantage of available numerical and physical models to investigate potential beach scour and overtopping on a site specific basis.

Box 8.8 *Estimating scour at vertical seawalls (Powell and Lowe, 1994)*

For the 2-dimensional case and a shingle sediment grading, toe scour is a function of the following variables:

- initial water depth at the toe of the seawall
- wave height and period
- number of waves
- sea wall geometry and type.

Figure 1 illustrates the relationship between scour depth (S), water depth (h_w) and the incident wave conditions (H_s, L_m) for vertical seawalls under orthogonal wave action.

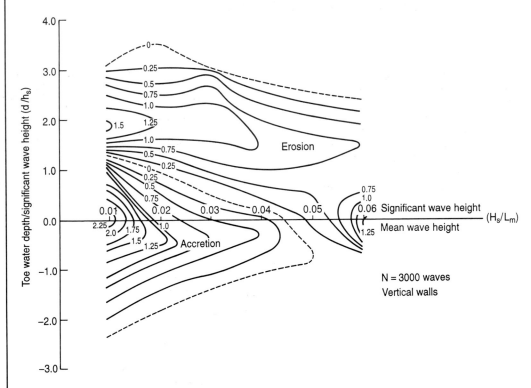

Figure 1 *Contours of dimensionless toe scour (S/H_s): vertical walls*

Two important comments can be made about Figure 1:

(i)   Maximum scour for $0.02 < H_s/L_m < 0.04$ is approximately equivalent to the wave height.

(ii)   Depending on wave steepness, maximum scour occurs when the water depth at the seawall h_w is in the range $2.0 < h_w/H_s < 0$.

The figure also clearly demonstrates the self-sustaining nature of the scouring process once the beach has been diminished to such an extent that waves can regularly reach the wall.

As an example, consider the situation where the beach crest level is above the waterline at the seawall with, say, $h_w/H_s = -0.5$. In this scenario accretion will occur for all wave conditions characterised by $H_s/L_m < 0.048$. If, however, a storm with $H_s/L_m = 0.06$ should occur, beach erosion will ensue and the resultant drop in beach level at the wall, according to Figure 1, will be 1.5 H_s. Following the storm the beach crest at the wall will lie below the waterline, $(h_w/H_s = 1.0)$ and erosion, or further scouring, will now occur for all wave conditions with a characteristic sea steepness in excess of 0.02. Furthermore, although more moderate seas $(H_s/L_m < 0.02)$ will promote accretion at the wall, the extent of this accretion will not necessarily be sufficient to return the beach to its original level.

Effect of sloping seawalls on shingle beaches

The general influence of seawall type on the scour development is shown in Figure 8.10. Here scour profiles are compared for a single input wave condition and water level, and the range of seawall cross-sections tested. It can be seen that scour is greatest for an impermeable vertical wall. As a slope is introduced, the scour depth decreases. A similar reduction also occurs if the slope is changed from impermeable to permeable (i.e. rock armour). For shallow angle rock armour slopes, toe scour is likely to be minimum.

Figure 8.11 indicates that seawall slope (and hence reflection coefficient K_r) is a very important variable in controlling the beach response in front of a seawall. To alter the reflection coefficient, and so influence the beach response, changes can be made to the characteristics of the seawall in terms of its profile and form of construction. The reflection coefficient, however, is also dependent on the incident wave conditions and the state of the beach levels. The beach response is therefore a complex interaction between the structure, the hydrodynamics and the previous development of the beach.

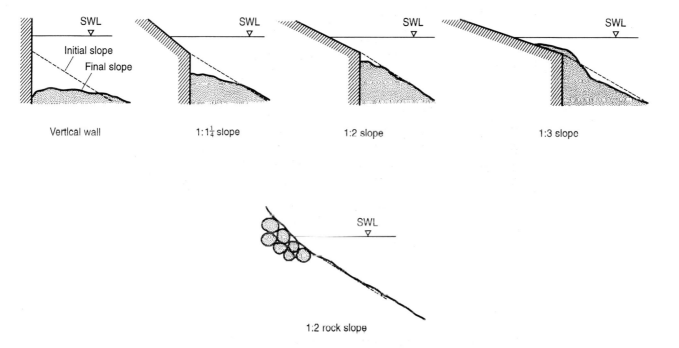

Figure 8.11   *Influence of seawall type on beach development*

8.5.3   Design considerations

Materials

Construction materials should be selected to achieve low reflections and overtopping. If the structure protects low-lying land then it may need to form an impermeable barrier, while in other situations a final defence against erosion is required. Many seawalls have to satisfy both of these criteria. Rock or concrete armour units can be used to form a porous front face, while single layer armour units or pitched stone can be used to provide a rougher face to structures. In both cases the aim is to absorb wave energy. Smooth vertical structures are not generally in favour because of their poor hydraulic performance.

Alignment

Many seawalls suffer unnecessary damage as a result of being built with a planshape which does not follow the natural beach orientation which itself changes with time. Sweeping curves or discontinuities which bring the wall toe forward of the natural beach line will create localised areas resulting in scour, outflanking or overtopping.

Dimensions

Face slopes will depend on the type of material used for construction and the likelihood of direct wave attack. Crest elevation is perhaps the single most important dimension. An estimation of the likely wave run-up level under the design storm provides a useful guide to this elevation. Numerical models can be used to determine overtopping rates for simple structures, but more complex cross-sections are better investigated using wave flume physical models. Acceptable overtopping rates, based on the sensitivity of the backshore area must be determined as a design objective. Rates must consider average overtopping and peak rates during storms. Peak overtopping rates are of importance to public safety, and in some cases can cause tructural damage. Time-averaged overtopping rates may also be important if the storage capacity of the area just behind the structure is limited.

End effects

The areas around both the updrift and downdrift ends of a seawall are often subject to localised erosion problems. It is good practice to reduce these problems by careful consideration of the transition from the seawall to the adjacent coast. Transition can be achieved by:

* gradually changing the orientation of the seawall along the coast
* terminating the seawall in solid rock
* beach control structures designed to gradually reduce the impact of the seawall on the beaches adjacent to it.

Problems can be particularly acute if the seawall orientation is not in line with the natural plan shape of the coastline.

Location

Many existing seawalls are now within the active foreshore zone and cannot be removed without substantial loss of hinterland. Managers should consider methods of reducing their negative impacts on the beach, while retaining their coast defence function. New seawalls can be sited to have a minimum impact on the foreshore while providing a secondary line of flood defence in the event of severe storms. Their function, in this case, will be to reduce the level of protection required from the beach. For example, a frontage requiring protection from a 1:200-year return period storm could be protected by a beach for events up to 1:10 years, while a wall set back from the beach crest could provide protection in the event of more extreme events. This wall would only normally face attack from the swash of waves which had already broken and would therefore not need to be of massive construction. They would have to be impermeable and able to withstand the loss of some beach material in the long-term.

8.6   OTHER APPROACHES

A range of other approaches to beach management and beach control structures may be possible in specific situations. For example, Pilarczyk (1994) has recently identified and evaluated some potential low-cost solutions for their applicability to the Dutch coastline.

Care needs to be taken, however, not to assume that techniques which have worked at sites overseas, often in micro-tidal environments, will necessarily be applicable in UK macro-tidal situations. For example, a development currently under evaluation by Goda (1995) for application in Japanese waters involving the use of wave interference shore perpendicular reefs.

These might well prove to be cost-effective, particularly since they could employ the pinned, sand-filled geotextile bags discussed by Pilarczyk (1994). However, since the technique requires the tidal range to be less than 2 metres for it to be effective, its applicability in the UK is likely to be very limited.

Another major issue with novel and apparently cheap systems is their probable life, which may be significantly lower than comparable conventional systems, and thus replacement/renewal costs will need to be included in any economic appraisal (see Section 6.5 and MAFF, 1993a). Conversely the adaptability of such systems may offer advantages in some situations, especially where the scheme may be somewhat experimental.

Two systems are discussed in more detail in this section, but as will be seen, both are more applicable to micro-tidal situations.

8.6.1   Sills

Sills, in contrast to detached breakwaters, are un-segmented, always or occasionally submerged, shore-parallel structures designed partly to reduce inshore wave climates and partly to act as physical barriers to the cross-shore transport of beach material. As a result, upper beach levels should be less liable to change. They are only able to significantly influence the sediment transport processes in their lee when they cause wave breaking, i.e. the depth of water over their crests is less than $H_s/0.55$. Information on appropriate crest widths is limited, but there appears to be little benefit in increasing the width beyond that needed for structural stability. Material retained shoreward of a sill may form a *perched beach*, with a distinct step in beach level across the structure. The perched beach will provide additional protection to the beach head. Sills are generally constructed from rock, but novel techniques such as the use of sand bags or old car bodies have been tried; if novel materials are proposed, then careful consideration should be given to their appearance, environmental impact and durability.

Experience in other parts of the world suggests that sills are most appropriate for low to moderate wave energy, micro tidal environments with low net longshore drift. Although the technique could be applied to shingle, most schemes have been built on sand beaches, and some guidance on their design in this situation is given in Box 8.9. To be effective in a macro-tidal situation, sills would have to be constructed with a crest level close to high water, and would therefore be exposed over most of the tide cycle; sills with lower crest elevations would still be effective in retaining part of the beach, but would not provide any significant shoreline protection during storm events at high water. Some recent work at HR Wallingford suggests that for a typical UK site with a spring tide range of the order of 4m to 5m subject to highwater surges of an additional metre, the crest elevation of such sills would have to be set at about mean high water Neap tide level to be effective. In high energy situations sills may suffer from a net loss of the perched beach material as the structure may act as a more effective barrier to onshore transport than to offshore. They can be used in conjunction with groynes or full-height detached breakwaters to retain pocket beaches.

Beach managers must consider the impact of sills as a navigation and recreational hazard. Small craft users and swimmers could be put at risk by construction of a submerged structure.

8.6.2   Beach drainage systems

Beach drainage systems are means by which the water table in the intertidal beach zone can be artificially lowered, thereby enhancing the natural wave energy absorbing capacity of a beach. In active drainage systems the lowering of the water table is achieved by pumping. Passive drainage systems increase the natural de-watering of a beach by the installation of drains.

Beach drainage is a recent technique developed from the discovery that pumping seawater landwards through a beach has a stabilising effect on the intertidal zone. The technique dates back to 1981, when a system of pipe drains and pumps was installed near Hirsthals harbour North Jutland, Denmark, to provide filtered sea water. A series of shore parallel pipes were set into the beach just below mean sea level. A fortnight after pumping began, water yield

Box 8.9 *Design of sand beach with rock sill in micro-tidal environment*

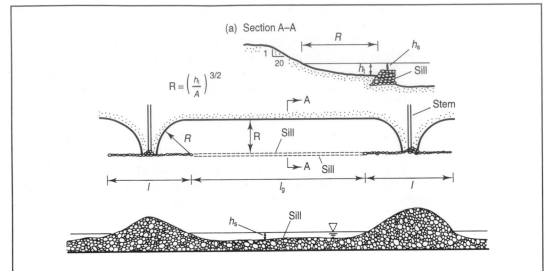

(a) Section A–A

$$R = \left(\frac{h_t}{A} \right)^{3/2}$$

Figure 1 *Definition sketch for rock sill and associated sand beach of relatively mild slope (Dean, 1988)*

Note: The beach profile scale parameter, *A*, may be obtained from formulae contained in Boxes 5.3 and 7.6.

decreased substantially and it was found that the beach had accreted. The discovery encouraged a full-scale experiment at Thorsminde in Jutland in 1985, on a sandy coast exposed to the North Sea waves. The coast at Thorsminde had experienced seasonal fluctuations in the shoreline position of +/- 15m, with an underlying trend of recession at 4m per year. Following installation, the coastline stabilised approximately 25m seawards of the drain line. Subsequently, beach retreat during storm events has been followed by accretion attributed to pumping. During 1988 the system was closed down and the coastline reverted back to erosion. Since this time there has been recovery following recommencement of pumping. Examples of active and passive beach drainage systems are presented in Boxes 8.10 and 8.11.

Box 8.10 *Active beach drainage - Hutchinson Island, USA*

At Hutchinson Island, Florida a drainage system was installed in 1988. The sandy beach is exposed to moderate wave activity, and has a small tidal range (0.9m on springs). Observations indicate that during north east swells, wave heights of 1.5m can occur in the nearshore zone. Conditions near the beach itself are somewhat calmer due to the protection afforded by a shore parallel coral reef. Over a monitoring period (July to November 1988) there was a net increase in beach volume in the drained beach area, with erosion to the north and south. No adverse impacts were identified and it is believed that the drained beach also acted as a "feeder" to the downdrift beach. Further monitoring has taken place subsequently; pumping being interspersed with significant periods of shut-down. Beach volume calculations indicate that up to the first shut-down period the beach had been slowly accreting. Thereafter a period of rapid erosion took place and, while there has been some recovery, the beach volume shows a net loss over the period 1988 to 1992. Over the same period the beach to the north has had much more substantial erosion. To the south, the downdrift beach, on the other hand, has had a net increase in volume over the same period, possibly gaining material from the drained area. Since the operation of the system resumed in late 1992 there has been evidence of recovery in the drained beach area; aerial photographs taken at low tide show a distinct bulge in the vicinity of the installation.

Box 8.11 *Passive beach drainage - Dee Why Beach, Australia*

A passive drainage system has been in operation in Australia, at Dee Why Beach, NSW. The beach is sandy and is part of a barrier system enclosing a small lagoon. The tidal range is small (2m) and wave action is moderate (deep water H_{rms} can exceed 2.5m on occasions). A system of gravity drains was installed in early 1991 and monitored over an 18-month period. The project proved that it is possible to lower the water-table by a system of gravity drains (i.e. without recourse to pumping). Analysis of morphological changes indicates that lowering the water table resulted in a significantly more stable beach within the drained area, with greater variance in the position of the beach contours outside the drained area than inside it. However, it was not possible to detect any actual increase in beach volume, because natural beach fluctuations due to cusps/rips, cycles of erosion/accretion had impacts which were of the same order of magnitude as the impacts of the drainage system.

There are varying opinions about the long-term effectiveness of beach drainage systems in UK waters. Few systems have been operational for long and there has been some difficulty in separating out their effect on beach behaviour from natural variations. Understanding of beach response is largely based on experience in areas of low tidal range and moderate wave activity. A trial scheme installed at Newquay, Cornwall, in 1994 will examine the performance of the system under conditions of large tidal range and storm dominated wave conditions.

Beach drainage systems have advantages over structural control works in terms of capital and maintenance costs, and low visual impact. However, they have yet to be proved in the UK and there are concerns over their ability to function under severe storm conditions when pipework could become exposed. It is likely that their use will be confined to improving amenity beaches which have existing, structurally sound seawalls that will provide the major defence against storm conditions. Pumped drainage systems are more likely to succeed than gravity drainage systems.

Monitoring

A careful analysis of beach processes needs to be carried out in order to separate the accretion caused by the drainage system from natural beach fluctuations. Monitoring needs to be carried out over a period of several years so as to:

* assess longer term improvements from natural trends
* assess the operability of the plant, the likely maintenance costs, etc.
* determine the impacts on beach amenity
* determine any potential adverse environmental impacts.

Once sufficient data are available, the performance of the system under a greater variety of conditions can be assessed by means of physical or numerical modelling.

8.7 COST OPTIMISATION

The overall cost optimisation process within the context of economic appraisal has been discussed in Section 6.5. This section sets out those aspects which are specific to beach control structures.

8.7.1 Overall costs

Scheme costs accrue from every aspect of a project from initial conception, through planning and construction to subsequent maintenance and monitoring.

In general, the major expenditure on a scheme occurs during the construction phase. The initial stages, comprising planning, design, investigation studies, etc. usually accrue relatively small costs in relation to the scheme as a whole (typically 5% to 15% of overall costs). However, investment in good investigation and design can greatly benefit a project by way of reduced construction costs and a reduced programme.

Costs will vary considerably between schemes because of different site conditions and the use of different types of beach control works. In general the overall cost of a scheme may be subdivided using the following categories:

* preliminaries
* planning and design
* construction
* land and property
* operational and maintenance costs.

Table 8.5 shows typical elements of cost associated with each of the above headings. Further details may be found in Section 8.5 of the CIRIA *Seawall Design* manual (Thomas and Hall, 1992).

8.7.2 Comparative costs

In general terms, beach control works involving over-water working will be more costly than those constructed using land-based techniques. This results from the higher mobilisation cost involved with the use of specialised floating plant and the difficulties associated with working over water. Consequently, where such over-water work is required in the construction of detached or shore connected breakwaters, their costs can be high, particularly on small schemes where mobilisation costs may be a significant percentage of the overall cost of the project.

Table 8.5 Typical elements of the cost of beach control works

Subject	Costs to be included
Preliminaries	Project co-ordination, management and administration
Planning and design	Survey, data collecting and investigations
	Model studies
	Design and contract preparation
	Statutory procedures and licences
	Economic appraisal
	Environmental impact assessment
	Safety planning supervision
Construction	Contract payments including adjustments, claims etc.
	Supervision (incl. safety) and administration costs
	Ancillary works for environmental improvement, amenity of services
Land or property	Purchase or lease of land and property either as part of the works or for construction
	Compensation payments to affected owners
Operation and maintenance	Operational activities
	Monitoring and maintenance, including replacement of elements having a shorter life than that of the overall scheme
	Repairs

The costs of schemes depend on the physical conditions at the site and sensitivity of the schemes to these factors. The costs of detached and shore connected structures are particularly sensitive to the nearshore bathymetry because of the effect water depth has on the material quantities. In comparison, the cost of shore structures, such as revetments, are more sensitive to the level of the foreshore.

8.8   ENVIRONMENTAL CONSIDERATIONS

Whereas beach recharge maintains the natural processes of beaches, control structures employed for beach management, as their name implies, are designed to resist and/or control natural processes. Consequently, the potential for significant environmental impact is greater with control structures than with recharge schemes. Groynes, for example, are designed to interrupt sediment movements in the longshore direction. This can lead to sediment starvation of downdrift shorelines, exacerbating erosion in these areas to the extent that the problem created may be greater than the one originally experienced at the protected site. Similarly, breakwaters are intended to reduce wave energy at the shore. Reduction in wave impact may reduce erosion and produce an imbalance in sediment budgets which may affect adjacent shores producing sediment starvation as a result. Accumulation of sediment in the lee of a breakwater, however, can be beneficial with regard to shore protection and/or amenity use of the beach. Negative impacts of such a phenomenon could include smothering of the indigenous biota and/or features of geological interest.

By their physical presence control structures are often visually intrusive and may prevent or inhibit access to or along the beach. They may also obliterate habitats, geological features and archaeological sites. Impermeable upper shore structures can eliminate or reduce sediment flux between beach and supra tidal habitats such as sand dunes.

Some other potential impacts of control structures are presented in Tables 8.6 and 8.7 respectively and a selection of possible mitigation measures are listed in Box 8.12. These lists are not intended to be exhaustive. The magnitude of the impact will depend, *inter alia*, on the sensitivity of the site and the type of construction.

Most of these impacts are equally relevant to recharge schemes and have, consequently, already been described in some detail in Section 7.9. Examples of mitigation measures identified in connection with groyne schemes at UK sites on the Holderness coast, Humberside, and at Eastbourne, East Sussex, are given in Boxes 8.13 and 8.14.

In addition to the mitigation measures shown in Box 8.12, other design modifications should also be considered to ensure that environmental enhancement opportunities are identified and maximised. A few examples of potential enhancement opportunities are given below:-

* the planting of dune-building vegetation can be carried out in order to enhance the landward side of a sandy beach (see Section 9.1)
* the quality of accesses can be improved in order to aid safe launching operations and encourage certain uses or users
* the material, and the type, size and location of sub-tidal structures can encourage crustaceans to use the habitat; possibly of value to commercial fisheries.

8.9   CONSTRUCTION

8.9.1   Introduction

The construction of beach control works falls into two broad categories. These are:

* works using land-based plant and techniques
* works using water-borne plant and techniques.

The decision as to the technique and plant to be used on a particular project is dependent on the following factors:

1.   Access and working areas - limited access to the site may prevent the use of heavy plant or the delivery of bulk materials by road. Within the site the use of heavy plant may be limited by a rocky or soft foreshore, the strength of existing structures or by a lack of suitable working areas.

2. Tidal range - the "tidal window" available for construction will determine whether land-based operations are practicable.

3. Foreshore and nearshore levels - the levels of the foreshore will determine whether land-based operations are possible and, for seaborne operations, determine the size (draught) of plant that can be deployed on the works.

4. Exposure of site - this will determine the size and type of plant that can be used and whether particular arrangements are required to safeguard equipment during storm conditions.

5. Environmental constraints - construction activities and techniques may be limited due to the potential effects on the public, and flora and fauna.

6. Availability of materials - haul distances and routes for bulk materials will determine whether deliveries by land or sea are appropriate.

8.9.2 Outline of construction methods

Construction techniques for the various types of beach control works covered in this section are discussed below.

Detached breakwaters

These structures may be constructed using either land-based or seaborne techniques. The decision as to the method is largely dependent upon the tidal range and foreshore levels at the site. Activities can be severely constrained by the tide. The tidal window can vary from a few hours per day upwards and where construction works remain exposed over the high water period it may be necessary to repair damage and clean up before work recommences.

Land-based operations may be possible where the breakwater is to be constructed on the foreshore. If required, the core and filter layers can simply be delivered in dump trucks running across the foreshore or along specially constructed causeways. The armourstone may be delivered using the same vehicles and placed using mechanical grabs. Alternatively armourstone may be delivered by seagoing barge and placed on the foreshore.

Alternatively it may be necessary to construct breakwaters using floating plant. If a composite structure is required, then the material for the core is commonly placed from self unloading barges. The construction of the filter layers is restricted to the use of side unloading or flat-deck barges which can place material with greater accuracy than split, bottom door or tilting barges. Alternatively, filter layers can be placed using rock trays. For the armour layer, particularly for rock over one tonne and concrete armour units, derrick barges or pontoon-mounted cranes are commonly used so that armour units are placed individually to achieve a stable structure of the required profile. For lighter armour the use of hydraulic grabs is a possibility.

Table 8.6 Examples of typical impacts of beach control structures during construction

POTENTIAL IMPACTS[1][2] DURING CONSTRUCTION	BEACH CONTROL STRUCTURES					
	Groynes	Detached Breakwater	Shore Connected Breakwater	Modified Seawalls/Revetment	Sills	Beach Drainage Systems
Natural Environment						
Disruption to fauna and flora due to machinery use, trampling and excavation	—		—	—	—	—
Smothering of fauna and flora due to deposition of material	—	—	—		—	
Smothering of fauna and flora due to increase in suspended sediment	—	—	—		—	
Destruction of habitat	—	—	—	—	—	
Noise disturbance to birds	—	—	—	—		
Impact on timber source	—					
Human Environment						
Restricted area for beach use	—	—	—	—	—	—
Restricted access onto or along beach	—	—	—	—	—	—
Public safety during plant movements	—	—	—	—	—	—
Unsightly and unconfined sites	—	—	—	—	—	—
Restricted access to inshore fishing ground	—	—	—		—	
Local economy, conflict with holiday tourist season	—	—	—	—	—	—
Disruption to commercial activities (e.g. local concessions)	—	—	—	—	—	—
Local employment generation	+	+	+	+		
Inshore navigational hazard	—	—	—		—	
Damage to designated archaeological sites	—	—	—	—	—	
Environmental Quality						
Increase in turbidity	—	—	—		—	
Accidental spillage of polluting material	—	—	—	—	—	—
Physical Environment						
Damage to designated geological sites	—	—	—	—	—	—

Notes: [1] Impacts will be dependent on the sensitivity of the resource
[2] — Adverse impact   + Beneficial impact

Table 8.7 Examples of typical impacts of beach control structures during scheme life

POTENTIAL IMPACTS[1][2] DURING SCHEME LIFE	Groynes	Detached Breakwater	Shore Connected Breakwater	Modified Seawalls/Revetment	Sills	Beach Drainage Systems
Natural Environment						
Change in wave climate and sedimentation rates affecting fauna and flora	±	±	±	±	±	
Erosion downdrift of works caused by disruption to natural sediment supply	—	—	—	—	—	
Barrier to passage of fish and invertebrates	—	—	—		—	
Creation of new habitat	+	+	+			
Disruption to benthos		—	—			—
Human Environment						
Restriction of access on to or along beach	—		—	—	—	
Creation of amenity facility				+		
Safety of beach users and swimmers	—	±	—		—	
Visual intrusion	±	±	±	±	±	
Reduction in inshore fishing grounds	—	—	—	—		
Reduced risk of flooding/coastal erosion	+	+	+	+	+	+
Nearshore navigation hazard	—	—	—		—	
Environmental Quality						
Litter and debris trap	—	—	—	—	—	
Substrate for algae	—	—	—	—	—	

Notes:
   (1)   Impacts will be dependent on the sensitivity of the resource
   (2)   — Negative   + Positive   ± Positive or negative

Box 8.12 *Examples of mitigation measures requiring consideration during the construction and operation of beach control structures*

A number of mitigation measures should be considered during each phase of development. These may include the following:

CONSTRUCTION PHASE

Natural Environment

- Avoid sensitive times of year for invertebrates, birds and fish
- Avoid designated sites
- Re-instate disturbed vegetation

Human Environment

- Confine and contain working sites
- Provide alternative access
- Avoid busy stretches of beach during holiday periods
- Patrol beach during plant and rock movements
- Avoid designated archaeological sites
- Use 'access corridors' and 'waiting areas' to control movement of construction shipping
- Ensure wide dissemination of information (e.g. local press, national fishing press, information boards)
- Use fishing liaison skippers on marine construction vessels
- Discuss with fishermen the appropriate timing or programming assignments of beach works
- Provide temporary coverage to exposed archaeological sites (e.g. matting) to prevent damage to site by construction plant

Physical Environment

- Create wave absorbing rather than wave reflecting structures
- Use permeable materials
- Minimise longshore effects of control structures

OPERATION PHASE

Natural Environment

- Create new habitats to replace those lost

Human Environment

- Provide handrailing on promenades and steps
- Provide notices explaining hazards
- Provide access over or around structures
- Provide navigation markers
- Disseminate information to inform coastal users of any new bathymetric conditions

Seaborne construction is more sensitive to weather and sea conditions and operations will be suspended when conditions are such that cranes and derricks cannot operate safely.

Further details on the construction of breakwaters may be found in the *Manual on the Use of Rock in Coastal and Shoreline Engineering* (CIRIA/CUR, 1991).

Shore connected breakwaters

The comments on the construction of detached breakwaters also apply to the shore connected breakwaters, although floating plant is not generally required.

Box 8.13   *Environmental mitigation measures - coast protection works along the Holderness Coast, Humberside*

Among the mitigation measures suggested for the construction of groynes at Great Cowden (Figure 1) and Hornsea (Figure 2) on the Holderness coast of Humberside were the following:

- reinstatement and landscaping new access point for plant to provide future foot access from the caravan park
- temporary access to be provided during construction with permanent points of access over completed groynes
- liaison with RAF Cowden to ensure target practice is suspended while barges are delivering rock
- prohibition on transport of rocks by road
- skipper to ensure protection of fisheries interests.

Figure 1   *Rock groynes and rock revetment at Mappleton, Humberside (1.5km north of Great Cowden) (courtesy Posford Duvivier)*

Figure 2   *Hornsea Terminal Service protecting the cliff slope/groyne intersection Humberside (courtesy Posford Duvivier)*

CIRIA Report 153

Box 8.14   *Environmental mitigation measures - coast protection scheme, Eastbourne, E. Sussex*

A review of the environmental implications of the various options for coastal defence at Eastbourne identified the following potential environmental mitigation measures associated with the construction of groynes:

- careful siting of site offices to reduce disruption to tourism
- safe means of access over the groynes
- marking of structures to ensure no risk to inshore navigation and fishing vessels
- use of timber (as existing) rather than rock to maintain current landscape characteristics.

Figure 1   *Aerial view of groyne field at the western end of Eastbourne*

Seawalls and revetments

These structures are generally constructed using land-based techniques. Construction of seawalls using concrete and steel sheet piling follows standard civil engineering construction techniques, however, access both to and along the site may limit the size and type of plant that can be deployed.

Armour for rock revetments can be delivered to site by either road transport or by seagoing barge. With both forms of transport it is common to stockpile rock adjacent to the site prior to placing using a grab attached to a crane or the bucket of a hydraulic excavator.

Groynes

Groynes may be constructed from rock, steel piling, concrete or timber and are, in general, built using land-based techniques. Comments covering the construction of seawalls and revetments apply equally to groynes and, in particular, the tidal window available to construct the seaward end of the groyne may be very limited.

9 Further management methods

9.1 DUNE MANAGEMENT

Active management of dunes can be a cost-effective and environmentally-friendly method of defence on sandy coasts. Indeed this is essentially the approach adopted over much of the length of the vulnerable coastline of The Netherlands. Dunes act both as a barrier against flooding by the sea, and as a reservoir of sand, replenished when beach levels are high, and able to provide a feed of extra material to the beach during winter storms (see Figure 9.1).

Dune management may consist of:

- reducing/eliminating damage to natural dunes by human activities
- improving the natural capacity of dunes to attract and store sand
- artificially adding material to dunes or creating new dunes.

Potential advantages of dune management are:

- producing an aesthetically pleasing and environmentally friendly beach
- reducing the need for expensive defence structures.

Potential disadvantages include:

- the need for regular monitoring and intervention
- labour-intensive management techniques (e.g. planting/fencing)
- public concerns about safety of dune/beach system in extreme events
- limitation of access and uses of beach (e.g. parking restrictions)
- nuisance of increased wind-blown sand where hinterland is developed.

Figure 9.1   *Sand dune material reservoir Barry Buddon, Tayside (courtesy HR Wallingford)*

9.1.1 Formation and maturation

Interaction between foreshore and dune system

The beach and dune systems are inter-related and thus management of one has repercussions for the other, material being naturally exchanged between the two systems. When sand dries on the foreshore, the particles are no longer cohesive and may be picked up and transported to the dunes by the wind. Conversely, the dune system acts as a sand reservoir. Sand released from dunes, eroded by wave action during storm events, replaces that lost from the foreshore and helps raise and flatten the beach profile.

Role of wind/wave energy

The nucleus for dune formation is often an obstacle on the strand line of the upper beach, such as a pile of driftwood or seaweed. Sand particles carried along by the wind are deposited on the windward side of the obstacle. The pile of sand increases in size until the tidal litter is buried and the surface of the pile is smooth and the wind resistance no longer enhanced. Further accumulation of sand is unlikely unless pioneer vegetation colonises the embryo dune.

Embryo dunes are highly unstable; their form and fate is governed by both wave and wind energies. Embryo dunes will only have a chance of maturing into vegetated stable dunes if they develop in an area above the mean high water spring mark. At elevations below this point, the time interval between successive tidal inundations is too short to allow colonisation by grass pioneers, such as sea lyme grass (*Elymus arenarius*). Without the presence of plants to stabilise the shifting sands and increase the accretion rate by trapping sand amongst their aerial shoots, the embryo dune cannot grow vertically or laterally. Furthermore, the unstabilised dune may be destroyed by the wave energy of the next tide that reaches it through the remobilisation of the sand and displacement of the litter nucleus.

A dune will grow in height as long as accretion outpaces erosion by wind. The degree of erosion of the crest depends on the climate and supply of sand. The velocity of winds tends to become stronger at higher elevations, hence the wind erosion on the dune crest increases as the dune accretes vertically. Humidity, rainfall and temperature are other climatic variables which effect dune morphology. In mild areas with adequate rain supply, erosion is reduced and the growing season is extended, thus enhancing the entrapment of wind-blown sand. Due to the differences in these aspects of climate and sand supply, the maximum height of dunes, and hence the degree of sea defence they can provide, varies markedly around the world.

The vertical growth of a dune may cease if a dune ridge develops in front of it and intercepts the wind-blown sand. This is particularly common on accreting sandy shores, where successive dune ridges are formed in front of the existing ones. The result is a series of relatively low, parallel ridges.

If the wind is variable in direction, the shape and movement of the dune is irregular. However, under conditions of more constant wind direction, its morphology and movement are more predictable. The windward side of the dune is steeper than the leeward side (see Figure 9.1) and the dune tends to creep in the direction of the wind, normally landwards, as the sand on the windward slopes is blown over the top of the dune to the leeward side. This process can have serious consequences for human settlements landwards of the dunes; burying buildings, infrastructure and croplands.

Role of vegetation

The grasses that colonise the mobile sands of the embryo dunes are crucial for the development of higher more stable dunes which provide better coastal protection. Colonisation begins by the establishment of plants from fragments of rhizomes or seeds which may be present in the litter layer which formed the nucleus of the embryo dune. Tidal litter aids the growth of these pioneers by ameliorating the natural factors which limit the establishment of dune vegetation i.e. through stabilising the mobile sands, acting as a source of nutrients and increasing the soil moisture of the embryo dune. Management techniques can enhance the development of embryo dunes by reproducing the effects of detritus on the strand line.

Figure 9.2 shows how grasses, such as marram grass (*Ammophila arenaria*), spread vegetatively as new tussocks of shoots sprouting from the rhizomes. These extra shoots increase the rate of accretion by enhancing wind resistance and sand trapping. To prevent the shoots being buried by the wind-blown sand, the rhizomes of the grass grow upwards and outwards to keep pace with accretion. This radiating network of rhizomes improves the stability of the sand heap to wind and wave action. Marram grass is thought to be able to cope with rates of dune accretion of up to 1 metre per year (Ranwell, 1981), but if accretion ceases, marram grass dies back.

The character of dunes changes with maturation (see Figure 9.3). Embryo dunes are highly unstable and have a high salt content. Conditions become more stable and less saline with the firm establishment of marram grass and the salt dissolving action of rainwater percolation; *yellow dune*, is a common term for this stage of dune development. Further maturation leads to an increase in the organic content of the substrate and an increase in plant species. Dunes of this age are described as *grey dunes*. Ageing is often accompanied by a reduction in nutrient concentrations due to leaching, and conditions are also more acidic than in younger dunes as the calcium rich shell fragments are dissolved and removed from the system.

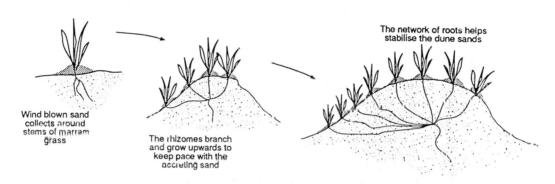

Figure 9.2   *Stylised diagram to illustrate the role of pioneer grasses in embryo dune formation*

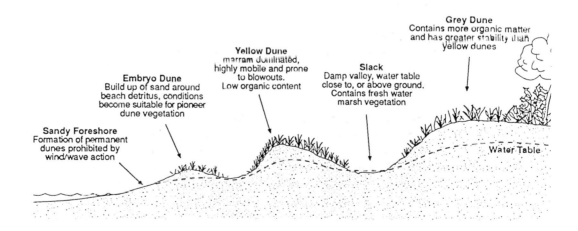

Figure 9.3   *Cross-section through an idealised dune system*

In the valleys between dune ridges, soil conditions are much more moist and freshwater ponds may be found when the piezometric surface is above the ground. These damp valley areas, known as *slacks*, support a distinct plant community and are important for amphibians and as a source of water to animals.

9.1.2 Types and causes of erosion

Although wind and wave energy are at the origin of the dune formation process, they can also cause the erosion of the dune system. There are two distinct types of erosion that result from these two driving forces: head erosion caused by wave energy and deflation produced by wind.

Head erosion

Head erosion occurs at the seaward edge of the dune system during episodic wave events. The waves erode the base of the dunes and the unsupported upper part then collapses, leaving a steep unvegetated surface which is vulnerable to wind erosion.

Even behind a healthy sandy beach, dunes can be severely eroded in a winter season or by an exceptional storm. Losses to the beach may reach 50 cubic metres per metre run, and take several years to be replaced during calmer conditions. If the beach itself is eroding, head erosion rates can reach 5 to 10 metres per year and continue at that rate for many years.

Deflation

Deflation is vertical, wind-driven erosion resulting in a lowering of the dune crest or blowouts (i.e. localised sites of major sand loss from unvegetated surfaces) on dune sides (see Figure 9.4). By far the most important factor leading to deflation is damage to dune vegetation. However, lowering the water table may also exacerbate wind erosion and lead to deflation. With the exception of episodic events of high wind velocity deflation is almost always generated by human activities rather than natural processes. In some respects, this is fortunate for coastal managers, as it is easier to modify human behaviour than natural events, and hence deflation should be controllable to a large extent. The following human activities can cause deflation:

- recreation - trampling by humans and livestock, off road vehicles, car parking
- military training
- pipeline installation
- sand extraction
- overgrazing by livestock/rabbits
- groundwater extraction which lowers the cohesive surface and causes salinisation.

The first five activities, and to a certain extent the last, all trigger deflation by damaging dune vegetation, and hence its ability to enhance accretion and prevent wind erosion by reducing surface wind speeds. Groundwater extraction from dune systems has been an important source of public water supply in Dutch coastal dune areas for more than a century. Excessive extraction increases the depth to which erosion is possible, by lowering the cohesive surface and adversely effecting plant growth, due to increased water stress and salt water incursion. Methods of avoiding or controlling these human impacts are given in Section 9.1.5.

9.1.3 Management techniques for dunes

In the first instance, possible options for controlling or managing the cause of erosion should be examined. If such control or management is not possible, reactive management of the dune system might be considered. Broadly speaking the task of managing dunes as part of a coastal defence can be divided into two types of activity. The primary task is to ensure that the dunes are not breached or overrun by the sea, which could lead to flooding or damage to the hinterland. The storm surge of 1953, for example, broke through dunes in a number of locations along the east coast of England, and in The Netherlands, with disastrous consequences. This type of dune management often has to be undertaken over substantial lengths of coast in order to produce a satisfactory standard of defence and is largely restricted to operations on the upper beach and most seaward parts of a dune system.

A supplementary but often vital management activity is to repair or prevent damage to dunes caused by wind action (e.g. localised blow-outs). Such work is often only required in specific

Figure 9.4   *Dune erosion by deflation, Traeth Harlech, Gwynedd (courtesy HR Wallingford)*

problem areas, for example in the vicinity of access tracks, although occasionally larger areas require treatment. This second type of management is closely related to environmental management of a dune system (see Section 9.1.5), and the techniques applied are often the same. From the viewpoint of coastal defence, the importance of such repairs is to avoid weak points in the dune belt, which might allow a breach to develop in extreme sea conditions.

In a few situations, however, a further problem caused by wind can arise which requires action. If a sandy beach accretes significantly, as a result of either natural processes or human intervention, then wind-blown sand can become a nuisance, accumulating on coastal roads or in seafront properties and gardens. In historical times, this phenomenon has ruined extensive areas of agricultural land, and even overwhelmed villages (e.g. Kenfig in South Wales). The same general management methods used to repair wind damage to established dunes have been used to tackle such problems (e.g. the use of fences and/or the planting of vegetation to trap and retain the wind blown sand).

As a first rule of thumb, it is unlikely that any attempt to maintain or strengthen a dune system will be successful if the beach in front of the dunes erodes. It is usually the case, therefore, that good dune management will be innately linked to good beach management. By increasing the width and height of the beach in front of dunes, it is likely that the dunes themselves will prosper. Many of the methods to protect dunes against the sea are therefore extensions to the methods described previously for managing sandy beaches. The following provides further information on methods where dunes are included in the overall management of a sandy coastline.

Dune nourishment

In The Netherlands, Germany and the USA, a large number of schemes to enlarge the dunes, and the beach in front of them, have been carried out. This approach to beach management now dominates the coast protection strategy in The Netherlands, where alternative methods such as the construction of seawalls have largely fallen out of favour. In many cases this approach relies on periodic, large-scale importation of sand to provide the basic materials for the defence scheme. As for beach recharge schemes (see Chapter 6), the nourishment of dunes requires an appropriate design to be developed in advance. The most important consideration is the resulting cross-section of the beach/dune system. Dunes tend to be naturally formed by the finer sand particles from the beach, and the question of a suitable grain size is therefore rather less important when considering dune construction or enhancement.

Groynes and breakwaters

The use of control structures to modify the hydraulic regime of a beach has been discussed in Chapter 8. Many of the considerations related to the use of these structures on sand beaches apply equally to the situation where dunes are present. For example, the use of groynes to reduce the rate of longshore sediment transport along a stretch of coastline, and hence to encourage beach accretion in a particular area, will provide a higher, wider beach which will normally lead to a healthier dune system quite naturally. However, the use of groynes could lead to problems elsewhere in the downdrift supply of sand. Shore connected breakwaters may be valuable when dealing with the management of dunes near the mouths of estuaries, acting to control the tidal currents which dominate the morphological development of the coast.

They may also be used to mitigate "end effect" problems, for example where a dune system adjoins a solid seawall. The whole issue of the interaction of dunes with adjacent stretches of coast and their defences, is considered in more detail in Section 9.1.4 below.

On an open and relatively straight stretch of coast, there is a need to take care of details at the point where a groyne meets the active face of a dune. It is good practice to ensure that the groyne berm level does not project significantly above the natural beach level. This will prevent the groyne interfering with the natural build-up of sand against the dune face. Thought should also be given to extending the groyne landward into the face of the dune system to prevent outflanking during severe storm events. Any necessary repairs to the dune system will need to be undertaken promptly if this option is pursued.

The use of detached breakwaters to control drift overcomes this latter problem, and also provides a measure of protection to the dune face against wave attack, especially if the breakwaters are situated on the upper part of the beach. Care is needed, however, to ensure that potential dune erosion, either in the gaps between breakwaters or at the end of the breakwater system, is anticipated and can be managed.

Armouring the dune face

At many sites around the UK coast, dune erosion has been tackled by direct armouring of the dune face, either by conventional solid seawalls, or by the use of more permeable revetments (e.g. of rock or gabions). Such armouring may be designed to protect just the lower part of the dune face, or extend a considerable distance up it. The obvious advantage of such a management option is to provide an increased safety margin against flooding or erosion. Where a dune system has largely disappeared, or the beach is likely to continue to erode, this may be a possible option (see also *Novel types of dune management* below).

However there are a number of disadvantages which have to be considered. Such armouring will usually separate the dunes from the beach, preventing the free interchange of sand. As a consequence the beach will be unable to draw upon a reservoir of extra sand in severe storms, often leading to beach lowering in front of the structure. There will also be changes in the character of dunes, with primary sand-binding grasses (e.g. marram) declining as the supply of fresh sand reduces. This will often lead to increased problems of wind damage, because the capacity of dunes to self-heal is diminished. Armouring the dune faces has adverse impacts on the environmental attributes of a coast (e.g. amenity, landscape, and ecology) and erosion problems often occur at the junction point between armoured and natural dune faces.

The extent to which problems arise as a result of armouring a dune face will vary greatly depending on the particular site and the extent of the armouring. In a few places, high concrete seawalls built between the dunes and the beach have been covered over by new dunes. At this stage, the wall continues to provide a second line of defence, but does not seriously interfere with natural beach and dune processes. However such examples are much less common than those where the beach in front of the wall has dropped in level, with little beach width above the high water mark. This situation prevents new dunes forming and greatly reduces the quantities of sand which can be dried and transported inshore by winds.

Lower, and sometimes temporary, protection to the dune face has been used in a number of places (e.g. brushwood thatching of the dune face, see Box 9.1). These act both to trap wind-blown sand and hence promote embryo dune formation, whilst protecting the backshore against modest wave action. Low rock revetments on the upper beach have also been successfully used to provide local protection to dunes, for example in front of access tracks to the beach (Colquhoun, 1968).

Use of sand fences and vegetation

The natural rate of dune rebuilding, following damage by a storm, can be accelerated by using sand fences and the planting of suitable vegetation. Both of these methods will decrease surface wind velocities. The same methods can also be used to repair localised damage to the dunes, caused by excessive trampling, or even to create a new dune system landward of a nourished beach. Guidance on the materials used and on the management methods can be found in a number of publications, notably Ranwell and Boar (1986). Guidance is also available from handbooks and information sheets have been produced by several organisations, including the British Trust for Conservation Volunteers (1979). Box 9.1 shows a recommended staged approach to dune building using permeable sand fences, based on experiments in the USA. Information on such methods can also be found in Section 9.1.4 below.

Box 9.1 *Sand fences*

Sand fences are erected to aid accretion. They should be positioned at a sharp angle to the direction of the prevailing winds, as sand will only be deposited if the fence is a barrier to air flow. The way in which the dune rebuilds can be manipulated by deploying fences in a time sequence. The positioning and timing of the fences determines whether the accretion will increase the width or height of the dune field (see figure below). Hence, the setting of fences is an ongoing process, which requires prior planning.

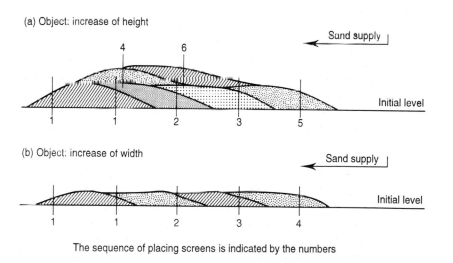

The sequence of placing screens is indicated by the numbers

Figure 1   *The utilisation of fences to: A - gain height; and B - increase the width of the dune field (from Blumenthal, 1964)*

Continued

Box 9.1   *Continued*

Solid fencing would cause scour of the sand on the windward side of the fence and around the ends. Permeable barriers are much more effective at accelerating accretion. The optimum porosity is approximately 50%, with effectiveness decreasing significantly as porosity increases to over 65%. Figures 2 and 3 show some of the various materials which have been used as sand fences, including old Christmas trees and wooden paling fences. It is best to select biodegradable materials as it is difficult to retrieve the fences due to burial.

The practical details of how to construct and position sand fences are competently covered by Brookes (1979).

Figure 2   *Sand fence at East Head, Chichester Harbour, Sussex (courtesy HR Wallingford)*

Figure 3   *Integrated attempt to repair a blow-out on a sand dune at Aberffrau, Anglesey (courtesy HR Wallingford)*

Figure 9.5   *Two views of a low fence of pine tree thinnings being used to encourage foreshore building near Allonby, Cumbria (courtesy HR Wallingford)*

Figure 9.6   *Sand fences, Prestatyn, Clwyd (courtesy HR Wallingford)*

From the viewpoint of managing a beach, this can be an environmentally attractive method of restoring an adequate standard of defence. However, these methods have limitations. Sand fences will only be effective if they can be established above the normal reach of tides and wave run-up. Even if a suitable wide area exists on the backshore, sand fences can be destroyed soon after their installation by storm wave action, along with the embryonic dunes they have created. So too can any recently planted vegetation, if it is within reach of the waves. It can be appreciated, therefore, that such works can rarely be regarded as permanent. For this reason, the general approach is to use low-cost materials for fencing (e.g. brushwood) rather than high-quality textile meshes or planked fence units (see Figures 9.5 and 9.6). Even so, the considerable labour costs involved in erecting and repairing the fences, and planting vegetation, often make this type of management difficult to organise. Many of the dune-restoration schemes around the UK coast have been carried out by conservation volunteers, largely because of the ecological value of the dunes, rather than as a pure coastal defence initiative.

Novel types of dune management

In recent years there have been a number of attempts to improve the standard of safety against flooding provided by dunes, whilst allowing them to develop as naturally as possible. The general idea has been to provide a hidden defence, set in place under or behind the dunes themselves.

Gabions (see also *Armouring the dune face* above) have been successfully used at a number of dune fields (e.g. Dawlish Warren, Devon and Hunstanton, Norfolk). They may be used to block off any small breaches of a dune ridge where the backshore is temporarily within reach of the highest tide. Gabions are also used to protect the seaward face of the dunes. The baskets are placed seawards of the dune field to give some protection against head erosion by dissipating wave energy before it reaches the dune face. As gabion revetments tend to be covered over by wind-blown sand, they may provide a second line of defence against erosion for many years. However, if they are placed in areas which suffer from frequent episodes of erosion, their lifespan will be greatly reduced, therefore they are only suitable in areas subject to infrequent wave attack.

Clay embankments have been used to protect hinterland flooding. These clay walls are normally situated at the back of the dune field as a secondary line of defence to protect human interests. A novel way of using clay was employed to protect the village of Sizewell, Suffolk (English Nature, 1992). The dune system fronting the village is its only form of sea defence, and the protection provided was decreasing due to erosion. Hard defences would have been detrimental to the wildlife interest of the site and so a hidden form of soft engineering was deemed to be more appropriate. To improve the degree of flood defence that the dunes provided, a dune at the back of the system was raised in height and made less permeable, by the insertion of a clay core. A trench was dug out of the dune and filled with clay, sand was replaced on top of the clay and stabilised by the replanting of marram grass and the erection of sand fences. At present, the scheme seems to be effective.

Effects on adjacent frontages

One of the major considerations in the active use and management of dunes is the interaction with adjacent stretches of coast. It is not possible to simply terminate a beach/dune system at one point and begin an alternative defence scheme. Where the situation has arisen in the past, there have been problems of dune erosion at the junction point, threatening to cause flooding behind both types of defence.

In many natural situations, dunes are restricted to pocket beaches, when the rocky headlands on either side act as natural end points to the beach/dune system. Here the active management of dunes can usually be carried out without risk to adjacent stretches of coast.

Elsewhere, however, a dune system may occupy a substantial length of coastline, only part of which may require a high standard of protection from flooding or erosion. A number of factors have to be considered in this situation as part of the consideration of managing a beach/dune system:

- effect of defences located on adjacent coast (e.g. groynes) on sand supply to beach/dune system

- consequences of sudden, temporary, retreat of dune/beach system on adjacent coast
- effects of wind-blown sand on adjacent frontage
- danger of access and disturbance to dunes (e.g. trampling) at junction point.

Typical solutions to these problems include a low rock revetment, a groyne system and/or periodic recharge or recycling. Wind-blown sand into roads or promenades can be reduced by fencing (perhaps during the winter season only), with the sweepings being returned to the beach.

9.1.4   Design considerations

Behaviour of dunes during storms

During a storm, waves will attack a dune if the tide and beach levels are such that waves can reach it. Under wave attack, sand is moved from the front of the dune into the nearshore zone where it is deposited as a bar. The larger waves break over this bar and the severity of attack is thereby reduced.

The volume of material moved from the dunes during a storm, therefore, depends upon the following:

- incident waves (height and period)
- duration of the storms
- water levels
- foreshore and nearshore slopes
- grading of the beach and dune sand
- changes in longshore transport along the coast (see Section 2.4).

In general, the following factors will encourage dune loss; high waves, long period waves, steep foreshore and nearshore slopes and long storm duration.

Dunes as a coastal defence

The performance of a dune and reliance on it as a coastal defence depends upon a number of factors including:

1. Sand supply - there should be at least as much sand supplied to the system as is being lost onshore through wind-blown transport and lost offshore and alongshore through wave-driven transport. If this is not the case, the dunes will erode or retreat inland and will not recover fully after storms.

2. Discontinuities in the longshore supply of sand (e.g. due to the presence of a groyne or seawall) - these will tend to reduce the ability of dunes to withstand wave attack immediately downdrift of the discontinuity.

3. Vegetation cover - this must be sufficient to trap a proportion of the sand being blown onshore.

4. Dune size - in general, the greater the volume of sand within the dune, the greater the storm the system can withstand.

5. Exposure - the exposure of the site may be such that dunes cannot fully recover after extreme events.

Assessing the performance of sand dunes as a coastal defence is an extremely difficult task. A considerable volume of research has been carried out into the response of natural and nourished dunes to severe sea conditions, particularly the effect of storm surges, in both The Netherlands and the USA. The first models were largely of simplified and empirical nature, but later advances have included a probabilistic approach to be adopted and a better representation of factors such as the duration of a storm event. Existing assessment methods assume that the front face of the dune, the beach, foreshore and nearshore zone attain an equilibrium profile. The profile is then located such that the volume of erosion equals the volume of deposition. The available methods include:

- a very simple empirical method by Hallermeier and Rhodes (1988)

- a more sophisticated empirical method by Vellinga *et al* (CUR/TAW, 1989), known as the CUR/TAW method, summarised in Box 5.3

- finite difference models developed in the United States by Kriebel (1986); these models solve simplified governing equations relating surf zone hydrodynamics and sediment transport.

The first method has been developed predominately from field data along the US Gulf and Atlantic coasts and it is questionable whether it is appropriate for use in other locations. The CUR/TAW method is a more generally applicable formula and, being relatively straightforward, can be readily applied. The third method is complex and should only be used with specialist advice.

Maintenance of dunes

Dune crests may be maintained using the techniques discussed in Section 11.6 for the control of wind blown sand on natural frontages. In addition, it may be appropriate to consider the use of beach recharge and/or beach control structures described in Chapters 7 and 8 to protect the dune front and foreshore.

9.1.5   Environmental management

Sand dunes are a valuable coastal habitat not only in terms of their coastal defence function but also because of their importance as a recreational source and as a natural habitat for a wide variety of plants and animals, including any rare species.

When managing, designing or modifying beaches in front of or up/downdrift of dune systems, various environmental requirements of the dune system must be considered. Some of these are outlined below:

1.   Dunes are essentially mobile features and require the space to migrate inland and/or to build out seaward during periods of increased sand supply (see Section 9.1.1).

2.   Any sand beach recharge must be consistent with the existing supply in terms of the physical and chemical composition. This is important when considering the type of vegetation communities present on the existing dune system. A change in physical composition (e.g. sediment size, distribution) or chemical composition (e.g. acidity of the sediment) brought about by introducing a different type of sand to the existing beach could have an adverse effect on existing dune vegetation.

3.   Trampling and vehicle movements, e.g. associated with the recreational use of an improved beach, will lead to a progressive degradation of the dune system and should be avoided through careful management (e.g. fencing to encourage visitors to use certain areas of the dune which are least sensitive to disturbance; the use of boardwalks to prevent trampling of vegetation; and the use of woodchippings or broken shells to reduce erosion of sand from footpaths).

4.   Any mechanical plant involved in beach or dune regrading must avoid areas which are vegetated. It should also avoid dune slacks (see Figure 9.3), which, as wetland areas, have a higher plant diversity than the surrounding mobile sand areas. Access points should be kept to a minimum and temporary paths should be constructed to minimise damage. Heavy mechanical plant should not be used within the duned areas and, if necessary, repairs should be carried out by manual labour.

5. Control of shrubs may be necessary in dune systems where certain species are becoming invasive. One such species in the United Kingdom is sea buckthorn, which was introduced into many dune systems for stabilisation purposes. Once established, this species can spread rapidly to become a nuisance.

   In some situations, however, scrub can be advantageous in that it stabilises dunes, controls access and provides shelter and nesting sites for birds, invertebrates and mammals. It is therefore important to consider the requirements of each dune system separately.

6. Certain dune systems support rare plant species which require specific conditions, such as bare sand, in order to colonise areas of dune habitat. This can be achieved using management techniques, such as destabilisation, where vegetation is removed from an area of dune, thereby allowing new species to colonise.

7. Controlled grazing can improve the diversity of vegetation by eliminating scrub and invasive species. The type of stock, density of stocking levels and season and length of grazing can all be varied to support or manage different vegetation types. Areas grazed extensively by rabbits encourage dune grassland to persist. Grazing is considered to be advantageous in that it encourages diversity of vegetation but can also be detrimental where numbers of rabbits are excessive and vegetation is eliminated leaving bare patches vulnerable to blow-outs.

9.2   ROCK BEACHES

A rock beach may be defined as a permeable slope or mound formed from quarried rock used for coast protection. The rock will generally be placed to seaward slopes shallower than 1:4, but is expected to move under wave attack, with the beach profile re-shaping under design wave conditions to shallower slopes. Even after this profile change, some rock on the slope will continue to move under wave attack, but the profile should reach equilibrium, when it is termed dynamically stable.

A rock beach may be attractive at sites where little conventional amenity use is made of the beach/inter-tidal area, and/or where the coastline is generally rocky. This form of construction may be most easily be considered as a rather coarser shingle beach, or as a shallower rock revetment or mound. Some of the advantages of this form of structure are discussed in Section 9.2.5.

The response of a rock beach to waves falls between that of an armoured mound or slope, and that of a shingle beach. Rock on such structures will generally fall between 50mm and 500mm. Rock above 500mm is more likely to be used for revetments or rock armoured slopes, although these larger sizes could potentially be used for a rock beach in very exposed situations. Rock below 50mm will behave as shingle/gravel and may be treated accordingly (see Chapter 7).

The engineering use of quarried rock in dynamically stable slopes is relatively recent, and data and experience available for the analysis/design of these structures are as yet much less than for statically stable armoured slopes or mounds. Much of the information available is based on laboratory experiments, often from hydraulic model tests in wave flumes, or, more rarely, in wave basins. Where possible, empirical design methods have been fitted to the model test data to give simple design formulae, or limiting values for key design parameters.

Information on long-term behaviour of such engineered structures is still relatively sparse. The performance of any new structure that approaches or exceeds limits suggested here should be checked by hydraulic model tests. Such studies may also be used to optimise the selection of beach material, provide data for probabilistic calculations of structure response and to provide estimates of structure performance to substantially higher levels of confidence than is possible for simple empirical methods. Some information on the response of coarse natural beaches is available in the field and, if analyzed, could be used to support the design of new structures.

9.2.1 Design concept

The principal role of a rock beach will be to dissipate wave energy. In doing so, the structure is expected to re-shape by adjusting its profile to the incident wave action, but must not allow excessive wave overtopping over the beach crest, significant seepage through the beach ridge; or significant depletion of the beach material itself. The main design problems are therefore to estimate:

- conditions for onset of profile re-shaping
- extent of profile changes during severe storm events, particularly to the beach crest level, and the minimum beach thickness
- wave run-up/overtopping and/or percolation performances
- long-term changes to the beach profile
- lateral or long-shore movement of rock along the coastline.

Re-shaping of the beach profile under wave action, particularly under severe storms, is generally beneficial as the beach crest will often build upwards under the more severe storms, increasing overtopping resistance under all but the most severe storms. This mobility is likely to reduce in time unless the relative beach material size is small. The key aspect of the design of a structure is to ensure that sufficient mobile material will always be available to allow the profile changes without eroding through the beach to a lower layer, or without significant overtopping of the beach crest.

The movement of rock will however have two potentially retrograde effects. Firstly abrasion/attrition of the rock by continuing movement under wave action may lead to material loss, and hence reduction in the mean rock size and possibly a widening of the grading. These processes will reduce the resistance of the beach to wave action. This may be mitigated by selecting a rock source which is relatively resistant to abrasion loss, and/or increasing the design rock size to reduce mobility under frequently occurring wave conditions.

The second potential problems arises if severe wave action is oblique to the shoreline. Under these conditions, movement of rock up and down the profile will be accompanied by some movement along the structure, following the direction of long-shore transport. If wave attack is generally from one direction, continuing longshore transport may lead to denudation of the up-drift part of the structure. Again, this may be reduced by selecting a larger rock size to reduce the frequency and/or rate of longshore transport, by re-shaping the plan shape of the beach to reduce the relative obliquity of the wave attack, or by placing additional material at the up-drift end of the structure to provide a sufficient supply.

The principal parameters that influence the hydraulic performance and beach stability are:

- median rock size, given by the equivalent sieve size, D_{e50}, or the nominal median size, D_{n50} (defined as $(M_{50}/\rho_r)^{1/3}$), where M_{50} is the mass of individual armour rocks not exceeded by 50% (by mass) of all the rocks in a given grading and ρ_r is the rock mass density)
- rock grading, D_{85}/D_{15}
- thickness of permeable beach material, t_a
- initial beach slope, $\cot\alpha$
- crest freeboard relative to design water level, R_c
- permeability of the beach to wave action, perhaps given by the internal penetration length, λ_i
- relative wave height, $N_s = H_s/\Delta D_{n50}$
- relative mean wave period, $T_o = T_m(g/D_{n50})^{1/2}$, or sometimes as relative peak period, $T_{op} = T_p(g/D_{n50})^{1/2}$
- wave obliquity to the shoreline, β
- strength/resistance of the rock material against attrition.

The simplest categorisation of likely beach behaviour is suggested by Van der Meer (1988), based on the relative wave height $N_s = H_s/\Delta D_{n50}$, and relative wave period, $T_o = T_m(g/D_{n50})^{1/2}$.

Within the range of material sizes considered in this section, up to four categories might be considered:

$H_s/\Delta D_{n50}$	Structure/beach type
1 - 4	Statically stable rock slopes/mounds
3 - 6	Re-shaping rock slopes
6 - 20	Mobile rock slopes/beaches
15 - 500	Shingle/gravel beaches.

Relatively few practical rock beaches will fall into the first or last category, so this section is chiefly concerned with re-shaping and mobile rock slopes, given by $3 < H_s/\Delta D_{n50} < 20$.

It is important to note that the permeability of the beach will significantly influence its stability and hydraulic performance. In turn, beach permeability is strongly influenced by the median rock size, grading and proportion of fines. The design/analysis methods discussed below have been derived for reasonably narrow-graded material, say $D_{85}/D_{15} < 4$, without significant levels of fines. Wider graded material is likely to show worse hydraulic performance due to the reduced permeability of the rock slope to wave action and possible greater levels of movement/ re-shaping and is therefore not likely to be favoured as potential armouring material for a rock beach. The relative permeabilities of alternative beach materials or profiles could however be tested by calculating the internal wave-generated pore pressure penetration length, λ_i, using the method of Box 65 of CIRIA/CUR (1991).

9.2.2   Profile response

Design/analysis methods for rock beaches require the definition of the beach profile geometry. The principal dimensions for the vertical section or profile shown in Figure 9.7 are all related to the intersection point between the outer surface of the beach and the water level:

- crest height, h_c
- run-up length, l_r
- step length, l_s
- transition length, l_t
- crest length, l_c
- step height, h_s
- transition height, h_t.

The beach profile will respond to the water level and incident wave conditions, principally the significant wave height H_s, mean wave period T_m, and the number of waves in a given storm event N. In general an initially steep slope will be eroded at the water line. Some rock will be washed up to form a new crest and the rest will roll down towards the toe. On shallow slopes, more material may be washed up-slope, building a crest to approximately the 0.5% run-up limit if sufficient material is available.

For preliminary design purposes, beach profile changes may be estimated using empirical relationships and/or by profile models, some of which are available as computational models on PCs. The most comprehensive empirical relationships are given by the models BREAKWAT by Van der Meer (1988) and SHINGLE by Powell (1990), and the Van der Meer simplified method, as described briefly in Boxes 9.2, 9.3 and 9.4. Each of these methods gives the geometry of the new profile for a given set of wave conditions and initial profile.

9.2.3   Longshore transport

Any mobile beach will respond to wave obliquity, β, with beach material tending to move in the direction of longshore movement. On many rock beaches, this longshore movement will be insignificant for much of the time as wave conditions remain below a threshold level, or as waves approach the beach at small relative angles, say $\beta < 15°$. Beach material can move significantly under storm conditions and/or if frequent wave conditions are oblique to the beach.

Excessive longshore movement may lead to local denudation of the beach, with consequential erosion to sub-strata and/or increased overtopping. A number of simple empirical methods have been suggested to estimate conditions at the outset of significant longshore transport.

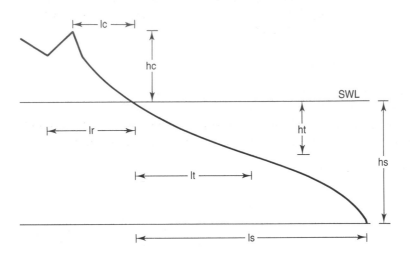

Figure 9.7   *Profile geometry parameters*

Burcharth and Frigaard (1988) tested longshore movements on the trunk and outer end of dynamically stable breakwaters under wave obliquities of $\beta = 15°$ to $30°$. They suggested simple limits for trunk section attacked by oblique waves of $H_s/\Delta D_{n50} < 3.5$ and $H_s/\Delta D_{n50} < 3.0$ for the roundhead. However, other unpublished tests carried out in a wave basin at HR Wallingford on a dynamically stable breakwater, showed significant longshore movement at $H_s/\Delta D_{n50} = 3.3$ and $\beta = 17°$. Comparison of these recommendations suggest that a limit might be set for the onset of longshore transport along the trunk section of $H_s/\Delta D_{n50} < 3.0$.

Box 9.2   *The BREAKWAT model*

The computational model of BREAKWAT uses empirical equations developed by Van der Meer (1988) for rock and riprap armouring on breakwaters, sea walls, and revetments. These relate the main geometrical parameters of the profile to wave conditions given by the wave parameters H_0 and T_0. The computational model may be used to calculate dynamically stable profiles where the manual method would be laborious. In each instance the beach profile is described by calculating the parameters outlined in Figure 9.4. The method is limited to different ranges for the main dimensionless parameters:

$0.01 < s_m = 2\pi H_s/gT_m^2 < 0.06$
$3 \leq H_s/\Delta D_{n50} \leq 500$ where $N_s = H_s/\Delta D_{n50}$ and $T_0 = T_m(g/D_{n50})^{1/2}$
$80 \leq N_s T_0 \leq 200,000$
$H_s/h_s \leq 0.6$.

The computational model has been fitted with warnings for when calculation parameters fall outside these or other ranges. Van der Meer (1988) reports that this model and the underlying equations have been verified against a number of experiments at small and large scales.

Experience of the use of this method, and supplementary studies on coarse rock mounds (Sievwright, 1994), suggests however that this method tends to over estimate the crest level and thus to under-predict wave overtopping. Where this aspect is important to the acceptable performance of the rock beach, additional studies using physical model tests will be required to give a reliable design.

Van der Meer and Veldman (1992) measured the number of stones moved per wave, $S(x)$, on a dynamically stable breakwater for $\beta = 25°$ and $50°$, and combine these results with those of Burcharth and Frigaard (1988). The transport rate $S(x)$ was then related to the relative wave height, N_s, and wave period T_{op} (where $N_s = H_s/\Delta D_{n50}$ and $T_{op} = T_p(g/D_{n50})^{1/2}$). This gave a limit for the onset of longshore movement, and then a rate of movement for more severe wave conditions for $15° < \beta < 35°$:

$$S(x) = 0 \text{ for } N_s T_{op} < 100 \tag{9.1}$$

$$S(x) = 0.000048 \ (N_s T_{op} - 100)^2 \text{ for } N_s T_{op} > 100 \tag{9.2}$$

At smaller or larger obliquities, that is for $\beta < 15°$, or $\beta > 35°$, the onset of longshore transport starts at more severe wave conditions, so the initial threshold rises:

$$S(x) = 0 \text{ for } N_s T_{op} < 180 \tag{9.3}$$

Box 9.3 *The SHINGLE model*

The SHINGLE model (see Box 5.4) was developed by Powell (1990) from the results of model tests and field data analysis on shingle-sized material. The empirical equations again relate the profile geometry to the initial profile and the main wave parameters.

The use of the equations, or of the computational model, is limited to different ranges, depending upon the wave steepness s_m. For $0.01 < s_m < 0.03$, use should be restricted to:

$20 \leq H_s/D_{e50} \leq 300$
$3000 \leq H_s T_m (g D_{e50}^3)^{1/2} \leq 55,000$
$1 \leq H_s^2/D_{e50}^3 L_m)^{1/2} \leq 1,200$
$1 \leq H_s^2/D_{e50} L_m \leq 18$

and for $0.03 < s_m < 0.06$, use should be restricted to:

$20 \leq H_s/D_{e50} \leq 300$
$5000 < H_s T_m (g D_{e50}^3)^{1/2} < 40,000$
$0.5 \leq H_s^2/D_{e50} L_m \leq 40$.

These methods, which are relatively simple, are based on a restricted series of studies and do not give any guidance on the response of structures that vary in the plan shape. Some measurements indicate higher rates of movements and/or onset of longshore transport at less severe wave conditions. Where these parameters are significant to the acceptable performance, physical model tests are recommended.

9.2.4   Use of analysis/design methods

The design of a rock beach, as of any other structure, requires the identification of the performance standards required and of the main restraints to its construction. The main numerically expressed parameters have been summarised above. Other particular restraints on the use of such structures are summarised in Section 9.2.5.

Three main levels of design tool may be used and they may be used at preliminary and/or detailed design phases. At its simplest, a rock beach may be specified on the basis of local experience, with rock sizes, layer thickness and plan layout based on similar structures with similar wave exposures. This however relies on there being sufficient experience available to allow interpolation to the new site, particularly of profile changes under storm conditions.

In some situations it may be possible to use the empirical methods outlined in Sections 9.2.2 and 9.2.3 above for both preliminary and detailed design stages, although limitations and uncertainties suggest that their use should be restricted to preliminary design only. Extrapolation of these methods outside of their ranges of validity is not recommended.

Box 9.4 *Van der Meer's simplified method*

A simplified method based on Van der Meer's equations is suggested in the CIRIA/CUR *Rock Manual* (1991) for $H_s/\Delta D_{n50}$ greater than about 10-15 to give a first estimate of the profile (see Figure 1). The crest length, l_c, step length l_s, run-up length, l_r, and transition height, h_t, are given by simple empirical expressions:

$$l_c = 0.041\, H_s\, T_m\, (gD_{n50})^{1/2} \tag{1}$$

$$l_r = l_s = 1.8\, l_c \tag{2}$$

$$h_t = 0.6\, l_c \tag{3}$$

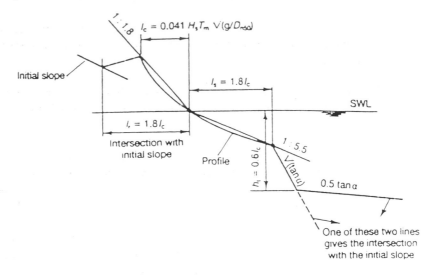

Figure 1 *Simplified profile prediction*

The position of the beach crest ridge is set by l_c and slope of 1:1.8 up from the intersection point with the water level. Similarly the transition point is set by l_s and a slope of 1:1.5 down from the intersection point with the water level.

Further information is available on profile changes for larger sized materials from studies on berm breakwaters, (e.g. by Kao and Hall, 1990), but this information is generally limited to $2 \le H_s/\Delta D_{n50} \le 7$.

Physical model tests remain a simple and reliable method to test the performance of a rock beach under a wide range of possible exposures. Such a structure should be modelled at a relatively large undistorted scale to ensure correct wave processes, although some distortion of the scaling of the mobile material may be demanded to ensure that mobility and permeability of the beach material are correctly reproduced at small scale.

Two-dimensional tests in a wave flume may be used to quantify the profile response to changes in wave conditions, water levels, or to the rock material and/or initial beach geometry. Three-dimensional tests will be needed if longshore movement may constitute a significant design restraint. In such tests, both profile changes and the rates of longshore movement should be measured.

9.2.5 Appropriate uses of rock beaches

There are many situations where the construction of a rock beach may offer significant advantages over the other solutions to coastal erosion and/or overtopping problems. There are also many more situations where a rock beach solution is simply inappropriate. The balance of advantage/disadvantage is strongly site specific, but in general the use of a dynamically stable solution may be most advantageous where a number of these factors apply:

1. The use of a rough and rocky beach is sympathetic to the local environmental and amenity constraints, for example, aesthetic and access considerations.
2. Quarried rock material is available in sufficient quantity locally, and/or can be transported to site at acceptable economic and environmental cost.

3. Larger rock material, placed in conventional rubble mounds or revetments to steeper slopes, is more difficult/expensive to obtain, transport, or place.
4. Oblique wave attack is limited, thus reducing potential longshore movement.

Typical examples of successful uses of rock beaches are given in Boxes 9.5 and 9.6.

9.3   MANAGED LANDWARD REALIGNMENT

In areas of the coastline experiencing relative sea level rise, management options other than maintaining a fixed line of defence are increasingly being considered. There are two main reasons for this:

1. Benefit cost considerations - in some low-lying rural areas the cost of maintaining the existing line of defence exceeds the benefits of avoided flooding and damage in the hinterland were the defence to fail.

2. Nature conservation - hard defences, including beaches fixed in position by control structures, interrupt the natural response of the shoreline to sea level rise (see Box 5.7) by restricting landward retreat. This results in a loss of the intertidal habitat and is termed *coastal squeeze*.

Managed landward realignment (managed retreat) is an alternative coastal management option which can yield favourable benefit-cost ratios, whilst conserving natural processes by minimising the impact of coastal squeeze. In addition, retreat will result in the promotion of coastal processes which can lead to improved flood defence and will enhance the sustainability of defences.

Managed landward realignment involves retreating inland from the existing line of flood defence or coast protection, while monitoring and maintaining an awareness of the consequences of the landward realignment (Brooke, 1992). "Management" of landward realignment need not necessarily entail physical intervention on the coastline (e.g. in the form of engineering works), but it implies an awareness of what is happening and provides an opportunity to intervene, if appropriate (Brooke, 1993).

Managed landward realignment in low-lying areas can take one of four forms, as shown in Figure 9.8. Set back (sub-figure 2) involves the maintenance of a defence but along a new line further inland. Controlled abandonment (sub-figure 3), on the other hand, refers to abandoning the existing line of defence and allowing a natural "water's edge" to develop at the high water mark. However, regular monitoring and possibly intervention will be required in this case to ensure that subsequent erosion problems do not develop at the upland edge. Controlled abandonment differs from the "do nothing" option, in that the latter involves abandoning the existing line of defence without any future monitoring or intervention. A deliberately reduced standard of defence (sub-figure 4) or a tiered defence system (sub-figure 5) are other examples of managed landward realignment.

Managed landward realignment can be exploited for its environmental benefits. On sites characterised by cohesive sediments, for example, managed landward realignment might be exploited to create saltmarsh or mudflats on former low-lying agricultural land. On sites characterised by non-cohesive sediments and/or on eroding coastlines, managed landward realignment may be used to re-instate or restore the natural sediment supply from an area which had previously been defended (e.g. a cliff front). It may also be used to facilitate the natural "rolling-back" of sand dune habitats. Through these types of initiative, it may also be possible to restore or develop recreational beaches.

Box 9.5   *Rock beach at Hilton Bay, Berwick on Tweed, Northumberland*

A rock beach was constructed to protect the base of an eroding boulder clay cliff below the East Coast Main (Railway) Line at Hilton Bay 7km north of Berwick on Tweed. Wave action was eroding the base of the cliff, threatening its stability, and that of the railway some 60m above. Physical hydraulic model tests at HR Wallingford measured the beach profile changes for a number of initial beach slopes, and two rock gradings.

The new rock beach was constructed in summer 1988 using rock between about 0.2 and 0.4m, placed to initial slopes of 1:6 on the lower slope, 1:5 on the upper slope, and with a crest ridge at 1:1.5 (see Figure 1). The cliff toe and beach are shown before and after construction of the new rock beach in Figure 2.

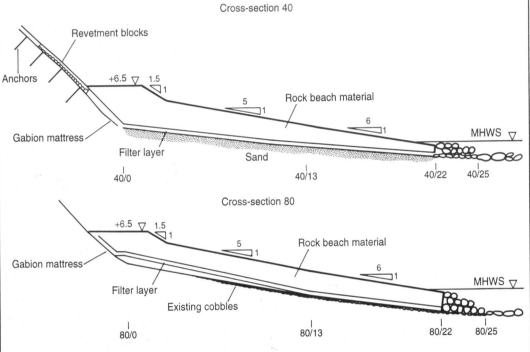

Figure 1   *Sections of rock beach at Hilton Bay*

Figure 2   *Hilton Bay, before and after construction of rock beach (courtesy HR Wallingford)*

Box 9.6   *Rock beach at Prestatyn, Clwyd*

At Prestatyn, N. Wales, a rock beach was used as a transition between the rock armour at the root of a rock groyne, forming the end of a conventional beach control scheme, and a natural shingle bank. The beach had a variable grading with coarser material at a steeper slope (1 in 5.5) near the groyne and finer material with a flatter slope near the shingle bank.

Figure 1   *Rock beach under construction (courtesy Babtie Dobbie)*

Part of the reasoning behind managed landward realignment is that it will encourage the development of a shoreline in equilibrium with the natural coastal processes. On or adjacent to dune systems, for example, applying the concept of managed landward realignment will involve using forms of beach management which can accommodate the tendency of the dune system to migrate inland, whilst ensuring at the same time that an adequate defence standard is provided and maintained. Management strategies should also consider the possibilities of managed landward realignment leading to the restoration or interruption of longshore transport and downdrift accretion or erosion.

On sensitive eroding coastlines the concept of managed landward realignment can similarly be applied by using beach management to slow rather than prevent erosion. This can help ensure, as far as possible, that some degree of natural sediment supply is maintained, geological exposures do not become covered with vegetation due to overprotection, archaeological features are protected and an adequate standard of coastal defence is achieved and maintained (Brooke and Thomas, 1993).

Managed landward realignment, on its own or supported by other beach management methods, should be reviewed as an option whenever coastal defence schemes are being considered. In some cases, particularly if the managed landward realignment has a coastal defence function or consequence, a scheme may be eligible for grant-aid from MAFF. An example of a set back scheme funded in this way is Dinas Dinlle, North Wales, shown in Box 9.7. In all cases a managed landward realignment scheme should be subject to the same technical, economic and

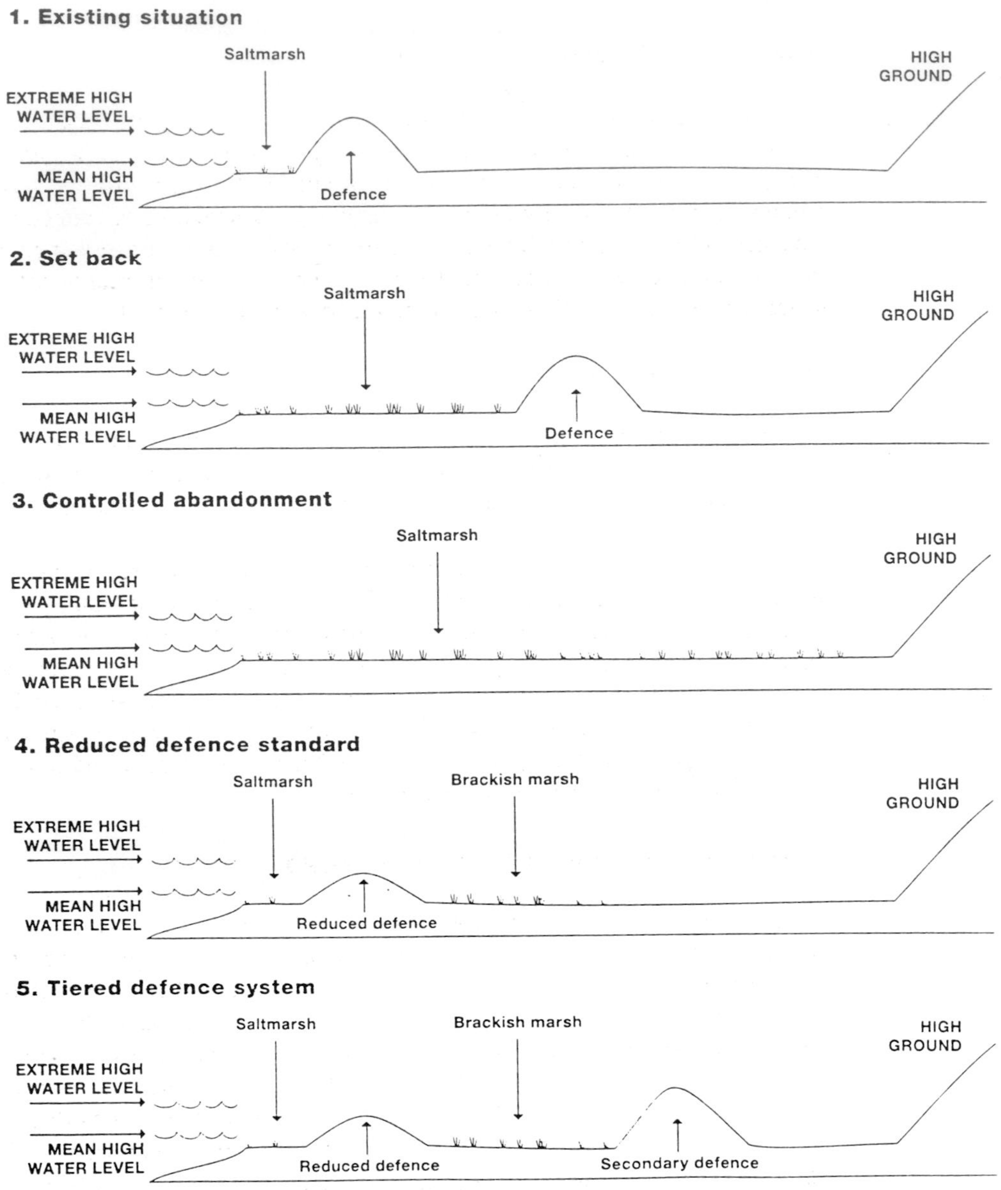

1. Existing situation

2. Set back

3. Controlled abandonment

4. Reduced defence standard

5. Tiered defence system

Figure 9.8   *Forms of managed landward realignment in low lying areas (Brooke, 1993)*

environmental evaluations as any other type of scheme. However, as discussed elsewhere, the environmental costs and benefits may be difficult to quantify in monetary terms. Techniques such as the contingent valuation method may therefore need to be employed (see Section 6.5).

9.4   RESTORATION OF NATURAL SUPPLY

The concept of beach management by restoration of littoral drift or reintroduction of the supply of material recognises the fundamental principle of continuity (e.g. restoring the balance within the sediment budget so as to maintain an even rate of littoral drift within the management unit).

Source of supply

The starting point of this approach is the identification of the sources of supply and the determination of how these may have been altered by man's intervention or by natural phenomena (i.e. sea level rise, climate change etc.). Supplies may have been derived from either offshore, alongshore or from inland sources. For further information on sediment supply, see Chapter 2.

Management of supply

The ephemeral nature of much of contemporary sediment supply means that a flexible approach to this form of beach management is necessary. Management can be carried out by the removal or adjustment of the height of revetments or cliff protection walls. The effects of such a removal may not be readily quantifiable and any prediction of the effectiveness of this form of management requires detailed studies of the coastal regime. Examination of historic records, field studies and mathematical modelling all play an important role in determining the fate of material released by cliff erosion and transported by littoral drift.

Management of drift

Management of littoral drift involves the release of material from an area of coast with a surplus of material to one which has deficit. It is becoming an increasingly important management method as the stocks of fresh beach material are reducing.

Management of littoral drift by the removal or adjustment of groyne systems has been carried out in the past at Sheringham, North Norfolk. In this particular case "gates" were constructed at the head of groynes to allow shingle to be passed into groyne compartments which, for one reason or another, became emptied faster than others. More often, management of drift over long coastal frontages is carried out by the removal or the addition of timber planking to alter the retaining capacity of groynes. Altering groyne length is more costly and requires a major change in the design philosophy. This method is less often practised in the UK. For further information on groyne design, see Chapter 8.

Areas suitable for restoration of natural supply

Areas of low land values and areas which have uncontrollable rates of cliff retreat are clearly candidate areas in which to allow the restoration of natural supply to occur. Within the context of an overall shoreline management plan, such areas could be considered as sacrificial. It is important to determine, however, how much benefit will be gained by allowing erosion to continue unchecked. If the eroding cliffs consist of silts and clays, the contribution to the local sediment budget may be small. On a regional scale, however, their contribution may be significant, as they may provide material for the development of mudflats in estuarine areas, for example. An appropriate scale for this type of management approach would therefore be a coastal cell which includes a grouping of several coast protection authorities or other bodies sharing common interest and encompassing a large physiographic unit. Sparsely developed areas where the backshore zone does not require hard defences, are also candidate areas, for a "do nothing" management policy.

Another significant category of areas in which some degree of restoration of natural supply could be permitted is that of heavily developed coastal areas which have an excessive number of groynes as a result of successive stages of groyne construction over the last century. Quite often a policy is adopted where new, long groynes are constructed between shorter older groynes, with a view to interrupting an increasingly large proportion of the natural drift to

Box 9.7 *Managed set back, Dinas Dinlle, Wales*

As part of a scheme to provide the village of Dinas Dinlle with protection, an earth flood embankment has been built on the landward edge of the shingle bank and, with a contribution from the Highway Authority, has been made wide enough to accommodate a new road when the existing highway is no longer maintainable. The existing shingle bank will be allowed to roll back and utilise all the material presently beneath the car park and existing road to re-establish a crest at its natural elevation (see Figure 1). The scheme at Dinas Dinlle is described further on pages 114 and 115 of the MAFF (1993c) publication *Coastal Defence and the Environment - a guide to good practice*.

Continued

Box 9.7   Continued

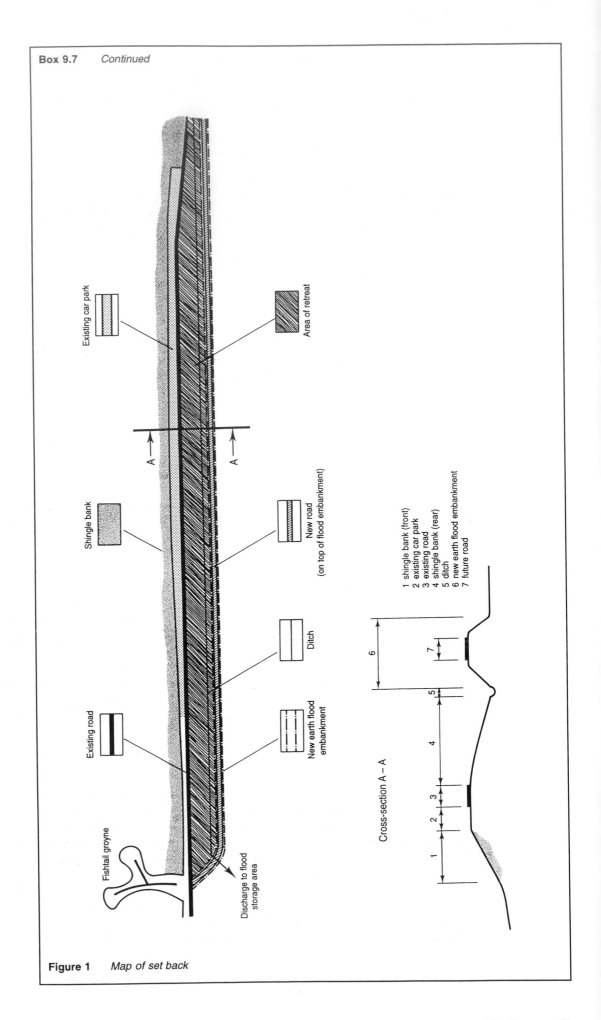

Figure 1   *Map of set back*

Cross-section A – A

1 shingle bank (front)
2 existing car park
3 existing road
4 shingle bank (rear)
5 ditch
6 new earth flood embankment
7 future road

Existing car park

Area of retreat

Shingle bank

New road
(on top of flood embankment)

Existing road

Ditch

New earth flood
embankment

Fishtail groyne

Discharge to flood
storage area

counteract the tendency of the coast to erode. Ultimately a stage is reached where downdrift stretches of coastline become severely depleted and even within the groyne system itself the proliferation of structures leads to a very uneven alongshore distribution of material. Problems can also arise as more and more groynes are built to counter the downdrift erosion caused by the existing updrift groynes.

Role of monitoring and mathematical modelling

Managing beaches by restoring natural supply clearly needs careful monitoring to determine whether the defined objectives are being achieved. Where possible, the impact of groyne removal/reduction or other measures on beach profiles and downdrift beaches should be assessed by means of mathematical or physical modelling (see Section 6.4).

9.5   SEDIMENT BYPASSING

The concept of sediment bypassing was developed in response to problems associated with tidal inlets. These problems include excessive accretion updrift of an inlet jetty, unwanted sedimentation seawards of the inlet and often acute erosion downdrift. In the case of flood tide dominated inlets, beach material may also be carried upstream, leading to a loss of navigable depth in the entrance. Sediment bypassing involves moving material from the areas of accumulation, to the eroding area.

Current techniques for sediment transfer include mechanical bypassing, hydraulic bypassing, bed fluidization, sediment traps and variations including one or more of these techniques.

Mechanical bypassing

Mechanical bypassing operations are not widely used, and in the USA, which has a long history of sand bypassing at tidal inlets, there are only a few examples of mechanical systems (see Box 9.8).

Box 9.8   *Mechanical bypassing - Shark Inlet, New Jersey*

A land-based bypassing scheme was carried out at Shark Inlet, New Jersey in 1958/9 which involved the transfer of sand over a distance in excess of 750m from the south to the north side of the inlet, using a trucking operation. This operation had the benefit of easy access to the "borrow" and "feeder" beaches via a bridge located across the inlet, in close proximity to the inlet mouth. The operation involved the recycling of some 190,000 m³ of sand over two successive winter periods (at times when the beach was not required for amenity). The volume of material transferred was of the same order of magnitude as the littoral drift in this area and proved successful in the short term. The process of bulldozing the material, transporting it and placing it onto the feeder beach resulted in a coarser and better graded fill than would have been obtained had the material been removed from submerged inlet shoals. The operation also proved to be cheaper than proposals to bypass material hydraulically. (During the bidding stage proposals included a price of $0.88 per cubic yard for trucking, as compared with a price of $1.42 per cubic yard for carrying out the work by a hydraulic dredge and discharge line).

Operations of this kind are often unacceptable in built-up areas on the grounds of nuisance, loss of public amenity and environmental considerations. This type of operation was considered at one stage, for bypassing at Viarregio harbour, in north-west Italy, but was found to be much more expensive than the hydraulic bypassing plant which was eventually decided upon. However they are in place in a limited number of locations, such as St Valéry-en-Caux in France.

Sediment bypassing associated with capital dredging operations at the entrances to major ports and estuaries, however, may prove to be an effective means of nourishing downdrift beaches. It requires the co operation of both harbour and coast protection authorities, who often have conflicting interests.

Hydraulic bypassing

Hydraulic bypassing of sediment can be carried out by fixed, floating or semi-mobile bypassing plant.

Fixed bypassing plant involves the transport of sand as a slurry via a system of suction pipes, using a centrifugal pump to a discharge pipeline (see Figure 9.9). Effective operations of this type have been taking place in Florida, USA, to transfer material across the relatively narrow inlets through barrier beaches (see Box 9.9).

Floating or semi-mobile operations allow the establishment of a fixed location for the pumping apparatus and for the discharge system, while allowing the intake system to be moved within a designated area. Operational costs with such systems are likely to be higher than those for fixed plant, because of higher maintenance costs, the greater number of personnel required to man the operations and due to the more complex plant. The system may also interfere with other users of the harbour or inlet system and the plant is generally more vulnerable to mechanical damage by wave action, etc. (see Box 9.10).

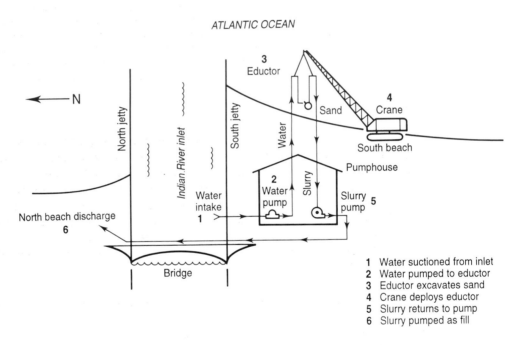

Figure 9.9   *Typical bypass system*

Box 9.9 *Hydraulic bypassing - Worth Inlet, Florida, USA*

At Lake Worth Inlet, Florida, the bypassing system consists of a 30cm suction pipe, a 400 horse power electric motor/pump combination and two 25cm discharge pipes laid across the channel bed. Monitoring of the system has shown that over the period 1967 to 1978 an average annual bypassing rate of about 100,000 m³ was achieved, this being equivalent to about 60% of the estimated nett littoral drift of sand in the area. The bypassing system was enhanced by maintenance dredging operations, which were necessary because the fixed plant could not "reach" all the sediment being transported in the inshore zone. The unit costs of bypassing averaged over the period 1967 to 1978, were $0.97 per cu yd at 1979 prices.

Box 9.10 *Semi-mobile bypassing - Viarregio, Italy*

Viarregio harbour, which is situated on the north-west coast of Italy has had a long history of beach erosion associated with the interruption of littoral drift. Fixed sand bypassing was attempted as far back as the 1930's but proved unable to cope with the transport of sand in large quantities. In 1980 a scheme was established consisting of a system of floating dredgers which could be connected up to a field pumping station sited on the downdrift side of the harbour. These dredgers can be used to remove material from the harbour itself, from the updrift beach or from a shoal at the entrance to the harbour. Over a period 1980 to 1985 the system achieved an average rate of transfer of 95,000 m³ per year. Despite the fact that the nett littoral drift in this area has been estimated at 200,000 m³ per year, surveys of the shoreline have shown that immediately downdrift of the harbour, at least, there has been considerable accretion. This form of bypassing has been estimated to be 50% less expensive than mechanical bypassing, by means of lorry, of this busy and large harbour. Success of the system of floating dredgers has been attributed to the low tidal range and the relatively modest wave conditions in the harbour area.

Seabed fluidisation

The amount of material which can be made available for bypassing can be increased by the use of so-called jet pumps or other means of bed fluidisation. A jet pump or eductor is essentially a hydraulically powered pump which uses water supplied under pressure. This is forced through a nozzle and the high velocity jet is buried in the sand bed, where it creates a sand/water slurry which is drawn into the discharge pipe and pushed to the discharge pump. A booster pump placed within the discharge line may then be used to push the slurry further down coast if necessary. Figure 9.10 shows the layout of the arrangements employed in a small so-called "dive dredger", an example of which is shown in operation in South Africa in Figure 9.11 (Prestedge and Bosman, 1994).

Larger scale operations are also underway. Details of one scheme are given in Box 9.11.

Similar systems are also being used in the USA (see Figure 9.12). At Oceanside harbour the fluidisation technique involves pumping water through a perforated pipe which is buried beneath the seabed surface. Once the sand overburden is liquified, the sand is able to flow more freely into the transport pump crater. These innovative schemes are still at an experimental stage and the cost effectiveness and long term viability have yet to be determined. No such systems have been tested under UK coastal conditions, where the tidal range is large and the level of wave activity is moderate to high.

Other bypassing methods

A number of other innovative bypassing systems are in operation in USA, including sediment traps, weir jetties, etc.. Essentially the design of all of these systems is site specific, and they have been tested under conditions of low tidal range and a moderate wave climate. It is considered that their design has not proceeded to such a stage that these systems could be employed under UK conditions without considerable further development.

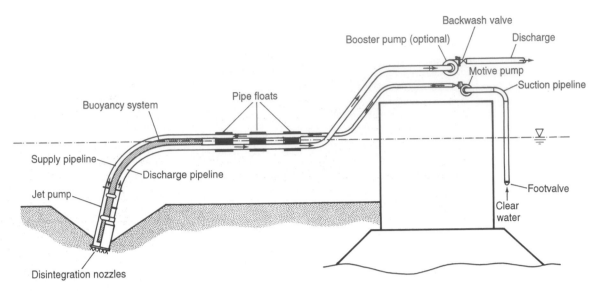

Figure 9.10   *Schematic illustration of mobile dive dredger*

Figure 9.11   *Mobile (60 tonnes solids/hour) dive dredger working at Gordon's Bay, near Cape Town, South Africa (courtesy G.K. Prestedge)*

Potential use in the UK

Only a few areas in the UK have sufficiently persistent and sustained rapid shoreline advance and accompanying downdrift erosion to make bypassing with fixed plant an economic proposition. It should be borne in mind that most parts of the UK coastline are subject to substantial variations in drift from year to year, not only as regards quantity but also direction. It would be difficult under these conditions to design an effective bypassing system, which could transport material in both alongshore directions.

CIRIA Report 153

Figure 9.12   *Prototype trials of a 300 tonnes solid per hour diver dredger for US Army Corps of Engineers (courtesy G.K. Prestedge)*

Box 9.11   *Seabed fluidisation - Gold Coast Seaway, Australia*

A large-scale bypassing scheme involving an array of jet pumps was put into operation to deal with a high rate of sand transport at the entrance of the Nerang river on the Queensland coast of Australia. Prior to stabilisation by means of twin training walls, the river entrance had tended to migrate. To prevent any potential migration of the river entrance, which now forms part of the important Gold Coast Seaway, a massive sand transfer plant was established. The system included an array of 10 jet pumps set on a trestle spanning a 300m width of littoral zone, with the jet pumps being located at about 11m below sea levels. The pumps are capable of transporting up to 500,000m^3 of sand per year which is of the same magnitude as the littoral rate. Since 1989 some reduction in the bypassing rate has been caused due to debris (e.g. tree trunks, etc.) being transported by storms into the large stilling craters from which the jet pumps collect the sand.

On the other hand sediment bypassing with mechanical plant may be economic, differing little from sediment recycling and, unlike fixed plant, allowing for changes in drift direction and quantity.

Areas which may be suitable for this type of management include the approaches to ports, navigation channels and areas of accumulation at harbour shoals. Bypassing operations as part of a capital dredging programme could be used to transfer material from an area of siltation in a harbour approach channel to downdrift coasts at a relatively low cost. However, it would be sensible to allow wave action to transport material into such areas from the updrift zone rather than disturbing the updrift beach. Extensive environmental impact studies are necessary to determine the ultimate fate of the dredged spoil, its environmental impact and its impact on beach quality and visual appearance.

There are a number of harbours in the UK (e.g. Harwich in Essex and Port Talbot in West Glamorgan) which require dredging on a regular basis, and which are candidate areas for beach feeding. There are also a number of harbours with well developed ebb deltas (e.g. Chichester

Harbour in West Sussex) which require maintenance dredging. In such cases, dredging operations will be the vehicle by which sediment bypassing takes place.

Longshore considerations

Sediment bypassing operations have a number of potential advantages in reducing the longshore environmental impacts of beach control structures (see Section 8.8). By maintaining the supply of material along the shore, sediment bypassing ensures that excessive downdrift erosion is avoided. Bypassing can also help to avoid potentially deleterious build up to the updrift side of a structure (e.g. preventing the exposure of an area of geological interest in a cliff face, because of the establishment of vegetation, creating a wide sand backshore subject to feed onshore wind transport), as shown by the example in Box 9.12.

In the case of sediment bypassing associated with dredging operations, there can be a risk of fines fouling the beaches with the consequential disruption to public amenity.

Box 9.12 *Sediment bypassing proposals at Easington, Humberside*

One of the main concerns expressed by the conservation agencies in respect of the proposed coast protection works at Easington on the UK's Holderness coast, was the possible build-up of beach material on the updrift (northern) side of the planned coastal defences. This was considered to be of particular importance because of the sensitive natural resources to the south, notably the lagoons SSSI, and Spurn Head. The coastal process studies undertaken as part of the Environmental Assessment indicated that any such build-up, at least in the short- to medium-term, would be negligible. Nonetheless, in order both to satisfy the concerns of the conservation agencies and to corroborate the modelling predictions, a comprehensive monitoring programme was recommended. This would involve:

- monitoring both cliff top positions and beach profiles
- monitoring positions to cover the coastline from 2km north of the neck of the Spurn peninsula over a distance of 5km to the south
- monitoring positions varying from 100m centres close to the works, to 500m-1000m centres at the furthest points
- monthly monitoring for the first 2-3 years and at six monthly intervals thereafter.

In addition, proposals were put in hand for a review committee to evaluate the results of the monitoring and, if appropriate, to authorise sediment bypassing. Bypassing could be achieved by either:

- bulldozing the excess build-up of the material into the sea in appropriate weather conditions for "natural" longshore transport past the coast protection works
- excavating and transporting the excess build up of material along the beach at low tide (or, if necessary, by road), to the southern limit of the works.

10 Project implementation

10.1 GENERAL

In broad terms the following steps are involved in the implementation of a project:

- obtaining approvals and funding
- preparation of contract documents
- tendering
- construction.

In addition, once a project has been constructed, it should be subject to post project monitoring and evaluation to assess its overall performance.

These aspects are discussed in the following sub-sections, largely in the context of UK practice, nevertheless, many of the principles raised will have wider application. A flow chart for the process, referencing the subsections of this chapter, is given in Figure 10.1 below.

10.2 APPROVALS AND FUNDING

10.2.1 Legislation

Coastal defence works may be subject to both specific legislation and more general planning and environmental legislation. When undertaking these works it is important that the necessary approvals and statutory requirements are considered at an early stage and, where doubt exists over the precise details, that specialist advice is sought. It should be noted that within the UK the statutory framework controlling the implementation of coastal defence works varies in England, Scotland, Wales and Northern Ireland.

Coastal defence legislation

In the UK coastal defence legislation generally empowers certain bodies to undertake works, subject to government approval. An outline of the legislation that applies within England and Wales at the time of preparation of this manual was given earlier in Box 1.1. Further details on the statutory framework may be found in Appendix A of the CIRIA document *Seawall Design* (Thomas and Hall, 1992), in the MAFF/Welsh Office (1993b) *Strategy for Flood and Coastal Defence*, and in MAFF grant memoranda issued from time to time.

Planning legislation

It is likely that coastal defence works will have to comply with the relevant planning legislation. In England and Wales planning permission is generally required under the Town and Country Planning Act 1990. Further details of UK requirements may be found in the references listed under *Coastal defence legislation*.

Environmental legislation

In the UK an environmental assessment will normally be required when the coastal defence works are likely to have significant effects on the environment by virtue of factors such as their nature, size or location. The statutory framework controlling the requirements and procedures for environmental assessment may be found in the references listed under *Coastal defence legislation* and in Section 6.6. Reference should also be made to MAFF (1993c) and MAFF (1993d).

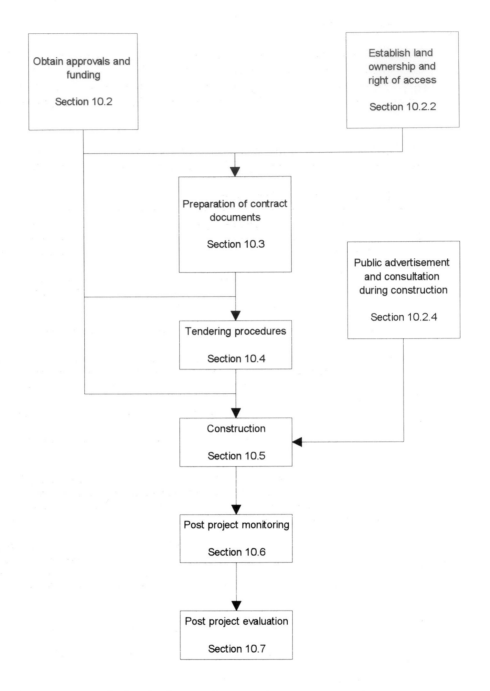

Figure 10.1   *Project implementation process*

10.2.2   Land ownership

It is important to establish the ownership of the beach and foreshore and to obtain permission from the owners, to place beach recharge material and/or construct beach control structures.

In the UK, the Crown Estate owns 55% of the foreshore (between high and low water marks), much of the remainder being owned by the Duchies of Lancaster and Cornwall, local authorities, private owners or public bodies.

CIRIA Report 153

10.2.3 Funding

Most coastal defence work is publicly funded and possible sources of funding should therefore be explored during the early stages of a project. This will ensure there is sufficient time available to comply with the funding agency's requirements. In addition to central governments, other sources include the European Regional Development Fund, international lending agencies and bilateral aid.

In England coastal defence works may be eligible for grants from MAFF. The procedures to be followed by applicants when applying to MAFF for grant aid are outlined in Box 10.1.

Box 10.1 *MAFF grant aid procedures*

In England coastal defence works may be eligible for grants from MAFF. MAFF is empowered under the Coast Protection Act 1949, and the Water Resources Act 1991 to pay grant to eligible authorities on those capital works which can be demonstrated to be environmentally acceptable, technically sound and economically worthwhile.

For beach nourishment schemes, MAFF will consider grant aiding both the initial recharge and subsequent maintenance recharges, recycling and monitoring of the beach provided that the scheme is part of a long-term management plan for the relevant stretch of coastline.

Formal approval (and grant aid) can only be obtained for a project when MAFF has received the following:

- completed grant aid application forms (there are separate forms for sea defence and coast protection works)
- an acceptable Engineer's Report/Project Appraisal prepared in accordance with (MAFF, 1993a). The report should include an engineering, environmental and economic assessment of the problem and potential solutions.
- the tender documents
- a tender appraisal report recommending award of contract (except in cases where the applicants own direct labour force is to be used)
- confirmation that Environmental Assessment procedures have been followed and that relevant statutory and environmental bodies are content with the proposals.

For flood or sea defence works two types of approval may be obtained; agreement in principle and formal approval. 'Agreement in principle' means that the objectives and outline solutions are generally accepted and an applicant may wish to obtain such an agreement before proceeding with detailed design. Formal approval is, however, required before grant can be paid. For coastal protection works only formal approval can be obtained.

Applicants are advised to discuss proposed schemes with the appropriate MAFF Regional Engineer at an early stage and then to liaise closely with MAFF throughout the development of the project. From receipt of an application, MAFF estimate that approval should take from about five weeks for schemes less than £0.5 million to about four months for schemes over £6 million which require additional consultation, though the actual time will depend on the complexity of the scheme and the degree of prior consultation.

The steps involved in obtaining formal approval and grant aid are essentially as follows:

1. Where appropriate, prepare and submit a Shoreline Management Plan to MAFF.
2. Prepare a Feasibility Study.
3. Undertake the detailed design of the proposed option.
4. Submit application and supporting documentation to MAFF for formal approval.
5. Prepare and submit tender documents to MAFF for approval.
6. Once approved, issue documents to tenderers.
7. Prepare tender appraisal report and revise economic analysis, as necessary.

A similar procedure is required to obtain grant aid from the Welsh Office for works in Wales. Further information on these procedures may be found in the grant memoranda issued by MAFF from time to time.

10.2.4 Public advertisement and consultation during construction

In order to minimise uncertainty and reduce many of the environmental impacts discussed in detail in Chapters 5 and 6 it is essential that the public and those groups likely to be affected by the implementation of the scheme are kept informed. There is, therefore, a need to develop and build on the consultation initiatives that will have been undertaken during the scheme development and project appraisal phases.

Residents, businesses and other interests (e.g. navigation) should be given clear information, preferably in writing, well in advance of the ensuing works. This may involve a letter drop prior to the commencement of the general works, followed by specific communication with those who will be directly affected, a few weeks in advance. The information thus presented should include the following:

- a timetable of works
- an explanation of how the works will be phased
- a schedule of working hours
- the area of works at a particular time
- a contact name, address and telephone number.

Local media should also be used, for example, articles in high circulation newspapers and features on local radio. Works affecting sensitive areas may require one or more public meetings.

An information board should be displayed prominently at all sites. By providing a contact name and telephone number to which the public can channel their questions and complaints, problems should be rectified quickly.

Throughout the construction period, residents should be kept informed about unavoidable disturbance such as noise, dust, extended working hours or disruption to traffic.

It is also important that, at the end of the construction work, the public are informed of its completion. At this stage a questionnaire asking for feedback on the effects of the operation could aid appraisal and ensure that any mistakes do not occur again.

10.3 PREPARATION OF CONTRACT DOCUMENTS

10.3.1 General

Contract documents are required to enable tenderers to realistically price the proposed work and subsequently to provide a framework for undertaking the contract. The primary objectives of the documents are to:

- describe accurately the work to be undertaken (including any constraints) and to clearly specify the character and quality of materials, standards of workmanship, tolerances etc. that are to be used

- set out the conditions under which the work will be carried out, including any inherent health and safety risks evident from the design process (see Section 6.2.7)

- provide a fair and equitable method of payment for work satisfactorily completed

- clearly define the distribution of responsibility and risk between the employer and the contractor.

In general a set of contract documents will comprise the following:

- Conditions of Contract
- Special Conditions of Contract
- Specification
- Pre-tender health and safety plan
- Bill of Quantities
- Drawings
- Forms of Tender
- Form of Agreement
- Form of Bond.

In addition to the above documents, Instructions to Tenderers are generally issued at the tender stage.

Each of the above items is described briefly in the following sections.

10.3.2 Instructions to Tenderers

The Instructions to Tenderers are provided to assist each tenderer in the preparation and submission of his tender. They provide instructions as to how the tender is to be completed and may ask for certain items of information to be supplied with the tender return. For a beach recharge scheme the Instructions to Tenderers are likely to ask for:

- a method statement - this should describe the tenderer's proposed working methods including the type of dredger(s) and pipeline(s) to be used, whether rehandling sites would be used, location of site compounds (particularly any pipeline fabrication yards) and techniques for placing material on the beach

- a programme for the completion of the works - this should indicate the tenderer's proposed sequence and rate of working and, where appropriate, indicate whether winter working would be undertaken

- details of major items of plant - this should include a full description of the dredgers and other major items of plant

- the source of beach recharge material (if not to be supplied by the client) - this should include a description of the proposed material (location, grading, colour, level of contaminations) and provide evidence that there is sufficient quantities available to undertake the work.

They may also provide additional information to assist the tenderer with the preparation of a tender. This may include wave and current conditions, survey results and data on any recharge material supplied by the client.

It should clearly state whether the information provided in the instructions and also the data supplied by the tenderers will form part of any subsequent contract; to this end, some data may be declared to be "for information only" (e.g. a preliminary programme). The Instructions to Tenderers would also not form part of the contract.

10.3.3 Conditions of Contract

The Conditions of Contract define the legal terms under which the work is to be carried out. There are a number of standard conditions of contract for civil engineering works. In the UK work is commonly carried out under the Institution of Civil Engineers (ICE) Conditions of Contract for Works of Civil Engineering (currently 6th Edition). Overseas, the Federation Internationale des Ingenieurs - Conseils (FIDIC) Conditions of Contract (currently 4th Edition) are widely used.

In recent years a number of new forms of contract have been prepared, these include the New Engineering Contract (NEC 2nd Edition) published in November 1995 by the Institution of Civil Engineers. The NEC is beginning to be recognised as an alternative to the ICE (6th Edition) and is being used for civil engineering works.

10.3.4 Special Conditions of Contract

In order to adapt the general Conditions of Contract (described in Section 10.3.3) for beach recharge works, it may be necessary to introduce a number of special conditions. In general these changes should be kept to a minimum as both the ICE and FIDIC conditions are well understood and are supported by extensive case law.

The main areas where special conditions may be required are:

- plant ownership   -   as dredgers are very expensive items of plant, ownership on determination of a contract should be carefully considered

- insurance   -   consideration should be given as to whether it is appropriate, or indeed possible, for the Contractor to insure the beach recharge works; as a minimum, the Contractor should be required to insure his dredging equipment against normal marine risk

- maintenance period   -   as sea conditions can vary rapidly, adjusting the nourished profile, it may not be appropriate to include a long maintenance period within the contract

- fluctuations in the cost of fuel   -   on projects involving dredging, fuel costs can account for a large proportion of the overall contract value; in these circumstances it may be appropriate to incorporate fuel price fluctuations within the contract

- weather risk   -   consideration should be given to the apportionment of risk for adverse weather conditions.

Guidance on special conditions may be found in Part II of the FIDIC Conditions and in the Users Guide to the 4th Edition of the FIDIC Conditions prepared by the International Association of Dredging Companies (IADC, 1990).

The preparation of special conditions effectively changes the standard form of contract and should therefore be drafted carefully to ensure that the requirements are workable and provide a reasonable apportionment of risk. For this reason it may be necessary to seek advice from an expert in contract preparation.

10.3.5 Specification

The objective of the Specification is to describe in detail the work to be executed, the character and quality of the materials and workmanship and any special responsibilities placed on the Contractor that are not covered by the Conditions of Contract.

For a beach recharge contract it is generally better to leave the actual method of winning and placing beach recharge material as open as possible, subject to it being environmentally acceptable. This allows a method to be chosen that is suited to the Contractor's particular resources and experience and should lead to more competitive and reliable pricing at the tender stage. Full details on this subject have been given in Chapter 7 and this should be reviewed in detail before preparing any specification.

The Specification will, in general, include clauses covering the items listed below. These items have been grouped under the headings *General*, *Materials* and *Execution* and comments generally relating to beach recharge works have been included. Details for beach control structures may be found in CIRIA/CUR (1991) and Thomas and Hall (1992).

General

1. Location of site and description of the works - attention should be drawn to sites of environmental interest and recreational use of the beaches.

2. Site access - points at which land access to the beach is permitted should be defined together with any restriction on seaborne and land-based delivery routes.

3. Safety Fencing - requirement for safety fencing and warning signs around working areas on the beach should be defined.

4. Delivery by road - the need to remove mud from roads, rocks from between lorry tyres, and cover backs, etc. should be identified.

5. Services - a description of public utilities and services affected by the works should be provided.

6. Tidiness - the need to keep the beach clear of construction debris and to remove sand contaminated by oil and diesel spillages from plant operating on the beach should be identified.

7. Maintenance of existing defences - the standard of defence that must be maintained during construction should be identified.

8. Programme of works - any key dates should be identified.

9. Working hours - it should be stated whether 24 hour working is permitted (both offshore and on the beach) and any special requirements covering noise and lighting identified.

10. Licences and consents - responsibility for obtaining necessary licences and consents should be clearly identified.

11. Liaison with third parties - responsibility for dealing with public and interested third parties should be clearly identified.

12. Fisheries liaison - the employer may decide to use the services of a fisheries liaison skipper. Responsibility for the remuneration of the skipper and provision of his or her accommodation and messing (meals) aboard the dredger should be identified.

Material (see also Section 7.4)

1. Materials for beach recharge - the Specification should clearly set out the options available for obtaining material and the required grading, i.e. whether material is to come from a client specified source or from a source proposed by the Contractor. It should also be stated whether the mixing of material of different gradings to produce a material that complies with the Specification will be permitted. If so, careful consideration should be given to the behaviour of the composite material after placing.

2. Testing of material - the requirements for grading and chemical testing of materials together with the rate at which samples are taken and tested should be defined. Sampling can either take place aboard the dredger or on the beach after placing. Typical rates may be 3 samples per hopper load and at 100 metre intervals along the beach. Beach samples should comprise sub-samples taken through the depth of the fill and at a number of locations down the beach slope. Where land-based sources are used, sampling may take place at either the quarry or on the beach.

3. Disposal of unsuitable material - arrangements for dealing with unsuitable material should be carefully considered and clearly defined. Where disposal at sea is contemplated, a licence will normally be required.

Execution

1. Method of working - any restrictions that apply to the Contractor's method of working should be defined, for example, whether or not material can be temporarily dumped on the seabed for subsequent rehandling; the maximum number of work areas; the provision of access for beach users; and any mitigating measures identified in the Environmental Statement.

2. Pipelines and boosters - any restrictions on the location of pipeline fabrication yards, the position of pipelines along frontage and the use of booster stations should be described. The requirements for marking pipelines and booster stations should be identified.

3. Dredging operations - if recharge material is to be dredged from an employers own licensed area the employer may wish to impose certain restrictions upon the Contractor's operations. These may include permitting the Contractor to work only specific parts of the area, only dredge to certain depths and take steps to minimise disturbance to the seabed outside the working area. In situations where material is taken from an area licensed to the Contractor or a third party, no restrictions would be applied through the contract.

4. Beach recharge profiles and placing tolerances - the permitted tolerances for placing the material to the profile defined in the drawings should be stated. In establishing tolerances account should be taken of the primary aim of beach recharge, namely to place a certain volume of material onto the beach. It is counterproductive to require the Contractor to place material to strict tolerances when the beach will quickly be reworked by the sea.

   The recharged profile should be surveyed at regular intervals, perhaps every 25 metres for measurement purposes and to confirm compliance with the Specification.

5. Completion of sections of beach - the Specification should state the lengths over which the beach may be handed over and become the responsibility of the employer. In this context consideration should be given as to whether a Maintenance Period/Defects Correction Period is appropriate in a beach recharge contract.

6. Removal of wrecks and debris - responsibility for the removal of wrecks and debris encountered during the execution of the works should be defined. Archaeologists should be advised if any artifacts of potential interest are discovered.

The above is not an exhaustive list of clauses required in the Specification, other project specific items are likely to be required.

10.3.6 Pre-tender health and safety plan

A pre-tender health and safety plan must be prepared under the CDM Regulations 1994 in order to inform the tenderer of the inherent construction risks that it has not been practical to overcome within the design process (see Section 6.2.7).

This health and safety plan should take the form of a framework which will lay down the parameters of the contract and the key safety issues that must be addressed.

10.3.7 Bill of Quantities

The Bill of Quantities essentially comprises a Preamble, a list of items giving quantities and a brief description of the works. In conjunction with the other contract documents the Bill of Quantities forms the basis on which tenders are obtained and subsequently on which payments are made to the Contractor.

The Preamble should clearly and precisely describe the Method of Measurement. It should define the distribution of risk between the Employer and the Contractor for such matters as weather downtime and standing time by stating the circumstances under which such payments would be made. It should also state who is responsible for any royalty payments due to the Crown Estate and payment of harbour dues.

It is suggested that items are included in the Bill of Quantities for dealing with key safety issues. This will assist the process of checking, under the CDM Regulations, that adequate resources have been allocated to these matters.

The actual techniques available to measure the quantity of material used for beach recharge are discussed in Section 7.7.1.

10.3.8 Drawings

Sufficient drawings should be prepared to enable the Contractor to complete the beach recharge works. In general the drawings should provide the following details:

- location and site plan, including working areas and any other geographical constraints
- results of hydrographic surveys of the nearshore
- plans illustrating restrictions on the location of pipelines and floating plant
- beach plans indicating the extent of the works, access points, services, etc.
- cross-sections showing the existing beach profiles and beach recharge profiles at regular interval along the frontage
- lead-in, and tail-off details at the ends of the recharge works.

If an Employer's own licensed area is to be used, then additional drawings will be required providing details of the site.

10.3.9 Form of Tender

The Form of Tender is the Contractor's written offer to execute the work in accordance with the Contract Documents for a sum to be determined in accordance with the Conditions of Contract and within the specified time for completion.

10.3.10 Form of Agreement

The Form of Agreement, if completed, is a legal undertaking between the Employer and the Contractor for the execution of the work in accordance with the other Contract Documents. A Form of Agreement is not essential if the Employer has written to the Contractor accepting his tender.

10.3.11 Form of Bond

A bond provides a sum of damages up to an agreed maximum figure in the event of the Contractor being in default of the Contract. The ICE Conditions of Contract provide a proforma for use with this contract, but alternative forms may be used.

10.4 TENDERING PROCEDURES

10.4.1 Tender list

General

The approach adopted in the preparation of a list of suitable tenderers varies depending upon the size of the project.

For small projects it is general for a tender list to be prepared using information held by the client or his technical advisors on the experience and performance of Contractors or similar projects.

For larger public works it is a requirement of European law to advertise the tender in the Official Journal of the European Communities (OJEC). In general terms the Council Directives allow either an open or restricted procedure to be adopted for the invitation of tenders. In the open procedure the advertisement in the OJEC invites tenders from all interested parties, whilst under the restricted procedure the advertisement asks for expressions of interest, from which a tender list will be prepared. The latter procedure effectively involves the pre-qualification of prospective tenderers.

Further details on these procedures together with the relevant Council Directives can be obtained from local European Business Information Centres located throughout the country or from:

Office for Official Publications of the EU
2 Rue Mercier
L-2098 Luxembourg

Tel: 00 352 499281
Fax: 00 352 490003/495719.

Pre-qualification

In addition to an outline description of the project, it is usual for the advertisement inviting contractors to submit expressions of interest to ask for the following information:

- details of similar relevant projects
- employee experience
- plant availability
- details of the company's safety policy
- bank references
- last three years accounts.

On receipt of the submission documents, an analysis of the information would be undertaken by the client or his advisors. One approach is to evaluate the submissions by assigning scores to the items listed above and ranking companies on the basis of their total score. This would then lead to a short list of contractors who are both technically and financially qualified to undertake the particular project. Under the CDM Regulations, it is essential to ensure that any short-listed contractor is competent to carry out the work.

10.4.2 Tender period

It is important that tenderers are given sufficient time to realistically price the task of carrying out of the works as described in the tender document. This will encourage the submission of competitive prices as tenderers will have had adequate time to properly evaluate the risks. A minimum of six weeks should be allowed for tendering, however, for large projects and beach recharge projects requiring the tenderer to source material, a considerably longer period (say up to 5 months) should be provided. In addition, advance notice (say 1 month) of the issue of a tender is helpful, because it will allow tenderers to make provision for the tender within their work programme.

10.4.3 Assessment of tenders

It is usual for a client or a client's advisor to complete a formal assessment of the tenders. For large contracts it may be appropriate to complete the assessment in two stages. This would involve two stages. Firstly an initial coarse assessment would be carried out to identify a shortlist of tenders which are both competitively priced and technically acceptable. This stage would be followed by a detailed assessment of those tenders which passed the first stage review, including an assessment of information supplied in respect of key safety issues.

The assessment of tenders involves an analysis of the submissions, an appraisal of any qualifications that have been introduced and a recommendation to award a contract to a particular contractor.

10.4.4 Evaluation of alternative tenders

Tenderers should always be required to submit a tender fully in accordance with the Contract Documents and be invited to submit an alternative tender where they consider that they can offer any savings or advantages. A conforming tender is required to enable a comparison both with other tenders and any alternatives.

During the assessment it is important to establish the implications that changes to the design and working methods proposed by the tenderer may have on approvals and consents necessary to undertake the work. This can be significant for beach recharge projects, for example, changes may invalidate the licence to place material in the sea issued by MAFF under the Food and Environmental Protection Act, 1985 (FEPA) or break agreements with organisations such as local councils, harbour boards and Trinity House. Changes may also have environmental effects that had not previously been considered and these may require further investigation and revisions to any Environmental Statement. It may also require further consultation with affected parties.

If a tenderer is proposing an alternative source for the supply of beach recharge material, then the following aspects need careful consideration:

- the security of the supply both for this contract and future renourishment contracts

- the consequences for the existing design and whether further design work is necessary to confirm the performance of the alternative material

- the health and safety risks associated with the alternative

- the grading of the alternative material

- the levels of contamination present in the alternative material

- the effect of the existing material on adjacent frontages.

If the alternative source is unlicensed at time of tender, then very careful consideration should be given prior to embarking on the tendering procedure to the likely time required to obtain a licence and the effects this may have on the contract programme.

10.5 CONSTRUCTION

10.5.1 Safe working

The UK CDM Regulations prohibit any client from allowing construction to commence until the contractor has adequately prepared the construction phase health and safety plan.

During the construction process, the contractor is then responsible for health and safety matters.

10.5.2 Sequencing of works

In cases where works to hard structures are to be carried out in conjunction with beach recharge or other beach management schemes then careful consideration must be given to the sequencing of contracts for these works. Where the structures form controls on the beach movement (e.g. groynes, breakwaters) then it is likely to be desirable to construct these in advance of beach recharge in order that the sand or shingle is retained when placed.

Groynes can, however, impede access along the beach. The sequencing of works must, therefore, recognise this and provisions made for access to facilitate future beach management.

10.5.3 Supervision

The purpose of supervision is to ensure that the contract is completed in accordance with the Specification and Conditions of Contract and also to programme.   Supervision, therefore, includes the following activities on site:

* monitoring, working methods adopted by the Contractor to ensure they comply with the Specification
* checking that the completed sections of work comply with the Specification and drawings (on a beach recharge contract this would involve checks on the grading of the recharge material, for absence of contaminants and on the line and level of the completed profile)
* authorising variations to the contract
* recording progress and all activities on site
* measuring, jointly with the Contractor, the quantity of work completed so that the employer may make interim payments
* cooperating closely with the Contractor on all matters of site safety.

On beach recharge projects the construction site is generally a public area and the Engineer's staff must ensure that the Contractor complies fully with the public safety provisions included in the Contract Documents. For the same reason it is also likely that the project will be of considerable interest to the public. The supervising staff will have an important role to play in liaising with and advising the public of activities on site. To assist with this role it may be appropriate for supervising staff or the client to hold weekly meetings at which the public may obtain information on the project or voice their concerns (see also Section 11.1.3).

Where a Contractor is working 24 hours per day, progress on site can be very rapid. In these circumstances it is important that the Engineer's representative is delegated sufficient powers under the Contract to quickly resolve any problems that may occur on site. If the Contractor has to continually refer back to the Engineer for decisions then costly delays may occur. There may also be a requirement for an ecologist or archaeologist to be on site to supervise certain aspects of the construction process.

10.5.4 Sampling and testing

The sampling and testing required to confirm that the beach recharge material complies with the Specification will have been set out in the Contract Documents. Typical requirements are described in Chapter 7, where the link between measurement and sampling is also discussed.

Over and above the sampling and testing required under the contract it may also be appropriate to undertake more extensive sampling of the beach to provide data for a long term monitoring programme. The requirements of such a monitoring programme are discussed in Chapter 4.

In order to assess impacts of a scheme it is necessary to obtain information on the existing environment at various stages throughout the scheme. Initially a sampling strategy should be devised which, ideally, is carried out several times during the year prior to the proposed works, although it should be noted that even a full year of sampling may not provide a fully representative baseline. This will enable the collation of a baseline dataset which accounts for natural seasonal fluctuations in community structure. Such sampling should be carried out in the proposed borrow area and the recharge area. Detailed survey requirements will vary depending on the scheme size, location and proximity to sensitive sites. Adequate surveys should be carried out to establish the existing environment in terms of the following, as applicable:

* infauna (animals living in the sediment)
* epifauna and epiflora (animals and plants living on the surface)
* pelagic fauna (animals living in the water column)
* planktonic organisms (zoo- and phyto-plankton).

Surveys will be required both in and around the area to be dredged to enable consideration of potential indirect impacts (e.g. smothering due to the resettlement of dredging induced suspended material). Chemical and physical analysis should also be carried out to establish the potential impacts due to any contaminant resuspension and increases in turbidity.

Comparable survey methods should be used to survey the same areas during the actual works. Any mitigation measures recommended in the Environmental Statement should be adhered to if impacts are identified. It is important that post project survey work is carried out to monitor the impact of the scheme on the environment and to ensure that all mitigation measures, where necessary, are successful. Post-project monitoring is also important to enable the collation of information to aid in the assessment of environmental impacts in future schemes.

10.5.5   Surveys and measurement

Beach profiles are necessary for measurement purposes to either establish the volume of material placed on the beach or, if hopper measurement is adopted, to confirm the material has been placed to the line and level specified. The interval at which beach surveys are required will have been set out in the Contract Documents and this aspect is discussed in Section 10.3.

Over and above the need to complete profiles for contract purposes it may also be appropriate to undertake additional survey work to contribute data to the long-term monitoring of the beach. In particular, beach profiles may be taken on both the up and downdrift sides of the recharge to monitor the longshore transport of material from the new beach.

10.5.6   Environmental management of the construction process

The environmental studies undertaken during the feasibility and design stages of a project, will have made recommendations as to methods of "management" designed to minimise environmental damage during the construction works (see Section 7.9). Such recommendations, or mitigating measures, are likely to include:

* thorough liaison with the public, interested bodies and users (e.g. fisheries interests)
* careful location of site compound to avoid visual impacts
* noise and vibration control
* dust minimisation
* waste water control
* lighting control
* protection of sensitive nature conservation, geological or landscape sites, possibly necessitating an ecologist on site to supervise operations in potentially vulnerable areas
* timing/seasonality or programming of works to avoid sensitive times of year including bank holidays and height of tourist season or bird breeding season (e.g. for beach nesting little terns)
* provision of adequate access and safety measures
* road traffic or navigation management
* monitoring where features of ecological or geological interest may be disturbed.

Two CIRIA handbooks provide practical guidance on the above measures to those concerned with the tender and construction phases of a civil engineering project (see Box 10.2).

10.6   POST-PROJECT MONITORING

It is important to demonstrate the performance of coastal defence structures and management methods after the event, and not only as a justification for those works.

The basis for such appraisals lies in the monitoring undertaken before and after the implementation of any scheme (capital or management), and the subsequent analysis of the results. It is crucial if there have been assumptions made about the expected performance and life-time of a scheme as part of the decision to implement it. In particular, the monitoring of

- Environmental handbook for building and civil engineering projects - Design and specification, Special Publication 97 (CIRIA, 1994a)

- Environmental handbook for building and civil engineering projects - Construction phase, Special Publication 98 (CIRIA 1994b)

A major objective of these Handbooks is to provide a checklist for and guidance on the environmental considerations required at the various stages in the life of construction projects, identifying key activities and decision-making stages which can have a significant impact on the environment. Legislative requirements and associated measurements and controls are also detailed.

beach levels and beach volumes is vitally important, but other factors may also have to be taken into account, depending on circumstances. As a general rule, monitoring should not start on completion of a particular scheme, but for some time before and during its implementation. Comparisons should not only be made between the present-day position and that at the beginning of the scheme, but also with the expected present-day situation had the scheme not been installed.

Wherever possible, monitoring should be carried out in a fashion which allows the effect of a scheme to be separated from the effects of the weather and changing hydraulic conditions. This will involve comparing different stretches of coast, with similar material and similar exposure to waves and tides, but with different management methods being applied. There will be few ideal sites for such control measurements, because of the nature of the UK coastline. Nevertheless it is important to provide a reasoned opinion on whether beach changes were the result of particular (storm) events or of the management methods used.

Within the UK, the NRA Anglian Region have developed a post-project monitoring programme that is integrated into a general coastal monitoring plan (see Box 4.1). Full details on these and other monitoring techniques and the analysis of results, including monitoring of both physical and environmental parameters, are given in Chapter 4.

10.7 POST-PROJECT EVALUATION

10.7.1 General

Post-project evaluation is the assessment of a project, either shortly after it has been completed or after it has been established for a number of years. The purpose of the evaluation is to enable improvements to be made to all aspects of the planning, design and implementation of future schemes based on the experience learnt from completed projects.

Evaluations will normally cover the engineering performance, and the environmental and economic aspects of a project.

Within the UK a useful guide to procedures can be found in the MAFF Procedural Guidelines for Post-Project Evaluation of Flood and Coastal Defence Schemes (MAFF, 1994). A summary of the MAFF procedures is given in Box 10.3.

10.7.2 Assessment of performance

In general, the main concern of a beach manager will be to ensure that the methods adopted are providing a satisfactory standard of defence. Prior to the implementation of any management strategy, even if it was to do nothing, there should have been an assessment of the requirements of the beach as a defence structure. This will have involved quantifying an acceptable beach volume, and perhaps crest levels or crest width, based on calculations under design storm conditions. The post-project appraisal should therefore include a simple comparison of the present-day beach against these specified criteria, for at least the most important sections of coast. Specifically, this will include:

Box 10.3 *MAFF Procedural Guidelines for Post Project Evaluation of flood and coastal defence schemes*

Each evaluation normally investigates the following aspects of a project:

* technical
* economical/financial
* environmental
* operation and maintenance
* public perception
* appraisal, design and contract procedures.

A *construction evaluation* is carried out within about 12 months after completion of the project. This addresses technical, financial and environmental issues.

A *performance evaluation* is undertaken after four or five years from the completion of the works. This consists of a technical, financial and environmental evaluation. The construction evaluation may recommend more frequent performance evaluations.

Meetings of the evaluator with key personnel from the scheme development and construction phases are organised to develop an insight into the project history and to enable the background to decisions to be fully understood

The site of the project is visited early in the evaluation process so that the evaluator can understand the environment in which the project was constructed and to get a better appreciation of the project.

* calculations of beach volumes
* comparisons of beach levels with expected values
* trends in these quantities, compared with expected trends
* rate of alongshore transport, compared with expected rate
* depth of cover to substrate, toe of seawalls, etc.
* effects on updrift or downdrift beaches.

In the case of sand beaches in particular, a substantial part of the "active" beach volume is below low water. Ideally, this volume would be assessed by hydrographic survey but routine surveys may not be favoured for budgetary reasons; moreover, there are sometimes practical difficulties in taking sounding in very shallow waters. In the USA low-cost systems for measuring berm profiles below low water have been devised. These use a simple staff fixed to a sled which is taken away from the shore in small boat, and then winched ashore whilst level measurements are taken.

In addition, a number of other aspects may need to be monitored and appraised, depending on circumstances. These include:

* changes in beach texture/material (e.g. mud accumulation)
* steep scarps/bluffs in beach or dune faces
* beach material being carried over seawalls, promenades, groynes
* current speeds and directions, especially near new breakwaters
* damage or displacement to any structures or defences
* effects on downdrift or updrift beaches.

Where the performance of works is worse than expected, further work will be necessary to understand the reason why and to reassess the scheme's cost-effectiveness. This may lead to consideration of supplementary works (e.g. enlarging groynes) to support the investment already made.

Wherever possible, as noted in Section 10.6, any such appraisal should be compared with other stretches of coast. Unusually severe weather conditions soon after implementation of a scheme may unfairly prejudice an appraisal if some type of control monitoring is not available. Alternatively, if such similar stretches of coast are not available, then previous experience at the site itself under similar extreme conditions might be used for comparison.

10.7.3 Environmental considerations

The Environmental Statement or similar environmental report should describe any post-project evaluation monitoring and surveillance requirements. Some examples are set out in Table 10.1.

Table 10.1   Examples of environmental monitoring and surveillance requirements

Environmental parameter(s)	Objectives of monitoring/surveillance
Flora and fauna	To ensure the ongoing protection of identified sensitive sites. To ensure adequate re-establishment of vegetation in areas which have experienced disturbance.
Access	To ensure adequate provision of alternative access and re-instatement of existing access to the same or higher quality.
Safety	To ensure adequate signposting of potential public hazards.
Archaeology	To ensure that relevant provisions have been made to secure the protection of any sensitive sites.

Following construction it is important to monitor and review various environmental parameters in order both to verify any predictions made in the Environmental Statement and to measure the adequacy of mitigation measures and the success of enhancement initiatives. Such a review or post-project study/report should evaluate the "environmental performance" of the project in terms of "environmental criteria" (e.g. has the original baseline proved valid for subsequent monitoring) and the "impact of the project" (e.g. on change to nature conservation, visual impacts, morphology, water quality, etc.). The investigation should also address the following questions: how environmental issues were incorporated into the design stage; whether the initial Environmental Statement was adequate; if materials, timing and extent of construction/site operations had an environmental impact? The study should also comment on public perception during construction and highlight any obvious omissions in the issues identified. If there is no record of monitoring or surveillance requirements, this should be stated. Finally, such a review will enable variations to be made if necessary, thus ensuring the continued environmental acceptability of the completed project. It is important that such surveillance requirements are written into the contract documents to assist the Contractor in their subsequent execution.

10.7.4 Economics

A post-project evaluation of the economics of a scheme should attempt to compare the actual costs of construction and maintenance, benefits and damages with those estimated during the planning stage of the project. The economic analysis presented in the original Project Appraisal/Engineer's Report should be reviewed using post-project data.

Actual construction and maintenance costs together with damages, if any, should be relatively straightforward to establish. The actual take up of benefits is likely to prove more difficult to establish. The post-project evaluation should also highlight any unexpected benefits/disbenefits and assess if the economic appraisal was a fair representation. It may also be pertinent to assess any other subsequent changes in land use or assets protected.

10.7.5 Conclusions

Once the post-project appraisal has been completed and compared with the original appraisal, the reasons for any discrepancies should be reviewed and lessons that can be learnt identified and disseminated to all interested parties.

11 Ongoing management and beach maintenance

The dynamic nature of beaches makes the ongoing management and maintenance of beaches and beach schemes essential. Even if the action necessary only involves ongoing monitoring (described in detail in Chapter 4), it is essential to manage a beach following its implementation.

This final chapter covers the issues that may need to be considered by the beach manager in implementing an ongoing maintenance strategy. It covers both specific activities in regard to the beach (such as periodic recharge, longshore recycling and profile regradings) and the maintenance of beach control structures (see also CIRIA/CUR, 1991). In addition the chapter describes a range of specific environmental management issues, including some details on the control of blown sand.

Authorities managing beaches should produce an operating manual for each beach under their control, setting out how, when and why the need for maintenance activities should be triggered (see also Chapter 4).

11.1 PERIODIC RECHARGE

Beach recharge is the process of directly increasing the volume of a beach using imported material usually to improve its capacity as a coastal defence. Normally recharge is used to make good losses which have occurred as a result of changes to the supply of material from updrift, or to make good losses caused, for example, by the erosion of soft substrate underlying the beach. More rarely it is used to compensate for the organised removal of material from a beach for industrial use or to improve the amenity value of the coastline. The general design considerations for beach recharge are covered in Chapter 7. These considerations apply equally to periodic recharge as part of ongoing beach maintenance.

11.1.1 Effectiveness

The effectiveness of beach recharge will depend on how badly beaches have deteriorated. For example whilst loss of volume can be restored if material of a similar nature can be found for recharge, erosion of the underlying pavement on which the beach lies generally cannot Certainly, the addition of relatively small quantities of material may result in little visible improvement. Sand recharge on a beach will be redistributed across the full active beach, including the nearshore zone, and therefore a small volume recharge will have negligible effect. As shingle tends to remain within a narrow zone along the upper beach, recharge requires smaller volumes to be effective. Recharge with material of a similar size, grading and shape will also tend to be more effective than using fine-grained material.

Beaches which may benefit from sand recharge are those with a relatively healthy upper beach where the waterline rarely, if ever, comes into contact with hard defences. Recharge is thus useful for making good backshore losses due to storm erosion and for healing gaps in the line of defence due to dune blow-outs. Sand recharge is rarely effective on a rapidly falling beach, unless it is carried out in conjunction with control structures (see Chapter 8). Even then there will often be a need for substantial and regular maintenance recharges. Most shingle beaches, on the other hand, will benefit even if only limited quantities of shingle are imported into the beach system. As a method of improving defences, beach recharge is often the most environmentally acceptable option available to the coastal manager.

11.1.2 Role of monitoring and modelling

The successful management of beach recharge schemes, as with other schemes which involve the rehandling or artificial redistribution of material on a beach, requires a commitment to regular beach monitoring. Measurement of changes in the volume of a beach together with information about the costs of adding quantities of material periodically, are needed to determine the cost-effectiveness of such operations. The rate at which material is lost from a recharge scheme, determined volumetrically, can be used to calibrate longshore transport mathematical models, which can then be used to refine future recharge schemes. It should be noted that overcharging a beach with fine material can lead to rapid dispersion and thus modelling has as important role to play in determining the optimum recharge material type and grading and the optimum frequency of recharge.

An interesting case was reported at San Onofre in California where a large volume of sand was placed on a relatively short length of straight, open coast. The material migrated quite rapidly (2m per day) along the coast as a hump, not only depriving the original area of its new beach, but also, by refracting waves towards it and causing a local reduction in longshore drift rates, provoking a "wave" of erosion in front of it. Such problems can be minimised by the prediction of beach planshape changes following recharge. Details of suitable modelling techniques can be found in Sections 5.3 and 6.4 of the manual.

11.1.3 Environmental considerations

Environmental impacts of beach recharge will essentially be the same as those associated with the initial nourishment (see Section 7.9).

11.2 LONGSHORE RECYCLING

Longshore recycling involves the mechanical movement of sediment from the downdrift end of a beach, back to the updrift end. Through this approach a degree of continuity of beach material supply and transport can be achieved.

Recycling operations are normally carried out immediately after winter or seasonal storms when littoral transport has passed its annual maximum. The updrift frontage often suffers most during winter weather as a result of the combination of rapid littoral transport and beach drawdown. During the summer period, public beach usage normally prohibits recycling. Consideration must also be given to factors such as road access and public disturbance, if recycling is to involve haulage by lorry.

11.2.1 Effectiveness

The effectiveness of shingle recycling operations has been proven on the south-east coast where the NRA regularly transport shingle by lorry. Indeed shingle recycling was pioneered in Kent and Sussex in the 1950's for maintaining adequate beach levels in front of existing hard defences which would otherwise have had to be rebuilt at high cost. An example of this technique is given in Box 11.1 below.

Recycling can have a number of potential advantages. It is relatively low cost in comparison with capital works schemes e.g. rebuilding a seawall. Apart from reducing downdrift problems, a rapid response can be made to changes in the littoral drift rate or to the impact of severe storms which might otherwise cause breaching of low-lying areas. The negative impacts which are associated with recharge with imported material, such as beach scarping and offshore losses, do not appear to be so great a problem with shingle recycling.

The high degree of flexibility of operations is particularly important on those coasts of the United Kingdom on which littoral drift rates not only fluctuate significantly on an annual basis but often reverse in direction, not only seasonally but occasionally for a period of several years (or more).

Box 11.1 *Shingle recycling - Pett, E. Sussex*

The Pett foreshore, to the west of Dungeness, has only a limited amount of beach feed at its western end, while the harbour arm of the River Rother at the eastern end traps most of the net eastward littoral drift of shingle. This frontage therefore forms a unit, ideally suited for recycling operations. Following persistent erosion and deterioration of existing flood defences on this frontage, access ramps were constructed over the existing seawall and an initial transfer of 150,000m^3 of shingle was made in 1970. This has been followed by annual recycling at the rate of 19,000m^3 per year and has proved to be successful. The shingle is dug from the beach face immediately updrift of the Rother and this operation has not only maintained the beaches to the west, but has also prevented the river mouth from blockage by shingle (though some blockage with sand does occur).

The main constraints with this type of operation are beach material size, access to the beach and transport routes. Recycling is best suited for shingle beaches. For flatter mixed sand/shingle beaches or for wide sand beaches, recycling not only poses difficulties because of the large scale of the loading and trucking operation required, but also because of the amenity and environmental hazards that may result e.g. damage to fragile dune systems, disruption of greater amenity usage, destruction of infauna. Beach recycling operations are thus best suited for relatively coarse materials which can be easily handled, for low to moderate rates of littoral drift and for recycling within relatively small coastal units.

There is limited scope for sand recycling in the UK except under very special circumstances. Such circumstances would include emergency restoration of beaches following extensive storm damage. Recycling is however commonplace on the east coast of the USA, for example, where emergency barrier island restoration has to be carried out quite regularly following severe storms and hurricanes. The cost-effectiveness of such measures is however a matter of some debate.

In terms of cost, recycling operations will be largely dependent upon the haulage distance, though factors such as the volume moved clearly are also important. In general, the cost of recycling operations for shingle will vary from about £1/m^3 to as much as £8/m^3 (1994 prices). The costs of recycling operations on sand beaches will clearly be much higher due to the more rapid rates of littoral drift.

Recycling can be carried out at relatively short notice in response to sudden demand. At Hayling Island, Hampshire, for example, recycling of the shingle recharge will significantly prolong the lifespan of the original scheme. Beach recycling in the UK is mainly carried out in response to changes in the pattern of littoral drift, caused by the strong impact of shifts in wave direction.

11.2.2   Environmental considerations

In terms of impact on the natural environment of recycling operations, since fresh material is not being won, many of the adverse impacts listed in Table 7.5, Section 7.9, for construction of beach recharge schemes will not apply. However, there will be an inevitable loss of or damage to some habitat as a result of transport and, to a certain extent from removal, placement and regrading.

In some cases, there may also be downdrift impacts which arise from the reduction of supply to the downdrift frontages, but these can often be designed out in an overall scheme.

Impacts on the human environment during recycling will include the majority of those listed in Table 7.5, but the impact can be significantly reduced where the haulage plant can use the beach itself to recycle the material and the works can be timed to avoid the summer tourist season. At Seaford in East Sussex, for example, periodic recycling of shingle plays an integral part in the management of the beach. Operations are normally carried out during the winter when up to 80,000m^3 may be transported within a 3 month period, with little effect on beach amenity.

11.2.3 Role of monitoring and modelling

The role of monitoring is of particular importance for beach recycling operations. On most coasts the littoral drift not only shows great seasonal variations but also major changes from year to year. This is especially true for coastal frontages which are exposed to a high level of wave activity and where the angle of incidence of the predominant waves to the beach contours is small. Under these conditions, any small change in the wave activity may result in a large change in the littoral transport rate and hence the recycling volumes. Monitoring therefore helps by determining the volume of sediment that has to be relocated to restore the beach to its desired position, and later to check that this has been achieved. A good example of this is the recharged beach at Seaford in East Sussex, where the main frontage is aligned almost perpendicular to the predominant south-westerly waves and hence small changes in the morphologically averaged wave direction (see Section 3.4.2) can lead to changes in drift direction as well as drift rate.

Numerical modelling can also play a significant role in the management of long stretches of coastline especially if verified by detailed measurement of beach volume changes. By the accumulation of monitoring results over many years, therefore, a great deal of light is shed on the sediment transport characteristics of the coastline. An example of monitoring for beach recycling operations is given in Box 11.2 below.

Box 11.2 *Monitoring recycling - Dungeness, Kent*

> Efficient management of beach recycling is carried out to protect the frontage of Dungeness Power Station, situated on the west face of the peninsula. After extensive studies of the historical evolution of the peninsula and mathematical modelling of littoral drift over the Power Station frontage, it was decided to maintain a protective beach width by means of recycling shingle from east to west. The recycling requirement was estimated at 20,000m³ per annum. Operations began in 1965 and have been continuing since. Detailed monitoring of beach volume changes has shown that the requirement for annual recycling has been at about 540m³ above first estimates. This shows that the requirement for recharge had been accurately determined. The discrepancy between the original estimates and actual recycling requirements is ascribed to a reducing supply from the west (i.e. updrift of the frontage).

11.3 BEACH PROFILE REGRADING

Beach profile regrading involves the adjustment of the beach profile from its natural condition to an artificial one. It is often used to slow down erosion or to aid beach recovery on amenity beaches following winter draw-down. It is carried out by land-based plant, such as bulldozers and haulage trucks, and is therefore a flexible method of management which can easily be tied into other methods (e.g. beach recycling). Regrading is generally only effective in the short term and does not solve underlying causes of erosion e.g. losses of beach material along the coast.

Regrading is normally carried out within the intertidal zone and results in a general steepening of the beach slope as a result of the transfer of material from seaward to landward. Beach regrading may also involve the addition of material to the backshore as a means of dune restoration.

11.3.1 Beach scraping

Beach scraping involves gathering material from a wide area of lower beach profile and transferring it mechanically to the upper beach. It is normally most beneficial in duned areas, where the addition of sand to the backshore significantly delays the onset of erosion and scarping of the underlying beach. By contrast, the exercise is likely to be least effective in front of vertical walls where it will have a very short residence period. An example of beach scraping is given in Box 11.3.

Beach regrading can play an important role in terms of storm berm maintenance and protection against flooding, particularly on shingle storm beaches which are deficient in material. Areas which are suitable for this form of management are, for example, rural areas which are relatively inaccessible and of low land value, where the costs of more traditional forms of protection are difficult to justify. Raising the shingle beach crest has been practised in conjunction with artificial recharge at Medmery, west of Selsey Bill (see Figure 11.1). This practice, while sometimes carried out in response to wave overtopping events, has certainly reduced the incidence of flooding the low-lying hinterland. The claimed advantage of the process is that it speeds beach recovery after storm damage. The new artificial profile then offers greater protection from the next storm.

Figure 11.1   *Beach scraping at Medmery, west of Selsey Bill, W. Sussex, (courtesy HR Wallingford)*

Advantages of this form of operation over other methods of beach manipulation include a low unit cost due to the short haul distance, and great flexibility allowing emergency works to be carried out at short notice. However, the repeated reworking of existing beach deposits may, in the long term, result in the removal of fines from the beach and possible damage to the beach sub-layers.

There may also be some scope for using mechanical regrading on extensive sand beaches, when the beach gradient is very low and where removal of material from the low tide mark does little to alter this gradient. It is recommended that only a thin sand layer is removed by scraping and this layer should be considerably less than the thickness of sand over the beach sub-strata.

It should be stressed that assessment of this form of beach management requires extensive profile monitoring to compare the performance against adjacent unaltered control areas.

Box 11.3   *Beach scraping - Topsail Beach, North Carolina*

Field trials at Topsail Beach, North Carolina, have been used to assess beach scraping performance. Changes after reprofiling were compared against the performance of an unaltered "control" beach. The beach at Topsail consists of medium-sized sand, sloping at about 1:17 from the toe of the dunes to mean low water. The mean tidal range is only 1m and the wave height averages at 0.6m to 0.9m in 5.1m water depth. The net longshore transport is northwards but has strong seasonal reversals. During the field trials, the coast was hit by two severe storms, including Hurricane Hugo. On average the control section lost a greater amount of its primary dune than the scraped section (2.82m³/m as compared with 2.06m³/m). However the two storms produced different beach response, with greater erosion in the scraped section than in the control section during the hurricane. It appears that a scraped beach is more susceptible to damage than a natural beach under catastrophic events but less so during calmer weather conditions. Over an annual cycle, the scraped beach retained a larger volume of sediment than the control beach, indicating no adverse impacts. The fears that beach handling itself may result in net losses does appear to be unjustified. After a year of monitoring, it was concluded that while beach reprofiling can be beneficial to protection of the backshore, oversteepening of the beach by reprofiling can have a locally destabilising effect on sand beaches. It is therefore recommended that controlled scraping should only be carried out for backshore protection and that it should only be carried out with simultaneous beach monitoring. Ideally material should be removed from the beach face at a slower rate than the expected rate of natural recovery (as determined by profile measurements).

11.4   MAINTAINING BEACH CONTROL STRUCTURES

All structures must be maintained. This is particularly true of beach control structures which are located in the exposed marine environment, where lack of maintenance could quickly lead to extensive damage and possibly failure of the structure.

Maintenance should therefore be addressed both at the design stage and throughout the operational life of the structure.

11.4.1   Design for maintenance

During the design of beach control structures, the following should be considered in relation to the future maintenance of the works:

1.   Detailing - structures should be detailed, bearing in mind that elements vulnerable to settlement, corrosion, abrasion, etc. may require repair or replacement in the future. Detailing should also ensure that in the event of damage, that it is progressive so that maintenance can be undertaken before the structure has failed totally.

2.   Access for maintenance - provision shall be made to enable plant and material to be brought to site to complete maintenance operations. Vulnerable elements of the structure likely to require repair or replacement should also be readily accessible so that maintenance can be undertaken.

3.   Stockpiling - where special materials are used for construction or where the supply of certain materials, such as heavy rock, involves substantial mobilisation costs, consideration should be given to stockpiling some materials at the end of construction for subsequent maintenance use.

4.   Monitoring and maintenance programme - a programme for monitoring and regular maintenance of the structure should be prepared by the designer and submitted to the owner. Monitoring and maintenance is discussed further in the following section.

Further details on this aspect of design may be found in Sections 6.8 and 6.9 of the *Seawall Design* manual (Thomas and Hall, 1992) and in Chapter 7 of the *Manual for the Use of Rock in Coastal and Shoreline Engineering* (CUR/CIRIA, 1991).

11.4.2 Structural monitoring and maintenance

Following completion of the works, regular structural monitoring should take place to ensure that the structure continues to perform satisfactorily, as well as monitoring of the beach/seabed levels adjacent to the structure. In addition, it may also be desirable to monitor the wind, wave and tidal climate at the site. This latter point is discussed in Section 4.5.

Structural monitoring enables planning of repair work and assessment of the actual long-term performance of the structure. It will also identify gradual deterioration of the structure which, without regular and systematic measurements, may continue unnoticed.

The frequency at which monitoring is undertaken is related to the consequences of failure, but, as a minimum, it is recommended that monitoring takes place:

• immediately after construction to provide baseline measurements
• immediately after extreme storms when beach draw-down may expose lower parts of the structure
• annually (and preferably in the spring) for all elements in the inter-tidal zone where exposure to wave action is greatest
• every five years for submerged elements.

Typical monitoring techniques for the structures discussed in Chapter 8 are given in Table 11.1. The table also gives an indication of the likely maintenance operations that will be required for each type of structure. It can be seen that erosion of the toe is a problem common to all of these structures and this mechanism is, in fact, one of the most likely causes of failure. Monitoring and maintenance of the toe is therefore vitally important.

Table 11.1   Monitoring and maintenance of beach control structures

Type of structure	Monitoring methods	Typical maintenance
Detached breakwaters and shore connected breakwaters	• Visual inspection at low water • General, fixed aspect and aerial photography • Profile surveys using land and/or bathymetric techniques • Side-scan sonar, for parts of structures permanently submerged	• Replace dislodged rocks • Repair/extend toe protection
Modified seawalls and revetments	• Visual inspection at low water • General, fixed aspect and aerial photography • Profile surveys of structure and foreshore • Inspection for voids	*All Types* • Repair/extend toe protection • Repair handrailing • Maintain drainage, eg. flap valves *Concrete* • Repair joints and cracks • Replace abraded and corroded sections *Rock* • As for detached breakwaters
Groynes	• Visual inspection at low water • General, fixed aspect and aerial photography	*Timber* • Replace fixings and damaged/rotten members *Steel and Concrete* • As for seawalls *Rock* • As for detached breakwaters

Construction methods used for maintenance will generally follow the techniques and equipment used for the original construction. Access arrangements may, however, limit the size of plant that can be deployed on maintenance work.

Further details on the monitoring and maintenance of rock structures may be found in Chapter 7 of the *Manual for the Use of Rock in Coastal and Shoreline Engineering* (CUR/CIRIA, 1991).

11.5   CONTROL OF BLOWN SAND

On a developed beach frontage, blown sand can cause the following problems:

- disruption to seafront traffic through the deposition of sand on roads, car parks, etc.
- damage to vehicles and buildings
- deposition against seafront properties
- blockage of drainage systems.

Beach recharge schemes can increase the problems associated with blown sand by increasing the area of dry sand above the high water mark. This possibility should be considered during the planning stages of a beach recharge project.

11.5.1   Analysis methods

In addition to wind speed and grain size, the more important factors governing the initiation of transport are those controlling the moisture content of the sand surface (i.e. tidal conditions, humidity, air temperatures and solar radiation). This is because sand is more cohesive when wet and thus greater wind velocities are required before sand grains become mobile. At a qualitative level, this process is well understood but there has been limited success in applying the theory to practical situations and in reliably calculating quantities.

R A Bagnold was the pioneer of experiments involving wind blown sand transport and his publication in 1941 provides a formula for quantifying this movement. His empirical formula was developed from field data and analysis. Subsequent researchers have modified Bagnold's formula following their own investigations. Formulae have been developed by:

- Kawamura (1951)
- Kadib (1964)
- Lettau K and H (see Fryberger and Dean, 1979).

In the absence of any site-specific data it is recommended that volumes calculated from these formulae are only used for comparative purposes. Where local knowledge and measurements are available, it may be possible to calibrate the formulae using actual site measurements and use them to predict transport volumes with some improved confidence.

11.5.2   Control methods

Most techniques for the control of wind-blown sand attempt to interrupt the flow of wind in some way. Fencing and temporary walls are commonly used. These impede wind flow causing a reduction in velocity and hence deposition of sand. Full details are given in Section 9.1.3.

Typical methods adopted for the control of blown sand are listed in Table 11.2. On a developed frontage it may only be practicable to set up fencing and temporary walls during the winter when use of the beach by the public is limited. This may be considered sufficient as blown sand problems are generally more severe during the winter months.

The build up of sand against vertical seawalls causes sand-laden wind to be deflected upwards and over the wall. It is therefore important that this build-up of material is removed on a regular basis providing that this does not jeopardise the seawall structure or hydraulic characteristics.

Table 11.2   Methods of controlling wind-blown sand

Developed frontage	Open frontage
• Fencing on beach or along backshore	• Planting of vegetation
• Temporary walls	• Fencing to trap and accumulate sand
• Closure of gaps in seawall	• Fencing to prevent damage to vegetation by the public and animals
• Remove build-up of sand against vertical walls	• Use of broadwalks to prevent erosion at points where public access is required

Control methods on natural frontages generally aim to encourage the growth of vegetation either by new planting or the protection of existing growth using such things as fencing, broadwalks. Fencing may also be used to trap and accumulate sand, techniques which are used in the development of dunes (see Section 9.1.3).

11.6   MANAGING THE BEACH ENVIRONMENT

Beach management may accompany or lead to changes (improvements) in other aspects of beach use. In particular, a well managed beach may lead to increased use, in turn requiring other forms of management (see Figure 11.2). Beach management thus needs to be carried out within a broad environmental management context. Since 1976, for example, there has been a concerted effort by the regional water companies to improve bathing water quality. The "Good Beach Guide" published annually identifies, *inter alia*, beaches which have been awarded a Blue Flag under the programme run by the Foundation for Environmental Education in Europe. The Blue Flag is awarded to resort beaches which, in addition to passing the requirements of the EC Bathing Water Directive (76\160\EC), have fulfilled 25 land based criteria on safety, cleanliness and other facilities, details of which are given in Box 11.4.

Figure 11.2   *Dawlish Warren: looking west to end of rock revetment (courtesy HR Wallingford)*

Box 11.4 *European Blue Flag: 1995 Award Criteria*

The European Blue Flag for beaches is awarded annually and is only valid for one year. To be eligible for the Blue Flag a bathing beach has to fulfil all requirements. The Blue Flag should be removed whilst any criterion is no longer satisfied.

The European Blue Flag refers to resort beaches. A 'resort beach' is one which actively encourages visitors, has developed its facilities and provides varied recreational opportunities. The beach must be adjacent or within easy and reasonable access to the urban community and typically would include all the following facilities: a café or restaurant, shop, toilets, public transport, supervision, first aid, public telephone.

Water Quality

1   The water must comply with the Guideline value of the appropriate microbiological parameters of the EC Bathing Water Directive 76/160/EC
Guideline water must meet the guideline standard for faecal coliform, total coliform and faecal streptococci parameters and the mandatory standard for the faecal and total coliform parameters. There should be at least 20 samples taken at regular intervals throughout the bathing season (15 May - 30 September)

a]	total coliform	< 500 per 100 ml	80% compliance
b]	faecal coliform	< 100 per 100 ml	80% compliance
c]	faecal streptococci	< 100 per 100 ml	90% compliance

2   No industrial or sewage discharges affecting the beach area

Beach and Intertidal Area

3   No gross pollution by sewage related or other waste including glass and litter, and no discharge of industrial or urban waste
4   No algal or other vegetation materials accumulating or decaying
5   No oil pollution

Management

6   The beach must be actively managed by the owners (local authority or private) as a tourist resort
7   Local emergency plans to cope with pollution incidents
8   Easy and safe access to the beach for all including disabled people where this is possible
9   Prohibition of unauthorised driving, dumping and camping
10   Manage the conflicting and incompatible needs of different users e.g. zoning for swimmers, windsurfers, nature conservation
11   Dogs must be banned throughout the summer season
12   A source of drinking water
13   Public telephones within easy access to the beach
14   Clean and regularly maintained toilet facilities
15   All buildings and equipment must be maintained to a high standard and there must be safe confinement of all construction work which must not detract from the enjoyment of the beach user

Cleansing

16   Provide regular and adequate cleansing of the beach
17   Litter bins in adequate numbers, properly secured and regularly maintained/emptied

Safety

18   Safe bathing under all normal weather conditions
19   Life guard(s) on duty during the summer season and/or adequate safety provision including lifesaving equipment
20   Clearly signposted First Aid facilities

Information and Education

21   Prompt public warning if the beach or part thereof has or is expected to become grossly polluted or unsafe
22   Evidence that the interests of protected sites and rare or protected species have been addressed with close liaison with recognised local conservation organisations
23   Laws covering each use and code of conduct easily available to the public (including in tourist offices, town hall) and must be strictly enforced
24   Public display of   -   Bathing Water Quality poster with updated information of water quality and location of sampling points
                          -   Blue Flag Criteria
25   The responsible authority should be able to demonstrate at least five educational activities relating to the coastal environment in the area

In addition, the Tidy Britain Group grants "Seaside Awards" for both resort and rural beaches. The objective of the "Seaside Awards" is to raise standards of hygiene, safety and environmental management as well as actively encouraging visitors. In 1995, 182 British beaches were granted "Seaside Awards", a prestigious award when the marketing of a resort is considered.

Irrespective of whether beach management contributes to maintaining existing uses of the beach or attracting new ones, there are a number of aspects of the maintenance of beaches, beach control structures and associated facilities which always need to be taken into account. Some of these are discussed below.

Safety

A number of measures can be employed to improve public safety on beaches. Some possible features worthy of consideration, depending on local conditions, are given in Table 11.3.

Protecting bathing water quality

The quality of imported beach recharge may jeopardise water quality either locally or downstream if contaminated material is used inadvertently, or if a high proportion of fine material results in increased turbidity.

Algae control

Algae and lichens are valuable forms of marine life. Removal of algae from structures should therefore only be undertaken where they become a public hazard. In the event of such a hazard, their removal should only be carried out using MAFF approved pesticides which are suitable for the marine environment.

Table 11.3   Possible safety features for beach management

Potential Hazard	Safety Feature
Drop from sea defences or promenades	Handrailing
Rock armour (e.g. access for children)	Handrailing
Steps (e.g. slippery when wet)	Shallow design with handrails
Slipways/ramps (e.g. congestion)	Gentle slope, adequate room for turning and manoeuvring, proper maintenance
Detached breakwaters (e.g. navigational problems and access)	Navigation marks
Build up of unconsolidated fine deposits	Warning notice
Offshore winds and inclement weather conditions (e.g. swimmers)	Lifesaving equipment (conforming to recommendations in ROSPA/RLSS, (1993) Times and areas patrolled by lifeguards clearly marked and defined using the nationally recognised flag zoning system. Information boards detailing hazards, weather conditions, zoning, etc.
Currents and Tides (e.g. swimmers)	Lifeguards on duty during summer season Lifesaving equipment Warning notices/flags
Shelving beach (e.g. for water access and swimming)	Gently shelving beach incorporated into design
Wave cut cliffing on recharged beaches (see Section 7.9.2	Blade down with mechanical plant as necessary

Zoning enforcement

Additional public use of a beach may result in conflicts between users, for example bathers and watersports. Active, water-based pursuits which rely on beach access can be accommodated by allocating exclusive water areas using buoys and access channels, and actively enforcing such zones.

Amenity facilities

Increased usage of a beach may also require additional facilities such as car parks, toilets, showers and changing rooms.

Provision of information boards

These should detail local weather and tidal conditions in addition to warnings about other hazards.

Oil removal

Clearance of oil pollution from beaches may be necessary at certain times of the year. Removal of oil from sandy beaches should be carried out using manual or mechanical clearance methods (e.g. scraping into temporary pits). Oil on shingle beaches should be left to degrade naturally following initial build up, with manual clearance undertaken where necessary.

Litter control

Once a nourished beach becomes operational, more formal and informal recreational use of the area will generally occur and lead to a progressive increase in the amount of litter/debris left on the beach. A significant increase in beach litter may require either the provision of more facilities, or additional management activities such as beach cleaning. Additional litter bins and collection may be required, as well as possible beach clearance by mechanical means, particularly if a wide inter-tidal beach is being managed.

Need for beach management

The implementation of the ongoing engineering and environmental management measures discussed in this chapter is essential if beaches are to be managed in a sustainable way to both provide an adequate defence against flooding and erosion, and maintain their amenity, recreational and conservation value.

References

ABRAHAM G, KARELSE M and VAN OS A G (1979)
On the magnitude of interfacial shear of sub-critical stratified flows in relation to interfacial stability.
publication
Journal of Hydraulic Research, Vol. 17, No. 4, 1979, pp273-284

ALLEN, R. S. (1994)
Current disposal practices
In: *ICE/CEDA Seminar, Dredged Material Disposal - Problems and Solutions*, Institution of Civil Engineers, London, April 1994

ALLSOP, N.W.H., JONES, R.J. and BRADBURY, A.P. (1995)
Design of Beach Control Structures on Shingle Beaches
In: *Coastal Structures and Breakwaters '95*, ICE Conf., April 95, Paper 14

APPLETON, R.N. (1991)
Dredging of Swash Channel, Poole
In: *ICE Conference on Capital Dredging*, Edinburgh, May 1991, Thomas Telford, London

ASH, J (1994)
The Beneficial Use of Dredgings in the Marine Environment
In: MAFF Conference of River and Coastal Engineers, Loughborough, July 1994

BAGNOLD, R.A. (1963)
Mechanics of Marine Sedimentation
The Sea, M.N. Hill (ed), Wiley - Interscience, NY, pp507-582

BAGNOLD, R.A. (1941, new edition 1954)
The physics of blown sand and desert dunes
Methuen & Co. Ltd., London

BARBER, P.C. and DAVIES, C. (1985)
Offshore breakwaters - Leasowe Bay
Proc. Institution of Civil Engineers, Vol. 77, February, pp85-109

BERENGUER, J.M. and ENRIQUEZ, J (1988)
Design of pocket beaches; the Spanish case
In: *Proc. 21st Int. Coastal Engineering Conf.*, American Soc. Civil Engs.

BIRD, P.A.D., DAVIDSON, M A , BULLOCK, G.N. and HUNTLEY, D.A.
Wave measurement near reflective structures
In: *Proc. Coastal Dynamics '94*, American Soc. Civil Engs., Barcelona, Spain

BAKKER, W.T., KLEIN BRETELER, E.H.J. and ROOS, A., (1970)
The dynamics of a coast with a groyne system
In: *Proc. 12th ASCE Coastal Engineering Conference*, Washington DC, pp1001-1020

BIRKEMEIER, A.W. (1985)
Field data of seaward limit of profile change
ASCE Journal of Waterway, Port, Coastal and Ocean Engineering, Vol. 11 No 3

BLUMENTHAL, K.P. (1964)
The construction of a drift-sand dyke on the Island Rottumerplaat
In: *Proc. of 9th Coastal Engineering Conf.*, Lisbon, Portugal, ASCE, New York, pp346-367

BODGE, K.R. (1989)
A literature review of the distribution of longshore sediment transport across the surf zone
Journal of Coastal Research, Vol. 5, No.2

BODGE, K.R. and KRAUS, N.C. (1991)
Critical examination of longshore transport rate magnitude
In: *Proc. Coastal Sediments '91 Conf.*, Seattle, WA., ASCE, New York, pp139-155

BRAMPTON, A.H. (1993)
UK South Coast Shingle Mobility Study: alongshore drift variability
Report SR 319, HR Wallingford

BRAMPTON, A.H. and GOLDBERG, D.G. (1991)
Mathematical model of groyned shingle beaches
In: *Proc. Coastal Sediments '91 Conf.*, Seattle, WA., ASCE, New York, pp1842-1855

BRAMPTON, A.H. and HAWKES, P.J. (1990)
Wave Data Around the Coast of England and Wales: a review of instrumentally recorded information
Report SR 113, HR Wallingford

BRAY, R.N. and TATHAM, P.F.B. (1992)
Old Waterfront Walls - management, maintenance and rehabilitation
CIRIA/E & FN Spon, London

BRETSCHNEIDER, C.L. and REID, R.O. (1953)
Changes in wave height due to bottom friction, percolation and refraction
Technical Memorandum No 45, Beach Erosion Board, US Army Corps of Engineers, Washington

BRETSCHNEIDER, C.L. (1954)
Field investigations of wave energy loss in shallow water ocean waves
Report TM-46, Beach Erosion Board, US Army Corps of Engineers, Washington

BRITISH STANDARDS INSTITUTION (1975 - revised 1991)
Sampling and testing of mineral aggregates, sands and fillers
BS 812

BRITISH STANDARDS INSTITUTION (1977)
The structural use of timber
BS 5268

BRITISH STANDARDS INSTITUTION (1981)
Code of practice for site investigations
BS 5930

BRITISH STANDARDS INSTITUTION (1984)
Code of practice for maritime structures
BS 6349

BRITISH STANDARDS INSTITUTION (1984)
Code of practice for maritime structures: Part 1 General Criteria
BS 6349

BRITISH STANDARDS INSTITUTION (1990)
Methods of test for soils for civil engineering purposes
BS 1377: Part 2. Classification tests

BRITISH STANDARDS INSTITUTION (1990)
Methods of test for soils for civil engineering purposes
BS 1377

BRITISH STANDARDS INSTITUTION (1991)
Code of Practice for Maritime Structures: Part 7 Guide to the design and construction of breakwaters
BS 6349 Part 7

BRITISH TRUST FOR CONSERVATION VOLUNTEERS (1979)
Sand Dunes - a practical handbook

BROOKE, J.S. (1992)
Coastal Defence: the retreat option
Journal of the Institution of Water and Environmental Management Vol. 6 No. 2, pp151-157

BROOKE, J.S. (1993)
Marine Update No. 10
Worldwide Fund for Nature

BROOKE, J.S. and THOMAS, R.S. (1993)
Managed Retreat on Eroding Coasts: environmental considerations
Presented to *Association of District Councils, Coastal Protection and Planning Conference*, Great Yarmouth, 11-12 October 1993

BROOKE, J.S. and WHITTLE, I.R. (1990)
The role of environmental assessment in the design and construction of flood defence works
In: *Proc. IWEM Conf.*, Glasgow

BROOKES, A. (1979)
Coastlands
British Trust for Conservation Volunteers Ltd., published by Zoological Gardens, Regents Park, London NW1 4RY

BRUUN, P.M. (1954)
Coast Erosion and the Development of Beach Profiles
Technical Memo No. 44, Beach Erosion Board, U.S. Army Corps of Engineers

BRUUN, P.M. (1962)
Sea-Level Rise as a Cause of Shore Erosion
Journal of the Waterways, Harbors and Coastal Engineering Division, ASCE, Vol. 88, No. WW1, pp117-130

BRUUN, P.M. (1983)
Review of conditions for uses of the Bruun Rule of erosion
Journal of Coastal Engineering, Vol. 7, No. 1, pp77-89

BURCHARTH, H.F. and FRIGAARD, P. (1988)
On the 3-dimensional stability of reshaping berm breakwaters
In: *Proc. 21st ICCE*, Malaga, ASCE, New York

CAMPBELL, J.A. (1993)
Guidelines for assessing marine aggregate extraction
Laboratory Leaflet Number 73, MAFF Directorate of Fisheries Research, Lowestoft, 1993

CARTER, D.J.T. (1993)
Estimating extreme wave heights in the NE Atlantic from GEOSAT data
Health and Safety Executive, Offshore Technology Report OTH 93 396, pp24

CERC (1973)
Shore Protection Manual
Coastal Engineering Research Center, US Army Corps of Engineers, 2nd Edition

CERC (1984)
Shore Protection Manual
Coastal Engineering Research Center, US Army Corps of Engineers, 4th Edition

CERC (1993)
Engineering design guidance for detached breakwaters as shoreline stabilization structures
Coastal Engineering Research Center, US Army Corps of Engineers, 1993

CHADWICK, A.J., FLEMING, C., SENIM, J.D., and BULLOCK, G.N. (1994)
Performance Evaluation of Offshore Breakwaters: a field and computational model
In: *Coastal Dynamics '94*, Barcelona, pp 950-957

CHADWICK, A.J. (1988)
The derivation of longshore transport rates and the calibration of a longshore transport formula from the Shoreham Beach field data
Dept. Civil Engineering, Brighton Polytechnic

CIRIA (1990)
Groynes in Coastal Engineering: data on performance of existing groyne systems
CIRIA Technical Note 135

CIRIA (1993)
Environmental Issues in Construction
Volumes 1 and 2

CIRIA (1994a)
Environmental Handbook for Building and Civil Engineering Projects
Special Publication 97, Vol. 1: Design and Specification

CIRIA (1994b)
Building and Civil Engineering Projects
Special Publication 98, Vol. 2: Construction phase

CIRIA (1994c)
Environmental Assessment
Special Publication 95, CIRIA (London)

CIRIA (1996)
Beach Recharge Material - demand and resources
CIRIA Report 154

CIRIA/CUR (1991)
Manual on the use of rock in coastal and shoreline engineering
CIRIA Special Publication 83/CUR Report 154

CLARE, M.J. (1988)
The performance of the Hayling Island beach replenishment scheme
In: *MAFF Conference of River and Coastal Engineers*, Loughborough

CLAYTON, K.M. (1977)
Beach Profiles, Form and Change
East Anglia Coastal Research Programme, Report No 5, Universtity of East Anglia, 44pp.

CLAYTON, C.R.I. (1993)
The Standard Penetration Test (SPT): methods and use
CIRIA Funders Report/CP/7

COATES, T.T. (1994)
Effectiveness of control structures on shingle beaches, physical model studies
Report SR 387, HR Wallingford

COATES, T.T. and LOWE, J.P. (1993)
Three-dimensional response of open and groyned shingle beaches
Report SR 288, HR Wallingford, January

COLES, S.G. and TAWN, J.A. (1990)
Statistics of coastal flood prevention
Philosophical Transactions of the Royal Society, Series A, No 332, pp457-476.

COLQUHOUN, R.S. (1968)
Dune erosion and protective works at Pendrine, Carmarthenshire, 1961-1968
In: *Proc. 11th Int. Coastal Eng. Conf.*, London, September 1968, Vol 1, pp 708-718

CRAWFORD, A.R., WALKDEN, M.J., BIRD, P.A.D. and BULLOCK G.N. (1994)
Wave Impacts on Sea Walls and Breakwaters
In: *Coastal Dynamics '94*, Barcelona, pp656-670

DAVISON, A.T., NICHOLLS, R.J. and LEATHERMAN, S.P. (1992)
Beach nourishment as a coastal management tool: an annotated bibliography on developments associated with the artificial nourishment of beaches
Journal of Coastal Research, Vol. 8, No. 4, pp984-1022

DeVIDI, D. and COATES, T.T. (1995)
L-shaped breakwaters
HR Wallingford Internal Report IT 463

DE VRIEND, H.J. (1991)
G6 Coastal Morphodynamics
In: *Proc. Coastal Sediments '91*, Seattle, WA., ASCE., New York, pp 356-370

DEAN, R.G. (1977)
Equilibrium beach profiles; U.S. Antlantic and Gulf coasts
Ocean Engineering Report No.12, Department of Civil Engineering, Univ. of Delaware

DEAN, R.G. (1986)
Coastal Armouring: effects, principles and mitigation
In: *Proc. 20th Int. Coastal Engineering. Conf.*, ASCE, pp1843-57

DEAN, R.G. (1987)
Coastal Sediment Processes: toward engineering solutions
In: *Proc. Coastal Sediments '87*, ASCE, pp1-24

DEAN, R.G. (1988)
Evaluation of shore protection structures (including beach nourishment)
Short course: Planning and designing maritime structures,
Malaga, Spain, ASCE

DEAN, R.G. (1991)
Equilibrium Beach Profiles: characteristics and applications
Journal of Coastal Research, Vol. 7, No.1, pp 53-84

DEPARTMENT OF ENERGY (1977)
Offshore Installations: guidance on design and construction. Part II, Section 2: Environmental conditions
HMSO, London

DEPARTMENT OF ENERGY (1984)
Environmental parameters on the United Kingdom Continental Shelf
Offshore Technology Report OTH 84 201, HMSO, London

DEPARTMENT OF ENERGY (1990)
Offshore Installations: guidance on design, construction and certification
HMSO, London

DEPARTMENT OF ENERGY (1991)
Wave climate atlas of the British Isles
Offshore Technology Report OTH 89 303, HMSO, London

DEPARTMENT OF THE ENVIRONMENT (1989)
Environmental Assessment - a guide to the procedures
HMSO

DEPARTMENT OF THE ENVIRONMENT (1994)
Planning policy guidance 9, Nature Conservation
HMSO

DEPARTMENT OF THE ENVIRONMENT (in press)
Floods, waves and reservoir safety: an engineering guide
Thomas Telford, London

DHÉRENT, C. and PETIT-RENAUD, G. (1994)
Using archival resources for climate history research
UNESCO, Paris

DODD, N., BOWERS, E.C. and BRAMPTON, A.H. (1995)
Non-linear modelling of surf zone processes: a project definition study
HR Wallingford Report SR 398

DRAPER, L. (1982)
MIAS catalogue of instrumentally-measured wave data
Institute of Oceanographic Sciences, 2nd Edition

DUMBLETON, M.J., and WEST, G. (1976)
Preliminary Sources of Information for Site Investigation in Britain
DOE Transport and Road Research Laboratory L403

DYER, K.R. (1979)
Estuaries Hydrographical Sedimentation
Cambridge University Press

ENGLISH NATURE (1992)
Coastal zone conservation   English Nature's rationale, objectives and practical recommendations
English Nature, Northminster House, Peterborough PE1 1UA

FLEMING, C.A. (1990)
Guide to the Use of Groynes in Castal Egineering
CIRIA Report 119

FRYBERGER, S.G. and DEAN, G. (1979)
Dune forms and wind regime
In: McKee, E.D. (ed) *A study of global sand seas*, US Geological Society Professional Paper 1052, pp137-169

GALVIN, C. J. (1990)
Importance of longshore drift
Shore and Beach, Vol. 58, No 1.

GAO, S., COLLINS, M.B., LANCKNEUS, J., DeMOOR, G. and VAN LANCKER, V (1994)
Grain size trends associated with net sediment transport patterns; an example of the Belgian Continental Shelf
Marine Geology, Vol. 121, pp171-185

GODA, Y. (1985)
Random seas and design of maritime structures
University of Tokyo Press, Tokyo

GODA, Y. (1995)
Wave damping characteristics of a horizontal reef system
In: *Proc. Conf. Coastal Structures and Breakwaters '95*, Institution of Civil Engineers

GRAFF, J. (1981)
An investigation of the frequency distributions of annual sea level maxima at ports around Great Britain
Estuarine, Coastal and Shelf Science, Vol. 12, pp389-449

GRIFFITH, D.H. and KING, R.F. (1985)
Applied Geophysics for Engineers and Geologists
Second edition, Pergamon Press

HALLERMEIER, R.J. (1978)
Uses for a calculated limited depth to beach erosion
In: *Proc. 16th ICCE*, ASCE, New York

HALLERMEIER, R J (1981)
Terminal settling velocity of commonly occurring sand grains
Sedimentology, Vol. 28, No. 6, pp859-865

HALLERMEIER, R.J. and RHODES, P.E. (1988)
Generic Treatment of Dune Erosion for 100-year Event
In: *Proc. 21st Coastal Engineering. Conf.*, American Soc. Civil Engs., pp1197-1211

HANSON, H. and KRAUS, N.C. (1989)
GENESIS - a Generalized Shoreline Change Numerical Model
Journal of Coastal Research, Vol. 5, No. 1, pp1-27

HARDISTY, J. (1994)
Beach and nearshore sediment transport
In: Pye, K. (Editor), *Sediment Transport and Depositional Processes*, Blackwell Scientific Publications,
Oxford, pp219-255

HASSELMANN, K., BARNETT, T.P., BOUWS, E., CARLSEN, H., CARTWRIGHT, D.E., ENKEE, K., EWING, J.A.,
GIENAPP, H., HASSELMANN, D.E., KRUSEMAN, P., MEERBURG, A., MÜLLER, P., OLBERS, D.J.,
RICHTER, K., SELL, W. and WALDEN, H. (1973)
Measurements of wind-wave growth and swell decay during the joint North Sea wave project (JONSWAP)
Deutsches Hydrographisches Zeitschrift, No A8 (12), pp95

HAWKES, P.J. (1987)
A wave hindcasting model
In: *Advances in Underwater Technology, Ocean Science and Offshore Engineering, Vol. 12: Modelling the Offshore
Environment*, Society for Underwater Technology

HAWKES, P.J. and HAGUE, R.C. (1994)
Validation of joint probability methods for large waves and high water levels
Report SR 347, HR Wallingford

HAWKES, P.J. and JELLIMAN, C.E. (1993)
Review and validation of models of wave generation and transformation
Report SR 318, HR Wallingford

HAWKES, P.J., BAGENHOLM, C. and EWING, J.A. (1995)
Swell wave climate around the coast of England and Wales
Report SR 409, HR Wallingford

HEDGES, T.S. (1987)
Combinations of waves and currents: an introduction
Proc. Institution of Civil Engineers, Part 1 Vol. 82, June 1987

HEDGES, T.S., BURROWS, R. and DICKINSON, P.J. (1991)
Coastal wave climate categorization during storms
Proc. Institution of Civil Engineers, Part 2, Vol. 91, pp631-644

HERBERT, D.M. and OWEN, M.W. (1995)
Wave overtopping of sea walls - further research
In: *Coastal Structures and Breakwaters '95*, ICE Conf., April 95, Paper 5

HM TREASURY (1991)
Economic appraisal in central government: a technical guide for government departments
HMSO, April 1991

HOEK, E. and BRAY, I.W. (1977)
Rock Slope Engineering IMM
IMM., London

HOGBEN, N., DACUNHA, N.M.C, and OLLIVER, G.F. (1986)
Global wave statistics
Unwin Brothers for British Maritime Technology Ltd

HOGBEN, N. and LUMB, F.E. (1967)
Ocean wave statistics
HMSO, London

HR WALLINGFORD (1988)
Wave prediction in reservoirs: comparison of available methods
Report EX 1809, HR Wallingford

HR WALLINGFORD (1994)
Application of appropriate wave transformation models
Report EX 2991, HR Wallingford

HR WALLINGFORD (1995)
Coastal cells in Scotland
Report EX 3176, HR Wallingford, August

HSU, J.R.C., SILVESTER, R. and XIA, Y.M. (1989)
Generalities on static equilibrium bays
Journal of Coastal Engineering, Vol. 12, No.4, pp353-369

IADC (1990)
Users Guide to the 4th edition of the FIDIC Conditions of Contract for Works of Civil Engineering Construction,
International Association of Dredging Companies, January

IAHR (1986)
List of sea state parameters
IAHR Report, January

ICE (1988)
Penetration Testing in the UK
Proc. of Geotechnology Conf., Thomas Telford

ICE (1991)
Slope Stability Engineering developments and applications
Proc. of Int. Conf. on slope stability

ICE (1995)
New Engineering Contract (2nd Edition)
Institution of Civil Engineers, London

ICE (1993) Site Investigations Steering Group
Site Investigation in Construction
Thomas Telford, London 1993

INT. GEOLOGICAL SOCIETY OF ENGINEERING GROUP (1988)
Engineering Geophysics Report by Institute of Geologists
Quart. Journal of Engineering and Geology. Vol. 21, No.3

INTERGOVERNMENTAL PANEL ON CLIMATE CHANGE (IPCC) (1990)
Climate Change. The IPCC scientific assessment
Cambridge University Press

JAMES, W.R. (1975)
Techniques in evaluating suitability of borrow material for beach nourishment
Tech. Memo No. 60, Coastal Engineering Research Center, US Army Corps of Engineers

JELLIMAN, C.E., HAWKES, P.J. and BRAMPTON, A.H. (1991)
Wave climate change and its impact on UK coastal management
Report SR 260, HR Wallingford

JONES, R.J. and ALLSOP, N.W.H. (1994)
Rock armoured beach control structures on steep beaches
In: *24th Int. Conf. on Coastal Engineering*, Kobe, Japan, October 1994

KADIB, A.L. (1964)
Sand movement by wind
Tech. Memo No. 1, US Army Corps of Engineers, Addendum II

KAMPHUIS, J.W. (1991)
Alongshore Sediment Transport Rate
Journal of Waterway, Port, Coastal and Ocean Engineering, ASCE, Vol. 117, No. WW6

KAMPHUIS, J.W., DAVIES, M.H., NAIRN, R.B. and SAYAO, O.J. (1986)
Calculation of littoral sand transoport rate
Coastal Engineering, Vol. 10, pp1 21

KAO, J.S. and HALL, K.R. (1990)
Trends in stability of dynamically stable breakwaters
In: *Proc. 22nd ICCE*, Delft, ASCE, New York

KAWAMURA, R. (1951)
Study of sand movement by wind
Rep. of the Institute of Science and Technology, University of Tokyo, Vol. 5, No. 3/4, pp 95-112

KEDDIE, R.G. (1995)
Coasts and Seas of the United Kingdom. Region 5 North-east England: Berwick-upon-Tweed to Filey Bay,
Chapter 7: Coastal protected sites. Barne, H.R., Robson, C.F., Kaznowska, S.S. and Doody, J.P., (eds.)
Peterborough, Joint Nature Conservation Committee

KING, C.A.M. (1972)
Beaches and Coasts
Arnold, London (2nd edition)

KIRKGOZ, M.S. (1995)
Breaking wave impact on vertical and sloping coastal structures
Ocean Engineering, Vol. 22, No. 1, pp35-48

KOMAR, P.D. (1976)
Beach processes and sedimentation
Prentice-Hall, Engelwood Cliffs, New Jersey

KRAUS, N.C. and PICKLEY, O.H. (eds.) (1988)
The effects of seawalls on the beach
Journal of Coastal Research, Special Issue No. 4

KRIEBEL, D.L. (1986)
Verification Study of a Dune Erosion Model
Shore and Beach, Vol. 54, No. 3, pp13-21

KRUMBEIN, W.C. and JAMES, W.R. (1965)
A log-normal size distribution model for estimating stability of beach fill material
Tech Memo No. 16, Coastal Engineering Research Center, US Army Corps of Engineers

LARSON, M. (1991)
Equilibrium profile of a beach with varying grain size
In: *Proc. Coastal Sediments '91*, Seattle, WA., ASCE, New York, pp 905-919

MAFF (1993a)
Flood and Coastal Defence: project appraisal guidance notes
Report PB 1214

MAFF (1993b)
Strategy for flood and coastal defence in England and Wales
Report PB 1471

MAFF (1993c)
Coastal defence and the environment - a guide to good practice
Report PB 1191

MAFF (1993d)
Coastal defence and the environment - a strategic guide for managers and decision makers in the National Rivers Authority, Local Authorities and other bodies with coastal responsibilities
Report PB 1192

MAFF (1995)
Shoreline Management Plans - a guide for coastal defence authorities, MAFF

MARINE INFORMATION AND ADVISORY SERVICE (MIAS) (1982)
MIAS catalogue of instrumentally-measured wave data
MIAS Reference Publication No 1, IOS, Wormley, Surrey

MCDOWELL, D.M. and O'CONNOR, B.A. (1977)
Hydraulic behaviour of estuaries
Macmillan Press Limited

MCQUILLIN, R., and ARDUS, D.A. (1977)
Exploring the geology of shelf seas
Graham & Trotman, 1977

MEIGH, A.C. (1987)
Core Penetration testing - methods and interpretations
CIRIA/Butterworth-Heinemann, London

MIDDLESEX UNIVERSITY FLOOD HAZARD RESEARCH CENTRE (1990)
FLAIR (Food Loss Assessment Information Report)
Available directly from the University at Queensway, Enfield EN3 4SF (tel 0181 362 5359)

MILES, J.W. (1957)
On the generation of surface waves by shear flows
Journal of Fluid Mechanics, Vol. 3, pp185-204

MOTYKA, J.M. and BRAMPTON, A.H. (1993)
Coastal management: mapping of littoral cells
Report SR 328, HR Wallingford

MURRAY, A.J. (1992)
The Provision of Marine Sediments for Beach Recharge
Coastal Zone Planning and Management, Thomas Telford, London 1992

NICHOLLS, R.J. (1985)
The Stability of the Shingle Beaches in the Eastern Half of Christchurch Bay
PhD Thesis, Univ. of Southampton

OHNAKA, S. and WATANABE, D. (1990)
Modelling of wave-current interaction and beach change
In: *Proc. 22nd ICCE.*, Delft., pp 2443-2456

OZASA, H. and BRAMPTON, A.H. (1980)
Mathematical modelling of beaches backed by seawalls
Journal of Coastal Engineering, Vol. 4, No. 1, pp47-63

PARKER, D.J., GREEN, C.H. and THOMPSON, P.M. (1987)
Urban flood protection benefits: a project appraisal guide
(the 'Red Manual'), Gower

PARRISH, F. (1989)
Marine Resources, Coastal Management
Thomas Telford, 1989

PENNING-ROWSELL, E.C., GREEN, C.H., THOMPSON, P.M., COKER, A.M., TUNSTALL, S.M., RICHARDS, C.
and PARKER, D.J. (1992)
The economics of coastal management: a manual of benefits assessment techniques
(the 'Yellow Manual'), Belhaven Press, London

PERLIN, M. and DEAN R.G. (1983)
A Numerical Model to Simulate Sediment Transport in the Vicinity of Coastal Structures
Miscellaneous Report No 83-10, Coastal Engineering Research Center, US Army Corps of Engineers

PHILLIPS, O.M. (1957)
On the generation of waves by turbulent wind
Journal of Fluid Mechanics, Vol. 2, pp417-445

PIERSON, W.J. and MOSKOWITZ, L. (1964)
A proposed spectral form for fully developed seas based on the similarity theory of S A Kitaigorodskii
Journal of Geophysical Research, Vol. 69, No 24

PILARCZYK, K.W. (1994)
Novel systems in coastal engineering: geotextile systems and other methods - an overview
Rijkwaterstaat, Netherlands

PILARCZYK, K.W., VAN OVEREEM, J. and BAKKER, W.T. (1986)
Design of beach nourishment scheme
In: *Proc. 20th Int. Conf. on Coastal Engineering*, Taiwan, 1986

POOLE, A.B. (1993)
Pensarn Coastal Protection Scheme, Degradation of Beach Nourishment Material
Queen Mary College, Ref 934/P

POWELL, K.A. (1990)
Predicting short term profile reponse for shingle beaches
Report SR 219, HR Wallingford, February 1990

POWELL, K.A. (1993)
Dissimilar sediments; model tests of replenished beaches using widely graded sediments
Report SR 350, HR Wallingford, October

POWELL, K.A. and LOWE, J.P. (1994)
The scouring of sediments at the toe of seawalls
In: *Proc. of the Hornafjördur Int. Symposium*, Iceland

PRESTEDGE, G.K. and BOSMAN, D.E. (1994)
Sand bypassing at navigation inlets: solution of small scale and large scale problems
In: *7th National Conf. on Beach Preservation Tech.*, American Shore & Beach Presvn. Assn., Tampa, Florida

PROUDMAN OCEANOGRAPHIC LABORATORY (POL) (1995)
Extreme sea-levels at the UK A-Class sites: Optimal site-by-site analyses and spatial analyses for the east coast
POL *Internal Document No. 72*. Proudman Oceanographic Laboratory

RAMSAY, D.L. and HARFORD, C.M. (1995)
A catalogue of synthetic wave data around the coast of England and Wales
Report SR 373, HR Wallingford

RANWELL, D.S. (1981)
Sand dune machair 2
Institute of Terrestrial Ecology, Cambridge

RANWELL, D.S. and BOAR, R. (1986)
Coast Dune Management Guide
Institute of Terrestrial Ecology, NERC, Grange-over-Sands, Cumbria

READERS DIGEST (1995)
Good Beach Guide
David & Charles, Frome

RENDEL GEOTECHNICS (1993)
Coastal planning and management: a review
HMSO

ROELVINK, J.A. and BRØKER, I. (1993)
Cross-shore profile models
Coastal Engineering Vol. 21, Special Issue, *Coastal morphodynamics: processes and modelling*, pp163-191

ROYAL SOCIETY FOR THE PREVENTION OF ACCIDENTS/ROYAL LIFE SAVING SOCIETY
(ROSPA/RLSS), (1993)
Safety on British beaches
ROSPA/RLSS, Birmingham/Strudley, Warwickshire

SIEVWRIGHT, M.J. (1994)
Development and verification of empirical models of profile evolution for dynamically stable rock slopes under wave action
Oxford Brookes University BEng. thesis report for HR Wallingford, March

SILVESTER, R. and HSU, J.R.C. (1993)
Coastal Stabilisation: Innovative Concepts
Prentice-Hall, Engelwood Cliffs, New Jersey

SOULSBY, R.L. (1994)
Manual of Marine Sands
Report SR 351, HR Wallingford, October

STANDING COMMITTEE OF ANALYSTS, (1981)
Methods for the examination of water and associated materials
HMSO, London

STRIDE, A.H. (editor) (1982)
Offshore Tidal Sands, Processes and Deposits
Chapman & Hall, London, 222pp

THOMAS, R.S. and HALL, B. (1992)
Seawall design
CIRIA/Butterworths, London

TUCKER, M.J. (1991)
Waves in ocean engineering: measurement, analysis, interpretation
Ellis Horwood, Chichester, England, 431pp

TUCKER, M.J. (1994)
Nearshore wave height during storms
Proudman Oceanographic Laboratory Internal Document No 71 (unpublished manuscript)

TURNER, N. (1994)
Recycling of Capital Dredging Arisings - The Bournemouth Experience
SCOPAC Seminar, Inshore Dredging for Beach Replenishment, Lymington, October 1994

VAN DER MEER, J.W. (1988)
Rock slopes and gravel beaches under wave attack
Delft Hydraulics Comm., No.396

VAN DER MEER, J.W. and VELDMAN, J.J. (1992)
Stability of the seaward slope of berm breakwater
Journal of Coastal Engineering, Vol. 16, September

VAN DER POST, K. and OLDFIELD, F. (1994)
Magnetic training of beach sand
In: *Coastal Dynamics '94*, Barcelona, Spain

VAN HIJUM, E. and PILARCZYK, K.W. (1982)
Equilibrium profile and longshore transport of coarse material under regular and irregular wave attack
Delft Hydraulics Laboratory, Publication No. 274

VELLINGA, P. (1982)
Beach and dune erosion during storm surges
Delft Hydraulics Laboratory, Publication, No. 276

VELLINGA *et al* (1989)
Guide to assessment of safety of dune to sea defence
CUR/TAW, Report 140, Gouda, The Netherlands

VERHAGEN, H.J. (1992)
Method for artificial beach nourishment
In: *Proc. 23rd Int. Conf. on Coastal Engineering, Venice*, pp2474-2485

VOULGARIS, G., WORKMAN, M. and COLLINS, M R (1994)
New techniques for the measurement of shingle transport rates in the nearshore zone
In: *Proc. 2nd Int. Conf. on the Geology of Siliclastic Shelf Seas*, May 1994, Gent

WATANABE, A., MARUYAMA, K., HSIMIZU, T. and SAKAKIYAMA, T. (1986)
Numerical prediction model of thre-dimensional beach deformation around a structure
Coastal Engineering in Japan, Vol. 29, pp179-194

WATANABE, A., SHIMUZU, T. AND KONDO, K. (1991)
Field appreciation of a numerical model of beach topography change
In: *Proc. Coastal Sediments '91*, Seattle, WA., ASCE, New York, pp184-1828

WELTMAN, A.J. and HEAD, J.M. (1983)
Site Investigation Manual
CIRIA special publication 25

WMO (WORLD METEOROLOGICAL ASSOCIATION) (1988)
Guide to wave forecasting and analysis
Report WMO-No702, Secretariat of WMO, Geneva, Switzerland

WORK P.A. and DEAN R.G. (1991)
Effect of varying sediment size on equilibrium beach profiles
In: *Proc. Coastal Sediments '91*, Seattle, WA., ASCE, New York, pp890-904

Appendix A   Obtaining a licence for offshore extraction

In Section 7.5 of this manual a brief outline was given of the procedure for obtaining material from a new offshore source. Of all the alternative sources a new offshore source is the most difficult to arrange and this section describes the required procedure in more detail. In addition, guidance is given for each stage of the process to enable scheme promoters and their development teams to avoid some of the pitfalls.

It should be noted that the procedures for obtaining licences for offshore aggregate dredging are currently under review and there is a strong possibility that these procedures will be modified at some time in the future. It is, therefore, recommended that the relevant authorities are contacted to ascertain the current position, prior to commencement of work in this area.

A.1   OVERALL PROCEDURE

The overall procedure is illustrated in Figures A1 and A2. Figure A1 describes the Pre-application and Exploratory Stage whilst Figure A2 essentially covers a subsequent phase, generally known as the Government View Procedure.

In its entirety the complete process; from identifying a potential source, prospecting, applying for a licence, carrying out necessary studies and consultations, to the eventual satisfactory completion of the Government View Procedure; is a lengthy business and may take up to three years or more. The overall timescale will have much to do with the environmental sensitivities of the extraction site and the availability of, or time taken to collect, baseline environmental data.

There are a number of points in the procedure where the applicant can take stock of the situation and decide not to proceed, for instance if the chances of an eventual production licence being issued appear to be too tenuous. Funding for exploratory work for beach recharge purposes of this nature, even if the eventual outcome is unproductive, is now available from MAFF under Grant Aid arrangements, since it is a condition that all reasonable alternative sources of beach recharge material be considered.

A.2   SELECTION OF SEARCH AREA

In the past, production licences have tended to be granted only when it could be shown that extraction of material offshore would have no general detrimental effects, and particularly no effect on the coastline. This so-called "nil-effect" policy generally restricted aggregate applications to areas of the seabed beyond the 18-metre depth contour line, as in shallower waters it was considered that there was a high risk of extraction causing coastal problems. With increased knowledge of coastal processes and improved predictive methods being developed, there is now a trend to try to license extraction areas for beach recharge which can be shown to have a "net benefit" to the community. This means that areas inside the 18-metre depth contour are now being considered.

Any review of potential search areas should take account of the following:

- inshore areas in the same coastal cell or sub-cell as the beach to be recharged may well contain materials of type and size similar to the existing beach material

- information on inshore sources and potential reserves may be available from local coastal groups (such as SCOPAC)

- inshore areas tend to be more environmentally sensitive than those areas further from the coast and may well require extensive environmental impact assessment, over long periods

- areas of poor aggregate quality, or contaminated by shell, lignite, clay, silt, chalk, etc. may prove to contain considerable reserves of material, since these areas tend to be avoided by the aggregate dredging companies

- for shingle recharges, the search area should extend to at least 25 nautical miles from the site if the water depths at the site restrict pumping ashore to the high water period. The search area can be increased without undue cost penalty if pump-ashore is not tidally restricted. However, screening and beach site bathymetry also affect cycle times and costs, and specialist advice should be sought on these matters.

- for sand recharges, tidal working has less effect since pumping distances can be increased. Thus, search areas are less likely to be tidally restricted except at very shallow sites

- search areas in very dynamic regions, such as the Bristol Channel, Humber Estuary, etc, are less suitable for fish spawning and thus may be less likely to conflict with fish conservation interests. However, fisheries and environmental concerns may still be of importance.

A.3 THE GRANTING OF PROSPECTING LICENCES

A prospecting licence will only be granted by the Crown Estate if, in the opinion of the CE Commissioners, its issue will not be detrimental to the best interests of the Crown and other interested parties. Before granting a licence the Crown Estate will confer with English Nature (or The Countryside Council for Wales) and MAFF to identify any environmental or fisheries concerns. If the area is outside the 12 mile limit the Joint Nature Conservation Council (JNCC) will also be consulted.

Prospecting licences are short-term, usually for one year or 18 months, and closely defined, both in area and activity permitted (Murray, 1992). Upon receipt of a licence, the licensee may carry out prospecting in the area by conventional marine investigation methods, such as sidescan sonar, seismic methods, grab sampling and vibrocoring, sometimes followed by trial dredging (subject to MAFF approval, detailed licence controls and observance of an agreed code of practice).

English Nature (or The Countryside Council for Wales) are only likely to object to the prospecting licence if the area of search contains or is very close to one of their 27 identified Sensitive Marine Areas (SMAs). However, for material only intended for beach recharge purposes they may be prepared to show some flexibility. In the future a new classification of Special Areas of Conservation (SAC) will be designated under the Habitats and Species Directive. As such, they will each be managed by a competent or relevant authority, whose scheme of management for the SAC will influence the response to any application for a prospecting licence.

MAFF consult with their Burnham and Lowestoft Fisheries Laboratories to ascertain the fish resource aspects of the proposed search area and contact District Fisheries Inspectorates and Sea Fisheries Committees, mainly to assess reasonable prospecting licence controls, but on rare occasions these consultations result in MAFF objecting to licences being granted.

To ensure that no delays occur in the granting of a prospecting licence, it is suggested that the applicant hold informal consultations with English Nature (or The Countryside Council for Wales) and MAFF Fisheries Division during the search area selection process, together with the JNCC if the area is outside the 12-mile limit. In addition, the managing body for any SAC, when appointed, should also be consulted.

A.4 PROSPECTING

Prospecting is a major and lengthy undertaking, often carried out as a two-stage exercise. In the first stage seismic profiling and grab sampling are used to identify the most promising zone in the search area. The second stage is used to obtain quantitative and qualitative information relating to the seabed material.

It is also an ideal opportunity to collect data on the benthos. However, to obtain useful benthic material, the sampling techniques used must be appropriate. For this reason the prospecting campaign should be planned and overseen with an adequate input from both engineers and marine biologists.

An indication of how the data obtained will be assessed by MAFF may be found in Campbell (1993).

A.5 ENVIRONMENTAL ASSESSMENT AND CONSULTATIONS

Environmental appraisals and assessments feature in various locations in the procedure for obtaining a new licence. In some cases they are optional. However, as part of the Government View Procedure the DoE/Welsh Office may insist on an Environmental Statement (ES) to enable a final decision to be taken. Since to commence an ES at that stage may put the whole process back by in excess of a year, it is strongly recommended that environmental appraisals and assessments be carried out as part of the preliminary planning and pre-application stages where shown in Figure A1. Potential impact of material extraction is described in Section 7.9.5.

Environmental data relating to offshore areas is often difficult to locate and time-consuming to collect or measure. A considerable amount of data relating to fisheries is held within MAFF but at busy times it may require a number of weeks for it to be produced in the right format. Information relating to inshore fisheries may be incomplete or even non-existent. A certain amount of confusion is also apparent in people's minds as to which organisation deals with what aspect, particularly with respect to fish and fisheries. Box 4.2 gives details of the main organisations to be consulted and their areas of interest. Essentially, English Nature (or the Countryside Council for Wales) have regard for the conservation of important fisheries, particularly in their relation to the wider health of the marine environment and contribution to biodiversity. Conservation of the commercial fishery is a matter for MAFF. The JNCC may also be able to provide information on the marine environment.

Both the mechanism for obtaining a new production licence and the associated environmental assessments are highly consultative activities and it is of prime importance that the consultations involved are as comprehensive and effective as possible. In particular, it is important that all concerns are addressed adequately and at an early enough stage of the process to enable them to be accommodated without undue disruption to the licensing procedures or modification to the proposed scheme.

Consultations will be most effective in a two-stage approach; a very broad scoping exercise, followed by comprehensive consultations with interested parties whose concerns are shown to be real. It is very important that all *bona fide* concerns are investigated fully and that none are ignored, since, if legitimate objections are raised at late stages of the process, considerable periods of time may be lost re-examining the situation, collecting additional data and modifying the proposed scheme to suit. In addition, objections to the proposed extraction may often be overcome by negotiation in the early stages, but not necessarily later, when positions have become more entrenched.

The final evaluation of the beach recharge scheme will involve examining its source of material and all the alternatives considered. Where relevant objections to these alternatives exist, positive evidence of the objections may need to be provided. Much of the value of consultation is lost if objections to alternative proposed sources are not made in writing by the objectors. For this reason it may be necessary to prompt interested parties into considering specific issues, to enable them to respond with relevant objections.

A.6 STUDY OF THE COAST PROTECTION IMPLICATIONS OF PROPOSED EXTRACTION

The Crown Estate consult with HR Wallingford (HR) as to the probable effect on the coastline of the proposed material extraction. In forming their opinion HR aims to answer the following questions (Parrish, 1989):

- Whether the area of dredging is far enough offshore to prevent beach drawdown into the deepened area

- whether the area to be dredged is sufficiently far offshore and in deep enough water to prevent changes in wave refraction pattern, since such changes may alter the longshore transport of beach material and affect shoreline stability

- whether the area of dredging includes offshore bars which are sufficiently high to give protection to the coastline from wave attack, since a reduction in crest height might increase wave action and lead to erosion

- whether the dredging to be carried out is in deep enough water to prevent it affecting the possible onshore movement of shingle.

The scope of the HR studies are decided by them and have been modified over the years to take account of developments in coastal engineering knowledge, advances in modelling techniques and coast protection philosophy. In the past, if there was any likelihood of the proposed extraction affecting the coast, the application was rejected on the "nil-effect" principle. Current attitudes to coastal management may allow some effect on the coast if it can be quantified, monitored and taken into account in the overall coast protection management policy, particularly if the effects will be felt on the coastline which is to be recharged.

In view of the significance of the HR opinion on the effects of the proposed material extraction it is prudent to hold informal consultations with them at an early stage. There are advantages to be gained from involving HR in the source selection process and the preliminary assessments, prior to application for a production licence, because:

- HR deal with all the Crown Estate licence applications and, thus, hold a large databank of coastal information which will be useful in determining possible source locations

- if they are involved in the preliminary studies, their review of the licence application is likely to be carried out in the most cost-effective manner.

However, it may be unwise to engage HR in detailed studies at too early a stage, since if the preliminary consultations with other bodies reveal serious environmental concerns, this work may be wasted.

It should be noted that in future most shoreline studies relating to licence applications are likely to be carried out on a cell, or sub-cell, basis and that, where appropriate, the cumulative effect of a number of licensed blocks adjacent to one cell will be studied.

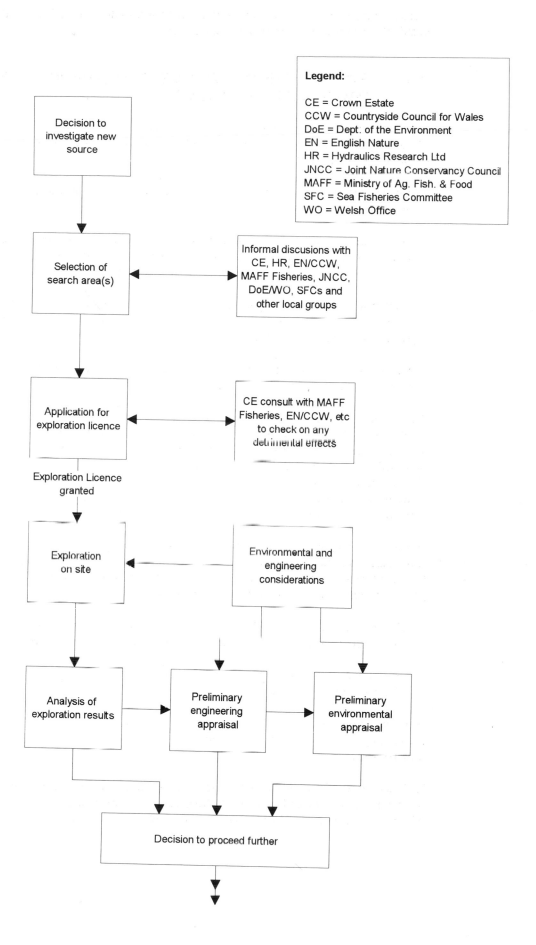

Figure A1 *Finding and licensing a new source - Part 1: prospecting and analysis*

CIRIA Report 153

A.7   THE LICENCE APPLICATION

The formal application for a Production Licence is made to the Crown Estate. Although the maximum annual extraction tonnage allowed is often in the region of 500,000 tonnes per year, it is a common misconception that the Crown Estate sets this figure. It is the applicant who decides on the volume for which he is to apply.

For any application to be successful, the Government View must be positive (see Section A8), which will only occur if no sustainable objections arise. To reduce the chances of objections being sustained, it is prudent to:

* carry out a full comprehensive Environmental Assessment at an early stage of the process

* provide agreed source management and monitoring plans which take account of environmental concerns

* leave no concern unaddressed at the time of application, and

* apply, initially, for a short licence period.

A.8   THE GOVERNMENT VIEW

The Government View is obtained by the Crown Estate submitting the licence application and all supporting documentation, including studies, results of consultations, HR's report and records of their discussions with the applicant to the Department of the Environment (or the Welsh Office) Minerals Division. The DoE/WO obtain their view by consulting all Departments and organisations whose interests might be affected by the proposal. These include:

* DoE Construction Industries Division
* DoE Rural Affairs Division
* MAFF Fisheries and Coast Protection Divisions
* English Nature/Countryside Council for Wales
* Joint Nature Conservation Council
* Department of Transport (Navigation)
* Ministry of Defence (Hydrographic and Naval)
* Department of Energy (oil, gas, etc.)
* Coastal authorities
* Other Welsh Office divisions.

Each of these bodies will in turn consult others, such as sea fishery committees, ports, NRA regional offices and other coast protection authorities. Only when no sustainable objections are raised by organisations consulted, can a favourable view be given. The procedure is, thus, essentially conservative by nature.

The Government View Procedure is also currently non-statutory. This means that although the initial consultation period may only take a few months, final resolution of contentious applications can take years to achieve. The Crown Estate will not issue a licence without a favourable Government View and all Government View conditions will be included in the licence.

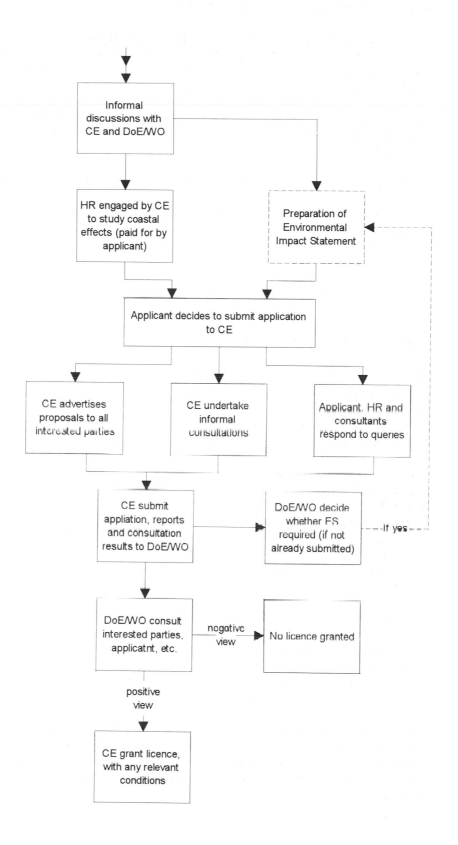

Figure A2 *Finding and licensing a new source - Part 2: extraction licensing procedure*

Index

Page numbers follow the relevant entry. References to Figures and Tables are given in *italics*, and a 'B' after the page number indicates that the material is presented in a Box.

Coastal Defence and the Environment, MAFF
  guidelines 249, 377-8B
coastal defence(s) 39, 40B, 135, 191, 194
  beach management for 143, 221
  beaches as 51-2, 197-9
  dunes as 365-6
  effect of human intervention 84
  Environmental Assessment in 249, *251*
  hydraulic modelling for schemes 147-51
  legislation 385
    and responsibilities, England and Wales
      39, 40B
  managed landward realignment 373-6
  protection by seawalls 334
  reduced standard of 373, *376*
  sea level rise to be taken into account 144
  use of seawalls 237, 239
Coastal Groups 155
coastal management 191-7
  terminology *197*
coastal modelling 147
coastal processes 165B, 170
  changed by detached breakwaters 237
  impact of beach recharge 306
coastal responses 151
  coastal response variable 142
  and joint probability contours 141
coastal squeeze 32, 86-7, 373
  minimization of 239
coastal structures 157
  overtopping and damage to 135
  wave/current measurements near to 176-7
  see also beach control structures
coastal sub-cells 93, *94*
coastal zone management 39, 191, *192*, 193
coastlines
  effects of solid geology on 79-83
  geometry affecting tides 100
coasts, open, large waves and high water
  levels 143
collector charts 172
Colwyn Bay, Clwyd 322
combined models, fully integrated 241B
commercial fishing 165B
  beach recharge, impacts on and mitigation
    measures 304-5
compensation, for beach recharge work 296
component life, beach management schemes
  213
Computer Aided Design (CAD) 155, 183
Conditions of Contract 389
  Special Conditions of Contract 389-90
cone penetration tests, static or dynamic drive
  mechanism 180-1
conservation, and beach management 39
construction
  beach control structures 347-54
  beach management schemes 395-7
  public advertisement and consultation

  during 387-8
  sampling and testing 396-7
  sequencing of work 395
  site supervision 396
  surveys and measurements 397
Construction (Design and Management)
  Regulations 1994 *see* CDM regulations
construction evaluation 399B
construction traffic, routes for 230
consultation, for Environmental Assessment
  249, 252
contingent valuation survey 246, 376
contract documents, preparation of 388-93
controlled abandonment 373, *376*
Coriolis force 105
cost optimisation, beach control structures
  345-6
cost-benefit analysis, for scheme comparison
  246-7
cost-benefit considerations, managed
  landward realignment 373
Covehithe, Suffolk, beach formed from glacial
  tills cliffs 60
crest heights 270
  seawalls 342
  shingle beaches 201-4
crest levels, groynes 316, 319, *320*
crest width 270
critical beach levels/cross-sectional areas 187
critical overfill ratio 271, 275B
cross-shore processes 204, *204*
  sills as a barrier to 343
cross-shore structures
  stability of under breaking waves 314
  see also breakwaters; groynes
Crown Estate 284, 386
  application for Production License 430
  granting of Prospecting Licenses 426
crushed rock nourishment 162
currents
  deflection by groynes 237
  derivation and measurement of 106-7
  estimation of 106
  flow and transport processes 106
  generation processes 104-5
  modulation of flow 105-6
  recording of 107
  round coastal structures 176-7
  shore-parallel 68, 70
  wind-induced 77
cuspate forelands (cusps/nesses) *80*, 81
cutter suction and suction dredgers 290B

data
  requirement for 153
  sources for historic extreme events 146-7
  storage and analysis 155-6, 182-6
  structured and unstructured 184, 185B
  vector and raster 184, 185B

foreshore building, Allonby, Cumbria *363*
Form of Agreement 393
Form of Bond 393
Form of Tender 393
freshwater sites, high standard of protection
 required 217
funding, for coastal defence work 387

gabions, in dune management 364
Geographical Information Systems (GIS) 155,
 184-6
Geological Conservation Review Sites 58
geological mapping 179
geological maps/memoirs (BGS) 178, 179
geology 165B
 and geomorphology 58-9, 170
 nearshore and backshore 157
 potential impacts of beach recharge 306
geophysical surveys 179, 181
GEOSAT, wave data from 126
geotechnical data collection 177-82
 methods 180-1
 site investigation 178-9
Global Positioning Systems (GPS) 173
 for beach profile surveys 159
global wave models, for swell data 124
Global Wave Statistics, Hogben *et al* 126
Gold Coast Seaway, Australia, seabed
 fluidisation 383B
Good Beach Guide 409
Government View Procedure 284, 285, *287*
 and Environmental Statements 426
 extraction licenses 425, 430, *431*
grading envelopes 278, 280B
 limits on undersize/oversize material 280-1
grading specification, shingle recharge
 scheme, Elmer, W. Sussex 279B
grain size
 and beach recharge 306-7
 in longshore drift 71
 see also particle size
gravel pits, source of recharge material 278
gravitational forces, Sun and Moon 100, 104
grazing, controlled, on dunes 367
Greenhouse effect 86-7
grey dunes 357
gross drift 70
ground conditions, required data 225
groundwater
 and cliff failure 60
 extraction from dunes causing erosion 358
 and shingle beaches 81
groundwater levels, beach and beach head 97
groyne bays, volume of beach material within
 200-1
groyne fields
 design of 319, 321
 recharge of 322
groyne head extension 319, *321*

groyne stability 135
groyne system, typical currents in *320*
groynes 36, 38, 84, 235, 237, *238*, *312*, 313-
 22, 347, 395
 affecting beach plan shape 74
 affecting sediment movement 73
 berm length 316, *320*
 berm level 360
 construction and maintenance 321
 construction methods 354
 definition/general guidelines 313
 design considerations 314-21
 in dune management 360
 effect on beach development 314
 length of 316, 319, 321, 377
 materials for 237, 314, *317*, 318B
 monitoring and maintenance *407*
 in restoration of natural supply 377
 rock 228-9, 319
 rock mound 316
 spacing of 319, 321
 terminal *310*, 313, 316
 timber *320*
 vertical 316, 319
Gugh-St Agnes sand bar 81
*Guide to the use of groynes in coastal
 engineering*, CIRIA 309
Gumbel distribution 117B

habitat loss 38
Habitats Directive (1992) 217
Harwich, beach recharge using navigational
 dredgings 285, 289B
Hayling Island
 hazard, excavation in shingle beach *303*
 overtopping of shingle beach 77, *78*
hazards
 during beach recharge 303, *303*
 sills as 343
head erosion, dunes 358
headland control 79, 333, 335-6B, *337*
headlands (nesses) 63
 as cell boundaries 90, 92
health and safety plan, pre-tender 392
Hengistbury Head, Dorset
 beach cusps *69*
 groynes and natural beach accumulation
 315
Heritage Coasts 39, 195
heritage interest 57, 165B, 168, 217
high water levels, timing of 104
Highcliffe, Dorset, beach coarsening 267B
Hilton Bay, Berwick on Tweed, rock beach
 374B
hindcast wave data 114, 115
hindcasting
 from wind records 118
 and joint probability assessment 142
 wave climate, long-term 121

coastal protection 359
New Engineering Contract (NEC 2nd Edition) 389
Newborough Warren, dune accretion rate 78
Newborough Warren National Nature Reserve 195
NGOs, source of information and statistics 164
"nil-effect" policy, extraction licenses 425
noise/nuisance restrictions 297
North Norfolk sub-cell 93, *94*
North Sea storm flood (1953) 39
NRA Anglian Region
  Hunstanton to Heacham flood defences 218, *219*
  Mablethorpe to Skegness
    analysis of beach profile monitoring 187, 188B
    environmental mitigation measures 301B
  ongoing beach and coast monitoring programme 157, 158B
  post-project monitoring programme 398
  regional database 145
  use of dredgings from Harwich Harbour 285, 289B
numerical models 240, 241-2, 241B, *243*, 404
  water levels and currents 148

Ocean Weather Ships 126
Official Journal of the European Communities (OJEC) 393
offshore (marine) extraction areas
  licensed 257B, 258, 260, 284
  newly licensed 284-5
  obtaining a license for 425-30, *431*
    environmental assessment and consultations 427-8
    granting of prospecting license 426
    selection of search area 425-6
    study of coastal protection implications of proposed extraction 428
  unlicensed 257B
offshore to breaker zone 76
offshore zone 50B
Old waterfront walls, CIRIA 334
one-way drift valves 84, 93
open beach drift rate 205
open beaches, profile lines 159
Ordnance Survey maps 178
Orford Ness 81
oscillatory wave action 67
overall still water level 103
"overfill factor" or "overfill ratio" methods 271
overtopping 135, 199, 215B, 225
  of beach crests 97
  of beaches 52, 198
  calculations of 243
  hindcasting rates of 142

prediction of 77
  of rock beaches 368
  of seawalls 176B, 221, *223*
  seawalls/revetments 342
Owers Bank, source for shingle recharge 279B

Pagham Beach, W. Sussex, rock groyne extension *321*
paleo-river valleys, infilling of 83
particle size 169
Peaks Over Threshold (POT) method 114
  storm wave height data 116
Penmaenmawr, Gwynedd, creation of artificial shingle beach *255*
Penrhyn Beach, Carboniferous limestone beach recharge weight loss *269*
perched beaches 237, *238*, 343
percolation
  shingle beaches 266
  of water through beaches 52, 81
performance assessment, post-project evaluation 398-9
performance evaluation 399B
periodicity, incoming waves 68
permeability, rock beaches 369
photogrammetry, and beach plan shape 161
photography
  aerial 178, 179
  for beach response near structures 162
  during site reconnaissance 178
  for site inspections 157, 160
physical environment
  data collection 170
  impact of beach control structures during construction *349*
  impact of beach recharge 306-7
  mitigation measures for beach control structures 351B
physical modelling
  of waves 151
  waves and currents 147, 148
physical models 202, 240-2, *242*, 242B, *243*, 243B, 372
Pierson-Moskowitz (P-M) spectrum 109, 118
pioneer grasses, in embryo dune formation 356, 357, *357*
planning legislation 385
plant ownership 390
pocket beaches *59*, 79, *80*, 322
  based on Spanish micro-tidal experience 328B
  North Shore, Llandudno 59, *59*
point measurements 177
pollution 412
  prevention of 217-18
Portland Bill 90
ports/harbours, and sediment bypassing 303, 379, 380, 381B

direction of 319
wave climate(s) 225
  altered by dredging 86
  change in directionality 210
  from joint waves and tides 143
  hindcasting, long-term 121
  inshore, reduced by sills 343
  long-term, methods for compilation 111
  nearshore 143
  UK coastline 95
  wave climate atlases 126-7
  wave climate prediction 121
wave conditions
  at breaker line 101
  in beach management projects 225
  changes in 86
  deep water 107-27
  depth-limited 135
  shallow cf. deep water 127
  shallow water 127-35
  types of 108-9
  see also extreme wave conditions
wave data
  measured and hindcast 147
  remote sensed 126
  sources of 124-7
    and modelling 135, *136*
  synthetic 126
  see also wave statistics
wave energy
  alternative sources 110
  dissipation of 51, 237, 368
  and dune formation 356
  reduced by breakwaters 347
wave gauges 125
wave height
  deep and shallow water forecasting curves *122*, 132
  and direction, long-term distribution 133
  increase in 145, *146*
  long-term distribution 133
  peak during storm 115
  and period, long-term distribution 133
  significant, analysis of extreme statistics 116-17
wave models
  choice of 148, 150
  site-specific data 147
wave observations, visual 125
wave period 142
  relationship between different measures of 117-18
  and storm peak wave height 115
wave prediction methods 121-3, 132
wave recording, commissioning of 124-5
wave rose *115*
wave set-up 99, 101, *102*, 103
wave statistics
  in deep water 110-12

in shallow water 133-5
wave transformation 151
  processes in shallow water 128-33, 135, 142
wave-current interaction, shallow water 130-1
wave/seawall interactions 334
waves
  breaking, oblique arrival of 71
  deep water breaking and diffraction 127
  depth-limited 143
  direction 142, 151
    changes in 86, 145
    importance of 112
    shift in, s. coast, UK 210
  generation by wind 118-24
  modified moving onshore 76
  numerical modelling of 148, 150
  response of rock beaches to 367
  sources of measurements 124-5
  spectral description 109, 134
  and water levels, joint probability of 135-43
  wave growth formulae 121
  wave processes near to coastal structures 176
  wave propagation velocity, changes in 129
weather records 146-7
weather risk 390
weathering, of cliff face 60
Weibull Distribution 111, 117, 133
  three-parameter 112B
  two-parameter *113*
weight loss, recharged beaches 268-9
Wentworth Classification *265*
wind, small changes, speed and direction 145
wind action, and loss of beach material 63, 77, 209B
wind climate data 119, *120*
  used in wave predictions 119-21
wind energy and dune formation 356
wind roses 119, *120*
wind set-up 99, 101, 103
wind statistics 118-21
wind stress, and current generation 104
wind velocities, over water 118
wind-blown sand 235
  control of 408-9
  a nuisance 359
  see also dune management
wind-sea 110
working areas, for beach management projects 229
working life, beach management schemes 213
working methods 391
Workington, industrial waste beach 61, *62*
Worth Inlet, Florida, hydraulic bypassing 381B

yellow dunes 357